MANAGERIAL FINANCE
Cases and readings

Managerial finance

CASES AND READINGS

George N. Engler
Assistant Professor of Finance and Business Economics
University of Southern California

 1973

BUSINESS PUBLICATIONS, INC. Dallas, Texas 75224
IRWIN-DORSEY INTERNATIONAL London, England WC2H 9NJ
IRWIN-DORSEY LIMITED Georgetown, Ontario L7G 4B3

© BUSINESS PUBLICATIONS, INC., 1973

First Printing, May 1973

ISBN 0-256-01454-X
Library of Congress Catalog Card No. 72-98127
Printed in the United States of America

Preface

CASES HAVE long been considered one of the best learning tools available to the instructor. This text is aimed at utilizing this vehicle to provide an opportunity for students to cross over into the realm of practical application of basic learning concepts. As such, the text could be utilized as a primary text in a course that is totally case-oriented or as a supplemental text in a more lecture-oriented framework.

The text examines a number of recent business experiences so that younger students can relate more effectively to the particular business situation. Industry and firm data are extensive enough so the student can limit his outside efforts to obtain external environmental data and concentrate more on the problem at hand. Readings are included to assist the student in his problem-solving task by providing information on a subject that is one level above what could be obtained from a basic textbook on finance. In addition to the cases and readings, a selected reference section is provided at the end of each section for the student who wishes to further pursue a particular topic or issue. The material in the text has been class tested so that the case analysis and presentation should flow fairly smoothly. Any suggestions from instructors and/or students as to the improvement of the cases are of course always welcome.

I am grateful to all of the authors and editors who have graciously consented to my reprinting their articles so that students can obtain a more meaningful learning experience. All references to the author and source are cited at the beginning of each article.

I am deeply indebted to Dean Jerry B. Poe of the School of Business Administration at Drury College; to Dr. Michael W. Keenan of the Graduate School of Business Administration at New York University;

v

and to Dr. John R. Kreidle of the College of Business Administration at Northern Illinois University for the time they spent in reviewing the manuscript and contributing to the improvement of the text. Special appreciation is extended to Dr. J. Fred Weston of the Graduate School of Management at the University of California at Los Angeles for his valuable guidance during the formative years of my intellectual development.

I would also like to express my appreciation to Messrs. Kapil Nada, Gurinder Sethi, Jack Seaquist, and Arnold Maddox who assisted in developing the computer programming aspects of some of the cases. Special appreciation is extended to Messrs. William Brown and Ray Payne, who worked extensively with the author in revising and editing the text. For typing the manuscript, I am grateful to Jean B. Schuster and Sandy Gregory.

Los Angeles   GEORGE N. ENGLER
April 1973

Contents

Part I
FINANCIAL ANALYSIS AND PROJECTIONS   1

A. Basic financial tools   3
AMC Corporation (Financial Forecasting), 3
North Plains Airlines (Ratio Analysis), 10
Optical Character Scanning, Inc. (Budgeting), 30

B. Quantitative Financial Tools 42
Westwind Senicruise Airlines (A) (Linear Programming), 42
Quality Appliance Company, Incorporated (A) (Linear
    Programming), 44
Quality Appliance Company, Incorporated (B) (Linear
    Programming), 46
Beamir Company (Goal Programming), 48
Selected references, 55

"Interest Rates, Credit Flows, and Monetary Aggregates since 1964,"
    Federal Reserve Bulletin, 56
"The Concept of Sustainable Growth," *Guilford C. Babcock*, 74
"An Introduction to Linear Programming: Concepts and Examples,"
    International Business Machines, 87
"Linear Programming versus Goal Programming,"
    James C. T. Mao, 104

Part II
CURRENT ASSET MANAGEMENT 109
Canama Corporation (Cash Management-Linear Programming), 111
G. & L Corporation (Cash Management), 115

Morgan Organ Company (Inventory Management), 121
Imperial Manufacturing Company (Accounts Receivable
    Management), 135
Selected references, 143

"Cash Management," *James McN. Stancill,* 146
"Use Your Hidden Cash Resources," *Frederick W. Searby,* 166
"Managerial Controls of Accounts Receivable: A Deterministic
    Approach," *Haskel Benishay,* 179

Part III
CAPITAL BUDGETING 199

Chemdrug Company (Conditions of Certainty), 201
Computer Logic Corporation (Conditions of Uncertainty), 215
H-S Astronautics (Conditions of Uncertainty), 224
Kay Machine Tools, Inc. (Conditions of Uncertainty), 228
Selected references, 231

"The Derivation of Probabilistic Information for the
    Evaluation of Risk Investments," *Frederick S. Hillier,* 239
"Decision Trees for Decision Making," *John J. Magee,* 256
"Abandonment Value and Capital Budgeting,"
    Alexander A. Robichek and *James C. Van Horne,* 271

Part IV
COST OF CAPITAL AND DIVIDEND POLICY 287

Pacific Telephone and Telegraph Company (Cost of Capital), 289
TSA Equipment Company (Dividend Policy), 231
Universe Airlines (Dividend Policy), 332
Selected references, 356

"Valuation and the Cost of Capital for Regulated Industries,"
    Edwin J. Elton and *Martin J. Gruber,* 359
"Fund Administration and Dividend Policy," *Robert H. Plattner,* 370
"Increasing Stream Hypothesis of Corporate Dividend Policy."
    Keith V. Smith, 381

Part V
REFINING THE DEBT AND CAPITAL STRUCTURE 395

United States Steel Corporation (Preferred Stock), 397
Associated Chemical Company (Preferred Stock), 409
Whittaker Corporation (Convertible Debentures), 421
Trans World Airlines, Inc. (Convertible Debentures), 430
Selected references, 444

"The Function of Preferred Stock in the Corporate Financial Plan,"
  Hussein H. Elsaid, 446
"Financing with Convertible Preferred Stock, 1960–1967,"
  George E. Pinches, 455
"An Analysis of Convertible Debentures: Theory and Some
  Empirical Evidence," *Eugene F. Brigham,* 467
"The Refunding Decision: Another Special Case in Capital
  Budgeting," *Oswald D. Bowlin,* 490

Part VI
RAISING LONG-TERM FUNDS 507

  Southern California Edison Company (Lessing versus
    Borrowing), 509
  UAL Incorporated (Debt versus Stock), 526
  National Housing Products (A) (Financing
    Diversification), 541
  National Housing Products (B) (Financing
    Diversification), 551
  AVCO Financial Services, Ltd. (Financing of Overseas
    Subsidiary), 554
  Selected references, 580

  "Valuation of Long-Term Leases," *William L. Ferrara* and
    Joseph F. Wojdak, 583
  "To Lease or Not to Lease?" *George L. Marrah,* 592
  "Yield-Risk Performance of Convertible Securities,"
    Robert M. Soldofsky, 602
  "The Euro-Dollar Market: Some First Principles,"
    Milton Friedman, 610
  "Euro-Dollars: A Changing Market," *Federal Reserve Bulletin,* 626

Part VII
VALUATION, MERGERS, AND ACQUISITIONS 645

  Telectro, Inc. (Valuation), 647
  Vostron Industries (Merger), 655
  McDonnel-Douglas (Merger), 668
  Litton Industries, 1965 (A) (Merger of Litton & Royal-McBee), 681
  Litton Industries, 1965 (B) (Merger with
    Antitrust Implications), 696
  Crocker-Citizens National Bank (A) (Merger), 708
  Crocker-Citizens National Bank (B) (Merger with
    Antitrust Implications), 720
  Selected references, 732

  "Corporate Growth as Affected by the Federal Antitrust Laws,"
    G. B. Haddock, 734

"U. S. Supreme Court Voids Merger of Philadelphia Banks,"
Banking, 743

Part VIII
MARKETS AND INTERMEDIARIES 747

Screen View Company (Going Public), 749
Eli Lilly and Company (Possible Listing on an Exchange), 755
Anheuser-Busch (Possible Listing on an Exchange), 766
Selected references, 778

"Does Listing Increase the Market Price of Common Stocks?"
Richard W. Furst, 780
"An Introduction to Going Public," *Brian Sullivan,* 790

Appendix 803

part I

Financial analysis and projections

A. BASIC FINANCIAL TOOLS

AMC CORPORATION

In November 1971, Dave Johnson, Mike Moore, and Bob Stills were discussing their progress toward starting a new manufacturing company. Each of the three had previously worked for United Machine and Tool Company, a large manufacturer of numerically controlled machine tools. The three formed the core management team for the new company, American Machine Control (AMC) Corporation.

Dave Johnson, president of AMC Corporation, had been the head of the research and development department. Working outside of United Machine and Tool Company, Dave had a patent on a new type of mini-computer control for machine tools called the computerized numerical control (CNC). The CNC is a promising substitute for numerical control.

Mike Moore's background was in the marketing and sales departments. He had personally developed the sales campaign for United Machine and Tool Company's latest numerically controlled welding machine which used a control produced by General Electric.

Bob Stills worked his way from a first-line supervisor to the vice president in charge of manufacturing for United Machine and Tool Company. Bob has years of experience in all phases of the manufacturing of controls and machine tools. Bob has also compiled extensive data on the various manufacturing costs involved in the production of the CNC control.

NUMERICALLY CONTROLLED (NC) MACHINES

History

Numerically controlled (NC) machine tools were first introduced in 1954 when M.I.T. developed the first practical NC milling machine.

3

The next major breakthrough occurred when Giddings & Lewis produced its profile skin milling machine.

During the later 1950s, due to the high cost of each NC machine, the major use of NC was in defense contracts where the government funded the programs. These first major uses were mainly in the complex contouring of aircraft components.

The first low-cost NC for nondefense use occurred during 1960 when Pratt & Whitney introduced their Tape-O-Matic drilling machine. By 1963, there were approximately 2,800 NC units in common use. The increase in the number of NC units accelerated to a yearly shipment of 2,900 units in 1968. Since 1968, the number of units has leveled off; however, the dollar value has increased to an average of $121,000. The total impact of NC units can be demonstrated when one realizes that they currently represent 25 percent of the total machine tool industry shipments.

NC units have become such an important factor in modern manufacturing because of the following basic advantages:

1. NC machines eliminate the use of templets, jigs, fixtures, and their necessary storage space.
2. NC units allow a reduction in setup time and changeover costs.
3. NC units can usually match the production of two or more conventional machines.
4. Machining time is reduced.
5. Greater accuracy and reproduction capabilities are possible.
6. Otherwise impossible part designs or methods are practical with NC.

Types of Numerically Controlled Machines

Boring machines. Numerically controlled boring machines accounted for approximately 14 percent of the total value of NC units shipped in 1970. NC boring units can be equipped with either point-to-point or continuous path controls with from two to eight axes of movement.

Drilling machines. Numerically controlled drilling machines represented 6 percent of the total value of all NC units shipped in 1970. However, they have the lowest value per unit of all major types of NC units. NC drilling units are usually two or three axes with point-to-point systems.

Milling machines. Numerically controlled milling machines represented 11 percent of value of the total NC units shipped in 1970. Milling units are usually sophisticated contouring control systems.

Machining centers. Numerically controlled machining centers represented the largest category of shipments in 1970 with 33 percent. NC machining centers were designed to obtain the greatest advantage from

NC and exist only as NC machines. NC machining centers usually represent the largest cost savings of all types of NC units for the purchase.

Lathes. Numerically controlled lathes represented 26 percent of the value of the total shipments of NC units in 1970. The NC lathes are available in practically all sizes and types of lathes. They utilize both continuous path and point-to-point control systems.

Other metal cutting types. This category of NC units mainly consists of special-purpose tools such as grinding, special metal cutting, punching, shearing, and pipe bending machines. This group totaled less than 7 percent of the total value of all NC units shipped in 1970.

AMC'S COMPUTERIZED NUMERICAL CONTROL PRODUCT (CNC)

AMC's CNC, as presently conceived, is designed to provide a low-cost, flexible, reliable, and powerful numerical control (NC) machine tool controller that can be economically justified on an individual machine basis. To achieve these objectives, AMC Corporation has developed a control exhibiting the following characteristics:

1. Use of an inexpensive, dedicated, stored program computer to perform the major system control functions
2. Simple but sturdy mechanical construction
3. Severe environmental operating specifications
4. Maximum utilization of system software techniques

It is significant to note that since at least 1965, the major Machine Tool Builders (MTB's), NC builders, and computer suppliers have been seeking similar objectives, but their strong commitment to specific technologies such as hard-wired controllers and general-purpose computers has precluded the development of systems with characteristics similar to AMC's CNC unit. As a result, none of these has been able to develop a low-cost NC system with the flexibility and reliability desired by the MTB's and users.

ENGINEERING SUPPORT PLAN

Dave Johnson had prepared an engineering support plan outlining the engineering objectives and presenting an engineering expense forecast covering development costs.

Engineering support plan summary

The engineering objective is to support entry into the NC business. The underlying specific objectives are:

1. Prepare functional product specifications.
2. Design an integrated, structured, quality product line for minimum cost, minimum product support engineering, and maximum adaptability to meet customer service and special functional requirements.

The following engineering effort is planned to support our business: Development (over six-month period)—$325,000

   a) Functional specification preparation
   b) Design development
   c) Applications engineering development
   d) Annual development cost after 1972

Year	Cost
1973	$50,000
1974	75,000
1975	100,000
1976	125,000

Marketing Support Engineering

   a) Application engineering (to requisition)
   b) Product engineering (to requisition)

MANUFACTURING SUPPORT

Bob Stills has produced an operations support plan which indicates that the product manufacturing cycle would be three months from receipt of order to shipment. (Inventories of finished goods were not normally held because of the need to provide specialized equipment for each order.) In addition, Bob has provided information regarding the costs of manufacturing and supporting the product based on his experience with the United Machine & Tool Company where a similar product was produced. A preliminary bill of materials was provided by Dave Johnson from which purchased material costs were determined.

Purchased Material Cost (PMC)	$6,900
Direct Assembly Labor (DAL)	220 hours
Test Labor (TL)	80 hours

Cost for 1 unit = PMC $\times$ 1.59 + DAL $\times$ $10.38 $\times$ 1.38 + TL $\times$ 13.96

It was also determined that a raw material inventory would be maintained to supply 9, 33, 74, 80, and 186 units, respectively in the years 1972–76.

MARKETING SUPPORT

Mike Moore's personal feeling was that by 1975, the served market for AMC's product would be over $100 million, but he desired a more precise estimate in order to provide a solid story to potential investors. To facilitate a more accurate forecast of demand, Mike had gathered some industry data published by the Department of Commerce (Exhibits 2, 3, and 4). Investigating current NC equipment on the market, he found that the Machine Tool Builder paid $18,000 for a basic system; however a typical system with the desired options sold for $29,000. Mike felt that the proprietary technology used in CNC would allow a sufficiently low cost to permit a low selling price and a market penetration of 1, 4, 8, 14, and 24 percent of total numerical control industry sales, respectively, during the years 1972–76. The rate of gross profit was expected to be 0, 10, 11.8, 15.9, and 20 percent during the same periods. He was aware, however, that Dave Johnson had mentioned that investors had been very firm on providing not more than $500,000 in funds. Advertising & Promotion expenses were forecast as $10,000, $40,000, $25,000, $20,000, and $20,000 during the 1972–76 period.

These three have been working for approximately six months preparing estimates for production facilities, finalizing production processes, and lining up tentative personnel for AMC Corporation. Presently, they are working on a complete financial package to present to various sources of venture capital. Bob estimated that they would need approximately $500,000 for initial working capital. This amount would pay for start-up costs and production on a limited scale.

Mike has prepared several detailed reports about the NC industry as a whole. He has showed Dave and Bob an article from *Manufacturing Automation News* where Dr. J. P. Richard estimated future NC sales to reach $25 million by 1975. What Mike needs to prepare are detailed sales projections for the CNC units for the next five years along with financial data to complete the venture capital proposal.

EXHIBIT 1
AMC CORPORATION
Value of U.S. shipments of metal cutting machine tools
(millions of dollars)

Year	Value	Year	Value	Year	Value
1905	25	1927	91	1949	298
1906	42	1928	100	1950	300
1907	27	1929	153	1951	339
1908	18	1930	191	1952	678
1909	28	1931	211	1953	1487
1910	38	1932	184	1954	870
1911	42	1933	100	1955	665
1912	38	1934	48	1956	892
1913	42	1935	49	1957	878
1914	48	1936	70	1958	436
1915	47	1937	98	1959	469
1916	36	1938	168	1960	539
1917	80	1939	198	1961	531
1918	238	1940	197	1962	627
1919	224	1941	247	1963	658
1920	183	1942	400	1964	875
1921	63	1943	538	1965	1048
1922	32	1944	138	1966	1232
1923	75	1945	1500	1967	1373
1924	76	1946	847	1968	1309
1925	83	1947	398	1969	1243
1926	94	1948	321	1970	1098

EXHIBIT 2
AMC CORPORATION
Numerically controlled and automatic mechanical metal-working machinery
(total shipments, 1964 to date)

	Shipments		
		Value in millions	
Total	*Number of machines*	*Machines and controls*	*Controls only*
1964	1,517	$105.5	$29.2
1965	2,100	159.3	43.9
1966	2,939	249.9	55.5
1967	2,957	284.9	69.4
1968	2,917	353.8	81.2
1969	2,376	193.9	70.2
1970 preliminary	1,904	209.3	50.0

Source: U.S. Department of Commerce, *Current Industrial Reports, Series MQ-35W, Metalworking Machinery* (quarterly and annual summaries).

EXHIBIT 3
AMC CORPORATION
Value of U.S. shipment of metal cutting machine tools
(millions of dollars)

	Quarterly figures		
Quarter	*1969*	*1970*	*1971*
February..........	$1,305	$1,195	$921
May.............	1,273	1,164	890
August..........	1,252	1,113	925
December.........	1,243	1,098	950 (est.)

EXHIBIT 4
AMC CORPORATION
Total served market forecast
(millions of dollars)

Year	*Value*
1970..................	$50.0
1971..................	48.0(est.)*
1972..................	51.0 "
1973..................	58.0 "
1974..................	67.5 "
1975..................	77.0 "
1976..................	88.0 "

* Indicates projected market.

NORTH PLAINS AIRLINES

DURING THE FINAL QUARTER of 1971 the president of North Plains Airlines commissioned a recently employed MBA to evaluate the industry competition which might be anticipated during 1972. It was felt that 1972, an election year, would be a period of prosperity and that the airlines would fully participate in this business expansion following the end of the recessionary period of 1969 to 1971.

The individual in question investigated the total industry and decided that the most significant threat to North Plains' share of the market's revenue passenger miles was presented by Trans Lift Airlines. He then submitted the following report concerning Trans Lift's 1972–73 intentions:

The prospect of a resurgent economic environment leading to a resumption of airline traffic growth, combined with Trans Lift's potential to capture a larger share of the available business through its new aircraft, suggests this carrier will experience above average traffic gains in 1972 and 1973. Trans Lift's domestic traffic increased 0.9 percent in 1971 compared with a gain of 1.7 percent for the industry. Moreover, with capacity reduced 4.6 percent, its domestic load factor rose 2.6 points to 48.1 percent. In contrast to Trans Lift's increase in load factor, the modest 3.9 percent expansion of capacity for the industry as a whole was sufficient—given the generally poor traffic background—to continue the declining trend in load factor experienced in more recent years. Trans Lift's excellent performance reflects, in part, the fact that unlike many carriers it was not burdened with the problem of absorbing substantial new wide-body capacity in a recessionary traffic environment. The only wide-body aircraft received in 1971 were two Boeing 747s, which were employed effectively in the airline's developing Pacific market. Since an airline's traffic growth in a competitive market is, all else being equal, largely a function of the capacity it offers, Trans Lift's success in substantially reducing capacity without experiencing a similar decline in traffic demonstrates the ability of its management to realize more fully the potential of its route structure through more effective marketing as shown in Exhibit 1.

The marketing strategy of Trans Lift's management, directed toward extending the airline's penetration of the international market, has focused essentially on two elements: (a) improved schedule planning, and (b) procurement of a fleet of aircraft designed to meet the operating requirements of the carrier's route structure. While improved schedule planning will assist the carrier in realizing and sustaining the optimum traffic potential of its route structure, it is felt that the major benefits from such a program have been realized and henceforth the principal factor in the carrier's anticipated superior traffic growth will be the emerging equipment strategy. In addition to the existing fleet, a decision was made to commit resources to the purchase of four Anglo-French SSTs (at $60 million each) during 1972–73 while phasing out obsolete aircraft. (See Exhibit 2.)

About 70 percent of Trans Lift's traffic is business related. High density and large exposure to business traffic, increases the economic effectiveness of a new generation of jets at this time. A high density market will be able to support the SST and at the same time increase Trans Lift's competitive position.

Given the expectation of a rapidly expanding traffic environment, the change to the SST should permit profitable incremental traffic. Trans Lift will have the flexibility to effect a meaningful increase in its available capacity beyond levels projected. The capacity offered should be sufficient to handle any reasonable increase in traffic forecast for the next couple of years as shown in Exhibit 3. Trans Lift's capacity, measured in terms of available seat miles will amount to 1.5 percent in 1972; because of the larger seating capacity of new aircraft the estimate of available seat miles will increase by 6.7 percent.

Financing of the new aircraft ($240 million) will be the result of internally generated funds which will largely obviate the need for any outside sources. Cash flow from depreciation and amortization will be more than sufficient to meet required debt repayments through 1973, and funds obtained from the sale of obsolete aircraft will cause a positive flow including the $240 million purchase.

In conclusion, if estimates and projections are accurate, the debt to equity ratio, presently 2.1, will approach 1.0, and Trans Lift's position will approach the strongest in the industry. (See Exhibit 4.)

After reading the report the president of North Plains Airlines called a meeting with the vice presidents of the company. Following a brief discussion it was concluded that the analysis was correct and that the threat by Trans Lift was real and imminent. The members were also of the opinion that the forecasts of expansion were accurate and concluded the meeting with the intention of investigating the feasibility of North Plains also purchasing SSTs to meet the competition.

At the time of the analysis to ascertain the advisability of purchasing SSTs, North Plain was suffering from several poor years. The airline lost $45.5 million in 1971 and management was not sure that the tide had been turned. It reported a $30.9 million loss during the first quarter of 1972 as compared to a loss of $23.9 million in the first quarter of 1971.

A return to profitability of the airline is a realistic objective. The major difficulty has been an increase in operating expenses. Efforts have continued to pare those costs. In the first quarter of 1972, revenues were up 6 percent, but expenses were up 14 percent. For the five-year period revenues were up 40 percent, while expenses outran revenues. Over the past year, interest expense on some of the outstanding debts had run as high as 11 percent.

In March 1972, 38 banks agreed to provide a $270 million one-year revolving credit loan to the airlines. The president of the North Plains feels that this loan could ease the financial problems such that with pro forma profits looking up, the airplane purchases (four in total) could be made.

Based upon industry trends as displayed in the accompanying data, would such an investment in new aircraft be wise?

EXHIBIT 1
NORTH PLAINS AIRLINES
Trans Lift Airlines and Domestic Trunk Airlines*
Comparison of domestic operations (50 states)
percent change from preceding similar period

	Scheduled revenue passenger-miles			Scheduled available seat-miles			Actual passenger load factor		
	Total trunks	Trans lift	Vari- ance	Total trunks	Trans lift	Vari- ance	Total trunks	Trans lift	Vari- ance
1970.............	0	+7.6	+7.6	+2.2	+12.4	+10.2	−1.0	−2.0	−1.0
1971									
1st quarter..........	−3.1	−7.0	−3.9	+3.1	−9.4	−12.5	−2.8	+1.1	+3.9
2nd quarter.........	−3.4	−0.7	−4.1	+7.7	−6.9	−14.6	−2.0	+3.1	+5.1
3rd quarter.........	0	−2.6	−2.6	+4.4	−6.4	−10.8	−2.2	+4.7	+6.9
4th quarter (est.)†...	+7.9	+7.2	−0.7	+1.6	+3.8	+2.2	+2.8	+1.6	−1.2

* Includes domestic operations of North Plains Airlines.
† Improvement in industry load factor in the fourth quarter of 1971 essentially reflects the benefits from the capacity limitation agreement which became effective in October 1971.

EXHIBIT 2
NORTH PLAINS AIRLINES
Trans Lift, Inc.—Aircraft fleet

	Passenger capacity	1970 O	1970 L	1971 O	1971 L	1972 est. O	1972 est. L	1973 projection O	1973 projection L
BAC 1–11............	63	13	0	8	0	0	0	0	0
Boeing 747.............	348	0	0	0	1	0	1	0	1
Boeing 727–100........	102	24	5	27	7	28	5	28	5
Boeing 727–200........	130	0	3	0	6	8	5	8	5
Boeing 707–138B.......	131	0	4	0	4	0	4	0	4
Boeing 720.............	124	5	0	5	0	3	0	0	0
Boeing 707–227........	125	4	0	0	0	0	0	0	0
Boeing 707–320–C......	144	8	0	3	0	0	0	0	0
Douglas DC 8–62.......	164	0	7	0	7	0	7	0	7
SST..................	150	0	0	0	0	2	0	4	0
Total.............		54	19	43	25	41	22	40	22

O = owned.
L = leased.

EXHIBIT 3
NORTH PLAINS AIRLINES
Trans Lift, Inc.—Traffic and capacity

	Percent change from preceding years								
	Revenue passenger-miles			Available seat-miles			Passenger load factor		
Market	1973 pro- jected	1972 esti- mate	1971	1973 pro- jected	1972 esti- mate	1971	1973 pro- jected	1972 esti- mate	1971
Domestic (48 states)	+11.5	+11.5	−1.3	+7.5	+7.1	−7.4	53.1	51.2	49.2
Hawaii...........	+15.0	+18.0	+20.8	0	0	+18.2	55.9	48.6	41.2
Mexico...........	+10.0	+9.0	−4.2	+10.5	0	−3.2	53.5	53.7	49.3
South America.....	+14.0	+17.0	+16.5	+8.3	+9.7	+0.9	52.9	50.2	47.1
System...........	+12.3	+13.1	+3.4	+7.0	+6.7	−3.5	53.3	50.8	47.9
System break-even passenger load factor							44.8	44.2	43.3

EXHIBIT 4
NORTH PLAINS AIRLINES
Trans Lift, Inc.—Cash flow analysis
(millions of dollars)

	1973 projection	*1972 estimate*	*1971 estimate*
Sources:			
Net income (loss)...............	$ 32.7	$ 22.3	$ 9.0
Minus (plus) deferred charges......	—	—	(2.3)
Deferred taxes (credit)...........	—	—	(.3)
Sales of aircraft and property.......	109.5	92.5	27.3
Depreciation and amortization......	26.2	25.5	27.6
Other.........................	—	—	11.1
Total Sources..............	$168.4	$140.3	$ 72.4
Uses:			
Aircraft purchases			
(net of deposits)..............	120.0	120.0	⎱18.5
Facilities......................	2.5	10.0	⎰
Debt repayments................	13.6	7.4	93.7
Other.........................	2.5	5.0	8.6
Total Uses................	$138.6	$142.4	$120.8
Cash Surplus (deficit).......	$ 29.8	($ 2.1)	($ 48.4)

EXHIBIT 5*
NORTH PLAINS AIRLINES
United Airlines—Selected financial data
(income statement data—millions of dollars)

Year	Net sales	Operating income	Depreciation amortization	Fixed charges	Income taxes	Net income	E.P.S. as reported
1960........	379.10	61.83	46.34	8.74	3.99	11.17	1.16
1961........	502.20	75.70	62.34	10.08	2.08	3.69	0.31
1962........	594.30	94.12	69.54	12.52	6.39	7.73	0.64
1963........	622.90	101.34	63.88	9.10	14.19	14.71	1.21
1964........	669.40	114.36	59.89	9.73	18.87	27.33	2.03
1965........	792.80	148.30	61.76	12.88	31.77	45.77	3.34
1966........	856.90	141.20	69.66	19.66	24.07	38.31	2.44
1967........	1,098.90	187.11	76.58	25.76	34.84	72.82	4.19
1968........	1,261.70	196.65	101.96	23.09	35.53	41.75	2.23
1969........	1,477.50	263.05	142.18	38.95	37.03	44.69	2.39
1970........	1,501.60	134.21	168.70	42.88	−9.38	−40.88	−2.33

(balance sheet data—millions of dollars)

Year	Cash and equivalent	Receivables	Inventory	Current assets	Net plant	Total assets	Funded debt	Common equity
1960....	32.70	52.90	18.60	106.80	392.00	508.80	242.10	155.36
1961....	30.00	75.90	27.50	135.90	499.80	644.70	309.90	170.18
1962....	34.60	72.10	27.80	138.40	487.80	630.80	279.40	176.55
1963....	31.70	71.10	29.00	134.10	497.20	635.40	224.80	213.59
1964....	28.50	80.60	33.90	146.90	577.00	730.10	281.20	234.58
1965....	176.80	89.10	36.40	308.60	658.50	974.70	435.80	275.02
1966....	247.10	117.40	48.60	419.10	780.60	1,207.70	502.20	412.15
1967....	300.40	144.10	63.40	516.90	970.50	1,495.90	623.20	541.17
1968....	61.60	155.50	74.20	301.30	1,478.40	1,796.80	832.90	564.80
1969....	52.30	175.10	77.10	317.60	1,605.50	1,945.70	880.10	593.23
1970....	55.63	199.65	77.79	363.43	1,609.27	2,179.69	1,045.75	463.30

* Data for all companies in this case was collected through *Moody's Transportation Manuals* and *Compustat Tapes* published by Standard & Poors. The ratio analysis and source and application of funds statement were obtained from computer programs (developed by Guilford C. Babcock, Associate Professor of Finance at U.S.C.), which utilized the basic data from Compustat.

EXHIBIT 5 (Continued)
(ratio analysis)

Year	Current ratio X	Quick ratio X	Gross operating margin (percent)	Net operating margin (percent)	Return on total capital (percent)	Return on common equity (percent)
1960........	1.25	1.03	16.31	6.30	5.65	7.19
1961........	1.21	0.96	15.07	3.16	2.98	1.91
1962........	1.16	0.93	15.84	4.48	5.21	3.89
1963........	1.06	0.83	16.27	6.10	7.47	6.50
1964........	1.11	0.85	17.08	8.36	9.36	11.31
1965........	1.81	1.60	18.71	11.41	11.24	16.36
1966........	2.21	1.95	16.48	9.57	8.06	9.11
1967........	2.35	2.06	17.03	12.14	10.46	13.32
1968........	1.18	0.89	15.58	7.96	6.51	7.27
1969........	1.08	0.82	17.80	8.17	7.31	7.43
1970........	1.11	0.87	24.88	−0.49	−0.40	−9.28
Mean........	1.41	1.16	17.37	7.01	6.71	6.82

Year	Debt to total assets (percent)	Debt to net worth (percent)	Times interest earned X	Cash turn-over X	Inven-tory turn-over X	Fixed assets turn-over X	Sales to net worth X	Total assets turn-over X	Aver-age collec-tion period (days)
1960........	64.39	210.87	2.73	11.59	20.38	0.97	2.44	0.75	50.93
1961........	65.53	227.05	1.57	16.74	18.26	1.00	2.70	0.78	55.16
1962........	63.17	207.60	2.13	17.18	21.38	1.22	3.10	0.94	44.28
1963........	55.37	153.97	4.18	19.65	21.48	1.25	2.73	0.98	41.66
1964........	56.64	166.01	5.75	23.49	19.75	1.16	2.69	0.92	43.95
1965........	62.18	209.70	7.02	4.48	21.78	1.20	2.74	0.81	41.02
1966........	57.29	162.55	4.17	3.47	17.63	1.10	2.01	0.71	50.01
1967........	56.38	152.19	5.18	3.66	17.33	1.13	1.98	0.73	47.86
1968........	60.59	188.57	4.35	20.48	17.00	0.85	2.19	0.70	44.98
1969........	60.38	194.36	3.10	28.25	19.16	0.92	2.44	0.76	43.26
1970........	62.97	241.31	−0.17	26.99	19.30	0.93	2.64	0.69	48.53
Mean........	60.44	192.20	3.64	16.00	19.41	1.07	2.51	0.80	46.51

EXHIBIT 5 *(Concluded)*
(source and application of funds—millions of dollars)

Year	Net income	Depreciation and amortization	Internal sources	New debt	New equity	Total sources	Dividends paid
1961.....	3.69	62.34	66.03	78.07	29.72	173.82	2.68
1962.....	7.73	69.54	77.27	−26.27	1.51	52.51	3.37
1963.....	14.71	63.88	78.59	−39.84	25.53	64.28	3.70
1964.....	27.33	59.89	87.22	68.81	3.88	159.91	10.62
1965.....	45.77	61.76	107.53	166.65	6.78	280.96	12.60
1966.....	38.31	69.66	107.97	76.97	113.57	298.52	15.26
1967.....	72.82	76.58	149.40	129.18	73.66	352.24	17.96
1968.....	41.75	101.96	143.71	242.27	0.47	386.45	19.09
1969.....	44.69	142.18	186.87	82.77	1.49	271.13	19.05
1970.....	−40.88	168.70	127.82	237.48	21.20	386.50	15.94

Year	Capital spending	Other investments	Increase in working capital	Total uses	Increase in cash	Increase in receivables	Increase in inventory
1961..........	146.40	22.74	2.00	173.82	−2.70	23.00	8.90
1962..........	55.60	−2.46	−4.00	52.51	4.60	−3.80	0.30
1963..........	74.30	−1.52	−12.20	64.28	−2.90	−1.00	1.20
1964..........	140.20	1.59	7.50	159.91	−3.20	9.50	4.90
1965..........	153.50	−8.84	123.70	280.96	148.30	8.50	2.50
1966..........	194.40	−2.24	91.10	298.52	70.30	28.30	12.20
1967..........	281.60	−14.62	67.30	352.24	53.30	26.70	14.80
1968..........	752.80	−134.34	−251.10	386.45	−238.80	11.40	10.80
1969..........	657.50	−382.72	−22.70	271.13	−9.30	19.60	2.90
1970..........	262.91	93.95	13.70	386.50	3.33	24.55	0.69

EXHIBIT 6
NORTH PLAINS AIRLINES
North Plains Airlines—Selected financial data
(income statement data—millions of dollars)

Year	Net sales	Operating income	Depreciation and amortization	Fixed charges	Income taxes	Net income	E.P.S. as reported
1960......	413.10	75.57	50.18	12.31	6.97	7.09	0.27
1961......	460.40	85.32	59.09	15.95	5.15	8.93	0.33
1962......	503.90	103.36	58.35	15.34	15.95	15.01	0.56
1963......	560.90	135.27	56.26	12.18	34.66	33.57	0.64
1964......	604.70	119.99	54.09	10.65	20.97	37.14	1.34
1965......	669.00	146.34	60.88	12.83	26.19	47.28	1.80
1966......	841.00	202.29	70.29	15.45	45.08	71.95	2.68
1967......	950.20	203.26	88.28	17.47	33.91	66.25	2.00
1968......	1,036.10	172.40	104.50	23.45	15.15	49.21	1.46
1969......	1,045.00	81.03	106.22	26.32	−18.42	−25.89	−0.75
1970......	1,125.70	93.42	121.18	45.91	−18.21	−47.93	−1.36

(balance sheet data—millions of dollars)

Year	Cash and equivalent	Receivables	Inventory	Current assets	Net plant	Total assets	Funded debt	Common equity
1960....	42.60	58.20	26.30	131.10	383.90	585.70	317.30	147.34
1961....	78.70	59.30	22.90	163.60	342.00	573.80	290.90	150.72
1962....	80.70	64.60	23.90	172.30	333.00	569.50	261.20	160.97
1963....	56.30	74.90	26.40	161.00	326.60	552.70	183.10	184.06
1964....	25.00	74.80	30.00	133.30	460.10	663.10	246.10	231.91
1965....	37.90	90.90	44.70	180.40	535.00	777.70	295.60	275.19
1966....	62.80	127.00	60.90	254.30	722.90	1,039.40	428.90	379.22
1967....	58.10	115.00	70.70	248.30	955.10	1,272.10	576.50	446.70
1968....	77.90	130.40	72.50	296.70	1,079.20	1,458.80	669.00	482.50
1969....	27.90	218.20	74.40	342.50	1,188.00	1,626.30	811.00	462.81
1970....	61.10	190.42	85.11	360.96	1,354.47	1,838.59	1,019.46	421.41

EXHIBIT 6 (Continued)

(ratio analysis)

Year	Current ratio X	Quick ratio X	Gross operating margin (percent)	Net operating margin (percent)	Return on total capital (percent)	Return on common equity (percent)
1960	1.32	1.05	18.29	6.38	5.42	4.81
1961	1.49	1.28	18.53	6.52	6.47	5.92
1962	1.41	1.21	20.51	9.19	10.35	9.32
1963	1.14	0.96	24.12	14.34	19.52	18.24
1964	1.03	0.80	19.84	11.37	12.89	16.01
1965	1.23	0.92	21.87	12.90	13.68	17.18
1966	1.62	1.23	18.70	15.75	15.02	18.97
1967	1.51	1.08	21.39	12.38	10.62	14.83
1968	1.51	1.14	16.64	8.48	6.96	10.20
1969	1.51	1.18	7.75	−1.72	−1.29	−5.59
1970	1.38	1.05	28.81	−1.80	−1.28	−11.37
Mean	1.38	1.08	19.68	8.53	8.94	8.96

Year	Debt to total assets (percent)	Debt to net worth (percent)	Times interest earned X	Cash turnover X	Inventory turnover X	Fixed assets turnover X	Sales to net worth X	Total assets turnover X	Average collection period (days)
1960	71.16	282.88	2.14	9.70	15.71	1.08	2.80	0.71	51.42
1961	69.82	265.79	1.88	5.85	20.10	1.35	3.05	0.80	47.01
1962	67.32	238.19	3.02	6.24	21.08	1.51	3.13	0.88	46.79
1963	58.60	175.97	6.60	9.96	21.25	1.72	3.05	1.01	48.74
1964	56.64	161.96	6.46	24.19	20.16	1.31	2.61	0.91	45.15
1965	56.89	160.76	6.73	17.65	14.97	1.25	2.43	0.86	49.59
1966	56.39	154.56	8.57	13.39	13.81	1.16	2.22	0.81	55.12
1967	58.28	165.97	6.73	16.35	13.44	0.99	2.13	0.75	44.17
1968	59.36	179.48	3.74	13.30	14.29	0.96	2.15	0.71	45.94
1969	63.82	224.26	−0.68	37.46	14.05	0.88	2.26	0.64	76.21
1970	69.70	304.10	−0.44	18.42	13.23	0.83	2.67	0.61	61.74
Mean	62.54	210.36	4.07	15.68	16.55	1.19	2.59	0.79	51.99

EXHIBIT 6 (*Concluded*)
(source and application of funds—millions of dollars)

Year	Net income	Depreciation and amortization	Internal sources	New debt	New equity	Total sources	Dividends paid
1961.....	8.93	59.09	68.02	−25.48	−0.24	42.30	5.31
1962.....	15.01	58.35	73.36	−27.05	0.59	46.90	5.35
1963.....	33.57	56.26	89.83	−58.49	−3.32	28.02	7.16
1964.....	37.14	54.09	91.23	73.85	17.05	182.13	6.34
1965.....	47.28	60.88	108.16	54.01	4.63	166.80	8.62
1966.....	71.95	70.29	142.24	147.28	41.40	330.92	9.33
1967.....	66.25	88.28	154.53	157.52	12.74	324.79	11.51
1968.....	49.21	104.50	153.71	118.80	0.07	272.58	13.48
1969.....	−25.89	106.22	80.33	157.29	13.03	250.65	6.83
1970.....	−47.93	121.18	73.25	218.52	6.53	298.30	0.0

Year	Capital spending	Other investments	Increase in working capital	Total uses	Increase in cash	Increase in receivables	Increase in inventory
1961..........	25.20	−10.51	22.30	42.30	36.10	1.10	−3.40
1962..........	66.30	−20.95	−3.80	46.90	2.00	5.30	1.00
1963..........	33.70	17.06	−29.90	28.02	−24.40	10.30	2.50
1964..........	172.30	19.89	−16.40	182.13	−31.30	−0.10	3.60
1965..........	143.10	−14.72	29.80	166.80	12.90	16.10	14.70
1966..........	227.50	30.59	63.50	330.92	24.90	36.10	16.20
1967..........	249.20	77.78	−13.70	324.79	−4.70	−12.00	9.80
1968..........	160.10	82.70	16.30	272.58	19.80	15.40	1.80
1969..........	243.60	−15.68	15.90	250.65	−50.00	87.80	1.90
1970..........	465.57	−150.56	−16.71	298.30	33.20	−27.78	10.71

EXHIBIT 7
NORTH PLAINS AIRLINES
Trans World Airlines—Selected financial data
(income statement data—millions of dollars)

Year	Net sales	Operating income	Depreciation and amortization	Fixed charges	Income taxes	Net income	E.P.S. as reported
1960........	378.30	53.52	37.47	4.15	8.93	6.47	0.97
1961........	363.10	46.06	58.07	16.89	−12.51	−14.75	−2.21
1962........	401.10	64.26	57.26	19.87	−4.06	−5.70	−0.85
1963........	476.50	90.50	51.86	22.18	−0.17	19.74	2.96
1964........	575.00	134.01	49.24	20.69	31.47	37.00	5.47
1965........	672.80	156.32	59.23	19.52	31.46	50.10	5.74
1966........	699.60	139.03	71.93	22.35	18.93	29.74	3.29
1967........	875.50	144.83	89.89	31.05	5.56	40.77	3.97
1968........	948.20	113.48	83.26	30.94	−6.11	21.54	1.78
1969........	1,098.40	121.45	96.36	20.87	−2.95	19.89	1.63
1970........	1,157.38	24.26	108.14	23.71	−26.63	−63.51	−6.39

(balance sheet data—millions of dollars)

Year	Cash and equivalent	Receivables	Inventory	Current assets	Net plant	Total assets	Funded debt	Common equity
1960.....	64.20	30.70	15.30	113.00	311.80	450.30	223.20	126.04
1961.....	46.50	44.10	12.70	109.20	339.10	477.20	281.10	87.33
1962.....	76.50	41.20	14.60	136.20	368.40	531.30	329.20	81.62
1963.....	71.50	46.00	16.80	136.80	367.10	511.50	310.80	102.00
1964.....	62.60	59.80	20.80	147.50	468.00	623.90	326.90	140.32
1965.....	43.90	68.40	27.80	142.10	538.20	688.20	276.50	233.69
1966.....	45.70	83.00	33.30	164.70	657.00	830.40	372.20	263.09
1967.....	95.70	98.20	38.80	238.30	798.40	1,069.10	529.20	276.95
1968.....	67.70	131.10	42.00	246.40	863.70	1,159.90	570.10	292.57
1969.....	145.40	188.50	40.80	387.00	948.30	1,421.90	757.20	311.86
1970.....	42.49	163.33	45.50	260.00	1,063.36	1,405.76	810.60	297.63

EXHIBIT 7 (Continued)

(ratio analysis)

Year	Current ratio X	Quick ratio X	Gross operating margin (percent)	Net operating margin (percent)	Return on total capital (percent)	Return on common equity (percent)
1960	1.48	1.28	14.15	5.17	5.23	5.14
1961	1.24	1.09	12.69	−2.86	−2.67	−16.88
1962	1.34	1.20	16.02	2.52	2.35	−6.99
1963	1.50	1.31	18.99	8.76	9.94	19.35
1964	1.21	1.04	23.31	15.51	17.75	26.37
1965	1.04	0.84	23.23	15.02	18.31	21.44
1966	1.12	0.90	19.87	10.15	10.39	11.30
1967	1.58	1.32	16.54	8.84	8.43	13.87
1968	1.45	1.20	11.97	4.89	4.68	6.53
1969	1.79	1.61	11.05	3.44	3.13	5.75
1970	1.11	0.92	22.76	−5.74	−5.67	−22.01
Mean	1.35	1.16	17.33	5.97	6.53	5.81

Year	Debt to total assets (percent)	Debt to net worth (percent)	Times interest earned X	Cash turnover X	Inventory turnover X	Fixed assets turnover X	Sales to net worth X	Total assets turnover X	Average collection period (days)
1960	66.58	237.86	4.71	5.89	24.73	1.21	3.00	0.84	29.62
1961	77.39	422.89	−0.61	7.81	28.59	1.07	4.16	0.76	44.33
1962	81.10	527.91	0.51	5.24	27.47	1.09	4.91	0.75	37.49
1963	78.61	394.23	1.88	6.66	28.36	1.30	4.67	0.93	35.24
1964	71.87	319.56	4.31	9.19	27.64	1.23	4.10	0.92	37.96
1965	59.95	176.56	5.18	15.33	24.20	1.25	2.88	0.98	37.11
1966	62.50	197.27	3.18	15.31	21.01	1.06	2.66	0.84	43.30
1967	63.61	209.81	2.49	9.15	22.56	1.10	2.70	0.82	40.94
1968	63.81	216.87	1.50	14.01	22.58	1.10	2.78	0.82	50.47
1969	68.42	268.86	1.81	7.55	26.92	1.16	3.04	0.77	62.64
1970	74.26	347.79	−2.80	27.24	25.43	1.09	3.86	0.82	51.51
Mean	69.83	301.78	2.01	11.22	25.41	1.15	3.52	0.84	42.78

EXHIBIT 7 (Concluded)
(source and application of funds—millions of dollars)

Year	Net income	Depreci- ation and amorti- zation	Internal sources	New debt	New equity	Total sources	Divi- dends paid
1961........	−14.75	58.07	43.32	54.01	−23.96	73.37	0.0
1962........	−5.70	57.26	51.56	46.30	−0.00	97.86	0.0
1963........	19.74	51.86	71.60	−29.77	0.63	42.46	0.0
1964........	37.00	49.24	86.24	43.88	1.32	131.44	0.0
1965........	50.10	59.23	109.33	−43.67	43.28	108.93	0.0
1966........	29.74	71.93	101.67	102.10	8.56	212.33	8.90
1967........	40.77	89.89	130.66	173.54	30.78	334.98	10.49
1968........	21.54	83.26	104.80	54.58	7.46	166.84	11.88
1969........	19.89	96.36	116.25	195.71	7.72	319.68	7.02
1970........	−63.51	108.14	44.63	27.97	3.82	76.42	2.01

Year	Capital spending	Other invest- ments	Increase in working capital	Total uses	Increase in cash	Increase in receiv- ables	Increase in inven- tory
1961..........	82.10	6.67	−15.40	73.37	−17.70	13.40	−2.60
1962..........	77.20	7.16	13.50	97.86	30.00	−2.90	1.90
1963..........	29.90	1.56	11.00	42.46	−5.00	4.80	2.20
1964..........	134.40	16.54	−19.50	131.44	−8.90	13.80	4.00
1965..........	88.00	40.93	−20.00	108.93	−18.70	8.60	7.00
1966..........	127.10	64.43	11.90	212.33	1.80	14.60	5.50
1967..........	224.60	30.39	69.50	334.98	50.00	15.20	5.50
1968..........	59.00	106.96	−11.00	166.84	−28.00	32.90	3.20
1969..........	197.40	20.36	94.90	319.68	77.70	57.40	−1.20
1970..........	272.59	−53.58	−144.60	76.42	−102.91	−25.17	4.71

EXHIBIT 8
NORTH PLAINS AIRLINES
Eastern Airlines—Selected financial data
(income statement data—millions of dollars)

Year	Net sales	Oper- ating income	Depreci- ation and amorti- zation	Fixed charges	Income taxes	Net income	E.P.S. as reported
1960	293.80	31.07	38.47	6.00	−4.18	−5.61	−0.56
1961	295.40	17.90	41.93	6.27	−13.00	−14.97	−1.48
1962	288.10	27.31	43.56	8.03	−4.11	−14.90	−2.06
1963	355.00	32.84	45.32	8.12	−0.40	−19.66	−5.83
1964	414.30	43.57	40.03	10.94	0.0	−5.83	−0.90
1965	507.50	89.47	48.93	11.90	0.0	29.67	3.52
1966	496.30	63.46	39.21	11.12	0.0	15.02	1.57
1967	657.80	92.22	48.15	15.15	7.62	24.11	2.24
1968	744.80	72.85	65.24	27.99	−3.94	−11.94	−1.06
1969	869.60	101.34	77.50	33.19	−0.91	−2.32	−0.27
1970	971.05	127.22	83.34	37.61	1.88	5.46	0.39

(balance sheet data—millions of dollars)

Year	Cash and equiv- alent	Receiv- ables	Inven- tory	Current assets	Net plant	Total assets	Funded debt	Common equity
1960	14.80	35.60	15.90	68.10	257.90	337.80	165.00	110.55
1961	16.70	29.10	15.90	63.30	264.00	342.40	195.00	100.16
1962	18.80	30.60	18.00	68.70	243.80	328.80	195.00	86.81
1963	28.40	30.40	24.60	85.20	222.00	318.70	217.00	49.07
1964	23.50	33.90	31.10	90.90	262.60	366.40	263.70	43.31
1965	55.10	39.70	27.20	126.70	313.60	445.80	251.50	122.89
1966	18.30	47.30	31.90	102.90	436.80	542.60	304.50	152.55
1967	92.20	74.50	39.80	213.80	586.80	829.20	443.40	221.04
1968	48.20	70.50	48.20	174.20	755.40	976.20	605.70	206.17
1969	47.60	84.10	52.70	194.00	783.30	1,030.30	626.10	203.25
1970	60.71	90.86	59.03	222.21	846.21	1,128.56	693.92	207.90

EXHIBIT 8 (*Continued*)
(ratio analysis)

Year	Current ratio X	Quick ratio X	Gross operating margin (*percent*)	Net operating margin (*percent*)	Return on total capital (*percent*)	Return on common equity (*percent*)
1960.............	1.73	1.33	10.58	−1.29	−1.27	−5.08
1961.............	1.48	1.11	6.06	−7.35	−7.24	−14.95
1962.............	1.53	1.13	9.48	−3.81	−3.87	−17.16
1963.............	1.65	1.18	9.25	−3.36	−4.47	−40.06
1964.............	1.66	1.09	10.52	1.23	1.64	−13.46
1965.............	1.90	1.49	17.63	8.19	10.97	24.14
1966.............	1.33	0.92	30.72	5.27	5.62	9.85
1967.............	1.71	1.39	31.69	7.13	6.66	10.54
1968.............	1.38	1.00	9.78	1.63	1.42	−6.19
1969.............	1.14	0.83	11.66	3.45	3.48	−1.54
1970.............	1.15	0.85	30.44	4.63	4.80	2.24
Mean............	1.52	1.12	16.16	1.43	1.61	−4.70

Year	Debt to total assets (*per-cent*)	Debt to net worth (*per-cent*)	Times interest earned X	Cash turn-over X	Inven-tory turn-over X	Fixed assets turn-over X	Sales to net worth X	Total assets turn-over X	Aver-age collec-tion period (*days*)
1960.........	60.48	184.80	−0.63	19.85	18.48	1.14	2.66	0.87	44.23
1961.........	69.45	237.42	−3.46	17.69	18.58	1.12	2.95	0.86	35.96
1962.........	72.96	276.35	−1.37	15.32	16.01	1.18	3.32	0.88	38.77
1963.........	84.25	547.20	−1.47	12.50	14.43	1.60	7.23	1.11	31.26
1964.........	86.93	735.31	0.47	17.63	13.32	1.58	9.56	1.13	29.87
1965.........	71.38	258.94	3.49	9.21	18.66	1.62	4.13	1.14	28.55
1966.........	70.35	250.21	2.35	27.12	15.56	1.14	3.25	0.91	34.79
1967.........	68.52	234.08	3.09	7.13	16.53	1.12	2.71	0.79	41.34
1968.........	74.93	321.01	0.43	15.45	15.45	0.99	3.27	0.76	34.55
1969.........	77.32	354.12	0.90	18.27	16.50	1.11	3.87	0.84	35.30
1970.........	78.56	386.19	1.20	16.00	16.45	1.15	4.23	0.86	34.15
Mean.........	74.10	344.15	0.46	16.02	16.36	1.25	4.29	0.92	35.34

EXHIBIT 8 (*Concluded*)

(source and application of funds—millions of dollars)

Year	Net income	Depreciation and amortization	Internal sources	New debt	New equity	Total sources	Dividends paid
1961......	−14.97	41.93	26.96	11.49	5.39	43.84	0.81
1962......	−14.90	43.56	28.66	−2.35	1.55	27.86	0.0
1963......	−19.66	45.32	25.66	21.04	−18.08	28.62	0.0
1964......	−5.83	40.03	34.20	50.15	0.08	84.43	0.0
1965......	29.67	48.93	78.60	−12.07	49.90	116.43	0.0
1966......	15.02	39.21	54.23	56.64	17.45	128.31	2.80
1967......	24.11	48.15	72.26	148.81	71.18	292.26	5.11
1968......	−11.94	65.24	53.30	160.86	3.68	217.84	6.60
1969......	−2.32	77.50	75.18	12.32	3.15	90.65	3.75
1970......	5.46	83.34	88.80	71.46	−0.03	160.24	0.81

Year	Capital spending	Other investments	Increase in working capital	Total uses	Increase in cash	Increase in receivables	Increase in inventory
1961........	51.00	0.33	−8.30	43.84	1.90	−6.50	0.0
1962........	27.00	−2.44	3.30	27.86	2.10	1.50	2.10
1963........	35.10	−16.38	9.90	28.62	9.60	−0.20	6.60
1964........	82.50	−0.47	2.40	84.43	−4.90	3.50	6.50
1965........	90.70	1.83	23.90	116.43	31.60	5.80	−3.90
1966........	159.70	0.11	−34.30	128.31	−36.80	7.60	4.70
1967........	195.50	28.35	63.30	292.26	73.90	27.20	7.90
1968........	232.40	19.44	−40.60	217.84	−44.00	−4.00	8.40
1969........	114.20	−2.40	−24.90	90.65	−0.60	13.60	4.50
1970........	210.29	−56.91	6.04	160.24	13.11	6.76	6.33

EXHIBIT 9
NORTH PLAINS AIRLINES
Trans Lift Airlines—Selected financial data
(income statement data—millions of dollars)

Year	Net sales	Operating income	Depreciation amortization	Fixed charges	Income taxes	Net income	E.P.S. as reported
1960.....	86.60	10.37	7.76	1.70	0.60	0.72	0.04
1961.....	89.40	10.23	7.72	2.07	0.47	0.74	0.07
1962.....	94.50	12.36	8.03	1.88	1.34	2.43	0.14
1963.....	98.50	12.02	8.12	1.77	1.07	1.26	0.07
1964.....	109.70	19.67	8.38	1.67	4.39	5.97	0.34
1965.....	129.30	23.78	10.01	1.86	3.60	9.45	0.53
1966.....	187.80	39.50	15.08	4.86	3.07	17.82	1.01
1967....	256.40	40.85	26.39	11.66	0.0	4.70	0.27
1968.....	294.10	51.77	24.97	13.39	2.98	10.41	0.58
1969.....	325.65	47.77	27.58	13.31	1.62	6.22	0.34
1970.....	325.59	286.53	27.92	12.77	−1.19	−2.64	−0.14

(balance sheet data—millions of dollars)

Year	Cash and equivalent	Receivables	Inventory	Current assets	Net plant	Total assets	Funded debt	Common equity
1960.....	5.70	8.90	3.90	19.60	69.20	91.50	40.00	36.71
1961.....	4.00	11.10	3.80	19.90	72.80	95.30	40.70	37.54
1962.....	7.50	9.50	4.20	22.30	71.60	95.90	35.70	38.79
1963.....	7.70	9.20	3.80	21.60	71.00	94.60	32.80	40.05
1964.....	8.80	10.70	3.60	24.10	72.20	98.80	29.90	45.72
1965.....	9.40	14.80	4.30	29.40	97.30	130.30	51.10	54.88
1966.....	23.40	28.20	7.90	60.40	210.50	309.70	204.80	83.22
1967.....	13.60	40.70	12.70	68.70	288.90	378.00	199.00	74.45
1968.....	13.90	43.90	17.80	78.30	270.70	372.50	213.90	83.74
1969.....	14.70	41.50	17.60	76.00	273.70	376.20	200.80	87.58
1970.....	18.87	46.11	16.32	84.97	244.52	367.02	194.98	81.68

EXHIBIT 9 *(Continued)*

(ratio analysis)

Year	Current ratio X	Quick ratio X	Gross operating margin (percent)	Net operating margin (percent)	Return on total capital (percent)	Return on common equity (percent)
1960..........	2.04	1.64	26.99	3.49	3.69	1.96
1961..........	1.91	1.55	26.54	3.67	3.86	1.98
1962..........	1.77	1.44	28.36	5.98	6.78	6.26
1963..........	1.77	1.46	27.47	4.16	4.98	3.14
1964..........	1.87	1.59	32.82	10.97	14.00	13.06
1965..........	2.10	1.79	34.35	11.53	12.82	17.22
1966..........	2.88	2.50	37.34	13.71	8.92	21.41
1967..........	0.80	0.65	32.45	6.38	5.61	6.32
1968..........	1.38	1.07	32.86	9.11	8.48	12.44
1969..........	1.09	0.84	29.47	6.50	6.90	7.10
1970..........	1.20	0.97	27.71	2.74	3.02	−3.23
Mean.........	1.71	1.41	30.58	7.11	7.19	7.97

Year	Debt to total assets (per-cent)	Debt to net worth (per-cent)	Times interest earned X	Cash turn-over X	Inven-tory turn-over X	Fixed assets turn-over X	Sales to net worth X	Total assets turn-over X	Average collection period (days)
1960...	54.21	135.13	1.78	15.19	22.21	1.25	2.36	0.95	37.51
1961...	53.62	136.13	1.58	22.35	23.53	1.23	2.38	0.94	45.32
1962...	50.36	124.52	3.01	12.60	22.50	1.32	2.44	0.99	36.69
1963...	47.57	112.37	2.32	12.79	25.92	1.39	2.46	1.04	34.09
1964...	43.32	93.61	7.20	12.47	30.47	1.52	2.40	1.11	35.60
1965...	49.96	118.63	8.02	13.76	30.07	1.33	2.36	0.99	41.78
1966...	72.91	271.34	5.30	8.03	23.77	0.89	2.26	0.61	54.81
1967...	75.50	383.36	1.40	18.85	20.19	0.89	3.44	0.68	57.94
1968...	72.62	323.04	2.00	21.16	16.52	1.09	3.51	0.79	54.48
1969...	71.88	308.76	1.59	22.15	18.50	1.19	3.72	0.87	46.51
1970...	72.46	325.61	0.70	17.26	19.95	1.33	3.99	0.89	51.69
Mean...	60.40	212.04	3.17	16.05	23.06	1.22	2.85	0.89	45.13

EXHIBIT 9 (Concluded)

(source and application of funds—millions of dollars)

Year	Net income	Depreciation amortization	Internal sources	New debt	New equity	Total sources	Dividends paid
1961....	0.74	7.72	8.46	2.17	0.53	11.16	0.44
1962....	2.43	8.03	10.46	−2.85	−0.00	7.61	1.18
1963....	1.26	8.12	9.38	−2.16	−0.00	7.22	0.0
1964....	5.97	8.38	14.35	−2.18	−0.00	12.17	0.29
1965....	9.45	10.01	19.46	21.25	−0.01	40.70	0.29
1966....	17.82	15.08	32.90	144.06	11.99	188.95	1.47
1967....	4.70	26.39	31.09	11.67	−12.00	30.76	1.47
1968....	10.41	24.97	35.38	15.01	0.03	50.42	1.15
1969....	6.22	27.58	33.80	−13.14	0.08	20.74	2.46
1970....	−2.64	27.92	25.28	−4.66	0.00	20.62	3.26

Year	Capital spending	Other investments	Increase in working capital	Total uses	Increase in cash	Increase in receivables	Increase in inventory
1961.......	−0.00	11.22	−0.50	11.16	−1.70	2.20	−0.10
1962.......	−0.00	6.23	0.20	7.61	3.50	−1.60	0.40
1963.......	−0.00	7.52	−0.30	7.22	0.20	−0.30	−0.40
1964.......	−0.00	10.08	1.80	12.17	1.10	1.50	−0.20
1965.......	36.10	0.11	4.20	40.70	0.60	4.10	0.70
1966.......	120.60	42.88	24.00	188.95	14.00	13.40	3.60
1967.......	112.60	−26.21	−57.10	30.76	−9.80	12.50	4.80
1968.......	−0.00	9.87	39.40	50.42	0.30	3.20	5.10
1969.......	23.70	9.88	−15.30	20.74	0.80	−2.40	−0.20
1970.......	12.23	−2.46	7.60	20.62	4.17	4.61	−1.28

OPTICAL CHARACTER SCANNING, INC.

Optical Character Scanning, Inc. (OCS) has developed a low-cost high-performance Optical Character Recognition machine (OCR) which now permits preparation of data for entry into computers, data processing systems, and communications links at costs as low as 1 percent of conventional means. As part of their financial planning efforts, the firm needs a budgeting system to assist in determining the firm's financial requirements over the next four years.

Optical Character Recognition machines (OCR) are devices which read ordinary typewriter print and hand-lettered numerical information. They are being used to read information from original documents (source documents) directly into data processing and communications systems.

A total of fewer than 1,000 OCR machines are estimated to be in service today. Of these, few read more than 70 percent of the available source documents. Almost all are priced in excess of $50,000—a large percentage in excess of $100,000.

Although electronic data processing was introduced in the early 1950's, general acceptance did not occur until the early 1960's. Today, an estimated 100,000 computer main frames are reported to be in operation with many authorities estimating as many as 400,000 by 1980. Data processing, the fastest growing large industry, has now become the third in size, exceeded only by the automotive and petroleum industries.

A typical electronic data processing installation consists of the computer main frame which must be augmented by peripherals such as magnetic tape and disk units which store and input-output large bulks of data; IBM card readers and punches for data input and output; printers, and an assortment of specialized input and output devices. The installation consumes data collected at a wide variety of locations from a wide variety of documents. Generally the data on these documents is retranscribed for entry into the data processor through manual entry of the data into a keyboard unit.

In the evolution of data processing and computing systems, different components successively became the limiting item in achieving more reliable and faster throughput. Initially the central processor was the limiting item. Then the several levels of memory systems became more important. At another period, the software systems received the major attention. In recent years continuing technological advances have resulted in minimizing the problems of the above areas and have emphasized the need for a better form of information input to the computer.

From the beginning, punched cards have represented the major form of data input. Recently key-to-tape and key-to-disk systems provided a modest improvement in decreasing cost in this area. It is quite clear, however, that the ultimate in efficiency and low cost would eliminate the keyboard step completely and provide a means of reading source documents directly. Optical character recognition provides this means, and it is broadly agreed that OCR will indeed be the ultimate method for widespread data processing input.

Since OCR machines have been in use for over 10 years, why then has this market not developed more strongly to date? The answer is partly based on the complexity of OCR technology and partly on computer system development—The problem of data input has not quite reached the crisis stage. The early OCR machines were inherently costly, due to the then available technology, and hence to justify the cost to the user, very high performance was built into the machines. There was almost a competition between suppliers to provide the highest possible reading rate coupled with flexibility to accommodate a wide variety of type fonts. The logic design permissible with the available semiconductor technology was relatively cumbersome and expensive. Long life sources of monochromatic light for document illumination, which permit low-cost optics, were not yet available.

As a result of the above, the major uses of OCR to date have been in those applications requiring extremely high-volume activity. For example, the oil companies have extensively used OCR to read individual charge tickets on machines which processed 20,000 or more tickets per hour. Other users included banks and insurance companies with large volumes of premium slips and payment coupons. Another significant substantial user is the utilities industry for monthly billing activities. While these volume users represent an appreciable market volume, it is clear that this market is limited.

OCS recognizes the need for a different approach to the use of OCR. With the data processing industry's present rate of growth, it is estimated that by 1975 an acute shortage will exist for keypunch and key-tape operators to prepare the vast quantities of data requiring processing. More than a half-million IBM keypunches are now in service with IBM's production continuing at an annual rate well in excess of 60,000. Keyboard to magnetic tape, now in its fourth year of production, has reached an annual rate of 20,000 units. To accommodate the anticipated needs of this exploding industry, a breakthrough is required in the methods for input of data to the data processing systems. With the technology now available, Optical Character Recognition (OCR) finally provides opportunity for the urgently required breakthrough. The Optical Character Scanning System Z/OCR will prove to be less costly than keyboarding of data at an estimated 20,000 data processing facilities now in operation throughout the nation.

OCS intends to mass-produce their SYSTEM Z using the very latest design concepts and components, including lasers and the latest integrated-circuits. The extremely flexible, modest speed, low-cost OCR machine will economically justify replacement of as few as three keypunch operations. Though of modest cost, the machine is still sufficiently powerful to be able to replace 100 or more keypunch operators in many single-shift installations. SYSTEM Z will sell for $25,000 to $35,000 with a factory cost for the first year's production averaging $10,750 and a production factory cost thereafter varying between $6,500 and $9,000 depending on the output options. An estimated 18,000 data processing systems today use six or more keypunches,[1] and as such are candidates for one or more SYSTEM Z.

The basic technical approach for the design of such a low-cost OCR machine susceptible to mass production has been demonstrated in the existing SYSTEM Z preproduction prototype. Unique optics and refined document handling coupled with the innovative automatic format controls permit SYSTEM Z to read a greater variety of source documents than previously has been considered practical.

To determine the cost savings possible through operation of SYSTEM Z consider the monthly cost of the machine to be one fortieth of a $30,000 purchase price ($34.50 per day), the cost of an operator to be $650 per month ($31 per day), and the cost of electricity and floor space to be $100 per month ($4.75 per day). The daily cost for a five-day week then becomes $70 per day. Operating seven hours out of a single eight-hour shift, the operating speeds of SYSTEM Z permit data to be transcribed from one-line documents for ½ cent per document and for double-spaced, 80 character lines on 8½ × 11 sheets of paper at 2½ cents per full page. The generally accepted cost of verified keypunched data in IBM cards is $1 to $1.50 per thousand characters. Thus, even

---

[1] Optical Character Recognition Industry 1968-73—Creative Strategies, Inc.

a document containing but one line of data with as few as four characters on that line could be processed as economically on SYSTEM Z as it could be keypunched, while data recorded on a full typewritten sheet could be processed for less than 1 cent per thousand characters—less than 1 percent of the accepted cost of keypunching. For further comparisons, the curves in Exhibit 1 have been prepared in the outline of Auerbach[2] using his keypunch cost figures and his typist costs for the manual retyping of documents when necessary to make them readable by an OCR machine.

In most industrial environments, particularly the smaller industries, management can discipline the personnel in the accounting, production and planning departments to use but one typewriter type style. Thus basic data from such departments for entry into a data processor may be produced as alphabetical and numerical information recorded on typewritten sheets of paper. Once the basic alphabetical descriptive information (i.e., employees name, inventory descriptions, etc.) has been entered into the data processor, transactions pertaining thereto are generally purely numeric, either as typewritten or hand-lettered numerical information. Hence SYSTEM Z was designed to recognize a single alphameric type font and the hand-lettered numerical digits. To increase throughput through any OCR machine, OCS recommends use of the type font which was optimized for machine recognition, OCR-A, in preference to other more common optional fonts. However SYSTEM Z can be provided for other fonts (Pica, Elite, and so forth) on special order at added cost. Although Auerbach does not expect OCR systems in general to process more than 30 percent of the source documents, OCS expects SYSTEM Z, with its automatic format provisions, to accurately process more than 50 percent of all submitted source documents without need for retyping.

THE MARKET

The OCS SYSTEM Z is intended to be used as a direct replacement for the present manual keyboard entry of data read from original source documents by a human operator. Direct automatic machine reading of a material percentage of such documents is expected with SYSTEM Z. More than 500,000 keypunches which produce the common Hollerith (or IBM) punched card are now in service, and it is understood that production is continuing at a rate in excess of 60,000 per year. In addition, key-to-tape units have reached an annual rate of 20,000. From the curves in Exhibit 1, it can be seen that the OCS unit can be economically justified for installations employing as few as three to five keypunch operators. When reading full typewritten sheets of paper, SYSTEM Z is also capable of reading data as fast as 50, 70-word-per-minute typists

---

[2] Auerbach Information, Philadelphia, Pennsylvania.

could produce it. Using the cost figures of Auerbach an installation where 25 keypunch operators were employed could effect a saving of $12,000 per month if 50 percent of the source documents could be read by SYSTEM Z without retyping. The full cost of the OCS/OCR machine in such an operation could be recovered within three months after its activation. In most installations where the machine work load justifies half of a second shift and where 50 percent of the source documents can be read, the full purchase price should be recovered in but one month of operation.

On a conservative basis, it is assumed that two OCS units should be the minimum installation so as to avoid a single failure disabling the user's entire operation. With this approach, all installations having six or more keypunch machines constitute a potential market for OCS. It is estimated by an independent market research organization that some 18,000 data processing centers use six or more keypunches, and hence are candidates for the OCS machines. The combination of these existing installations, the continuing large sales of keypunch, key-to-tape, and key-to-disk units, and the tremendous continuing growth of the entire data processing industry, all lead to a very substantial existing market plus a rapidly expanding future one. The financial projections in a later section of this presentation are based on shipments of approximately 100, 400, 1,000, and 2,400 units in the years 1972, 1973, 1974, and 1975. With the early start and planned aggressive marketing program, these figures may be overly conservative, based on both the total OCR market and on a reasonable share of that market.

The highly effective introduction of key-tape units during the past few years must be recognized as a superb marketing accomplishment. The pioneer in this field, Mohawk Data Sciences, accomplished phenomenal growth in its formative years by successfully marketing the key-to-tape concept to the very large existing keypunch users market. Although providing only a relatively modest (25 percent) throughput advantage over keypunch machines, the marketing force was able to expand sales from zero to the present rate of 20,000 per year in only a few years.

THE PRODUCT

SYSTEM Z is a compact optical character recognition machine designed to read information typewritten on sheets of paper using a single typewriter font (preferably OCR-A). Automatic self-programming of the machine is provided by preceding each run of data with a conditioning document that indicates where data is located on the succeeding stack of forms. Data is read at a maximum rate of five lines per second from forms preprinted from a wide selection of printing inks. Input hoppers and output stackers are designed to accommodate documents of almost any size up to legal size sheets and of thickness varying from onion skin to card stock. SYSTEM Z may be operated unattended when the completeness of the source documents so justifies. The machine reads the complete upper case alphabet (A through Z), numerics 0 through 9, plus 20 typewritten control codes from documents containing up to 80 characters per line. In addition, SYSTEM Z reads up to 40 characters per line of handwritten numerical data, digits 0 through 9 and control symbols.

FINANCING

The total equity financing requirements of the proposed company for 1971 through 1975 are forcasted at $2,050,000. In July 1971, the founders contributed $300,000 and received 300,000 shares at a par value of $1 per share. They also received warrants to purchase an additional 1,500,000 shares at the same rate for a period of 10 years. The warrants were issued to compensate the founders for starting the firm. They brought to the firm (1) an expertise in data processing and OCR technology, and (2) a cohesive management team used to working together and making a direct labor contribution to the extent of $1,000,000 in value without salary reimbursements.

Of the $300,000 contribution, $26,000 was used to purchase testing and office equipment as shown in Exhibit 7. As of December 31, 1971, the equipment had been depreciated for six months and $274,000 remained in the cash account.

A private placement to investors will be made January 1972 for 750,000 shares at a $1 par value. $750,000 will be realized. In addition, the investors will receive warrants to be exercised for 1,000,000 shares of stock at $1 par value. It is assumed that the warrants will be exercised by the fourth quarter of 1972, and that the firm will realize an additional $1,000,000 at that time.

In addition, the founders agree not to exercise their warrants until a cash dividend of at least $4 per share is paid, and no earlier than the first quarter of 1976. It should be noted that short-term borrowing is not limited, but salaries and bonus payments to officers must be approved by the investors.

THE COMPANY

OCS follows the general pattern of peripheral equipment manufacturers in the data processing industry. Extremely high marketing costs and engineering costs, low manufacturing costs and relatively low capital equipment investment. Inventories are high and receivables are somewhat slow due to various acceptance criteria by the industry. There is a significant trend toward third-party leasing which means that much equipment is sold rather than leased. This is beneficial to the smaller firm just starting out in business that has little cash to invest in long-term leases.

The unit selling price is expected to average $30,000 from 1972–74. In 1975, the firm expects to market a machine that will double in speed and throughput without affecting manufacturing costs. The average price is then expected to rise to $36,000 per unit.

To assist in the development of the product, an engineering staff of 14 people will be hired in 1972. This will increase to 20 persons by 1975. Their area of emphasis is in new product design and product improvement. Their salaries will range from $164,000 plus 10 percent fringe benefits in 1972 to $321,000 by 1975. Their expenses are considered part of the manufacturing overhead account shown in Exhibit 10.

The marketing areas will be directed by a vice president of marketing to be hired in early 1972. OCS products will be sold through a national organization of direct factory salesmen. Direct sales commissions of $2,250 or 7½ percent of total sales will be paid to salesmen. They will receive a draw of $14,000 per year and will receive expenses commensurate with the territory. They are expected to earn an average of $28,000 per year. Each sales district will be supervised by a district manager who is expected to function as both manager and key account salesman. He is expected to earn an average of $35,000 per year.

Twelve major sales offices will be established over a three-and-a-half-year period. Each office, in addition to sales personnel, will have a salaried sales secretary and sufficient technical support to install and maintain the equipment in that particular territory.

To assist in the sales effort, an advertising budget is set forth in Exhibit 9 that will cover trade shows, magazine literature, and institutional advertising. Other associated selling costs are also shown in Exhibit 9.

Sales commissions will be paid salesmen at the time funds are received from sales. Since this is anticipated to take some time after shipment, it is assumed that accruals for commission will equal commissions earned during the last two months of each year.

Salaries will be accrued at the rate of 10 percent to compensate for one-week holdback, plus a week's separation fund per year of service, plus vacation pay, plus sick and other personnel-oriented activities. There will be no accrual on direct labor since the production labor cost is paid weekly and benefits are paid directly to the union to be disbursed to the production employees.

Given the information in the following exhibits, management must now develop a cash budget and pro forma income statements and balance sheets for the years 1972–75.

EXHIBIT 1
OCS., INC.
Monthly cost versus work load for keypunching and OCS-OCR

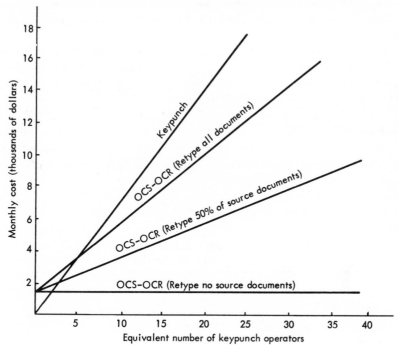

EXHIBIT 2
OCS., INC.
Sales forecast
(figures in units and dollars)

Month	1972	1973	1974	1975
January.................		15	50	125
February...............		15	50	125
March.................	2	20	70	150
April..................	3	20	70	150
May...................	5	30	70	150
June..................	5	30	70	150
July..................	10	30	70	200
August................	10	40	100	250
September.............	10	50	100	250
October...............	12	50	100	250
November.............	12	50	100	300
December.............	12	50	100	300
Total Units.........	81	400	950	2,400
Average Sales price per unit.................	$ 30,000	$ 30,000	$ 30,000	$ 36,000
Total Annual Sales...	$2,430,000	$12,000,000	$28,500,000	$86,400,000

1. Assume a 50 percent tax rate when developing the Income Statements.
2. Assume all taxes for one year paid in the following year.

EXHIBIT 3
OCS., INC.
Cash collection from sales

Items	1972	1973	1974	1975
Collection from sales of goods from November and December of previous year.......	0	$ 720,000	$ 3,000,000	$ 6,000,000
Collections from sales of goods sold from January–October of current year............	$1,710,000	$9,000,000	$22,500,000	$64,800,000
Total Annual Collections.....	$1,710,000	$9,720,000	$25,500,000	$70,800,000
Year-end Accounts Receivable balance..................	$ 720,000	$3,000,000	$ 6,000,000	$ 600,000

1. Collections lag behind sales by 60 days due to shipping installation delays.
2. No bad debt account is considered due to the high credit rating demanded by OCS for credit extensions.

EXHIBIT 4
OCS., INC.
Production budget and finished goods inventory
(figures in units)

Finished goods	1972	1973	1974	1975
Annual sales..................	81	400	950	2,400
Desired ending inventory.......	30	100	250	300
Delete beginning inventory......	0	30	100	250
Yearly production.............	111	470	1,100	2,450

1. Year-end inventory equals January and February sales of the following year.
2. No provision is made for work in process inventory.
3. FIFO method of inventory valuation is used.

EXHIBIT 5
OCS., INC.
Estimated unit cost breakdown

Item	1972	1973	1974	1975
Direct labor.....................	$ 1,500	$1,200	$1,100	$1,000
Recognition circuits..............	4,000	3,500	2,300	2,900
Documentary track..............	700	700	650	600
Cabinets.......................	600	500	500	450
Controls.......................	1,000	900	750	650
Fibre optics....................	150	150	120	110
Lasers.........................	300	300	250	225
Power supply...................	500	500	450	410
Tape drive.....................	2,000	1,800	1,500	1,300
Total Labor and Materials........	$10,750	$9,550	$8,520	$7,645
Units produced.................	111	470	1,100	2,450

1. Assume all material purchases are paid in month they are incurred.
2. Assume a raw material ending inventory equal to 30, 100, 250, and 300 units, respectively, in 1972–74. These are also equivalent in number to the units of finished goods ending inventory.

EXHIBIT 6
OCS., INC.
Wage expenses schedule

	1972	*1973*	*1974*	*1975*	*1976*
General and administrative:					
Wages.................	$82,800	$187,100	$287,200	$406,800	
10 percent fringe.......	8,300	18,700	28,700	40,700	
Total Wages..........	$91,100	$205,800	$315,900	$447,500	
Disbursed accruals from previous year........	—	9,100	20,600	31,600	$44,800
Current year salaries disbursed...........	82,000	185,200	284,300	402,700	
Total Disbursements....	$82,000	$194,300	$304,900	$434,300	
Marketing:					
Wages.................	$342,000	$1,110,800	$2,785,900	$6,909,000	
10 percent fringe	34,200	111,100	278,600	691,000	
Total Wages	$376,200	$1,221,900	$3,064,500	$7,600,000	
Disbursed accruals from previous year........	—	37,600	122,200	306,500	$760,000
Current year salaries disbursed...........	338,600	1,099,700	2,758,000	6,840,000	
Total Disbursements....	$338,600	$1,137,300	$2,880,200	$7,146,500	
Direct labor:					
Wages.................	$166,500	$564,000	$1,210,000	$2,450,000	
Engineering:					
Wages.................	$152,400	$222,500	$266,500	$316,300	
10 percent fringe	15,200	22,300	26,700	31,700	
Total Wages	$167,600	$244,800	$293,200	$348,000	
Disbursed accruals from previous year........	—	16,800	24,500	29,300	$34,800
Current year salaries disbursed...........	150,800	220,300	263,900	313,200	
Total Disbursements....	$150,800	$237,100	$288,400	$342,500	
Material control:					
Wages.................	—	$64,800	$ 97,200	$171,100	
10 percent fringe.......	—	6,500	9,700	17,100	
Total Wages	—	$71,300	$106,900	$188,200	
Disbursed accruals from previous year........	—	—	7,100	10,600	$18,800
Current year salaries disbursed...........	—	64,200	96,200	169,400	
Total Disbursements....	—	$64,200	$103,300	$180,000	
Sales commissions:					
Sales.................	$2,430,000	$12,000,000	$28,500,000	$86,400,000	
Commissions earned at 7.5 percent of sales....	$ 182,250	$ 900,000	$ 2,137,500	$ 6,480,000	
Sales commissions paid...	$ 128,250	$ 729,000	$ 1,912,250	$ 5,310,000	
Sales commission accrued at December 31st.....	$ 54,000	$ 171,000	$ 225,000	$ 1,170,000	

EXHIBIT 7
OCS., INC.
Annual capital expenditures

Equipment	1971	1972	1973	1974	1975	Totals
Test gear.........	$20,000	$ 40,000	$100,000	$ 50,000	—	$210,000
Tooling...........	—	210,000	—	—	$ 30,000	240,000
Production........	—	30,000	60,000	60,000	—	150,000
Line equipment....	—	10,000	25,000	25,000	—	60,000
Office equipment ...	6,000	25,000	15,000	30,000	60,000	136,000
Computer.........	—	—	—	—	75,000	75,000
Total.............	$26,000	$315.000	$200,000	$165,000	$165,000	$871,000

1. All equipment is depreciated for five years using straight-line depreciation.
2. Office equipment is assumed to be used in the factory for indirect labor. Thus all depreciation is applied to the Factory Overhead account.
3. Assume all assets are purchased January 1 of each year and at the end of the year 1 full year of depreciation can be taken.

EXHIBIT 8
OCS., INC.
Other general and administrative expenses

	1972	1973	1974	1975
Travel..........................	$2,000	$3,000	$4,000	$ 5,000
Telephone......................	2,000	3,000	4,000	5,000
Office supplies..................	1,000	2,000	3,000	5,000
General counsel.................	2,000	4,000	8,000	10,000
Miscellaneous expenses...........	1,000	4,000	8,000	10,000
Auditors.......................	2,000	3,000	8,000	10,000

1. Note that in developing the Income Statement and Cash Budget, general and administrative salaries must also be considered.

EXHIBIT 9
OCS., INC.
Other selling expenses

	1972	1973	1974	1975
Travel and entertainment....	$ 1,000	$ 5,000	$ 10,000	$ 20,000
Telephone...............	2,000	6,000	12,000	24,000
Automobile expense........	5,000	8,000	12,000	24,000
Freight and installation......	10,000	20,000	40,000	80,000
Advertising..............	50,000	120,000	300,000	600,000

1. Note that in developing the Cash Budget and Income Statement, selling and distribution salaries as well as sales commissions must be considered.

EXHIBIT 10
OCS., INC.
Manufacturing overhead

	1972	1973	1974	1975
Indirect Materials:				
Used in production.......	$ 810	$ 4,000	$ 9,500	$ 24,000
Office supplies...........	810	4,000	9,500	24,000
Other expenses:				
Rent...................	40,000	200,000	400,000	700,000
Utilities...............	1,200	6,000	12,000	24,000
Insurance..............	2,430	12,000	28,500	86,400
Machine maintenance.....	4,000	8,000	12,000	12,000

1. When developing the manufacturing overhead schedule for the Cash Budget and Income Statement, one must include depreciation, and the indirect labor of engineering and material control.

B. QUANTITATIVE FINANCIAL TOOLS

WESTWIND SENICRUISE AIRLINES

WESTWIND SENICRUISE AIRLINES, a Southern California-based supplemental carrier, has just taken delivery of a new McDonnell Douglas DC-10 trijet airbus. The new plane is expected to substantially reduce seat mile costs and other direct operating costs for the airline's charter operations; but Mr. Russ Packer, vice president of operations is wondering what mix of first-class, coach, and economy seats will maximize the luxury jet's 2,100 square feet of floor space.

COMPANY BACKGROUND

Westwind was organized in July 1971 by two men, Russ Packer and Bruce Jones. Mr. Packer had been an aerospace engineer with NASA; and Mr. Jones an airline consultant. Early in 1971, Mr. Packer was laid off from NASA as the Apollo program slowed, and Mr. Jones had trouble finding consulting work as airline profits began to sag. By combining personal funds and bank loans, they were able to purchase a 145-passenger used Boeing 707 aircraft from Trans World Airlines for $2.5 million in August 1971. Pilots were easily obtained due to recent airline flight crew layoffs.

In September 1971, the CAB granted the carrier a supplemental certificate to carry passengers between Los Angeles, San Diego and San Francisco and Hawaii by charter agreement. At the same time, a maintenance agreement was signed with Continental Airlines in Los Angeles. Other overhead costs remained at low levels while the charter sales advanced dramatically as the economy expanded in late 1971. Through extensive marketing to travel agents, social clubs, and student groups, traffic had picked up by mid-1972 and a larger airplane was needed to handle the demand. Consequently, the 707 was sold and a new 250-seat DC-10 was purchased.

PRESENT DILEMMA

As he sat in his office, Mr. Packer knew that the seat mix decision must be made today. Mr. Jones had determined from recent market studies that an average of 80 first-class, 100 coach, and 200 economy seats could be sold for each flight at $170, $140, and $135, respectively. In evaluating various interior combinations, Mr. Packer had determined that setup costs and varying area allotments would have to be $25 and 10 square feet for first class, $20 and 8 square feet for coach, and $17 and 6 square feet for economy. The total cost of the plane was $16.5 million, excluding galley costs of $1.5 million, extra navigational equipment of $400,000, landing fees of $4,000 per flight, fuel and maintenance fees of $10,000 per flight, and pilot and crew salaries of $100,000 per year. In addition, Mr. Jones had budgeted only $5,000 for interior setup costs.

PART B

In November 1973, Mr. Jones was asked to give a talk before the Southern California Financial Analysts Society to discuss the 1974 outlook for Westwind. He felt he should be prepared to give a sales estimate for each DC-10 flight, but he wanted to use only 90 percent capacity in each section of the plane so that if traffic sagged from the 100 percent figure he wouldn't be placed in a poor competitive view with other airlines.

PART C

In January 1974, the CAB granted a 3 percent fare increase; and Mr. Packer was debating whether or not to spend an additional $2,000 to change the seating mix of the company's plane.

QUALITY APPLIANCE COMPANY, INCORPORATED (A)

QUALITY APPLIANCE COMPANY, INC. (QACI) was a small, fairly sophisticated manufacturing company producing refrigerators and dishwashers. Being a small company, they were constantly in strong competition with the larger manufacturers. Because of their size and volume production methods, the larger companies could generally produce these items more cheaply than QACI.

As a result of this, QACI did not attempt to compete on a volume-price basis with the larger firms in the industry, but instead exploited any technological modifications in the products as fully as possible before the larger firms developed the same. QACI's resourcefulness and technical know-how kept them well ahead in their struggle for survival in the appliance business.

The sustained demand for the company's products during the first three quarters of 1972 plus the efforts of the employees had brought sales to an all time high.

Mr. Tom Price, the vice president of manufacturing was planning his production for the last quarter. He had the burden of keeping up the efficient optimum operation of the previous quarters.

The success of the last quarter had resulted in a total sellout and the company was left with hardly any inventory. The supply for the high demand for QACI's products was only restricted by the company's own operational and financial constraints.

Mr. Price was faced with the immediate task of ordering raw materials for the next quarter. Next year some further technical changes in the refrigerators and dishwashers were expected. While these continued, some slack in the operation was expected. Mr. Price, in his planning, decided to have in stock an ending inventory of 300 refrigerators and 100 dishwashers.

For the next 13 weeks, a 40-hour week, one shift a day was envisaged. Each product went through two processes; namely manufacturing and assembly. The manufacturing division employed 10 men while the assembly employed 6. Typically, for the refrigerator, each unit required two hours of manufacturing time and one hour of assembly time. Similarly, a dishwasher could be produced with 1.5 hour of manufacturing time and 1.5 hour of assembly time.

The labor rates in the two departments also varied. The manufacturing labor rates were $4.20 per hour and assembly labor rates were $3.80 per hour. These labor rates included a 28 percent provision for FICA and SDI payments which were made after the end of the quarter. The wages, however, were paid weekly and could be accrued for one week.

The refrigerator sold at the wholesale price of $97.50 and the dishwasher at $87. The company followed the industry practice of n/30 collection terms for refrigerators and n/45 for dishwashers. No bad debts were expected.

The raw materials for the refrigerator and the dishwasher ran at $42 and $39 per unit, respectively. Commonly, the trade accounts were payable on the n/30 terms. The suppliers to QACI would provide a maximum line of credit of $37,000. The other variable costs, including selling expenses, paid out at production time included $18 for refrigerators and $16 for dishwashers.

At the beginning of the quarter, Mr. Price looked at the balance sheet and considered the following figures relevant to analysis:

Beginning Cash Balance............	$58,000
Accounts Receivable...............	72,000
Trade Accounts Payable............	30,000
Notes Payable....................	42,000
Wages Payable...................	3,000

Mr. Price also wanted to provide for an ending cash balance of $130,000 in his planning. Upon consultation with the bank, he learned that for the last quarter's operation he would be able to borrow up to a ceiling amount (including notes payable of $42,000) of $110,000, if necessary. Mr. Price preferred to maintain a quick ratio of at least 1.00 as this was the industry practice and one of the requirements of the trade credit suppliers.

With all the above facts in mind, Mr. Price called in a hired MBA graduate. He was assigned the task of determining the optimum number of dishwashers and refrigerators to be produced in the next 13 weeks which would maximize the contribution to overhead and profits.

QUALITY APPLIANCE COMPANY, INCORPORATED (B)

AN OUTSIDE CONTRACTOR approached Mr. Price with two propositions as follows:

a) The contractor would provide an additional 1,000 hours of assembly time at $7 per hour. He suggested that this might improve QACI's capabilities further.

b) The second offer by the contractor was to facilitate extra manufacturing hours at $8.20 per hour. It would be up to Mr. Price to specify the extra hours needed.

The contractor, however, could not supply both the assembly and manufacturing times simultaneously.

Mr. Price had just received the solution to Part A from the new MBA employee. He decided to assign him the task of evaluating the above propositions.

In the meantime, QACI's marketing vice president had come up with the suggestion that the company should engage in assembling electric stoves as a subcontractor for a major producer in the field. The contract was for the next quarter. This, he argued, would better utilize the existing capacity of the assembly division. The job would be done on a strict cash basis (payment at delivery) without any outlays for raw material.

In order to get an idea of the proposal's impact on profitability, Mr. Price decided to simplify the computational effort by keeping financial constraints such as bank lending, trade credit limits, and payroll, the same as Part A. He did, however, have to consider the extra factors as follows:

1. The contribution to profit and overhead was expected to be $4 per stove.
2. Some manufacturing time (0.1 hours) per stove will be necessary.
3. Each stove needed an assembly time of 0.5 hours.

Mr. Price was faced with the problem of introducing stoves in his analysis to maximize the profits.

The decision of subcontracting for stoves was to be made independent of the proposals for excess outside manufacturing and assembly time mentioned earlier.

BEAMIR COMPANY

In late October 1971, Charles Lane, treasurer of Beamir Company was reviewing the effect of company policies on company profits. Mr. Lane expected to propose to management a plan which would ultimately be reflected in the production rates, product mix, and profits. It was his intention to determine the optimum production and financial mix which conformed to current management policies and to estimate the effect of changes in management goals on the production and financial mix.

COMPANY HISTORY

The Beamir Company was founded in 1956 by Michael Beamir. The firm currently mass-produces three types of water control valves which are used by municipal and private waterworks. The firm began its relationship with the waterworks industry with a job shop machining operation. By 1962, Beamir had discontinued the job shop operation and had begun producing 20 types of waterworks products. These were various valves, fittings and linkages used primarily in housing construction.

In 1968, Craig Dana, a mechanical engineer was hired by Beamir. Mr. Dana had designed a water control valve, which though not new in concept, was more adaptable to mass production than earlier types. It was decided by management to phase out the other products and to phase in the mass production of the three valves.

In order to raise the capital required to initiate the mass production Beamir decided to incorporate the firm. In 1969, 120,000 shares had been sold at a $1 par value. These shares were all held by Michael Beamir and company management. The funds were used to purchase two special-purpose machines at a cost of $40,000 each. The machines were installed in late 1970 and began full operation in 1971.

MANUFACTURING

A new manufacturing facility was constructed in 1963 at a cost of $400,000. The 50,000-square foot structure occupied a portion of a five-acre site. Beamirs products were processed through a production line made up of four machining areas. Before the purchase of the two special-purpose machines in 1970, all the machining had been done on standard turret lathes and drill presses. In late 1972, Beamir added two more special-purpose machines which completely eliminated the need for any turret lathes or drill presses.

Beamir's labor force of 160 men consisted of foundry workers, machinists, factory helpers, shippers, truckers, clerks, and foremen. They had a 40-hour workweek and they worked 50 weeks per year.

Craig Dana, who was in charge of mechanical engineering, was requested by Mr. Lane to conduct a study on Beamir's production capacity with the four special-purpose machines. Mr. Lane also assigned the company accountant to assist Mr. Dana in the cost analysis. Mr. Lane reminded Dana that management would firmly oppose further reduction in the labor force but would permit an increase, although it was not advisable because of the training requirements. It was suggested that these restrictions be incorporated into the analysis.

During the study it became obvious that although the two original machines had been rated at an 80,000 product-hours capacity per year when new, by 1972 the capacity was down to 60,000 product-hours. It was determined that minimum service would be required as long as the reduced capacity rate was not exceeded.

The two machines purchased in 1972 had a 120,000 product-hours capacity. These two machines, if properly maintained, should be capable of holding a constant production rate. Exhibit 1 displays the capacity rates for the four special-purpose machines. Data was also collected on the time required on each type machine to produce each of the three valves. (See Exhibit 2.)

The analysis of the production capacity also disclosed the number of labor hours required per product. The hours are shown in Exhibit 3.

The cost analysis as constructed by the accountant is shown on Exhibit 4. The selling price noted on the exhibit is net after sales returns and allowances.

SALES

Beamir's sales force had recently been increased by two and by 1972 Beamir had five salesmen. According to Jim Phelps, the sales manager, the two salesmen were added following an analysis of the potential sales in the territories to which they were assigned.

COMPETITION

There were five major competitors in the production of the specialty valves which Beamir produced. The largest competitor held approximately 30 percent of the market. The balance was about evenly shared by the other four producers.

Various factors helped to break up the distribution into regional markets.

1. Numerous potential applications required that the district salesmen should be in close contact with the customers and the mechanical engineering section of the firm.
2. The weight of these valves tended to raise the price due to increased transportation costs.
3. Because of the direct sales approach, customers tended to stay with their original supplier given that the valve quality remained the same and the price was lower than that of another producer who would have to ship from a greater distance.

PRICING POLICY

The factors mentioned above all contributed in keeping the prices relatively constant. Dropping of prices would only lower the revenue within a region. In order to draw sales from another region prices would have to be dropped enough to offset the added shipping expense and to be lower than the regional competitor. Raising the prices would only make the existing market available to competition. Consequently prices remain relatively constant. (See Exhibit 4.)

FINANCIAL REQUIREMENTS

In the examination of the income statements and the balance sheets from 1969 through 1972 it was found that the working capital to net sales requirement was approximately 30 percent. (See Exhibit 5.) Working capital for 1972 was $533,027. Mr. Lane determined that as related to the financial mix, management would be firmly opposed to having insufficient working capital and though not advisable, they would accept an overage in working capital.

Mr. Lane requested that the shipping foreman, the office manager and the sales manager should submit their budgets for 1973. These are shown as fixed expenses in Exhibit 6.

In addition to the fixed expenses mentioned above, an additional $15,166 was expected to be paid out in interest during 1973. After the fixed expenses have been deducted, the net earnings before tax in 1973 will be subject to a tax rate of 48 percent.

In Exhibit 7, the percent of total debt to net worth from 1969 through 1972 is displayed. Beamir's management has not formed a firm policy on the acceptable level of debt, but the general management concensus is that hopefully it will remain at approximately 22 percent. Total debt and net stockholder's equity for 1972 were $199,527 and $908,272, respectively. In order to provide additional short-term funding if needed, an additional line of credit of $50,000 at 6 percent has been made available by Beamir's bankers.

MANAGEMENT'S DIVIDEND POLICY

Based on the increase in earnings before taxes from 1970 to 1971 when the first two machines went into full operation, management fully expects that a similar increase in earnings before taxes between 1972 to 1973 will exist. Management has strongly indicated that the minimum they expect is $150,000 before taxes. Estimated dividend payout for the period was $50,000. Of course, any income greater than this amount is wholly welcomed.

Charles Lane fully expected that through the optimization of the product and financial mix within the flexible but weighted management goals, the profit goal could easily be satisfied. (See Exhibit 8.)

EXHIBIT 1
BEAMIR COMPANY
Machine capacity

Machine	Date purchase	Capacity in product-hours per year
I	1968	60,000
II	1972	120,000
III	1972	120,000
IV	1968	60,000

EXHIBIT 2
BEAMIR COMPANY
Hours required by product per machine

	Machine			
	I	*II*	*III*	*IV*
Valve A	1	0	3	2
Valve B	2	4	4	2
Valve C	2	6	3	1

EXHIBIT 3
BEAMIR COMPANY
Labor hours required per product

Valve A	4
Valve B	7
Valve C	15

EXHIBIT 4
BEAMIR COMPANY
Per valve cost

	A	*B*	*C*
Direct labor	12.60	22.05	47.25
Materials	1.40	5.95	1.75
Total Variable Costs	14.00	28.00	49.00
Net selling price	23.00	46.00	70.00

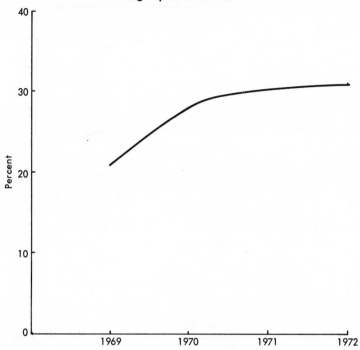

EXHIBIT 5
BEAMIR COMPANY
Working capital to net sales

EXHIBIT 6
BEAMIR COMPANY
Fixed expenses

Selling expense..............	$115,854
Shipping expense............	62,944
Administrative expense.......	182,605
	$361,403

EXHIBIT 7
BEAMIR COMPANY
Total debt to net worth

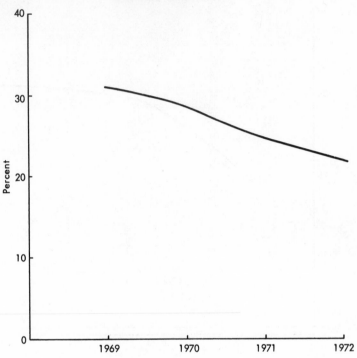

EXHIBIT 8
BEAMIR COMPANY
Weights assigned by management for their selected goals

1. Profit before tax
   A. It is perfectly acceptable to have excess profits
   $$\alpha_1 = 0$$
   B. It is of paramount importance to accomplish the profit objective
   $$\alpha_2 = 10^6$$
2. Net Working Capital to Sales Ratio
   A. An excess in working capital is acceptable but not desired
   $$\beta_1 = 10^2$$
   B. A deficit of working capital is the second most unacceptable result
   $$\beta_2 = 10^3$$
3. Labor Hours to Be Used
   A. An excess of labor hours is acceptable but not desired
   $$\gamma_1 = 10^2$$
   B. A deficit in the labor used is strongly opposed
   $$\gamma_2 = 10^3$$
4. Debt to Net Worth Ratio
   A. Excess debt is not desired
   $$\delta_1 = 10$$
   B. Lack of debt is an indication of being underleveraged and is to be avoided
   $$\delta_2 = 10$$

SELECTED REFERENCES
FOR PART ONE

CROXTON, FREDERICK and COWDEN, DUDLEY. *Applied General Statistics*. Englewood Cliffs, N.J.: Prentice-Hall, Inc., 1955.

DI ROCCAFERRERA, GIUESEPPE M. FERRERO. *Introduction to Linear Programming Processes*. Cincinnati, O.: South-Western Publishing Co., 1967.

GRUNEWALD, A. E. and NEMMERS, E. E. *Basic Managerial Finance*. New York: Holt, Rinehart & Winston, Inc., 1970.

HADLEY, G. *Linear Programming*. Reading, Mass.: Addison-Wesley Publishing Co., Inc., 1962.

HUNT, PEARSON; WILLIAMS, CHARLES M.; and DONALDSON, GORDON. *Basic Business Finance*. Homewood, Ill.: Richard. D. Irwin, Inc., 1971.

LEWIS, J. P. and TURNER, R. C. *Business Conditions Analysis*. McGraw-Hill Book Co., 1967.

LINDSAY, J. ROBERT and SAMETZ, ARNOLD W. *Financial Management*. Homewood, Ill.: Richard D. Irwin, Inc., 1967.

MAO, JAMES C. T. *Quantitative Analysis of Financial Decisions*. New York: The Macmillan Co., 1969.

MOCK, EDWARD J.; SCHULTZ, ROBERT E.; SCHULTZ, RAYMOND G.; and SHUCKETT, DONALD H. *Basic Financial Management*. Scranton, Pa.: International Textbook Co., 1968.

VAN HORNE, JAMES C. *Financial Management and Policy*. Englewood Cliffs, N.J.: Prentice-Hall, Inc., 1971.

WAGNER, HARVEY. *Principles of Operations Research with Applications to Managerial Decisions*. Englewood Cliffs, N.J.: Prentice-Hall, Inc., 1969.

WESTON, J. FRED and BRIGHAM, EUGENE F. *Managerial Finance*. New York: Holt, Rinehart & Winston, Inc., 1972.

Interest Rates, Credit Flows, and Monetary Aggregates Since 1964*

INTEREST RATES in securities markets have fluctuated very sharply over the past half-decade, although the trend in yields has generally been upward. In 1969 and early 1970, when inflationary expectations were strong and bank credit expansion was curtailed, market rates reached levels as high as any in U.S. history. Then during 1970 and early 1971, as economic activity slowed and monetary policy eased, interest rates dropped more sharply than in most earlier periods of decline.

Most recently, interest rates have tended up again, reversing some of their preceding decline. These recent yield increases—which occurred in the aftermath of a rapid expansion of gross national product during the first quarter of 1971—were accompanied by large credit demands in long-term financial markets. They also came during a time when a flow of private short-term investment funds into foreign money market centers—indicating in part expectations of upward revaluations of some European currencies—had exerted some pressures to bring short-term U.S. rates somewhat closer into alignment with higher interest rates in foreign centers.

The factors that account for the behavior of interest rates at any point in time are highly complex—reflecting, in addition to current developments, lagged responses to past events and expectations of future events. To try to sort out more persisting underlying relationships among interest rates, credit flows, and monetary aggregates, this article reviews interest rate movements from 1964 to early 1971.

* Reprinted from the *Federal Reserve Bulletin*, Vol. 57, No. 6 (June 1971), pp. 425–40, by permission of the publisher.

Selected interest rate (in percent)

Rates	Earlier highs*	1971 lows*	June 15, 1971
Short-term:			
Treasury bills, 3-months............	7.87	3.38	4.95
	(January 1970)	(March)	
Commercial paper, 4 to 6 months.....	8.84	4.19	5.50
	(December 1969)	(March)	
Long-term:			
10-year U.S. government†	7.91	5.70	6.70
	(May 1970)	(March)	
Corporate Aaa new issues‡............	9.12	7.00	7.90‡
	(July 1970)	(February)	

* Monthly averages.
† Estimated from yield curve.
‡ Estimated by First National City Bank, except latest figure which is Federal Reserve estimate for week ending June 18, 1971.

The review starts with the years just prior to the escalation of U.S. involvement in the Vietnamese conflict—that is, early 1964 to mid-1965. In those years, while short-term rates had risen appreciably from the lows reached in the 1960–61 recession, interest rates in general remained remarkably stable by present standards, particularly in long-term markets. Moreover, the levels of rates prevailing—with long-term bonds generally yielding somewhat above 4 percent and rates in short-term markets running a bit lower—were not unusual in terms of previous U.S. financial history.

After mid-1965, however, interest rates began to trend sharply upward and to show much greater volatility. The 6-year span since mid-1965 divides logically into several subperiods that represent fairly distinct patterns of increasing or decreasing yield movements.

Data in Chart 1 and Table 1 differentiate these various subperiods and show summary measures of interest rate changes and some other economic data. The interest rates selected for these exhibits are two relatively sensitive market series showing borrowing costs for major corporations—namely, the rate on 4- to 6-month prime commercial paper and the average rate on newly issued corporate bonds of Aaa quality. These two series are broadly representative of yields in short- and long-term financial markets, although any single interest rate series on a particular type of debt will, of course, occasionally show divergencies from the general pattern of rate changes.

The yield on new corporate bonds was selected as the most representative measure for long-term market yields. Interest rates on long-term Treasury bonds tended to move more sluggishly during this time span, because the 4½ percent interest rate ceiling foreclosed new Treasury debt offering of long maturity during most of the period under review.

TABLE 1

Summary data for seven periods of interest rate changes end 1963 to early 1971 (in per cent unless otherwise indicated)

Item	Q_1 1964–Q_2 1965	Q_3 1965–Q_4 1966	1st half 1967	Q_3 1967–Q_2 1968	2d half 1968	Year 1969	Q_1 1970–Q_1 1971
Interest rate levels, end of period:							
Commercial paper	4.38	6.00	4.72	6.08	5.96	8.62	4.59
Corporate Aaa, new issues	4.48	5.76	5.58	6.56	6.69	8.41	7.05
Interest rate changes:							
Commercial paper	.47	1.62	−1.28	1.36	−.12	2.66	−4.03
Corporate bonds	.14	1.28	−.18	.98	.13	1.72	−1.36
Annual rates of increase:							
Real GNP	5.6	6.2	1.1	5.0	3.5	1.6	.4
GNP deflator	1.8	2.8	2.4	4.2	4.3	5.0	5.4
Current-dollar GNP	7.4	9.2	3.6	9.4	7.9	6.8	5.8
Money stock (M_1)	4.1	3.5	6.8	7.2	7.7	3.1	6.2
Average level during period:							
High-employment budget surplus (in billions of dollars at annual rates)	3.9	−5.4	−13.0	−15.5	−4.4	3.9	−.4

Note.—Based on quarterly data for terminal quarters in each period, except growth rate of M_1—which is calculated from averages for terminal months in the periods—and high-employment budget surplus—which shows average levels for the entire span of each period. Data for yields on Aaa newly issued corporate bonds are First National City Bank estimates and data for high-employment budget surplus (NIA basis) are unpublished estimates by the Division of Research and Statistics at the Federal Reserve.

CHART 1
Subperiods showing different patterns of yield movement

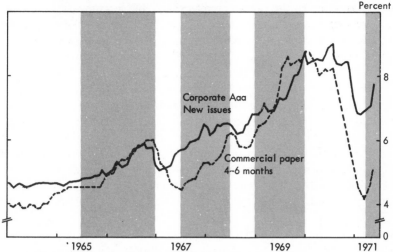

Monthly averages. First National City Bank estimates of average investor yield on new issues of high-grade corporate bonds adjusted to Aaa basis; prime commercial paper, dealer offering rates.

To facilitate comparisons between long- and short-term rates on debt of comparable quality, the short-term rate used in the analysis is the rate on commercial paper.

SKETCH OF SUBPERIODS

The relevant subperiods of rising and falling interest rates can be readily identified on Chart 1. The large extent of interest rate stability during the period from early 1964 to mid-1965 has already been mentioned, although on balance yields did tend to rise slowly during this period. Market yields rose sharply in the next period—from mid-1965 through the so-called "credit crunch" of 1966. As is usually the case, changes in long-term rates were in the same direction as short-term rates, but were smaller. Most yields reached their peaks at the height of the credit crunch in the fall of 1966. These interest rate increases partly reflected an unusually rapid pace of economic growth during late 1965 and early 1966. Defense contracts and payrolls mounted quickly, on top of spending demands by private economic sectors that had been stimulated by the income tax cuts of 1964. While the growth rate of real economic activity became less rapid over the course of 1966, readily available manpower and capital resources had been absorbed by that time and inflationary pressures had set in. To deal with the thrust of these excess demands, monetary policy became restrictive.

The succeeding subperiod of declining interest rates covers the first half of 1967. In this period growth of economic activity slowed briefly, partly in reaction to the earlier credit crunch and a temporary suspension of investment tax credits that took place in late 1966. Interest rate declines were also encouraged by a shift to an expansive monetary policy. In short-term markets, the general rate decline continued through mid-1967, but in bond markets, rates reached their lows as early as February 1967 and then started moving up. This latter upturn was partly anticipatory; it reflected concern among market participants that the income surtax requested by the administration would not be enacted and this would lead to large Federal deficit spending on top of a renewal of strength already expected for the private economy. At the same time, the volume of long-term borrowing—in contrast to short-term financing—increased substantially (Table 2) as borrowers tried to make up for capital market financing foregone during the credit crunch and to anticipate possible future shortages of funds.

Expectations of rising interest rates were in fact confirmed after mid-1967, and rates continued to advance through the next subperiod. Excess demand in the domestic economy and adverse expectations engendered by events in the foreign exchange and gold markets—beginning with the devaluation of sterling in late 1967—were among the factors that encouraged interest rates to rise above the peaks reached earlier during the 1966 credit crunch.

The long-delayed passage of the Revenue and Expenditure Control Act in June 1968—which provided for a 10 percent surcharge on income taxes and a ceiling on Federal spending in the fiscal year 1969—considerably improved the outlook of credit market participants. A temporary decline in interest rates occurred during the summer and early fall of 1968. As in the first half of 1967, however, the rate decline in long-term markets was reversed sooner than that in short-term markets. With borrowers seeking to cover previously delayed financing as credit market conditions eased, the volume of long-term debt offerings expanded sharply (Table 2). In part, this enlarged volume of capital market financing also came about when borrowers sought funds in anticipation of future needs, once it became evident that the mid-1968 fiscal actions were not fully curbing excess spending demands.

During 1969, interest rates moved to new record highs as the sharp increases in rates that had begun in late 1968 continued throughout the year with only minor interruptions. The year 1969 had larger rate increases, both absolutely and in relative terms, than any of the other periods considered here. These rate increases were accompanied by a restrictive monetary policy that resulted in a marked slowdown in the growth rate of bank credit and the monetary aggregates. At the same time the high employment Federal budget moved into surplus—a process which had

TABLE 2

Net borrowing in short- and long-term markets selected periods, 1964 to 1971

(in billions of dollars at seasonally adjusted annual rates unless otherwise indicated)

Item	Q_1 1964–Q_2 1965	Q_3 1965–Q_4 1966	1st half 1967	Q_3 1967–Q_2 1968	2d half 1968	Year 1969	Q_1 1970–Q_1 1971ᵖ
Total net borrowing[1]	61.4	62.9	62.8	84.8	96.5	73.4	83.3
Less: Funds supplied by Federal Reserve	3.4	3.7	6.0	5.5	–.4	4.2	7.1
Equals: Funds supplied by private sectors:	58.0	59.1	56.8	79.3	96.9	69.2	76.2
In short-term markets[2]	17.4	27.1	20.5	38.0	36.0	38.9	18.8
In *long-term markets—by type of instrument:*	40.6	32.0	36.3	41.3	60.9	30.3	57.4
Corporate and foreign bonds[3]	7.6	10.7	15.9	16.4	15.9	14.8	25.0
Mortgages, net of government housing-credit support	24.7	20.1	20.9	21.7	25.9	18.7	20.7
State and local bonds	5.6	5.7	8.0	5.7	13.0	5.0	10.1
U.S. government and government-sponsored agencies, over 5 years[4]	2.7	–4.5	–8.4	–2.5	6.1	–8.2	1.5
Share (in percent) of total supply by private sectors:							
Short-term	30.0	45.9	36.1	47.9	37.2	56.2	24.7
Long-term	70.0	54.1	63.9	52.1	62.8	43.8	75.3

[1] For derivation, see Table 3.

[2] Includes mainly nonfinancial borrowing in the form of bank loans, consumer credit, open market paper, State and local securities maturing within 1 year, and U.S. government as well as government-sponsored agency debt maturing within 5 years.

[3] In addition to bonds issued by nonfinancial sectors, includes bonds issued by sales finance companies and commercial banks. The proceeds of such bond sales by financial sectors are netted out in calculating short-term borrowing on the assumption that the proceeds are used to finance short-term debt.

[4] Abrupt shifts in maturity classification—that arise when securities pass from the over-5-year to the under-5-year category as a result of the passage of time—have been phased in gradually. The smoothing technique spreads the shift over a 2-year period.

Source.—Federal Reserve flow of funds accounts.

ᵖ preliminary.

already begun after mid-1968. While initially this shift in fiscal policy had seemed to have little effect, it subsequently contributed to the dampening of aggregate demand, and its effect on interest rates was in the direction of moderating upward rate pressures.

Economic expansion came to a halt in late 1969, and the following year was marked by recessive tendencies in output, sales, and employment. This slowdown was counteracted by measures that made fiscal policy more expansive—such as the expiration of the surtax—by a quickening of growth rates in monetary aggregates, and by substantial decreases in interest rates that continued until late winter 1971; all this helped to set the stage for the resumption of economic growth that has been observable in recent months. Although the most dramatic interest rate decreases occurred in the short-term sector, long-term rates also declined significantly during this last period, but only after first climbing further to reach new highs toward the middle of 1970—as pressures to rebuild depleted corporate liquidity positions had mounted in the spring of 1970. Thus the declines in long-term rates started much later than those of short-term rates. Also, the level of long-term rates were still unusually high relative to short-term rates in the spring of 1971.

INTEREST RATES AND CREDIT MARKET FLOWS

In explaining interest rate trends over long periods of time, economists usually stress the influence of expected rates of return on investment in physical capital and the willingness of the various economic sectors to supply savings. A consideration of these variables was implicit in some of the preceding discussion of GNP and Federal budget developments. However, for short cyclical periods analysts often relate interest rate movements to shifting demand and supply conditions in the credit markets or in the stock of liquid assets, such as money.

Evaluating the relationship of interest rate movements in the seven subperiods to changing demand and supply conditions in the credit markets is a complex undertaking. It is difficult to distinguish between shifts in the demand for and shifts in the supply of loanable funds in the *ex post* data on fund flows. For example, an increased volume of credit may at times signify an upward shift in demand for funds that would lead to higher interest rates, whereas at other times an expanded flow of credit may reflect an increased supply that would lead to lower interest cates. Even without a separate identification of demand and supply factors, however, an examination of developments in credit flows may still contribute to an understanding of interest rate behavior.

Total borrowing.   Table 3 shows the major borrowing flows at annual rates during the seven subperiods under discussion. Total net borrowing (line F) reflects major types of borrowing by nonfinancial sectors in the economy. Total credit expansion was substantial in all of the sub-periods under review, ranging between 7.9 and 10.9 percent of current-dollar GNP. The flows appear to be largest in the periods when the economy was in the early or middle phase of an upswing, as in 1964—early 1965 and the two periods from mid-1967 to the end of 1968. Relative to GNP, credit flows were smallest in 1969 and in the latter half of 1966 (Table 3, footnote 5), when the economy was nearing the end of an upswing and when monetary policy was most restrictive.

In the periods when tendencies of recession and incipient recovery were present, as in early 1967 and in the 1970–71 period, credit flows were slightly larger than in the immediately preceding phases of expansion. It may also be noted that the large increase in Federal borrowing in fiscal year 1968—at a time of substantial budget deficit at high employment—was reflected in an expansion of total credit flows and was succeeded by an unusually large expansion of non-Federal borrowing in the latter half of 1968.

Given the pattern of relatively small credit flows and rapidly rising interest rates found in the late expansion phase of the business cycle, and intermediate-size credit flows accompanied by falling interest rates in the two periods when the economy slowed substantially, it is apparent that no simple relation can be formulated between the size of total credit flows and movements in interest rates. The explanation would seem to lie in an interaction of supply and demand conditions.

Although total demands for credit tend to shrink when the economy weakens, monetary policy at such times has generally contributed to easier credit supply conditions. Hence total borrowing tended to expand even while the economy was still sluggish. Lagged policy effects and the upturn of economic activity have tended to lead to a more rapid increase in total credit flows once economic expansion was well under way. Finally, in the late expansion phases, total borrowing showed declines while interest rates reached high levels, and credit availability was most restricted in relation to efforts by monetary policy to restrain excess demands.

Sectors supplying funds. There is a general association of interest rate movements with the sectoral composition of the supply of funds in credit markets, as discussed below and shown in Table 4. In periods when commercial banks, thrift institutions, and the Federal Reserve System supplied the predominant portion of total credit, interest rates eased or tended to be stable. But when other domestic sectors—especially households, nonfinancial business, and State and local governments—had to be attracted into the securities markets to meet borrowers' demands for funds, interest rates increased.

Major shifts of this type in the sources of lending may develop initially from either the demand or the supply side of credit. For example, if

TABLE 3

Borrowing in major credit markets selected periods, 1964 to 1971

(in billions of dollars at seasonally adjusted annual rates unless otherwise indicated)

Line	Item	Q_1 1964–Q_2 1965	Q_3 1965–Q_4 1966	1st half 1967	Q_3 1967–Q_2 1968	2d half 1968	Year 1969	Q_1 1970–Q_1 1971ᵖ
A.	U.S. government securities................	5.0	2.8	4.0	20.5	7.2	-3.6	9.2
B.	Sponsored credit agencies..............	1.1	3.8	-3.0	3.3	2.2	8.8	5.7
C.	Short-term non-Federal[1]............	20.2	21.0	18.3	18.5	33.3	31.4	15.0
D.	Long-term non-Federal[2]............	36.2	38.7	40.7	47.0	56.3	46.0	58.6
E.	*Less:* Government housing-credit support[3]........	1.1	3.5	-2.9	4.5	2.4	9.2	5.2
F.	*Equals:* Total net borrowing by nonfinancial sectors and sponsored credit agencies[4]...........	61.4	62.9	62.8	84.8	96.5	73.4	83.3
G.	Total borrowing as percent of GNP[5]........	9.5	8.6	8.1	10.2	10.9	7.9	8.5

[1] Borrowing by nonfinancial sectors in the form of bank loans, consumer credit, open market paper, and State and local securities under 1 year.

[2] Borrowing by nonfinancial sectors in the form of State and local securities other than short-term, corporate and foreign bonds, and mortgages.

[3] Net mortgage purchases of U.S. budget agencies, Federal National Mortgage Association, and Federal land banks; and Federal home loan bank loans to savings and loan associations.

[4] Borrowing by government-sponsored credit agencies is included as a component of total borrowing and is shown in line B. However, to the extent that such borrowing finances home mortgage lending it is deducted in line E, since total mortgage borrowing has been included in line D.

[5] During the last half of 1966, total borrowing amounted to 6.7 per cent of GNP.

Source.—Federal Reserve flow of funds accounts.

ᵖ preliminary.

TABLE 4

Sectors supplying funds in major credit markets selected periods, 1964 to 1971

(in billions of dollars at seasonally adjusted annual rates unless otherwise indicated)

Item	$Q_1 1964-$ $Q_2 1965$	$Q_3 1965-$ $Q_4 1966$	1st half 1967	$Q_3 1967-$ $Q_2 1968$	2d half 1968	Year 1969	$Q_1 1970-$ $Q_1 1971^p$
Total net lending (or borrowing)	61.4	62.9	62.8	84.8	96.5	73.4	83.3
Funds supplied directly by:							
Federal Reserve Banks	3.4	3.7	6.0	5.5	−.4	4.2	7.1
Commercial banks, net[1]	23.9	20.7	33.9	32.1	54.1	12.2	34.9
Thrift institutions, net[2]	15.2	9.6	16.5	15.4	14.7	10.2	20.3
Foreign[3]	.4	.2	2.4	−.6	3.8	−.3	10.9
All other domestic sectors[4]	18.5	28.6	4.0	32.4	24.3	47.1	10.1
Share (in percent) provided by:[5]							
Federal Reserve, commercial banks, and thrift institutions	69.2	54.1	89.8	62.5	70.9	36.2	74.8
All other domestic sectors	30.1	45.5	6.4	38.2	25.2	64.2	12.1

[1] Net of bank borrowing in commercial paper market and securities market. Bank borrowing from foreign branches has not been deducted in evaluating funds supplied by commercial banks.

[2] Credit market lending by mutual savings banks, savings and loan associations, and credit unions, net of borrowing from commercial banks and Federal home loan banks.

[3] Does not include funds lent to U.S banks by foreign branches, which in the last two periods amounted to $7.0 and $8.0 billion, respectively.

[4] Mainly reflects private domestic nonfinancial sectors (such as households, business, and State and local funds) and insurance companies as well as minor differences between funds lent and borrowed by finance companies, dealers and brokers, and Government-sponsored agencies.

[5] The percentages do not add to 100 because the share of foreign net lending has been omitted.

Source: Federal Reserve flow of funds accounts.

ᵖ preliminary.

demands for credit experience an autonomous increase, market interest rates would tend to rise. Such rate increases on market securities would need to be large enough to attract additional lending from the "other domestic sectors." These higher rate levels would tend to make market securities more attractive relative to holdings of deposits. Nominal interest rates on demand deposits are fixed at zero, while rates paid on savings accounts at commercial banks and thrift institutions tend to fluctuate much less than rates on market securities, as illustrated in Chart 2. More-

CHART 2
Rates on savings accounts respond very slowly to market rates

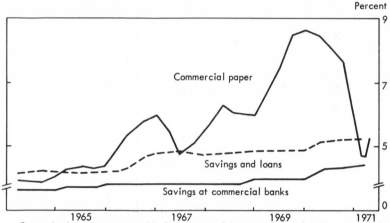

Quarterly data, except monthly for commercial paper and savings at commercial banks in April and May 1971. Weighted average offering rates on savings and loan accounts estimated by Federal Reserve from the FHLBB quarterly survey. Weighted average interest rates paid on savings deposits by commercial banks in the 7th District.

over, regulated rate ceilings on time and savings deposits have at times constrained the ability of banks and other depositary institutions to offer interest rates on such deposits that are competitive with the market. In the case of depositary institutions specializing in mortgage lending, such as savings and loan associations, competitive interest rates often could not be offered on savings accounts when market interest rates rose, since the earnings of these institutions reflected in large part the lower returns obtained on mortgages that had been acquired before the increase in market interest rates.

As a result, the more market interest rates rise, the more extensive the process of "disintermediation" becomes. The recent patterns of Euro-dollar borrowings by commercial banks from foreign branches can be viewed as an exception to this generalization. In this case, U.S. commercial banks were bidding aggressively for Euro-dollar loans when interest rates rose rapidly in 1969, thus offsetting some of the curtailment of bank credit. But in 1970–71, when U.S. interest rates declined below the levels of foreign rates, banks were repaying large amounts of Euro-dollar borrowing.

The nonfinancial domestic sectors attracted to the securities markets in periods of rising rates typically acquire a different type of market instrument from those purchased by thrift institutions and banks; therefore, a particular scarcity of funds tends to develop for certain types of loans. Mortgage funds, especially, are not readily provided by the nonfinancial sectors; thus housing credit is curtailed when "disintermediation" occurs. Federal and federally sponsored credit programs have amelioerated some of this unevenness of credit flows, as is indicated by the offsetting fluctuations in the volume of housing-credit-support lending by the Government, particularly in periods of general credit restraint such as in 1969 (Table 3).

Major shifts in the share of lending being provided by different sectors can also be initiated from the supply side. For example, monetary policy can inject more reserves into the banking system, thus fostering more bank credit and in this way exerting downward pressures on interest rates, at least in the short run. The domestic nonfinancial sectors are then encouraged to part with securities and to channel their financial assets into deposits and shares at savings institutions.

SHORT-TERM INTEREST RATES AND MONETARY AGGREGATES

The process just described—in which the nonfinancial sectors become important direct lenders in credit markets when interest rates are rising and high, while banks and savings institutions become more predominant in supplying credit funds when rates are falling and low—is reflected for the most part in movements of the monetary aggregates that measure selected sets of liabilities of banks and thrift institutions.

A rough correspondence in movements between measures of credit supplied by banks and thrift institutions and the monetary aggregates is to be expected, since there is a considerable amount of overlap between data taken from the credit side of these institutions' balance sheets and data that represent their major liabilities. However, the monetary aggregates also measure particular types of liquid assets held by the public, and this is the major focus of the various concepts of money stock.

The narrowly defined money stock (M_1)—that is, currency and demand deposits (other than U.S. Government and interbank)—has the least direct correspondence to credit data on the asset side of the balance sheet, since commercial bank time and savings deposits constitute a major share of the total liabilities of the banking system. However, since the narrowly defined money stock has the special characteristic of comprising the generally accepted medium of exchange, economists have been particularly interested in investigating the association between this type of liquid asset and other economic magnitudes.

Short-term market interest rates are frequently considered as the opportunity cost of holding or obtaining money, both for potential financial investors and for borrowers. Borrowers have to pay this rate as the price for money, and lenders can earn this rate if they are willing to give up money. Since short-term debt instruments are relatively free of market price risk, they are also considered "liquid" and hence are good money substitutes.

For some types of investors, however, savings accounts may be better substitutes for M_1 than are market securities. A 1968 FDIC survey showed that 35 percent of the dollar amount of demand deposits held by individuals, partnerships, and corporations were in accounts smaller than $10,000; for many of these holders savings accounts would tend to be a more realistic alternative to demand deposit holdings than short-term marketable instruments. Rates on savings accounts for those holders would be a better measure of the cost of holding money than the yields on short-term market securities.

The public's demand for money balances can be thought of as depending on transaction needs and interest rate levels as well as on a number of other specific influences, some of which are difficult to isolate and will not be considered here. Transaction needs can be represented in a very rough fashion by the current-dollar value of GNP on the simplifying assumption that financial and intermediate transactions that are not included in GNP would tend to grow at a similar rate to GNP. When GNP is divided by the current stock of money, the "income velocity" of money is obtained and this velocity ratio then provides some rough allowance for the volume of transactions for which money is used. Data for money velocity, as shown in Table 5, permit a direct examination of the relationship between money stock and interest rates.

When velocity increased substantially, during the subperiods in Table 5, short-term interest rates were tending to increase also. In periods when velocity increased only moderately, remained unchanged, or declined, short-term interest rates remained about unchanged or tended to fall. During the entire period from the end of 1963 to the first quarter of 1971, velocity increased at an annual rate of 2.4 percent but short-term interest rates at their recent lows were only slightly higher than in later 1963. This may indicate, in a rough manner, that there were some economies in the use of money over this period so that some of the increasing trend in velocity could represent efficiencies in the management of cash balances. Alternatively, some of the increasing trend in velocity could also reflect the general rise in the interest rates paid on time and savings accounts.

TABLE 5
Changes in the income velocity of money and short-term interest rate movements

Time period	Velocity of M_1[1]	Rate of increase in velocity[2]	Movement in short-term interest rates
Q₄ 1963....................	3.95		
Q₁ 1964–Q₂ 1965............	4.16	3.5	slightly increasing
Q₃ 1965–Q₄ 1966...........	4.50	5.5	increasing
1st H 1967.................	4.46	− .2	decreasing
Q₃ 1967–Q₂ 1968...........	4.55	2.0	increasing
2nd H 1968.................	4.55	....	about unchanged
Year 1969.................	4.68	2.9	increasing
Q₁ 1970–Q₁ 1971............	4.70	.3	decreasing
Q₄ 1963–Q₁ 1971............	4.70	2.4	slightly increasing

[1] Terminal quarter GNP, at annual rates, divided by average stock of currency and demand deposits for that quarter.
[2] Percentage change at annual rate.

It should be noted that the relationships among GNP, money stock, and short-term interest rates represent a complex interaction. All of these three variables act on one another rather than having only bilateral relationships. Growth in the money stock has a short-run effect in reducing interest rates, making credit more easily available, and making the asset

CHART 3
Broad conformity of movement appears despite diversities in short-term rates

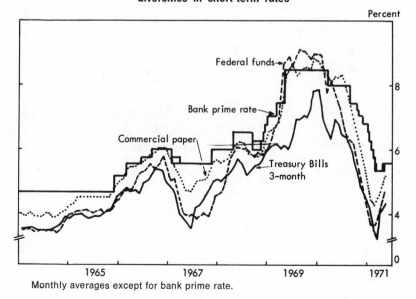

Percent

Federal funds

Bank prime rate

Commercial paper

Treasury Bills 3–month

8

6

4

0

1965   1967   1969   1971

Monthly averages except for bank prime rate.

holdings of the public more liquid. These effects stimulate transactions and GNP. The larger GNP—whether in the form of additional product or higher prices—in turn increases interest rates and money demand.

Of course, the presentation in Table 5 has been oversimplified in many respects. Lagged relationships have been neglected, although most econometric work has found that actions by holders of money to adjust their balances lag behind growth in the volume of transactions as well as changes in interest rates. Table 5 thus is merely illustrative of a general approach taken in investigating the relationship between money stock and interest rates.

Expectations represent still other factors that influence the demand for money and short-term interest rates. For instance, expectations about economic developments or about monetary policy influence short-term rates. The strong reaction sometimes observable in short-term rates to changes in the Federal Reserve discount rate, for example, takes place largely because a discount rate change may at times be viewed by the market as an indicator of the likely future course of monetary policy.

Inflationary expectations, however, have a smaller impact on short-term rates than on long-term interest rates. To the extent that large investors consider deposit holdings and short-term marketable instruments as their major alternatives for the placement of liquid reserves, neither of these

CHART 4
Long-term rates exhibit a common trend

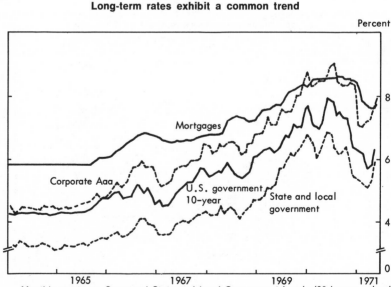

Monthly averages. Seasoned State and local Government bonds (20 issues, mixed quality), Bond Buyer; FHA series (new homes) on average contract interest rates on conventional first mortgages in primary markets; U.S. Government security yields as estimated from yield curve.

alternative holdings offers protection against inflation. Thus the influence of inflation on short-term interest rates is exerted mainly by the expansion of the current dollar value of transactions, rather than by changing the incentives to substitute between deposits and short-term securities.

MOVEMENTS IN LONG-TERM INTEREST RATES

On the average, the level of long-term rates has been historically somewhat higher than that of short-term rates due to a preference for liquidity by lenders. In general, long-term market rates have tended to move in the same direction as short-term rates, but their amplitude of change has been smaller. As a result of the greater volatility of short-term rates, long-term rates for instruments that are similar in all respects except maturity have frequently been below the corresponding short-term rates during periods when interest rates were at cyclical peaks, and they have been substantially higher than short-term rates when interest rates were unusually low.

This standard pattern of relationships between long- and short-term rates prevailed in the period from 1963 to late 1966. As shown in Chart 5, the spreads between long- and short-term rates declined significantly during this period as short-term rates were rising. Thereafter, however, the standard relationship did not hold up well. Long-term yields remained higher than short-term interest rates in mid-1968, even though short-term rates had reached a new peak. In 1970 and early 1971, when short-term interest rates were falling, some of the large increase in yield spreads did conform to the usual relationships between long-term and short-term rates. However, the extent to which spreads have widened has been unusually large. In summary, it would seem that long-term rates have had an upward shift relative to short-term rates since early 1967 in comparison to their usual historical relationship.

The wider spread between short- and long-term rates in recent years is frequently attributed to changed expectations about the future course of prices of goods and services. When entering into financial contracts that terminate many years hence, lenders and borrowers must naturally make some evaluation of the range of possible alternatives over the life of the contract. In making such evaluations during the past few years, investors appear to have become more concerned about expected general price increases. When such concerns are strong, investors believe it to be unprofitable to advance funds to bond markets except at high yields.

The pattern of credit demands by borrowers is, of course, also influenced by expectations. In 1970 and early 1971 large demands for long-term funds by borrowers have contributed to the relatively high levels of long-term yields. As is shown in Table 2, the demand for long-term funds has been unusually large in the period from 1970 to early 1971,

CHART 5
Spreads between long- and short-term rates alter over time

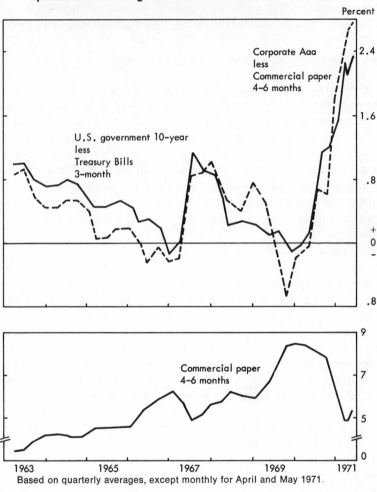

Based on quarterly averages, except monthly for April and May 1971.

especially in comparison to the quantity of short-term funds demanded. As was noted earlier, demands in the long-term sectors of the credit market also had increased substantially in early 1967 and late 1968 when interest rates were declining from their preceding peaks. In these earlier periods the declines in interest rates became short-lived: markets had tightened initially in reaction to backlog and anticipatory borrowing demands in the long-term sector; somewhat later short-term borrowing demands also had increased due to vigorous expansion of the economy that provided full-potential activity and intensified inflationary pressures.

Recent yield behavior suggests that inflationary expectations are probably imbedded to a considerable extent in the yield spreads between long- and short-term maturities and to a lesser extent in the level of all interest rates, as already indicated. Investors in short-term marketable assets frequently are anxious to maintain the liquidity of their investment, and there are no good outlets for investment of short-term funds that hedge against inflation. Some long-term investors, however, can find alternative inflation-hedged assets, such as corporate equities and real estate—and can also shift temporarily to short-term assets, when they become apprehensive about the risk of capital losses in the bond markets.

Another feature of current yield spreads is the large difference between the rates on prime- and lower-grade bonds. The yield spread between Baa-rated corporate bonds and Aaa-rated bonds, in the market for seasoned issues, increased since about the time of the filing for bankruptcy of a major railroad last year (see Chart 6). These spreads usually

CHART 6
Lower-grade bonds still demand sizable yield premiums

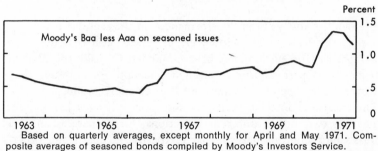

Based on quarterly averages, except monthly for April and May 1971. Composite averages of seasoned bonds compiled by Moody's Investors Service.

increase in periods of economic recession when uncertainty increases; during the most recent months—perhaps as a reaction to the signs of economic recovery—these spreads have narrowed.

The Concept of Sustainable Growth*

Guilford C. Babcock†

THE WORD has always been "performance" in the sense of price appreciation plus dividend yield.[1] However, in recent years, higher taxes and higher prices (for everything) have combined to make the dividend the less important part of this total-yield concept. As a result, the word performance has become a synonym for price appreciation.

The increased interest in prices and price changes has led security analysts in two rather different directions. First, there is an increased emphasis on technical analysis, that is, the use of charts and other techniques to develop patterns of price and volume which have some predictive value.[2] Second, there is beginning a more systematic analysis of the basic elements of price appreciation, namely, higher earnings and higher multiples. Such analysis, of course, has taken place for years; what is new is the systematic approach to the problem and the explicit recogni-

*Reprinted from *Financial Analysts Journal*, vol. 26, no. 3, (May–June 1970), pp. 108–14, by permission of the author and the publisher.

† Guilford C. Babcock is Associate Professor, School of Business Administration, University of Southern California. Gratitude is hereby expressed to Standard Statistics Company, a subsidiary of Standard & Poor's Corporation, for the use of their compustat tapes and to Mr. Gifford Fong for his excellent programming.

[1] For example, see Irving Fisher (ed.), *How to Invest When Prices Are Rising* (G. Lynn Summer & Co., 1912); and Edgar Lawrence Smith, *Common Stocks as Long Term Investments* (New York: Macmillan, 1923).

[2] For example, see Paul Cootner (ed.), *The Random Character of Stock Market Prices* (Cambridge, Mass.: The M.I.T. Press, 1964); Tabell and Tabell, "The Case for Technical Analysis," *Financial Analyst Journal*, Vol. XX, No. 2 (March–April 1964); and Robert A. Levy, "Random Walks: Reality or Myth," *Financial Analyst Journal*, Vol. XXIII, No. 6 (November–December 1967).

tion that these elements are only a means to the goal of price appreciation, both long term and short term.[3]

The price of any stock can be expressed as:

$$P = m \times E \qquad (1)$$

where m stands for the multiplier or price-earnings ratio, and E stands for earnings per share for some annual period. It follows that the price movement of any stock from one period to another can be expressed as:

$$\frac{P_2}{P_1} = \frac{m_2 \times E_2}{m_1 \times E_1} = \left(\frac{m_2}{m_1}\right)\left(\frac{E_2}{E_1}\right) \qquad (2)$$

where subscripts denote successive period of time. Equation (2) makes it clear, at least in theory, that stock-price changes stand equally on two elements. This fact is also shown in the chart below where points along each downward-sloping line represent equal price appreciation.

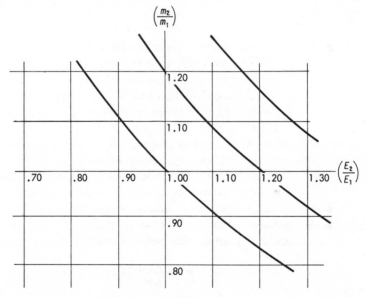

Which element, (m_2/m_1) or (E_2/E_1), is more volatile and/or more predictable is an important, empirical question;[4] however, it is beyond the scope of the present article. The chart, of course, is intended as

---

[3] For example, see S. Francis Nicholson, "Price Ratios," *Financial Analysts Journal*, Vol. XXIV, No. 1 (January–February 1968); and J. E. Murphy, Jr. and J. Russell Nelson, "Stability of P/E Ratios," *Financial Analysts Journal*, Vol. XXV, No. 2 (March–April 1969).

[4] Murphy and Nelson, "Note on the Stability of P/E Ratios," pp. 77–80.

a general framework for price-change analysis; however, this article will only deal with one aspect of price change, namely, changes in earnings per share.

THE BASIC EQUATION

The earnings per share of any company for any period of time may be expressed directly as the product of five variables:

$$M \times T \times L \times U \times B = E, \qquad (3)$$

where M stands for the margin of profit on sales,
      T for the turnover ratio of sales to total capital,
      L for the effect of any leverage employed,
      U for the after-tax rate, that is, $U = 1 - t$
         where t is the tax rate, and
      B for the equity or book value of a common share

Actually, Equation (3) is an identity which has the useful property of relating the traditional ratios of financial analysis to the earnings per share for the period.

It follows that any change in earnings can be expressed as changes in these five variables:

$$\left(\frac{M_2}{M_1}\right) \left(\frac{T_2}{T_1}\right) \left(\frac{L_2}{L_1}\right) \left(\frac{U_2}{U_1}\right) \left(\frac{B_2}{B_1}\right) = \left(\frac{E_2}{E_1}\right) \qquad (4)$$

However, changes in M, T, L, and U cannot be relied upon to sustain growth over a long period of time. Specifically, *changes in margin* will always occur, but upward movements will be limited by the degree of competition in the industry. Similarly, *changes in turnover* are almost inevitable, but plant capacity or the state of technology will limit the volume of sales relative to total capital. Likewise, the degree of *leverage* available to a company is limited, either by the willingness of creditors or by the prudence of management. And certainly the government at all levels may be relied upon to limit the number of *tax cuts* as a continuing source of growth. In any one period, changes in these four variables may be critical in determining the level of earnings; however, over time, they all have a tendency to fluctuate about some normal value depending on the nature of the industry and the level of the economy.

In contrast to this, *changes in book value* can occur regularly in an upward direction through the retention of earnings. Indeed, this is the only sustainable source of growth available to a company.[5] Moreover,

---

[5] The concept of "Sustainable Growth" is essentially the same as the concept of "Supportable Growth" developed by Manown Kisor, Jr., "The Financial Aspects of Growth," *Financial Analysts Journal*, Vol. XX, No. 2 (March–April 1964). The present article, however, is more general in its treatment of leverage and tax, and more formal in the development.

it will be shown that changes in B can be expressed directly in terms of M, T, L, and U. Thus, *changes in earnings per share* depend directly on changes in M, T, L, and U and also on the absolute value of these same variables.

The remainder of this paper will define the terms in Equation (3) and then develop Equation (4) as an analytical tool which can breakdown the growth rate in reported earnings into *sustainable* and *unsustainable* components. The sustainable component will be associated with the normal earning power of the company, based on the current level of margin, turnover, leverage, and taxes. The unsustainable component will be shown to represent fluctuations above or below the sustainable rate. Admittedly, there is no substitute for a detailed knowledge of the period in question; however, it is possible to isolate the important variables in a manner that facilitates a more detailed analysis. That is the purpose of this paper.

SOME BASIC DEFINITIONS

TA   Total assets.

CL   Current liabilities.

TC   Total capital is equal to total assets less current liabilities. It is made up of long-term liabilities plus the net worth of the stockholders.

LTL   Long-term liabilities is made up of funded debt, deferred items and other non-current liabilities, including reserves.

NW   Net worth represents the total dollar interest of both preferred and common stockholders.

CE   Common equity represents the total dollar interest of the common stockholders. It includes the par value of their stock, paid-in surplus, and retained earnings.

B   Book value per share is equal to common equity divided by the number of common shares outstanding at the end of the period.

TR   Total revenue is an aggregate measure which includes total sales.

EBIT   Earnings before interest and taxes is derived by adding back income taxes and interest payments on LTL to the net income reported for the period. If non-recurring gains or losses are included in net income, they will also be included in EBIT.

EBT   Earnings before taxes is derived from the concept of EBIT above. Hence, it may differ from the accounting concept of taxable income.

EAT   Earnings after taxes is simply the net income reported for the period.

EAC   Earnings available for common stockholders is equal to EAT less any preferred dividend payments.

E   Earnings per share is equal to earnings available for common divided by the number of common shares outstanding at the end of the period.

MARGIN × TURNOVER = RETURN

Margin is herewith defined as the ratio of earnings before interest and taxes to the total revenue for the period:

$$M = EBIT/TR \tag{5}$$

Since M holds total "profit" up against total "revenue," it is an aggregate measure of profitability per dollar of revenue. Turnover is defined as the ratio of total revenue to total capital:

$$T = TR/TC \tag{6}$$

Hence, T is an aggregate measure of revenue per dollar of capital. It follows that return on total capital, which is defined as the ratio of $EBIT$ to total capital, may be written as:

$$R_{TC} = EBIT/TC = M \times T \tag{7}$$

This is one of the most basic relationships in the field of finance. It is perhaps best known as the "duPont formula" for appraising divisional performance.

It should be noted that return here is measured against the total capital existing at the *end of the period*. This is an arbitrary decision based largely on the convenience of obtaining and interpreting year-end data. Incidentally, the same convention is followed by *Fortune* magazine in reporting rate of return on equity for the 500 largest U.S. industrial companies. However, this is only a simplifying convention and not a necessary one. Indeed, a good case can be made for using some measure of average invested capital and the same relationships can be derived.

Equation (7) is important for two reasons. First, it distinguishes between the concept of return and the concept of margin. The former always refers to profit in relation to *investment*, while the latter always refers to profit in relation to *sales* or revenue. Second, the formula properly puts the focus on return as the goal of investment and only on margin as a means to that goal. In other words, a low profit margin is not necessarily bad if it is combined with a high turnover ratio. For example, a 2% margin and 10× turnover will yield a 20% rate of return. However, a low rate of return usually indicates a bad state of affairs.

However, the rate of return on total capital is only one measure of return and certainly not the one of most interest to the investor-stockholder. The typical investor is assumed to have a primary interest in the rate of return on his own investment, which is in the stock market, and not on the brick and mortar, which is in the plant. Therefore, it must be shown that R, as defined above, has a direct bearing on the growth in earnings which underlies the stock market investment.

THE EFFECT OF LEVERAGE

If the total capital of a company is provided by stockholder's equity, the rate of return on total capital is, of course, equal to the rate of return on equity. In a subsequent section it will be shown that the rate of return on equity has a direct bearing on the growth rate of earnings; however, we must first face the fact that capital is usually provided by some combination of debt and equity which tends to lever the rate of return on equity.

The term "leverage" simply refers to the "advantage" of using debt together with equity. The intended effect is to raise the rate of return on the equity. Therefore, a useful measure of leverage is one which indicates "how much" the rate of return has been (or could be) raised. For example, if the rate of return on total capital is $R_{TC} = 20\%$, and one-half the capital is provided by debt at a cost of 8%, the pretax return on net worth is:

$$\tfrac{1}{2}(8\%) + \tfrac{1}{2}(R_{NW}) = 20\%$$
$$R_{NW} = 32\%$$

where R_{NW} represents the rate of return (before taxes) on net worth. Hence the use of debt raised the rate of return from 20% on total capital to 32% on net worth (or equity), that is, by a factor:

$$L_B = \frac{R_{NW}}{R_{TC}} = \frac{EBT/NW}{EBIT/TC} = 1.60 \text{ times} \qquad (8)$$

Here L_B stands for the leverage effect (before taxes) of long-term liabilities.

This is the basic definition of the leverage effect which will be used throughout this paper. However, it will be useful to recognize an after-tax leverage effect which will exist if any preferred stock is outstanding. Whereas L_B shows "how much" the rate of return (before taxes) will be raised by the use of long-term liabilities, L_A shows "how much" the rate of return (after taxes) will be raised by the use of preferred stock:

$$L_A = \frac{r_{CE}}{r_{NW}} = \frac{EAC/CE}{EAT/NW} \qquad (9)$$

where r_{CE} represents the rate of return on common equity, and r_{NW} represents the rate of return on net worth, that is, the equity of both preferred and common stockholders.

So defined, L_B and L_A are direct measures of the effect of using some-one else's money. They not only take the amount of money used into account, they also take the cost of using that money into account.

Furthermore, it should be noted that L_B will only be greater than 1.0 if the rate of return on total capital is greater than the interest cost of borrowing. Similarly, L_A will only be greater than 1.0 if the rate of return on total equity (net worth) is greater than the preferred dividend re-quirements. Otherwise, both L_B and L_A will be less than 1.0 and the lever-age effect will be called "negative."

THE EFFECT OF INCOME TAXES

Whereas the usual effect of leverage is positive, that is, to raise the rate of return to the stockholders, the inevitable effect of taxes is to lower that rate of return. For example, if we assume that taxes claim a fraction $t = .50$ of earnings before taxes, the after-tax rate of return will be lowered by a factor $U = (1 - t)$, from 32% to 16%. In general, this relationship can be written:

$$R_{NW}(1 - t) = r_{NW}$$

or, $\qquad\qquad\qquad\qquad\qquad\qquad\qquad\qquad\qquad\qquad$ (10)

$$R_{NW} \times U = r_{NW}$$

where $U = (1 - t)$ denotes the fraction earnings before taxes which are pulled through to net income.

RETURN ON COMMON EQUITY

It will be helpful at this point to show how the concepts of margin, turnover, leverage, and taxes combine to yield return on common equity:

$$M = \text{margin of profit on sales,} \qquad\qquad\qquad (5)$$
$$M \times T = \text{return on total capital,} \qquad\qquad\qquad (7)$$
$$M \times T \times L_B = \text{return on net worth (before taxes),} \qquad (8)$$
$$M \times T \times L_B \times U = \text{return on net worth (after taxes),} \qquad (10)$$
$$M \times T \times L_B \times U \times L_A = \text{return on common equity.} \qquad (9)$$

This last expression can be simplified if we let $L = L_B \times L_A$ represent the total leverage effect of long-term debt and preferred stock,[6] and if we let r (without subscript) $= r_{CE}$:

$$M \times T \times L \times U = r \qquad\qquad\qquad\qquad (11)$$

---

[6] This definition of over-all leverage is identical to the concept of "trading on the equity" developed by Pearson Hunt, "A Proposal for Precise Definitions of 'Trading on the Equity' and 'Leverage,'" *Journal of Finance*, Vol. XVI (1961).

In other words, margin, turnover, leverage, and taxes have a direct effect on r, and (as we shall see) on E, the earnings per share of the common stockholders.

Return on common equity has already been defined as the ratio of total earnings available for the common stockholders to the total equity of the common stockholders. This ratio may be easily re-expressed on a per share basis:

$$r = \frac{EAC}{CE} = \frac{E}{B} \tag{12}$$

where E represents earnings per share and B represents books value per share. Combining this result with Equation (11), we can write our basic equation for earnings per share:

$$M \times T \times L \times U \times B = E \tag{3}$$

It should be remembered that this equation is an identity, that is, the two sides of it are equal by definition. Therefore, M, T, L, and U are not independent variables and the equation cannot be used mechanically as a forecasting tool. However, M, T, L, and U do correspond to the variables which corporate managers seek to control and financial analysts seek to forecast. Hence, Equation (3) does provide a logical framework for analyzing the traditional variables and their relationship to earnings per share. Exhibit 1 shows the application of this basic equation to the 30 stocks which make up the Dow Jones Industrial Average.

CHANGES IN EARNINGS PER SHARE

Since Equation (3) holds for every period, it follows that:

$$\left(\frac{M_2}{M_1}\right)\left(\frac{T_2}{T_1}\right)\left(\frac{L_2}{L_1}\right)\left(\frac{U_2}{U_1}\right)\left(\frac{B_2}{B_1}\right) = \left(\frac{E_2}{E_1}\right) \tag{4}$$

This is our basic equation for changes in earnings. It simply says that any change in earnings per share will depend on changes in the underlying variables. However, as noted earlier, changes in M, T, L, and U cannot be relied upon to sustain growth, although they will almost certainly introduce fluctuations (upward and downward) into the earnings stream. Changes in book value, on the other hand, can sustain growth, that is, move upward as long as the company earns a profit and retains a portion of it.

CHANGES IN BOOK VALUE

Any change in book value can be attributed to retained earnings and/or all other sources, such as new equity financing. Hence, the differ-

EXHIBIT 1
The DJIA Stocks: Ratio analysis of 1965 earnings

	M	$\times$ T	$(=R)$	$\times L$	$\times U$	$(=r)$	$\times$ B	$= E$
Allied Chemical.........	12.7	1.00	2.6	1.58	.64	12.8	24.00	$3.08
Alcoa..................	12.3	.77	10.7	1.44	.63	8.7	39.39	3.41
American Can..........	9.8	1.43	14.0	1.42	.54	10.8	33.51	3.61
AT&T.................	32.5	.37	12.1	1.40	.55	9.3	36.61	3.39
American Tobacco......	22.9	1.07	24.5	1.07	.51	13.3	22.84	3.05
Anaconda..............	17.7	.82	14.5	1.07	.46	7.2	101.25	7.27
Bethlehem Steel.........	10.6	1.27	15.9	1.15	.57	8.8	37.13	3.26
Chrysler...............	8.6	2.69	23.1	1.27	.52	15.3	33.78	5.16
duPont................	25.7	1.28	32.9	1.21	.52	20.8	41.58	8.63
Eastman Kodak.........	32.4	1.40	45.3	1.02	.52	24.2	12.71	3.07
General Electric.........	11.8	2.27	26.9	1.24	.50	16.7	23.36	3.90
General Foods..........	12.0	2.44	29.3	1.14	.51	17.0	21.99	3.73
General Motors.......	19.8	2.28	45.2	1.16	.52	27.3	27.13	7.40
Goodyear Tire..........	9.6	1.75	16.9	1.32	.55	12.1	25.20	3.06
International Harvester...	8.7	1.73	15.1	1.11	.54	9.1	38.16	3.46
International Nickel......	37.4	.73	27.2	1.09	.61	18.1	26.86	4.85
International Paper......	11.6	1.31	15.3	1.02	.58	9.1	22.16	2.02
Johns-Manville..........	13.2	1.45	19.2	1.02	.54	10.5	38.29	4.03
Owens Illinois..........	11.6	1.17	13.7	1.22	.57	9.5	35.55	3.38
Procter & Gamble.......	12.6	1.92	24.1	1.11	.53	16.3	21.76	3.08
Sears..................	10.2	2.44	24.9	1.08	.55	14.9	14.27	2.12
Standard Oil, Calif.......	19.1	.69	13.2	1.06	.86	12.0	42.54	5.10
Standard Oil, (N.J.).....	15.4	1.08	16.6	1.16	.62	11.9	40.27	4.81
Swift..................	1.1	5.13	5.8	1.10	.63	3.9	68.56	2.70
Texaco................	19.7	.81	16.0	1.11	.88	15.6	30.31	4.71
Union Carbide..........	19.1	1.04	20.0	1.39	.61	16.9	22.29	3.76
United Aircraft.........	6.8	3.05	20.7	1.18	.55	13.2	32.84	4.33
U.S. Steel..............	12.3	.98	12.1	1.14	.54	7.4	62.48	4.62
Westinghouse...........	8.6	1.77	15.2	1.29	.54	10.7	26.69	2.86
Woolworth.............	7.5	1.15	8.6	1.10	.72	6.8	36.68	2.51
Average.......	15.1	1.58	19.7	1.19	.58	13.0	34.66	4.03

ence in book value between one period and the next can be expressed as:

$$B_2 - B_1 = b_2 E_2 + X_2 \qquad (13)$$

where b_2 stands for the fraction of earnings retained, $b_2 E_2$ for the dollar amount retained (per share), and X_2 for the dollar amount of change due to all other sources. This latter category will include new equity financing, merger activity, or simply a shift in accounting procedures. In other words, X_2 is a catch-all for "external" factors—hence the letter "X."

The ratio of B_2 to B_1 can now be written:

$$\frac{B_2}{B_1} = \left(\frac{B_1 + X_2}{B_1}\right)\left(\frac{B_2}{B_2 - b_2 E_2}\right) \qquad (14)$$

since $(B_1 + X_2) = (B_2 - b_2E_2)$ from Equation (13) above. This expression has the advantage of separating the external component of change, which is non-recurring, from the retained-earnings component, which is sustainable. Indeed, in theory this second factor is the mainspring of earnings growth, and, happily enough, initial tests of the DJIA show that it seems to correlate with both performance (price appreciation) recognition (the multiplier). This is shown in Exhibit 2.

However, it is useful to rearrange the terms of Equation (14), and then by substitution from Equations (13) and (11) to write:

$$\frac{B_2}{B_1} = \left(1 + \frac{X_2}{B_1}\right)\left(\frac{1}{1 - b_2E_2/B_2}\right) = \left(1 + \frac{X_2}{B_1}\right)\left(\frac{1}{1 - r_2b_2}\right)$$

$$= \left(1 + \frac{X_2}{B_1}\right)\left(\frac{1}{1 - M_2T_2L_2U_2b_2}\right). \quad (15)$$

In other words, any change in book value is fully explained by non-recurring, external factors, by the absolute value of M, T, L, and U, and by the retention rate b.[7]

IN CONCLUSION

Substituting the results of Equation (15) into Equation (4), we have our final expression for changes in earnings per share:

$$\left(\frac{M_2}{M_1}\right)\left(\frac{T_2}{T_1}\right)\left(\frac{L_2}{L_1}\right)\left(\frac{U_2}{U_1}\right)\left(1 + \frac{X_2}{B_1}\right)\left(\frac{1}{1 - M_2T_2L_2U_2b_2}\right) = \left(\frac{E_2}{E_1}\right) \quad (16)$$

Hence, any change in earnings per share is a function of six variables:

1. margin and changes in margin,
2. turnover and changes in turnover,
3. leverage and changes in leverage,
4. tax rates and changes in tax rates,
5. "external" factors, which affect the book value of a common share, and
6. the retention rate.

The first four factors of Equation (16), which represent changes in the key variables, will introduce fluctuations into the earnings stream, as will the fifth term, which represents "external" factors. Only the final factor, which depends on the absolute value of the key variables, can be viewed as a sustainable source of growth.

---

[7] This expression for sustainable growth $\frac{1}{1 - rb}$ differs from the more familiar expression (rb) only because return is here calculated on the *ending* amount of equity and not on *beginning* amount. Although the latter convention has certain advantages in theory, it makes the practical problem of gathering and interpreting data much more difficult.

EXHIBIT 2

The DJIA stocks: Sustainable growth, $g_s = \dfrac{rb}{1 - rb}$,

based on 1965 data and 1954–1965 data

	1965 data			1954–1965 data				1965
	r	b	g_s	$\bar{r}$	$\bar{b}$	$\bar{g}_s$	$\bar{g}_p$	P/E
Texaco........................	15.6	.48	8.1	15.1	.54	8.9	15.6	17.1
General Foods.................	17.0	.44	8.0	17.1	.46	8.5	15.5	22.4
Goodyear Tire.................	12.1	.61	8.0	12.7	.62	8.4	13.8	16.2
Eastman Kodak................	24.2	.42	11.2	17.9	.41	7.9	19.8	30.4
Standard Oil, Calif.............	12.0	.56	7.2	13.1	.56	7.9	9.7	14.3
General Motors................	27.3	.29	8.6	21.6	.33	7.6	13.1	13.8
Sears.........................	14.9	.47	7.5	14.2	.49	7.5	18.1	32.8
Procter & Gamble..............	16.3	.41	6.2	15.0	.44	7.2	14.9	24.5
International Nickel............	18.1	.37	7.2	16.9	.38	6.8	12.7	18.0
Alcoa.........................	8.7	.59	5.4	9.6	.55	5.6	5.8	20.5
Top 10 Average........	16.6	.46	7.7	15.3	.48	7.6	13.9	21.0
General Electric................	16.7	.39	7.0	17.1	.30	5.4	9.6	27.1
Chrysler......................	15.3	.77	13.2	8.4	.61	5.4	11.7	10.0
American Tobacco.............	13.3	.46	6.5	12.6	.40	5.3	8.4	12.1
Union Carbide.................	16.9	.47	8.6	15.8	.30	5.0	4.8	17.8
International Paper............	9.1	.38	3.6	10.3	.46	4.9	5.1	15.9
Standard Oil, (N.J.)............	11.9	.34	4.3	12.1	.38	4.8	9.4	17.0
duPont.......................	20.8	.30	6.8	19.6	.22	4.5	55.4	28.2
United Aircraft................	13.2	.70	10.2	13.1	.33	4.5	10.2	15.5
Owens Illinois.................	9.5	.60	6.1	8.7	.46	4.2	8.9	17.3
Allied Chemical................	12.8	.40	5.4	11.4	.34	4.0	2.3	16.4
Middle Average........	14.0	.48	7.2	12.9	.39	4.8	7.6	17.7
Johns-Manville................	10.5	.49	5.4	10.3	.36	3.9	3.8	14.3
U.S. Steel.....................	7.4	.57	4.4	8.9	.41	3.8	5.5	11.0
AT&T........................	9.3	.40	3.8	8.8	.35	3.2	8.0	19.2
Bethlehem Steel...............	8.8	.54	5.0	9.2	.29	2.7	6.0	11.7
Westinghouse..................	10.7	.57	6.5	7.3	.37	2.7	4.4	18.3
International Harvester..........	9.1	.57	5.4	6.6	.39	2.6	8.5	11.6
Anaconda.....................	7.2	.48	3.6	6.2	.40	2.5	5.0	9.6
American Can.................	10.8	.43	4.9	9.2	.27	2.5	1.6	14.0
Woolworth....................	6.8	.60	4.3	4.9	.44	2.2	5.9	11.8
Swift.........................	3.9	.26	1.0	4.3	.25	1.1	1.5	20.3
Bottom Average........	8.5	.49	4.4	7.6	.35	2.7	5.0	14.2
30 Stock Average	13.0	.48	6.5	11.9	.41	5.0	8.8	17.6

However, such growth is only sustainable to the extent margin, turnover, leverage, and taxes are maintained at current levels. The data, of course, contain no such guarantee for the future, although a look at the historical values of M, T, L, and U may help define the "normal" earning power of the company. What the data of Equation (16) do contain is a growth rate which will prevail "other things being equal." Whether or not other things are "equal" remains within the purview of the analyst who has a working knowledge of the company, the industry, and so forth.

A NUMERICAL EXAMPLE

Since Equation (16) is rather formidable without reference to any data, it may be useful to illustrate its application. Shown below is the relevant data for a company whose earnings increased by 11%, 76%, and 18% in three successive years.

	1966	1967	1968	1969
Margin..............	.02	.02	.03	.03
Turnover	10×	10×	10×	10×
Leverage............	1.60	1.60	1.60	1.60
$U = (1 - t)$........	.50	.50	.50	.50
r.................	.16	.16	.24	.24
Book Value	$9.00	$10.00	$11.76	$13.84
E................	1.44	1.60	2.82	3.32
D................	−.54	−.60	−1.06	−1.24
Retained...........	$ .90	$ 1.00	$ 1.76	$ 2.08
b................	⅝	⅝	⅝	⅝
rb..............	.10	.10	.15	.15
$\left(\dfrac{1}{1 - rb}\right)$..........	1.11	1.11	1.18	1.18
$\left(\dfrac{E_2}{E_1}\right)$............		1.11	1.76	1.18

During the first year, earnings growth and sustainable growth are equal as no change occurs in M, T, L, and U. During the second year, margin is allowed to increase by a factor of 1.50, that is, from .02 to .03. As a result, earnings increase by a factor of 1.76, that is, 1.50 times the "new" sustainable growth factor of 1.18. During the third year, earnings growth and sustainable growth are again equal, as M, T, L, and U are held constant; however, it should be noted that they are equal at the rate of 18% which was "discovered" during the previous year. In other words, the 76% growth rate of the second year came with its own "caveat investor."

It can also be shown that earnings will decline by 26% on a year-to-year basis, if margin now drops back to .02. Nonetheless, the final term in Equation (16) will reveal the old growth potential of 11% per annum, based on the old levels of M, T, L, and U. Hence, Equation (16) not only contains a warning if earnings rise too fast, it also contains a promise if they do not rise fast enough.

Finally, the relationship of these variables to the stock market itself should be noted, although this goes beyond the scope of work intended here. Exhibit 1 provides ratio analysis for the stocks in the Dow Jones Industrial Average based on 1965 data. Exhibit 2 ranks the 30 stocks on the basis of sustainable growth calculated over an eleven-year period from 1954 to 1965. It shows that the top ten stocks on this basis not only had the greatest price appreciation for the period, 13.9% per annum compared to 5.0% for the lowest group, they also continued to sell at the highest price in relation to 1965 earnings, 21.0 times earnings compared to 14.2 times for the lowest group. Whether or not this type of analysis can be profitably adapted to shorter periods of investment is an open question; however, the results here certainly argue its merits for the long-term investor.

An Introduction to Linear Programming: Concepts and Examples*

LINEAR PROGRAMMING is a mathematical technique for determining the optimum allocation of resources (such as capital, raw materials, manpower, plant or other facilities) to obtain a particular objective (such as minimum cost or maximum profit) when there are alternative uses for the resources. Linear programming can also be used to analyze the economics of alternate availability of resources, alternate objectives, and so on.

A few brief examples may serve to indicate more concretely what can be achieved with linear programming:

1. A manufacturer makes a number of different products. Each product uses certain production resources, each of which is available in a limited amount. The manufacturer knows how much profit he makes from each product. How much of each product should he produce in order to make the maximum total profit?

2. A producer of livestock feed is required to provide certain amounts of various nutritional elements in each sack of feed. He can obtain the various elements from different grains and supplements, and he knows the cost of each. What combination of grains and supplements should he use to meet the requirements at least cost?

3. The manager of an oil refinery is considering expanding the production of his plant by adding capacity at some point in the refining process. Of the many different processes involved in refining, which one should have its capacity increased so as to bring the greatest return on the capital expenditure?

* Reprinted from *An Introduction to Linear Programming*, Chap. 1 (White Plains, N.Y.: International Business Machines, 1964), pp. 1–8. © 1964 by International Business Machines Corporation.

4. Another manufacturer uses a large number of raw materials in the production of a line of products. The prices of his raw materials are subject to market fluctuations, and in some cases there are significant price breaks for large orders. He has a choice of which raw materials to use. One of the materials he is not using at the moment might profitably be used if the price were lower. How much would the price have to drop before he could make a greater profit by using it instead of something else?

5. This same manufacturer is faced with another problem: one of the raw materials he is now using will be unavailable for a while because of a fire at the plant of one of his suppliers. Of the various alternative raw materials that he could use to replace it, which one will cause the least decrease in profit, considering that the introduction of a different material may change the mixture of other materials he uses?

These examples emphasize the importance of linear programming. When a large number of interrelated choices exist, the best choice may be far from obvious. An intuitive solution may never uncover the best approach, and there is seldom any guarantee that what appears to be a fairly good policy is really the best.

Such problems often involve large amounts of money. A rational approach to the problems requires:

• A systematic way to represent the goal, or *objective*, of the system under study.

• A systematic way to describe the limitations, or *constraints*, under which the system must operate—for instance, the limited amount of production resources in the first example given, and the minimum nutritional requirements in the second example.

• Some way to arrive at one policy out of the many possibilities, and to be sure that it is the best.

• Some way to explore the ramifications of changes in the stated problem (assuming, of course, that the best, or *optimum*, policy for the original objective and the original constraints has been determined).

In the third example, the refinery manager needed to know which capacity limitation could most profitably be relaxed. In the fourth example, the manufacturer needed to know the effect on his best policy of a change in the costs of materials. In the fifth example, the manufacturer needed to know how the nonavailability of one raw material would affect his profit and how to choose a new policy that would minimize this effect.

"Linear programming," as the term is used today, includes the formulation of the problem, the solution (finding the optimum policy), and the exploration of the effects of changes. Such large-scale work almost always involves a computer, for any problem small enough to be done "by hand" could probably be solved without resorting to linear programming. Because computers are so important for large-scale work, special application systems have been developed to assist in the practical use of linear programming methods. Thus the user is not required to write the complex program of instructions needed to tell the computer how to solve linear programming problems. The user is required, however, to formulate his problem in the proper form of a linear programming solution and to prepare the necessary input data for the computer. The solution (best policy) is then found by the computer. Most systems also contain at least some features to allow investigation of the effects of problem changes of various sorts. The user must also know enough about linear programming to interpret the results printed by the computer, and to decide what changes should be explored.

Ordinarily, the user does not need to know a great deal about how the computer finds the optimum policy or how it arrives at the effect of changes. He does, however, need to know the elements of these methods in order to formulate his problem most effectively and to interpret the results intelligently.

The three examples that follow are designed to serve four essential purposes for the user who wants to employ linear programming intelligently but who needs only a minimum knowledge of the methods of solution.

1.   The examples introduce the characteristics of a problem that can be handled with linear programming. The technique is not the universal remedy for all management problems; it is important to know not only what can be done with linear programming, but also what cannot.

2.   They introduce the idea of problem formulation. Linear programming requires that the problem be stated in a specific manner (in terms of the objective and the constraints mentioned earlier). There is usually a certain amount of work involved in transforming a problem, as initially stated, into the form required for linear programming solution.

3.   They indicate the method of computation of the optimum policy.

4.   They reveal some of the information that can be derived from the solution to a linear programming problem, and they aid in interpreting the results.

EXAMPLE OF PRODUCTION CAPACITY ALLOCATION

We can get an idea of the characteristics of a problem that can be attacked effectively with linear programming by considering a simplified example. The illustration is realistic to the extent that businessmen do face such problems, but the problem presented is much smaller than the linear programming problems that are handled with computer systems.

A small machine shop manufactures two models, standard and deluxe, of an unspecified product. Each standard model requires four hours of grinding and two hours of polishing; each deluxe model requires two hours of grinding and five hours of polishing. The manufacturer has two grinders and three polishers; in his 40-hour week, therefore, he has 80 hours of grinding capacity and 120 hours of polishing capacity. He makes a profit of $3 on each standard model and $4 on each deluxe model. He can sell all he can make of both.

How should the manufacturer allocate his production capacity to standard and deluxe models; that is, how many of each model should he make in order to maximize his profit?

Let us begin by converting this problem statement into a mathematical form. Assign the symbol S to the number of standard models manufactured in a week, and the symbol D to the number of deluxe models. The profit from making S standard models and D deluxe models in a week, then, is

$$3S + 4D \text{ dollars}$$

For instance, if five standard models ($S = 5$) and seven deluxe models ($D = 7$) are built in a week, the profit is $(3 \times 5) + (4 \times 7) = \$43$; if the manufacturer could make 25 standard models and 20 deluxe models, the profit would be $155.

How can we express the restrictions on machine capacity? The manufacture of each standard uses four hours of grinding. Making S standard models therefore uses $4S$ hours. Similarly, the manufacture of D deluxe models uses $2D$ hours of grinding time, since the manufacture of one deluxe uses two hours. The total number of hours of grinding capacity used in a week, therefore, is

$$4S + 2D$$

We said previously that 80 hours of grinding time was available, so we might be tempted to write

$$4S + 2D = 80$$

This would not be correct, however, because at this point we have no assurance that the greatest profit lies in using all the grinding time. All we know is that the total hours of grinding time must not exceed 80. "Must not exceed" can also be expressed as "must be less than or equal to," a more convenient expression. The mathematical symbol for "less than or equal to" is $\leq$. The correct formula for the restriction on grinding capacity would be

$$4S + 2D \leq 80 \text{ hours}$$

In the same manner, we arrive at the limitation on polisher capacity:

$$2S + 5D \leq 120 \text{ hours}$$

In view of the higher profit on the deluxe models, one might suggest that the optimum policy would be to make as many deluxe models as possible and forget the standard models. Let us calculate how many deluxe models alone could be made, and record the corresponding profit for future reference. The limitation on grinder time provides that two times the number of deluxe models must not exceed 80, and the limitation on polisher time provides that five times the number of deluxe models must not exceed 120. Grinder capacity permits 40 deluxe models to be made; polisher capacity permits no more than 24 to be made. Therefore, 24 is the maximum number of deluxe models that could be made, even though this policy would consume only 48 hours of grinder time out of the 80 available. The profit with this policy is $96, since there is a $4 profit on each of the 24 deluxe models.

Let us now explore what the constraints (restrictions, or limitations) on machine time mean in geometrical terms. We shall draw a graph on which the vertical axis represents S (the number of standard models made in a week) and on which the horizontal axis represents D (the number of deluxe models). Now remember the first constraint that on grinder capacity $4S + 2D \leq 80$ hours. Let us consider only the "equal" part of the symbol for the moment, and rearrange the statement of the constraint:

$$4S + 2D = 80$$

so

$$2D = 80 - 4S$$

and

$$D = 40 - 2S$$

This equation lets us draw up a table of a few values of S and the corresponding values of D:

S	D
0	40
5	30
10	20
15	10
20	0

If we plot these points on a graph, the results would be those shown in Figure 1.

FIGURE 1
Five points that satisfy the equation 4S + 2D = 80

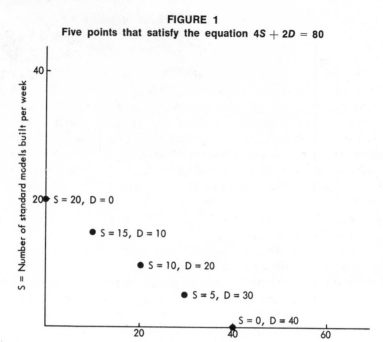

D = Number of deluxe models built per week

These five points lie on a line. We say that the equation $4S + 2D = 80$ is linear. In geometrical terms, this means that all points that satisfy the equation lie on a straight line. In algebraic terms, it means that S and D both appear in the equation multiplied only by a constant coefficient; that is, they are not squared, multiplied together, and so on.

Reviewing what the graph of our equation means, we have a straight line which "represents" the equation in the sense that any point on the line corresponds to some specific combination of values of S and D, and these values satisfy the equation. With this meaning in mind, we can plot the equation of the constraint under consideration simply as a line, without identifying any of the specific points, as in Figure 2.

But our constraint is not an equation; it is an inequality: $4S + 2D \leq 80$ hours. Graphically, this means that the inequality is represented in the picture by any point on the line or below it. We can make this explicit by shading in the region that is covered by the inequality (see Figure 3).

It is important to realize that any point on the line or below it still represents some specific combination of a value of S and a value of D; points below the line will be the "less than" part of the "less than or equal to" symbol.

In Figure 4 we also plot the constraint on the polishing capacity

FIGURE 2
Graph of the equation $4S + 2D = 80$

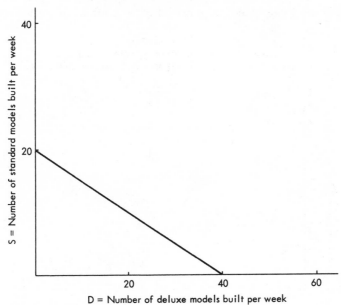

FIGURE 3
Graphical representation of the inequality $4S + 2D \leq 80$

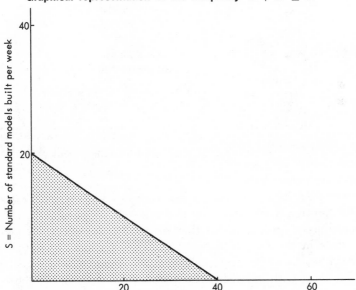

Any point on the line or in the shaded region satisfies the inequality.

$(2S + 5D \leq 120)$, but we now have shaded only the part of the graph that is "below" both lines.

In Figure 4 the shaded region reflects the effect of both constraints.

FIGURE 4
Graphical representation of both constraints
The small shaded region violates neither constraint and is called the feasible region.

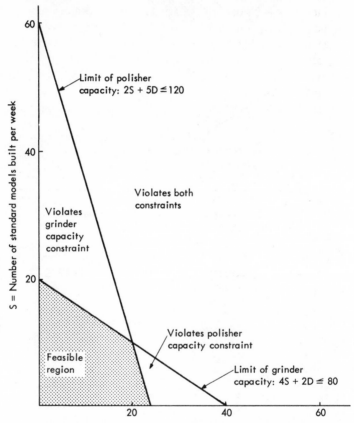

D = Number of deluxe models built per week

The parts of the graph within the triangles violate one or the other of the constraints; the part outside both lines violates both; the shaded region violates neither, and is therefore called feasible. This means that any point in the feasible region represents a combination of so many standard models and so many deluxe models, the combination being possible (feasible) with due regard for the amount of machine time available. From now on, we shall display only the feasible region on such graphs, since this area is all that really interests us.

How would we take into account the profit? We already know that the profit is $3S + 4D$ dollars; in other words, any point anywhere on the graph represents some specific profit. Some of these points will, of course, lie outside the feasible region and therefore will not represent possibilities for the best policy. What we are looking for is the point in the feasible region that represents the policy with the greatest profit. (In fact, the essence of the linear programming computation is the search for this point.) In a computer the location of the optimum point is reached by algebraic methods, rather than by graphical ones.

Here, we will see what can be done by graphical methods. We know that the profit for any particular point is $3S + 4D$ dollars. What would happen if we set this expression equal to some specific profit level, say $60? The answer is that we would have a linear equation, which we could plot as the broken line in Figure 5. This line includes such points

FIGURE 5
Graph of the constraints, the feasible region, and the profit line for $60: $3S + 4D = 60$

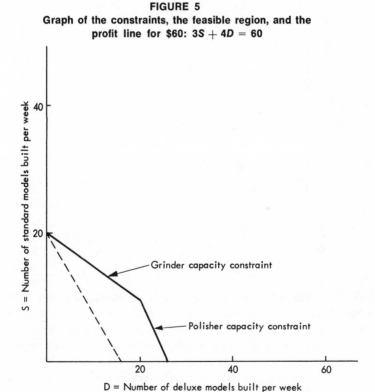

D = Number of deluxe models built per week

as 20 standard and zero deluxe models, 16 standard and three deluxe models, 12 standard and six deluxe models, eight standard and nine deluxe models, or zero standard and 15 deluxe models.

All points on this profit line are feasible; there is no violation of either machine capacity constraint anywhere on this line. Any point on this line thus represents a feasible policy, and all such points would return a $60 profit.

This policy, however, is not the best one. If, for instance, we try plotting the profit line $3S + 4D = \$96$, we find proof that there is a better policy (see Figure 6).

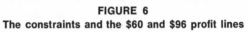

FIGURE 6
The constraints and the $60 and $96 profit lines

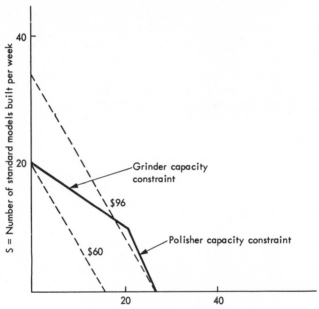

D = Number of deluxe models built per week

Not all points on this profit line are feasible. We cannot make 36 standard models and zero deluxe models, even though this point is on the line, because there is not enough grinder capacity to permit it. Some points on the line are feasible, however; for instance, the combination of twelve standard models and 15 deluxe models violates neither constraint and is therefore a feasible combination.

At $60, all points on the profit line were feasible; at $96 some points are feasible. The question that interests us now is the extent to which we can go and still have at least one feasible point on the profit line. This point represents the optimum policy. To find it is the fundamental goal of linear programming, and we shall see that there are ways of working with algebra to arrive at it.

Staying with the graphical approach for now, we notice in Figure

6 that the two profit lines are parallel, an observation that can be proved mathematically. Furthermore, all profit lines will be parallel for the problem as stated. This suggests a method of attack; look for the line parallel to the ones we have already drawn that goes as "far out" as possible but that still keeps one point in the feasible region. This will be the line that goes through the "corner" of the feasible region where the two constraint lines meet. It is shown in Figure 7. This is the profit line for $110, made from 10 standard models and 20 deluxe models.

FIGURE 7
The constraints and the $60, $96 and $110 profit lines

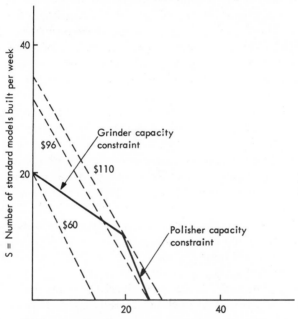

D = Number of deluxe models built per week

It should be clear from Figure 7 that striving for any profit greater than $110 would involve a profit line with all points outside the feasible region. We have therefore established that $110 is the best profit that can be made under the original objective and constraints.

We see that getting the maximum profit possible does require manufacture of some of the less profitable standard models, because that policy makes the best use of machine capacity. Thus one of the most important things this example shows is that maximizing profit may require a tradeoff between exclusive manufacture of the most profitable item and the full use of facilities. In other words, the manufacturer's most profitable policy was determined not only by his unit profit on each product, but also by the constraints on his production capacity.

The problem of maximizing profit is representative of a large class of problems that can be solved by linear programming. Such problems are characterized by the allocation of limited resources to products of different profitability.

It need not always happen, however, that the most profitable policy will require a combination of products. Suppose that the profit on each standard model was still $3, but that each deluxe model brought in $9 profit. When we search for the line with the greatest profit that still has at least one feasible point, we get the situation shown in Figure 8.

Here the profit line for the greatest profit that contains one feasible point still intersects the feasible region at one of its vertices (corners), but now it is a vertex formed of one of the constraint lines and one of the axes. This means that it is indeed most profitable to make all deluxe models (24 in this instance) and zero standard models, even though this policy will leave 32 hours of grinder time unused.

It will be instructive to explore what the best policy would be if each standard model brought in $6 profit and each deluxe model brought in $3 profit. When we seek the greatest profit line that contains a feasible point, we get a profit line that coincides with one of the constraint lines, as in Figure 9.

The manufacturer has several choices of the best policy. He can make 20 standard and zero deluxe models, 15 standard and ten deluxe models, 10 standard and 20 deluxe models, since each combination brings in the same profit of $120. Any of these combinations can be taken as the "best" policy; they are all equally good. This type of solution occasionally appears in practical applications.

In each of the preceding examples, we have taken it for granted that S and D are either zero or positive; there is no way to make a negative quantity of anything. We reject such quantities without thinking; however, when we discuss the algebraic method of finding the maximum profit line subject to constraints, we will have to include an explicit requirement that no variable be negative, because ordinary algebraic methods do permit negative numbers. This nonnegativity requirement becomes an integral part of the algebraic approach, but a person using a computer program based on such an algebraic method does not have to go to any extra effort because of the requirement.

We are now in a position to state the original example in the standard form for a problem that can be handled with linear programming.

Maximize	$3S + 4D$	the objective function (profit)	(1)
Subject to	$4S + 2D \leq 80$	the problem constraints	(2)
	$2S + 5D \leq 120$		
And subject to	$S \geq 0, D \geq 0$	the nonnegativity constraints	(3)

FIGURE 8
The constraints and the $216 profit line when the
profit on a standard model is $3 and the
profit on a deluxe model is $9

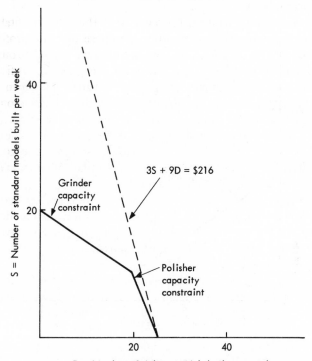

D = Number of deluxe models built per week

We shall refer frequently to the parts of the mathematical statement of a problem for linear programming solution. Figure 10 shows the terminology that will be used in this manual. Note that the objective function has been set equal to Z as a convenience in later operations. Observe that a *row* refers to one constraint or to the objective function; one *column* refers to one activity or to the right-hand side. The values of the variables are called *activity levels.*

We shall see that the standard form of a problem suitable for linear programming is characteristic, although there are important variations: we often want to minimize a cost rather than maximize a profit, and we often have constraints that state a "greater than or equal to" condition rather than a "less than or equal to" condition.

EXAMPLE OF FEED BLENDING

A poultry farmer needs to supplement the vitamins in the feed he buys. He is considering two products, each of which contains the four

FIGURE 9
The constraints and the best profit line when the
profit on each standard model is $6 and the
profit on each deluxe model is $3

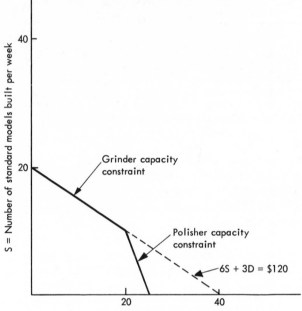

D = Number of deluxe models built per week

FIGURE 10
The terminology used in describing the normal
formulation of a linear programming problem

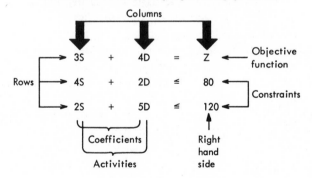

vitamins required, but in differing amounts. Naturally, he wants to meet (or exceed) the minimum vitamin requirements at least cost. Should he buy one product or the other, or should he mix the two? The facts are summarized in the table below.

	Product 1	Product 2
Cost per ounce..............	3 cents	4 cents
Vitamin 1 per ounce..........	5 units	25 units
Vitamin 2 per ounce..........	25 units	10 units
Vitamin 3 per ounce..........	10 units	10 units
Vitamin 4 per ounce..........	35 units	20 units

The farmer must provide, per hundred pounds of feed, at least 50 units of vitamin 1; 100 units of vitamin 2; 60 units of vitamin 3; and 180 units of vitamin 4.

Let us state the problem in the standard form described near the end of the previous example.

The objective in this case is to minimize the cost of obtaining the required vitamins. Let $P1$ represent the number of ounces of product 1 purchased, and let $P2$ represent the number of ounces of product 2. Then the objective is to minimize

$$3P1 + 4P2$$

The constraints this time are the minimum requirements. Each of the four vitamins can be obtained in varying amounts from either product. Whatever combination of products is bought, the sum of the units of a given vitamin in the two must equal or exceed the minimum requirement for that vitamin. We thus get the following four "greater than or equal to" constraints:

$$5P1 + 25P2 \geq 50$$
$$25P1 + 10P2 \geq 100$$
$$10P1 + 10P2 \geq 60$$
$$35P1 + 20P2 \geq 180$$

As always, we have the nonnegativity requirement on the variables, in this case the number of ounces of $P1$ and of $P2$ bought.

How does this problem compare with the earlier one? Before, we were trying to maximize profit; now we want to minimize cost. Before, we had two activities (manufacture of standard and deluxe models); now, we also have two activities (buying of two types of product). Before, there were two constraints; now there are four. The nonnegativity requirement on each activity level never changes.

The situation is graphed in Figure 11.

FIGURE 11
Graph of the constraints in the feed additive problem

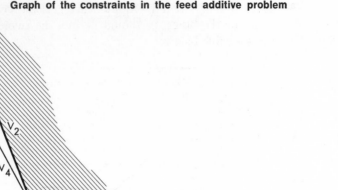

P1 = Number of ounces of product 1 bought

The feasible region in this case is on the right-hand side of the lines, since the constraints are all "greater than or equal to"; there is no restriction on the amount by which the minimum can be exceeded. The feasible region consists of all combinations of products that do not violate any of the constraints.

In Figure 12 we have shown only that part of each constraint line that is on the border of the feasible region, and we have plotted four total-cost lines.

We see that the 12 cent line is not feasible anywhere and that the 40 cent line is feasible everywhere. Since the 19 cent line is the lowest-cost line that touches the feasible region, there is no possibility of getting the required vitamin content for less than 19 cents. This corresponds to five ounces of $P1$ and one ounce of $P2$, which minimizes the cost and still satisfies all four constraints.

One of the most valuable features of the methods used to solve general linear programming problems is that the methods guarantee that the optimum solution is the best. We have, of course, not proved this fact by

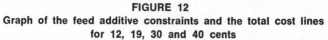

FIGURE 12
Graph of the feed additive constraints and the total cost lines
for 12, 19, 30 and 40 cents

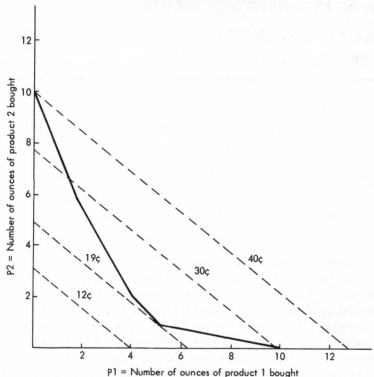

the graphical demonstrations here, but the procedures used in linear programming guarantee optimality.

It might be interesting to see what the cost would be if the poultry farmer bought only one type of product. These numbers can be derived rather simply from the graph: they are the number of ounces at the points where the feasible region intersects the $P1$ and $P2$ axes. It happens, by coincidence, that it would take 10 ounces either way. Ten ounces of $P1$ would satisfy exactly the requirement for the first vitamin and would exceed the requirements for the others in varying amounts; the cost would be 30 cents. Ten ounces of $P2$ would satisfy exactly the requirement for the second vitamin and would cost 40 cents. Note that once again the optimum occurred at a vertex of the feasible region.

Linear Programming versus Goal Programming*

James C. T. Mao †

BEFORE APPLYING goal programming to break-even analysis, it will be useful to explain the nature of goal programming and its relationship to linear programming. Goal programming is a special type of linear programming developed and extended by A. Charnes, W. W. Cooper, and Yuji Ijiri.[1] We should distinguish the term *goals*, which refers to management desires, from the term *constraints*, which refers to the environmental conditions under which the management makes its decisions. In ordinary linear programming, only one goal is incorporated into the objective function to be maximized or minimized. If management has multiple goals, then the goals not incorporated into the objective function are treated as constraints of the problem. The computational procedure then picks from the set of all solutions that satisfy the constraints the one (or ones) that maximizes or minimizes the objective function. Since the firm is striving for the highest value of the objective function, it is said to be adopting an optimizing behavior. In goal programming, all goals, whether one or many, are incorporated into the objective function, and only the true environmental conditions are treated as constraints. Moreover, each goal is set at a value that is judged satisfactory by the

* Reprinted with permission of The Macmillan Company from *Quantitative Analysis of Financial Decisions*, by James C. T. Mao. Copyright © 1969 by James C. T. Mao.

† Professor of Finance, University of British Columbia.

[1] The basic references on goal programming are the following: A. Charnes and W. W. Cooper, *Management Models and Industrial Applications of Linear Programming* (New York: John Wiley & Sons, Inc., 1961), pp. 219 ff; and Y. Ijiri, *Management Goals and Accounting for Control* (Amsterdam, Neths.: North-Holland Publishing Company, 1965).

management, but that is not necessarily the best attainable. The computational procedure then picks from the set of all solutions that satisfy the constraints the one (or ones) that best fulfills the management's announced targets. Since the objective here is to produce "satisfactory" results, rather than the best possible results, the firm is said to be adopting a "satisficing" behavior.

To illustrate the technique of goal programming, let us refer back to the hypothetical TV–radio manufacturer of Chapter 3. The reader will recall that the problem is to determine the values of x_1 and x_2 (production rates) that satisfy the constraints (1) and nonnegativity conditions (2) and at the same time maximize the objective function (3):

$$x_1 + x_2 \leq 4 \quad \text{(capacity constraint)}$$
$$3x_1 + x_2 \leq 10 \quad \text{(capacity constraint)} \tag{4–1}$$
$$x_1 + 4x_2 \leq 12 \quad \text{(financial constraint)}$$
$$x_i \geq 0 \quad (i = 1, 2) \quad \text{(nonnegativity conditions)} \tag{4–2}$$
$$\text{Maximize } f = x_1 + 2x_2 \quad \text{(objective function)} \tag{4–3}$$

The optimal values of x_1 and x_2 are $\frac{4}{3}$ and $\frac{8}{3}$, respectively. Hence, if the firm's objective is to maximize profit, it can make a profit as high as $6.67.

Although $6.67 is the maximum profit, the management of the firm for various reasons may wish to set a profit target in excess of $6.67. For example, management may set the target at $8 to evoke maximum effort from its employees or to serve as a criterion for judging the performance of its employees. To incorporate the $8 profit target into a goal programming model, we first define the surplus variable y^+ and the slack variable y^- as follows:

$$y^+ \times y^- = 0$$
$$y^+, y^- \geq 0 \tag{4–4}$$
$$x_1 + 2x_2 - 8 = y^+ - y^-$$

The equations in (4) state that (1) either one or both of these variables are zero, (2) both of these variables are nonnegative, and (3) the expression $y^+ - y^-$ is a measure of the divergence of realizable profit $x_1 + 2x_2$ from the target profit of $8.

Observe that if realizable profit $x_1 + 2x_2$ equals the target profit of $8, $y^+ - y^- = 0$. According to the equation $y^+ \times y^- = 0$, at least one of the y's must be zero. Therefore, $y^+ - y^- = 0$ implies that both slack and surplus variables are equal to zero. If $x_1 + 2x_2 > 8, y^+ - y^- > 0$. Since one of the y's must be zero and the other y zero or positive, $y^+ - y^- > 0$ implies that $y^- = 0$ and $y^+ > 0$. The variable y^+, therefore, measures the amount by which realizable profit exceeds the target profit, and this is the reason for the $+$ in y^+. Similarly, if $x_1 + 2x_2 < \$8$, then $y^+ - y^- < 0$ and $y^- > 0$ and $y^+ = 0$. The variable y^-, therefore, measures the amount by which realizable profit falls short of target profit and this is the reason for the — in y^-.

With the variables y^+ and y^- thus defined, the problem facing the TV-radio manufacturer takes the following goal programming formulation:

$$\begin{aligned}
x_1 + x_2 &\leq 4 &&\text{(capacity constraint)} \\
3x_1 + x_2 &\leq 10 &&\text{(capacity constraint)} \\
x_1 + 4x_2 &\leq 12 &&\text{(liquidity constraint)} \\
x_1 + 2x_2 - y^+ + y^- &= 8 &&\text{(profit target)}
\end{aligned}$$
(4-5)

$$x_i, y^+, y^- \geq 0 \quad (i = 1, 2) \quad \text{(nonnegativity conditions)} \tag{4-6}$$

$$\text{Minimize } f = y^+ + y^- \quad \text{(objective function)} \tag{4-7}$$

Three aspects of this formulation deserve comment. First, the objective is to minimize $y^+ + y^-$. Since prior knowledge tells us that the profit target of \$8 is unattainable, we expect that in the optimal solution y^+ would be zero and y^- would be positive. Second, the fact that y^+ and y^- both appear in the objective function means that the management wants both variables to have the value of zero, implying exact attainment of its profit goal. The fact that y^+ and y^- are equally weighted means that the management is equally willing to accept a positive or negative deviation in order to come as close to the target as possible, if it cannot be attained exactly. Third, although $y^+ \times y^- = 0$ does not appear as a constraint in this formulation, the simplex solution guarantees that at least one of the two variables will be zero.[2]

To solve the goal programming problem above by the simplex method, we convert the constraints in (5) into a set of equations by introducing slack variables wherever necessary. The problem then becomes

$$\begin{aligned}
x_1 + x_2 + x_3 &&&= 4 \\
3x_1 + x_2 &+ x_4 &&= 10 \\
x_1 + 4x_2 &&+ x_5 &= 12 \\
x_1 + 2x_2 &&- y^+ + y^- &= 8
\end{aligned}$$
(4-8)

$$x_i, y^+, y^- \geq 0 \quad (i = 1, 2, 3, 4, 5) \tag{4-9}$$

$$\text{Minimize } f = y^+ + y^- \tag{4-10}$$

The simplex solution in this case consists of the three tableaus presented in Table 4-1.[3] At the optimum, $x_1 = 1\frac{1}{3}$, $x_2 = 2\frac{2}{3}$, $x_3 = 0$, $x_4 = 3\frac{1}{3}$, $y^- = \frac{4}{3}$, and $y^+ = 0$. The fact that $y^+ = 0$ and $y^- = \frac{4}{3}$ means that the

---

[2] If the rectangular array of coefficients in constraints (8) is viewed as a set of column vectors, then the vectors with which y^+ and y^- are associated are linearly dependent. Hence, y^+ and y^- cannot both appear as basic variables in a solution to the system of equations in (8). For a more detailed explanation, see Charnes and Cooper, *Management Models and Industrial Applications of Linear Programming*, p. 219.

[3] For purposes of computation, the objective function in (10) is to be interpreted as $f = y^+ + y^- + ox_1 + ox_2 + ox_3 + ox_4 + ox_5$.

TABLE 1
Simplex solution of goal programming problem

Tableau 1

	x_1	x_2	x_3	x_4	x_5	y^+	y^-	
x_3	1	1	1	0	0	0	0	4
x_4	3	1	0	1	0	0	0	10
x_5	1	4	0	0	1	0	0	12
y^-	1	2	0	0	0	-1	1	8
Δf	-1	-2	0	0	0	2	0	

$$f = y^+ + y^- = 8$$

Tableau 2

	x_1	x_2	x_3	x_4	x_5	y^+	y^-	
x_3	$\tfrac{3}{4}$	0	1	0	$-\tfrac{1}{4}$	0	0	1
x_4	$1\tfrac{1}{4}$	0	0	1	$-\tfrac{1}{4}$	0	0	7
x_2	$\tfrac{1}{4}$	1	0	0	$\tfrac{1}{4}$	0	0	3
y^-	$\tfrac{1}{2}$	0	0	0	$-\tfrac{1}{2}$	-1	1	2
Δf	$-\tfrac{1}{2}$	0	0	0	$\tfrac{1}{2}$	2	0	

$$f = y^+ + y^- = 2$$

Tableau 3

	x_1	x_2	x_3	x_4	x_5	y^+	y^-	
x_1	1	0	$\tfrac{4}{3}$	0	$-\tfrac{1}{3}$	0	0	$\tfrac{4}{3}$
x_4	0	0	$-1\tfrac{1}{3}$	1	$\tfrac{2}{3}$	0	0	$10\tfrac{2}{3}$
x_2	0	1	$-\tfrac{1}{3}$	0	$\tfrac{1}{3}$	0	0	$\tfrac{8}{3}$
y^-	0	0	$-\tfrac{2}{3}$	0	$-\tfrac{1}{3}$	-1	1	$\tfrac{4}{3}$
Δf	0	0	$\tfrac{2}{3}$	0	$\tfrac{1}{3}$	2	0	

$$f = y^+ + y^- = \tfrac{4}{3}$$

firm's goal cannot be achieved: The best attainable profit of $6.67 is $1.33 below the target profit of $8. So, in this case, the solution obtained by goal programming is identical to that obtained by the original method of linear programming.

In the preceding example the management's goal was unattainable. Goal programming could be illustrated equally well by an example in which the management's goal is attainable. But whether the goal is attainable or not, it may be asked what advantages there are in converting an ordinary linear programming problem into a goal programming problem. That is, for which situations is goal programming more appropriate than ordinary linear programming? First, goal programming can be used to further the coordination of activities within a firm. If the marketing executive forecasts sales of 100 units per month, the production executive takes this figure as his goal and the financial executive must in turn provide the necessary funds. When such a specific sales objective is set, the different departments are able to plan their activities in coordination.

A second situation in which goal programming is especially useful is one in which the manager of a firm is a "satisficer" rather than an optimizer. A useful discussion of the principle of satisficing may be found in Y. Ijiri, *Management Goals and Accounting for Control*.[4] For example, a sales manager, who has been capturing 50 percent of the industry sales for many years, may regard the difference between 48 and 50 percent as considerably more significant than the difference between 58 and 60 percent. Instead of striving for an ever-expanding market share, the sales manager may simply aim at maintaining his current market share, which he regards as "satisfactory enough." Similarly, the owner of a business, who has been making $10,000 of yearly profit for a number of years, may for psychological reasons attach particular significance to the profit figure of $10,000. Instead of striving for maximum profit, he may simply aim at a profit of $10,000, which he regards as "good enough."

Third, even when the overall aim of the firm is to maximize profit, goal programming is still preferable in cases in which there are multiple goals. As mentioned earlier, when management has multiple goals, ordinary linear programming incorporates only one of these goals in the objective function and treats the remaining goals as constraints. Since the optimal solution must fully satisfy all constraints, this structuring of the problem implies that (1) the several goals within the constraining equations are of equal importance to the management and (2) these goals have absolute priority over the goal incorporated into the objective function. But what if, instead of incorporating only one goal, the management wishes to incorporate, e.g., three goals in its objective function? Moreover, assume that management ranks its goals such that goal A has absolute priority over goal B and B has absolute priority over goal C. Ordinary linear programming cannot solve problems of this kind, whereas goal programming can. This flexibility of goal programming in dealing with multiple goals is especially important in situations in which management goals are conflicting and hence cannot all be fully satisfied.

---

[4] See Y. Ijiri, *Management Goals and Accounting for Control*, pp. 9–13 (see footnote 1, this chapter); see also H. Simon, *Models of Man* (New York: John Wiley & Sons, Inc., 1957), pp. 204–206.

part II

Current asset management

CANAMA CORPORATION

In June of 1972, Mr. John Flannery, Canama's newly appointed director of banking operations, began a reappraisal of the firms banking activities which had evolved over a long period. During that time, no attempt at optimizing banking efficiency at the corporate level had been made. Canama's banking operations in 1972 were confined to two large banks: (1) Citizens National Bank (CNB), and (2) Trans National Bank (TNB).

THE COST OF BANKING SERVICES

Canama incurred three types of charges for banking services: (1) a charge per check deposited by Canama; (2) a charge per check paid out by Canama; and (3) other monthly charges, generally small amounts, such as wire transfer charges, account reconciliation fees, and postage costs.

Canama's customer receipts were deposited into both banks (depending on product line and location). The charges per check deposited in CNB and TNB were $0.02 and $0.03, respectively.

Based on careful records of the average size of the checks deposited in each bank, Mr. Flannery estimated that the number of checks deposited in CNB during the next month would be equal to: the total dollar amount of all deposits in CNB for the next month *times* .00095. In other words, the average check size for CNB deposits was $1,052.63.[1] For TNB, Mr. Flannery estimated that the number of checks deposited would equal:

---

[1] That is, if anticipated deposits for the month totaled, say, $1,052.63, then the expected number of checks deposited would be ($1,052.63) × (.00095) = 1.

the total dollar amount deposited *times* .000145. That is, TNB deposits averaged $6,896.55 per check.

Both banks charged $0.05 per check paid out. Using the approach applied previously with regard to deposits, and past records, Mr. Flannery then derived a parameter, for each bank, which relates *the dollar amount of disbursements to the number of checks written*. An estimate of the number of checks which will be drawn on a particular bank is obtained by multiplying the expected dollar amount of disbursements for the month for that bank, by the bank's parameter.

Table 1 below shows the "disbursement" for each bank. For instance, the expected number of checks paid out from CNB monthly is equal to: the expected dollar amount of monthly disbursements from CNB *times* .000517.

TABLE 1
Disbursement parameters
number of checks
dollar amount of
disbursements

Bank	Payout parameter
CNB...........	.000517
TNB...........	.002709

Derived from records of Canama
over a number of years.

Anticipated "other monthly charges" for each bank for the coming month were:

Bank	Anticipated other monthly charges
CNB............	$ 90
TNB............	$145

THE BANKS' COMPENSATION

The banks received compensation in two forms: (1) cash fees and (2) use of net collected balances.

Net collected balances for a particular bank are defined as (1) the company's cash book balance, plus (2) a fraction of monthly disbursements through the bank (equal to "the float,") minus (3) an estimate of the dollar amount of (deposited) checks in transit which have not yet reached the bank.

The "float factor" (i.e., the fraction of disbursements assumed, on the average, to be still in the account) for each bank is as follows:

Bank	Float factor
CNB..............	.19459
TNB..............	.18189

Dollar amounts of checks in transit for CNB and TNB are assumed to be respectively .05063 and .032877 *times* the dollar amounts of deposits in each of the two banks.

Both banks granted a service charge credit on funds available for investment. These credits (as fractions of net collected balances) were:

Bank	Service charge credit *net collected balance*
CNB..........	.003566
TNB..........	.001667

The rate for CNB, for instance, was derived as follows: The bank granted a credit of $5\frac{1}{8}$ percent[2] of funds available for investment. The reserve requirement reduced this amount to .835 *times* net collected balances. The monthly rate is $(\frac{1}{12})$ (.835) (.05125) = .003566.

RESTRICTIONS ON FLANNERY'S MANAGEMENT DECISIONS

The primary restriction with regard to Canama's banking operations was that the value of the compensation received by each bank (from cash fees, and net collected balances) must be at least as great as the cost of the services provided to Canama by each bank.

Canama's policy was to maintain positive company cash book balances for each bank at all times. Mr. Flannery accepted this policy initially. In the future, however, he intended to relax this constraint to see the effects of "playing the float."

Mr. Flannery estimated that deposits in TNB and CNB combined would total $9,223,000 next month. He based his figure on sales forecasts supplied to him by the marketing department. Estimated disbursement from the banks combined for the same period were $4 million.

THE FIRM'S OBJECTIVE: COST MINIMIZATION

Mr. Flannery recognized two economic costs of banking: (1) cash fee payments to banks, and (2) the opportunity cost of the average ledger balances maintained for each bank. Mr. Flannery assigned a cost of 20 percent per year, before income taxes, to the company's cash book balances. The 20 percent rate reflects Mr. Flannery's view of the firm's cash holdings in banks as a long-term investment. An alternative would be to use short-term money market rates as the cost of the balances. Mr. Flannery noted, however, that as long as the service credit rate allowed by banks was below the short-term money market rate, the

---

[2] Annual rate.

optimal banking policy was relatively insensitive to the choice of opportunity cost rate. In such cases, a strong incentive for minimizing cash balances was operative regardless of the choice among alternative rates. The 20 percent annual rate corresponds to a monthly rate of 1.667 percent.

SUMMARY

Mr. Flannery intended to determine the company's optimal (1) average cash book balances, (2) deposits, (3) disbursements, and (4) cash fees.

G & L CORPORATION

In January 1971, Mr. Robert Woods, newly appointed vice president of banking and credit for G & L Corporation, was confronted with the task of conserving and more effectively utilizing the cash balances of the company's divisions and subsidiaries across the nation. G & L Corporation has been profitable since its inception, and future growth and profitability is expected to continue. The working capital position has been sound in the past and no problems in this regard are expected in the future. It is Mr. Woods' feeling that although the management of the company's cash is not a problem in terms of normal operations, more effective utilization of this resource could be obtained through a formal cash management program.

COMPANY BACKGROUND

G & L Corporation was formed in June of 1916 in the state of Ohio. The company is a diversified, technically oriented, manufacturing firm. Its principal business is the manufacture and sale of products and the performance of services through its four operating divisions, as described below:

1. Electronic Components, Systems and Services
    Major products:
    Components—transistors, resistors, capacitors.
    Systems—advanced defense/space electronic systems, including communications, guidance, navigation, oil, power generation, electrooptical, lasers, and computers.

Computer-based services—software, programming and analysis, including mission planning and trajectory analysis.

2. Vehicle Components

    Major products:

    Original equipment—engine and chassis parts and related equipment. Replacement parts—complete line for use in passenger cars and trucks.

3. Aerospace Components, Systems and Services

    Major products:

    Components—jet engine blades, valves, aircraft fuel pumps, and mechanical subsystems.

    Systems and service—systems engineering for defense and space programs; design, development and manufacture of communication, scientific and defense satellites.

4. Industrial Components, Equipment and Systems

    Major products:

    Components—antifrictional bearings, steam and gas turbine components.

    Equipment and systems—drills and related equipment for petrochemical and mining industries.

G & L Corporation is a highly diversified, multidivision company. Their divisions and subsidiaries are geographically dispersed throughout the continental United States. As shown in Exhibit 1, the divisional contributions to both sales and earnings are somewhat evenly distributed among the four operating divisions. As indicated in Exhibit 2, the company has shown continuous growth in sales and earnings since 1961. Approximately 30 percent of G & L Corporation's net sales over the past seven years has been generated by contracts in affiliation with the U.S. government, either as prime contractor or as subcontractor. Accordingly, the strain on the cash and working capital of those divisions involved in such work is somewhat alleviated through the inflow of funds from government progress payments and the use of the percentage-of-completion method of accounting for their cost-plus contracts, which allows monthly and/or weekly billings. Future company growth will continue both internally and externally by means of acquisitions and new product development.

CASH MANAGEMENT PROCEDURES

At the present time, the company's policies and procedures relating to the control and administration of cash in excess of divisional needs is relatively lax. Within each of the four major divisions there are a number of operating subdivisions and subsidiaries which are autonomous and therefore control their own cash funds. In addition, there are a number of small field operations utilizing field imprest accounts which account for approximately 6 percent of G & L Corporation's total cash balances.

The organizational structure of one of the larger autonomous units, felt to be a scale representation of the other units, is broken down as follows (as relates to the management and control of cash):

1. Manager of Finance
   The principal duties are to ensure the timeliness of financial reports to management, to present such statements to the Operations Review Committee, to maintain good banking relations, and to oversee the finance department.
2. Manager of Banking and Credit
   The principal duties include the responsibility for opening and closing bank accounts, the supervision of the finance department employees and the responsibility for analyzing the cash position of the company unit and the determination of their credit policies.
3. Finance Department
   The employees of the finance department are responsible for preparing cash forecasts, followup on past due accounts receivable, corresponding with the banks on disputed items, initiating the requests for reimbursement to the field imprest accounts and providing the accounting department with input and support on daily receipts and deposits.

Under the present procedures of the company, each autonomous unit is required to project their own cash needs on a weekly basis. These cash forecasts were designed to inform the corporate office of cash needs in the immediate future rather than to indicate an excess cash position. If a need for cash were to be apparent, then the unit would formally request from the corporate office sufficient funds to meet its projected requirements. This transaction would be handled through the intercompany account. To avoid the constant need for such requests of the corporate office, it became the operating unit's policy to maintain a cash balance sufficient to cover immediate requirements as well as future needs. The corporate policy also stated that "excess cash" was to be remitted to the corporate office as often as practicable, and the operating units were to submit daily cash reports to the corporate office using conventional mail. However, the corporate office did not employ staff to monitor this policy and assure that such reports were being submitted on a timely basis, nor did they have the means to determine that excess cash was being properly remitted. Exhibit 3 shows the major operating units within the four divisions and their cash balance on hand as of December 31, 1970.

Only those operating units which had large amounts of cash on hand were in a position to invest in short-term marketable securities, such as Treasury bills or short-term commercial paper. Although such investments were made by only a few of the largest units, the other units retained their excess cash in order to avoid making constant requests for cash to the corporate office.

Presented in Exhibits 4 and 5 are a balance sheet and a summary of several relevant financial ratios indicating the current cash position in relationship to the overall financial position of G & L Corporation. Based on the thorough review of the entire situation, Mr. Wood must determine if steps need to be taken to implement a new system for the management of the corporation's cash balance, and if so, what procedures should be enacted to accomplish such a goal.

EXHIBIT 1
G&L CORPORATION
Source of net sales

Division	Sales (percent) 1970	Sales (percent) 1969	Earnings before taxes (percent) 1970	Earnings before taxes (percent) 1969
Electronic Components, systems and services.....	27	29	20	20
Vehicle components.........................	31	28	29	29
Aerospace components, systems and services......	23	23	25	23
Industrial components, equipment and systems....	19	20	26	28
Total.............................	100	100	100	100

EXHIBIT 2
G&L CORPORATION
Record of earnings
(dollar figures in thousands)

	Net sales	Net income	Depreciation and amortization	Common stock earnings per share
1960...........	$ 420,421	$10,177	Not available	$3.13
1961...........	409,077	6,495		1.84
1962...........	460,314	12,454		3.23
1963...........	482,639	15,165		3.95
1964...........	553,420	23,409	$15,419	2.49
1965...........	664,510	28,976	18,486	3.17
1966...........	863,866	35,154	21,321	3.61
1967...........	1,214,408	54,207	34,526	4.04
1968...........	1,487,547	72,193	43,187	2.22
1969...........	1,588,396	78,230	40,459	2.43
1970...........	1,595,188	79,315	44,012	2.47

EXHIBIT 3
G&L CORPORATION
Analysis of cash by division as of December 31, 1970
(dollar figures in thousands)

		Cash balances
Electronic Companies		
Colorado, Denver.................	$1,011	
Arizona, Phoenix.................	684	
Ohio, Cleveland..................	2,619	
Pennsylvania, Philadelphia.........	1,392	
Illinois, Forest Park..............	1,352	
California, Sunnyvale.............	842	
California, Los Angeles............	4,722	
Other states.....................	2,354	$14,976
Vehicle Companies		
Michigan, Detroit.................	$2,723	
Indiana, Gary....................	1,986	
Ohio, Dayton....................	2,571	
New York, Rochester.............	1,814	
Pennsylvania, Erie................	947	
Tennessee, Memphis.............	1,731	
Other states.....................	2,615	$14,387
Aerospace		
California, Los Angeles............	$3,149	
California, Anaheim..............	842	
Texas, Houston..................	935	
Florida, Cocoa Beach.............	2,679	
Washington, D.C.................	1,244	
Utah, Ogden....................	1,568	
Connecticut, Danbury.............	1,597	
Other states.....................	2,137	$14,151
Industrial		
North Carolina, Greensboro........	$1,123	
Missouri, Kansas City............	797	
Ohio, Cincinnati.................	1,345	
Pennsylvania, Pittsburgh...........	1,836	
Georgia, Atlanta.................	592	
Virginia, Norfolk.................	822	
Massachusetts, Boston.............	1,429	
Illinois, Springfield...............	1,138	
Other States.....................	1,844	$10,926
Total cash..............		$54,440

EXHIBIT 4
G&L CORPORATION
Consolidation balance sheet December 31, 1970
(dollar figures in thousands)

ASSETS

Cash......................................	$ 53,440
Marketable securities........................	5,399
Receivables................................	202,154
Inventories................................	281,908
Prepayments...............................	17,468
Total Current Assets...................	$ 560,369
Fixed assets...............................	$ 330,860
Other assets...............................	60,219
Intangibles................................	122,656
Total Assets.........................	$1,074,104

LIABILITIES AND STOCKHOLDERS' EQUITY

Notes payable..............................	$ 40,697
Accounts payable...........................	155,733
Dividends payable..........................	10,750
Income taxes...............................	34,100
Total Current Liabilities................	$ 241,280
Long-term debt............................	$ 272,378
Deferred income tax........................	8,567
Minority interest...........................	2,129
Total Liabilities......................	$ 524,354

STOCKHOLDERS' EQUITY

4% preferred (par $100).....................	$ 1,823
$4.25 preferred A..........................	16,725
$5.00 preferred B..........................	7,835
$4.40 preferred series 1.....................	4,958
Common stock.............................	30,895
$4.50 preferred series 3.....................	5,655
Capital surplus............................	90,415
Retained earnings..........................	391,444
Total Stockholder's Equity..............	$ 549,750
Total Liabilities and Stockholders' Equity..........	$1,074,104

The 1970 capital expenditures totaled $69,022,000 of which
$21,000,000 was used for expenditures in international subsidiaries.

EXHIBIT 5
G&L CORPORATION
Supplementary financial data

	1970	*1969*
Percent cash to current assets..............	9.54%	11.64%
Percent securities to current assets.........	0.96	0.92
Percent inventory to current assets.........	50.31	45.95
Percent net current assets to net worth......	58.04	66.60
Inventory turnover......................	5.66X	6.04X
Receivables turnover.....................	7.89X	7.21X
Percent net income to total assets...........	7.38%	7.61%
Percent net income to net worth............	14.43	15.26

THE MORGAN ORGAN
COMPANY

In April 1971, Mr. John Abbot was considering the recommendations he should make to Mr. King, the president of the Morgan Organ Company, to provide better control over the accumulation of inventories and to reduce the size of existing inventories held by the Morgan Company. Mr. Abbot had been transferred from the financial staff of Midwestern White Goods Company in January to serve as assistant to Mr. King. The Morgan Organ Company was a subsidiary of Midwestern White Goods Company. Mr. Abbot's newly assigned responsibilities included financial analysis, planning, and business systems developed for the Morgan Company. While he previously had only a short time to review Morgan's operations, he was convinced that if the company were to again make reasonable profits, management would have to learn how to operate with smaller inventories.

THE COMPANY

Morgan Organ Company was founded in 1954 by Walter Morgan, an accordianist of some repute. Mr. Morgan's original plan was to design an electronic accordian, but the resulting instrument proved to be too bulky for practical use. While he was experimenting without the bellows, he realized that what he had really invented was an electronic organ. The company never prospered under Mr. Morgan's guidance, and in 1958 he sold all the assets to the Brown Goods Corporation, a small manufacturer of televisions, radios, and phonographs. The company began to grow with Brown Goods' control and technological support.

In 1960, a majority interest in Brown Goods was obtained by Midwestern White Goods, Inc., a leading manufacturer of home appliances. Mid-western gradually increased its ownership in Brown Goods to about 85 percent in 1970. It was also able to obtain options for the balance of the outstanding stock, so that by 1972 it would wholly own Brown Goods.

Midwestern channeled the efforts of Brown Goods to the private label market. This substantially increased Brown Goods' sales. By 1970, except for Morgan's sales, virtually all the sales of Brown Goods were made to a major retailer. Financial statements for the parent companies are presented in Exhibits 1 and 2.

PRODUCT LINES

Electronic organs are manufactured by Morgan primarily for the home entertainment market. Morgan produces all electronic subassemblies and builds its own cabinets. Its products are sold worldwide. A Netherlands subsidiary, Morgan Muziek-Instrumenten N.V., distributes the products in Europe. Other distribution is made from the home factory.

Morgan also distributes electric guitars, organs, and amplifiers produced by an Italian subsidiary, Bender Electronica Musicale, S.P.A. These items are sold under the Bender name. The Bender organs are of the portable type, and require the use of an amplifier and speakers. Morgan organs are self-contained units. The Bender line is rounded out by a group of acoustic (nonelectric) guitars manufactured to Morgan's specifications in Japan. Morgan and Bender products are of a high quality and have been well received by both the general public and professional musicians.

INDUSTRY OUTLOOK

In 1970, the organ industry experienced its first year of significant sales decline in the last 15 years. Early indications were that sales for the industry declined almost 20 percent from the record sales in 1969 of $211 million. In the economic slowdown of 1970, it was only the big ticket items of pianos and organs in the musical instruments industry that registered large declines. This caused Morgan's management to believe that there is a demand being built up for their products, and that sales would significantly increase when a greater degree of optimism returned to the consuming public.

In the past, electronic organ sales have increased at a greater rate than musical instruments in general. This has been due to both the growing affluence of the consumers and the technological advances of the organ industry. The product has been improved considerably over recent years, making it more versatile, reliable, and easier to play. Recent innovations include self-teaching courses programmed into the organ's electronic system, and the incorporation of synthesizers in some models. Morgan has always been among the leaders in product development.

CORPORATE GOALS

Prior to moving to this new assignment, Mr. Abbot attended a meeting with the financial vice presidents of Brown Goods and Midwestern. At this meeting some of the financial goals for Morgan were mentioned, that is, a return to profitable operations and a reduction of the intercompany debt. He was aware that both parent companies had experienced poor years and were strapped for funds. While profitable operations were of great importance, Mr. Abbot left with the impression that a reduction of the parents' investment in the Morgan Company was a more immediate concern.

Morgan's only source of long-term funds is through intercompany debt. Interest is charged to Morgan at usually ½ percent above the prevailing prime rate. Normally, about half of the intercompany payables represented on the balance sheet is this long-term borrowing. The balance of the intercompany payables are for services performed by the parent, such as warehousing, shipping, transfer of materials, and interest. Morgan's intercompany debt to Brown Goods had increased by over $8 million since 1967 (Exhibit 3).

Mr. Abbot also learned that Morgan's problems seemed to revolve around inventories. After studying Morgan's financial statements (Exhibits 3 and 4) and comparing them to other organ manufacturers (Exhibits 5 and 6), he decided that he could concentrate his attention on this area. He could see no reason why the ratio of inventory to sales should be so much higher for Morgan than for its competitors. He reasoned that if Morgan's inventory-to-sales ratio could be brought into line with the other firms, its inventories and in turn its debt to Brown Goods might be reduced by $4 million or $5 million. He also felt that eliminating the cost of carrying excess inventory would help the company in its efforts to return to profitable operations.

FINISHED GOODS INVENTORY

A summary of the finished goods inventory by line and model is presented in Exhibit 7. A line refers to the organs containing the same physical components. A model is the organ's components in a specific cabinet for that organ. An X160 Spanish organ is differentiated from the other X160 organs only by cabinet (there are slight variations in cost and selling price resulting from the cabinet type).

Every year or two a line of organs is either improved or replaced by a new product in the same price range. The introduction of a new line is planned for the third quarter of the year to enable dealers to build up inventories for the prime Christmas selling season (about 40 percent of retail organ sales occur in the fourth quarter, and about a third of Morgan's sales are recorded in this period). Morgan's practice has been to hold introduction of a new line to dealers until all of the models of the old line have been sold. It has found that if a new model is released, dealers won't buy the balance of the old line as they fear being stuck with less-marketable merchandise.

In 1970, declining sales delayed the introduction of many new lines until late in the fourth quarter. Certain lines had not yet been introduced at year-end. Morgan's sales manager felt that not having the latest line available early and having voids in some lines adversely affected the fourth quarter sales by a minimum of 10 percent. He felt that the remaining models of each line could be sold at reductions of 15–20 percent in a matter of weeks, thus permitting a smooth and timely release of the new line. There is concern that delayed introduction of the new models could happen again in 1971.

One element of the Bender inventory poses a special problem. There are guitars and amplifiers with a carrying value of about $220,000 that the company has not released on the market because of a design defect. The items have been in inventory for over a year. The defect can be corrected by installing a $9 part. Installation of the part requires about $50 in labor. The entire rework can be done at the factory in Italy for a total cost of about $60 a unit, including parts and roundtrip transportation. As this is not a current model, there is a 50 percent possibility that the sales price to dealers would have to be reduced by an average of 20 percent to dispose of the entire lot in the event it is reworked. It would be strictly against company policy to sell the units on an "as is" basis since most Bender sales are to professional musicians, and the company zealously controls the quality of its products.

Mr. Carter, Brown Goods' financial vice president, has discussed donating the instruments to servicemen overseas through a charitable organization. Under his plan, the replacement part and rework instructions would be provided with the instruments. Mr. Carter estimates that about a third of the cost would be recovered through current year tax savings, and the balance in the next year. The units were originally planned to retail at about $450, of which 50 percent would represent the retailers gross profit. Morgan's gross margin was 20 percent on the items.

The balance of Morgan's finished goods inventory is salable merchandise.

SALES FORECASTING

Sales forecasting has been the responsibility of the sales department. The sales manager has complained that the "best guess" method now employed is less than adequate, and more sophisticated techniques should be employed. He has suggested that through an initial cost of around $15,000 and annual maintenance costs of about $25,000, a simulation model could be developed based on certain industry and economic indicators that would project sales by line and model. The projections would be updated monthly as actual sales data became available. As it stood, the best estimate for 1971 sales was $21,787,000.

The adverse affects of poor sales forecasting on the introductions of new organ lines was already indicated. The production manager suggested that he would be able to save a large amount through reduced overtime if an effective sales forecast became available, although he couldn't estimate how much. He added that a reliable forecast would aid in the development of more realistic standard costs. Due to the reduction of 1970 production, there was underabsorbed burden at the end of the year of about $700,000.

The sales manager was also of the opinion that the finished goods inventory could be substantially reduced if the company could get a better handle on when and where sales were coming from. He alleged that it had always been a selling point that Morgan could fill orders faster than the competition, but they could continue to do so with less inventory if planning could be improved. He felt that a 15–20 percent decrease would be possible. In an unguarded moment he told Mr. Abbot that finished goods could be reduced over 10 percent right now, but he wasn't going to let his salesmen miss a single sale because of a "can't" deliver. He later denied making the statement.

PRODUCTION SCHEDULING

The company uses a production lot release scheduling system. Lot sizes are in multiples of 10 units representing quantities equivalent to one week's production of chassis, keyboards, and cabinets, and four weeks' production of electronic subassemblies. The orders are scheduled so that sales requirements can be met and the minimum desired inventory maintained. Subassemblies are scheduled based on the elapsed times shown in Exhibit 8. Production orders are released about a month in advance of requirements to provide the production units a backlog to enable them to level their work loads.

Under this scheduling arrangement, a typical electronic module assembly would be built in lot quantities of 150 to 250 units. The cost of purchased components would range from $2.50 to $7.50 per module.

The setup time for the lot would be about 2 hours and assembly would require about 0.2 hours per unit. (Labor rates averaged $3.25 per hour and factory burden was 10 percent of direct labor costs). Mr. Abbot's preliminary review indicated that while these typical values suggested that the lot sizes used were approximately optimum when calculated by standard formulas, he believed that some steps should be taken to reduce the length of storage periods found in the schedule. He observed that the work-in-process inventory was running about $3,000,000.

Over the next four quarters, management felt that it would be important to strive for even quarterly production and raw material purchases. It was felt that accessories and Bender Guitar inventory would increase to $1.5 million in the first quarter, decrease to $1.3 million in the second quarter, $1.1 million in the third quarter, and $1.0 million in the fourth quarter.

PRODUCTION CONTROL

Materials used in production are of two types—controlled and usage. Controlled items are all individual items with a cost of 25 cents or more per unit. They may not leave the stores department without proper requisition. Usage items are those costing less than 25 cents a unit; or items purchased in bulk quantities, such as wire, tape, and finishing materials. Usage items are furnished the production departments on a blanket requisition, and each department maintains limited inventories of usage items it employs in production.

Physical inventories have resulted in adjustments to the book inventory at each year-end ranging from $300,000 to $600,000. This has prompted the production manager to suggest that the production control system be revised, and all controlled materials be subject to computer control. The controller has estimated that this would involve about $150,000 of start-up costs and would increase operating costs about $100,000 per year. The production manager stated that the tighter control should significantly reduce inventory adjustments and work stoppage caused by the shortage of parts. It would also permit refinements in the scheduling system that could reduce the amount of storage built into the production schedule by about 30 percent. He also implied that if the purchasing department could be plugged into the system, even further savings would be possible.

MATERIAL PROCUREMENT

Purchases of components and raw materials totaled $7.6 million in 1970. The purchasing agent was cognizant of the savings available by purchasing in large lots, and instructed the persons in his department to use their judgment and take advantage of quantity discounts whenever feasible. He also stated that it costs the company about $60 to place the order, receive the goods, and process the bill. Reductions in the number of orders represented dollars in the bank, according to him. There had been earlier discussion concerning implementation of an economic order quantity system, but the purchasing agent stated that it would be a waste of time and money, because he was already buying at the most economical prices. He also stated that the system would not be effective because only about two thirds of the items could be ordered and used in quantities where the savings could exceed 10 percent.

The material control supervisor cited several instances in which excessive amounts of raw materials had been purchased. On one occasion, a two-year supply of a certain copper wire had been purchased in anticipation of impending price increases. Unfortunately, all the new organ lines did not use this wire, and after three years over half of the purchase remained in inventory. Another time, an unusually good price was obtained on a year and a half's supply of a packaging cardboard. There was no adequate storage space for this large quantity, and a large portion was lost as a result of its being outside during a weekend rainstorm. The material control supervisor felt that more attention should be given to the costs of holding large raw material inventories. He estimated that a cost of 25 percent of the purchase price per year was incurred to hold material in inventory. The 25 percent covered the average cost of material handling, storage, deterioration, obsolescence, loss, and the cost of capital tied up in the inventory.

A system that ties in with the proposed system for production control of controlled parts to automatically produce purchase orders had been suggested. This system could also be applied to usage items based upon the establishment of economic order quantities and order points. The cost of installing this system involved an initial expenditure for software of $40,000 and an increase in annual operating costs of about $10,000. Under the system, prices for the purchase orders would be established by annual agreements with major suppliers, but the system also provided for negotiation of prices on individual orders where desired. The purchasing agent suggested that for the money involved, he would rather buy engraving equipment and send his suppliers engraved purchase orders. He indicated that the present system was working satisfactorily as far as he was concerned.

EXHIBIT 1
THE MORGAN ORGAN COMPANY
Consolidated balance sheet of parent companies as of December 31, 1969–70
(dollar figures in thousands)

	Midwestern White Goods, Inc.		Brown Goods Corp.	
	1970	1969	1970	1969
ASSETS				
Cash..................................	$ 31,024	$ 18,960	$ 6,086	$ 3,787
Accounts receivable....................	68,933	77,535	10,277	9,831
Inventories (FIFO, Cost or Market)........				
Finished goods......................	105,550	147,940	27,546	39,339
Raw materials and work-in process.....	94,843	90,583	18,236	22,445
	$200,393	$238,523	$45,782	$61,784
Prepaid expenses........................	3,955	3,065	755	662
Deferred taxes..........................	11,747	7,614	—	—
Current Assets..................	$316,052	$345,697	$62,900	$76,064
Investments in subsidiaries not consolidated..	19,762	17,984	—	—
Other assets............................	2,501	2,673	288	363
Property, plant, and equipment (net)........	139,395	132,665	22,313	21,104
Excess of cost over assets of subs...........	17,527	17,527	—	—
Total Assets....................	$495,237	$516,546	$85,501	$97,531
LIABILITIES				
Notes payable..........................	$ 43,997	$ 45,477	$ 5,886	$14,980
Accounts payable.......................	41,506	64,516	10,349	6,195
Accrued expenses.......................	28,656	31,588	6,965	6,009
Warranty reserve.......................	35,089	24,877	—	—
Income taxes payable....................	8,970	10,835	116	94
Current portion of long-term debt..........	4,671	3,434	2,395	2,349
Current Liabilities...............	$162,889	$180,727	$25,711	$29,627
Loans from parent and customer............			25,000	25,000
Long-term debt.........................	93,406	98,890	29,344	31,715
Deferred taxes..........................	8,421	6,290	—	—
Minority interest in subsidiaries............	773	4,950	—	—
Stockholders' equity:.....................				
Common stock......................	26,714	26,699	2,173	2,172
Additional paid-in capital..............	15,982	14,346	2,400	2,399
Retained earnings (deficit)............	187,052	184,644	873	6,618
Total Liabilities and Equity.......	$495,236	$516,546	$85,501	$97,531
Shares common stock outstanding..........	10,685	10,639	4,346	4,345

Brown Goods owns 100 percent of the stock of Morgan, a consolidated subsidiary. Midwestern White Goods owns 82 percent of Brown Goods outstanding stock, and has options to acquire the balance through 1972. Brown Goods is a consolidated subsidiary.

EXHIBIT 2

THE MORGAN ORGAN COMPANY
Consolidated income statements of parent companies
for years ended December 31, 1969–70
(dollar figures in thousands)

	Midwestern White Goods, Inc.*		Brown Goods Corp.†	
	1970	1969	1970	1969
Sales....................	$1,077,161	$1,038,177	$184,912	$166,396
Other income............	4,567	4,781	551	574
	$1,081,728	$1,042,958	$185,463	$166,970
Cost of goods sold........	891,009	848,491	164,516	142,347
Selling, general, and administrative expenses.......	107,925	98,084	20,862	20,849
Interest on long-term debt.................	5,449	5,908	3,508	3,881
Interest—other...........	6,680	2,957	1,614	749
	$ 70,665	$ 87,518	$ (5,037)	$ (856)
Income taxes.............	38,610	47,070	—	—
Operating Income.....	32,055	40,448	$ (5,037)	$ (856)
Extraordinary losses.......	12,600§		708‡	
Net Income......	$ 19,455	$ 40,448	$ (5,745)	$ (856)
Earnings (loss) per share before extraordinary losses.................	$ 3.01	$ 3.80	$ (1.16)	$ (.20)
Extraordinary loss........	(1.18)		(.16)	
Net earnings (loss) per share................	1.83	3.80	(1.32)	(.20)

* Includes the operations of Brown Goods.
† Includes the operations of Morgan Organ Company.
‡ Casualty loss.
§ Loss from discontinuation of division.

EXHIBIT 3

THE MORGAN ORGAN COMPANY
Balance sheets as of December 31, 1966–70
(dollar figures in thousands)

	1970	1969	1968	1967	1966
ASSETS					
Cash........................	$ 543	$ 321	$ 685	$ 501	$ 413
Accounts receivable...........	2,318	3,491	3,787	2,086	1,879
Inventories:					
Finished goods..............	5,409	5,604	4,321	2,463	2,521
Raw materials and work-in-					
process..................	4,312	5,036	5,086	3,188	2,839
	$ 9,721	$10,640	$ 9,407	$ 5,651	$5,360
Prepaid expenses.............	541	611	342	518	78
Recoverable federal income					
tax*.......................	747	679			
Current Assets.......	$13,870	$15,742	$14,221	$ 8,756	$7,730
Investment in foreign					
subsidiaries................	1,008	952	909	762	485
	47	38	38	104	43
Property, plant, and equipment,					
net.......................	1,319	1,517	1,732	1,110	1,274
Total Assets..........	$16,244	$18,249	$16,900	$10,732	$9,532
LIABILITIES					
Accounts payable..............	$ 821	$ 937	$ 628	$ 437	$ 349
Accrued expenses.............	1,374	1,149	1,841	981	718
Income taxes.................			137	319	270
Current Liabilities.....	$ 2,195	$ 2,086	$ 2,606	$ 1,737	$1,337
Due Brown Goods†...........	14,927	14,511	11,817	6,870	6,818
Stockholder's equity:					
Commons stock, $0.50 par....	200	200	200	200	200
Additional paid-in capital.....	300	300	300	300	300
Retained earnings (deficit)....	(1,378)	1,152	1,977	1,625	877
	$16,244	$18,249	$16,900	$10,732	$9,532

* Resulting from Net Operating loss carry-back.
† Approximately half the amount due Brown Goods bears interest at ½ to 1 % above the prevailing prime rate. The balance of the intercompany account represent transfers of materials, services, etc.

EXHIBIT 4
THE MORGAN ORGAN COMPANY
Income statements for year ended December 31, 1966–70
(dollar figures in thousands)

	1970	1969	1968	1967	1966
Sales*	$17,211	$21,583	$18,119	$13,327	$12,581
Cost of goods sold	15,893	17,643	13,118	9,073	8,658
	$ 1,318	$ 3,940	$ 5,001	$ 4,254	$ 3,923
Selling, general, and administrative expenses:					
Engineering	623	631	537	298	282
Selling	2,874	3,683	2,942	1,974	1,917
Administrative	603	618	571	421	402
Interest	495	512	311	176	186
Net income before taxes	$(3,277)	$(1,504)	640	1,385	1,136
Federal income taxes (recovery of taxes previously paid)	(747)	(679)	288	637	501
Net Income	$(2,530)	$ (825)	$ 352	$ 748	$ 635

* First and second quarter sales have historically averaged 17 percent and 20 percent of total net sales.

EXHIBIT 5
THE MORGAN ORGAN COMPANY
Selected balance sheet data for organ manufacturers
(dollar figures in thousands)

December 31, 1970	Allen Organ Co.	Baldwin (D.H.) Co.	Hammond Corp.*	Wurlitzer Co.*
Cash and marketable securities	$1,069	$ 8,373	$ 2,353	$ 3,633
Accounts receivable	722	22,570	17,497	30,406
Inventories	2,459	18,229†	26,138‡	18,258
Prepaid expenses	8	1,566	658	
Current Assets	$4,258	$50,738	$46,646	$52,297
Property	1,656	6,332	9,376	13,918
Investments	145	39,875	1,429	
Other	403	363	224	2,027
Total assets	$6,462	$97,308	$57,675	$68,242
Notes payable	$ 114	$12,908	$ 4,949	$ 9,269
Accounts payable	118	3,070	3,464	3,483
Accrued expenses	306	4,411	4,477	2,326
Income taxes payable	28	3,190	283	3,023
Current Liabilities	$ 566	$23,579	$13,173	$18,101
Long-term debt	767	23,600	9,918	12,100
Other liabilities		1,649	1,331	6,104
Preferred stock		14,414	5,145	
Common stock	528	4,715	3,499	12,340
Additional paid in capital	2,931	1,546	1,056	
Retained earnings	1,706	28,086	25,553	19,597
Treasury stock	(36)	(281)	(2,000)	
Total Liabilities and Net Worth	$6,462	$97,308	$57,675	$68,242

* Balance sheet for fiscal year end of March 31, 1971
† Finished goods = $7,622; Raw materials and work-in-process = $10,607
‡ Finished goods = $12,239; Raw materials and work-in-process = $13,899

EXHIBIT 6

THE MORGAN ORGAN COMPANY

Selected operating data for organ manufacturers (dollar figures in thousands)

	Allen Organ Co.	*Baldwin (D.H.) Co.*	*Hammond Corp.**	*Wurlitzer Co.**
1970				
Sales......................	$8,327	$59,480	$96,100	$63,407
Net income.................	441	5,024	272	1,247
Inventory as percent of sales....	29%	32%	27%	29%
1969				
Sales......................	$8,669	$64,028	$96,355	$59,942
Net income.................	507	4,494	4,697	880
Inventory as percent of sales....	29%	31%	35%	29%
1968				
Sales......................	$7,334	$66,555	$90,490	$63,563
Net income.................	340	3,742	5,276	2,158
Inventory as percent of sales....	28%	27%	30%	30%
1967				
Sales......................	$6,474	$61,891	$83,992	$62,246
Net income.................	334	2,210	4,565	2,037
Inventory as percent of sales....	36%	38%	26%	30%

* Data for fiscal years ending March 31, 1971–68

EXHIBIT 7

THE MORGAN ORGAN COMPANY

Finished goods inventory at December 31, 1970

Electronic organs	Number of units						Standard cost*	Dealer cost†	Approx. retail‡	Inventory amount
	Contemporary	Spanish	Early American	French Provincial	Rosewood and other	Total				
X140	308	284	47	N/A	N/A	639	$ 372	$ 405	$ 695	$ 237,708
X10 (old)	14	–0–	12	–0–	7	33	464	510	850	15,312
XA150 (new model)	243	297	37	30	12	619	467	510	850	289,073
X160	274	318	28	40	N/A	660	515	590	995	339,900
X170 (old)	117	93	3	21	4	238	597	710	1,200	142,086
XA170 (new)	149	180	48	16	49	442	604	720	1,200	266,968
X180	269	301	10	15	N/A	595	800	895	1,500	476,000
X190 (old)	204	–0–	–0–	4	–0–	208	997	1,160	1,995	207,376
XA190 (new)	156	173	11	19	17	376	984	1,160	1,995	369,984
X200	199	195	N/A	N/A	10	404	1,100	1,500	2,500	444,400
X210	43	138	4	7	11	203	1,335	1,850	3,600	271,005
X220 (old)	41	–0–	N/A	N/A	–0–	41	2,065	2,900	4,500	84,665
XA220 (new)	–0–	49	N/A	N/A	8	57	2,063	2,900	4,800	117,591
X230	N/A	43	N/A	N/A	7	50	3,375	4,200	6,900	168,750
Organ accessories										791,477
Bender guitars, organs and amplifiers										1,187,023
Total Finished Goods										$5,409,318

* Average standard cost. Actual varies according to cabinet.
† Average dealer cost. There is a great variation in actual selling prices due to liberal quantity discounts and other incentives.
‡ Dealers are free to determine selling price.

EXHIBIT 8
THE MORGAN ORGAN COMPANY
Scheduled flow through manufacturing operations

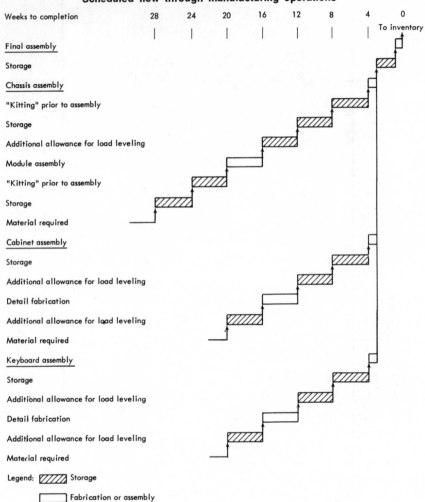

Weeks to completion   28   24   20   16   12   8   4   0

To inventory

Final assembly

Storage

Chassis assembly

"Kitting" prior to assembly

Storage

Additional allowance for load leveling

Module assembly

"Kitting" prior to assembly

Storage

Material required

Cabinet assembly

Storage

Additional allowance for load leveling

Detail fabrication

Additional allowance for load leveling

Material required

Keyboard assembly

Storage

Additional allowance for load leveling

Detail fabrication

Additional allowance for load leveling

Material required

Legend: ⧄ Storage

☐ Fabrication or assembly

IMPERIAL MANUFACTURING COMPANY

IN EARLY 1971, Imperial Manufacturing Company of St. Louis, Missouri, was experiencing working capital problems. The firm recently retained Mr. Dave Carter, a financial consultant and according to Mr. Craig Dunlop, president of Imperial Manufacturing, his task would be to improve the firm's liquidity position.

COMPANY BACKGROUND

Imperial Manufacturing Company was founded by the present Chairman of the Board, Mr. Bob Dunlop, in 1931. The firm now manufactures alternating and direct current motors, generators, generator sets, gear motors, and inverted rotary converters in sizes from $\frac{1}{20}$ to 500 horsepower. Imperial Foundry Company, a wholly owned subsidiary, produces gray iron and ferrous alloy castings, mostly for outside customers.[1]

The bulk of Imperial's manufacturing plants are located in St. Louis, Missouri, and consists of 15 buildings with the combined floor area of 25 acres. All of these buildings, with the exception of one which is occupied under a long-term lease, are owned by the firm. Other manufacturing facilities are located in Tennessee and Mississippi. Imperial Manufacturing markets its products through its own offices and through various agencies. The firm maintains warehouses and sales offices in 33 principal cities of the United States, and in over 70 cities throughout the world.

---

[1] Imperial Foundry Company is considered to be an independent profit center. It has not been consolidated into the financial data provided as exhibits.

EXTERNAL ENVIRONMENT

The electric motor portion of the electrical machinery industry is very competitive. There are many small firms concentrating on local markets, as well as the largest nationwide producers of electrical equipment such as General Electric and Westinghouse. The generator portion of the industry has a similar wide variety of producers, with Imperial representing only a very minor factor in this section.

The industry is one of derived demand, highly dependent upon the general health of the economy. The nation has been in the grips of a recession since late 1969, but indications are that business conditions are slowly improving. The Federal Reserve noted that industrial production edged up slightly in March. Retail sales, credit, money supply and deposits also increased. For the last half of the year the economy was predicted to return to record levels.

PROBLEM DEVELOPMENT

In early 1967, Imperial's newly appointed vice president of finance, Mr. Terry Brown, convinced the remainder of the firm's management that if the firm were to maintain or increase its share of the market, it was necessary to liberalize the firm's credit policies. Armed with his experience gained while employed with several other electrical machinery and equipment manufacturers, and with the knowledge of Imperial's relative position to the industry (presented in Exhibits 1 to 3), Mr. Brown changed the firm's credit terms from $\frac{1}{10}$ net 30 to $\frac{2}{10}$ net 60. Mr. Brown also decided that the firm could profit by being more liberal in extending credit to customers. With this in mind, he empowered the marketing department to extend credit to any potential customer who had earned profits and maintained a 1.2 current ratio for the past five years.

These changes were not unanimous decisions on the part of Imperial's management and met with much criticism. Mr. Brown responded to this criticism by declaring that with these changes, both sales and profits could be expanded without endangering Imperial's long-range liquidity position. One specific complaint that Mr. Brown faced from some members of the management team was that Imperial was operating near capacity and that any increase in sales would require an expansion of facilities. However, Mr. Brown was quick to point out that the firm was operating at only around 70 percent of capacity with a regular work schedule, and that an increase in sales would not require short-run expansion of facilities.

PRESENT SITUATION

Within nine months from the time that Mr. Brown instituted these changes, Imperial began to experience difficulty in responding to its accounts payable obligations. At this point Mr. Dunlop estimated that approximately 94 percent of all purchase orders placed by the company offered a cash discount as an incentive for prompt payment. The majority of the firm's vendors adhered to the $\frac{2}{10}$ net 30 terms, which were standard for the entire industry. With the firm's cash flow problems, Imperial was unable to pay its obligations before the end of the discount period, although it was able to pay before the end of the net period.

Since the end of the first half of 1970, however, Imperial Manufacturing was frequently unable to meet its accounts payable obligations even at the end of the net period. Rather than allowing obligations to become delinquent which would damage the firm's credit worthiness and its relationship with vendors, Imperial adopted the policy of requesting that accounts payable items which were in danger of becoming overdue, be converted into 90-day notes to be held by the creditor. Mr. Dunlop estimated that the effective annual interest rate on these notes was around 12 percent. Because of the expense of this type of financing, Mr. Dunlop hoped that it would only be a temporary measure used until the firm could improve its liquidity position.

Because of the resulting liquidity problems, Mr. Dunlop revealed his misgivings over the use of liberal credit terms and discounts to boost sales. While the firm had certainly experienced an increase in sales and profits since the new policies were adopted in 1967, Mr. Dunlop was not sure what portion of these increases were accounted for by the changes made by Mr. Brown. He felt that the lenient credit terms attracted a large percentage of late or nonpayers to deal with Imperial Manufacturing. A cursory examination of accounts receivable (Exhibit 6) revealed a significant change in the average age and composition of accounts. He also noted that the firm's bad debt expense had risen in the past few years to 3 percent of outstanding accounts from a relatively stable level of 1 percent.

Ever since Mr. Brown resigned in October 1970, Mr. Dunlop had become very concerned with the firm's working capital problems, and felt that the present crisis was similar to "the many that Imperial had somehow managed to survive in the past." His personal feeling was that the best source of funds would be those that are internally generated. He believed that because of both internal factors, such as the cost of carrying higher inventory levels to support sales and the increased bad debt expense, and external factors, such as industry and economic changes, a revision in the company's credit policy could be made that would result in the freeing up of resources for alternative uses.

In discussing Mr. Carter's area of responsibility, Mr. Dunlop described two obstacles involving the possible utilization of external sources of funds. The first problem was that the bank, which the company was currently doing business with, had expressed a reluctance to extend any further funds until a marked improvement in the firm's financial position had been demonstrated. The second problem was that the option of choosing a public stock offering was not available. Even if such an offering were economically feasible, it would be rigorously opposed by the Chairman of the Board, Mr. Bob Dunlop. The senior Dunlop had built Imperial Manufacturing Company from a garage shop into a major competitor within the industry, and he had stated that he would not chance the loss of control by diluting his equity position. Currently, approximately 51 percent of the outstanding common stock was closely held.

EXHIBIT 1

IMPERIAL MANUFACTURING
COMPANY

Income statement for the electrical machinery,
equipment and supplies industry for 1970
(dollar figures in millions)

Net sales......................	$70,309
Costs and expenses..............	65,529
Operating profit.................	$ 4,780
Other deductions................	472
Income before taxes.............	$ 4,308
Federal income tax..............	1,960
Net Income............	$ 2,348

EXHIBIT 2

IMPERIAL MANUFACTURING COMPANY

Balance sheet for the electrical machinery, equipment and supplies
industry as of December 31, 1970

(dollar figures in millions)

ASSETS

Cash	$ 2,194
Securities and notes	219
Receivables from U.S. government	1,258
Other receivables	10,907
Inventories	16,193
Other current assets	2,812
Total Current Assets	$33,583
Property, plant and equipment—net	15,847
Other assets	5,960
Total Assets	$55,390

LIABILITIES AND STOCKHOLDERS' EQUITY

Bank loans	$ 4,500
Advances and prepayments	1,025
Trade and notes payable	4,676
Accrued taxes	1,047
Other current liabilities	6,369
Total Current Liabilities	$17,617
Long-term debt	9,485
Other liabilities	1,588
Total Liabilities	$28,690
Capital stock and surplus	10,585
Earned surplus and reserves	16,115
Total Stockholders' Equity	$26,700
Total Liabilities and Stockholders' Equity	$55,390
Net working capital	$15,966

EXHIBIT 3

IMPERIAL MANUFACTURING COMPANY

Selected data—1970

(dollar figures in millions)

	Reliance Electric	General Electric	Bendix	Westing-house
Net sales	$326.4	$8,726.7	$1,442.9	$4,313.4
Net income	14.1	328.5	29.1	127.0
Accounts receivable	64.0	1,573.7	261.8	911.5
Current assets	142.9	3,334.8	663.4	2,041.5
Total assets	226.2	6,198.5	1,037.1	3,358.2
Current liabilities	60.4	2,650.3	299.6	1,139.8
Long-term debts	46.4	573.5	176.6	621.0
Stockholders' equity	117.4	2,553.6	523.0	1,487.4

EXHIBIT 4

IMPERIAL MANUFACTURING COMPANY

Income statements for the year ended December 31, 1966–70

	1966	1967	1968	1969	1970
New sales	$40,683,968	$44,045,367	$46,613,222	$54,752,029	$59,200,915
Other income	93,812	177,495	54,923	73,437	108,113
Total	$40,777,780	$44,222,862	$46,668,145	$54,825,466	$59,309,028
Cost of sales	33,741,486	36,645,062	39,669,636	44,781,799	48,357,030
Selling, general and administrative expense	3,699,650	3,987,318	3,918,177	4,609,232	4,889,106
Depreciation and amortization	962,041	962,059	1,009,279	1,543,023	1,690,485
Interest	217,853	501,299	592,473	538,944	810,116
Income taxes	920,000	875,000	560,000	1,611,000	1,650,000
Deferred income taxes	57,000	45,000	145,000	133,000	140,000
Net Income	$ 1,179,750	$ 1,207,124	$ 773,580	$ 1,608,468	$ 1,772,291
Dividends—Cash	365,836	376,075	376,084	376,099	395,315
Dividends—Stock	325,814				750,462
Net Income retained	$ 488,100	$ 831,049	$ 397,496	$ 1,232,369	$ 626,514
Earnings per share	$1.88	$1.93	$1.23	$2.56	$2.72
Common shares outstanding (authorized = 750,000 shares)	626,768	626,807	626,827	626,847	651,655

EXHIBIT 5

IMPERIAL MANUFACTURING COMPANY
Balance sheets as of December 31, for 1966–70

ASSETS

	1966	1967	1968	1969	1970
Cash and securities	$ 514,152	$ 334,267	$ 807,933	$ 1,249,741	$ 844,041
Accounts receivable—net	4,669,687	5,727,089	5,701,119	7,572,493	7,178,233
Inventory	9,067,977	10,356,423	9,094,750	11,467,587	12,139,543
Prepayments	135,591	294,621	412,751	171,009	170,976
Total Current Assets	$14,387,407	$16,712,400	$16,016,553	$20,460,830	$20,332,793
Property, plant and equipment—net	8,982,999	11,584,946	11,545,908	11,950,164	13,562,645
Municipal bonds	728,533	715,933	699,693	686,433	456,933
Other investments		459,838	428,192	408,606	422,121
Plant location deposits	318,241	349,010	349,010	349,010	349,010
Deferred changes	205,123	356,940	394,928	242,052	286,849
Total Assets	$24,622,303	$30,179,067	$29,434,284	$34,097,095	$35,410,351

LIABILITIES AND STOCKHOLDERS' EQUITY

	1966	1967	1968	1969	1970
Notes payable	$ 2,295,379	$ 4,287,000	$ 805,500	$ 779,500	$ 3,217,500
Accounts payable	2,320,953	2,314,683	1,841,269	3,786,135	1,922,784
Accruals	321,531	376,181	417,140	595,426	615,017
Employee retirement fund	855,255	790,779	866,017	1,458,442	1,126,351
Federal income tax	805,921	417,789	284,555	1,452,324	728,788
Total current liabilities	$ 6,599,039	$ 8,186,432	$ 4,214,481	$ 8,071,827	$ 7,610,440
Long-term debt	1,586,833	4,679,833	7,364,333	6,684,833	6,942,500
Deferred federal income tax	453,800	498,800	643,800	753,800	893,800
Total Liabilities	$ 8,639,672	$13,365,065	$12,222,614	$15,510,460	$15,446,740
Capital stock (par $10)	6,472,300	6,472,300	6,472,300	6,472,300	6,720,380
Paid-in surplus	382,522	382,522	382,522	382,522	884,884
Retained earnings	9,316,079	10,147,128	10,544,624	11,919,417	12,545,951
Stockholders' equity	$16,170,901	$17,001,950	$17,399,446	$18,774,239	$20,151,215
Reacquired stock	188,270	187,948	187,776	187,604	187,604
Total Stockholders' Equity	$15,982,631	$16,814,002	$17,211,670	$18,586,635	$19,963,611
Total Liabilities and Stockholders' Equity	$24,622,303	$30,179,067	$29,434,284	$34,097,095	$35,410,351

EXHIBIT 6

IMPERIAL MANUFACTURING COMPANY
Accounts receivable schedule

	1966	*1967*	*1968*	*1969*	*1970*
Accounts receivable—net....	$4,669,700	$5,727,100	$5,701,100	$7,572,500	$7,178,20
Allowance for bad debts....	47,200	57,800	86,800	170,300	214,40
Total............	$4,716,900	$5,784,900	$5,787,900	$7,742,800	$7,392,60
Age of Accounts:					
Over 120 days..........	$ 44,810	$ 54,380	$ 56,950	$ 76,650	$ 71,71
90 to 120 days..........	158,960	276,520	243,090	321,330	311,97
60 to 90 days..........	372,160	518,900	494,290	669,750	632,81
30 to 60 days..........	1,672,600	2,179,200	2,176,250	2,841,670	2,942,25
Less than 30 days.......	2,468,370	2,755,900	2,817,320	3,833,400	3,433,86
Total............	$4,716,900	$5,784,900	$5,787,900	$7,742,800	$7,392.60

EXHIBIT 7

IMPERIAL MANUFACTURING COMPANY
**Common stock price range—
American Stock Exchange**

Year	*High*	*Low*
1970........	$33\frac{7}{8}$	16
1969........	$27\frac{3}{8}$	$16\frac{1}{2}$
1968........	$29\frac{3}{4}$	$18\frac{3}{8}$
1967........	25	$14\frac{1}{8}$
1966........	$19\frac{5}{8}$	$11\frac{3}{8}$
1965........	$21\frac{1}{8}$	$10\frac{3}{8}$

SELECTED REFERENCES
FOR PART TWO

ARCHER, STEPHEN H. "A Model for the Determination of Firm Cash Balances," *Journal of Financial and Quantitative Analysis*, Vol. 1 (March 1966), pp. 1–11.

BAUMOL, WILLIAM J. "The Transactions Demand for Cash: An Inventory Theoretic Approach," *Quarterly Journal of Economics*, Vol. 66 (November 1952).

BAXTER, NEVINS D. "Marketability, Default Risk, and Yields on Money-Market Instruments," *Journal of Financial and Quantitative Analysis*, Vol. 3 (March 1968), pp. 75–85.

BEAN, VIRGINIA L., and GIFFITH, REYNOLDS. "Risk and Return in Working Capital Management," *Mississippi Valley Journal of Business and Economics*, Vol. 1 (Fall 1966), pp. 28–48.

BENISHAY, HASKEL. "Managerial Control of Accounts Receivable—A Deterministic Approach," *Journal of Accounting Research*, Vol. 3 (Spring 1965), pp. 114–33.

BERANEK, WILLIAM. *Analysis for Financial Decisions*. Homewood, Ill.: Irwin, 1963, chap. 10.

BERANEK, WILLIAM. *Working Capital Management*. Belmont, Calif.: Wadsworth, 1968.

BIERMAN, HAROLD, JR. *Financial Policy Decisions*. New York: Macmillan, 1970, chap. 3.

BLOCH, ERNEST. "Short Cycles in Corporate Demand for Government Securities and Cash," *American Economic Review*, Vol. 53 (December 1963), pp. 1058–77.

BROSKY, JOHN J. *The Implicit Cost of Trade Credit and Theory of Optimal Terms of Safe*. New York: Credit Research Foundation, 1969.

CALMAN, ROBERT F. *Linear Programming and Cash Management/CASH ALPHA*. Cambridge, Mass.: M.I.T., 1968.

CYERT, R. M., DAVIDSON, H. J., and THOMPSON, G. L. "Estimation of the Allowance for Doubtful Accounts by Markov Chains," *Management Science*, Vol. 8 (April 1962), pp. 287–303.

D'AGOSTINO, R. S. "Accounts Receivable Loans—Worthless Collateral?" *Journal of Commercial Bank Lending*, Vol. 52 (March 1970), pp. 34–42.

EPPEN, GARY D., and FAMA, EUGENE F. "Solutions for Cash-Balance and Simple Dynamic-Portfolio Problems," *Journal of Business*, Vol. 41, No. 1 (January 1968), pp. 94–112.

FRIEDLAND, SEYMOUR. *Economics of Corporate Finance*. Englewood Cliffs, N.J.: Prentice-Hall, 1966, chap. 4.

GREER, CARL C. "The Optimal Credit Acceptance Policy," *Journal of Financial and Quantitative Analysis*, Vol. 2 (December 1967), pp. 399–415.

HORN, FREDERICK E. "Managing Cash," *Journal of Accountancy*, Vol. 117. *Instruments of the Money Market*. Richmond, Va.: Federal Reserve Bank of Richmond, 1968.

JEFFERS, JAMES R., and KWON, JENE. "A Portfolio Approach to Corporate Demands for Government Securities," *Journal of Finance*, Vol. 24 (December 1969), pp. 905–20.

KING, ALFRED M. *Increasing the Productivity of Company Cash*. Englewood Cliffs, N.J.: Prentice-Hall, 1969, chaps. 4 and 5.

LEVY, FERDINAND K. "An Application of Heuristic Problem Solving to Accounts Receivable Management," *Management Science*, Vol. 12 (February 1966), pp. 236–44.

"Lock Box Banking—Key to Faster Collections," *Credit and Financial Management*, Vol. 69 (June 1967), pp. 16–21.

MANAGER, CHARLES C. "A Yardstick for Cost of Investment in Accounts Receivable," *Credit and Financial Management*, Vol. 69 (June 1967), pp. 24–26.

MAO, JAMES C. T. *Quantitative Analysis of Financial Decisions*. New York: Macmillan, 1969, chaps. 13 and 14.

MARRAH, GEORGE L. "Managing Receivables," *Financial Executive*, Vol. 38 (July 1970), pp. 40–44.

MEHTA, DILEEP. "The Formulation of Credit Policy Models," *Management Science*, Vol. 15 (October 1968), pp. 30–50.

MEHTA, DILEEP. "Optimal Credit Policy Selection: A Dynamic Approach," *Journal of Financial and Quantitative Analysis*, Vol. 5 (December 1970).

MILLER, MERTON H., and ORR, DANIEL. *An Application of Control Limit Models to the Management of Corporate Cash Balances*, Proceedings of the Conference on Financial Research and Its Implications for Management, Stanford University, Alexander A. Robichek, ed. (New York: Wiley, 1967).

MILLER, MERTON H., and ORR, DANIEL. "A Model of the Demand for Money by Firms," *Quarterly Journal of Economics*, Vol. 80 (August 1966), pp. 413–35.

MILLER, MERTON H., and ORR, DANIEL. "The Demand for Money by Firms: Extension of Analytic Results," *Journal of Finance*, Vol. 23 (December 1968), pp. 735–59.

MYERS, JAMES H., and FORGY, EDWARD W. "The Development of Numerical

Credit Evaluation Systems," *Journal of the American Statistical Association*, Vol. 58 (September 1963), pp. 799–806.

NEAVE, EDWIN H. "The Stochastic Cash-Balance Problem with Fixed Costs for Increases and Decreases," *Management Science*, Vol. 16 (March 1970), pp. 472–90.

ORGLER, YAIR E. "An Unequal-Period Model for Cash-Management Decisions," *Management Science*, Vol. 16 (October 1969), pp. 77–92.

ORGLER, YAIR E. *Cash Management*. Belmont, Calif.: Wadsworth Publishing Co., 1970.

PARK, COLIN, and GLADSON, JOHN W. *Working Capital*. New York: Macmillan, 1963.

PETTWAY, RICHARD H., and WALKER, ERNEST W. "Asset Mix, Capital Structure, and the Cost of Capital," *Southern Journal of Business*, April 1968, pp. 34–43.

ROBBINS, SIDNEY M. "Getting More Mileage out of Cash," *NAA Bulletin*, September 1960.

SEARBY, FREDERICK W. "Use Your Hidden Cash Resources," *Harvard Business Review*, Vol. 46 (March–April 1968), pp. 74–75.

TINSLEY, P. A. "Capital Structure, Precautionary Balances, and Valuation of the Firm: The Problem of Financial Risk," *Journal of Financial and Quantitative Analysis*, Vol. 5 (March 1970), pp. 33–62.

VAN HORNE, JAMES C. "A Risk-Return Analysis of a Firm's Working Capital Position," *Engineering Economist*, Vol. 14 (Winter 1969), pp. 71–89.

WHITE, D. J., and NORMAN, J. M. "Control of Cash Reserves," *Operational Research Quarterly*, Vol. 16, No. 3 (September 1965).

Cash Management[*]
James McN. Stancill[†]

OF ALL THE ASSET ACCOUNTS of a firm, the cash and marketable securities accounts are usually the only ones solely under the discretion of the finance manager. After reviewing the present and past treatments of the management of cash and marketable securities, a model is presented which attempts to provide a workable answer to the elusive question of how much a firm should carry in cash and marketable securities.

THE TRADITIONAL APPROACH TO CASH MANAGEMENT

The earliest approaches to cash management[1] were couched in terms of ratio analysis and were epitomized by the adage that a firm should keep so many days' worth of payables in their cash account or a certain percentage of sales. Thirty days or two weeks come to mind as rather typical rules of thumb.[2] If a percentage of sales approach was taken,

---

[*] Reprinted from *The Management of Working Capital*, chap. 2 (Scranton, Pa.: International Textbook Company, 1971), pp. 8–28, by permission of the author and the publisher.

This chapter is based largely on my article, "The Determination of Corporate Holdings of Cash and Marketable Securities," in Edward J. Mock (ed.), Financial Decision Making (Scranton, Pa.: International Textbook Company, 1967), pp. 269–83.

[†] Associate Professor of Finance, University of Southern California.

[1] In this chapter the word "cash" is meant to define the firm's demand deposit (checking) account at a bank. Currency on hand will be referred to as "till cash," and marketable securities will include those securities which a firm holds as "near-cash" items. Later each of these categories will be accorded separate treatment. The composition of the marketable securities portfolio is treated in Chapter 3.

[2] At least twenty basic finance and accounting texts published in the 1920's and early 1930's were checked for an explicit citation, but either the subject of cash was ignored or only a passing perfunctory reference was made to it.

then the industry average was usually suggested. In other cases the discussion of "How much?" was answered only in the most general way by stating some of the most basic determinants of the cash balance (such as "It depends on the industry") or stating that cash should be sufficient to pay the bills as they accrue.[3] But this ratio approach suffers from the same deficiencies as all ratio analyses. "What is" is construed to be "What should be."

Following this "descriptive" or ratio approach, some basic textbooks in corporation finance adopted a Keynesian "liquidity preference" approach.[4] In the framework of Keynes' General Theory,[5] the motives for holding cash were trichotomized as (1) transactions balances, (2) speculative balances, and (3) precautionary balances. A fourth motive, the "finance" motive, was added by Keynes in a later article.[6] Expressed in corporate finance terms, these motives may be roughly defined, in order, as (1) the cash balances needed to transact the day-to-day activities of the firm, (2) balances set aside in anticipation of price declines (of inventory items, for example), (3) "safety stocks"—balances motivated by possible business declines, and (4) those cash balances set aside in anticipation of a major expenditure—for example, an extraordinary capital budgeting item.

While of questionable value in explaining the theory of interest,[7] this approach helps, in a theoretical way, to explain why firms hold cash, but it is quite insufficient in establishing *how much* cash to hold.

As shown in Figure 1, the usual depiction of the liquidity-preference function, the cash balance is shown to be an inverse function of the interest rate, i. But is it? As Hicks pointed out in an article in 1937,[8]

---

[3] Dauten, for example, made the following statement in his finance text: "In determining the amount of cash which a business needs, it is necessary to understand fully all of the factors that affect the cash account and to consider the effect which the trend, the seasonal, and the irregular movements have on each of them." Carl A. Dauten, *Business Finance* (Englewood Cliffs, N.J.: Prentice-Hall, Inc., 1948), p. 292.

[4] Cf. Pearson Hunt et al., *Basic Business Finance* (rev. ed.; Homewood, Ill.: Richard D. Irwin, Inc., 1961), pp. 89–90, and more recently Seymour Friedland, *The Economics of Corporate Finance* (Englewood Cliffs, N.J.: Prentice-Hall, Inc., 1966), pp. 99–119. Others, e.g., Alvin F. Donaldson and J. K. Pfahl, *Corporate Finance* (New York, Ronald Press, 1963), p. 482, and J. Fred Weston, *Managerial Finance* (New York: Holt, Rinehart & Winston Co., Inc., 1962), pp. 98–99, while not following the Keynesian terminology, couch their explanation of the desirable cash balance in motivational terms (i.e., the motives for holding cash such as for "safety stocks" or "financing stocks."

[5] John M. Keynes, *The General Theory of Employment, Interest and Money.* (New York: Harcourt, Brace & World, Inc., 1935), p. 170.

[6] John M. Keynes, "Alternative Theories of the Rate of Interest," *Economic Journal*, January 1937, pp. 241–252.

[7] At least in today's world of an institutionalized capital market.

[8] J. R. Hicks, "Mr. Keynes and the 'Classics': A Suggested Interpretation," *Econometrical*, April 1937, pp. 147–159.

the "transactions" demand for cash, L_i, presumes a given interest rate. Thus Keynes was guilty of the logical error of *hysteron proteron*, or more simply, circularity. From a more pragmatic approach, however, Keynes' theory, while introspectively plausible, seems to ignore business-men's thinking with respect to their cash and marketable securities account. Admittedly, at *very* low short-term rates of interest, businessmen may be reluctant or slow to switch redundant cash into marketable securities, and at high rates they may be more conscious of the opportunity cost of retaining redundant cash. But to give short-term interest rates

FIGURE 1
Liquidity preference

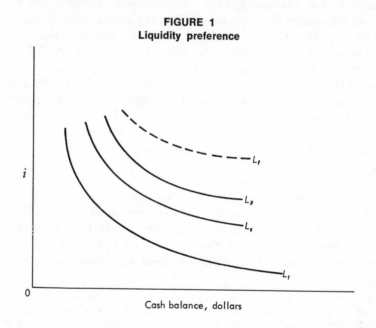

Cash balance, dollars

a place of dominant importance in a theory that attempted to be *positive* in nature is unrealistic. Keynes' liquidity-preference theory simply ignores the indigenous factors at work within the firm.

Tackling just the transactions demand for cash by business firms, Baumol, Beranek, and more recently Whalen have developed some interesting models to attempt to answer the "how much" aspect of the subject. Baumol[9] attempted a union between "inventory theory and monetary theory"[10] in a mathematical model—but without explicit recognition of probabilistic variance. In general, Baumol concludes that even in a sta-

---

[9] William J. Baumol, "The Transactions Demand for Cash: An Inventory Theoretic Approach," *Quarterly Journal of Economics*, November 1952, pp. 545–556.
[10] Ibid., p. 545.

tionary state "some" cash should be held and, secondly, "that the transactions demand for cash will vary approximately in proportion with the money value of transactions."[11]

Beranek[12] like Baumol, dealt only with the "transactions demand" for cash, but advanced his model in a probabilistic framework. In particular, Beranek's work is commendable for this probabilistic approach and for isolating salient variables in the process of determining a firm's cash balance. In his words, the "Factors in the decision are (1) behavior and magnitude of cash flows, (2) size of 'critical' minimum, (3) amount of 'short' cost, (4) returns from marketable securities, and (5) length of cash balance planning period."[13] The "short cost" comes about when the balance falls below the "critical minimum" and is defined to consist of the cash discount foregone on the firm's accounts payable, and the deterioration in credit rating.[14] To include these two aspects of the "short cost" in his probabilistic model of the "critical balance," Beranek had to quantify each, and in so doing made his model difficult to apply. It is unrealistic to suggest that a firm quantify "deterioration in credit" position. Credit position is a function of many variables, and to isolate this variable in a "transactions balances only" approach is theoretically convenient but a gross simplification. Also unrealistic is the presumption that cash discounts will be foregone if the critical balance is violated. This may indeed happen, but for a well-managed firm short-term loans are a less costly alternative.

Edmund Whalen, the third author cited, tried to follow up Baumol's work and directed his paper[15] to an empirical examination of whether the mechanistic assumption of the more pure Keynesian liquidity-preference theory (the relationship between the transactions and the precautionary balances) or the Baumol[16] Tobin[17] approach, which set forth nonproportionate hypotheses,[18] was more plausible. In short, "Do transactions and precautionary cash balances of nonfinancial business corporations vary proportionately or less than in proportion to changes in the volume of their sales?"[19]

---

[11] In other words, if cash balances were used as a regressor with sales, the slope of the regression line would be positive and approximately unitary.

[12] William Beranek, *Analysis, op. cit.*, pp. 345–387.

[13] Ibid., p. 385.

[14] Ibid., pp. 385, 360–362.

[15] Edward L. Whalen, "A Cross-Section Study of Business Demand for Cash," *Journal of Finance*, September 1965, pp. 423–443.

[16] Baumol, "The Transactions Demand for Cash."

[17] James Tobin, "The Interest Elasticity of Transactions Demand for Cash," *Review of Economics and Statistics*, August 1956, pp. 241–247.

[18] Or, in the jargon of economic theory, "nonunitary elasticity."

[19] Whalen, "A Cross-Section Study of Business Demand for Cash," p. 423.

In this macro approach, Whelan's findings seem to indicate that cash balances in some industries appear to increase "more than in proportion to sales." While of interest, this study still leaves the determination of a realistic, micro approach to the determination of a firm's cash and marketable securities balance unanswered. It is only normative, i.e., it deals with "what is" rather than "what should be." It is a worthwhile study, however, and should provide ground for further empirical examinations at a macroeconomic level.

Delineating the problem

All firms are faced with the problem of how much to keep as till cash and how much to keep in their checking account at a bank—although too many firms are unwilling to rigorously face up to the problem. For those firms that pass a certain point in their development where they are considered "middle-sized" or "large," a third aspect must be reckoned with—investment in marketable securities.[20] For some firms, a separate payroll and/or dividend account is maintained, and since this is a logical subset of the whole problem an approach to the management of this account will be suggested.

For most nonfinancial, noncommercial firms, the problem of how much to keep in "till cash," i.e., their cash registers or cash drawers, is of substantially less magnitude than the other two aspects of the problem. While till cash will be ignored for the rest of this book, it is hoped that more rigorous, stochastic reasoning will be devoted to the matter where relevant.

With respect to the demand deposit (general corporate checking) account—and what will henceforth be called the *cash* account—the usual purposes for maintaining it are: (1) to use it to pay "accounts payable," and (2) to use it for a depository for the checks received through the firm's credit sales—"accounts receivable." When payroll checks are issued, often a charge is made to the general account and the amount of the payroll deposited in a separate payroll account—usually at the same bank (or banks) as the general account. Lacking perfect synchronization in the inflows and outflows of the general account, all firms

---

[20] This is so because most money-market instruments come "packaged" in rather large denominations, e.g., $10,000, $50,000, or even $100,000. To buy such instruments a firm needs, perforce, rather substantial sums. I hasten to add, however, that "marketable securities" should be construed to include all *interest-bearing* or *dividend-paying* assets—Treasury bills, commercial paper, certificates of deposit (CD's), deposits in savings and loans, time deposits, and certain stocks. In this respect, therefore, even small firms may have marketable securities in the form of deposits in their local savings bank or a time (savings) deposit at their bank. Furthermore, the model suggested and the discussion in this chapter could include the problem faced by small firms, too. Chapter 3 deals extensively with money-market instruments.

find that the desirable balance is other than zero—the theoretically most profitable balance because no money is earned on demand deposits.

The purpose of maintaining a marketable-securities account is assumed in this book to be an interest-earning cushion which could be used to sop up redundant cash or, alternately, to supplement cash when the account dips below the optimal level. With this purpose in mind, consideration will not be given to a determination of how much "other" securities (subsequently defined as "free" marketable securities) a firm may happen to have included in its balance-sheet item "marketable securities."[21] Payroll, tax payments, and extraordinary purchases (e.g., a building, a major capital expenditure, or a purchase of another firm) are factors to reckon with, and subsequently will be included in the discussion of the question.

Stated as directly as possible, a firm must have *enough* in its cash account to meet the claims presented against such account. This does not mean that for every dollar in checks written (or drawn) today there must be a dollar on deposit. Not at all! Barring a state law to the contrary, a firm must have *on deposit* only the amount *presented* (charged) to its account. This is true also of the firm's payroll account, and failure to be aware of this might result in the maintenance of an excessive amount in the cash (or payroll) account. Similarly, the amount held in the marketable securities account should be enough to absorb the usual shocks in the cash account, but the rest ("free" marketable securities) should be put to use more profitably to finance other accounts, e.g., inventories, receivables, or fixed assets. If opportunities for investment in these other assets—and for most viable firms this implies at greater rates of return than are usually realizable in marketable securities—are not available at any point in time, then the marketable-securities account would swell to that extent. But what is the "unneeded" (free) amount in this account? Furthermore, how should the optimal amount be determined? Likewise, what is the optimal cash balance for a firm at any point in time, and how should this amount be determined? To seek a deterministic approach to these questions it is first necessary to deal with the optimal cash balance for it is the cash account (or rather the behavior of the cash account) that logically should determine the marketable securities balance.

DETERMINING THE OPTIMAL CASH BALANCE

In order to approach the question of how much to have in a cash account, it is useful to categorize the various inflows and outflows in

---

[21] It is because of his "grossing" problem, i.e., the inclusion of marketable securities—for the above-mentioned purpose—and "other," e.g., investment securities, in the balance-sheet account that empirical studies utilizing published statements only are on questionable ground.

the account. While not pretending to be exhaustive, the following seem to be the most common and important: [22]

1. Inflows
    A. Accounts Receivable
    B. "Cash sales" receipts
2. Outflows
    A. Accounts payable
    B. Taxes
    C. Payroll
    D. Extraordinary expenditures,
        e.g., large capital outlays

Further classifications of these accounts, however, suggests this dichotomization:

Random variables
    1A. Accounts receivable
    1B. Cash sales
    2A. Accounts payable
Controllable (known) variables
    2B. Taxes
    2C. Payroll
    2D. Extraordinary expenditures
    2E. Cash dividends

Viewing the activity of the cash account in this way, the problem resolves to this: (i) have enough cash to compensate for the *lack of perfect synchronization* in the random variables (the inflows and the outflows), and (ii) provide a way in which 2B, 2C, 2D, and 2E expenditures (controllable outflows) can be "covered," i.e., a balance sufficient to take care of the random, routine activity *and* these substantial but controllable (known?) withdrawals.

Assuming daily rectification of the cash account at the bank, and that the bank posts deposits before withdrawals, if the inflows were exactly equal to the outflows the account could be opened with $1, and this would be the daily closing balance. Since this is not the case, obviously, what the firm really must do is to provide for the *dissynchronization* of these inflows and outflows. To do this, it is possible to construct a probability distribution of the firm's day-to-day *change* in their cash

---

[22] A somewhat similar approach was taken by Archer and D'Ambrosio (Stephen H. Archer and Charles D'Ambrosio, *Business Finance: Theory and Management* [New York: Macmillan Co. 1966], p. 331) in their treatment of the management of cash. I am particularly indebted to Professor Archer for stimulating my interest in this subject and for providing a useful framework of analysis, particularly with respect to the payroll model presented later in this chapter.

account *sans* the amounts attributable to the "controllable variable" items. Of course this distribution should be as independent as possible of seasonal factors, such as Christmas, Easter, and the Fall "busy" period. To do this it appears possible to take separate periods (by seasons, for example) and construct a distribution for each season, or to devise a "seasonal index" that could be used as a deflator or inflator for each season's activity. Figure 2 illustrates the former approach.

FIGURE 2
Day-to-day change in cash account after removal of "controllable" changes in the account (this distribution would not be a continuous function, but rather a discrete one. It is shown as continuous for purposes of exposition and convenience only.)

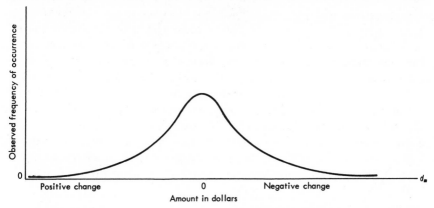

Having constructed such a distribution, our next problem is to formulate a decision rule for the daily opening balance. Since the major problem is not having sufficient cash, we are concerned with the negative side only. If the opening balance is greater than the desired opening balance, the excess[23] may be used to purchase marketable securities.

Looking therefore at the "negative change" side of the distribution, a first approximation to the optimal cash balance, which is now called the desired opening balance, may be had by deciding on the *chance* to be taken of not having enough cash on any given day (Figure 3). If, for example, management elects to take a 1 percent chance of "running short," its *decision rule* is found by merely selecting that dollar amount to the right of which includes 1 percent of the observations.

The *larger* the desired opening balance, the *smaller* the chance of running short, and vice versa. Exactly what dollar limit the firm selects as its decision rule would be a function of many factors, but the two

---

[23] More specifically, the excess beyond a second amount somewhat greater than the desired opening balance. This is the "indifference band" and is discussed in the next section.

FIGURE 3
Illustration of the decision rule for the desired opening balance

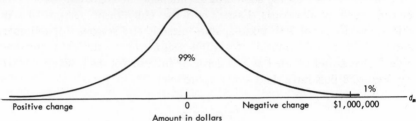

that seem of greatest moment are (i) management's aversion to a tight cash situation, and (ii), on a more *ad hominem* basis, the relationship the firm has with the bank. If, for example, the bank is made cognizant of what the firm is trying to do, it might agree to give the firm until the next morning to sell some marketable securities and through, say, telegraphic transfer or even intrabank transfer thus cover the deficiency.[24]

If it is possible to establish a line of credit with a bank that would automatically become effective with an overdraft, the absolute size of the desired opening balance could be lowered. This implies, of course, a greater chance of running short of cash. This backup line of credit would be most advisable if the firm did not have marketable securities in a sufficient amount as described below. One very progressive bank, with which the author is familiar, has developed a model of this type for its customers' convenience.

The indifference band

Primarily because of the cost of effecting a purchase of marketable securities (say Treasury bills), the desired opening balance should be construed to be the lower limit of a range—called the *indifference band*. The width of the band is thus a function of this transaction (purchase) cost, translated into the daily interest on a given increment of marketable securities. On a $100,000 lot of Treasury bills, the daily interest is, currently, approximately $16–$20. If the cost of making a purchase is construed to be $15, then the width of the indifference band would thus be about $100,000.

---

[24] With the current state of competition among banks this is not an unrealistic suggestion. Furthermore, the oft-expressed suggestion after World War II that firms should keep healthy balances with their bank is now quite unrealistic.

If perchance the firm has a loan agreement with the bank to maintain a minimum-level balance, this situation could be accounted for by *raising* the desired opening balance to meet this restriction. If this balance is less than the desired opening balance, the desired opening balance amount should supersede the smaller "required" amount.

Viewing the lower limit of this indifference band as the "reorder point," we see that the problem of the width of the band has some aspects of an inventory problem. In fact, Miller and Orr[25] have considered this to be the case and applied an EOQ (economic order quantity)—square root—formula for the solution. To do this, however, they have to assume a "purchase cost," as was done above, and, additionally, a constant issuance rate. The cost of carrying the inventory is, of course, the daily interest lost—$16 to $20 on a $100,000 block of bills in the above example. The trouble with this approach, however, is that it is unreasonable to assume a constant issuance—i.e., withdrawal or decrease in the cash account. Miller and Orr go well beyond this naive approach, however, and have developed an interesting stochastic model for the width of the band and the desired cash balance.

Cash is allowed to vary in the cash account until it hits an upper limit h, at which time securities are bought (in an amount of hz) in order to reduce the balance to z, which represents that Miller and Orr call the *return point* and is similar to d_m. If the balance falls below z, no action is taken until a dollar balance r is reached. At that point, money-market securities are sold in an amount rz in order to return the balance to the level z.

In the Miller and Orr model,

$$z = \left(\frac{3\gamma\sigma^2}{4v}\right)^{1/3} \tag{1}$$

$$h = 3z \tag{2}$$

for the special case where p = the probability that the cash balance will increase = .5, and q = the probability that the cash balance will decrease = .5. In the above equation σ^2 represents the variance of the daily change in the cash balance, γ = cost per transfer (presumably either into cash or into securities), and v = daily interest rate on securities.[26]

The object of the Miller and Orr model is to minimize the cost function $\epsilon(c)$ by choice of the variables z and h. The cost function[27] is defined as

$$\epsilon(c) = \gamma\frac{\epsilon(N)}{T} + v\epsilon(M) \tag{3}$$

where $\epsilon(N)$ = expected number of transfers between cash account and marketable securities during the upcoming period
T = number of days in period
$\epsilon(M)$ = expected average daily balance

[25] Merton H. Miller and Daniel Orr, "A Model of the Demand for Money by Firms," *Quarterly Journal of Economics*, August 1966, pp. 413–435.
[26] Ibid., p. 423.
[27] Ibid., p. 420.

Provision for controllable variables

The term "first approximation" of the desired opening balance was used above advisedly, however, for the preceding model accounts only for what was described as random-variable flows. How could the firm provide for the controllable-variable amounts, such as taxes, payroll, dividends, and capital expenditures? If the firm wants strictly to observe the profit motive it should provide for such demands, which presumably would be through a gradual accumulation, by increases earmarked for such purposes in the *marketable securities* account. In this way the funds could be kept working at interest and not lying fallow in the cash account. If on the other hand the firm's management expresses a personal propensity to play it safe, it may decide to keep such balances (i.e., gradually accumulate such balances) in its cash account. But if it chooses the latter course, it must add to the desired opening balance periodic (or occasional) amounts to accomplish this purpose (Figure 4).

FIGURE 4
Illustration of how the "desired opening balance" could be increased for various purposes

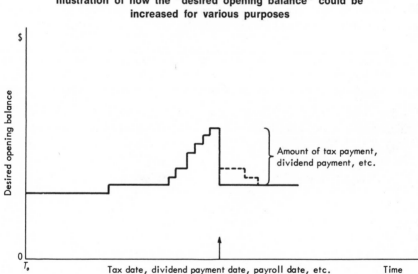

Of course, if the firm elects this procedure it will incur an opportunity cost to the extent of lost interest. But if the firm is quite small and feels it is preempted from carrying marketable securities because of minimum purchase requirements, or because it cannot leave the balance on deposit at a savings and loan or commercial bank for the minimum period on which interest is paid, or simply because of the aforementioned problem of interest earned versus purchase cost, it may elect this course of action.

Before continuing to the next section, and to anticipate the preceptive reader who questions the possibility of *successive* negative changes in the cash account, it is well to add here that this is a factor in the determination of the optimal marketable securities account, and not the cash account. The presumption here is that if the opening balance is not up to the desired opening balance (within the constraints of the "indifference band") on any given day, the firm will sell marketable securities and that day bolster its balance up to the desired opening balance.[28]

DETERMINING THE OPTIMAL BALANCE FOR PAYROLL AND DIVIDEND SUBACCOUNTS

Many firms have found it convenient to maintain, in addition to their general (cash) account, subordinate accounts to service their payroll and dividend checks. Assuming such accounts, it is possible to devise a probabilistic model to assist in the management of such accounts.

The basic principle operative in these cases is the same as in the preceding treatment: the debits (withdrawals) made to such an account can be depicted by a probability distribution, and the use of such a distribution will provide the decision rule on how much to have in the account at any given point in time. But unlike the former model, the assumption of "independent trials" is quite tenuous. What happens the first day after a payroll is issued has a pronounced effect on what happens the second day, and the second day's activity affects the third, and so on. Thus the model presented here must be construed as only a first approximation to the solution. If the dollar volume involved warranted extensive analysis, the approach that seems to be most promising is a computerized simulation of the account utilizing a Markov chain process of conditional probabilities.

Barring a state law to the contrary, a firm that issues a given amount of payroll or dividend checks on, say, Friday need not have *that* amount in the account on *Friday*. In fact, not all the checks will be presented for payment to the firm's bank on Monday. If presented to another bank on Monday, it may be Tuesday before the check clears the firm's bank—possibly longer in the case of dividend checks, as there is a more pronounced float situation with respect to such checks. The latter case assumes, of course, more geographic distribution of the recipients of dividend checks than of payroll checks. But if a firm does not have to have the amount of the total payroll (or total dividend) on deposit immediately

---

[28] While the models set forth here are predicated on time intervals of one day, expansion to some other longer time interval might be accommodated. Again, this seems to turn on the relationship and agreement the firm has with its bank.

after issuance, how much should it have? The model (Figure 5) will illustrate this, but since it is a probabilistic decision, the same *caveat* as earlier applies: what chance is the firm willing to take of not having enough?

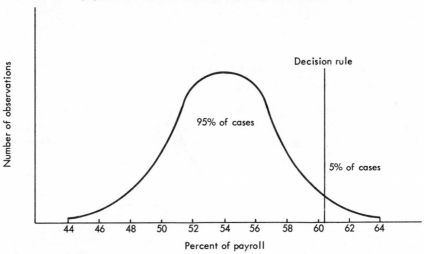

FIGURE 5
Frequency distribution of the percent of total payroll checks presented for payment to a firm's bank on Monday, last five years

To help reach a decision rule on how much to have on deposit on the first (business) day after issuance of the checks (what ever day that might be), it should be useful to examine the experience of this account over time—say, the past three to five years. Assuming that there are not serious factors at work tending to change the pattern at least for the near future, a study of the recent past should be quite sufficient for near-term forecasting. Having constructed such a distribution for the first day (and Monday was used in the illustration), a decision rule can be chosen for the desired amount to be held on the first day, *given the risk* assumed. This process can then be repeated for each successive day until a new payroll date is reached: for example, there would be ten such distributions if the firm paid its employees every two weeks. Each successive distribution would be like the first, except that its modal value probably would be centered over a lower percentage-of-payroll figure, and presumably each successive decision rule (desired balance) would be smaller.

Once these respective distributions have been plotted and decision rules reached for each day in the interpayroll period, a model can then be constructed which will depict the desired dollar amount to be held for the whole period. Figure 6 illustrates such a composite (but naive) model.

As previously mentioned, this same type of model could be constructed for a dividend account. In either case the reason for constructing such a model is the same: to keep funds invested in interest-earning assets as long as possible. While the firm would only be keeping some of their funds working a day or two or three longer, if this process were *repeated* 52 times a year (assuming a weekly payroll) it would amount to keeping,

FIGURE 6
Composite model of desired balances in payroll account for period following issuance of check

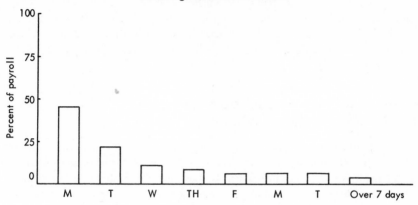

say 20–40 percent of their total payroll (or dividend payment) earning interest for 50–150 days a year. If the amounts involved are in the order of tens of millions of dollars, the interest earned will help pay the expense of the treasurer and his staff. If the amounts are smaller, the returns will be smaller, but it would still add to the firm's profit.

While on the subject of the firm's payroll it may be well at this point to remember that the longer the pay period, the greater the credit extended to the firm by the employees. In the past century daily pay was not uncommon, and even up to World War II weekly pay was the rule for most plants. It was in the early postwar period that checks were first widely used in paying employees. Were it not for the use of checks, and the fact that often many if not most of the employees have checking accounts at other banks, the preceding model would not be possible.[29]

Recently it was brought to the writer's attention that a firm's bank had worked out an innovation to assist a firm in handling its payroll

---

[29] Not only would the interest income be lost, but the firm would have to incur substantial expense in filling the pay envelopes for all employees. It is a wonder that some firms still pay in currency, and weekly at that.

account. No longer did the firm have to issue thousands of checks to its employees. Instead, it could transfer one sum from its general account, and the bank would set up individual accounts for *all* the employees. Each employee then had one "free" check per pay period. In this say, he could write a check for the amount of his pay and deposit it with his bank, or—and, in part this is what the bank hoped—he would use this account as his regular checking account. What the bank was trying to do obviously was the same thing suggested above for the business firm. It had the use of the unexpected balance until it was completely drawn down—and many new customers in addition! On the other hand, the firm gained the advantage of not issuing all the payroll checks, but it lost the interest that could be earned on the amounts in question. Since this firm had automated equipment for producing the checks, the cost would be rather low, but since the payroll amounted to millions of dollars, the small cost savings should have been overshadowed by the interest income foregone.[30]

DETERMINING THE OPTIMUM BALANCE IN THE MARKETABLE SECURITIES ACCOUNT

As previously stated, the purpose of maintaining a marketable-securities account as here defined is that it acts as a reserve for the cash account. When the cash account needs funds, because the daily opening balance is less than the desired opening balance, some securities are quickly sold and the cash account bolstered accordingly. If there is redundant cash (i.e., if the opening balance is above the upper limit of the indifference band) then securities can be purchased with the redundancy.

Within this frame of reference, therefore, some optimum balance of marketable securities should be carried to take care of the probable deficiencies in the cash account, but above this amount the marketable securities thus become redundant for the purpose at hand.

Before pursuing this matter further, let us remember that there are other purposes for holding marketable securities. As mentioned in the section on cash-balance determination, funds must be provided for meeting the controllable (known) outflows such as taxes and dividends. The accumulation of these outflows would thus cause the marketable securities account to rise above the desired daily level. And as the model to be formulated below will show, it is important that these funds be held

---

[30] In California there is an interesting state law that prescribes that employers *must* pay employees at least every 26 days. Also, another California law states that in the case of termination an employee must be paid the balance of the amount in the original offer of employment. If that is monthly, and termination takes place on the first day of a new month, then a whole month's pay must be given to the employee. Such a law as this obviously mediates against stretching the pay period too far.

in addition to the balance held for the primary purpose. This is so because it is entirely possible (but not "probable") that the day a large tax payment is due, for example, would be just the day when the cash balance took a maximum downturn.

If more marketable securities (defined as "free" marketable securities) are present in the firm's account than needed (i) to service the cash account, and (ii) to accommodate the controllable outlays then this excess amount would be available for financing other assets in the firm, e.g., receivables, inventory, and fixed assets. Of course if the firm does not have any immediate use for the funds in such other assets, it is better to keep these funds in marketable securities than in the cash account. But in this way a financial manager at least *knows* what his "free" balance of marketable securities is, and can act accordingly. If he does not estimate his needs, he may deny more profitable "other" investments—suffering in the process an opportunity cost. On the other hand, he may think he has more "free" marketable securities than he does and approve commitments that would require the liquidation of marketable securities. Here the opportunity cost may be the interest forgone and the interest incurred *if* he finds he needs the marketable securities that he unwisely sold.

Let us return now to the immediate question, How can a firm determine how much to hold in its marketable securities account for the primary purpose—i.e., the optimal (desired) balance? Having set up the model for the cash balance the approach to the solution to this question is at first easy, but becomes more complicated as it is made dynamic.

If all we were to consider was a *one-period* (e.g., one-day) analysis, the answer to how much marketable securities would be simply enough to cover the accepted maximum probable deficit in the cash account, or in other words, it would *equal* the opening balance. If the desired opening balance were set (on the basis of Figure 3) at say, $1,000,000, then this would be the amount of the (basic) optimal balance in the marketable securities account. The reason, of course, is that management has determined this to be the maximum decrease for which they are going to provide. If in those few cases the marketable securities account were insufficient to cover the daily decrease, then the logical alternative would be to borrow—for example, through a short-term loan. But if the firm does not have some sort of automatic loan arrangement[31] it would involve some trouble and effort to take out such loans frequently, and furthermore it may cause a deterioration in rapport and relationship with the bank. Such frequent borrowing would be necessary, however, if the firm forgets that it is possible to have *successive* decreases *in the short run* of various amounts just through what we have called random

---

[31] Such as an overdraft arrangement, or a line of credit they can draw upon at will.

events. Furthermore, as will subsequently be discussed, if the firm is expanding or contracting sales volume to any appreciable extent, it will introduce into the system a force that is not provided for. In this case estimates of the future flows should be made using accounts receivables as a regressor with sales, and "cash sales" (if material) as a regressor with sales; an estimate of accounts payable can be made by regressing this account with the estimated cost-of-goods-sold account.

Referring only to a short-run analysis, however, a probabilistic approach (Table 1) can be used to help determine the expected drain that would be put on the marketable securities account if successive maximum probable decreases were experienced.[32]

TABLE 1
Computation of the summation of successive maximum probable decreases assuming $1,000,000 as desired opening balance

	Maximum decrease in d_m	Probability of successive decreases	Summation of successive decreases
	(1)	(2)	(1) × (2)
Starting value, t_0	$1,000,000	1.00	$1,000,000
Expected value, t_1	1,000,000	.50	500,000
t_2	1,000,000	$.50^2$	250,000
t_3	1,000,000	$.50^3$	125,000
t_4	1,000,000	$.50^4$	62,500
t_5	1,000,000	$.50^5$	31,250
t_6	1,000,000	$.50^6$	15,630
t_7	1,000,000	$.50^7$	7,810
t_8	1,000,000	$.50^8$	3,910
.	.	.	.
.	.	.	.
.	.	.	.
t_{15}	1,000,000	$.50^{15}$	20
Present value of successive decreases =			$1,996,100

While $1,000,000 is the illustrative maximum probable decrease, it is unrealistic merely to double this to take account of two successive decreases, etc. This is so because we must consider the probabiltiy of two successive decreases. If the probability of a decrease (any decrease) is $p = .5$, then to the $1,000,000 a firm holds to take care of the first day (t_0) maximum decrease we must add $1,000,000 (.5) to take account of a decrease in day t_1. To take account of a whole chain of successive

---

[32] As in the case of the payroll model, an alternative approach to the model that follows is to devise a simulation model utilizing a Markov chain process. In fact, the matrix approach used in Markov chains is quite similar to the chain used here. The situation here, however, is rather unlike the preceding discussion regarding the conditional probabilities in the payroll model. *Less* autocorrelation is assumed here.

decreases, we would have to continue the process. Symbolically, if d_m is the maximum probable decrease, and m_o is the optimal marketable securities balance, then

$$m_o = d_m + \sum_{i=1}^{i=n} d_m p^i, \qquad p = .50 \tag{4}$$

Notice that the d_m used in this case was \$1,000,000, the maximum probable decrease, and not the "expected" decrease.[33] This was done because of the express concern for successive *maximum* probable decreases. The weighted average decrease thus has little meaning here except to remind us that if we have a decrease it will probably be quite a lot less than \$1,000,000. In other words, most of the day-to-day changes will be fairly close to the modal point of the distribution, and zero was assumed to be the modal value here. For the illustration at hand, therefore, the optimal balance of marketable securities, m_0, would be approximately \$2,000,000.

While a "normal" distribution with the mode = 0 was used in the preceding illustration, the reader is cautioned against assuming a normal distribution with the mode = 0. If the firm is in the course of expanding, the distribution of the changes in the cash account probably would be skewed to the right, as in Figure 7, with the mode centered over some negative change.

FIGURE 7
Illustrative distribution of daily changes in cash account (d_m), assuming expanding sales

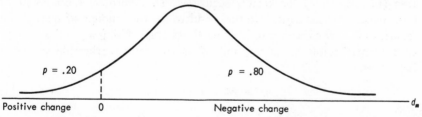

If the firm's sales are not expanding but retrenching, the distribution of d_m would probably be as depicted in Figure 8.

---

[33] The expected decrease could be determined by an "expected-gain" model in which Figure 2 would be redrawn with the horizontal axis segregated into \$200,000 increments. The area under the curve for each increment would be the probability of that change (and here we would be concerned only with a decrease). Taking a weighted average of all such decrements (with the probability of that decrement as the respective weights) would be the average expected decrease. In the illustration at hand, and assuming weights, respectively, of $p = .12$, $p = .08$, $p = .05$, and $p = .03$ plus $p = .02$ for an all-over \$1,000,000 decrease, the expected decrease would be \$226,000.

FIGURE 8
Illustrative distribution of daily changes in cash account (d_m), assuming
contracting sales

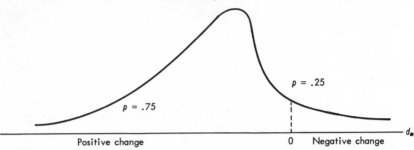

Now the purpose of Figures 7 and 8 is to remind the reader that the probability coefficient used in determining m_0, i.e., p in Equation 4 and column (2) in Table 1, will be determined by each respective distribution of d_m. If, for example, $p > .50$, then $m_0 > \$2{,}000{,}000$ for the assumed \$1,000,000 maximum decrease. Conversely, if the area in the "negative" tail of the d_m distribution is less than $p = .50$, then $m_0 \mid < \$2{,}000{,}000$.

Determination of free marketable securities

As noted earlier, one of the important by-products of the determination of the m_0 balance is that it assists in the determination of the firm's free (i.e., available) marketable securities. To determine the amount of free marketable securities, we must add to m_0 the amount of marketable securities held for the controllable outflows (m_c). Using m_f as the amount of free marketable securities, and M as the total marketable securities held, then

$$m_f = M - (m_0 + m_c). \tag{5}$$

Summary

In this chapter the problem of "cash management" was decomposed into two basic areas: (i) a determination of the optimal cash balance, and once this was done, (ii) a determination of the optimal balance for marketable securities. The payroll and dividend models were treated together owing to their similarities, but the determination of the optimal daily balance following issuance of the checks was not necessary in the determination of the other two major models. The problem of providing for the requisite tax, payroll, dividend and other controllable amounts was considered a subset of the marketable securities account. Unlike

Beranek's functions, it was shown that the logical optimal level of marketable securities depended on the maximum expected change in the cash account and not on the "returns from marketable securities."

Summarizing the models in symbolic form, the first determination is the maximum expected change in the cash account, d_m, given the probability p management is willing to accept of not having enough cash:

$$f(d_m) = 1 - p, \qquad p \; given \qquad (6)$$

Having determining d_m for a single period, the next problem is to take account of successive maximum probable decreases in order to determine the optimal amount of marketable securities, m_0:

$$m_0 = d_m + \sum_{i=1}^{i=n} d_m p^i \qquad (4)$$

where $p = .50$ as an example.

To determine the total required amount of marketable securities, m', the firm must add to m_0 the amount accumulated for such controllable purposes as tax dates (x_t), payroll dates (w_t), dividend dates (I_t), and so forth. Thus:

$$m' = m_0 + m_c \qquad (7)$$

where

$$m_c = f(x_t, w_t, I_t, \ldots, N_t) \qquad (8)$$

If the firm wishes to determine "how much" of its marketable securities are free for investment elsewhere (usually in the firm), it may do so by the following:

$$m_f = M - (m_0 + m_c). \qquad (5)$$

Use Your Hidden Cash Resources*

Frederick Wright Searby

MYSTERY STORY BUFFS and Humphrey Bogart fans alike will remember Dashiell Hammett's superb tale *The Maltese Falcon*, later made into a suspenseful movie. The title object in Hammett's story was a foot-high gold statute of a bird, encrusted from head to foot with precious stones. Painted over with black enamel to disguise its value, the falcon had been passed from hand to hand for centuries. Few of its possessors even guessed its true value, and none was perceptive enough to scratch its enameled surface to bare the treasure underneath.

Hammett's story provides a moral for today's top management and senior financial officers. For most companies have in their own possession a treasure of which they are unaware. They have failed to look beneath the surface of a familiar, everyday reality—the company's own cash gathering and disbursing system—little suspecting the wealth it may conceal.

To be sure, the high interest rates of the past two years have stimulated many companies to whittle down some of their cash balances or take another look at the length of their receivables. By and large, however, these belt-tightening efforts have been carried out piecemeal by individual departments. Only in rare cases has a chief executive, perceiving the profit potential in reducing his company's fallow cash assets, set in motion an across-the-board, multidepartmental review of cash gathering and disbursing processes. Yet, where this has happened, the results have often been astonishing. Consider these recent examples:

* Reprinted from *Harvard Business Review*, Vol. 46, No. 2 (March–April 1968), pp. 71–80. © 1968 by the President and Fellows of Harvard College; all rights reserved.

• A major oil company reduced the cash in its gathering and disbursing system by 75%, providing over $25 million for marketing and refining expansion.

• A large railroad that showed cash balances of only $9 million drew a total of $17 million out of its cash gathering and disbursing system to help finance a major equipment acquisition program.

• A leading insurance company that showed cash balances of $8 million discovered an additional $18 million which could be profitably extracted and put to work.

Solely by tapping the previously unrecognized potential in its cash gathering and disbursing systems, each of the first two companies avoided substantial outside financing at an unfavorable time, without weakening its working capital position or its relationships with outside financial institutions, and saved approximately $1 million in interest charges. The insurance company in the third example profited by a sizable expansion of its loan portfolio.

The recurring savings to manufacturing companies with $100 million or more in assets from much less spectacular cash balance reductions—say, 20% of cash deposits held at year-end 1967—would be about $144 million annually, assuming that the $2.4 billion thus released was invested at 6%.

REASONS FOR DORMANCY

Why has such a substantial resource lain dormant, like the treasure of the Maltese falcon, in so many companies? There are at least three reasons:

1. *Accounting treatments usually understate the size of cash balances.* A substantial portion of the cash available seldom appears as cash on a company's balance sheet, if indeed it appears at all. The two principal sources of this hidden cash are (*a*) receipts by an agency of the company that have not yet reached a dispersing bank (cash-in-transit), and (*b*) cash in a bank on which checks have been drawn but not charged to a company bank account (float). Such items thus understate the true amount of money to be managed and explain the paradox of the railroad and the insurance company mentioned above that were able to withdraw more cash than their cash balances showed.

2. *Scorekeeping practices of the financial function hinder imaginative cash management.* Frequently, the treasurer or other financial officer most able to improve cash management processes is evaluated primarily by his ability to produce funds on short call and to obtain the prime rate on commercial bank loans. Obviously, both of these factors are important to the financial health of a company. However, the first measurement can encourage money managers to maintain unnecessarily large

reserve balances or excessive standby lines of credit which require sizable compensating balances with commercial banks. As for the second measurement—the rate at which money can be borrowed—it is almost always calculated at the simple interest rate, masking the true cost of borrowing when compensating balances are required by the lending bank, as they usually are.

For example, if the treasurer must maintain a 20% compensating balance to obtain the current prime rate of, let us say, 6% on a commercial bank line of credit, then the company's true cost is not 6%, but 7.5%.

3. *Corporate management has not come to grips with the substance of its cash gathering and disbursing processes.* Frequently in the past, top management has shied away from examining the company's cash processes because of their assumed complexity, preferring to leave "technical details" to the bank officers and the company's accountants—none of whom is concerned with more than a fraction of the total picture. Instead of using a cash management system designed to free cash resources for other uses, such a company is operating with a conglomeration of processes and procedures that have evolved piecemeal in response to various historical circumstances, practices, and pressures. Today, however, more and more companies are reclaiming the initiative in cash management and applying the same systematic, problem-solving approaches here that they use elsewhere in their businesses.

Basically, the process of "finding" interest-free funds within the company merely entails thorough fact gathering and analysis. But the opportunities thus identified almost always involve making tradeoffs among mutually related variables. This calls for careful analysis of the overall, interrelated, long-term profit impact of alternative decisions on the system as a whole. Moreover, some of the improvement opportunities fall in the controller's domain, while others are in the province of the treasurer—a split of responsibility that underscores the need for top management attention. Effective cash management, therefore, requires the concerted attention of talented personnel whose top management sponsorship and direction gives them the authority to cross organization lines.

INTERWOVEN OPPORTUNITIES

In real life, a company's cash gathering and cash disbursing activities are two sides of an interwoven system in which changes to one must be evaluated for their impact on the other. For the purposes of this article, however, it will be useful to consider cash gathering and cash disbursing opportunities separately.

Exhibit 1 illustrates a total cash management control system covering 85% to 90% of the expected cash flow for a typical company and shows in visual form how the various facets of cash management fit together.

EXHIBIT 1
Schematic diagram of total cash management control system

Cash forecast

Receipts
Disbursements
Securities maturing

Lender banks

Security portfolio

Borrow and repay

Buy and sell

Disbursement accounts

Automatic movement
of funds into zero
balance accounts

Vendors
Employees
Government
Others

Central bank account

Automatic wire transfers

Regional lockboxes

Concentration banks

Depository transfer checks

Local depository banks

Field offices

Customers

Cash gathering

An obvious but easily overlooked way to speed incoming cash is getting bills to customers earlier. Consider these examples:

• Simply by installing and enforcing standards, a Midwestern oil company cut several days off the time branch offices were taking to process retail customers' credit card invoices and forward them to the home office. In the home office further time was saved by mechanizing the invoice-processing operation and eliminating an auditing step that turned out to be costing more than the errors it was intended to uncover. Altogether, the company has saved $150,000 annually by taking these steps to speed up the mailing of its bills.

• American Telephone & Telegraph Company is working on two ways of speeding its billing processes: computerized processing of receivables and billing through customers' banks. For most of the 350,000,000 collect and credit calls handled annually by the Bell System's 1,500 U.S. operating offices, an operator writes a ticket, which is then mailed to one of 108 local accounting offices that prepare customer bills. But in the area served by Southern Bell, where 100,000 credit and collect calls are made daily, the same call records are now collected in 11 computer centers and transmitted at high speed over existing telephone lines to a processing center in Atlanta, where the billing data are swiftly sorted and relayed to the proper accounting offices, again over telephone lines. The system has cut a day or more from receivables, which in this one area alone will release cash assets conservatively estimated at $200,000 a year. AT&T expects to extend the system nationwide within a few years.

AT&T is also trying out an automatic bill payment plan under which the customer authorizes his bank to pay drafts drawn on his account by a Bell company. Along with the usual bill, AT&T's computer-based accounts receivable processes automatically produce a draft which is presented directly to the customer's bank for payment. In addition to speeding collection of AT&T receivables, this plan reduces the customer's cost of administering accounts payable.

• Smaller companies have speeded up their billing in simpler, but no less effective, ways. A well-known shipping company found it had been losing from 2 to 13 working days in billing to various classes of customers, partly because data required for bill preparation were received unnecessarily late, and partly because a few accounting supervisors did not appreciate the time value of money. By improving the flow of data and installing elementary controls, the company was able to free $400,000 that had been tied up in receivables.

From the time the customer puts his check in the mail, the financial manager has four important opportunities: (*a*) to cut down cash-in-transit time; (*b*) to minimize "uncollected funds"—that is, recently deposited checks drawn on other banks and not yet credited to the company's account; (*c*) to reduce balances in collection banks and speed the movement of funds to disbursing locations; and (*d*) to optimize the balances necessary to compensate banks for depository and movement services.

The financial manager can avail himself of four principal devices for accelerating his company's inward cash flow: depository transfer checks, wire transfers, lockboxes, and relocation of gathering banks.

Depository transfer checks. Used to move funds to concentration or disbursing banks, depository transfer checks are nonnegotiable, usually unsigned, and payable only to a single company account in a specific bank.

In a representative situation shown in Exhibit 2, the company's local agent deposits his day's receipts in a local bank and immediately mails

EXHIBIT 2
Use of depository transfer checks

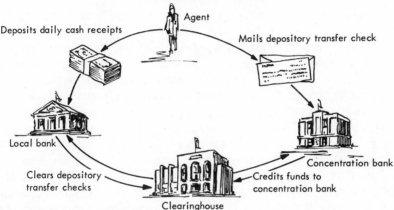

Deposits daily cash receipts

Agent

Mails depository transfer check

Local bank

Clears depository transfer checks

Clearinghouse

Concentration bank

Credits funds to concentration bank

Deposit credited to company account becomes good when check is cleared.

a depository transfer check for the same amount to a designated concentration bank. Receiving the depository transfer check in the next day's mail, the concentration bank puts it into collection that same day, either through the Federal Reserve System or by forwarding it directly to the local depository bank.

By use of this device, funds received at field points are moved directly into concentration banks without requiring action first by headquarters' financial officers. And, although anyone in the local organization may issue a depository transfer check, since the check is nonnegotiable, it cannot be misapplied.

Depository transfer checks cost only 5 to 10 cents apiece, but they are not so fast as wire transfers and may offer no advantage when more than a day is required for mailing or clearing.

Wire transfers. Available in approximately 60 U.S. cities, wire transfers are the fastest way to move money between banks. On order, a bank will transfer a specified amount of a customer's funds by telegram to a designated bank. The funds are considered collected on receipt of the wire notice.

Frequently, a bank is given standing instructions to wire transfer routinely any funds above a stated bank balance to a specified bank. In this case the movement of funds is automatic, while balances are held at the level necessary to compensate the bank fairly for its services.

Wire transfers require that both the sending and the receiving banks have access to the bank wire system. And, of course, they are uneconomical unless the value of having money available as early as possible exceeds the extra cost of the wire transfer (the price is generally about $1.50 a transfer). In general, wire transfers for amounts under $2,000 are not practical.

Lockboxes. Cash gathering can often be expedited by having remittances mailed directly to a post office box that is opened by a bank. The use of lockboxes speeds the collection of checks as well as the movement of remittances, since the checks are deposited before, rather than after, the accounting is done. On occasion, however—especially where only checks for small amounts are involved—the cost of a lockbox may outweigh its benefits. One company, for example, found that by using a lockbox it could speed up remittances from its customers by an average of 3 days. But the average remittance was only $5, while the additional per-check cost of a lockbox was 2 cents, or 8 times the incremental value of receiving the money 3 days early—$0.0025 (i.e., $5 × .06 × 3 ÷ 356, where 6% represents the value of money). Wisely, the company kept on making local deposits. But it did start using depository transfer checks to move customer remittances to gathering banks.

Installing lockboxes can also require major changes in accounting and control systems if cash receipts have to be processed at different locations.

Selection of gathering banks. Frequently, the cash gathering system can be made more effective by selecting more advantageously located banks for use as local depositors or concentration points.

A concentration bank—as well as the local depository bank, if possible—should meet five criteria:

1. The bank should be in the Federal Reserve city which is serving the collection area.
2. It should be on the bank wire system.
3. It should receive 90% of deposited checks one day after they are mailed.
4. Its check availability schedule should average less than one and a half days for normal deposits.
5. Its service charge, earnings allowance rate and reserve requirements should be competitive.

Many large industrial companies use several cash gathering systems, depending on the size regularity, type, and origin of their receipts, as well as on the availability of bank services. They may use, for example, alternative combinations of the four devices just mentioned, tailoring the appropriate cash gathering system for each area in the light of such factors as mailing time statistics for the area, and local bank availability schedules, service charges, earnings allowances, and reserve requirements. Exhibit 3 shows how one company selected appropriate cash gathering systems for different areas.

Systems chosen

Description	Used where	Effect on field and home office operations
Local cash receipt and deposit	Payments made on locally maintained accounts receivable	200 field locations mail their deposits to new, relocated regional banks
Depository transfer check to regional concentration bank	Average local receipts less than $2,500 per day *or* . . .	Regional banks receive mail overnight from 90% of locations
Automatic wire transfer to disbursing bank	Wire transfer not available	Intransit cash reduced by $750,000
Local cash receipt and deposit	Payments made on locally maintained accounts receivable	Can be used in 20 field locations controlling 50% of deposits
Automatic wire transfer to central bank	Average local receipts exceed $2,500	Intransit cash reduced by $1,250,000
Direct mailing of checks to regional post office box cleared by concentration bank	Payments made on centrally maintained credit card receivables	2 regional lockboxes established
Automatic wire transfer to central bank		Intransit cash reduced by $800,000
		Home office clerical costs reduced by $25,000 per year

Cash disbursing

The principal opportunities available to the financial manager for improving his company's disbursing procedures and freeing more funds for investment include synchronizing transfers with clearings, delaying check mailings, and eliminating field working funds.

Synchronizing transfers with clearings. Financial managers recognize that the funds actually available in banks are generally greater than the balances shown on the company's books. This difference (float) is caused by the delay between the time a check is written and its clearing by the bank—due to mailing time, handling by payee, and normal collection time. Exhibit 4 shows the sizable amount of float which built up in one oil company's royalty disbursing account.

If a financial manager can accurately estimate the size of float and

EXHIBIT 3
Alternative retail cash gathering systems, Company X
Systems considered

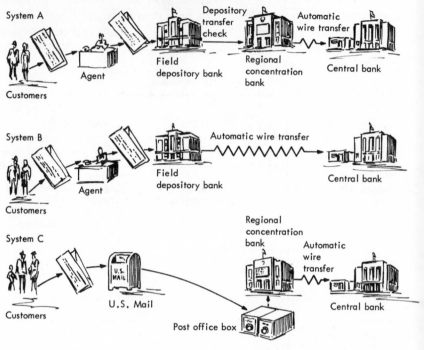

predict when checks will clear, he can maintain a negative book balance and invest the float. He does not have to reimburse the disbursement account until shortly before the checks are presented for payment. Often, he can synchronize transfers into disbursement accounts with check clearings if an accurate clearing projection has been developed.

One device that may help the financial manager forecast and control float is the zero balance account. Under this system, no balance is maintained in the disbursing accounts. Instead, all funds are held in a single general account, and the bank is authorized to transfer funds from the general account into each zero balance account as disbursement checks actually clear. In this way the forecasting and control problem is centralized in the single general account.

Some money managers may be reluctant to have a consistently negative book balance position at disbursing banks. This problem can be overcome by realigning the disbursing system so that major portions of the check float are generated at the banks that require the largest compensating balances. When this is done, the float balances at these important banks usually are sufficient to cover the compensation needs while the book balances can be held at a small positive figure.

EXHIBIT 4
Actual funds available while Company Y's
books showed zero balances

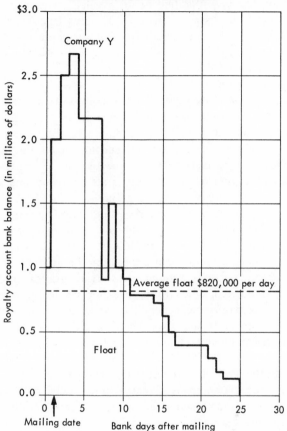

Delaying check mailings. Without the loss of prompt-payment discounts, credit rating, of supplier goodwill, substantial free credit and
cost savings can often be realized from better timing of accounts payable.
For example, input data can be date-coded to trigger printing by computer and mailing on the latest possible date. (In many states, payments
mailed on the discount expiration date legally qualify for the discount.)
Nondiscount suppliers, such as transportation companies or joint venture
partners, can be paid at the latest possible date which is consistent with
legal and competitive conditions.

The oil company referred to in Exhibit 4 not only found ways to
minimize its royalty payment float, but was also able to delay its royalty
check mailings each month. Following a thorough study, this company
discovered that it was sending out $10 million in oil royalty payments

each month 12 days ahead of industry practice and 15 days ahead of legal requirements in most states. On the basis of an analysis of mailing times, the company began coding its oil royalty accounts so as to release computer-printed checks an average of 12 days later than before. The recurring savings to the company from this relatively easy change were $237,000 a year (or $10,000 $\times$ $12\%_{365}$ $\times$ 12 $\times$ .06, with the first 12 representing the number of days; the second 12, the number of months; and 6%, the value of money).

Eliminating field working funds.   Many companies maintain small bank balances in field locations for convenience in paying small local bills. In total these funds frequently create unnecessarily large cash balances because of "cushions" maintained for contingencies. For example, one company with a large marketing organization in 25 states reduced its cash balances $3 million by substituting draft payments and a centralized disbursement account for field working funds.

Draft payment plans and centralized field disbursement accounts are two devices which can be used to improve field disbursing procedures. Payments to local vendors can be made with drafts drawn by themselves on a designated bank. Limits can be set on the amount of drafts, and payment may be refused. Among the advantages of drafts are that cushions are eliminated, since funds are not needed until the draft is presented; one reimbursement per day covers all drafts; bank service charges for cashing drafts are lower than for checks; and clerical costs of preparing checks and maintaining individual working funds are eliminated.

However, some of the disadvantages are that many smaller banks do not accept drafts; their use requires the cooperation of suppliers; and drafts may reduce the company's float. Alternatively, a centralized, zero-balance account can be maintained to pay local vendors. Checks are issued locally but drawn on the central account. The checks can be coded to show the disbursing location and purpose, and the bank can provide periodic listings, by code and amount, of the checks that have cleared.

This system also eliminates working fund cushions and the clerical costs of maintaining individual working funds. Furthermore, check float is centralized in a single account, simplifying the control problem.

IMPACT ON BANKS

Better corporate cash management has obvious portents for commercial banks. Sometimes, such as in the case of a receivables reduction, its effects are confined to a shifting of deposits from one company to another. At other times, say, when a company begins using automatic wire transfers to reduce cash-in-transit, the result is a shift of deposits from one bank to another bank. Overall, however, there can be no doubt that the systematic analysis and overhauling of cash management systems as described in this article will reduce (and, in fact, are currently reducing) the amount of interest-free demand deposits available to commercial banks.

How are the banks reacting to all this? Naturally enough, many are reluctant to initiate a process that in the short run results in a partial drying up of their traditional source of raw material, and in the long run may well require substantial changes in "product line" and pricing policies.

Positive view

Increasingly, however, most of the nation's biggest and most farsighted banks are taking a positive approach. Recognizing the legitimacy of their customers' concern with the profit improvement opportunities concealed in their cash management systems, these banks are taking the view—a real sign, perhaps, of the much-heralded marketing revolution in banking—that the long-term health of their institutions depends on how well they serve the best interest of their customers. And they know that this means more than simply adding new services. It means being willing to drop old services—and to look for new and more flexible pricing practices.

In fact, many banks are working actively with large corporate customers to help them design more effective cash gathering and disbursing systems—thereby, not surprisingly, strengthening greatly their working relationships with these customers. In at least one case, the bank in question inherited some of the customers' deposits from other banks less eager to assist in improving cash management, emerging with only slightly lower overall deposits. But even those whose deposits have been substantially drawn down have found themselves, thanks to their new and deeper knowledge of their customers' businesses, in a far better competitive position to develop profitable new business.

SUMMARY

Companies searching for additional cash sources or profit improvement would do well to remember Dashiell Hammett's Maltese falcon and first take a look close to home.

The opportunities for capital generation or for profit improvement in cash management are often impressive. For a company representing the mean of *Fortune's* "500," for example, even a day's reduction in cash-in-transit would be worth well over $100,000 in recurring annual savings. For a small company, the dollar figure will be smaller but relatively no less significant. (Company managers can estimate, on a rough basis, the value of reducing a day's cash-in-transit by dividing their sales by 365 and multiplying the result by 6%. The resulting figure, of course, represents not the cash freed up, but the savings recurring annually from the cash freed up.) And this, as we have seen, is only one of a number of ways of freeing idle funds. In other words, it is only a fraction of the total opportunity.

To take advantage of the total opportunity, all that is needed to begin with is a systematic, tough-minded examination of cash processes to uncover profit opportunities such as those indicated by the symptoms listed below.

Clues to Improvement Opportunity

Decentralized responsibility for processing cash receipts, disbursing funds, and maintaining relationships with banks.
Absence of a reasonably accurate, daily cash forecasting system.
Use of gathering or concentration banks in cities which are non-Federal Reserve or have no bank wire facilities.
Lack of current figures on:
  Float in major disbursing accounts.
  Cash-in-transit in parts of cash gathering system.
No record for individual accounts showing purpose, activity, tangible and intangible services, and average bank ledger balance.
No current analysis of the cost to the company, and the profitability to the bank, of each major banking relationship.
Limited use of the administrative services provided by banks, such as draft payment plans, lockboxes, depository transfer checks, zero balance accounts, and automatic wire transfers.
Maintenance of balances in a large number of banks and/or accounts for disbursing purposes.

Once these opportunities are identified and the savings targets are established, the financial manager can proceed, with top management's support and encouragement, to implement the changes needed to reduce costs and free corporate cash reserves for profitable uses. Some of these may be independent, such as closing out inactive accounts; others may be interdependent, such as modifying cash collection procedures and setting cash balance minimums at concentration banks.

A company can expect both immediate and long-range benefits from appraising its cash handling practices and capitalizing on the unveiled potential. Not only can clerical costs in cash gathering and disbursing be minimized, but, more important, large sources of funds can be tapped for business growth.

Managerial Controls of Accounts Receivable: A Deterministic Approach*

Haskel Benishay †

In this paper an analytical framework for the interpretation and evaluation of accounts receivable is constructed. Its purpose is to provide accountants and managers with general insights into the dynamics of the credit sales-accounts receivable process. Within the assumptions of the framework, the mean collection period is evaluated, and empirical measures for its direct and indirect representation are provided.

The mean collection period is an "interval measure" of the type discussed by Sorter and Benston.[1] It emerges as a meaningful concept directly related to both external and internal considerations of the payment patterns of a firm's customers. The turnover rate of accounts receivable, which is sometimes offered as an alternative to the mean collection period, appears to have no place in the analysis; it does not provide a valid means for evaluating the credit policies of a firm. The mean collection period is deemed more appropriate than the receivables turnover concept for reasons of relevance and meaningfulness. These reasons are similar

* Reprinted from *Journal of Accounting Research*, Vol. 3, No. 1 (Spring 1965), pp. 114–32, by permission of the author and the publisher.

An earlier version of this paper was presented in the Harvard Business School Research Workshop in Business Finance, sponsored by the Ford Foundation in summer 1964. It was further developed and extended in the workshop during that summer. My thanks are extended to Professors Burt Fox and Eli Shapiro for valuable editorial comments, to Professors John Lintner and Charles Christenson for stimulating discussions, to Professor Gordon Donaldson for practical suggestions and to Dick Bower for lending his ear.

† Professor of Finance and Management Sciences, State University of New York at Buffalo.

[1] G. H. Sorter and G. Benston, "Appraising the Defensive Position of a Firm The Interval Measure," *The Accounting Review*, October 1960.

in content to those expressed by Davidson, Sorter, and Kalle in their evaluation of the defensive interval measure vis-à-vis the current ratio.[2]

The type of control mechanism proposed is statistical and is known variously as quality control in production, and as management by exception[3] in the accounting controls area. In this control system, the exception, i.e., the deviation from the norm, triggers managerial diagnosis and, when required, remedial action. The mechanism is best suited to the needs of top management since it conserves their energies for nonroutine problems. That is, it allows management's attention to be "focused on the relatively small number of items in which actual performance is significantly different from the standard so that little or no attention need be given to the relatively large number of situations where performance has been satisfactory."[4]

The traditional literature dealing with accounts receivable and their evaluation and control seems deficient in this respect, since it is short on analysis and long on description of practices and traditions. Thus, the receivables process and the rationale for some of the control measures commonly used receive insufficient or inadequate attention. Chapin, for example, devotes only a few lines to the method of computing the average (mean) collection period from sales and receivables data and omits an accompanying rationale. He writes: "The collection turnover may be obtained by dividing average receivables outstanding by the average daily sales. . . . Thus with annual sales of $360,000 and average receivables of $40,000 there are 360000/4000 or nine turnovers, or one-ninth of the year's business on the books at one time. . . ."[5] In a later edition he does not elaborate.[6] Beckman and Bartels give, what will appear to be from the vantage point of this paper, an inconsistent account of receivables control measures and an improper distinction between the concept of mean collection period and number of days sales outstanding.[7] In more recent works, the receivables process has been more closely examined both as a population process[8] and as an absorbing Markov pro-

[2] S. Davidson, G. H. Sorter, and H. Kalle, "Measuring and Defensive Position of the Firm," *Financial Analyst Journal*, January–February 1964, pp. 2–8.

[3] The objective is to provide supervisors with appropriate information for "comparing actual results with plans, and taking corrective action where appropriate." John Dearden, "Can Management Information Be Automated?" *Harvard Business Review*, March–April 1964, p. 130.

[4] Robert N. Anthony, *Management Accounting* (Homewood, Ill.: Richard D. Irwin, Inc., 1956), p. 277.

[5] Albert F. Chapin, *Credit and Collections Principles and Practices* (New York: McGraw-Hill Book Co., 1953), p. 422.

[6] Ibid., (1960), p. 359.

[7] T. N. Beckman and R. M. Bartels, *Credit and Collections in Theory and Practice* (New York: McGraw-Hill Book Co., 1955), pp. 580–581, 586.

[8] H. Benishay, "Neglected Areas of Accounts Receivable," *Business and Society*, Vol. 2 (Autumn 1961), p. 29.

cess.[9] Both approaches provide a more comprehensive view of the receivables process, and, if used judiciously, they provide a framework for analysis and for data processing applications in the accounts receivable area.

Do businessmen and managers have a verbal understanding of the receivables process that can be turned to advantage? I believe not. They have some rules-of-thumb, determined in interviews and described in the study by Thompson and Langer.[10] For example 51 interviews; 48 respondents indicated an aging schedule as some measure of control, 27 used a turnover measure, and 17 a collection index. An awareness of the accounts receivable process as a whole and an understanding of what the control ratios represented exactly was not exhibited by these businessmen respondents. They might benefit from reading a general receivables analysis such as that suggested by Ewing.[11]

There are two main subareas within the domain of credit sales and accounts receivable. These are a decision making area and a process control area. This paper is concerned with the understanding and control of what happens, once a particular optimal credit policy has been decided upon. The credit department can behave non-optimally in two ways: it can be either too zealous or too lax in maintaining a given credit policy. Both extremes are non-optimal. Therefore, top management must have a proper means of controlling the receivables process if it is to guard against the occurrence of either extreme.

With respect to control measures, the main conclusions which develop from the analysis are as follows:

1. The ratio of the stock of receivables outstanding to credit sales provides a direct and meaningful measure of the effective and actual *mean collection period*. It makes better sense than its reciprocal, the so-called receivables turnover ratio, since it is a *direct* measurement of the *time* concept relevant to the firm's decision making problems.

2. The ratio of the stock of receivables outstanding to collections is also a direct measure of the mean collection period. It measures mean collection time *directly* and in this sense is a better choice than its reciprocal, the so-called collection index.

3. The aging schedule is an *indirect* but effective method of measuring collection patterns. It must be handled and interpreted with care.

4. The mean age of the receivables outstanding is an *indirect* measure

[9] R. M. Cyert, H. J. Davidson and G. L. Thomson, "Estimation of the Allowance for Doubtful Accounts," *Management Science*, Vol. 8 (April 1962), pp. 287–303.

[10] L. E. Thompson and L. C. R. Langer, *A Study on the Measurement of Credit Department Effectiveness* (New York: Credit Research Foundation, Inc., 1957), p. 41.

[11] David W. Ewing, "The Knowledge of an Executive," *Harvard Business Review*, March–April 1964.

of the average collection period. *Contrary to popular notions it is not exactly equal to one-half of the collection period.*

5. The most neglected of all possible measures is the distribution of collections by their age at the time of collection. This distribution provides a direct estimate of the *actual* percentages of credit sales paying after various length of time.

6. The *mean* age of collections at the time of collection is another direct measure of the mean collection period. Although mean age is easy to compute it is not commonly used.

The first step here is to develop a simple, deterministic receivables model where the receivables process is stable over time, and the variables are stable or nonvariant. From this, we learn about the receivables process and the possible control measures. Then we relax the assumption of non-variance, consider the phenomenon of normal variability in the basic variables, and suggest that the control measures are also subject to normal variability. Next, a mechanism for control of the receivables process will be prescribed. Its essence: As long as the divergence of the control measures is within some prescribed upper and lower bound, there is no need for alarm—the process is under control. When the control measures step out of these bounds it is to be interpreted as a danger signal. Finally, the essence of the model and the control scheme will be demonstrated in a simulated example.

THE DETERMINISTIC RECEIVABLES MODEL

The notation and the underlying assumptions of the receivables model are as follows.

Let S be credit sales (or new loans) made in an interval of time, and let S in any time interval be equal to S in any other time interval. Let the dollar amounts of collections and bad debts in an interval of time be, respectively, C and B.

Let the time *interval* (day, month, etc.) from point in time $T - 1$ to point in time T (from dawn to dawn, Monday noon to Monday noon, etc.) be t.

Let i be the possible collection period in intervals of time and the maximum collection period be n intervals of time such that $i \leq n$ for any portion of credit sales.

n can be thought of as the period from the time a credit sale is made to the time the resulting account receivable is declared a "bad debt" by the company. The length of this period is usually determined by the firm's experience. It assumed that the firm classifies the receivable as a bad debt by the criterion that it has grown older than n periods, a common practice.

Let the portion of credit sales paid (collected) on the ith interval after the interval in which the sales were made be P_i, the ith interval itself be D_i, and the whole pattern of the possible duration of collection periods and their associated P_i proportions be D. Clearly P_n refers both to collections after n periods and to receivables deemed bad debts.

Let D be constant over time, i.e., both D_i and P_i are constant over time.

The mean, M, of the duration of collection periods, D, assuming that the periods are counted from 1 to n, will be

$$M = \sum_{i=1}^{n} P_i i \qquad (1.00)$$

Finally let the total value of receivables outstanding (credit sales made but not yet paid) at time T be V_T.

Note that this is a deterministic model where the exogenous variables are *not* random. The S is constant over time with variance zero between the periods, and the P_i are constant proportions through time (not constant probabilities), so that if P_1 is 20%, then exactly 20% of S pay on the first interval after the interval in which they are made. Later we deal with a stochastic or probabilistic model and obtain, by simulation, some notion of its properties.

A. Volume of receivables in equilibrium

In equilibrium, when

$$S_t = S_{t-1};$$

$$D_t = D_{t-1}$$

i.e., P_i at t equal to P_i at $t - 1$, and if trade credit has been granted for at least n periods, the volume of receivables can be written at any time T, looking backwards at a sequence of time intervals, as follows:

$$V_T = S_t(1) + S_{t-1}(1 - P_1) + S_{t-2}(1 - P_1 - P_2) + \cdots + S_{t-n+1}(P_n)$$
$$(1.01)$$

the first term on the right denoting the credit sales of the period t, of which none were paid yet; the second term, the credit sales of the period before last, which were not yet paid, etc. In the pictorial representation of time which follows, the asterisked sub-segments, beginning at point in time T at extreme right, identify the time periods associated with expression (1.01) above.

$t - n$	$t - n + 1$			$t - 3$	$t - 2$	$t - 1$	t	
	*	...		*	*	*	*	

T

Expression (1.01) is the sum of the amounts in the various age categories. If V_{ci} represents directly the ith category (age group) of the volume of receivables outstanding where i ranges between 1 to n, than (1.01) can be first viewed simply as the sum of its age categories:

$$V_T = V_{c1} + V_{c2} + V_{c3} + \cdots + V_{cn} \qquad (1.01a)$$

However, when the various age categories are expressed in terms of the *uncollected portions of past credit sales* with the appropriate S_i and P_i, symbols, expression (1.01) emerges. Expression (1.01) can be rewritten as:

$$V_T = S[1 + (1 - P_1) + (1 - P_1 - P_2) + \cdots + P_n] \qquad (1.02)$$

since $S_t = S_{t-1}$ by assumption. Expression (1.02) can be rewritten in turn as:

$$V_T = S[(P_1 + P_2 + P_3 + \cdots + P_n) + (P_2 + P_3 + \cdots + P_n) + \cdots \\ + (P_{n-1} + P_n) + (P_n)] \qquad (1.03)$$

since the difference in the inner parentheses above can be written as sums of the remaining P_i.

Now note that:

$$P_n \text{ is in } n \text{ expressions}$$
$$P_{n-1} \text{ is in } n - 1 \text{ expressions}$$
$$\cdots$$

and finally,

P_1 is in only one expression. Hence, adding the P_i, (1.03) can be written:

$$V_T = S[1P_1 + 2P_2 + 3P_3 + \cdots + nP_n] \qquad (1.04)$$

and utilizing summation notation and expression (0.1) above

$$V_T = S\left[\sum_{i=1}^{n} P_i i \right] = SM \qquad (1.05)$$

which is the expression of the equilibrium receivables volume outstanding in terms of the product of credit sales and mean collection period. Consequently, by algebraic manipulation,

$$M = V_T/S \qquad (1.06)$$

and

$$S = V_T/M \qquad (1.07)$$

Equation (1.05) demonstrates that the amount of funds tied up in receivables depends on total credit sales, resulting conditions of demand from the credit granting policy of the firm, and the mean collection period. Equation (1.06), which is derived from (1.05), shows that, in equilibrium, the mean collection period is represented by the ratio of receivables to credit sales. This provides a quick control measure to estimate directly the mean collection period. Equation (1.07) shows that, in equilibrium, credit sales may be represented by the ratio of receivables to the mean collection period.

B. The aging schedule and mean age of receivables

The aging schedule refers to the proportions of accounts receivable in the various age categories. Referring to expression (1.01) we see that the proportion of receivables in a particular age category to total receivables volume at time T can be expressed as

$$S_t(1)/SM \tag{2.01}$$

$$S_{t-1}(1 - P_1)/SM \tag{2.02}$$

$$S_{t-2}(1 - P_1 - P_2)/SM \tag{2.03}$$

$$\cdot$$

$$S_{t-n+1}(P_n)/SM \tag{2.04}$$

Since credit sales are assumed constant over time, the S in the previous expressions cancels out, and the differences inside the parentheses can be expressed as sums. Hence, the expressions can be rewritten as follows:

$$(P_1 + P_2 + P_3 + \cdots + P_n)/M \tag{2.11}$$

$$(P_2 + P_3 + \cdots + P_n)/M \tag{2.12}$$

$$(P_3 + \cdots + P_n)/M \tag{2.13}$$

$$\cdot \qquad \cdot$$

$$(P_n)/M \tag{2.14}$$

Note that the sum of proportions in the numerators of the expressions above is the proportion of incoming credit sales which does not pay within i periods. Sales are thereby dichotomously divided into those customers who pay after $i(i = 1, 2 \ldots n)$ and those who do not. For example, in (2.11) 100% of sales do not pay before 1 period from the time they are made $(i = 1)$, in (2.12), $(P_2 + P_3 + \cdots + P_n)$ do not pay before 2 periods from the time they are made, etc., in (2.14) P_n do not pay before n periods.

Clearly if the younger age categories become weightier over time relative to the older ones, it means that the proportion of credit sales paying after shorter time spans increases relative to those paying after longer time spans. For example if P_1 increases at the expense of P_n alone, all age groups but the oldest will have increased. It follows that the relation between the proportions in the various age categories is an *indirect but useful reflection of the basic payment patterns expressed in the separate P_i, i.e., $P_1, P_2 \ldots P_n$.*

Other uses may be made from the information contained in the aging schedule. The mean age of receivables outstanding can be easily computed. For this purpose, note that the mean age of the various age categories 0 to 1, 1 to 2, 2 to 3, . . . , $(n-1)$ to (n), is respectively $\frac{1}{2}$, $\frac{3}{2}$, $\frac{5}{2}$, . . . $((n-1) + (n))/2$; i.e., halfway between the maximum and minimum ages in the category since the inflow of credit sales is assumed evenly distributed over time. The mean age of receivables outstanding is then simply the sum for all age categories of the products of the proportion of receivables in each age category to total receivables times the mean age of this category. In terms of (2.11), (2.12), (2.13), (2.14), each of the expressions should be multipled by $\frac{1}{2}$, $\frac{3}{2}$, $\frac{5}{2}$, etc., respectively. The products thus formed are summed up as follows:

$$
\begin{aligned}
(P_1(\tfrac{1}{2}) + P_2(\tfrac{1}{2}) + P_3(\tfrac{1}{2}) + \cdots + P_n(\tfrac{1}{2}))/M + \\
(P_2(\tfrac{3}{2}) + P_3(\tfrac{3}{2}) + \cdots + P_n(\tfrac{3}{2}))/M + \\
(P_3(\tfrac{5}{2}) + \cdots + P_n(\tfrac{5}{2}))/M + \\
\cdot \qquad \cdot \qquad \cdot \\
(P_n(n + - 1)/2)/M \qquad (2.15)
\end{aligned}
$$

Rearranging terms and simplifying, results in an expression for the mean age of receivables, as follows:

$$
\frac{P_1 1^2 + P_2 2^2 + P_3 3^2 + \cdots + P_n n^2}{2M} \qquad (2.16)
$$

This result can be evaluated by means of a well known theorem in statistics[12] and it can be shown that it yields the result:

$$
\frac{P_1 1^2 + P_2 2^2 + P_3 3^3 + \cdots + P_n n^2}{2M} = \frac{V_d + M^2}{2M}
$$

$$
= \frac{V_d}{2M} + \frac{M}{2} \qquad (2.17)
$$

where V_d is the variance of the collection periods. This states that the mean receivables age consists of two components: $M/2$, i.e., one-half of the mean collection period, plus $V_d/2M$, the ratio of the variance of the collection period to twice its mean. The mean receivables age rises with the variance of the collection periods V_d, and with the mean collection period M. This result is especially interesting since there seems to be a common-sense tendency to assume that the mean age of the outstanding receivables is one-half the mean collection period.[13] It may

---

[12] The second moment about zero equals the second moment about the mean + the square of the mean. In this case the numerator in (2.16) above is the second moment about zero of the collection period variable, D.

[13] My conversations with businessmen indicated that the usual "businessman insights" analysis in this connection was something like this: If it takes an average of x months to pay, the receivables outstanding should be, on the average, $\frac{1}{2}$ of x months old.

be useful to ascertain the magnitude of V_d and M from other sources, say from the distribution of the collections by age or from actual sampling, and then adjust the average age derived from the aging schedule to yield a second estimate of M.

If, however, the mean age is taken as a measure of $\frac{1}{2}$ the mean collection period and therefore multiplied by 2 to get the mean collection period, serious overestimates may be the result. Suppose D_i ranges between 1 and 30 periods and the P_i are equal, i.e., people pay with equal probability after 1, 2, 3 $\cdots$ 30 periods. V_d equals 74.916 in this case, M equals 15.5, $V_d/2M$ the "overestimate" referred to above will be $74.196/2(15.5) = 2.38$ which, if not taken into account, will produce a 15% error in the estimate of M.

C. The aging schedule and bad debts

Previously, P_n had been defined as the sum of P_{nc}, or the collections after n periods, and P_{nb}, or the bad debts ascertained after n periods. Expressing the dollar amounts in each age category of the outstanding receivables[14] and incorporating the decomposition of P_n into its P_{nc} and P_{nb} components results in:

$$(P_1 + P_2 + P_3 + \cdots + P_{nc} + P_{nb})S \qquad (3.01)$$
$$(P_2 + P_3 + \cdots + P_{nc} + P_{nb})S \qquad (3.02)$$
$$(P_3 + \cdots + P_{nc} + P_{nb})S \qquad (3.03)$$

$$(P_{nc} + P_{nb})S \qquad (3.04)$$

This shows, as expected, that bad debts become a larger and larger proportion of the total in an age category as age increases. Comparing the extremes, (3.01) and (3.04), the differences in the bad debt proportions between the age categories are evident.

$$\frac{SP_{nb}}{SP_{nc} + SP_{nb}} > \frac{SP_{nb}}{SP_1 + SP_2 + SP_3 + \cdots + SP_{nc} + SP_{nb}} \qquad (3.05)$$

D. The collection patterns expressed as proportions paying next period of amounts in age categories now

The collection patterns were expressed hitherto by the P_i which expressed the amounts collected as *proportions of the initial sales* batch of which they were a part. Many practitioners in the receivables area are in the habit of expressing the collection patterns as proportions col-

---

[14] See section B above for a more extended explanation.

lected during the next period of the various amounts in the age groups of the receivables outstanding. Put differently, they are proportions collected during the next period $t + 1$, from the uncollected sales as of now, at t; for example, if the collection patterns as expressed by the ordinary P_i are 50 cents of a dollar pay after one period, 40 after two, and 10 after three the alternative way of stating the above is a mere translation as follows:

$$50/100 = 0.5$$
$$40/(100-50) = 0.8$$
$$10/(100-50-40) = 1.0$$

Here, 0.5, 0.8, 1.0 are the proportions collected next period from last period's amounts in the various receivables age categories.[15]

The conversion from the "ordinary" P_i used in the paper to the proportions collected next period from the various age categories, designated as Q_i, can be generalized as follows:

$$P_1/(P_1 + P_2 + P_3 + \cdots + P_n) = Q_1 \qquad (4.01)$$
$$P_2/(P_2 + P_3 + \cdots + P_n) = Q_2 \qquad (4.02)$$
$$P_3/(P_3 + \cdots + P_n) = Q_3 \qquad (4.03)$$

$$P_n/(P_n) = Q_n \qquad (4.04)$$

E. Collections

Next it will be shown that in equilibrium (when S and D with its associated P_i are constant and the credit granting process has been in operation for at least n periods) credit sales equal collections plus bad debts.

Collections, C, plus bad debts, B, during a time interval t can be visualized as the sum of payments from a sequence of past credit sales and can be written as follows:

$$C + B = S(P_1) + S(P_2) + \cdots + SP_{n-1} + SP_n \qquad (5.01)$$

where the first term on the right denotes collections from sales in the previous period, i.e., during $t - 1$, the second term, collections from sales two periods ago, i.e., during $t - 2$, etc.; and the last term, collections and bad debts from sales n periods ago, i.e., during $t - n$. A pictorial representation of expression (5.01) may facilitate visualization of the concept embodied in the expression.

---

[15] The Markov chain approach mentioned previously utilizes this particular way of expressing the collection patterns.

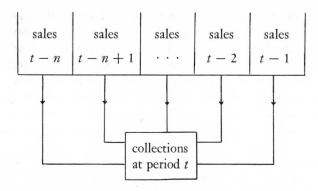

To aid visualization, collections (and bad debts) can first be viewed directly as the sum of the various age categories of which they consist, from the youngest category, one period old, to the oldest, n periods old. If C_{ci} represents an age category of collections (where small c stands for category and i ranges from 1 to n) collections and bad debts can be simply written as a sum of age categories:

$$C + B = C_{c1} + C_{c2} + \cdots + C_{c(n-1)} + C_{cn} \qquad (5.01\text{a})$$

When the various age categories are in turn expressed in terms of previous credit sales, S, and the collection patterns, P_i, expression (5.01) emerges.

That is expression (5.01) can be written as:

$$C + B = S(P_1 + P_2 + \cdots + P_{n-1} + P_n) = S(1) = S \qquad (5.02)$$

since $P_1 + P_2 + \cdots + P_{n-1} + P_n = 1$ by definition. Hence in equilibrium, collections plus bad debts equal credit sales. As a corollary, therefore, since (1.06) and (5.02) are true

$$M = V_T/(C + B) \qquad (5.03)$$

Thus, the mean collection period can be represented by the ratio of the receivables volume to collections and bad debts.

F. Distribution of collections by age

More detailed information about the distribution of the collection period for "incoming" credit sales may be provided by distributing, by age, the collections plus bad debts (outgoing sales) in period t. The distribution by age of collections and bad debts in this model is a mirror image of the distribution of collection periods, D, applicable to credit sales.

Each of the SP_i terms in (5.01) above provides the dollar amount of the different age groups among the paid or written-off receivables.

This term divided by either total credit sales or by total collections plus bad debts for a period will produce the original P_i since equation (5.02), which merely states the equality of S and $(C + B)$, is true

$$(SP_i)/S = P_i \qquad (6.01)$$

$$(SP_i)/(C + B) = P_i \qquad (6.02)$$

The implication is that, being provided with information about the dollar amounts in the various categories of collections and taking these as proportions of total sales or proportions of total collections, one ends up with a representation of the sales proportions paying after i intervals.

And to get the mean collection period, the resultant P_i computed from the proportions of the age categories are used as weights for a weighted mean of the various ages at collection. If P_i computed in (6.01) and (6.02) above is designated as P_i', then M can be simply written as:

$$M = \sum_{i=1}^{n} P_i'i \qquad (6.01\text{a}, 6.02\text{a})$$

Summary of model results

In preceding sections it was shown that the mean collection period can be represented by four expressions: (1.06), (5.03), (6.01a), (6.02a).

In Section F we saw that the distribution of collection periods of credit sales dollars can be represented by the distribution of collections (and bad debts) by age if, in computing the separate P_i, we take the amounts in the various age categories as a percentage of either collections or of credit sales.

In equations (2.11) to (2.14) we focused on the fact that each age category in the aging schedule represents the portion which has not yet been paid from sales of a particular past period. Consequently, it became evident that one can get as many estimates of collection patterns as there are age categories. These estimates are, of course, estimates of proportions of sales paying after i periods, where i is the age of the category under consideration.

In equation (2.17) we expressed algebraically the relation between the mean age of receivables and the mean collection period. This relation turns out *not* to be an obvious one.

In viewing bad debts analytically as a part of the total receivables picture, it became clear why age is positively associated with bad debts proportions. It was also possible to show how the collection proportions may be expressed in an alternative form which seems different, but contains the same basic information. Furthermore, we pointed out that given any two of the three quantities, V_t, S and M, the third can be deduced.

Generally, the analysis produced hitherto-neglected estimates of the mean collection periods and of the distribution of collections in toto. These estimates were found useful for the purpose of shedding light on the interaction between the various components and subcomponents of the credit sales-receivables process.

A "REALISTIC" EXAMPLE

Until now, credit sales and the pattern of collections were assumed exact and stable variables over time. Under these assumptions, no variability was allowed in the control measures. Strictly interpreted, given constant sales, any divergence of the control measures from their habitual and exact values constituted a priori a change in collection patterns. In reality, however, sales and the collection patterns are random variables. Consequently the control measures themselves are random variables varying within a "normal" range. The question arises: how can their variances be computed so as to enable us to construct the "quality control bounds" we have referred to previously? Obviously, these control measures must be computed over a period of time in a consistent manner, say every month, so as to provide a backlog of information about the past variability of our control measures. Once we accumulate enough information to provide a quantitative estimate of past variability, and assuming a normal distribution, we can set control limits around the mean. These control limits at some distance from their mean, say two or three standard deviations, will serve as "our management by exception apparatus."

A small-scale, hand simulation of a receivables process, the computation of control statistics, and the estimation of their variances may provide a general understanding of the nature of the receivables process and the nature of its control by the exception mechanism. Using actual figures, a receivables process is illustrated below which is very similar to the one described in the previous model. Credit-sales is assumed to be a *random variable* in order to lend some reality to our example. For the sake of convenience, assume that sales can take on only two values, 110 and 90, with one-half probability for each. To make the example more realistic, assume that the collection period is also a random variable. And for the sake of simplicity, again, assume only two possibilities for i, 1 and 2, i.e., customers pay either after one period or after two periods. No other possibilities are admitted. Suppose, too, that the proportion paying after one period from the time the sale is made can be either .4 or .6 with probability of one-half for each. This, of course, implies a probability pattern of paying after 2 periods, i.e., there is a probability of .5 that 60% will pay after 2 periods, and of .5 that 40% will pay after 2 periods. Those who do not pay after one period must, by assumption, pay after two. We make no provision for Bad Debts.

Given the above assumptions the mean collection period is implied and is equal to:

$$.5(1(.4) + 2(.6)) + .5(1(.6) + 2(.4)) = \qquad (7.01)$$
$$1(.5(.4) + .5(.6)) + 2(.5(.6) + .5(.4)) = \qquad (7.02)$$
$$1(.5) + 2(.5) = 1.5 \qquad (7.03)$$

Expression (7.01) above computes the mean collection period utilizing the following logic: given the previous assumptions, visualize two mixed distributions each one of which having one-half weight (probability) in the total. The first one is where 40% of credit sales pay after 1 period, 60% after 2 periods. The second one is where 60% of credit sales pay after 1 period, 40% after 2. The two properly combined produce expression (7.01) for the mean collection period. Expression (7.03) is a summary of all the forces; it yields 50% proportions paying after one, and 50% after two periods. Consistent with the point of view expressed earlier, the pattern of collections assumed in this example is the equivalent of the resultant collection pattern of a particular credit policy decided upon by top management.

The mean of sales implied by the assumption above is:

$$.5(110) + .5(90) = 100 \qquad (7.04)$$

From equation (1.05) of the deterministic model, we know in advance that the volume of receivables will average around $100(1.5) = 150$, and, from equation (5.02), that collections will also average around 100.

The hypothetical receivables process is simulated below in Table 1A.

TABLE 1A
Hand simulation of a receivables process

Period	Sales S_t	Collections from 1 month ago C_{c2}	Collection from 2 months ago C_{c1}	Total collections C_t	End of period receivables volume V_T	Category of .5 periods mean age V_{c1}	Category of 1.5 periods mean age V_{c2}
1........	110			0	110	110	
2........	90	66		66	134	90	44
3........	90	54	44	98	126	90	36
4........	110	54	36	90	146	110	36
5........	110	44	36	80	176	110	66
6........	90	44	66	110	156	90	66
7........	90	54	66	120	126	90	36
8........	90	54	36	90	126	90	36
9........	110	54	36	90	146	110	36
10........	90	66	36	102	134	90	44
11........	110	54	44	98	146	110	36
12........	90	44	36	80	156	90	66
13........		36	66				
14........			54				

The procedure is as follows. The period's sales were simulated by drawing from a table of random numbers in which 1, 2, 3, 4, 5, were defined as 90; and 6, 7, 8, 9, 0, as 110 to fit the stochastic assumptions about sales. A similar process was used to simulate the proportions paying after 1 period, i.e., 40% or 60%. Similarly 1, 2, 3, 4, 5 were defined as 40%; and 6, 7, 8, 9, 0 as 60% to fit the assumptions made about collections. In each period, the simulated sales figure multiplied by the simulated collection proportion determines collections during the following period. What remains from these sales is collected during the second next period. These sales-collection combinations are generated for 12 periods to provide 10 sets of equilibrium values of the receivables process (recall that it takes n periods, in this case $n = 2$, to bring the process to a stable equilibrium). The results generated are presented in Table 1A. The means and standard deviations of the various variables for the ten periods 3–12 are summarized in Table 1B. Note that in equilibrium, for the receivables

TABLE 1B
Means and standard deviations of Table 1A columns for periods 3 to 12 inclusive

	S_t	C_{c1}	C_{c2}	C_t	V_T	V_{c1}	V_{c2}
Mean..........	90.00	52.20	43.60	95.80	143.80	98.00	45.80
S.D...........	10.33	6.77	12.25	12.63	16.31	10.33	14.16

TABLE 2
Control statistics, means, standard deviation and control bounds, computed from data generated in Table 1

Period	V_T/S_t	V_T/C_t	C_{c1}/C_t $+$ $2C_{c2}/C_t$	C_{c1}/S_t $+$ $2C_{c2}/S_t$	C_{c1}/C_t	V_{c1}/V_T	$.5V_{c1}/$ $V_T +$ $1.5V_{c2}/$ V_T
3..............	1.40	1.29	1.44	1.58	.55	.71	.79
4..............	1.33	1.62	1.40	1.15	.60	.75	.75
5..............	1.60	2.20	1.45	1.06	.55	.63	.88
6..............	1.73	1.41	1.60	1.96	.40	.58	.92
7..............	1.40	1.05	1.55	2.07	.45	.71	.79
8..............	1.40	1.40	1.40	1.40	.60	.71	.79
9..............	1.33	1.62	1.40	1.15	.60	.75	.75
10..............	1.49	1.31	1.35	1.53	.65	.67	.83
11..............	1.33	1.49	1.45	1.29	.55	.75	.75
12..............	1.73	1.95	1.45	1.29	.55	.58	.92
Mean............	1.47	1.54	1.45	1.45	.55	.69	.81
S.D..............	.16	.33	.07	.34	.07	.07	.07
Mean − 2 S.D. Lower Limit.....	1.15	.84	1.30	.76	.40	.55	.68
Mean + 2 S.D. Upper Limit.....	1.79	2.20	1.60	2.13	.70	.82	.95

process during periods 3–12, the mean of the receivables volume is 143.8 which is not far from the expected mean of 150.[16] Also note, that sales and collections are both reasonably close to 100, the expected values (mean) of the assumed sales distribution.

Table 2 provides the periodic computations of the various control statistics for periods 3 through 12 when the system is in equilibrium. The means and the standard deviations of the various control statistics based on these 10 observations are provided at the bottom of the table. Also included are the ranges of two standard deviations around the means.

The estimated standard deviations in conjunction with the estimated means could be used for a quality control scheme.[17] For example, a control statistic for (V_T/S_t), or receivables outstanding over credit sales, could be set at possibly two estimated standard deviations around the estimated mean. Setting these limits means that as long as this control statistic is observed to remain between $1.4737 \pm 2(0.1604)$ there is no cause for concern about the management of the credit department or about the manner in which credit policy is maintained by the salesmen. Action is taken only if the control statistic steps out of bounds. The same procedure may be applied to other control statistics. Estimates of the normal range of a control statistic are computed from past data. When a control statistic is out of the normal range, an effort is made by top management to determine why. If it is decided that the reason for the divergence is negligence on the part of the departments which are responsible for the maintenance of the company's credit policy, then remedial action must follow.[18]

---

[16] Considering the fact that the estimated standard deviation is 16.31, 150 is well within the range of just one standard deviation.

[17] The control measures' longer run means (their expectations) may in principle be deduced rather than estimated from *a priori* knowledge of the collection patterns implied by a given predetermined credit policy if these patterns are known with a high degree of confidence. In our example, our assumed collection patterns summarized in expressions (7.01)–(7.03) representing the patterns of collections implied by some given credit policy in a real situation, and in our example known with certainty, enable us to compute, via methods developed in Section A-F, the expected values (long term means) of the control measures around which the control measures will cluster through time. In our example they will be 1.5 for those control measures which purport to measure the mean collection period, i.e., for (V_T/S_t), (V_T/C_t), $(1C_{c1} + 2C_{c2})/C_t$, $(1C_{c1} + 2C_{c2})/S_t$; .50 for (C_{c1}/C_t), the proportion paying after 1 period; .66 for (V_{c1}/V_T), the proportion in the age category 'less than one period,' and .83 for $(V_{c1}(.5) + V_{c2}(1.5))/V_T$, the mean age of the receivables outstanding. In practice however a period in the past in which the prescribed credit policy was adhered to reasonably faithfully may provide a direct estimate of the long term means. This is the procedure adopted in the paper.

[18] In a real case where nothing is known except an upward change in the observed control statistics, one cannot determine *automatically* that the cause for the change is a lengthening in the collection periods. A shift in the average level of sales may produce similar results. We shall treat this point in greater detail in the last section of this paper.

AN INSTANCE OF DEVIATION FROM THE NORM DUE TO A CHANGE IN COLLECTION PATTERNS

Table 3 shows what happens to the variables in the receivables process when the collection period, all other things equal, lengthens across the board. Assume that the properties previously assigned to the collection periods 1 and 2 are now assigned to collection periods 2 and 3 respec-

TABLE 3
Hand simulation of Table 1 receivables process after collection period lengthens by one period

Period	Sales S_t	Collections from 1 period ago C_{c1}	Collections from 2 periods ago C_{c2}	Collections from 3 periods ago C_{c3}	Total collections C_t	End of period volumes V_T	.5 period Mean age V_{c1}	1.5 periods Mean age V_{c2}	2.5 periods Mean age V_{c3}
13......	110	36	66		102	164	110	54	0
14......	110		54		54	220	110	110	0
15......	110		66		66	264	110	110	44
16......	90		44	44	88	266	90	110	66
17......	90		44	66	110	246	90	90	66
18......	110		36	66	102	254	110	90	54
19......	90		54	54	108	236	90	110	36
20......	90			36					

tively. This implies an across the board addition of one period to the collection period variable. Under this assumption the new mean collection period is 2.5 and the new figure expected for the receivables volume is 250. No account ever pays before 2 periods from the time it came into being, and no account ever lingers on unpaid for more than 3 periods. Thus accounts pay either after 2 or after 3 periods.

The assumed shift in the collection period and its effects on the various accounts receivable components are hand-simulated in Table 3 in a fashion similar to that used for Table 1A. It will be noted that the receivables volume outstanding (in Table 3) rises to around the expected level of 250. Also note, that, in comparison with Table 1A, a lengthening of the collection periods from the values 1, 2 to the values 2, 3 required an additional column for the third age category whose average age is 2.5 periods. That is, collections from one period ago are completely ruled out, and collections from 3 periods ago are introduced in an additional column.

Control statistics for the data in Table 3 are provided in Table 4.

The question is, as usual, are they within their normal ranges, i.e., within the upper and lower bounds computed at the bottom of Table 2? The control output emerging in Table 4 clearly reflects the increase in the

TABLE 4
Control statistics computed from data generated in Table 3

Period	(V_T/S_t)	(V_T/C_t)	C_{c1}/C_t $+$ $2C_{c2}/C_t$ $+$ $3C_{c3}/C_t$	C_{c1}/S_t $+$ $2C_{c2}/S_t$ $+$ $3C_{c3}/S_t$	(C_{c1}/C_t)	(V_{c1}/V_T)	$.5V_{c1}/V_T$ $+$ $1.5V_{c2}/V_T$ $+$ $2.5V_{c3}/V_T$
13......	1.49	1.61	1.65	1.53	.35	.67	.83
14......	2.00	4.07	2.00	.98	.00	.50	1.00
15......	2.40	4.00	2.00	1.20	.00	.42	1.25
16......	2.95	3.02	2.50	2.44	.00	.34	1.41
17......	2.73	2.24	2.60	3.18	.00	.37	1.40
18......	2.31	2.49	2.65	2.45	.00	.43	1.28
19......	2.62	2.19	2.50	3.00	.00	.38	1.27

collection period assumed and incorporated in Table 3. The control statistics are unequivocally out of the predetermined normalcy bounds at the bottom of Table 2, thereby being exceptions to the standard. Detecting these divergences creates a presumption of a change in the underlying process and calls for an investigation of the causes which brought the change about.

PRECAUTIONS REGARDING CHANGE

Unfortunately a significant change in a control statistic does not necessarily imply, in and of itself, a change in collection patterns. The change in the control statistic could result from a shift in the collection patterns or in the average level of credit sales. If a permanent change occurs in the length of the collection period, the control statistics will reflect the change both initially and permanently. They will settle after a few "adjustment periods" to their new and permanent level reflecting the changes in the "new norm" of the collection patterns. If however the change in the underlying process is a permanent shift in the mean level of sales, the control statistics will change only temporarily. They will revert after a few adjustment periods to their prechange levels or their new equilibrium. The fact that temporary changes occur in the control statistics as a result of either one of the underlying changes poses a problem for the short-run decision-making process of the control scheme. A mere change in the control statistics does not *automatically* indicate deviate behavior on the part of the credit and sales departments. First it must be ascertained that the change in the control statistics is not caused by a change in sales. If no clear trend in sales emerges, remedial action should follow. The responsibility for failure to maintain credit policy must be determined, and corrective changes instituted. On the other hand if it is discovered that sales have shifted, the change in the control statistics should be considered temporary.

The following statements summarize the effect of a change in sales on the various control statistics. These may facilitate the evaluation of deviations from standards. The statements are based on the assumption that the control statistics are computed from current data with no averaging or smoothing over time.

For the duration of a few adjustment periods (and in comparison to the average equilibrium values), a permanent (and one shot) increase in sales (ceteris paribus)

1. Will reduce the measured ratio of the receivables volume to credit sales (V_T/S_t);

2. Will increase the measured ratio of the receivables volume to collections (V_T/C_t);

3. Will diminish slightly the estimate of the mean collection period as computed by

$$\sum_{i=1}^{n} i(C_{ci}/C_t)$$

4. Will decrease the estimate of mean collection period as computed by

$$\sum_{i=1}^{n} i(C_{ci}/S_t)$$

5. Will increase the relative weight of the younger categories of collections, decrease the relative weight of the older categories, relative to the average relative weights of both in equilibrium;

6. Will increase the weight of the younger age categories of the receivables volume outstanding, decrease the weight of the older categories, relative to the expected weights of both in equilibrium;

7. Will reduce the measured mean age of the volume of receivables outstanding.

Generally speaking, the reverse will hold true for a downward change in sales.

If a deviation of a control statistic can be traced to a shift in sales, it should not be interpreted as cause for remedial action. Only when sales have *not* shifted can the change be attributed to a change in collection patterns.

SUMMARY

An analytical framework has been developed to provide insights into the process of creation and the main determinents of accounts receivable. This framework should prove useful for decision-making and managerial functions in the area of accounts receivable. Utilized for managerial control of a given credit granting policy, this model produces a control mechanism of the quality control variety. A number of control statistics have been derived to measure, directly or indirectly, the results of a given credit policy. Finally, to provide a more realistic illustration of the practical applications of this approach, a simple stochastic example of a receivables process was developed. The analytical model developed should prove useful as a framework for analyzing decisions in the area of credit sales and accounts receivables.

part III

Capital budgeting

CHEMDRUG COMPANY

In early January 1971, George Petri, vice president and treasurer of Chemdrug Company, was preparing a presentation for the board of directors concerning potential investment opportunities. Mr. Petri was convinced that the future growth of the company was dependent upon continued emphasis on extensive research and development and concommitant introduction of new products into the company's product line. In addition, he was concerned with the necessity of future plant construction. The chairman of the board had already expressed his opinion relative to the desirability of locating a new product plant near his hometown of Dayton, Ohio. Mr. Petri, however, knew that the industry had recently invested heavily in Puerto Rico and that several of Chemdrug's competitors had located new plants there and had reaped substantial tax benefits as a consequence. Also, the ratio of rates of return on sales outside the United States to those within was about 4 to 1 due to U.S. drug trade restrictions. Chemdrug to date had only invested in the continental United States, Europe, and South America.

COMPANY BACKGROUND

Chemdrug Company was incorporated in California on March 1, 1952, as successor by a merger of a New York corporation of the same name organized in 1920.

In April 1955, Chemdrug acquired a majority interest in a large South American manufacturer and distributor of pharmaceuticals and cosmetics. In February 1957, Chemdrug acquired Pharmco Co. of New England in Exchange for 350,000 common shares.

Chemdrug manufactures and markets ethical drug products, consisting of antibiotics, antidiabetics, steroids, nutritional, and other pharmacological products. Drug products account for 68 percent of its worldwide sales. The company also produces and sells agricultural products which account for 15 percent of worldwide sales. This line includes seeds and veterinary, plant and animal health items. The chemical division accounts for 15 percent of sales, marketing bulk pharmaceuticals and related intermediates, urethane foam and other isocyanate specialties. Its medical testing laboratories are 2 percent of sales, and provide a highly automated testing service for physicians and hospitals. They also have an employment service which provides professional and family nursing services for hospitals, institutions, and private homes. (Exhibit 1.)

The company's general office buildings and manufacturing plants in California contain approximately 1,950,000 square feet. Other buildings and plants are located in numerous cities throughout the world.

Total capital spending for 1969 amounted to over $8 million compared with about $12 million in 1968, and $10 million in 1967. Expenditures for 1970 totaled over $12 million.

THE DRUG INDUSTRY

Growth characteristics

Chemdrug belongs to the ethical drug industry which has been and remains one of the fastest growing and most profitable industries in the United States. Recently, however, there has been substantial evidence that growth in the domestic markets is slowing due to increasingly tighter federal regulations. This trend is being offset by the expansion of many industry leaders into less mature foreign markets, at a projected growth rate of 11 percent annually. This compares with a 1971 expected industry sales rise of 10 percent.

The 10 percent increase figure is characteristic of the annual industry growth rate over the past decade. The Department of Commerce compared 1970 sales of $7,100 million with $3,311 million in 1961, which does not include sales by foreign subsidiaries. The Federal Trade Commission and the Securities and Exchange Commission show total sales of $12,952 million for 1970 and $4,165 million in 1961. Likewise, on the basis of total sales, profit as a percentage of sales for the 10 years has been on the average 10.1 percent, with $1,213 million for 1971 and $410 million for 1961.

Sales for the industry, excluding foreign subsidiaries, in 1971 are expected to be $7.7 billion, increasing to $10.8 billion by 1975, and $15.4 billion by 1980. This represents an annual compound growth rate of 8.1 percent and indicates the expectation of passage of some form of national health insurance in the next few years, of continued expansion into foreign markets, of developments in the treatment of heretofore incurable diseases and ailments, and of growth in the field of preventive medicine.

The nature of the industry

Government reports show that the drug industry has the second highest net profit on sales among major industries in the United States. This reflects the specialized nature of the industry's products, the low cost of labor and raw materials, and the relative price weakness which occurs in the drug industry's product lines only after the expiration of patents. It also reflects the tax-free benefits available from investments in facilities in Puerto Rico and other foreign countries (Exhibit 2). For example, 30 percent of one firm's 1970 profits came from Puerto Rican tax savings, and of another's 1970 earnings per share of $2.80, about $0.48 was attributable to its tax-free Puerto Rican operations.

More than for any other industry, including Aerospace and Chemicals, research is the key to healthy growth in the drug industry. The development of new drug products in the United States is becoming more expensive every year. In 1970, the development of a new major drug ran about $7 million. In an effort to counter this trend, drug companies are concentrating their time and funds only in promising areas of research. They are also introducing drugs in foreign markets, where drug regulation and control is less sophisticated than in the United States. The development of a major drug begins with the organic synthesizing of a new chemical structure. It is estimated that only eight out of every thousand of these new chemical structures will ever be tested clinically in humans. Following the synthesis, the chemical is tested in animals for biological activity, pharmacologic action, absorption and excretion, and safety. According to the Department of Commerce, research outlays of U.S. drug firms totaled $625 million in 1970, a 14 percent rise from the $549 million spent the prior year. For many years research outlays by drug-oriented firms have approximated 11 percent of total sales of drug-oriented operations (Exhibit 3).

Actual new product introduction for 1970 included 16 new individual drugs. While this was up from the 11 of 1969, it was still relatively low compared to the highly productive research of the 1950s. Twenty-eight new products were introduced in 1950 and 63 in 1959. The 1970s are expected to continue to be slow, unless there are momentous discoveries of cures for cancer, heart disease, and the common cold. Breakthroughs in preventive medicine might also be significant. The other major hope for the 1970s is the new area of prostaglandins, which are hormonelike compounds related to the prostate gland and which act to regulate blood pressure, gastric and respiratory functions, and most importantly reproduction. Chemdrug is the acknowledged leader in this area in research and market potential.

The expiration of patents on major drug products and the pressure of government and consumer demand for reduced drug prices should encourage the growth of generics in the future. On the regulatory side, pressure has already been placed by congressional leaders on various government agencies to prescribe generic drugs where applicable. As generic drugs are generally ones whose patents have expired, their market share for the 1970s is forcasted to increase substantially beyond their present 10 percent of total U.S. prescriptions. While the drug industry is not dominated by any one company and the market share of the largest producer is only 7 percent, the increasing reliance on generics should prompt the larger drug companies to try to consolidate their positions.

Diversification, overseas expansion, strong government health program demand, and tax benefits should permit the industry to maintain good profit returns. In the future, regulatory problems, generic prescribing, and a slowing in new product development may dampen overall growth trends, but these do not appear to be a serious threat in the near future.

Industry stock market activity

The price-earnings ratio of the drug industry has generally been above those of the Standard and Poor industrial composite throughout the decade of the 1960s and in 1970. The appeal of the industry seems to lie in the above average growth potential and in the prospect of significant new products emerging from the research labs. Also, price action has generally followed a more steady upward pattern than that of the general market. However, due to the nature of the products and the high appraisal of earnings, unjustified optimism is also a frequent factor in the industry's market price.

In the long bear market of 1969–70, the drug issues initially outperformed the overall market, since equities were generally regarded as a haven from the downturns in the economic cycle. However, as the market weakness expanded, these issues declined in line with the general market. More recently, the drug stocks have regained some of the lost ground, reflecting a favorable profit outlook.

Through the end of 1970, the drug equities have been advancing at about the same rate as the general market. There is no apparent reason why the drug issues should differ greatly from the general market performance in the months ahead. As they are currently being accorded liberal price-earnings ratios, significant relative price appreciation from where they are at present would seem difficult. However, despite some difficulties in the first quarter, earnings prospects for the balance of the year seem favorable, and the drug equities should participate in any general market advance.

CHEMDRUG'S COMPETITION

Chemdrug generally compares favorably with the rest of the drug industry, when looking at the Standard and Poor drug index (Exhibit 4). In terms of yields, the drug industry has been behind the Standard and Poor 425 Industrials throughout the past decade, and Chemdrug, while lagging behind the industry until 1967, has been second in the industry since 1968. From the position of price-earnings ratios, drugs have been ahead of the Standard and Poor 425 at least since 1961, and although Chemdrug was above the industry average until 1968, it has since been substantially below (Exhibit 4). Profit margins for drugs have been above the 425 for the past decade but Chemdrug has been consistently behind the industry, ranking about ninth in 1970. Looking at dividends as a percentage of earnings, drugs were ahead of the 425 for the decade, and Chemdrug has been among the higher for the industry (Exhibit 5). For net income as a percentage of sales, the drugs have been far above the 425, and Chemdrug had been slightly behind the industry. Finally, with regard to capital expenditures as a percentage of gross plant, Chemdrug has spent less than the industry average during the past decade.

CURRENT SITUATION

As discussed in the industry survey, an expenditure of about $7 million is necessary for the research and development of a new drug product. The study also indicates that the drug industry channels nearly 16 percent of its total R.&D. commitment into basic research. Between 1940 and 1967, the industry introduced 848 new drug entities in 41 separate categories. Some observers believe a plateau has been reached in the discovery of new drugs, but others say that research has ups and downs, and that the industry has just left a low point in the cycle. Chemdrug research and development expenditures for the past five years are shown in Exhibit 6.

A late 1969 FDA recall of Alacin, a Chemdrug analgesic, was considered to be a significant setback for Chemdrug, as it was responsible for about $0.23 net earnings per share for 1969. This recall was the result of a series of FDA actions against similar drugs. Since passage of the Food, Drug, and Cosmetic Act of 1938, drug products have been required to meet certain criteria for safety. The Kefauver-Harris Amendments of 1962 opened the door for the imposition of criteria that turned out to be far more stringent. The main thrust of the amendments required drugs to be effective as well as safe. That its implementation is, in fact, not so simple is due mainly to the relationship between safety and efficacy or the risk-benefit ratio. Virtually no drug is risk-free. However, in the case of Alacin, the FDA determined that there was sufficient evidence to link the drug with heart disease.

INVESTMENT ALTERNATIVES

Mr. Petri planned to include in his presentation some of the new products proposed to him by the Research and Development Division. These included a new prostaglandin drug which could be used in inducing labor in pregnancy, and Panocine, a new broad-spectrum antibiotic. Mr. Petri had researched industry trends and found that 1970 sales for labor-inducing drugs were in excess of $5 million, and are expected to grow at a rate of 25 percent per year. Chemdrug's introduction of this new prostaglandin drug was estimated to capture over 15 percent of the available market by 1973. Broad-spectrum antibiotic sales for the industry are expected to grow 15 percent annually from the current level of $10.3 million (Exhibit 7).

Chemdrug had also planned for capital expenditures of up to $10 million for plant construction beginning in 1971 to be completed in early 1972. This project was aimed at increasing foreign sales and fit in with plans to considerably expand overseas operations throughout the 1970s. It was estimated that total Chemdrug production capacity would be increased by 15 percent during the first year of operation.

If the plant was built in Ohio, as the chairman of the board wished, Mr. Petri estimated that it would cost about $8 million for the facilities. Annual operating expenses would be 25 percent of incremental new product sales, based on past company experience. Locating the plant in Puerto Rico would cost about $10 million due to construction costs, and annual operating expenses would be about 75 percent of the costs in an Ohio plant. The plant itself would be constructed so that it could produce either of the two new product proposals or new products as these were phased out. The expected product life for the two new products is approximately eight years due to competitive forecasts within the industry. The cost of equipment to peculiarize the plant to the mode of operation necessary to produce either of these two products would be about $500,000 in Ohio and about $750,000 in Puerto Rico due to the increased cost of materials. It is estimated that the plants would have a life of 40 years.

FINANCING ALTERNATIVES

Chemdrug's financial position continued strong throughout 1970. The major sources and uses of funds are shown in Exhibit 8. Increases in working capital and capital expenditures required for current operations and as a basis for future growth resulted in an increase in short-term bank loans from $4.2 million at the close of 1969 to $4.9 million by December 31, 1970. In addition to established lines of credit, the company, during 1970, entered into a revolving credit agreement with several banks. This agreement provided for borrowings up to $36,000,000 through October 1973. Interest per annum is at the prime rate through October 1971, and one-quarter of one percent over the prime rate, thereafter, on amounts borrowed. The prime rate on January 18, 1971, was 6 percent. One-half percent per annum is charged on the unused portion of the credit line. The credit line is convertible at any time prior to October 29, 1973, into four-year term notes payable in equal semiannual installments bearing interest at one-half of one percent over the prime rate. The agreement contains certain restrictive covenants including a requirement that consolidated current assets shall not be less than 175 percent of consolidated current liabilities. At the end of 1970, the long-term debt was $10.98 million. Chemdrug had a policy of not taking on funded debt prior to 1970.

Chemdrug's common stock is listed and traded on the New York, Detroit, Boston, Midwest, Pacific Cost, and Philadelphia-Baltimore-Washington Stock Exchanges. At the end of 1970, 7,359,588 of the 10,000,000 authorized shares had been issued. This represents an increase of only 6.5 percent over the number of shares issued in 1952. Most of the additional shares were used in the acquisition of other companies. At the end of 1969, 110 institutions held 1,043,000 shares or 14 percent of the outstanding stock. An additional 35 percent of the stock is closely held. Thus, only about 51 percent of the stock is available for conventional trading.

Mr. Petri was concerned that his presentation might lack decisiveness if he did not have some concrete proposals to present relative to the new product introduction and the location and advisability of new plants.

EXHIBIT 1
CHEMDRUG COMPANY
Sales by product areas

	1966	*1967*	*1968*	*1969*	*1970*
Antibiotics..............	23	23	25	23	23
Steroids................	18	18	19	19	18
Antidiabetics............	16	16	16	15	14
Pharmacologicals........	15	15	15	14	13
Medical services.........	1	1	1	1	2
Agricultural.............	14	14	14	15	15
Chemical...............	13	13	10	13	15

EXHIBIT 2
CHEMDRUG COMPANY
Tax advantages to doing business in Puerto Rico

There are tax advantages to doing business in Puerto Rico due to provisions of the Federal Tax Code and due to the Puerto Rican laws. The federal tax advantages can be summarized as:

A U.S. citizen or a domestic corporation engaged in the active conduct of a trade or business within a U.S. possession is exempt from tax on income from sources outside the United States if: (1) 50% or more of gross income during the 3-year period ending with the close of the taxable year is from that business and (2) 80% of gross income for the same period was received from any source within a possession.[1]

The Puerto Rican tax advantages are due to the fact that Puerto Rico allows "flexible depreciation" and because it exempts the earnings of certain companies from tax.

An exempt industry is one engaged in the manufacture of either (1) "designated articles," or (2) products not produced on a commercial scale in Puerto Rico on or before January 2, 1947. The period of exemption varies, depending on where the exempt industry is established:

High Industrial Development Zone	10 years
Outside both the High Industrial Development Zone and the Underdeveloped Zone	12 years
Underdeveloped Industrial Zone	17 years
Underdeveloped Industrial Zone in adjacent Commonwealth Islands	17 years[2]

[1] Commerce Clearing House, Inc. *1971 U.S. Master Tax Guide* (Chicago, Ill. 60646) p. 467.
[2] Haskins and Sells. *Taxation in Puerto Rico*, (New York: International Taxation and Business Service. Vol. 3, 1965, p. 11.

EXHIBIT 3
CHEMDRUG COMPANY
Relationship of research and development expenditures, sales, and income in the prescription drug industry, 1969
(dollar figures in millions)

Company	R. & D. expenditures	Expenditures as a percent of total sales	Net sales	Net income after taxes
A.........	$20.5	6.7%	$303.3	$28.1
B.........	40.7	10.0	408.4	53.7
C.........	47.7	9.0	528.1	89.6
D.........	16.5	6.9	239.0	21.0
E.........	23.9	3.7	638.0	57.5
F.........	12.0	4.5	100.9	21.0
Chemdrug*......	18.5	10.0	185.5	18.7

* For Chemdrug, based on total sales, not just drug-oriented operations.

EXHIBIT 4
CHEMDRUG COMPANY
Stock price and S&P Drug Index closing prices

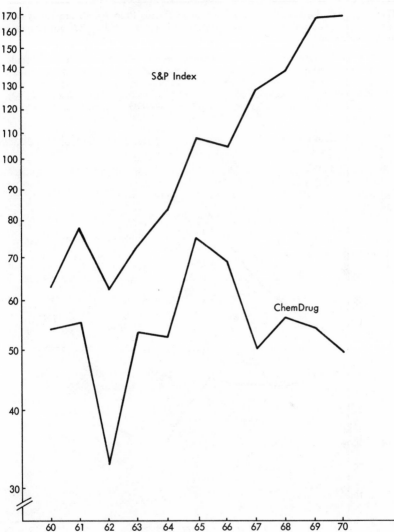

EXHIBIT 5
CHEMDRUG COMPANY
Earnings per share and dividend retention rates

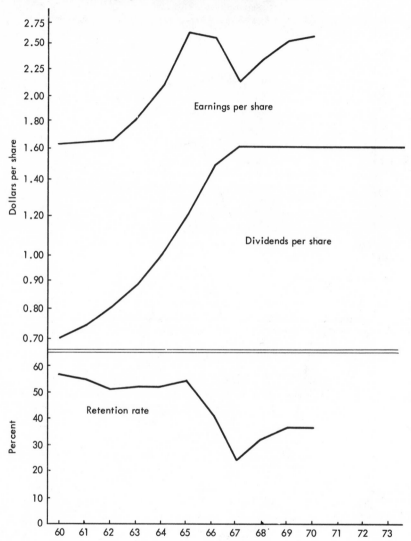

EXHIBIT 6
CHEMDRUG COMPANY
Research and Development
expenditures 1966–70
(dollar figures in millions)

Year	*Total expenditure*
1966.............	$13.50
1967.............	$15.11
1968.............	$16.95
1969.............	$18.52
1970.............	$21.03

EXHIBIT 7
CHEMDRUG COMPANY
Projected sales for investment alternatives
For labor-inducing pharmacologicals

Year	*Industry*	*Chemdrug*
1971........	$ 6,250,000	$ 440,000
1972........	7,813,000	1,120,000
1973........	9,766,000	1,510,000
1974........	12,207,000	1,980,000
1975........	10,000,000	1,700,000
1976........	8,000,000	1,300,000
1977........	6,000,000	1,000,000
1978........	3,000,000	500,000
1979........	—	—

For orally administered antibiotics

Year	*Industry*	*Chemdrug*
1971........	$11,845,000	$ 680,000
1972........	13,622,000	1,110,000
1973........	15,665,000	1,560,000
1974........	18,015,000	1,900,000
1975........	20,717,000	2,400,000
1976........	15,000,000	1,600,000
1977........	10,000,000	1,000,000
1978........	5,000,000	500,000
1979........	—	—

EXHIBIT 8

CHEMDRUG COMPANY

Statement of consolidated source and application of funds
for the year ended December 31, 1970
(dollar figures in thousands)

Source of Funds:

Net earnings................................	$18,837
Minority interests share of earnings............	1,561
Total.....................................	20,398
Noncash charges against earnings:	
Depreciation and amortization..............	6,035
Deferred taxes on income..................	955
Funds provided by operations................	$27,388
Book value of fixed assets sold or retired.......	813
Decrease (increase) in cash and securities.......	(92)
Increase in current liabilities.................	1,796
Long-term borrowing.......................	10,980
Total Sources......................	$40,885

Application of Funds:

Dividends to shareholders...................	$11,761
Dividends to minority interest...............	945
Property, plant and equipment...............	12,258
Increase in receivables.....................	4,974
Increase in inventories.....................	7,447
All other (net)...........................	3,500
Total Applications..................	$40,885

EXHIBIT 9
CHEMDRUG COMPANY
Year-end balance sheet
(dollar figures in thousands)

ASSETS	1966	1967	1968	1969	1970
Cash......................	$ 4,769	$ 7,161	$ 8,037	$ 5,856	$ 10,140
Marketable securities.........	17,272	7,476	4,835	4,192	—
Accounts receivable (net).....	20,590	25,462	35,669	41,070	46,044
Inventories.................	20,778	24,076	35,730	40,960	48,407
Prepaid expenses............	2,240	2,850	4,011	5,983	7,848
Total Current Assets....	$ 65,649	$ 67,025	$ 88,282	$ 98,061	$112,439
Property, plant and equipment...............	101,290	111,695	123,219	131,339	142,784
Less: accumulated depreciation...............	38,526	42,218	48,512	52,836	56,919
Net property, plant and equipment...............	$ 62,764	$ 69,477	$ 74,707	$ 78,503	$ 85,865
Excess cost acquisitions.......	1,036	1,088	2,502	1,956	2,314
Other assets................	1,360	1,316	1,493	1,891	2,025
Total Assets..........	$130,809	$138,906	$166,984	$180,411	$202,643

LIABILITIES AND STOCKHOLDERS' EQUITY	1966	1967	1968	1969	1970
Accounts payable............	$ 4,868	$ 4,866	$ 6,524	$ 9,206	$ 10,130
Bank loans payable..........	—	—	3,471	4,168	4,891
Accrued liabilities............	8,342	9,607	12,739	14,582	15,166
Dividends payable..........	2,838	2,847	2,934	2,937	2,944
Federal and Foreign income taxes payable..............	2,611	4,642	6,072	6,668	6,226
Total Current Liabilities..........	$ 18,659	$ 21,962	$ 31,740	$ 37,561	$ 39,357
Long-term debt..............	—	—	—	—	10,980
Deferred income tax..........	2,180	2,300	4,668	6,407	7,702
Minority interests...........	1,449	1,990	3,045	3,613	4,136
Other liabilities..............	387	410	767	649	854
Total Liabilities.......	$ 22,675	$ 26,662	$ 40,220	$ 48,230	$ 63,029
Common stock ($1 par)......	7,267	7,290	7,333	7,342	7,360
Paid-in capital..............	22,573	23,041	26,411	26,562	26,545
Retained earnings............	78,294	81,913	93,020	98,277	105,709
Total Stockholders' Equity.............	$108,134	$112,244	$126,764	$132,181	$139,614
Total Equity and Liabilities..........	$130,809	$138,906	$166,984	$180,411	$202,643

EXHIBIT 10
CHEMDRUG COMPANY
Income statements
(dollar figures in thousands)

	1966	1967	1968	1969	1970
Net sales..................	$128,778	$136,485	$166,620	$185,506	$198,847
Cost of goods sold...........	33,506	37,707	51,471	58,849	63,719
Selling, general and administrative expense...........	50,015	56,193	62,233	69,134	76,892
Research and development....	13,503	15,114	16,952	18,520	21,026
Operating profit.............	$ 31,754	$ 27,471	$ 35,964	$ 39,003	$ 37,210
Other income..............	2,054	1,685	2,252	2,691	3,121
Total Operating Income......	$ 33,808	$ 29,156	$ 38,216	$ 41,694	$ 40,331
Other expenses..............	948	1,231	1,392	1,686	2,758
Income before taxes..........	$ 32,860	$ 27,925	$ 36,824	$ 40,008	$ 37,573
Federal income tax...........	11,040	8,725	18,515	19,955	17,175
Foreign income tax..........	3,185	3,505	—	—	—
Minority interest............	461	667	1,089	1,372	1,561
Net Income........	$ 18,174	$ 15,028	$ 17,220	$ 18,681	$ 18,837

COMPUTER LOGIC
CORPORATION

In August 1969, Computer Logic Corporation was in the process of developing a new line of computers. All of the company resources were currently being utilized near full capacity. This is one of the primary reasons why outside software consulting services were being seriously considered. CLC solicited proposals from 30 software companies. Each proposal was analyzed for technical content while also considering the consulting firm's experience and competence in the field. After a thorough analysis, CLC selected three firms for final consideration. One of these three firms, or the CLC Programming Division, would be awarded the final responsibility for the development of the software which would complement the new line of computers.

COMPANY BACKGROUND

In September 1963, 10 computer professionals, headed by CLC President Jim Anderson founded the Computer Logic Corporation on the premise that a company dedicated to translating advanced technology into highly reliable computer products would find a ready market. Beginning on this premise, they developed real-time, special-purpose computers for the scientific market.

In the year following its inception, CLC had delivered its first computer, the Model 527, with unique design and real-time capabilities which were readily accepted by the scientific and industrial communities. Six additional computer models, including the third-generation Kappa 7, have since been developed by CLC.

Many of these computers represented industry firsts. CLC was first to deliver a computer using all-silicon semiconductors, giving higher computer reliability. CLC was also first to deliver a computer using monolithic integrated circuits, which further improved reliability and operating speeds. Moreover, the company pioneered the development of a multiuse computer specifically designed for time-sharing in a real-time environment, the CLC Kappa 7.

CLC was now beginning to broaden its product line to include general-purpose computers for commercial time-sharing applications. The company anticipated that this new market segment would offer enormous potentials for future sales growth. The company had assets totaling over $14 million, employed more than 400 and had delivered more than 150 computers and computer systems to customers throughout the world. Exhibits 1–3 give some of the company's financial statistics for the past two years.

The men primarily responsible for planning and implementing the successful products of the company were CLC President Jim Anderson, executive vice president Jeff Albert, and vice president of finance and administration, John Walsh. Key company executives were also located in the areas of marketing, manufacturing, development and administration.

Development, manufacturing and inventory problems attendant to the introduction of a new line of computers were well in hand at the beginning of 1969. However, the decision for developing the software for the new line was still up in the air. Mr. Walsh had been somewhat dissatisfied with the in-house development of software for previous CLC computers.

DEVELOPING THE NEW PRODUCT LINE

CLC's new computer line, which would be known as the Maxima series, represented a multimillion dollar developmental effort. To increase the productivity of CLC manufacturing, reduce overhead costs and inventories and elevate the reliability of the total CLC product line, many automatic assembly and testing devices had been added throughout the company's production facilities. A pin-straightening machine and several automatic back-panel wiring machines had been installed. An automatic conveyor, logic module assembly line had been designed and implemented. Final assembly and testing programs for fully integrated systems were modified and, as a result, both equipment delivery time and inventory requirements had been markedly reduced. Improved quality assurance procedures had been emphasized, such as the detection of problems at the logic and subassembly level of production. These procedures should prove invaluable in limiting the number of problems encountered at the system level, where they are most difficult and costly to isolate and correct. The new CLC product line would have widespread ramifications which directly related to the future success of CLC. It was of paramount importance, therefore, that all relevant costs be carefully controlled.

FINANCING DECISIONS

The financing of the Maxima line was another major problem facing CLC. In 1967, a large quantity of common stock was issued in order to provide additional funds for development of the Kappa series of computers. The board felt, therefore, that an additional common stock issue at this time would have a depressing effect upon the market price. The possibility of issuing preferred stock had been discussed at several board meetings, but Messrs. Albert and Walsh were quite adamant about maintaining a high dividend payout to the common shareholders.

After discussing financial alternatives with several investment bankers, Mr. Walsh concluded that issuing subordinated convertible debentures would be most advantageous at this time. It appeared that there would be no problem in issuing $4 million worth of debentures, which would be adequate to finance the hardware and software development for the Maxima line. However, in order to ensure that the issue would be fully subscribed, it would be necessary for the debentures to carry an interest rate of 7.5 percent. In addition, the issuance costs would increase the effective interest rate to 8.0 percent. Thus, it was decided that the latter figure would be used as the effective discount rate. The debentures would be convertible into common stock at a price of $95 per share until February 29, 1972 and $100 until August 29, 1974. In 1969, CLC common sold at a high of $80 per share.

SOFTWARE DEVELOPMENT

The system software, which is the logical step-by-step instructions that a computer must follow to solve a given problem or combination of problems, is the most important and difficult task faced by any computer manufacturer. The complexity of the development is illustrated by the fact that the company's development expenses for programming increased twentyfold over the past four years. During the period 1966–68, CLC spent over $6 million developing software for the Kappa line of computers.

Mr. Albert had suggested a realignment of the Programming Division, incorporating a new management approach to the development of software and successfully implementing new planning, monitoring, control and reporting procedures. In the past, the company had experienced problems in debugging the COBOL compiler.

The introduction of the new Maxima line would require an expansion of company services to the customer. The number of CLC personnel who assist customers in applying computers to various tasks was estimated to have increased by 30 percent, and the number of CLC customer engineering personnel who support the company's products in the field was estimated to have increased by more than 25 percent. By 1971, the company expected to have approximately 20 percent of its total personnel involved in Maxima customer-oriented activities.

Jim Anderson was very much in favor of developing the Maxima software within the company. He insisted that CLC had the capability of doing the job, although he admitted that it probably could be done more rapidly by an outside contractor. To reinforce his argument, he stated that the CLC version of Extended FORTRAN had been very satisfactory. Three contractors were also being seriously considered to perform the software task. Both the Cirrus and Delta companies had established reputations within the computer industry for object code efficiency and excellence in compiler design. The Beta company was a new company which had attracted many of the top senior programmers from the software industry. Many of these persons were experts in the development of systems programming packages.

Mr. Walsh and Mr. Albert felt that the risks associated with internal development were of such a magnitude that CLC could very likely be forced into bankruptcy if an improper decision were made. To support their position, they prepared, with the aid of the company's key design personnel, Exhibits 4–7 to illustrate the projected cash flows associated with in-house development and with each of the three contractors under consideration. In these exhibits, the States of Nature refer to the various possible conditions which can occur in each year being considered. The R_js are the returns associated with each State of Nature and the P_js are the probabilities that these returns will actually occur.

In-house development was by far the most expensive in terms of initial cash outlays. In addition, no returns would be realized until the second year. The Beta Company had proposed the lowest cost for software development. However, this company was new in the industry and therefore the results of the project were somewhat questionable. Cash inflows were less predictable with the Beta Company than with either Cirrus or Delta. The Cirrus Company, if chosen, would require a larger initial cash outlay to accomplish the task, but the results were not quite as uncertain as they were with Beta. The Delta Company's proposal was even higher in cost than the other two contractors, but cash inflows appeared more advantageous.

Mr. Walsh assigned the detailed analysis of the four alternative approaches to developing the software to a new employee who recently obtained his MBA degree. In an effort to provide the proper guidelines, he defined the analysis to be a problem of capital budgeting under conditions of uncertainty. He further suggested that graphs be plotted showing the probability distributions of the expected present values and a cumulative probability analysis of profitability index levels. With this information, management should be able to make a well-considered decision regarding the development of the Maxima software.

EXHIBIT 1

COMPUTER LOGIC CORPORATION

Balance sheet for years ending December 31, 1968 and 1969

ASSETS

	1969	*1968*
Current Assets		
Cash...	$ 396,920	$ 316,970
Marketable securities (at lower of cost or market)..	44,130	7,280
Receivables....................................		
Current accounts...........................	2,682,860	2,125,420
Installment accounts.......................	1,136,430	1,105,310
	$ 3,819,290	$ 3,230,730
Less—provision for doubtful accounts...........	82,650	74,190
Net Receivables.......................	$ 3,736,640	$ 3,156,540
Inventories (at lower of cost or market)...........		
Raw stock and production supplies.............	709,640	535,300
Work in process...........................	1,664,930	1,310,550
Finished goods............................	2,314,370	1,845,720
	$ 4,688,940	$ 3,691,570
Prepaid expenses.............................	212,710	170,030
Total Current Assets....................	$ 9,079,340	$ 7,342,390
Property, Plant and Equipment		
Land...	$ 124,130	$ 113,410
Buildings.....................................	1,366,220	1,254,340
Machinery and equipment.....................	4,043,790	3,519,480
	$ 5,534,140	$ 4,887,230
Less—accumulated depreciation................	2,599,660	2,326,750
	$ 2,934,480	$ 2,560,480
Rental equipment.............................	4,071,270	3,061,170
Less—accumulated depreciation................	1,894,860	1,476,200
	$ 2,176,410	$ 1,584,970
Other assets.................................	255,050	116,530
Total Assets........................	$14,445,280	$11,604,370

EXHIBIT 1 *(Continued)*

LIABILITIES AND STOCKHOLDERS' EQUITY

Current Liabilities	1969	1968
Notes payable..............................	$ 1,768,750	$ 916,350
Accounts payable..........................	430,660	445,100
Accrued taxes..............................	440,400	347,030
Accrued payroll............................	425,020	443,520
Other accrued liabilities.....................	875,060	684,860
Customers' deposits and service prepayments....	662,390	590,760
Total Current Liabilities.................	$ 4,602,280	$ 3,427,620
Long-Term Liabilities		
Long-term debt (exclusive of installments due in one year).........................	$ 3,514,410	$ 2,318,370
Lease purchase obligations...................	19,000	20,000
Deferred income taxes......................	110,070	23,650
International employees' pension and indemnity reserve........................	190,720	187,470
International operations reserve...............	86,090	80,910
Minority interests.........................	161,610	142,700
Total Liabilities......................	$ 8,684,180	$ 6,200,720
Stockholders' Equity		
Common stock, represented in 1969 by 107,018 shares (106,046 in 1968) of a total of 140,000 authorized shares, $5 par value............................	$ 2,959,100	$ 2,916,150
Retained earnings..........................	2,802,000	2,487,500
Total Stockholders' Equity...............	$ 5,761,100	$ 5,403,650
Total Liabilities and Stockholders' Equity..........	$14,445,280	$11,604,370

EXHIBIT 2

COMPUTER LOGIC CORPORATION

Income statement for the years 1968 and 1969

	1969	1968
Net sales..	$12,546,410	$11,271,500
Cost of goods sold.............................	7,360,830	6,672,350
Gross profit.............................	$ 5,185,580	$ 4,599,150
Selling, general and administrative expense...........	4,295,810	3,857,240
Interest expense................................	262,410	217,760
Minority interest in net earnings of subsidiaries......	33,670	30,800
Income from Operations..................	$ 593,690	$ 493,350
Other income...................................	209,460	202,160
Net Income Before Taxes..................	$ 803,150	$ 695,510
Federal and foreign income taxes..................	362,000	319,670
Net Income after Taxes...................	$ 441,150	$ 375,840

EXHIBIT 3
COMPUTER LOGIC CORPORATION
Statement of changes in working capital for the years 1968 and 1969

	1969	*1968*
Working Capital was Provided by:		
Net income for the year..........................	$ 441,150	$ 375,840
Depreciation:		
Property, plant and equipment...................	422,080	386,470
Rental equipment.............................	596,200	536,970
	$1,018,280	$ 923,440
Sale of property and rental equipment..............	63,380	162,020
Sale of common stock..........................	40,130	37,980
Proceeds from debentures and mortgages............	1,315,020	396,080
Increase in minority interests.....................	18,910	34,000
	$2,896,870	$1,929,360
Working Capital was Used for:		
Cash dividends to stockholders.....................	$ 126,650	$ 115,320
Expenditures for:		
Property, plant and equipment...................	812,870	655,580
Rental equipment.............................	1,239,230	902,640
	$2,052,100	$1,558,220
Reduction of long-term debt......................	118,980	65,720
Other......................................	41,850	7,550
	$2,339,580	$1,746,810
Net increase in working capital....................	557,290	182,550
Working capital at beginning of year..............	3,914,770	3,732,220
Working capital at end of year...................	$4,472,060	$3,914,770

EXHIBIT 4

COMPUTER LOGIC CORPORATION

Projected cash flows for in-house
software development

(dollar figures in thousands)

Cash Outflow = $10,000
(at the beginning of Year 1)

	State of nature (j)	R_{ji}	P_{ji}
Year 1	1	0	1.0
	2	No return possible	
	3	for the entire year	
	4		
Year 2	1	0	0.20
	2	$2,000	0.30
	3	$5,000	0.35
	4	$8,500	0.15
Year 3	1	$4,000	0.20
	2	$5,000	0.30
	3	$6,500	0.35
	4	$9,000	0.15

EXHIBIT 5
COMPUTER LOGIC CORPORATION
Projected cash flows
for software contractor "beta"
(dollar figures in thousands)

Cash Outflow = $5,000
(at the beginning of Year 1)

	State of nature (j)	R_{ji}	P_{ji}
Year 1	1	0	0.15
	2	$ 1,000	0.25
	3	$ 3,000	0.35
	4	$ 7,000	0.25
Year 2	1	0	0.20
	2	$ 2,500	0.30
	3	$ 7,000	0.30
	4	$10,000	0.20
Year 3	1	0	0.40
	2	$ 1,000	0.30
	3	$ 6,000	0.20
	4	$ 7,000	0.10

EXHIBIT 6
COMPUTER LOGIC CORPORATION
Projected cash flows
for software contractor "cirrus"
(dollar figures in thousands)

Cash Outflow = $10,000
(at the beginning of Year 1)

	State of nature (j)	R_{ji}	P_{ji}
Year 1	1	0	0.10
	2	$ 2,000	0.40
	3	$ 6,000	0.30
	4	$ 9,000	0.20
Year 2	1	$ 1,000	0.25
	2	$ 3,000	0.35
	3	$ 8,000	0.20
	4	$10,000	0.20
Year 3	1	$ 1,000	0.30
	2	$ 2,000	0.40
	3	$ 5,000	0.20
	4	$ 8,000	0.10

EXHIBIT 7
COMPUTER LOGIC CORPORATION
Projected cash flows
for software contractor "delta"
(dollar figures in thousands)

Cash Outflow = $11,000
(at the beginning of Year 1)

	State of nature (*j*)	R_{ji}	P_{ji}
Year 1	1	0	0.05
	2	$ 4,000	0.35
	3	$ 7,000	0.30
	4	$10,000	0.30
Year 2	1	$ 2,000	0.20
	2	$ 5,000	0.30
	3	$ 7,000	0.30
	4	$11,000	0.20
Year 3	1	$ 1,000	0.20
	2	$ 3,000	0.40
	3	$ 6,000	0.20
	4	$ 8,000	0.20

H-S ASTRONAUTICS

H-S ASTRONAUTICS was a small but highly regarded manufacturing firm in the Southern California area which specialized in the design and production of flight instruments for both private and commercial aircraft. The company was founded in 1962 by two young, energetic engineers who foresaw a rapid growth in the aerospace industry in general and in the light aircraft industry in particular. Initially only a small design shop, they eventually obtained a production facility and expanded into the manufacture of their own products. By 1971, the company had grown to the point where the present plant was being utilized at its maximum capacity.

In November 1971, Jack Farnsworth, treasurer of H-S Astronautics, was asked to analyze the alternatives available concerning construction of a new production plant into which the company might move. These alternatives had been narrowed down to either building a large facility in 1972 or to building a small facility in 1972 with the option of expanding the plant two years later in 1974 if the sales demand were high enough to warrant it. It was obvious to the company's owners that if recently designed instruments were eventually to be produced in large scale and if sales were to grow, a new plant was required. An added incentive to move arose when another firm made an attractive offer to purchase the present plant.

During the decade of the sixties, the growth of the light airplane industry had been substantial. The number of private pilot licenses issued had quadrupled during the period and with it the number of privately owned light aircraft had grown also. In addition to privately owned planes, many corporations were purchasing aircraft for executive use.

Flying clubs were being formed throughout the country to make aircraft available to many without the funds or the necessity to own their own plane. An integral part of each airplane, whether it was for private, commercial, or military use, was the flight instrumentation system. These instruments provided altitude and basic navigational information, and the system varied in complexity with the use to which the airplane would be put.

The entry of H-S Astronautics into the industry had been timely. The company grew in conjunction with the growth in flight traffic. The company's growth was also stimulated by some innovative designs and production techniques plus a talented sales force. As a result, the company was able to put out products which were highly reliable and very competitively priced. In the past the products were being sold primarily to manufacturers of light aircraft and, to a limited extent, to producers of commercial aircraft. These sales alone had enabled the company to utilize its production facility to capacity. By late 1971, the company was considering expanding its product line and entering the military aircraft market as well. To do so would necessitate a new production facility.

In analyzing the new plant alternatives, Mr. Farnsworth had available several cost estimates for construction of the new plant. These estimates called for a large plant to cost approximately $2,500,000. A small plant with the capability of being expanded at a later date would initially cost approximately $1 million. The production capacity of this smaller plant was expected to just handle the lowest sales demand estimate over the next 10 years. If additions were required, two options were available. A large addition would cost $2 million while a small addition would be approximately $1 million. These latter two figures were based on the constraint that the additions would be constructed in 1974, two years after initial construction of the basic facility.

In recent years the economy of the country in general and particularly the aerospace industry had been uncertain. Although the company had been successful in the past, it was difficult to predict what the demand would be for its products in the future. This demand was dependent on the continued growth of the light aircraft industry and the company's part in that market, and in the inroads the company would make into the military aircraft market. Several new military aircraft contracts were to be let during the next year and if the company could get the subcontracts for these projects their product demand would be high for a number of years to come.

Reflecting on the probabilities associated with the various levels of demand, Mr. Farnsworth estimated that the probability of high demand was about 50 percent. He felt that the probabilities of medium and low levels of demand were about 30 percent and 20 percent, respectively.

If the large plant were built, high demand would result in a yield of approximately $1 million per year for 10 years. For the large plant, medium demand would yield approximately $700,000 annually for 10 years and low demand would yield $300,000 per year, again for 10 years. If the small plant were built, the yield would be the same amount of $300,000 annually for 10 years independent of whether the demand were low, medium, or high. However, if demand were high, at the two-year point the company would be in a better position to decide which of the two building additions should be constructed, if indeed any should be built. If demand were high through 1974, then the probability that it would continue high for another eight years was estimated to be 80 percent. The probabilities that demand would be medium or low for the next eight years were estimated to be 20 percent and zero respectively. If it were decided to construct the larger addition in 1974, then yield per year for the next eight years with high demand would be $800,000, with medium demand $600,000, and with low demand $400,000. If the smaller addition were built in 1974, yield per year for eight years with high demand would be $600,000, with medium demand $500,000, and with low demand $400,000. If it were decided not to construct the addition to the small plant, a yield of $300,000 per year for eight years would be realized regardless of demand within reasonable limits.

In analyzing the alternatives, Mr. Farnsworth put the demand probabilities and expected yields in matrix form (Exhibit 2) and considered using decision tree quantitative analysis techniques in solving his problem. He felt that the discount rate for investment evaluations by the firm was 10 percent.

EXHIBIT 1

H-S ASTRONAUTICS

Income statements of years ended December 31, 1968–70

(dollar figures in thousands)

	1968	1969	1970
Net sales..	$1,346	$2,610	$3,473
Cost of goods sold............................	917	1,724	2,098
Gross profit..............................	$ 429	$ 886	$1,375
Research and development expense..........	121	290	397
Selling, general, and administrative expense ...	172	291	451
Interest expense.........................	10	17	23
Income from operations...................	$ 126	$ 288	$ 504
Other income................................	1	3	9
Income before tax........................	$ 127	$ 291	$ 513
Federal income tax........................	55	140	241
Net income.............................	$ 72	$ 151	$ 272

EXHIBIT 2
H-S ASTRONAUTICS
Demand levels and their associated probabilities

Plant size	Demand	Probability	Demand: year point	Probability
Large	High	0.50	—	—
	Medium	0.30	—	—
	Low	0.20	—	—
Small	High	0.50	Continue high	0.80
			Medium	0.20
			Low	0.00
	Medium	0.30	—	—
	Low	0.20	—	—

KAY MACHINE TOOLS, INC.

On September 30, 1972, Mr. Howard Abrams, vice president of Kay Machine Tools, Inc. was considering several investment opportunities for the company for the coming year. Among these various projects were two which Mr. Abrams felt deserved special attention due to the sales volitality of the associated product line.

Kay Machine Tools, Inc. is a small manufacturer of high-speed drills and drill presses used in the aerospace industry as well as in numerous light manufacturing companies located in the West. With manufacturing facilities located in Los Angeles and sales offices located in Los Angeles, San Francisco, and Seattle, the firm can service the 11 western states. In addition to carrying its own line of drills and drill presses, the firm is also a manufacturer's representative for numerous items such as wrenches, reamers, drill rods, sanding papers, and other items sold to wholesale and retail hardware outlets.

One of the investments under consideration is a project that would cost $10,000. Since the project is subject to conditions of uncertainty, Mr. Abrams has obtained a list of possible cash flows for the two-year life of the project under different projected demand levels.

Mr. Abrams determined from similar projects that the cash flows were not independent. With the assistance of others in the firm, he was able to develop a probability distribution of the returns for the first and second year. Both the cash flows and associated probabilities are presented in Exhibit 1.

Because of the fluctuating nature of the product line, an analysis must be made to decide whether the project should be continued after

228

the first year. The estimated abandonment value of this project after the first year is $8,000.

A similar decision has to be made for another project under consideration that has a three-year economic life and calls for an investment of $1,600. As with the previous project, the cash flows are subject to conditions of uncertainty and are not independent. Cash flows for the three years and their associated probabilities under different demand levels are presented in Exhibit 2.

With the sales volitality associated with the second project, Mr. Abrams must decide (1) whether to abandon the project at the end of the first year, (2) whether to abandon the project at the end of the second year, or (3) to keep the project for its entire economic life. The estimated abandonment value of the project after the first year would be $1,450 and after the second year would be $1,380.

Mr. Abrams felt that he could make a recommendation concerning the effect of the abandonment decision on the profitability of the projects by first analyzing the expected net present value and the expected standard deviation (as a measure of risk) of the projects without considering the abandonment decision. He would then repeat the analysis with the abandonment decision being taken into account. At this time, the cost of capital for the firm is 10 percent.

EXHIBIT 1
KAY MACHINE TOOLS, INC.
Cash flows for Project 1

	Year 1				*Year 2*		
Demand level	*Cash flow*	*Initial probability (PI)*		*Demand level*	*Cash flow*	*Conditional probability P(2/I)*	
Low..........	$ 8,000	0.3		Low..........	$ 6,000	0.3	
				Medium........	$ 8,000	0.5	
				High..........	$10,000	0.2	
Medium.......	$10,000	0.4		Low..........	$ 8,000	0.3	
				Medium........	$10,000	0.4	
				High..........	$12,000	0.3	
High..........	$12,000	0.3		Low..........	$10,000	0.2	
				Medium........	$12,000	0.5	
				High..........	$14,000	0.3	

EXHIBIT 2
KAY MACHINE TOOLS, INC.
Cash flows for Project 2

	Year 1			*Year 2*			*Year 3*	
Cash flow	*Demand level*	*Initial probability*	*Cash flow*	*Demand level*	*Conditional probability*	*Cash flow*	*Demand level*	*Conditional probability*
$ 800	Low	0.3	$ 700	Low	0.3	$ 600	Low	0.2
						$ 700	Medium	0.5
						$ 800	High	0.3
			$ 800	Medium	0.4	$ 700	Low	0.2
						$ 800	Medium	0.5
						$ 900	High	0.3
			$ 900	High	0.3	$ 800	Low	0.2
						$ 900	Medium	0.5
						$1,000	High	0.3
$1,600	Medium	0.4	$1,300	Low	0.3	$1,200	Low	0.2
						$1,300	Medium	0.5
						$1,400	High	0.3
			$1,600	Medium	0.4	$1,500	Low	0.2
						$1,600	Medium	0.5
						$1,700	High	0.3
			$1,700	High	0.3	$1,600	Low	0.2
						$1,700	Medium	0.5
						$1,800	High	0.3
$2,400	High	0.3	$2,300	Low	0.3	$2,200	Low	0.2
						$2,300	Medium	0.5
						$2,400	High	0.3
			$2,400	Medium	0.4	$2,300	Low	0.2
						$2,400	Medium	0.5
						$2,500	High	0.3
			$2,500	High	0.3	$2,400	Low	0.2
						$2,500	Medium	0.5
						$2,600	High	0.3

SELECTED REFERENCES
FOR PART THREE

ADELSON, R. M. "Criteria for Capital Investment: An Approach through Decision Theory," *Operational Research Quarterly,* Vol. 16 (March 1965), pp. 19–50.

ADLER, MICHAEL. "On Risk-Adjusted Capitalization Rates and Valuation by Individuals," *Journal of Finance,* Vol. 25 (September 1970), pp. 819–36.

ANTHONY, R. N. "Some Fallacies in Figuring Return on Investment," *NAA Bulletin,* Vol. 42 (December 1960), pp. 5–13.

ARDITTI, F. D. "Risk and the Required Return on Equity," *Journal of Finance,* Vol. 22 (March 1967), pp. 14–36.

BAILEY, MARTIN J. "Formal Criteria for Investment Decisions," *Journal of Political Economy,* Vol. 67 (October 1959), pp. 476–88.

BAUMAN, W. SCOTT. "Evaluation of Prospective Investment Performance," *Journal of Finance,* Vol. 23, No. 2 (May 1968), pp. 276–95.

BAUMOL, WILLIAM J., and QUANDT, RICHARD E. "Investment and Discount Rates under Capital Rationing—A Programming Approach," *The Economic Journal,* Vol. 75 (June 1965), pp. 317–29.

BAXTER, NEVINS D. "Marketability, Default Risk, and Yields on Money Market Instruments," *Journal of Financial and Quantitative Analysis,* Vol. 4 (March 1968), pp. 75–86.

BENNION, E. G. "Capital Budgeting and Game Theory," *Harvard Business Review,* Vol. 34 (November–December 1956), pp. 115–23.

BEN-SHAHAR, HAIM, and SARNAT, MARSHALL. "Reinvestment and the Rate of Return on Common Stocks," *Journal of Finance,* Vol. 21 (December 1966), pp. 737–42.

BERNHARD, RICHARD H. "Mathematical Programming Models for Capital Budgeting—A Survey, Generalization, and Critique," *Journal of Financial and Quantitative Analysis,* Vol. 4 (June 1969), pp. 111–58.

BIERMAN, HAROLD, JR., and SMIDT, SEYMOUR. *The Capital Budgeting Decision.* New York: The Macmillan Company, 1966.

BLUME, MARSHALL E. "On the Assessment of Risk," *Journal of Finance,* Vol. 26 (March 1971), pp. 1–10.

BODENHORN, DIRAN. "On the Problem of Capital Budgeting," *Journal of Finance*, Vol. 14 (December 1959), pp. 473–92.

BYRNE, R., CHARNES, A., COOPER, A., and KORTANEK, K. "Some New Approaches to Risk," *Accounting Review*, Vol. 63 (January, 1968), pp. 18–37.

CHEN, HOUNG-YHI. "Valuation under Uncertainty," *Journal of Financial and Quantitative Analysis*, Vol. 2 (September 1967), pp. 313–25.

CHENG, PAO L., and SHELTON, JOHN P. "A Contribution to the Theory of Capital Budgeting—The Multi-Investment Case," *Journal of Finance*, Vol. 69 (December 1963), pp. 622–36.

COHEN, KALMAN J., and ELTON, EDWIN J. "Inter-temporal Portfolio Analysis Based on Simulation of Joint Returns," *Management Science*, Vol. 14 (September 1967), pp. 5–18.

CORD, JOEL. "A Method for Allocating Funds to Investment Projects When Returns Are Subject to Uncertainty," *Management Science*, Vol. 10 (January 1964), pp. 335–41.

DEAN, JOEL. *Capital Budgeting*. New York: Columbia University Press, 1951.

DEAN, JOEL. "Measuring the Productivity of Capital," *Harvard Business Review*, Vol. 32 (January–February 1954), pp. 120–30.

DIETZ, PETER O. "Measurement of Performance of Security Portfolios Components of a Measurement Model: Rate of Return, Risk and Timing," *The Journal of Finance*, Vol. 23, No. 2 (May 1968), pp. 267–75.

DOUGALL, HERBERT E. "Payback as an Aid in Capital Budgeting," *Controller*, Vol. 29 (February 1961), pp. 67–72.

EDELMAN, FRANZ, and GREENBERG, JOEL S. "Venture Analysis: The Assessment of Uncertainty and Risk," *Financial Executive*, Vol. 37 (August, 1969), pp. 56–62.

EDGE, C. G. "Capital Budgeting: Principles and Projection," *Financial Executive*, Vol. 33 (September 1965), p. 50 ff.

EDSON, HARVEY O. "Setting a Standard for Your Company's Return on Investment," *Controller*, Vol. 26 (September 1958), pp. 411–15.

ELTON, EDWIN J. "Capital Rationing and External Discount Rates," *Journal of Finance*, Vol. 25 (June 1970), pp. 573–84.

ENGLISH, J. M. "Economic Comparison of Projects Incorporating a Utility Criterion in the Rate of Return," *Engineering Economist*, Vol. 10 (Winter 1965), pp. 1–14.

FARRAR, DONALD F. *The Investment Decision under Uncertainty*. Englewood Cliffs, N.J.: Prentice-Hall, 1962.

FISHBURN, PETER C. "Utility Theory," *Management Science*, Vol. 14 (January, 1968), pp. 335–78.

FREUND, RUDOLF J. "The Introduction of Risk in a Programming Model," *Econometrica*, Vol. 24 (July 1956), pp. 253–63.

GENTRY, JAMES, and PIKE, JOHN. "An Empirical Study of the Risk-Return Hypothesis Using Common Stock Portfolios of Life Insurance Companies," *Journal of Financial and Quantitative Analysis,* Vol. 5 (June 1970), pp. 179–86.

GORDON, MYRON J., and SHAPIRO, ELI. "Capital Equipment Analysis: The Required Rate of Profit," *Management Science,* Vol. 3 (October 1956), pp. 102–10.

GRANT, L. C. "Monitoring Capital Investments," *Financial Executive,* Vol. 31 (April 1963), pp. 19–24.

GRAYSON, C. JACKSON, JR. *Decisions under Uncertainty: Drilling Decisions by Oil and Gas Operators.* Boston, Mass.: Division of Research, Harvard Business School, 1960.

GRAYSON, C. JACKSON, JR. "Introduction of Uncertainty into Capital Budgeting Decisions," *N.A.A. Bulletin,* Vol. 43 (January 1962), pp. 79–80.

GREER, WILLIS R., JR. "Capital Budgeting Analysis with the Timing of Events Uncertain," *Accounting Review,* Vol. 45 (January 1970), pp. 103–14.

HAYNES, W. WARREN, and SOLOMON, MARTIN B., JR. "A Misplaced Emphasis in Capital Budgeting," *Quarterly Review of Economics and Business,* February 1962, pp. 39–46.

HEEBINK, DAVID V. "Postcompletion Audits of Capital Investment Decisions," *California Management Review,* Vol. 6 (Spring 1964), pp. 47–52.

HERTZ, DAVID B. "Risk Analysis in Capital Investment," *Harvard Business Review,* Vol. 42 (January–February 1964), pp. 95–106.

HERTZ, DAVID B. "Investment Policies That Pay Off," *Harvard Business Review,* Vol. 46 (January–February 1968), pp. 96–108.

HESPOS, RICHARD F., and STRASSMANN, PAUL A. "Stochastic Decision Trees for the Analysis of Investment Decisions," *Management Science,* Vol. 11 (August 1965), pp. 244–59.

HILLIER, FREDERICK S. "The Derivation of Probabalistic Information for the Evaluation of Risky Investments," *Management Science,* Vol. 9 (April 1963), pp. 443–57.

HILLIER, FREDERICK S., and HEEBINK, DAVID V. "Evaluation of Risky Capital Investments," *California Management Review,* Vol. 8 (Winter 1965), pp. 71–80.

HIRSHLEIFER, JACK. "On the Theory of Optimal Investment Decision," *Journal of Political Economy,* Vol. 66 (August 1958), pp. 329–52.

HIRSHLEIFER, JACK. "Risk, the Discount Rate and Investment Decisions," *American Economic Review,* Vol. 51 (May 1961), pp. 112–20.

HIRSHLEIFER, JACK. "Efficient Allocation of Capital in an Uncertain World," *American Economic Review,* Vol. 54 (May 1964), pp. 77–85.

HIRSHLEIFER, JACK. "Investment Decision under Uncertainty: Choice-Theoretic Approaches," *Quarterly Journal of Economics,* Vol. 79 (November 1965), pp. 509–536.

HOROWITZ, I. *An Introduction to Quantitative Business Analysis.* New York: McGraw-Hill Book Company, 1965.

HUNT, PEARSON. *Financial Analysis in Capital Budgeting.* Boston: Graduate School of Business Administration, Harvard University, 1964.

JEAN, WILLIAM H. "On Multiple Rates of Return," *Journal of Finance,* Vol. 23, No. 1 (March 1968), pp. 187-92.

JEAN, WILLIAM H. *Capital Budgeting.* Scranton, Pa.: International Textbook Company, 1969.

JEAN, WILLIAM H. "Terminal Value or Present Value in Capital Budgeting Programs," *Journal of Financial and Quantitative Analysis,* Vol. 6 (January 1971), pp. 649-52.

JEYNES, PAUL H. "The Significance of Reinvestment Rate," *Engineering Economist,* Vol. 11 (Fall 1965), pp. 1-9.

KLAUSNER, ROBERT F. "The Evaluation of Risk in Marine Capital Investments," *Engineering Economist,* Vol. 14 (Summer 1969), pp. 183-214.

KRAINER, ROBERT E. "A Neglected Issue in Capital Rationing—The Asset Demand for Money," *Journal of Finance,* Vol. 21 (December 1966), pp. 731-36.

LATANE, H. A. "Criteria for Choice among Risky Ventures," *Journal of Political Economy,* Vol. 67 (April 1959), pp. 144-55.

LATANE, H. A., and TUTTLE, DONALD L. "Decision Theory and Financial Management," *Journal of Finance,* Vol. 21, No. 2 (May 1966), pp. 228-44.

LERNER, EUGENE M. "The Integration of Capital Budgeting and Stock Valuation," *American Economic Review,* Vol. 54 (September 1964), pp. 682-702.

LERNER, EUGENE M. and CARLETON, WILLARD T. *A Theory of Financial Analysis.* New York: Harcourt, 1966.

LERNER, EUGENE M., and CARLETON, WILLARD T. "Capital Budgeting and Financial Management." In Alexander A. Robichek (Ed.), *Financial Research and Managerial Decisions.* New York: Wiley, 1967, pp. 72-89.

LERNER, EUGENE M., and RAPPAPORT, ALFRED. "Limit DCF in Capital Budgeting," *Harvard Business Review,* Vol. 46 (July–August 1968), pp. 133-39.

LEVY, HAIM, and SARNAT, MARSHALL. "Diversification, Portfolio Analysis and the Uneasy Case for Conglomerate Mergers," *Journal of Finance,* Vol. 25 (September 1970), pp. 795-80.

LINDSAY, J. R., and SAMETZ, A. W. *Financial Management: An Analytical Approach.* Homewood, Ill.: Irwin, 1967.

LINTNER, JOHN. "The Evaluation of Risk Assets and the Selection of Risky Investments in Stock Portfolios and Capital Budgets," *Review of Economics and Statistics,* Vol. 47 (February 1965), pp. 13-37.

LINTNER, JOHN. "Security Prices, Risk and Maximal Gains from Diversification." *Journal of Finance,* Vol. 20 (December 1965), pp. 587-616.

LITZENBERGER, ROBERT H., and BUDD, ALAN P. "Corporate Investment Criteria and the Valuation of Risk Assets," Vol. 5 (December 1970), pp. 395-420.

LITZENBERGER, ROBERT H., and JOY, O. M. "Target Rates of Return and Corporate Asset and Liability Structure under Uncertainty," *Journal of Financial and Quantitative Analysis,* Vol. 6 (March 1971), pp. 675-86.

LOCKETT, A. GEOFFREY, and TOMKINS, CYRIL. "The Discount Rate Problem in Capital Rationing Situations: Comment," *Journal of Financial and Quantitative Analysis*, Vol. 5 (June 1970), pp. 245–60.

LORIE, JAMES H., and SAVAGE, LEONARD J. "Three Problems in Rationing Capital," *Journal of Business*, Vol. 28 (October 1955), pp. 229–39.

LUTZ, FRIEDERICH, and LUTZ, VERA. *The Story of the Theory of Investment of the Firm*. Princeton, N.J.: Princeton University Press, 1951.

MAGEE, J. F. "How to Use Decision Trees in Capital Investment," *Harvard Business Review*. Vol. 42 (September–October 1964), pp. 79–96.

MAO, JAMES C. T. "The Internal Rate of Return as a Ranking Criterion," *Engineering Economist*, Vol. 11 (Winter 1966), pp. 1–13.

MAO, JAMES C. T. "Survey of Capital Budgeting: Theory and Practice," *Journal of Finance*, Vol. 25 (May 1970), pp. 349–60.

MAO, JAMES C. T., and BREWSTER, JOHN F. "An E-S$_n$ Model of Capital Budgeting," *Engineering Economist*, Vol. 15 (Winter 1970), pp. 103–21.

MAO, JAMES C. T., and HELLIWELL, JOHN F. "Investment Decisions under Uncertainty: Theory and Practice," *Journal of Finance*, Vol. 24 (May 1969), pp. 323–38.

MARKOWITZ, H. "Portfolio Selection," *Journal of Finance*, Vol. 7 (March 1952), pp. 77–91.

MASSÉ, PIERRE. *Optimal Investment Decisions*. Englewood Cliffs, N.J.: Prentice-Hall, 1962.

MAURIEL, J. J., and ANTHONY, R. N. "Misevaluation of Investment Center Performance," *Harvard Business Review*, Vol. 44 (March–April 1966), pp. 98–105.

MERRETT, A. J., and SYKES, ALLEN. *Capital Budgeting and Company Finance*. London: Longmans, Green & Company, Ltd., 1966.

MOAG, JOSEPH S., and LERNER, EUGENE M. "Capital Budgeting Decisions under Imperfect Market Conditions—A Systems Framework," *Journal of Finance*, Vol. 24 (September 1969), pp. 613–21.

MURDICK, ROBERT G., and DEMING, DONALD D. *The Management of Corporate Expenditures*. New York: McGraw-Hill Book Co., 1968.

MYERS, STEWART C. "Procedures for Capital Budgeting under Uncertainty," *Industrial Management Review*, Vol. 9 (Spring 1968), pp. 1–15.

NÄSLUND, BERTIL, and WHINSTON, ANDREW. "A Model of Multi-period Investment Under Uncertainty," *Management Science*, Vol. 9 (January 1962), pp. 184–200.

NÄSLUND, BERTIL, and WHINSTON, ANDREW. "A Model of Capital Budgeting under Risk," *Journal of Business*, Vol. 39 (April 1966), pp. 257–271.

PAGE, ALFRED N. (ed.). *Utility Theory*. New York: Wiley, 1968.

PAINE, NEIL R. "Uncertainty and Capital Budgeting," *Accounting Review*, Vol. 39 (April, 1964), pp. 330–32.

PERDUNN, R. F. "Capital Investment and Large Projects," *Financial Executive*, Vol. 33 (June 1965), p. 11 ff.

PULLARA, S. J., and WALKER, L. R. "The Evaluation of Capital Expenditure

Proposals: A Survey of Firms in the Chemical Industry," *Journal of Business*, Vol. 38 (October 1965), pp. 403–08.

QUIRIN, G. DAVID. *The Capital Expenditure Decision*. Homewood, Ill.: Irwin, 1967.

ROBICHEK, A., and MYERS, S. *Optimal Financing Decisions*. Englewood Cliffs, N.J.: Prentice-Hall, 1965, chap. 5.

ROBICHEK, A., and MYERS, S. "Risk Adjusted Discount Rates," *Journal of Finance*, Vol. 21, No. 4 (December 1966), pp. 727–30.

ROBICHEK, A., and VAN HORNE, JAMES C. "Abandonment Value and Capital Budgeting," *Journal of Finance*, Vol. 22 (December 1967), pp. 577–589. Edward A. Dyl and Hugh W. Long, "Comment," *Journal of Finance*, Vol. 24 (March 1969), 88–95; and Robichek and Van Horne, "Reply," *ibid.*, 96–97.

SALAZAR, RUDOLFO C., and SEN, SUBRATA K. "A Simulation Model of Capital Budgeting under Uncertainty," *Management Science*, Vol. 15 (December 1968), pp. 161–79.

SARNAT, MARSHALL, and BEN-SHAHAR, H. "Reinvestment and the Rate of Return on Common Stocks," *Journal of Finance*, Vol. 23, No. 1 (December 1966), pp. 737–42.

SARNAT, MARSHALL, and LEVY, HAIM. "The Relationship of Rules of Thumb to the Internal Rate of Return: A Restatement and Generalization," *Journal of Finance*, Vol. 24 (June 1969), pp. 479–89.

SCHWAB, BERNHARD, and LUSZTIG, PETER. "A Comparative Analysis of the Net Present Value and the Benefit-Cost Ratios as Measures of the Economic Desirability of Investments," *Journal of Finance*, Vol. 24 (June 1969), pp. 507–16.

SCHWAB, BERNHARD, and SCHWAB, HELMUT. "A Method of Investment Evaluation for Smaller Companies," *Management Services*, July–August 1969, pp. 43–53.

SCHWAB, BERNHARD, and SCHWAB, HELMUT. "A Note on Abandonment Value and Capital Budgeting," *Journal of Financial and Quantitative Analysis*, Vol. 5 (September 1970), pp. 377–80.

SHARPE, W. F. "Capital Asset Prices: A Theory of Market Equilibrium," *Journal of Finance*, Vol. 19 (September 1964), pp. 425–42.

SHARPE, W. F. "Security Prices, Risk, and Maximal Gains from Diversification," *Journal of Finance*, Vol. 21, No. 4 (December 1966), pp. 743–44.

SOLOMON, EZRA. "The Arithmetic of Capital-Budgeting Decisions," *Journal of Business*, Vol. 29 (April 1956).

SOLOMON, EZRA. *The Management of Corporate Capital*. New York: The Free Press of Glencoe, Inc., 1959.

SOLOMON, EZRA. *The Theory of Financial Management*. New York: Columbia University Press, 1963.

SOLOMON, EZRA, and LAYA, J. C. *Measuring Profitability*. Englewood Cliffs, N.J.: Prentice-Hall, 1969.

SOLOMON, EZRA, and LAYA, J. C. "Alternative Rate of Return Concepts and Their Implications for Utility Regulation," *Bell Journal of Economics and Management Science*, Vol. I (Spring 1970), pp. 65–81.

SWALM, RALPH O. "Utility Theory—Insights into Risk Taking," *Harvard Business Review*, Vol. 44 (November–December 1966), pp. 123–36.

TEICHROEW, DANIEL. "Mathematical Analysis of Rates of Return under Certainty," *Management Science*, Vol. 11 (January 1965), pp. 395–403.

TEICHPOEW, DANIEL, ROBICHEK, ALEXANDER A., and MONTALBANO, MICHAEL. "An Analysis of Criteria for Investment and Financing Decisions under Certainty," *Management Science*, Vol. 12 (November 1965), pp. 151–79.

TUTTLE, DONALD L., and LITZENBERGER, ROBERT H. "Leverage, Diversification and Capital Market Effects on a Risk-Adjusted Capital Budgeting Framework," *Journal of Finance*, Vol. 23 (June 1968), pp. 427–44.

U.S. CONGRESS, SUBCOMMITTEE ON ECONOMY IN GOVERNMENT OF THE JOINT ECONOMIC COMMITTEE. *Economic Analysis of Public Investment Decisions: Interest Rate Policy and Discounting Analysis*. Washington, D.C.: U.S. Government Printing Office, 1968.

VAN HORNE, JAMES. "Capital Budgeting for the Liquid Company," *Financial Executive*, Vol. 34 (April 1966), pp. 50–52, 60.

VAN HORNE, JAMES. "Capital Budgeting Decisions Involving Combinations of Risky Investments," *Management Science*, Vol. 13 (October 1966), pp. 84–92.

VAN HORNE, JAMES. "The Analysis of Uncertainty Resolution in Capital Budgeting for New Products," *Management Science*, Vol. 15 (April 1969), pp. 376–86.

VAN HORNE, JAMES. "A Note on Biases in Capital Budgeting Introduced by Inflation," *Journal of Financial and Quantitative Analysis*, Vol. 6 (March 1971).

VAN HORNE, JAMES. *Financial Management and Policy*. Englewood Cliffs, N.J.: Prentice-Hall, 1971.

VICKERS, DOUGLAS. "Profitability and Reinvestment Rates: A Note on the Gordon Paradox," *Journal of Business*, Vol. 39 (July 1966), pp. 366–70.

VICKERS, DOUGLAS. *The Theory of the Firm: Production, Capital and Finance*. New York: McGraw-Hill, 1968.

WALLINGFORD, B. A. "A Survey and Comparison of Portfolio Selection Models," *Journal of Financial and Quantitative Analysis*, Vol. 3 (June 1967), pp. 85–106.

WEINGARTNER, H. MARTIN. "The Excess Present Value Index—A Theoretical Basis and Critique," *Journal of Accounting Research*, Vol. 1 (Autumn 1963), pp. 213–24.

WEINGARTNER, H. MARTIN. *Mathematical Programming and the Analysis of Capital Budgeting Problems*. Copyright © H. Martin Weingartner, 1963.

WEINGARTNER, H. MARTIN. "Capital Budgeting of Interrelated Projects: Survey and Synthesis," *Management Science*, Vol. 12 (March 1966), pp. 485–516.

WEINGARTNER, H. MARTIN. "The Generalized Rate of Return," *Journal of Financial and Quantitative Analysis*. Vol. 1 (September 1966), pp. 1–29.

WEINGARTNER, H. MARTIN. "Some New Views on the Payback Period and Capital Budgeting Decisions," *Management Science*, Vol. 15 (August 1969), pp. 594–607.

WESTON, G. FRED, and BRIGHAM, EUGENE F. *Managerial Finance*. New York: Holt, Rinehart & Winston, 1972.

WOODS, DONALD H. "Improving Estimates That Involve Uncertainty," *Harvard Business Review*, Vol. 45 (July–August 1966), pp. 91–98.

WOODWORTH, G. WALTER, and OLSON, ALDEN C. "Discussion," *Journal of Finance*, Vol. 23, No. 2 (May 1968), pp. 296–302.

The Derivation of Probabilistic Information for the Evaluation of Risky Investments*

Frederick S. Hillier†

INTRODUCTION

THE AMOUNT of risk involved is often one of the important considerations in the evaluation of proposed investments. Thus, a reasonably safe investment with a certain expected rate of return will often be preferred to a much more risky investment with a somewhat higher expected rate of return. This is especially true when the risky investment is so large that the failure to achieve expectations could significantly affect the financial position of the individual or firm. Moreover, despite theoretical arguments against it, research [8] has indicated that many executives maintain this preference even when the personal or corporate resources are more than ample to meet the contingency of adverse events. On the other hand, the prosperity of Las Vegas attests to the fact that some individuals have risk preference rather than risk aversion, i.e., they often select a risky investment with a low or negative expected rate of return because of the possibility of an extremely high return.

Unfortunately, not many expository papers have appeared on practical ways of deriving the type of explicit, well-defined, and comprehensive information that is essential for an accurate appraisal of a risky investment. It is the purpose of this presentation to indicate how, under certain assumptions, such information in the form of the probability distribution of the internal rate of return, present worth, or annual cost of a proposed investment can be derived.

* Reprinted from *Management Science*, Vol. 9, No. 3 (April 1963), pp. 443–57, by permission of the author and the publisher.

† Stanford University, Stanford, California.

EXISTING PROCEDURES FOR CONSIDERING RISK

Capital budgeting literature has not yet given much consideration to the analysis of risk; and such procedures as have been suggested for dealing with risk have tended to be either quite simplified or somewhat theoretical. Thus, these procedures have tended either to provide management with only a portion of the information required for a sound decision, or they have assumed the availability of information which is almost impossible to obtain.

The simplified procedures usually amount to reducing the estimates of the possible values of the prospective cash flow during each time period to a single expected value, in either an intuitive or statistical sense, and then analyzing the problem as if each of these expected values were certain to occur.[1] Risk is sometimes included in this analysis by using an interest rate appropriate for the associated degree of risk as the standard for the minimum acceptable internal rate of return or for discounting the cash flow for a particular year. These procedures are the ones generally selected for use currently. However, they suffer the disadvantage of supressing the information regarding the risk of the proposed investment. Thus, while optimistic and pessimistic predictions have both been averaged in to obtain the single measure of the merit of the investment, the executive is not provided with any explicit measure of the risk of the investment. For example, he might be provided with an estimate of the expected rate of return of an investment but not its variance, even though the executive would probably have a distinct preference for an investment with a small variance of the rate of return over another investment with the same expected rate of return and larger variance. As a result, these procedures require the executive to resort to his own intuition for the ultimate consideration of risk.

A useful technique for considering risk which is sometimes used in conjunction with the simplified procedures is sensitivity analysis.[2] This technique involves revising uncertain estimates of prospective cash flows and investigating the sensitivity of the measure of the merit of the investment to such revisions in the estimates. This gives some indication of the effect if one of the original estimates were either too optimistic or too pessimistic. However, sensitivity analysis is quite limited in the amount of information it can provide. For example, it is difficult to draw precise conclusions about the possible effects of combinations of errors in the estimates, even though this is the typical situation of concern. For statistical reasons, it would usually be misleading to consider the case where all the estimates are too optimistic or where all are too pessi-

---

[1] See, for example, [7], Ch. 13; [2], Ch. 9; [11], pp. 210–13.

[2] See, for example, [7], Ch. 13.

mistic. In short, sensitivity analysis is useful but its conclusions tend to suffer from a lack of conciseness, precision and comprehensiveness.

A theoretical procedure occasionally suggested would determine the "utility" or degree of merit of each of the possible outcomes of an investment and then determine the expected value of the utility to use as a measure of the merit of the investment.[3] Assuming that valid utilities and associated probabilities are used, this procedure properly weights the merit of both the better and the poorer possible outcomes of an investment so that it accurately and completely takes risk into account. Thus, expected utility is an ideal measure of the merit of an investment from a theoretical point of view. Unfortunately, utility is a subtle concept, so that the measurement of utility is a difficult task. Therefore, it would be extremely difficult to determine explicitly, with the needed precision, the utility to management of all the possible outcomes of an investment. From a practical point of view, management usually would have neither the time nor the inclination to participate in such a monumental task in a formal manner. Another procedure which has been suggested by certain economists [10] involves selecting those investments whose expected rate of return exceeds the firm's average cost of capital, including both stocks and bonds, where this cost is a function of the risk associated with the industry and thus (by implication) the investments. However, practical objections can be made regarding the underlying assumptions, including the premise that executives will act solely in the long-run interests of the stockholders, and the difficulty of determining the prospective rate of return of stock. Another interesting approach to this type of problem has recently been reported [12] in the form of a model for investment in the stock market. However, it does not appear that this approach, involving the maximization of expected monetary gains subject to probabilistic constraints on maximum loss during the various periods, can be extended to the general problem of investment under uncertainty.

Finally, mention should be made of the work of Markowitz [9] concerning the analysis of portfolios containing large numbers of securities. Markowitz shows how to determine the portfolio which provides the most suitable combination of expected rate of return and standard deviation of rate of return. While the nature of scope of this problem differs somewhat from the problem dealt with here, there are similarities in the two approaches to the problem of evaluating risky investments. The primary similarities are in the use of the expected value and standard deviation of rate of return and in the treatment of covariances. Furthermore, [9] contains considerable theoretical material which is relevant to the problem posed here. Especially important is the justification given

---

[3] See, for example, [11], pp. 204–16, and [13], Ch. 2.

for the use of both the expected value and the standard deviation of rate of return as decision parameters. For example, it is shown that properly using these decision parameters is essentially equivalent to maximizing a quadratic utility function of rate of return.

COMPARISON OF PROPOSED PROCEDURE WITH EXISTING PROCEDURES

The procedure that will be recommended here is something of a compromise between the simplified procedures and the theoretical procedures described above. While it has some of the same deficiencies, it also enjoys many of the advantages of both types of procedures. It goes beyond the simplified approach to provide additional information, namely, the probability distribution of the selected measure of the merit of the investments. At the same time, this information enables the executive to quickly apply, in an intuitive and implicit sense, the theoretical procedure of evaluating expected utility. Therefore, the techniques that will now be developed are actually tools for more clearly exhibiting the risk involved and should complement, rather than supersede, most current procedures for evaluating investments.

FORMULATION OF PROBLEM

Consider an investment which will result in cash flows during at least some of the next n years. Let X_j be the random variable which takes on the value of the net cash flow during the j-th year, where $j = 0, 1, 2, \ldots, n$. Assume that X_j has a normal distribution with known mean, μ_j, and known standard deviation, σ_j.

It is recognized that these assumptions regarding X_j will not often be completely justified. In particular, the probability distribution of X_j may not be normal. On the other hand, it would seem that, for many types of prospective cash flows, one's best subjective probability distribution would be nearly a symmetrical distribution resembling the normal distribution. Furthermore, by the Central Limit Theorem, the actual distribution of X_j can sometimes deviate considerably from the normal distribution without significantly affecting the final results. More precisely, looking ahead to Equation 1, if $X_j/(1 + i)^j, j = 0, 1, \ldots, n$, are mutually independent random variables, with finite means and variances, which are either identically distributed or uniformly bounded then (by the Lindeberg Theorem) the Central Limit Theorem will hold and the sum of these random variables will be approximately normal if n is large. If this holds, the probability distribution of the measures of the merit of an investment considered in the following sections will be approximately normal, regardless of whether the X_j random variables are normal or not. Finally, even if the X_j random variables are not normal and the Central Limit Theorem is not applicable, all of the subsequent equations (Equations 1, 2, . . . , 13) will still hold. Thus, the mean and variance of the measures of merit will be the same (or nearly the same in the case of internal rate of return) regardless of the normality of X_j. The mean and variance (or standard deviation) of these measures, by themselves, provide a substantial basis for evaluating and comparing prospective investments; furthermore, certain weak probability statements can be made by using the Tchebycheff inequality. The only consequence of non-normality is that, without knowledge of the distribution of the measures of merit, precise probability statements cannot be made.

Regarding the other assumptions, present procedures already assume that some measure of the central tendency of each prospective cash flow is known since they require a single forecast of the cash flow. This measure usually corresponds roughly either to μ_j or to the mode ("most likely value"), which, for the normal distribution, equals μ_j. It should not be much more difficult to estimate σ_j than μ_j. Merely keep in mind that about 68% of the probability distribution will lie within $\mu_j \pm \sigma_j$, about 95% within $\mu_j \pm 2\sigma_j$, and about 99.73% within $\mu_j \pm 3\sigma_j$. Thus, estimating σ_j is just a more definitive version of that aspect of sensitivity analysis involving the investigation of reasonably likely values of X_j.

Some assumption needs to be specified regarding the relationship between the X_j random variables for different values of j. The two simplest assumptions are that all the X_j random variables are mutually independent or that they are all completely correlated. Actually, there will be many cases where a compromise between these assumptions is needed since some of the cash flows are reasonably independent whereas others are closely correlated. Therefore, what will be done is to consider the two cases individually and then show how they can be combined.

The desirability of an investment is not always a question that can be answered entirely independently of other investments. The performance of one investment is instead often interrelated with the performance of others. Therefore, for a truly satisfactory investment decision, it would sometimes be desirable to introduce into the analysis some measure or measures of covariance between the investment's merit and that of alternatives or complementary investments. Indeed, Markowitz [9] includes a thorough development of the use of covariance of returns in his analysis. However, this refinement is beyond the scope of this paper. Instead, the problem is confined to describing the desirability of individual prospective investments.

A large number of methods have been advocated for evaluating investments. While it is felt that the approach to be developed here can be applied to most of these methods, only compound interest methods (presently favored by most writers) will be considered. In particular, the three widely advocated discounting procedures—the present worth method, the annual cost method and the internal rate of return method—as defined by Grant and Ireson [7] will be explored. The objective will be to demonstrate how to obtain a probability distribution for each of these three measures of the merit of an investment.

PROBABILITY DISTRIBUTION OF PRESENT WORTH

The present worth, P, for a proposed productive investment may be defined as:

$$P = \sum_{j=0}^{n} \left[\frac{X_j}{(1 + i)^j} \right] \tag{1}$$

where i is the rate of interest which properly reflects the investor's time value of money. The value of i is often described as the minimum attractive rate of return or the cost of capital.

A more general definition of P is sometimes given by specifying possibly distinct values of i for each of the n periods. The following results can be applied with no increased difficulty to the more general case. However, since uniform values of i are almost always used in actual applications, only this simplest case will be considered, so as to concentrate attention on the new features of the proposed procedure.

It should be recognized that, as defined, P is actually a random variable rather than a constant. For purposes of evaluating a proposed investment, the usual procedure is to examine the expected value of P,

$$\mu_P = \sum_{j=0}^{n} \left[\frac{\mu_j}{(1 + i)^j} \right] \tag{2}$$

although this is often referred to as "the" present worth. Then, if $\mu_P > 0$, the investment would be made since this would increase the expected total wealth of the firm more than investing the same money elsewhere at the marginal rate of return i. When comparing mutually exclusive alternatives for the same investment funds, the alternative with the largest value of μ_P would be preferred, assuming no compensating intangible factors.

Assume initially that X_0, X_1, . . . , X_n are mutually independent. Therefore, it is well-known that P would have a normal distribution, where the mean is given by Equation 2 and the variance is

$$\sigma_P^2 = \sum_{j=0}^{n} \frac{\sigma_j^2}{(1 + i)^{2j}} \tag{3}$$

Before illustrating the use of this information, other assumptions leading to different variances will be considered. Assume that $X_0, X_1, \ldots, X_n$ are perfectly correlated. That is, if the value that X_m takes on is $\mu_m + C\sigma_m$, then the value that X_j takes on must be $\mu_j + C\sigma_j$ for $j = 0, 1, \ldots, m, \ldots, n$. Thus, this assumption states, in effect, that if circumstances cause the actual net cash flow during one period to deviate from expectations, then these same circumstances will also affect the net cash flow in all other periods in an exactly comparable manner. For this case, it is clear that P has a normal distribution with a mean as given by Equation 2 and a standard deviation,

$$\sigma_P = \sum_{j=0}^{n} \left[\frac{\sigma_j}{(1+i)^j} \right] \tag{4}$$

A more realistic model is one which combines the two assumptions considered above. This model would recognize and make allowance for the fact that, often, some of the cash flows are closely related while the others are reasonably independent. Therefore, the assumption is made that Y_j, $Z_j^{(1)}$, $Z_j^{(2)}, \ldots$, and $Z_j^{(m)}$ are the normally distributed random variables such that

$$X_j = Y_j + Z_j^{(1)} + Z_j^{(2)} + \cdots + Z_j^{(m)} \tag{5}$$

where the new random variables are mutually independent with the exception that $Z_0^{(k)}, Z_1^{(k)}, \ldots, Z_n^{(k)}$ are perfectly correlated for $k = 1, 2, \ldots, m$. In other words, the net cash flow for each period consists of an independent cash flow plus m distinct cash flows which are each perfectly correlated with the corresponding cash flows in the other periods. Therefore, it follows that P has a normal distribution with

$$\mu_P = \sum_{j=0}^{n} \left[\frac{\mu_j}{(1+i)^j} \right] = \sum_{j=0}^{n} \frac{E(Y_j) + \sum_{k=1}^{m} E(Z_j^{(k)})}{(1+i)^j} \tag{6}$$

and

$$\sigma_P{}^2 = \sum_{j=0}^{n} \left[\frac{\mathrm{Var}(Y_j)}{(1+i)^{2j}} \right] = \sum_{k=1}^{m} \left(\sum_{j=0}^{n} \left[\frac{\sqrt{\mathrm{Var}(Z_j^{(k)})}}{(1+i)^j} \right] \right)^2 \tag{7}$$

It is easily seen that the first two cases treated are actually only special cases of this model combining the two assumptions. The first case of complete independence is obtained by setting $m = 0$. The second case of complete correlation is obtained by setting $m = 1$ and $Y_j = 0$. The essential difference between the various special cases is reflected in Equation 7. In particular, given fixed values of σ_j, σ_P is smallest for the case of complete independence and largest for the case of complete correlation.

An even more precise model, from a theoretical point of view, would be one which admitted the possibility of relationship between random variables which falls somewhere between mutual independence and complete correlation. Ideally, one would be given the covariance matrix for $X_0, X_1, \ldots, X_n$, so that μ_P would be given by Equation 2 and σ_P^2 would be the weighted sum of the elements of the covariance matrix, where σ_{jk} is weighted by $(1 + i)^{-(j+k)}$. Unfortunately, it does not yet appear to be realistic to expect investment analysts to develop reliable estimates for covariances. Therefore, attention will be concentrated on the model summarized by Equation 5.

Having thus obtained the probability distribution of P, this information now provides the executive with some basis for evaluating the risk aspect of the investment decision. For example, suppose that, on the basis of the forecasts regarding prospective cash flow from a proposed investment of $10,000, it is determined that $\mu_P = \$1,000$ and $\sigma_P = \$2,000$. Ordinarily, the current procedure would be to approve the investment since $\mu_P > 0$. However, with additional information available ($\sigma_P = \$2,000$) regarding the considerable risk of the investment, the executive can analyze the situation further. Using widely available tables for the normal distribution, he could note (or be given the information on a drawing of the cumulative distribution function) that the probability that $P < 0$, so that the investment won't pay, is 0.31. Furthermore, the probability is 0.16, 0.023, and 0.0013, respectively, that the investment will lose the present worth equivalent of at least $1,000, $3,000, and $5,000, respectively. Considering the financial status of the firm, the executive can use this and similar information to make his decision. Suppose, instead, that the executive is attempting to choose between this investment and a second investment with $\mu_P = \$500$ and $\sigma_P = \$500$. By conducting a similar analysis for the second investment, the executive can decide whether the greater expected earnings of the first investment justifies the greater risk. A useful technique for making this comparison is to superimpose the drawing of the probability distribution of P for the second investment upon the corresponding drawing for the first investment. This same approach generalizes to the comparison of more than two investments.

PROBABILITY DISTRIBUTION OF ANNUAL COST

The equivalent uniform annual cost, A, for a proposed investment is shown by Grant and Ireson [7] to be

$$A = - \sum_{j=1}^{n} \left[\frac{X_j}{(1 + i)^j} \right] \left[\frac{i(1 + i)^n}{(1 + i)^n - 1} \right] = P \left[\frac{i(1 + i)^n}{(1 + i)^n - 1} \right] \quad (8)$$

Thus, for given values of i and n, A differs from P only by a constant factor. Therefore, the probability distribution of A is found by finding the probability distribution of P, as described above, and then multiplying P by this constant factor. The analysis of the risk would also correspond to the analysis when using the present worth method.

PROBABILITY DISTRIBUTION OF INTERNAL RATE OF RETURN

The internal rate of return, R, may be defined as the value of i such that $P = 0$. It is used as a measure of the merit of proposed investments. The highest priority is given to those investments with the highest values of R. If adequate funds are available, an established minimum attractive rate of return is often used as a standard for comparison, proposed investments being approved only if their value of R exceeds this standard.

Several writers, including Bernhard [1] and Bierman and Smidt [2], have recently voiced their opinion that the internal rate of return method is inferior to the present worth method. This article is intended to be an introductory exposition of a specific technique for evaluating risk, so the issues raised by these writers will be ignored. Thus, it will be assumed that the circumstances are appropriate for the use of the internal rate of return method, so that, for example, there is a unique value for R with probability essentially one.

The proposed procedure for finding the probability distribution of R is a relatively straight-forward one. It involves finding the probability distribution of P for various values of i in order to find the cumulative distribution function of R, and then, if desired, deriving the probability density function of R from its cumulative distribution function. This procedure will now be outlined.

Selecting an arbitrary value of i, find the probability distribution of P as described previously. Find the probability that $P < 0$. Then, except under unusual circumstances such as [1] discusses, this is just the probability that $R < i$. This result should be readily apparent since $R = i$ only if $P = 0$ and R normally increases as P increases for a given investment and a fixed value of i. Summarizing in equation form,

$$\text{Prob}\{R < i\} = \text{Prob}\{P < 0 \mid i\} \qquad (9)$$

Therefore, to find the cumulative distribution function of R, one need merely repeat the calculation of $\text{Prob}\{P < 0 \mid i\}$ for as many values of i as desired. The calculation of these values provides the basis for a graphical presentation of the cumulative distribution function of R. This procedure for deriving the probability distribution of R is illustrated by the example of the following section.

The cumulative distribution function of R can readily be used directly for evaluating an investment. It has a meaningful, yet simple, interpretation which is well-suited for this purpose. However, if desired, the cumulative distribution function can be transformed into the probability density function. Simply recall that the value of the probability density function at a certain i is just the first derivative of the cumulative distribution function at that value of i. Alternatively, since the probability distribution of R will usually approximate the normal distribution, the normal curve can be used as an approximate probability density function, where the mean and the standard deviation would be estimated from an examination of the cumulative distribution function.

The assertion that, under the prevailing asumption of the normality of P, the probability distribution of R will usually approximate the normal distribution is supported by the following argument. Assume the usual situation that $\mu_o < 0$ and $\mu_j > 0$ for $j = 1, 2, \ldots, n$. Therefore, the first derivative of μ_P with respect to i, μ_P', is obviously negative (see Equation 6). Assume, as an approximation, that μ_P' and σ_P are constants for all values of i. Then, for any numbers, Δ and i_o,

$$\text{Prob}\{P < -\mu_P'\Delta \mid i = i_o\} = \text{Prob}\{P < 0 \mid i = i_0 + \Delta\}$$

and therefore,

$$\text{Prob}\{R < i_o + \Delta\} = \text{Prob}\{P < -\mu_P'\Delta \mid i = i_o\}$$

Hence, R and P are identically distributed except for the location and scale parameters, mean and standard deviation. Since P is normal, it now follows that the probability distribution of R is the normal distribution. The one shortcoming in this argument is that, in fact, μ_P' and σ_P are not constants. However, the fact that $\mu_P' > 0$, whereas $\sigma_P' < 0$, means that these two discrepancies tend to cancel each other out.

It would be sometimes desirable, when comparing mutually exclusive investments requiring differing amounts of investment funds, to determine the probability distribution of the internal rate of return on each increment in investment. To illustrate how this would be done, consider two such mutually exclusive investments which can be described by the model involving Equation 5. Let $P(S)$, $P(L)$, and $P(\Delta)$ denote the present worths of the smaller investment, the larger investment, and the incremental investment, respectively. Let $R(\Delta)$ denote the internal rate of return on the incremental investment. Assume that $P(S)$ and $P(L)$ are mutually independent. Therefore, since

$$P(\Delta) = P(L) - P(S) \tag{10}$$

it is clear that $P(\Delta)$ has a normal distribution with

$$E\{P(\Delta)\} = E\{P(L)\} - E\{P(S)\} \tag{11}$$

and

$$\text{Var}\{P(\Delta)\} = \text{Var}\{P(L)\} + \text{Var}\{P(S)\} \tag{12}$$

Thus, just as before,

$$\text{Prob}\{R(\Delta) < i\} = \text{Prob}\{P(\Delta) < 0 \mid i\}, \qquad (13)$$

so that the same procedure is now used for finding the probability distribution of $R(\Delta)$ as for R.

EXAMPLE

The XYZ Company is primarily engaged in the manufacture of cameras. They will soon be discontinuing the production of one of their older models, and they are now investigating what should be done with the extra productive capacity that will consequently become available. Two attractive alternatives appear to be available. The first alternative is to expand the production of model A, one of their latest and most popular models. This model was initially marketed last year, and its successful reception plus favorable marketing research indicates that there is and will continue to be a market for this extra production. The second alternative is to initiate the production of model B. Model B would involve a number of revolutionary changes which the research department has developed. While no comparable model is now on the market, rumors in the industry indicate that a number of other companies might now have similar models on their drawing boards. Marketing research indicates an exciting but uncertain potential for such a model. Uncertainty regarding the reliability of the proposed new devices, lack of production experience on such a model, and the possibility that the market might be vigorously invaded by competing models at any time, all add to the risk involved in this alternative. In short, the decision is between the safe, conservative investment in model A, or the risky but promising investment in model B. It is felt that both of these models will be marketable for the next five years. Due to a lack of investment funds and productive capacity, it has been decided that only one of these alternatives can be selected. It is assumed that the production of model B would not affect the market for the presently scheduled production of model A.

Detailed studies have been made regarding the after tax cash flow consequences of the two alternatives. The analysis of the investment required in model A indicates that considerable new equipment, tooling, and modification of existing production processes will be needed. It was estimated that the difference in the immediate cash flow because of the investment in model A would be ($-\$400,000$). However, it is recognized that this estimate is only approximate, so that it is appropriate to estimate the standard deviation for this cash flow. Recalling that the probability is 0.6827, 0.9545, and 0.9973, respectively, that the actual cash flow will be within one, two, and three standard deviations, respectively, of the expected cash flow, it was decided that an estimate of $20,000 was the most appropriate one. In other words, the judgment was that, letting Y_o be the cash flow,

$$\text{Prob}\{-\$400,000 - \sigma \leqq Y_o \leqq -\$400,000 + \sigma\} = 0.6827$$
$$\text{Prob}\{-\$400,000 - 2\sigma \leqq Y_o \leqq -\$400,000 + 2\sigma\} = 0.9545$$
$$\text{Prob}\{-\$400,000 - 3\sigma \leqq Y_o \leqq -\$400,000 + 3\sigma\} = 0.9973$$

most accurately reflects the estimator's subjective probabilities of σ is chosen as $20,000.

Proceeding with a similar analysis, the expected values and standard deviations of the net cash flow for each of the next five years were estimated. Due to the previous experience with model A, these standard deviations were considered to be small. The variation that does exist largely arises from the variation in the production costs, such as maintenance, equipment replacement, and rework costs, and in the state of the economy. Since these conditions tend to vary randomly from year to year, it was decided that the appropriate assumption is that the net cash flows in the various years are mutually independent. One special problem was encountered in determining the standard deviation for the fifth year since this net cash flow combines the regular cash flow for the fifth year plus the effective salvage value of the equipment being used. This standard deviation was obtained by assuming independence, so that the variance of the sum equals the sum of the variances of these cash flows. Thus, even though the standard deviation for the salvage value was estimated at $30,000 and the standard deviation for the rest of the net cash flow at $40,000, the estimated standard deviation of the total net cash flow for the fifth year is $50,000.

Table 1 summarizes the results of the estimating process for model A.

TABLE 1
Estimated net cash flow data in thousands of
dollars for model A

Year	Corresponding symbol in Eq. 5	Expected value	Standard deviation
0...............	Y_0	-400	20
1...............	Y_1	$+120$	10
2...............	Y_2	$+120$	15
3...............	Y_3	$+120$	20
4...............	Y_4	$+110$	30
5...............	Y_5	$+200$	50

The procedure for describing the investment in model B was similar. The primary difference was that this investment was considered to generate both a series of correlated cash flows and a series of independent cash flows. Thus, in Equation 5, $m = 1$ instead of $m = 0$ as for the investment in model A. This difference arose because of the uncertainty regarding the reception of model B on the market. Thus, it was felt that if the reception exceeded expectations during the first year or two, it would continue to exceed present expectations thereafter, and vice versa. The resulting conclusion was that the net marketing cash flow, i.e., the net cash flow resulting from the sales income minus the expenses due to the marketing effort and advertising required, for each of the five years should be assumed to be perfectly correlated. On the other hand, it was felt the analysis of the production expenses involved was sufficiently reliable that any deviation from expectations for a given year would be primarily attributable to random fluctuations in production costs, especially in such irregular items as maintenance costs. Therefore, it was concluded that the net production cash flow for each of the five years should be assumed to be mutually independent. The effective equipment salvage value, being essentially independent of the other cash flows, was included in the net production cash flow for the fifth year.

Detailed analyses of the various components of total cash flow led, as for model A, to the desired estimates of the expectations and standard deviations of net cash flow for marketing and for production for each of the five years, as well as for the immediate investment required. These results are summarized in Table 2.

TABLE 2
Estimated net cash flow data in thousands of dollars for model B

Year	Source of cash flow	Corresponding symbol in Eq. 5	Expected value	Standard deviation
0.........	Initial Investment	Y_0	-600	50
1.........	Production	Y_1	-250	20
2.........	Production	Y_2	-200	10
3.........	Production	Y_3	-200	10
4.........	Production	Y_4	-200	10
5.........	Production, salvage value	Y_5	-100	$10\sqrt{10}$
1.........	Marketing	$Z_1^{(1)}$	$+300$	50
2.........	Marketing	$Z_2^{(1)}$	$+600$	100
3.........	Marketing	$Z_3^{(1)}$	$+500$	100
4.........	Marketing	$Z_4^{(1)}$	$+400$	100
5.........	Marketing	$Z_5^{(1)}$	$+300$	100

The procedure for using these data to derive the probability distribution of present worth will now be illustrated. For this particular company, the appropriate value of i is considered to be $i = 10\%$.

For the investment in model A, Equations 6 and 7 indicate that, since $m = 0$,

$$\mu_P = \sum_{j=0}^{5} \frac{E(Y_j)}{(1.1)^j} = -400 + \cdots + \frac{200}{(1.1)^2} = +95$$

$$\sigma_P{}^2 = \sum_{j=0}^{5} \frac{\text{Var}(Y_j)}{(1.1)^{2j}} = (20)^2 + \cdots + \frac{(50)^2}{(1.1)^{10}} = 2{,}247$$

so that $\sigma_P = 47.4$. Therefore, the probability distribution of present worth of the investment in model A is a normal distribution with a mean of 95 and a standard deviation of 47.4 (in units of thousands of dollars). Thus, referring to probability tables for the normal distribution to find what proportion of the population is less than the mean minus 95/47.4 standard deviations, it is concluded that

$$\text{Prob}\{P < 0 \mid i = 10\%\} = 0.023.$$

Preceding similarly for the investment in model B, Equations 6 and 7 indicate that, since $m = 1$,

$$\mu_P = \sum_{j=0}^{5} \frac{E(Y_j) + E(Z_j{}^{(1)})}{(1.1)^j} = -600 + \frac{50}{1.1} + \cdots + \frac{200}{(1.1)^5} = +262$$

$$\sigma_P{}^2 = \sum_{j=0}^{5} \frac{\text{Var}(Y_j)}{(1.1)^{2j}} + \left(\sum_{j=0}^{5} \left[\frac{\sqrt{\text{Var}(Z_j{}^{(1)})}}{(1.1)^j} \right] \right)^2$$

$$= 2{,}500 + \cdots + \frac{1{,}000}{(1.1)^{10}} + \left(\frac{50}{1.1} + \cdots + \frac{100}{(1.1)^5} \right)^2$$

$$= 114{,}700,$$

so that $\sigma_P = 339$. Therefore,

$$\text{Prob }\{P < 0 \mid i = 10\%\} = 0.22$$

This information regarding the probability distribution of present worth permits a precise probabilistic comparison of the two alternative investments. In order to facilitate this comparison, it is sometimes useful to superimpose the two normal curves (or the corresponding cumulative distribution functions) on the same graph.

If the company had desired to use the internal rate of return criterion, the procedure would have been a straight-forward extension of the above procedure for present worth. Thus, given the preceding information regarding present worth, Equation 9 immediately indicates that, for the investment in model A,

$$\text{Prob}\{R < 10\%\} = 0.023$$

and for the investment in model B

$$\text{Prob}\{R < 10\%\} = 0.22$$

Using the same procedure for various other values of i, the cumulative distribution function of R can be obtained for each of the investments. They are presented subsequently in Figure 1. Comparing these cumula-

FIGURE 1

Comparison of the cumulative distribution functions of R for the investments in model A and in model B

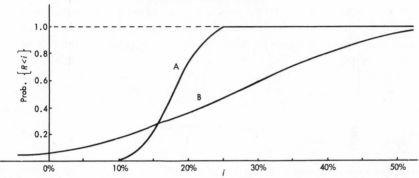

tive distribution functions with the cumulative distribution function for the normal distribution, a close similarity is noticed. Thus, a brief examination reveals that, for the investment in model A, the distribution of R is approximately normal with a mean of about 18.5% and a standard deviation of about 4%. For the investment in model B, the distribution of R is approximately normal with a mean of about 25% and a standard deviation of about 20%. This leads to the normal curves given in Figure 2 as the approximate probability density functions of R for the two investments.

Figure 2, or a reasonable facsimile, could also have been obtained directly by determining the slope of the corresponding curves in Figure 1.

If desired, similar information regarding the incremental investment could have been derived from Equations 10, 11, 12, and 13.

The impressive feature of this example is that the decision between the two investments is not an easy one. This is true despite the fact that there is a difference of about $167,000 in the expected present worth and of about 6.5% in the expected rate of return. The great difference in the risk involved compels management to examine carefully the financial position of the firm and evaluate the seriousness of the consequences should the riskier investment fail to achieve expectations. Then, considering the probabilities involved, management would, in effect, implicitly

FIGURE 2
Comparison of the approximate probability density functions of R for the
investments in model A and model B

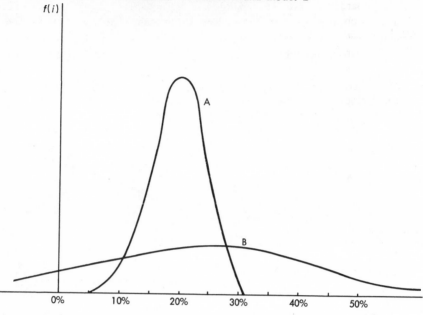

assign utilities to the possible outcomes of the investments and select
the investment with the larger expected utility.

CONCLUSIONS

The risk factor is often an important consideration in the evaluation
of a proposed investment. Unfortunately, present procedures for considering risk have not been entirely satisfactory. They have tended either
to provide insufficient information or to require the use of essentially
unobtainable information. The procedure proposed here appears to largely
avoid both of these pitfalls while simultaneously retaining some of the
best features of these two types of existing procedures. It requires only
that, in addition to an estimate of the expected value of a prospective
cash flow, the inexactitude of the estimate be described by an estimate
of the standard deviation. On this basis, it then generates an explicit
and complete description of the risk involved in terms of the probability
distribution of the internal rate of return, present worth, or annual cost.
This information then permits management to weigh precisely the possible consequences of the proposed investment and thereby make a sound
decision regarding the proposal.

REFERENCES

1. Bernhard, Richard H. "Discount Methods for Expenditure Evaluation—A Clarification of Their Assumptions," *The Journal of Industrial Engineering*, January–February 1962, pp. 19–27.

2. Bierman, Harold, Jr., and Smidt, Seymour. *The Capital Budgeting Decision*. New York: The Macmillan Company, 1960.

3. Bowker, Albert H., and Lieberman, Gerald J. *Engineering Statistics*. Englewood Cliffs, N.J.: Prentice-Hall, 1959.

4. Degarmo, E. Paul. *Engineering Economy*. 3d ed. New York: The Macmillan Company, 1960.

5. English, J. Morley. "New Approaches to Economic Comparison for Engineering Projects," *The Journal of Industrial Engineering*, November–December 1961, pp. 375–78.

6. Gordon, Myron J., and Shapiro, Eli. "Capital Equipment Analysis: The Required Rate of Profit," *Management Science*, October 1956, pp. 102–10.

7. Grant, Eugene L., and Ireson, W. Grant. *Principles of Engineering Economy*. 4th ed. New York: The Ronald Press, 1960.

8. Green, Paul E. "The Derivation of Utility Functions in a Large Industrial Firm," paper given at the First Joint National Meeting of the Operations Research Society of America and the Institute of Management Sciences, 1961.

9. Markowitz, Harry M. *Portfolio Selection*. New York: John Wiley & Sons, 1959.

10. Modigliani, Franco, and Miller, Merton H. "The Cost of Capital, Corporation Finance, and the Theory of Investment," *American Economic Review*, Vol. 48, No. 2 (June 1958).

11. Morris, William T. *Engineering Economy*. Homewood, Ill.: Richard D. Irwin, 1960.

12. Naslund, Bertil, and Whinston, Andrew. "A Model of Multi-Period Investment under Uncertainty," *Management Science*, January 1962, pp. 184–200.

13. Schlaifer, Robert. *Probability and Statistics for Business Decisions*. New York: McGraw-Hill, 1959.

Decision Trees for Decision Making*

John F. Magee†

THE MANAGEMENT of a company that I shall call Stygian Chemical Industries, Ltd., must decide whether to build a small plant or a large one to manufacture a new product with an expected market life of ten years. The decision hinges on what size the market for the product will be.

Possibly demand will be high during the initial two years but, if many initial users find the product unsatisfactory, will fall to a low level thereafter. Or high initial demand might indicate the possibility of a sustained high-volume market. If demand is high and the company does not expand within the first two years, competitive products will surely be introduced.

If the company builds a big plant, it must live with it whatever the size of market demand. If it builds a small plant, management has the option of expanding the plant in two years in the event that demand is high during the introductory period; while in the event that demand is low during the introductory period, the company will maintain operations in the small plant and make a tidy profit on the low volume.

Management is uncertain what to do. The company grew rapidly during the 1950's; it kept pace with the chemical industry generally. The new product, if the market turns out to be large, offers the present management a chance to push the company into a new period of profitable growth. The development department, particularly the development project engineer, is pushing to build the large-scale plant to exploit the

---

* Reprinted from *Harvard Business Review*, Vol. 42, No. 4 (July–August 1964), pp. 126–35, by permission of the author and © 1964, by The President and Fellows of Harvard College; all rights reserved.

† Vice president, Management Services Division, Arthur D. Little, Inc.

first major product development the department has produced in some years.

The chairman, a principal stockholder, is wary of the possibility of large unneeded plant capacity. He favors a smaller plant commitment, but recognizes that later expansion to meet high-volume demand would require more investment and be less efficient to operate. The chairman also recognizes that unless the company moves promptly to fill the demand which develops, competitors will be tempted to move in with equivalent products.

The Stygian Chemical problem, oversimplified as it is, illustrates the uncertainties and issues that business management must resolve in making investment decisions. (I use the term "investment" in a broad sense, referring to outlays not only for new plants and equipment but also for large, risky orders, special marketing facilities, research programs, and other purposes.) These decisions are growing more important at the same time that they are increasing in complexity. Countless executives want to make them better—but how?

In this article I shall present one recently developed concept called the "decision tree," which has tremendous potential as a decision-making tool. The decision tree can clarify for management, as can no other analytical tool that I know of, the choices, risks, objectives, monetary gains, and information needs involved in an investment problem. We shall be hearing a great deal about decision trees in the years ahead. Although a novelty to most businessmen today, they will surely be in common management parlance before many more years have passed.

Later in this article we shall return to the problem facing Stygian Chemical and see how management can proceed to solve it by using decision trees. First, however, a simpler example will illustrate some characteristics of the decision-tree approach.

DISPLAYING ALTERNATIVES

Let us suppose it is a rather overcast Saturday morning, and you have 75 people coming for cocktails in the afternoon. You have a pleasant garden and your house is not too large; so if the weather permits, you would like to set up the refreshments in the garden and have the party there. It would be more pleasant, and your guests would be more comfortable. On the other hand, if you set up the party for the garden and after all the guests are assembled it begins to rain, the refreshments will be ruined, your guests will get damp, and you will heartily wish you had decided to have the party in the house. (We could complicate this problem by considering the possibility of a partial commitment to one course or another and opportunities to adjust estimates of the weather as the day goes on, but the simple problem is all we need.)

This particular decision can be represented in the form of a "payoff" table:

	Events and results	
Choices..................	*Rain*	*No Rain*
Outdoors...............	Disaster	Real comfort
Indoors.................	Mild discomfort, but happy	Mild discomfort, but regrets

Much more complex decision questions can be portrayed in payoff table form. However, particularly for complex investment decisions, a different representation of the information pertinent to the problem—the decision tree—is useful to show the routes by which the various possible outcomes are achieved. Pierre Massé, Commissioner General of the National Agency for Productivity and Equipment Planning in France, notes:

> The decision problem is not posed in terms of an isolated decision (because today's decision depends on the one we shall make tomorrow) nor yet in terms of a sequence of decisions (because under uncertainty, decisions taken in the future will be influenced by what we have learned in the meanwhile). The problem is posed in terms of a tree of decisions."[1]

Exhibit 1 illustrates a decision tree for the cocktail party problem. This tree is a different way of displaying the same information shown in the payoff table. However, as later examples will show, in complex decisions the decision tree is frequently a much more lucid means of presenting the relevant information than is a payoff table.

The tree is made up of a series of nodes and branches. At the first node on the left, the host has the choice of having the party inside or outside. Each branch represents an alternative course of action or decision. At the end of each branch or alternative course is another node representing a chance event—whether or not it will rain. Each subsequent alternative course to the right represents an alternative outcome of this chance event. Associated with each complete alternative course through the tree is a payoff, shown at the end of the rightmost or terminal branch of the course.

When I am drawing decision trees, I like to indicate the action or decision forks with square nodes and the chance-event forks with round ones. Other symbols may be used instead, such as single-line and double-line branches, special letters, or colors. It does not matter so much which method of distinguishing you use so long as you do employ one or another. A decision tree of any size will always combine (*a*) *action* choices

---

[1] *Optimal Investment Decisions: Rules for Action and Criteria for Choice* (Englewood Cliffs, N.J.: Prentice-Hall, Inc., 1962), p. 250.

EXHIBIT 1
Decision tree for cocktail party

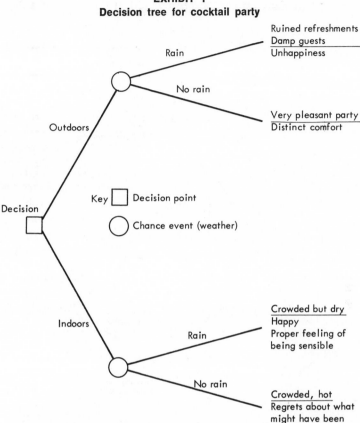

Rain
Ruined refreshments
Damp guests
Unhappiness

No rain
Very pleasant party
Distinct comfort

Outdoors

Key ☐ Decision point

Decision

◯ Chance event (weather)

Indoors

Rain
Crowded but dry
Happy
Proper feeling of
being sensible

No rain
Crowded, hot
Regrets about what
might have been

with (*b*) different possible *events* or *results* of action which are partially affected by chance or other uncontrollable circumstances.

Decision-event chains

The previous example, though involving only a single stage of decision, illustrates the elementary principles on which larger, more complex decision trees are built. Let us take a slightly more complicated situation:

You are trying to decide whether to approve a development budget for an improved product. You are urged to do so on the grounds that the development, if successful, will give you a competitive edge, but if you do not develop the product, your competitor may—and may seriously damage your market share. You sketch out a decision tree that looks something like the one in Exhibit 2.

Your initial decision is shown at the left. Following a decision to proceed

EXHIBIT 2
Decision tree with chains of actions and events

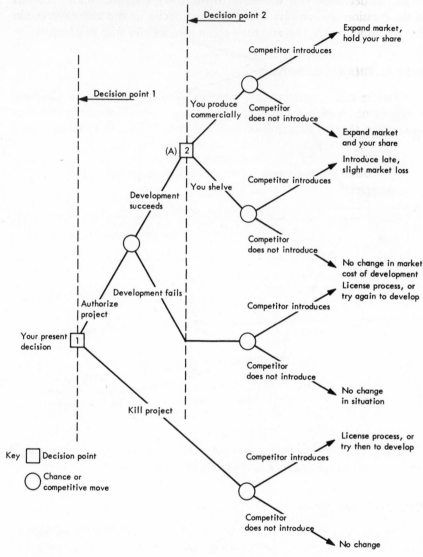

with the project, if development is successful, is a second stage of decision at Point A. Assuming no important change in the situation between now and the time of Point A, you decide now what alternatives will be important to you at that time. At the right of the tree are the outcomes of different sequences of decisions and events. These outcomes, too, are based on your present information. In effect you say, "If what I know now is true then, this is what will happen."

Of course, you do not try to identify all the events that can happen or all the decisions you will have to make on a subject under analysis. In the decision tree you lay out only those decisions and events or results that are important to you and have consequences you wish to compare.

ADDING FINANCIAL DATA

Now we can return to the problems faced by the Stygian Chemical management. A decision tree characterizing the investment problem as outlined in the introduction is shown in Exhibit 3. At Decision No. 1

EXHIBIT 3
Decisions and events for Stygian Chemical Industries, Ltd.

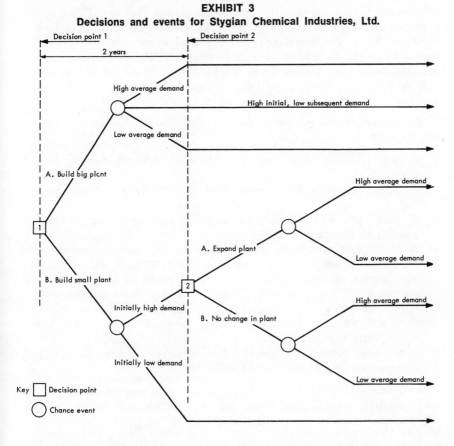

the company must decide between a large and a small plant. This is all that must be decided *now*. But if the company chooses to build a small plant and then finds demand high during the initial period, it can in two years—a Decision No. 2—choose to expand its plant.

But let us go beyond a bare outline of alternatives. In making decisions, executives must take account of the probabilities, costs, and returns which appear likely. On the basis of the data now available to them, and assuming no important change in the company's situation, they reason as follows:

Marketing estimates indicate a 60% chance of a large market in the long run and a 40% chance of a low demand, developing initially as follows:

Initially high demand, sustained high: 60%
Initially high demand, long-term low: 10% } Low = 40%
Initially low and continuing low: 30% }
Initially low and subsequently high: 0%

Therefore, the chance that demand initially will be high is 70% (60 + 10). *If* demand is high initially, the company estimates that the chance it will continue at a high level is 86% (60 ÷ 70). Comparing 86% to 60%, it is apparent that a high initial level of sales changes the estimated chance of high sales in the subsequent periods. Similarly, if sales in the initial period are low, the chances are 100% (30 ÷ 30) that sales in the subsequent periods will be low. Thus the level of sales in the initial period is expected to be a rather accurate indicator of the level of sales in the subsequent periods.

Estimates of annual income are made under the assumption of each alternative outcome:

1. A large plant with high volume would yield $1,000,000 annually in cash flow.
2. A large plant with low volume would yield only $100,000 because of high fixed costs and inefficiencies.
3. A small plant with low demand would be economical and would yield annual cash income of $400,000.
4. A small plant, during an initial period of high demand, would yield $450,000 per year, but this would drop to $300,000 yearly in the long run because of competition. (The market would be larger than under Alternative 3, but would be divided up among more competitors.)
5. If the small plant were expanded to meet sustained high demand, it would yield $700,000 cash flow annually, and so would be less efficient than a large plant built initially.
6. If the small plant were expanded but high demand were not sustained, estimated annual cash flow would be $50,000.

It is estimated further that a large plant would cost $3 million to put into operation, a small plant would cost $1.3 million, and the expansion of the small plant would cost an additional $2.2 million.

When the foregoing data are incorporated we have the decision tree shown in Exhibit 4. Bear in mind that nothing is shown here which Stygian Chemical's executives did not know before; no numbers have been pulled out of hats. However, we are beginning to see dramatic evidence of the value of decision trees in *laying out* what management knows in a way that enables more systematic analysis and leads to better

EXHIBIT 4
Decision tree with financial data

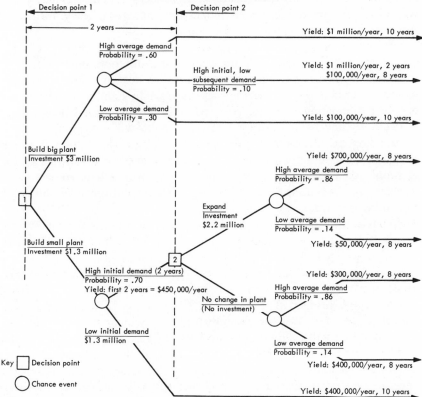
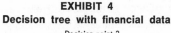

decisions. To sum up the requirements of making a decision tree, management must:

1. Identify the points of decision and alternatives available at each point.
2. Identify the points of uncertainty and the type or range of alternative outcomes at each point.
3. Estimate the values needed to make the analysts, especially the probabilities of different events or results of action and the costs and gains of various events and actions.
4. Analyze the alternative values to choose a course.

CHOOSING COURSE OF ACTION

We are now ready for the next step in the analysis—to compare the consequences of different courses of action. A decision tree does not give management the answer to an investment problem; rather, it helps management determine which alternative at any particular choice point will yield the greatest expected monetary gain, given the information and alternatives pertinent to the decision.

Of course, the gains must be viewed with the risks. At Stygian Chemical, as at many corporations, managers have different points of view toward risk; hence they will draw different conclusions in the circumstances described by the decision tree shown in Exhibit 4. The many people participating in a decision—those supplying capital, ideas, data, or decisions, and having different values at risk—will see the uncertainty surrounding the decision in different ways. Unless these differences are recognized and dealt with, those who must make the decision, pay for it, supply data and analyses to it, and live with it will judge the issue, relevance of data, need for analysis, and criterion and success in different and conflicting ways.

For example, company stockholders may treat a particular investment as one of a series of possibilities, some of which will work out, others of which will fail. A major investment may pose risks to a middle manager—to his job and career—no matter what decision is made. Another participant may have a lot to gain from success, but little to lose from failure of the project. The nature of the risk—as each individual sees it—will affect not only the assumptions he is willing to make but also the strategy he will follow in dealing with the risk.

The existence of multiple, unstated, and conflicting objectives will certainly contribute to the "politics" of Stygian Chemical's decision, and one can be certain that the political element exists whenever the lives and ambitions of people are affected. Here, as in similar cases, it is not a bad exercise to think through who the parties to an investment decision are and to try to make these assessments:

What is at risk? Is it profit or equity value, survival of the business, maintenance of a job, opportunity for a major career?

Who is bearing the risk? The stockholder is usually bearing risk in one form. Management, employees, the community—all may be bearing different risks.

What is the character of the risk that each person bears? Is it, *in his terms,* unique, once-in-a-lifetime, sequential, insurable? Does it affect the economy, the industry, the company, or a portion of the company?

Considerations such as the foregoing will surely enter into top management's thinking, and the decision tree in Exhibit 4 will not eliminate them. But the tree will show management what decision today will contribute most to its long-term goals. The tool for this next step in the analysis is the concept of "rollback."

"Rollback" concept

Here is how rollback works in the situation described. At the time of making Decision No. 1 (see Exhibit 4), management does not have to make Decision No. 2 and does not even know if it will have the occasion to do so. But if it *were* to have the option at Decision No. 2, the company would expand the plant, in view of its current knowledge. The analysis is shown in Exhibit 5. (I shall ignore for the moment the

EXHIBIT 5
Analysis of possible decision no. 2
(using maximum expected total cash flow as criterion)

Choice	Chance event	Probability (1)	Total yield, 8 years (thousands of dollars) (2)	Expected value (thousands of dollars) (1) x (2)
Expansion..........	High average demand	.86	$5,600	$4,816
	Low average demand	.14	400	56
			Total	$4,872
			Less investment	2,200
			Net	$2,672
No Expansion.......	High average demand	.86	$2,400	$2,064
	Low average demand	.14	3,200	448
			Total	$2,512
			Less investment	0
			Net	$2,512

question of discounting future profits; that is introduced later.) We see that the total expected value of the expansion alternative is $160,000 greater than the no-expansion alternative, over the eight-year life remaining. Hence that is the alternative management would choose if faced with Decision No. 2 with its existing information (and thinking only of monetary gain as a standard of choice).

Readers may wonder why we started with Decision No. 2 when to-day's problem is Decision No. 1. The reason is the following: We need to be able to put a monetary value on Decision No. 2 in order to "roll back" to Decision No. 1 and compare the gain from taking the lower branch ("Build Small Plant") with the gain from taking the upper branch ("Build Big Plant"). Let us call that monetary value for Decision No. 2 its *position value*. The position value of a decision is the expected value of the preferred branch (in this case, the plant-expansion fork). The expected value is simply a kind of average of the results you would expect if you were to repeat the situation over and over—getting a $5,600 thousand yield 86% of the time and a $400 thousand yield 14% of the time.

Stated in another way, it is worth $2,672 thousand to Stygian Chemical to get to the position where it can make Decision No. 2. The question is: Given this value and the other data shown in Exhibit 4, what now appears to be the best action at Decision No. 1?

Turn now to Exhibit 6. At the right of the branches in the top half

EXHIBIT 6
Cash flow analysis for decision no. 1

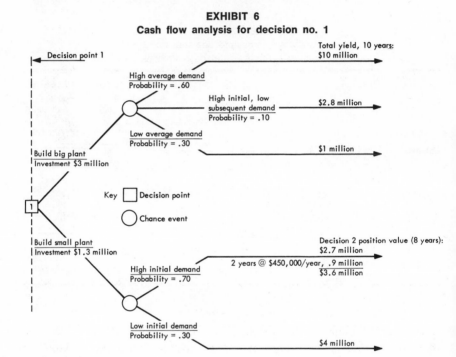

we see the yields for various events if a big plant is built (these are simply the figures in Exhibit 4 multiplied out). In the bottom half we see the small plant figures, including Decision No. 2 position value plus the yield for the two years prior to Decision No. 2. If we reduce all these yields by their probabilities, we get the following comparison:

Build big plant: ($10 × .60) + ($2.8 × .10) +
($1 × .30) − $3 = $3,600 thousand
Build small plant: ($3.6 × .70) + ($4 × .30) −
$1.3 = $2,400 thousand

The choice which maximizes expected total cash yield at Decision No. 1, therefore, is to build the big plant initially.

ACCOUNTING FOR TIME

What about taking differences in the *time* of future earnings into account? The time between successive decision stages on a decision tree may be substantial. At any stage, we may have to weigh differences in immediate cost or revenue against differences in value at the next stage. Whatever standard of choice is applied, we can put the two alternatives on a comparable basis if we discount the value assigned to the next stage by an appropriate percentage. The discount percentage is, in effect, an allowance for the cost of capital and is similar to the use of a discount rate in the present value or discounted cash flow techniques already well known to businessmen.

When decision trees are used, the discounting procedure can be applied one stage at a time. Both cash flows and position values are discounted.

For simplicity, let us assume that a discount rate of 10% per year for all stages is decided on by Stygian Chemical's management. Applying the rollback principle, we again begin with Decision No. 2. Taking the same figures used in previous exhibits and discounting the cash flows at 10%, we get the data shown in Part A of Exhibit 7. Note particularly that these are the present values *as of the time Decision No. 2 is made.*

Now we want to go through the same procedure used in Exhibit 5 when we obtained expected values, only this time using the discounted yield figures and obtaining a discounted expected value. The results are shown in Part B of Exhibit 7. Since the discounted expected value of the no-expansion alternative is higher, *that* figure becomes the position value of Decision No. 2 this time.

Having done this, we go back to work through Decision No. 1 again, repeating the same analytical procedure as before only with discounting. The calculations are shown in Exhibit 8. Note that the Decision No. 2 position value is treated at the time of Decision No. 1 as if it were a lump sum received at the end of the two years.

The large-plant alternative is again the preferred one on the basis of discounted expected cash flow. But the margin of difference over the small-plant alternative ($290 thousand) is smaller than it was without discounting.

UNCERTAINTY ALTERNATIVES

In illustrating the decision-tree concept, I have treated uncertainty alternatives as if they were discrete, well-defined possibilities. For my examples I have made use of uncertain situations depending basically on a single variable, such as the level of demand or the success or failure of a development project. I have sought to avoid unnecessary complication

EXHIBIT 7
Analysis of decision no. 2 with discounting
A. Present values of cash flows

Choice—outcome	Yield	Present value (in thousands)
Expand—high demand	$700,000 per year, 8 years	$4,100
Expand—low demand	50,000 per year, 8 years	300
No change—high demand	300,000 per year, 8 years	1,800
No change—low demand	400,000 per year, 8 years	2,300

B. Obtaining discounted expected values

Choice	Chance event	Probability (1)	Present value yield (in thousands) (2)	Discounted expected value (in thousands) (1) × (2)
Expansion.........	High average demand	0.86	$4,100	$3,526
	Low average demand	0.14	300	42
			Total	$3,568
			Less investment	2,200
			Net	$1,368
No expansion......	High average demand	0.86	$1,800	$1,548
	Low average demand	0.14	2,300	322
			Total	$1,870
			Less investment	0
			Net	$1,870

Note: For simplicity, the first year cash flow is not discounted, the second year cash flow is discounted one year, and so on.

while putting emphasis on the key interrelationships among the present decision, future choices, and the intervening uncertainties.

In many cases, the uncertain elements do take the form of discrete, single-variable alternatives. In others, however, the possibilities for cash flow during a stage may range through a whole spectrum and may depend on a number of independent or partially related variables subject to chance influences—cost, demand, yield, economic climate, and so forth. In these cases, we have found that the range of variability or the likelihood of the cash flow falling in a given range during a stage can be calculated readily from knowledge of the key variables and the uncertainties surrounding them. Then the range of cash-flow possibilities during the stage can be broken down into two, three, or more "subsets," which can be used as discrete chance alternatives.

CONCLUSION

Peter F. Drucker has succinctly expressed the relation between present planning and future events: "Long-range planning does not deal with

EXHIBIT 8
Analysis of decision no. 1

Choice	Chance event	Probability (*I*)	Yield (*in thousands*)	Discounted value of yield (*in thousands*) (2)	Discounted expected yield (*in thousands*) (*I*) × (2)
Build big plant....	High average demand	0.60	$1,000 per year, 10 years	$6,700	$4,020
	High initial, low average demand	0.10	1,000 per year, 2 years 100 per year, 8 years	2,400	240
	Low average demand	0.30	100 per year, 10 years	700	210
				Total	$4,470
				Less investment	3,000
				Net	$1,470
Build small plant....	High initial demand	0.70	$ 450 per year, 2 years Decision No. 2 value, $1,870 at end of 2 years	$ 860 1,530	$ 600 1,070
	Low initial demand	0.30	$ 400 per year, 10 years	2,690	810
				Total	$2,480
				Less investment	1,300
				Net	$1,180

future decisions. It deals with the futurity of present decisions."[2] Today's decision should be made in light of the anticipated effect it and the outcome of uncertain events will have on future values and decisions. Since today's decision sets the stage for tomorrow's decision, today's decision must balance economy with flexibility; it must balance the need to capitalize on profit opportunities that may exist with the capacity to react to future circumstances and needs.

The unique feature of the decision tree is that it allows management to combine analytical techniques such as discounted cash flow and present value methods with a clear portrayal of the impact of future decision alternatives and events. Using the decision tree, management can consider various courses of action with greater ease and clarity. The interactions between present decision alternatives, uncertain events, and future choices and their results become more visible.

---

[2] "Long Range Planning," *Management Science*, April 1959, p. 239.

Of course, there are many practical aspects of decision trees in addition to those that could be covered in the space of just one article. When these other aspects are discussed in subsequent articles,[3] the whole range of possible gains for management will be seen in greater detail.

Surely the decision-tree concept does not offer final answers to managements making investment decisions in the face of uncertainty. We have not reached that stage, and perhaps we never will. Nevertheless, the concept is valuable for illustrating the structure of investment decisions, and it can likewise provide excellent help in the evaluation of capital investment *opportunities*.

---

[3] We are expecting another article by Mr. Magee in a forthcoming issue—the editors.

Abandonment Value and Capital Budgeting*

Alexander A. Robichek and James C. Van Horne †

In the appraisal of investment proposals, insufficient attention in the literature is paid to the possibility of future abandonment. Customarily, projects are analyzed as though the firm were committed to the project over its entire estimated life. However, many projects have significant abandonment value over their economic lives; and this factor must be considered in the capital-budgeting process if capital is to be allocated optimally. This paper will examine the importance of abandonment value to capital budgeting, analyze how it can affect a project's expected return and risk, and propose a framework for taking account of this seldom-considered dimension. In this regard, a simulation method is developed for incorporating the effects of abandonment into the information provided for the investment decision.

I. THE INVESTMENT DECISION

The current literature in the field of capital budgeting favors the use of the discounted cash-flow approach to project selection. The basic decision rule given by this approach can be stated in one of two ways:

---

*Reprinted from *The Journal of Finance*, Vol. 22, No. 4 (December 1967), pp. 577–89, by permission of the authors and the publisher.

This study was supported, in part, by funds made available by the Ford Foundation to the Graduate School of Business, Stanford University. The conclusions, opinions and other statements in this paper are those of the authors and are not necessarily those of the Ford Foundation.

† The authors are, respectively, Professor of Business Administration and Associate Professor of Finance, Graduate School of Business, Stanford University. The assistance and helpful suggestions of W. David Neibuhr and Stewart C. Myers are gratefully acknowledged.

(1) accept a project if the present value of all expected cash flows, discounted at the cost-of-capital rate, is greater than, or equal to, zero; and (2) accept a project if the internal rate of return (i.e., the discount rate which equates the present value of expected cash inflows with the present value of expected cash outflows) is greater than, or equal to, the firm's cost of capital.[1]

These two rules will lead to the same optimal selection of investment proposals if the following conditions hold:

1. A meaningful cost-of-capital rate does exist in the sense that the firm has access to capital at this cost.
2. There is no capital rationing. If a project meets the acceptance criterion, capital is available at the cost-of-capital rate to finance the project.
3. All projects, existing as well as proposed, have the same degree of risk, so that the acceptance or rejection of any project does not affect the cost of capital.
4. A meaningful, unique internal rate of return exists.

In the absence of these assumptions, the capital-budgeting decision becomes considerably more complex.[2] Inasmuch as the resulting problems do not affect the central thesis of this paper, we assume initially all four of the conditions listed above.

II. THE ABANDONMENT OPTION

The economic rationale behind the capital-budgeting decision rule can be applied directly to the abandonment decision. We submit that a project should be abandoned at that point in time when its abandonment value exceeds the net-present value of the project's subsequent expected future cash flows discounted at the cost-of-capital rate.[3] Using the internal rate-of-return method, the decision rule would be to abandon when the rate of return on abandonment value is less than the cost of capital. In either case, funds will be removed from a project whenever their incremental return is less than the minimum acceptable standard—namely, the cost of capital.[4]

Although the abandonment concept itself is quite simple, problems of measurement exist in estimating cash flows and abandonment value.

[1] See, for example, Solomon [13] and Bierman and Smidt [1], especially Chapters 2 and 3.

[2] See Lorie and Savage [6], Teichroew, Robichek, and Montalbano [14], and Weingartner [16].

[3] Dean [2] discusses this problem in the Appendix to his book.

[4] The existence of the abandonment possibility may affect the "riskiness" of the project. This aspect is considered in detail later in the paper.

Fortunately, the measurement of these factors has been analyzed ably elsewhere;[5] consequently, in this paper we shall not be concerned with how they may be determined. "Cash flows" are assumed to be all cash revenues that would be lost by abandonment less all cash expenses avoided. Abandonment value is assumed to represent the net disposal value of the project that would be available to the company in either cash or cash savings.[6]

III. EFFECT OF ABANDONMENT

When the possibility of future abandonment is recognized, what effect does it have upon project selection? We suggest that the effect may be quite dramatic and that altogether different selection decisions may be reached when abandonment is considered explicitly. To illustrate, consider the following example: Project A, costing $4,800 at time 0, is expected to generate cash flows over three years, after which time, there is no expected salvage value. The cash flows and their respective probabilities are shown in Table 1.[7] There are 27 possible sequences (or branches) of cash flows over the three-year period. For instance, sequence No. 11 represents a cash-flow pattern of $2,000 in year 1, $1,000 in year 2, and $1,000 in year 3. The joint probability of each sequence of cash flows is shown in the last column of the table. For sequence No. 11, the probability of occurrence is $(\frac{1}{2} \times \frac{1}{4} \times \frac{1}{2} = \frac{1}{16} = \frac{4}{64})$. The abandonment value at the end of each period is shown below the cash flows; this value is $3,000 at the end of the first year, $1,900 at the end of the second, and zero at the end of the third year.[8] After the

---

[5] For an excellent discussion on measuring cash flows and abandonment value, see Shillinglaw's two articles [11] and [12]. For a somewhat related discussion involving replacement, see Moore [9].

[6] See Shillinglaw [11], p. 270.

[7] For additional discussion of decision trees, see Magee [7].

[8] For simplicity, we assume that the abandonment values over time are known and invariant with respect to the cash-flow patterns. For many projects, these assumptions are not unreasonable. For example, general-purpose buildings and machine tools are likely to have abandonment values that are, to a great extent, invariant with the results of operations for which they are used. When the assumptions are inappropriate, the proposed approach can be modified by specifying probability distributions for the abandonment values.

The modifications would fall into two basic categories depending on whether the abandonment values: (a) vary independently of the expected cash-flow patterns; or (b) are correlated in some measure with them. In the first case, the decision rule is to abandon the project at that point in time when the *expected* abandonment value at the end of time *t* exceeds the present value of the project's expected subsequent cash flows. In the second case, different expected abandonment values would be projected for the different "branches" of cash flows. The decision rule would be to abandon a project at that point in time when the expected abandonment value *for the particular cash flow branch* exceeds the present value of expected subsequent cash flows for that branch.

TABLE 1
Expected future cash flows for Project A

Period 1		Period 2		Period 3			
Cash flow	Probability	Cash flow	Conditional probability	Cash flow	Conditional probability	Cash flow sequence number	Probability of sequence (in 64ths)
		0	.25	−$1,000	.25	1	1/64
				− 500	.50	2	2/64
				0	.25	3	1/64
$1,000	.25	$ 500	.50	− 500	.25	4	2/64
				0	.50	5	4/64
				500	.25	6	2/64
		1,000	.25	0	.25	7	1/64
				1,000	.50	8	2/64
				2,000	.25	9	1/64
		1,000	.25	0	.25	10	2/64
				1,000	.50	11	4/64
				2,000	.25	12	2/64
2,000	.50	2,000	.50	1,000	.25	13	4/64
				2,000	.50	14	8/64
				3,000	.25	15	4/64
		3,000	.25	2,000	.25	16	2/64
				3,000	.50	17	4/64
				4,000	.25	18	2/64
		2,000	.25	1,000	.25	19	1/64
				2,000	.50	20	2/64
				3,000	.25	21	1/64
3,000	.25	3,000	.50	2,000	.25	22	2/64
				3,000	.50	23	4/64
				4,000	.25	24	2/64
		3,500	.25	3,000	.25	25	1/64
				3,500	.50	26	2/64
				4,000	.25	27	1/64
Abandonment Value at End of Period $3,000		$1,900					

third year, the project is not expected to provide any cash flow or residual value.

If we assume that the firm's cost of capital is 10 percent, then the expected net-present value of Project A can be computed.[9] The proce-

---

[9] While this example is analyzed in terms of the net-present value, it also could be analyzed in terms of the internal rate of return.

dure involves the following steps: (1) compute the net-present value for each cash flow sequence; (2) obtain the *expected* net-present value by multiplying the computed net-present value by the probability of occurrence of the sequence;[10] and (3) add the expected net-present values for all sequences.

When we follow this procedure for Project A, we find that the expected net-present value is —$144.23. Since this value is less than zero, the project is unacceptable under conventional standards. However, when we allow for abandonment, the results for the project are changed. Recall that the decision rule is to abandon a project if the abandonment value exceeds the expected cash flows for all subsequent periods, discounted at the cost-of-capital rate. Applying this rule to Project A, a revised set of relevant expected cash-flow sequences is obtained.[11] For example, if the cash flow in period 1 turned out to be $1,000, the only relevant cash-flow sequences would be 1 through 9 in Table 1. The project would be abandonment at the end of period 1 because the sum of the expected net-present value of cash flows for sequences 1 through 9 for periods 2 and 3 discounted to period 1 ($577.86) is less than the abandonment value at the end of period 1 ($3,000). Consequently, for the "branch" encompassing sequences 1 through 9 in Table 1, the cash flow for period 1 becomes $4,000 (i.e., the sum of the $1,000 cash flow during the period plus the abandonment value of $3,000); and there are no cash flows in the remaining two periods. Similarly, it is found that abandonment takes place at the end of period 2 for the cash-flow sequences 10 through 12, 13 through 15, and 19 through 21 in Table 1. The expected net-present values of cash flows for the above three "branches" for period 3 discounted to period 2 ($909.09, $1,818.18, and $1,818.18, respectively) are less than the abandonment value at the end of period 2 ($1,900). For the branch encompassing cash-flow sequences 10 through 12, the cash flow for period 2 becomes $2,900; and for the two branches encompassing sequences 13 through 15 and 19 through 21, the cash flow becomes $3,900 for each branch. Taking account of these changes, the revised cash-flow sequences are shown in Table 2.

Based upon the cash-flow information in Table 2, the expected net-present value for Project A is now recalculated and found to be $535.25—a considerable improvement over the —$144.23 calculated before. Whereas the project would have been rejected previously, the con-

---

[10] For example, the expected net-present value for sequence No. 11 ($E(NPV_{11})$) is determined as follows:

$$E(NPV_{11}) = \left[-4,800 + \frac{2,000}{(1+.10)} + \frac{1,000}{(1+.10)^2} + \frac{1,000}{(1+.10)^3} \right] (\tfrac{4}{64}) = -87.76.$$

[11] If the project is abandoned, the cash flows lost are those in Table 1.

TABLE 2
Expected future cash flows for Project A with the consideration of
abandonment values

Period 1		Period 2		Period 3		Cash flow sequence number	Probability of sequence (in 64ths)
Cash flow	Probability	Cash flow	Conditional probability	Cash flow	Conditional probability		
$4,000	.25	0		0		1	16/64
		2,900	.25	0		2	8/64
2,000	.50	3,900	.50	0		3	16/64
				2,000	.25	4	2/64
		3,000	.25	3,000	.50	5	4/64
				4,000	.25	6	2/64
		3,900	.25	0		7	4/64
				2,000	.25	8	2/64
3,000	.25	3,000	.50	3,000	.50	9	4/64
				4,000	.25	10	2/64
				3,000	.25	11	1/64
		3,500	.25	3,500	.50	12	2/64
				4,000	.25	13	1/64

sideration of the abandonment option results in the acceptance of the project.

The discussion so far serves to illustrate the importance of considering abandonment value when evaluating projects. The funds committed to some projects may be far more flexible than those committed to others. Not to take account of the possible mobility of funds and to regard all outlays as sunk overlooks an extremely important dimension. Such an omission may provide very misleading information for decision making and may result in capital-budgeting decisions that are sub-optimal.

IV. SIMULATION AND THE ABANDONMENT OPTION

In the preceding section of this paper, the attempt was made to show how the possibility of abandonment may affect the investment decision. To illustrate the problem, a relatively simple example was used—Project A, which had a total of 27 possible cash-flow sequences. While this Project was useful for purposes of illustration, most projects under consideration are considerably more complex with respect to the possible number of cash-flow sequences. As a result, the approach illustrated above that evaluates each separate cash-flow sequence becomes unfeasible.

In practice, it is often true that management has reasonably good knowledge of the possible range of cash flows to be expected from a project.[12] If probability distributions of these cash flows over time can

---

[12] For example, Grayson [3] has been successful in obtaining probabilistic information relating to possible cash flows of oil exploration projects.

be specified, Monte Carlo simulation[13] may serve as a practical substitute for the "all inclusive" approach described earlier. To illustrate the application of simulation techniques to the problem at hand, consider Project B, which has an estimated life of ten years, no expected salvage value, and expected cash flows and abandonment values as shown in Table 3.

TABLE 3
Expected cash flows and abandonment values for Project B (dollars)

					Year					
0	*1*	*2*	*3*	*4*	*5*	*6*	*7*	*8*	*9*	*10*
Expected Cash Flow										
−6,145	1,000	1,000	1,000	1,000	1,000	1,000	1,000	1,000	1,000	1,000
Expected Abandonment Value										
—	6,200	5,700	5,180	4,580	3,980	3,300	2,570	1,780	920	0

If no account is taken of the possibility of abandonment, the internal rate of return for this Project is 10 percent. If a discount rate of 8 percent is assumed, the Project has an expected net-present value of $565.

Assume now that the abandonment values and the cash outflow in year 0, shown in Table 3, are known with certainty, but that the expected cash flows for years 1 through 10 are random variables distributed normally with a constant standard deviation of $100. We must specify also whether the yearly cash flows are independent of each other (i.e., the "actual" cash flows in any one period do not affect the cash flows of subsequent periods) or whether, in some measure, they are correlated over time.[14] The latter relationship is considered to be more representative of the real world; consequently, we specify in our simulation approach a provision to generate revised cash forecasts as "actual" simulated cash flows deviate from expected cash flows. The particular manner in which forecasts are revised is described fully in the Appendix.[15]

The net-present value and the internal rate of return for Project B are simulated 100 times with the consideration of abandonment and 100 times without the abandonment option. We specified that in simulating with the abandonment option, the decision rule to abandon was identical

---

[13] Monte Carlo simulation is a technique which investigates the implications of uncertainty in a systematic manner. The readers who are unfamiliar with this approach will find it described in most basic Operations Research texts. For one such description, see Sasieni, Yaspan, and Friedman [10], pp. 58–67.

[14] See Hillier [5], especially pp. 447–449.

[15] The form of the cash-forecast revision rule was selected solely to illustrate the methodology of Monte Carlo simulation. We were not concerned particularly with the rule's realism, because in practice each project faces a distinct set of circumstances.

in form to the one described in connection with Project A—abandon the project at the end of year t if the revised expected cash flows for years t + 1 through 10, discounted at 8 percent to year t, are less than the abandonment value at year t. A detailed description of this rule is given in the Appendix. The simulation results are summarized in Table 4.

TABLE 4
Results of simulation for Project B

	Net present value		Internal rate of return	
	Without abandonment	*With abandonment*	*Without abandonment*	*With abandonment*
Expected Value........	$672	$991	9.83%	13.62%

Note that for the "without abandonment" option there are differences between the simulated expected values in Table 4 and the calculated expected values based upon the data in Table 3. For the net-present value case, the simulated mean value is $672, as compared with a calculated value of $565; for the internal rate of return, the simulated mean value is 9.83 percent, while the computed value is 10.0 percent. These differences are insignificant statistically,[16] and we conclude that the simulation technique described approximates fairly the actual distributions of net-present value and internal rate of return for Project B.

It is seen in Table 4 that explicit consideration of the abandonment option results in a significant increase in Project B's expected value of return, whether this return is measured in terms of the net-present value or of the internal rate of return. Based upon the simulation undertaken, Figure 1 shows the frequency with which abandonment takes place for each year of Project B's life. For this particular simulation, the project is abandoned before the end of its originally estimated useful life in 70 percent of the cases. Clearly, the abandonment results would be different under alternative assumptions as to: abandonment values; expected cash flows; distribution of cash flows; the manner in which forecasts are revised; and the discount rate.

V. THE ABANDONMENT OPTION AND PROJECT RISK

Our discussion thus far has been limited to capital-budgeting decisions solely based upon expected net-present value or internal rate of return. This limitation was in order because of our assumption that all projects

---

[16] The differences in means between simulated and calculated value is less than .08 standard deviations for the net-present value and about .03 standard deviations for the internal rate of return.

FIGURE 1
Frequency of abandonment of Project B before end of
estimated useful life

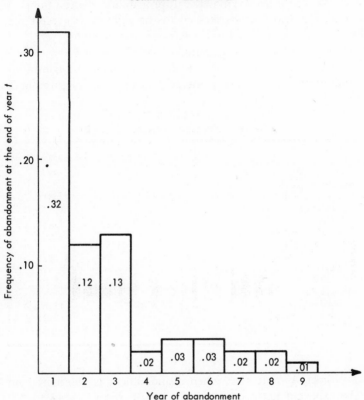

Year of abandonment

are of "equal risk." Specifically, Projects A and B are assumed to be
"equally risky," whether evaluated with or without the abandonment option. In this section it is demonstrated that the presence of abandonment value may reduce the "risk" of a project over that which would
be present if there were no abandonment value. By a reduction in risk,
we mean either or both of the following: (1) A lower variance of the
probability distribution around the expected value of returns;[17] and (2)
a shift in the skewness of the probability distribution toward the right,
reducing both the range and the magnitude of undesirable returns, i.e.,
those to the left of the expected value of returns.

In order to evaluate the effect that abandonment value has upon risk,
let us consider Projects A and B both with and without the abandonment
option. In this regard, we can compute such measures of risk as the

[17] For a discussion of expected return and variance as they relate to capital
budgeting, see Hertz [4], Hillier [5], and Van Horne [15].

variance, V, the standard deviation, S, and the semi-variance, SV.[18] In addition, a measure of relative skewness can be obtained by computing the ratio V/2SV. For symmetrical probability distributions, V/2SV equals one; for distributions skewed to the right, it is greater than one; and for distributions skewed to the left, it is less than one.

In addition to the expected value of returns, S and the ratio V/2SV were computed for Projects A and B and without the consideration of the abandonment option. The principal results are summarized in Table 5.

TABLE 5
Selected values for Projects A and B

	Without abandonment	*With abandonment*
Project A		
Net Present Value:		
Expected Value................	$—144	$ 535
Standard Deviation.............	2,372	1,522
V/2SV......................	.945	1.29
Project B (Simulated Values)		
Net Present Value:		
Expected Value................	$ 672	$ 991
Standard Deviation.............	1,422	888
V/2SV......................	1.01	2.96
Internal Rate of Return:		
Expected Rate................	$9.83%	13.62%
Standard Deviation.............	5.31	2.25
V/2SV......................	.75	1.25

For Project A, note that when abandonment is considered not only does the expected net-present value increase from —$144 to $535, but the standard deviation decreases from $2,372 to $1,522. Also, the skewness of the probability distribution of net-present values changes from slightly negative to positive. This latter result suggests that much of the downside risk can be eliminated if the Project is abandoned when events turn unfavorable. Figure 2 illustrates this point graphically—it depicts the cumulative probability distribution for Project A with and without the consideration of abandonment. For example, with abandonment, there is a 48/64 probability that the Project will provide an expected net-present value of more than zero; without abandonment, the probability

---

[18] Semi-variance is the variance of the probability distribution to the left of expected net-present value and may be thought to represent a measure of downside risk. Mathematically, it can be expressed as

$$SV(X) = \sum_{i=1}^{m} \{[X_i - E(X)]^2 P(X)_i\}$$

where X_i is the observation, $E(X)$ is the expected net-present value, $P(X_i)$ the probability of the event X_i, and m denotes the number of observations to the left of the mean. See Markowitz [8], p. 191.

is only 40/64 that the net present value will be greater than zero. Moreover, with abandonment, there is no probability that the expected net-present value will be less than —$1,164; while without abandonment, there is an 18/64 probability that it will be less than this amount.[19] For a given probability, the expected net-present value is higher with abandonment value than without through probability 27/64, after which the expected net-present values are about the same for both distributions.[20]

For Project B, a comparison of the simulation results, with and without the abandonment option, yields conclusions similar to those arrived at from the analysis of data for Project A. Again, consideration of the abandonment option results in a number of desirable occurrences: the expected value of returns (either net-present value or internal rate of return) increases; the standard deviation decreases; and the skewness of the probability distributions shifts to the right. The distributions of individual simulation values for Project B follow the general pattern illustrated in Figure 2 for Project A, and we shall not reproduce them here.

In our analysis, the acceptance or rejection of any project was assumed not to change the discount rate, i.e., the firm's cost of capital. The effect that the acceptance of a project will have on the discount rate will depend upon the characteristics of existing investments, the manner in which the project's expected returns are related to the expected returns of other projects, and the expectations and preferences of investors and lenders. The determination of this effect is extremely complex; and, inasmuch as it does not invalidate any of the basic tenets of this paper, we do not attempt to deal with it here.[21] We would suggest, however, that the acceptance of Project A (or B) with the possibility of abandonment is likely to result in a more favorable change (if a change takes place) in the discount rate then would occur from the acceptance of Project A (or B) without the abandonment option.

VI. CONCLUSIONS

Any estimate of future cash flows implies that a particular operating strategy will be followed. All too often, however, this strategy is not stated explicitly. Specifically, the consideration of possible abandonment is a dimension frequently omitted from capital-budgeting analysis. As illustrated in our examples, significant abandonment values for a project may result in a higher expected net-present value or internal rate of

---

[19] Since Figure 2 is in terms of discrete probability distributions this probability is denoted by the first dot to the left of the point where net-present value equals zero.

[20] For illustrative purposes, the same cost of capital rate was used to discount the subsequent cash flows for each event-tree. In practice, there may be situations when this approach is not completely appropriate.

[21] In this paper, we do not consider the portfolio problem of risk to the firm as a whole. For an analysis of this problem, see Van Horne [15].

FIGURE 2
Cumulative probability distributions—Project A

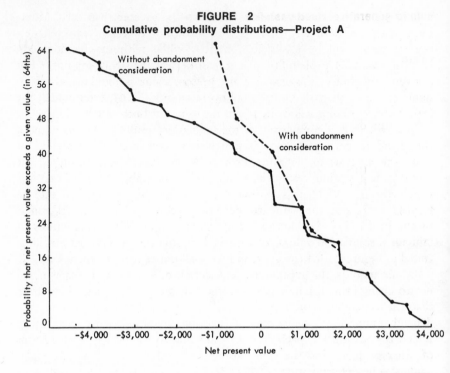

return and lower expected risk than would be the case if the project had no abandonment value over its economic life. It is important to take account of the fact that different investment projects provide different degrees of flexibility with respect to the possible mobility of funds if the project turns bad. To ignore these differences may result in sub-optimal investment decision. Since having the option to abandon never decreases project value, the typical consequences of ignoring the option would be to underestimate the value of a project. The framework proposed in this paper allows the firm to incorporate the possibility of abandonment into its capital-budgeting procedures.

APPENDIX

Description of the simulation model

Let

$EC_{t.\tau}$ = expected cash flow in year t as of year τ.

AV_t = abandonment value in year t.

AC_t = "actual" simulated cash flow in year t.

The values for AV_t and $EC_{t.o}$ are input as given in Table 3.

Rule to generate revised cash flow forecasts

$$EC_{t.\tau} = EC_{t.\tau-1}[1 + X\alpha],\qquad(1)$$

where

$$X = \frac{AC_\tau - EC_{\tau.\tau-1}}{EC_{\tau.\tau-1}},$$

and α varies depending on the values of X as shown below.

	If	$-.05 \le X \le .05$	then	$\alpha = 0$
If $-.10 \le \alpha < -.05$	or	$.05 < X \le .10$	then	$\alpha = .5$
If $-.15 \le \alpha < -.10$	or	$.10 < X \le .15$	then	$\alpha = 1.0$
If $-.20 \le \alpha < -.15$	or	$.15 < X \le .20$	then	$\alpha = 1.5$
If $-.20 > X$	or	$X > .20$	then	$\alpha = 2.0$

In words, the above rule revises the expected cash flow forecasts as of year τ for subsequent years if $(X\alpha)$ differs from zero, where X represents the percentage difference between "actual" simulated cash flows and "expected" cash flows and α is a parameter dependent upon X. For example, if the "actual" cash flow in year 5 were 4 percent greater than the "expected" cash flow for year 5 as of year 4, α would be zero, and the expected cash flows for all subsequent years (as of year 5) would remain the same as of year 4. On the other hand, if the "actual" cash flows were 18 percent less than the "expected" cash flows, all subsequent cash flows would be revised downward by 27 percent.

$$[X\alpha = (-.18)(1.5) = -.27].$$

Decision rule to abandon

Given all $EC_{t.\tau}$ for $\tau < t \le 10$, compute for all $\tau < 10$ the discounted present value of cash flows in Eq. 2:

$$PV_\tau = \sum_{t=\tau+1}^{10} \frac{EC_{t.\tau}}{(1 + .08)^{(t-\tau)}}\qquad(2)$$

If PV_τ M AV_τ then continue simulation.

If $PV_\tau < AV_\tau$ abandon project; in this case AC_τ (final) $= AC_\tau + AV_\tau$ and all $EC_{t.\tau} = 0$ for $t > \tau$.

Compute net-present value and rate of return

After all the final cash flows are determined for each run j, compute the net-present value in (Eq. 3) and rate of return from (Eq. 4):

$$NPV_j = -6145 + \sum_{t=1}^{10} \frac{AC_t}{(1 + .08)^t}; \tag{3}$$

Solve for R_j in (Eq. 4)

$$6145 = \sum_{t=1}^{10} \frac{AC_t}{(1 + R_j)^t}. \tag{4}$$

Complete simulation

Go to next simulation run. Run simulation 100 times and compute mean, variance, standard deviation, and semi-variance.

REFERENCES

1. H. Bierman, Jr., and S. Smidt, *The Capital Budgeting Decision*. New York: Macmillan Co., 1966.
2. J. Dean. *Capital Budgeting*. New York: Columbia University Press, 1951, pp. 163–68.
3. C. J. Grayson. *Decision under Uncertainty*. Cambridge, Mass.: Harvard University, 1960.
4. D. B. Hertz. "Risk Analysis in Capital Budgeting," *Harvard Business Review*, Vol. 42 (January–February 1964), pp. 95–106.
5. F. S. Hillier. "The Derivation of Probabilistic Information for the Evaluation of Risky Investments," *Management Science*, Vol. 9 (April 1963), pp. 443–57.
6. J. H. Lorie and L. J. Savage. "Three Problems in Rationing Capital," *Journal of Business*, Vol. 28 (October 1955), pp. 229–39.
7. J. F. Magee. "How to Use Decision Trees in Capital Investment," *Harvard Business Review*, Vol. 42 (September–October 1964), pp. 79–96.
8. H. M. Markowitz. *Portfolio Selection*. New York: John Wiley & Sons, 1959.
9. C. L. Moore. "The Present-Value Method and the Replacement Decision," *Accounting Review*, Vol. 39 (January 1964), pp. 94–102.
10. M. Sasieni, A. Yaspan, and L. Friedman. *Operations Research—Methods and Problems*. New York: John Wiley & Sons, Inc., 1959.
11. G. Shillinglaw. "Profit Analysis for Abandonment Decisions," reprinted in E. Solomon, (ed.), *The Management of Corporate Capital*. Glencoe, Ill.: The Free Press of Glencoe, 1959, pp. 269–81.
12. G. Shillinglaw. "Residual Values in Investment Analysis," reprinted in E. Solomon, (ed.), *The Management of Corporate Capital*. Glencoe, Ill.: The Free Press of Glencoe, 1959, pp. 259–68.

13. E. Solomon. "The Arithmetic of Capital—Budgeting Decisions," *Journal of Business*, Vol. 29 (April 1956), pp. 124–29.

14. D. Teichroew, A. A. Robichek, and M. Montalbano. "An Analysis of Criteria for Investment and Financing Decisions under Certainty," *Management Science*, Vol. 12 (November, 1965), pp. 151–79.

15. J. C. Van Horne. "The Capital-Budgeting Decision Involving Combinations of Risky Investments," *Management Science*, Vol. 13 (October 1966), pp. B84–92.

16. H. M. Weingartner. *Mathematical Programming and the Analysis of Capital Budgeting Problems.* Englewood Cliffs, N.J.: Prentice-Hall, Inc., 1963.

part IV
Cost of capital and dividend policy

PACIFIC TELEPHONE AND TELEGRAPH COMPANY

The Pacific Telephone and Telegraph Company[1] filed an application on February 10, 1967 with the California Public Utilities Commission (CPUC), seeking authority to increase rates and charges for telephone service provided by them within the state of California. The increase asked for by Pacific would raise their revenues by approximately $181,356,000 annually.

In the course of the proceedings, the five members of the CPUC heard testimony from 83 witnesses, who presented 221 exhibits. The actual record before them as they began final deliberations contained 12,600 pages in 86 volumes. Their task was to evaluate the evidence and reach a final majority decision that would establish a rate of return for Pacific. They felt that the rate of return to be assigned would have to meet the test of reasonableness prescribed by the U.S. Supreme Court[2] and give adequate and fair compensation to the suppliers of capital without unnecessarily burdening the ratepayers.

Each of the commissioners realized that in arriving at his decision he would have to consider a great many factors including investment in plant, cost of money, dividend price and earning price ratios, territory served, growth factor, comparative rate levels, diversification of revenues, public relations, management, financial policies, reasonable construction requirements, prevailing interest rates and other economic conditions, the trend of rate of return, past financing success, future outlook for the utility, outstanding securities and those proposed to be issued. Additional factors to be considered were adequacy of the service, rate history, customer acceptance and usage developed under existing rates, value of the

---

[1] Referred to hereafter as Pacific.

[2] *FPC* v. *Hope Natural Gas Co.*, 320 U.S. 591, 603 (1944).

service, and cost to serve. No one of these factors would be solely determinative of what might constitute reasonableness of earnings, rates, or rate of return.

The CPUC had analyzed the operations of Pacific on a number of occasions. In fact, in the period 1946–67, Pacific had presented a series of rate increase requests and other requests that had occupied the CPUC and its staff almost continuously. Among these proceedings had been 10 major rate cases applied for by Pacific and one exhaustive investigation undertaken by the CPUC's own motion. The last case submitted by Pacific was on July 26, 1962, with an interim decision issued by the CPUC in 1964, and a final decision being issued on November 23, 1966. This decision granted Pacific a rate increase of $6,100,000 annually and set the rate of return Pacific was allowed to earn at 6.3 percent of the adopted rate base.[3]

The Pacific Telephone and Telegraph Company was one of 21 principal telephone operating subsidiaries of American Telephone and Telegraph Company. The operating subsidiaries, together with two operating companies in the United States in which the American company owns less than a majority interest, were termed Associated Companies. AT&T also owned Western Electric Company, Inc., which manufactured and installed equipment for the Associated Companies and Long Lines Department (connects operating companies) of AT&T.

A.T.&T. and Western Electric each owned 50 percent of the outstanding capital stock of Bell Telephone Laboratories, Inc., which was the research and development organization for the Bell System. The Associated Companies, Western Electric, and Bell Telephone Laboratories together with the American company formed the Bell System.

The Pacific Telephone and Telegraph Company was incorporated under the laws of the state of California on December 31, 1906, as a reorganization of Pacific States Telephone and Telegraph Company, following the fire of that year.

The earliest predecessors of the present Pacific Company are considered to be the Gold and Stock Telegraph Company and the National Bell Telephone Company of San Francisco. The Gold and Stock Telegraph Company, which was a subsidiary of the Western Union Telegraph Company, installed the first exchange switchboard in California at 222 Sansome Street, San Francisco, early in 1878. Shortly after this first exchange was installed by the Gold and Stock Company, the National Bell Telephone Company of San Francisco was organized as a licensee of the National Bell Telephone Company of Boston, Massachusetts, the latter being the first telephone corporation formed by Alexander Graham Bell and his associates. After about two years of intense competition

---

[3] Rate base is the average net plant, cash, and materials and supplies.

in San Francisco, the National Bell Telephone Company of San Francisco and the Gold and Stock Telegraph Company, together with the latter's subsidiary, the American Speaking Telephone Company, were consolidated in 1880 to form the Pacific Bell Telephone Company.

In this same year of 1880, the first exchange in Los Angeles was inaugurated by the Los Angeles Telephone Company, serving only seven telephones for a population of 10,000 people. This company was acquired in 1883 by the Sunset Telephone-Telegraph Company, which was organized in that year under the same management as Pacific Bell Telephone Company, for the purpose of operating in the Pacific Coast territory outside of San Francisco.

In 1889, the Pacific Bell Telephone Company was reincorporated as the Pacific Telephone and Telegraph Company, which acquired Pacific Bell's interest in the Sunset Telephone and Telegraph Company, the latter having succeeded the majority of the stock in the Oregon, and the Inland Telephone and Telegraph Company, operating in eastern Washington.

The first Pacific Telephone and Telegraph Company was succeeded in 1900 by the Pacific States Telephone and Telegraph Company, which was later reorganized on December 31, 1906 as the present corporation, the Pacific Telephone and Telegraph Company. At the time of the formation of the latter company, the Pacific States Company owned and operated telephone systems in western Idaho, eastern Washington, northern Oregon, and in San Francisco. Pacific States Company owned all but directors' qualifying shares of the stock of the Sunset Company, which owned and operated telephone systems in western Washington, southern Oregon, the state of Nevada, and the state of California outside of San Francisco.

A number of independent competitive telephone companies were organized in the Pacific Coast states, beginning apparently in Sacramento in 1895. Among these were the Home Telephone Company of San Francisco and the Home Telephone Company of Alameda County, later combined into the Bay Cities Home Telephone Company. The Home Telephone and Telegraph Company of Los Angeles began operation in September 1903 in and about that city, employing a dial system installed by the Empire Construction Company. Over the years, a series of purchases and sales agreements finally resulted in the formation by the Pacific Company, on April 19, 1916, of the Southern California Telephone Company, a wholly owned subsidiary. The latter took over the properties of the Home Company and of the Sunset Company in and around Los Angeles and in 1930 acquired the properties and franchises of the Pacific Company in Southern California. Some of the latter had been purchased directly by the Pacific Company while others had been a part of the Sunset Company or had been acquired by this company.

Also in 1916, the Pacific Company took direct control over all the properties of the Sunset Company not included in the territory assigned to Southern California Telephone Company, with the exception of the Nevada operations. The latter had been transferred in 1913 to the Bell Telephone Company of Nevada, wholly owned by the Pacific Company and organized for this purpose.

On March 31, 1947, the Southern California Telephone Company was merged with the Pacific Telephone and Telegraph Company.

Pursuant to a plan of reorganization approved by its shareholders on March 24, 1961, Pacific transferred its business and properties in Washington, Oregon, and Idaho to Pacific Northwest Bell Telephone Company on June 30, 1961. In consideration, Pacific Northwest Bell Telephone Company issued 30,460,000 shares of its common stock with an aggregate par value of $334,950,000 and a 4½ percent demand note for $200,000,000. The Pacific Company had purchased 10,000 shares for $110,000 cash at the time of incorporation, March 27, 1961. The plan provided that within about three years after the transfer of assets, and at time related to its needs for new capital, the company would offer for sale to its shareholders the common stock of Pacific Northwest Bell Telephone Company. An initial offering was made in September 1961, and 17,446,031 shares were sold at $16 per share, with American Telephone and Telegraph purchasing 15,548,140, representing 51 percent of the total common stock. A second offering was made in June 1963, and the remaining 13,013,969 shares were sold at $16 per share. The plan also provided that within about three years after the transfer of assets, Pacific Northwest Bell Telephone Company would sell publicly several issues of debentures for the purpose of refunding $200 million demand note. Four $50 million debenture issues were sold during 1961, 1962, and 1963 and the final payment on the note was made in December 1963.

The growth of Pacific and the extension of its service facilities had been closely tied in with the expansion of population and business on the Pacific Coast. In recent decades, California had become the most populous state in the nation. While its population had grown, it had continued its vigorous economic development. California was the nation's largest defense and space contractor. It led all other states in retail sales and was first in total personal income. It ranked first in agriculture. It was also continuing its progress toward becoming the foremost manufacturing state.

Pacific's utility operations and service responsibilities were among the largest in the United States. Seventy-seven percent of California's 19 million population was served by Pacific. The capital invested in Pacific was greater than that of any telephone company in any other state or that of any other California utility.

Pacific spent more than $1,300,000,000 for new construction in the period 1964 to 1966 to keep abreast of California's population growth and economics development. The demand for service remained high, and Pacific felt that an additional outlay of about $2,100,000,000 would be required in the following three years.

By the end of 1966, Pacific had 8,855,830 telephones in service. Sixty-seven percent of 5,932,144 of these telephones were concentrated in the Los Angeles, San Francisco, East Bay, and San Diego metropolitan areas.

On December 31, 1966, Pacific's total assets exceeded $3,966 million (Exhibit 1). Total revenues for 1966 were over $1,454 million (Exhibit 2). Although this was a 9 percent increase over the previous year, earnings per share decreased for the second year in a row. Earnings per share were $1.18 compared to $1.24 in 1965, and $1.47 in 1964. Nevertheless, Pacific continued with its dividend policy and paid $1.20 per share of average common stock outstanding during the year. The decline in earnings and the constant dividend had caused the market price in Pacific's stock to decline substantially.

Pacific's application for a rate increase asked for earnings in the range of 7.5 to 8.5 percent on its net investment and earnings on equity capital in the range of 9.5 to 11.5 percent. They claimed such a range would bolster the market value of their stock and bring it equal with other investments of corresponding risks. Their rate proposals would increase its intrastate revenues (excluding toll) by about $168,000,000 and revenues from directories by about $13,000,000 and would produce a rate of return of 8.35 percent on its claimed and estimated 1967 rate base of $2,964,079,000.

The state of California required an application for rate increase to be based on a "test year." This could be any period selected by the applicant and could be a period previous to the application, a period based partially on actual and partially on estimated or it could be totally based on an estimated year. Pacific chose to base their operations on the "estimated year 1967." The Commission staff also used the same estimated period for its presentation. Exhibit 3 reflects the results of operations for this test year for Pacific.

The CPUC had heard three[4] expert witnesses offer opinion testimony on the subject of a proper intrastate rate of return for Pacific. Robert W. Mason, assistant vice president in charge of financial research in

---

[4] There were actually four witnesses who specifically offered testimony on the subject of rate of return. The fourth witness proposed a rate of return of 6.4 to 6.6 percent based on an earnings-price ratio analysis. This approach was based on the assumption that the average investor buys current earnings and near future earnings. The 6.4 to 6.6 percent rate of return was computed by taking the ratios of other Bell operating companies (6.26 percent) and applying a one-year lead, as a recognition of Pacific's recent decline in earnings. The lead was the relationship of average 1966 market price to estimated earnings per share for the year 1967. Since this approach differs from the other three approaches, it is entered only as a footnote for the student who wishes to analyze other avenues in his consideration of this case.

the secretary and treasury department of Pacific presented two variations of his interpretation of a "comparable earnings test" to recommend a rate of return of 7.5 to 8.5 percent. A CPUC staff witness recommended a return within the range of 6.85 to 7.10 percent on the basis of his judgment, relying primarily on his experience in dealing with the cost of money and rate of return studies in the regulatory field. Manual Kroman, a senior public utilities engineer in the Department of Public Utilities and Transportation, City of Los Angeles, concluded the appropriate rate of return should be 6.75 percent. His conclusion was reached by analyzing Pacific's individual risk and the changes which had occurred in financial conditions since the CPUC's last finding as to a reasonable return for Pacific.

The members of the CPUC agreed that the issues raised by these witnesses were the most important and they felt a final conclusion would be reached after a careful review of their testimony and exhibits.

Mason claimed that Pacific's earnings were the lowest among major telephone companies in the United States. He presented considerable evidence to show that Pacific's earnings did not meet the comparable earnings standard established by the U.S. Supreme Court. To set the stage for his two earnings tests, he explored some of the changes in financial conditions since 1962, which he thought warranted a new look at the current adequacy of the 6.3 percent rate of return.

Exhibit 4 showed yield at market price on high-grade public utility bonds (Moody's Aaa), Pacific's and U.S. government long-term maturities for the previous five years. The data reflected an increase of about 20 percent in bond costs over the 1962 level. This sharp rise was attributed to a growing shortage in the supply of investment funds relative to demand and to investors' fear of further inflation which would reduce the purchasing power of their bond investments at maturity.

Exhibit 5 showed Pacific's outstanding debentures and corresponding interest and amortization expense. Since 1962 Pacific had sold three additional debenture issues. The effect of these sales of additional debentures, at a cost considerably higher than the imbedded cost of bonds outstanding in 1962, had been to raise the current imbedded costs of Pacific's debentures by 11 percent over the 1962 level.

Exhibit 6 reflected the cost of Pacific's short-term borrowings and the prime rate for business loans. The data shows that Pacific's interest rate had risen 20 percent over the 1962 level. To show that the market for common stock had been affected by the sharp increase in debt costs, Mason introduced Exhibit 7. He felt that the decline in market values of about 15 percent indicated that investors were seeking higher returns on common equity investments because of the new higher bond costs and the associated increased risks to common equity brought on by these higher costs. He also pointed out that Pacific's common stock had followed a downward trend somewhat greater than that of other utilities due to the reduction in the earnings level of Pacific as contrasted with the continued upward trend in common equity earnings generally. As shown in Exhibit 8 the average return for 250 of the largest companies in the United States increased by over 10 percent, while Pacific's earnings on common equity declined 14 percent.

Having pointed out the changes in capital costs, Mason set about applying his first comparable earnings test. He selected data from 250 companies with comparable common equity risks. The companies he used included the 50 largest electric, 50 largest gas and 50 largest telephone companies, the 50 largest banks and the 50 largest industrial companies in the United States.

Mason measured risk by applying the definition given in Webster's Dictionary, i.e., risk is the "probability of loss." Exhibit 9 shows how he determined the probability of decline in the percent return on common equity. His measurement equated risk to the probability of a decrease in earnings from one period to the next. He had decided not to show increases because he had done so in his testimony for Pacific's last application and he had been severely ridiculed by rebuttal testimony for doing so. Mason applied his theory to each of the 250 companies and determined that as risk increases, return increases. He also concluded from his analysis that the 25 companies with an average risk corresponding to Pacific's earned an average 10.83 percent from 1962 to 1967 with a high of 11.14 percent in 1965. He, therefore, thought Pacific should have a 10–11 percent return.

Mason's second approach toward applying the test of comparable earnings was to use a "comparable operating characteristics" test. He presented the earnings of 20 other Bell System companies over the past five-year period and compared these with Pacific's earnings over the same period. (See Exhibit 10.) He concluded that Pacific would need to earn 9.50 to 10.25 percent on its common equity in order to realize the average return on total capital reflected by the other Bell companies.

Mason did not stop there. In a third test, he measured corresponding risks in terms of corresponding capital structure, i.e., companies with common equity ratios of 50 to 70 percent. His analysis shows (Exhibit 11) that the companies received average common equity returns ranging from 9.5 percent for the period 1961–65 to 11 percent in 1965.

The next rate of return witness to provide testimony was the Commission Staff witness who stated that "a proper rate of return recommendation cannot be based solely on the study of comparable companies." He felt that it should be determined by the particular circumstances of the individual utility. Earnings of other utilities could be an indication of what a company should earn, but such information should only be a starting point toward the determination of the overall cost of capital in a test for a reasonable rate of return on the rate base. He also considered cost of capital an important part of a fair rate of return study but it was not necessarily synonymous with a fair rate of return. Other things which he thought worthy of consideration were: (1) Capital structure of the specific utility, (2) Relationship between net investment or rate base, on one hand, and total capital on the other, (3) Plant requirements of the utility in the immediate future, (4) Availability of internally generated financing, and (5) Estimated amount and nature of external financing in the immediate future and the interest rates and terms of such financing.

A fair summary of his basic ideas was: "There is no simple cost of capital or other mathematical formula which can be strictly followed, and in the end careful and informal judgment must be utilized." Exhibit 12 summarizes the effects of various assumed rates of returns on common equity plus the imbedded costs of long-term debt and preferred stock to produce expected rates of return. Then, using the same kind of analysis, the staff witness shows (Exhibit 13) the range of recommended rates of return based on his analysis of the specific historical data of Pacific as applied to an adjusted rate base (Exhibit 14). This range, he felt, would "achieve the goal of capital attraction and adequately compensate for risk."

In arriving at his adjusted rate base, he considered intrastate versus interstate operations, prices paid for equipment purchased from Western Electric, an AT&T subsidiary, state tax expense adjustment, adjustments in relief and pension fund interest rates, and the change which would result if Pacific used accelerated depreciation methods.

The last rate of return witness was the witness for the City of Los Angeles, Manual Kroman. He began his testimony by evaluating the risk factor as presented by Pacific's witness. Kroman points out that the probable magnitude of earnings decline, illustrated by Exhibit 9, is a function of only one variable and is nothing more than the sum of earnings declines divided by the number of observations. He argued that it was necessary to give recognition to the level of earnings, to the trend of earnings, to the sequence of changes in earnings and to increases in earnings. He used hypothetical examples to support his argument. (See Exhibits 15 and 16.)

Turning to Mason's calculation of a common equity risk factor for each of the 250 companies, Kroman asserts that Pacific has a risk factor that is less than the median risk of each group. This is illustrated by Exhibit 17 which also shows that out of 250 companies, 187 have a common equity risk higher than Pacific's. Kroman also interjected disparities in the operating and financial characteristics of the 25 companies having common equity risk corresponding to Pacific's (Exhibit 18). To further dispute Mason's recommended rate of return, Kroman introduced rates of return allowed other Bell System companies in the previous decade. (See Exhibit 19.) He found the median of these allowed rates of return to be 6.50 percent.

Kroman's approach toward reaching a recommendation for a rate of return differed from that of all the other witnesses. He started with the 6.3 percent rate of return last found by the CPUC to be fair and reasonable for Pacific and reviewed the effects of that rate of return in the light of Pacific's present claims and circumstances which had occurred since such rate was determined. He felt the extensive amount of evidence presented in the last rate of return case and the fact that the CPUC's decision was affirmed by the California Supreme Court made the 6.3 percent rate particularly significant as a starting point for his current recommendation. The capital costs and ratios imputed to the last decision are shown in Exhibit 20.

With that background, Kroman proceeded to update the imbedded cost of Pacific's debt and the cost of advances from AT&T to Pacific. He calculated that the new weighted capital cost[5] based on the increased cost of debt would require an increase in rate of return from 6.3 to 6.478. However, he didn't believe that the increase in interest rates he computed was the sole basis for determining an increased rate of return.

Another consideration Kroman thought important was the relationship between Pacific's intrastate and interstate rates of return. He felt there should be substantial differences between intrastate and interstate rates of return, with the intrastate rate of return being lower to reflect the greater stability and lesser risk of such business.[6] His opinion, based on studies in this area, was that interstate operations were much more sensitive to changes in business conditions and were also increasingly competitive.

The last factor Kroman determined important to his recommendation was Pacific's earnings per share and dividend policy. Exhibit 21 shows a 10-year record of Pacific's common stock earnings and dividends per share and the percent dividend payout. Based on the 1967 estimated earnings at actual rate of return the current allowed rate of return, and a 6.50 percent and a 6.75 percent rate of return, Kroman concluded that a 6.75 percent rate of return would result in earnings per share and dividend coverage in line with Pacific's experience in the early 1960s and much improved over its experience in the past few years.

In determining the allowed rate of return, the Commission had to weigh the many tangible and intangible economic factors presented by the witnesses covering that subject. Each set of testimony had to be considered not as conclusive in and of itself, but as an attempt by each

---

[5] The cost of debt for Pacific as for all utility firms is computed on a before tax basis. This unusual measure is necessary to avoid considering tax twice in determining with the amount of required earnings.

[6] In July 1967, the Federal Communications Commission allowed a 7 to 7½ percent rate of return on the interstate operations of AT&T and the Associated Bell System Companies.

witness to advise the Commission as to how the matter should be settled. By sorting out the differences and reconciling them, a pattern for reaching a conclusion could be developed. The final conclusion by the Commission was to be an "optimization" of the interests and goals of Pacific, its management and its investors on the one hand and those of consumers on the other hand. In general the goal of all utility regulation by public bodies was to maintain the best possible services for consumers at reasonable prices. At the same time, however, the Commission knew that merely setting "reasonable" prices would not automatically enable Pacific to obtain adequate financing to actually provide the required level of services. Pacific's success in financing its operation could not be "legislated" by the Commission. It would be a result of both Pacific's financial management skill and the desire of the capital market to provide capital to Pacific at costs which would allow satisfactory operations. For these reasons it was necessary to pay particular attention to the cost of capital, earning on equity and Pacific's dividend policy. Of course, theoretically, service should be maintained adequately even if the returns to Pacific's investors had to be reduced, but the Commission was well aware of the possibility of both returns and service being reduced if Pacific's financing proved inadequate.

EXHIBIT 1

PACIFIC TELEPHONE AND TELEGRAPH COMPANY

Balance sheet

as of December 31, 1966

ASSETS

Plant and other investments:

Telephone plant in service	$4,287,013,730
Telephone plant under construction	116,614,302
Property held for future telephone use	3,386,648
Telephone plant acquisition adjustment	112,116
	4,407,126,796
Less: Depreciation reserve	808,594,980
	3,598,531,816
Investments in, and advances to affiliated companies	80,100,000
Other investments	65,003
Miscellaneous physical property	1,097,024
	$3,679,793,843

Current Assets:

Cash	21,869,389
Special cash deposits	982,559
Working funds	641,253
Accounts receivable	188,106,433
Material and supplies	16,041,388
	$ 227,641,022

Prepaid Accounts and Deferred Charges:

Prepayments	41,363,836
Other deferred charges	17,306,886
	58,670,722
Total Assets	$3,966,105,587

EXHIBIT 1 (*Continued*)

LIABILITIES

Capital Stock and Surplus:	
Common stock—par value (14\frac{2}{7}$ per share) (Authorized—140,000,000 shares; Outstanding—125,715,921 shares)	$1,795,941,816
Preferred Stock—par value ($100 per share) 6 percent cumulative (authorized and outstanding 820,000 shares)	82,000,000
Premium on capital stock	97,906,489
Other capital surplus	146,989,667
Unappropriated earned surplus	264,484,809
	$2,387,322,781
Funded Debt:	
Thirty-Year 3$\frac{1}{4}$ percent debentures due March 1, 1978	75,000,000
Twenty-Seven Year 3$\frac{1}{4}$ percent debentures due November 15, 1979	35,000,000
Twenty-Three Year 5$\frac{1}{8}$ percent debentures due August 1, 1980	90,000,000
Thirty Year 3$\frac{1}{2}$ percent debentures due November 15, 1981	30,000,000
Thirty-Five Year 3$\frac{1}{8}$ percent debentures due September 15, 1983	75,000,000
Forty Year 2$\frac{3}{4}$ percent debentures due December 1, 1985	75,000,000
Forty Year 2$\frac{7}{8}$ percent debentures due October 1, 1986	75,000,000
Forty Year 3$\frac{1}{8}$ percent debentures due October 1, 1987	100,000,000
Thirty-Two Year 4$\frac{3}{8}$ percent debentures due August 15, 1988	78,000,000
Thirty-Five Year 3$\frac{1}{8}$ percent debentures due November 15, 1989	50,000,000
Thirty-Two Year 4$\frac{5}{8}$ percent debentures due November 1, 1990	80,000,000
Thirty-Six Year 3$\frac{5}{8}$ percent debentures due August 15, 1991	67,000,000
Thirty-Three Year 5$\frac{1}{8}$ percent debentures due February 1, 1993	72,000,000
Thirty-Five Year 4$\frac{5}{8}$ percent debentures due April 1, 1999	100,000,000
Thirty-Five Year 4$\frac{5}{8}$ percent debentures due May 1, 2000	125,000,000
Thirty-Six Year 6 percent debentures due November 1, 2002	130,000,000
	$1,257,000,000
Advances from American Telephone and Telegraph Company	9,000,000
Current and Accrued Liabilities:	
Advance billing for service and customers' deposits	24,370,675
Accounts payable and other current liabilities	127,404,964
Accrued liabilities not due:	
Taxes	61,609,939
Interest	13,382,091
Dividends	35,665,911
Rents	2,645
	$ 262,436,225
Deferred Credits:	
Unextinguished premium on funded debt—Net	7,809,394
Unamortized investment credits	37,042,581
Other deferred credits	5,494,606
	50,346,581
Total Liabilities	$3,966,105,587

EXHIBIT 2

PACIFIC TELEPHONE AND TELEGRAPH COMPANY

Comparative consolidated income statements

(dollar figures in thousands)

	1966	1965	1964	1963	1962
Operating Revenues					
Local revenue....	$ 759,948	$ 714,369	$ 708,280	$ 672,134	$ 624,471
Toll revenue.....	632,731	559,610	510,189	443,979	401,576
Miscellaneous revenues......	74,726	70,510	65,559	61,144	56,990
Uncollectibles....	(12,664)	(9,877)	(8,491)	(7,332)	(6,334)
Total revenues..	$1,454,741	$1,334,612	$1,275,537	$1,169,925	$1,076,703
Operating Expenses					
Maintenance.....	289,871	261,401	235,505	210,878	189,550
Depreciation.....	218,811	201,630	187,357	157,785	144,970
Traffic..........	150,863	132,174	119,698	110,936	103,213
Commercial......	132,344	122,443	116,307	107,567	98,371
Operating rents..	9,822	8,636	7,861	7,051	6,238
Miscellaneous and general....	151,707	137,191	124,441	104,260	95,237
Total expenses..	953,418	863,475	791,169	698,477	637,579
Net operating revenues......	501,258	471,134	484,366	471,446	439,122
Miscellaneous income deduction......	738	10,713	748	cr 404	cr 11,383
Balance...	500,520	460,421	483,618	471,850	450,505
Social security taxes........	23,320	17,490	16,828	16,162	14,594
Federal income tax..........	127,930	112,447	141,320	144,154	134,965
Other taxes......	145,662	139,213	130,123	121,365	114,874
Balance...	203,608	191,271	195,347	190,169	186,072
Interest on funded debt....	44,969	41,780	36,827	33,718	33,718
Other interest....	9,912	6,220	4,121	3,629	2,659
Interest charged..	cr 4,491	cr 3,756	cr 4,685	cr 4,018	cr 3,266
Other fixed charges.......	cr 383	cr 370	cr 326	cr 287	cr 287
Net Income...	$ 153,601	$ 147,397	$ 159,410	$ 157,127	$ 153,248

EXHIBIT 3
PACIFIC TELEPHONE AND TELEGRAPH COMPANY
**State of California intrastate operations reflecting the effects of the
FCC separations changes* estimated year 1967**
(thousands of dollars)

	Intrastate operations	*Annual effect of FCC separations changes*	*Recast intrastate operations*
	(a)	*(b)*	*(c) = (a) + (b)*
A. Estimated Year 1967			
1. Revenues	$1,241,107	$ —	$1,241,107
2. Expenses and taxes	1,086,706	(9,032)	1,077,674
3. Balance net revenues	154,401	9,032	163,433
4. Average net plant, cash and material and supplies	3,065,178	(85,599)	2,979,579
5. Percent balance net revenues to average net plant, cash and material and supplies (rate of return)	5.04%		5.49%
B. Effect of Proposed Rates			
6. Revenues	$ 168,756	—	$ 168,756
7. Expenses and taxes	84,733	—	84,733
8. Balance net revenues	84,023	—	84,023
9. Average net plant, cash and material and supplies	(15,500)	—	(15,500)
C. Including Effect on Proposed Rates (A + B)			
10. Revenues	$1,409,863	$ —	$1,409,863
11. Expenses and taxes	1,171,439	(9,032)	1,162,407
12. Balance net revenues	238,424	9,032	247,456
13. Average net plant, cash and material and supplies	3,049,678	(85,599)	2,964,079
14. Percent balance net revenues to average net plant, cash and material and supplies (rate of return)	7.82%		8.35%

* FCC July 5, 1967, Interim Decision and Order, Docket 16258. Since Pacific's plant in California is used to furnish both interstate service and intrastate toll and exchange service, the revenues, expenses and plant must be separated between intrastate and interstate operations.

EXHIBIT 4
PACIFIC TELEPHONE AND TELEGRAPH COMPANY
Bond yields to maturity at market price

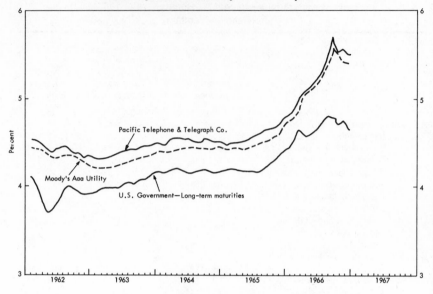

EXHIBIT 4 (Continued)
PACIFIC TELEPHONE AND TELEGRAPH COMPANY
Bond yields to maturity at market price
The Pacific Telephone and Telegraph Company bonds
(selected yield data)

	1962	1963	1964	1965	1966
January..............	4.53	4.31	4.51	4.49	4.83
February.............	4.52	4.30	4.47	4.50	4.91
March...............	4.62	4.30	4.53	4.50	5.03
April...............	4.42	4.33	4.55	4.50	5.08
May.................	4.36	4.36	4.54	4.53	5.12
June................	4.43	4.38	4.54	4.55	5.20
July................	4.46	4.41	4.52	4.60	5.30
August..............	4.46	4.41	4.51	4.64	5.49
September...........	4.38	4.44	4.54	4.65	5.67
October.............	4.37	4.45	4.51	4.65	5.51
November............	4.32	4.47	4.52	4.69	5.55
December............	4.34	4.50	4.52	4.79	5.48
Average........	4.42	4.39	4.52	4.59	5.26

EXHIBIT 4 (Continued)
Bond yields to maturity at market price
Moody's Aaa Public Utility Bonds

	1962	1963	1964	1965	1966
January	4.44	4.19	4.40	4.41	4.76
February	4.45	4.19	4.38	4.42	4.82
March	4.42	4.20	4.39	4.43	4.98
April	4.38	4.21	4.41	4.42	5.08
May	4.34	4.23	4.42	4.45	5.10
June	4.32	4.25	4.44	4.47	5.17
July	4.35	4.29	4.43	4.48	5.22
August	4.36	4.31	4.43	4.50	5.34
September	4.35	4.33	4.43	4.54	5.56
October	4.30	4.33	4.42	4.57	5.50
November	4.25	4.34	4.43	4.61	5.40
December	4.22	4.37	4.44	4.72	5.39
Average	4.35	4.27	4.42	4.50	5.19

EXHIBIT 4 (Concluded)
Bond yields to maturity at market price U.S. government bonds*
(long-term maturities)

	1962	1963	1964	1965	1966
January	4.11	3.93	4.17	4.18	4.45
February	4.02	3.96	4.16	4.19	4.63
March	3.88	3.96	4.19	4.18	4.65
April	3.71	3.99	4.21	4.18	4.57
May	3.71	3.99	4.18	4.18	4.60
June	3.80	4.02	4.15	4.18	4.65
July	3.94	4.05	4.16	4.18	4.74
August	4.01	4.02	4.17	4.22	4.80
September	3.93	4.07	4.18	4.28	4.78
October	3.93	4.09	4.18	4.30	4.70
November	3.91	4.13	4.15	4.36	4.74
December	3.92	.17	4.16	4.44	4.65
Average	3.98	4.03	4.17	4.24	4.65

* Moody's Bond Survey.

EXHIBIT 5
PACIFIC TELEPHONE AND TELEGRAPH COMPANY
Interest and amortization cost of
The Pacific Telephone and Telegraph Company debentures
as of November 30, 1966

	Month and year issued	Amount outstanding	Annual interest and amortization
3-¼% Debs. due 3-1-1978.......	March 1948	$ 75,000,000	$ 2,393,738
3-¼% Debs. due 11-15-1979.....	November 1952	35,000,000	1,122,906
5-⅛% Debs. due 8-1-1980.......	August 1957	90,000,000	4,559,018
3-½% Debs. due 11-15-1981.....	November 1951	30,000,000	1,031,215
3-⅛% Debs. due 9-15-1983......	September 1948	75,000,000	2,347,784
2-¾% Debs. due 12-1-1985......	December 1945	75,000,000	2,028,681
2-⅞% Debs. due 10-1-1986......	October 1946	75,000,000	2,113,963
3-⅛% Debs. due 10-1-1987......	October 1947	100,000,000	3,122,863
4-⅜% Debs. due 8-15-1988......	August 1956	78,000,000	3,382,283
3-⅛% Debs. due 11-15-1989.....	November 1954	50,000,000	1,548,859
4-⅝% Debs. due 11-1-1990......	November 1958	80,000,000	3,662,698
3-⅝% Debs. due 8-15-1991......	August 1955	67,000,000	2,400,311
5-⅛% Debs. due 2-1-1993.......	February 1960	72,000,000	3,684,400
Subtotal..............		$ 902,000,000	$33,398,719
4-⅝% Debs. due 4-1-1999.......	April 1964	100,000,000	4,573,631
4-⅝% Debs. due 5-1-2000.......	May 1965	125,000,000	5,733,954
6% Debs. due 11-1-2002.........	November 1966	130,000,000	7,819,444
Total................		$1,257,000,000	$51,525,748

EXHIBIT 6
PACIFIC TELEPHONE AND TELEGRAPH COMPANY
Prime rate and interest rate on AT&T Co. advances year 1962 to date

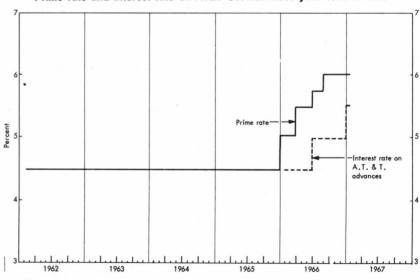

EXHIBIT 7
PACIFIC TELEPHONE AND TELEGRAPH COMPANY
Percent market value price of book value of common stocks

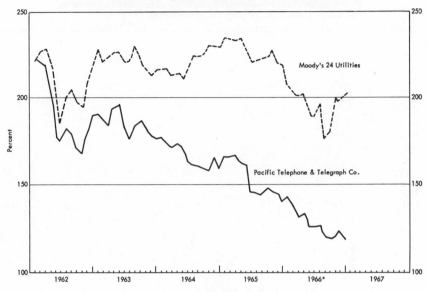

EXHIBIT 8
PACIFIC TELEPHONE AND TELEGRAPH COMPANY
Percent return on average common equity
(for various industry categories)

	1962	*1963*	*1964*	*1965*
50 Largest electric operating companies......................	12.13%	12.41%	12.90%	13.25%
50 Largest gas operating companies.....	12.05	12.29	12.77	12.84
50 Largest telephone operating companies......................	9.95	10.21	10.67	11.08
50 Largest banking companies........	10.10	9.97	10.11	10.36
50 Largest industrial companies........	10.22	10.83	11.83	12.53
Average 250 Companies......	10.89	11.11	11.66	12.01
Pacific Telephone...................	8.29%	8.29%	7.64%	7.12%

EXHIBIT 9
PACIFIC TELEPHONE AND TELEGRAPH COMPANY
Common equity risk
(probable magnitude of earnings decline)

Year	Percent return on common equity	Earnings declines
1946...............	5.93	
1947...............	2.78	3.15
1948...............	6.68	
1949...............	6.62	0.06
1950...............	8.62	
1951...............	7.77	0.85
1952...............	7.83	
1953...............	7.30	0.53
1954...............	8.42	
1955...............	9.15	
1956...............	8.83	0.32
1957...............	7.86	0.97
1958...............	8.18	
1959...............	9.31	
1960...............	8.89	0.42
1961...............	8.68	0.21
1962...............	8.29	0.39
1963...............	8.29	
1964...............	7.64	0.65
1965...............	7.12	0.52
Total......		8.07

Number of observations..................... 19
Number of declines......................... 11
Probability of decline (11 ÷ 19).............. 57.9%
Average magnitude of declines (8.07 ÷ 11)...... 0.73
Probable magnitude of decline (57.9% + .73).... 0.42

EXHIBIT 10
PACIFIC TELEPHONE AND TELEGRAPH COMPANY
Bell system companies
(percent return on average total capital)

		1961	*1962*	*1963*	*1964*	*1965*
1.	Bell Tel. of Pennsylvania..........	7.18%	7.24%	7.53%	7.95%	8.28%
2.	C. & P. Tel.—Maryland...........	7.06	7.24	6.93	6.65	7.12
3.	C. & P. Tel.—Virginia...........	7.49	7.57	7.57	7.74	7.81
4.	C. & P. Tel.—Washington, D.C.....	7.52	6.96	5.93	5.70	6.84
5.	C. & P. Tel.—West Virginia.......	6.76	7.00	7.33	7.57	7.80
6.	Cincinnati & Suburban Bell Tel.....	7.95	7.64	7.49	7.76	8.32
7.	Diamond State Tel................	7.57	7.73	7.89	8.04	8.22
8.	Illinois Bell Tel..................	8.37	8.33	8.12	8.57	8.71
9.	Indiana Bell Tel.................	7.98	8.06	8.25	8.16	8.19
10.	Michigan Bell Tel................	7.36	7.36	7.75	8.43	8.46
11.	Mountain States Tel. & Tel........	7.48	7.68	7.73	7.63	7.73
12.	New England Tel. & Tel..........	7.37	7.41	7.37	7.47	7.68
13.	New Jersey Bell Tel.............	7.83	7.71	7.82	7.87	8.03
14.	New York Tel...................	7.40	7.18	7.00	7.14	7.03
15.	Northwestern Bell Tel............	7.84	7.66	7.94	8.12	8.07
16.	Ohio Bell Tel...................	8.01	7.93	7.93	8.19	8.09
17.	Southern Bell Tel. & Tel..........	7.15	7.45	7.45	7.52	7.60
18.	Southern New England Tel.........	6.98	6.45	6.52	6.83	6.94
19.	Southwestern Bell Tel.............	8.06	8.12	8.06	8.39	8.47
20.	Wisconsin Tel...................	7.17	7.27	6.94	7.29	7.64
	Median.....................	7.45	7.51	7.55	7.75	7.92

EXHIBIT 11
PACIFIC TELEPHONE AND TELEGRAPH COMPANY
Common equity earnings of companies having from 50 to 69.9 percent common equity ratio (years 1961 through 1965)

		Common equity ratio	Percent return on average common equity
1.	United Gas Improvement	50.3%	8.99%
2.	General American Transportation	51.1	10.83
3.	Western Massachusetts Electric	51.4	9.15
4.	Wisconsin Natural Gas	51.4	11.21
5.	Sperry Rand	51.8	6.53
6.	Michigan Gas and Electric	52.5	14.84
7.	Intermountain Telephone	53.9	8.90
8.	U.S. Rubber	54.0	7.89
9.	Central Indiana Gas	54.5	13.46
10.	Southern Countries Gas of California	54.6	8.31
11.	Mississippi River Corporation	54.9	12.15
12.	Armour and Company	55.8	7.73
13.	DiGiorgio Corporation	56.4	7.99
14.	West Ohio Gas	56.7	13.10
15.	Arkansas Western Gas	57.4	13.96
16.	Radio Corporation of America	57.7	15.54
17.	Boston Gas	58.3	7.35
18.	Carolina Telephone and Telegraph	58.4	9.77
19.	General Tire and Rubber	58.4	15.75
20.	Aluminum Company of America	59.3	7.40
21.	Tidewater Oil	59.8	7.55
22.	National Distillers and Chemical	59.9	7.07
23.	Anderson Clayton	60.5	4.61
24.	New Haven Gas	61.1	7.84
25.	Schenley Industries	61.4	4.79
26.	Cities Service	61.9	8.28
27.	Colorado Fuel and Iron	62.3	−1.62
28.	Owens-Illinois Incorporated	62.3	13.70
29.	Southern New England Telephone	62.4	8.60
30.	United Aircraft	63.6	8.57
31.	American Can	64.7	9.12
32.	Elizabethtown Consolidated Gas	65.1	10.42
33.	New England Telephone and Telegraph	65.2	9.49
34.	Burlington Industries	66.1	11.09
35.	New York Telephone	66.2	8.98
36.	North American Aviation	66.3	15.23
37.	Cincinnati and Suburban Bell Telephone	66.5	9.51
38.	National Cash Register	67.6	9.60
39.	FMC Corporation	68.4	14.34
40.	May Department Stores	68.4	11.48
41.	Monsanto Company	69.1	11.92
42.	Union Carbide	69.4	16.09
43.	Michigan Bell Telephone	69.5	9.60
	Median	59.9	9.49

EXHIBIT 11 (Continued)
Common equity earnings of companies having from 50 to 59.9 percent
common equity ratio (year 1965)

		Common equity ratio	Percent return on average common equity
1.	Southern California Gas	50.0%	10.58%
2.	U.S. Rubber	50.0	10.20
3.	Commonwealth Edison	51.2	12.59
4.	Detroit Edison	51.2	12.46
5.	Central Indiana Gas	51.2	13.38
6.	Minneapolis Gas	51.2	13.48
7.	Mississippi River Corporation	51.4	11.68
8.	Rio Grande Valley Gas	51.4	7.71
9.	Western Massachusetts Electric	51.6	9.81
10.	Montana Power	51.7	13.84
11.	Citizens Utilities	52.3	16.66
12.	Cleveland Electric Illuminating	53.6	13.76
13.	Southern Counties Gas of California	54.0	9.83
14.	Carolina Telegraph and Telegraph	55.6	10.70
15.	Arkansas Western Gas	56.3	14.83
16.	Aluminum Company of America	56.8	8.88
17.	Sperry Rand	57.3	8.19
18.	Armour and Company	57.7	6.58
19.	Michigan Gas and Electric	58.6	13.23
20.	West Ohio Gas	58.8	15.44
21.	Sears Roebuck	59.1	15.43
22.	New Haven Gas	59.6	8.07
23.	General Tire and Rubber	62.1	15.57
24.	Schenley Industries	62.5	9.15
25.	General Dynamics	62.8	17.44
26.	Southern New England Telephone	62.9	8.83
27.	National Distillers and Chemical	63.4	8.46
28.	Elizabethtown Consolidated Gas	63.8	11.06
29.	New England Telephone and Telegraph	64.1	9.86
30.	Anderson Clayton	64.7	5.87
31.	Allis Chalmers Mfgr	64.9	7.03
32.	Deere and Company	65.3	11.30
33.	New York Telephone	65.6	8.74
34.	Dow Chemical	65.7	13.67
35.	Colorado Fuel and Iron	65.7	11.82
36.	Radio Corporation of America	66.0	18.87
37.	United Aircraft	66.1	14.95
38.	Burlington Industries	66.3	15.27
39.	Cincinnati and Suburban Bell Telephone	66.8	10.12
40.	FMC Corporation	67.5	18.15
41.	American Can	67.5	10.96
42.	Cities Service	68.0	10.23
43.	May Department Stores	68.1	13.29
44.	Union Oil of California	68.1	9.54
45.	Owens-Illinois Incorporated	68.7	18.53
46.	Tidewater Oil	68.7	9.11
47.	National Cash Register	68.9	9.28
48.	Monsanto Company	69.3	13.28
49.	Singer Company	69.3	10.32
50.	Stevens, J. P. and Company	69.6	10.58
51.	Chespeake and Potomac Telephone—Maryland	69.7	8.83
	Median	62.9	10.96

EXHIBIT 12
PACIFIC TELEPHONE AND TELEGRAPH COMPANY
Assumed rates of return on common equity used together with imbedded costs of long-term debt and preferred stock to produce various rates of return on total capital as of December 31, 1967

	Capital ratios	Cost factor	Weighted cost totals							
			Assumed earnings on common equity							
			7.00%	7.50%	7.75%	8.00%	8.25%	8.50%	8.75%	9.00%
Long-term debt	32.24%	4.10%	1.32%	1.32%	1.32%	1.32%	1.32%	1.32%	1.32%	1.32%
Advances from American Telephone & Telegraph Company	6.10	5.50	0.34	0.34	0.34	0.34	0.34	0.34	0.34	0.34
Preferred stock	2.10	6.55	0.14	0.14	0.14	0.14	0.14	0.14	0.14	0.14
Common stock equity	59.56	—	4.17	4.47	4.62	4.76	4.91	5.06	5.21	5.36
Total Return	100.00%		5.97%	6.27%	6.42%	6.56%	6.71%	6.86%	7.01%	7.16%

EXHIBIT 13

PACIFIC TELEPHONE AND TELEGRAPH COMPANY

Recommended range of return intrastate

	Capital ratios Dec. 31, 1967	*Cost factor*	*Weighted cost totals* Ascribed earnings to common equity					
			8.48%	*8.56%*	*8.65%*	*8.73%*	*8.81%*	*8.90%*
Long-term debt................	32.24%	4.10%	1.32%	1.32%	1.32%	1.32%	1.32%	1.32%
Advances....................	6.10	5.50	0.34	0.34	0.34	0.34	0.34	0.34
Preferred stock..............	2.10	6.55	0.14	0.14	0.14	0.14	0.14	0.14
Common stock equity........	59.56	—	5.05	5.10	5.15	5.20	5.25	5.30
Total Return............	100.00%		6.85%	6.90%	6.95%	7.00%	7.05%	7.10%

EXHIBIT 14
PACIFIC TELEPHONE AND TELEGRAPH COMPANY
Intrastate results of operations estimated year 1967
(thousands of dollars)

Operating Revenues
1. Local service revenues..................... $ 804,870
2. Toll service revenues..................... 371,422
3. Miscellaneous revenues................... 77,820
4. Less: Uncollectibles..................... 11,212

5.   Total............................. $1,242,900
Operating Expenses and Taxes
6. Maintenance........................... 237,500
7. Depreciation........................... 198,200
8. Traffic................................ 125,600
9. Commercial............................ 122,900
10. General office salaries and expenses......... 77,300
11. Operating rents....................... 9,600
12. General services and licenses.............. 11,400
13. Balance: Other operating expenses.......... 45,900
14.   Total Operating Expenses............. 828,400
15. Operating Taxes—Federal income.......... 104,200
16.   —Other................. 120,700
17.   —California Bank......... 17,500

18. Total Expenses and Taxes................ $1,070,800
19. Balance net revenues.................... $ 172,100
Average Net Plant, Cash and
Material and Supplies
20. Telephone plant in service................ $3,580,800
21. Property held for future telephone use........ 2,200
22. Telephone plant, acquired adjustment........ —
23. Cash................................. 62,100
24. Material and supplies.................... 12,000
25. Less: Depreciation reserve................ 708,200
26. Modifications to rate base................ (54,100)

27.   Total............................. $2,894,800
28. Percent balance, net revenue to average net
    plant, cash and materials and supplies
    (rate of return)........................ 5.95%

* At Pacific's proposed rates operating revenues would increase by $179,700 and operating expenses would increase $92,800. This would have the effect of raising the rate of return to 8.9 percent.

EXHIBIT 15
PACIFIC TELEPHONE AND TELEGRAPH COMPANY
Six hypothetical companies with zero common equity risk
(following witness Mason's method of Exhibit No. 7, Table 4)

Year	*Percent return on common equity*					
	(1)	*(2)*	*(3)*	*(4)*	*(5)*	*(6)*
1	−9%	0%	9%	0%	0%	0%
2	−9	0	9	0	1	2
3	−9	0	9	0	2	4
4	−9	0	9	0	3	6
5	−9	0	9	0	4	8
6	−9	0	9	0	5	10
7	−9	0	9	0	6	12
8	−9	0	9	0	7	14
9	−9	0	9	0	8	16
10	−9	0	9	0	9	18
11	−9	0	9	9	10	20
12	−9	0	9	9	11	22
13	−9	0	9	9	12	24
14	−9	0	9	9	13	26
15	−9	0	9	9	14	28
16	−9	0	9	9	15	30
17	−9	0	9	9	16	32
18	−9	0	9	9	17	34
19	−9	0	9	9	18	36
20	−9	0	9	9	19	38

EXHIBIT 16
PACIFIC TELEPHONE AND TELEGRAPH COMPANY
Four hypothetical companies with identical common equity risk
(following witness Mason's method of Exhibit No. 7, Table 4)

	Percent return on common equity				*Earnings declines*			
Year	*(1)*	*(2)*	*(3)*	*(4)*	*(1)*	*(2)*	*(3)*	*(4)*
1	28	28	28	0				
2	9	9	27	3	19	19	1	
3	9	10	26	0			1	3
4	9	11	25	4			1	
5	9	12	24	2			1	2
6	9	13	23	5			1	
7	9	14	22	3			1	2
8	9	15	21	6			1	
9	9	16	20	4			1	2
10	9	17	19	7			1	
11	9	18	18	5			1	2
12	9	19	17	8			1	
13	9	20	16	6			1	2
14	9	21	15	9			1	
15	9	22	14	7			1	2
16	9	23	13	10			1	
17	9	24	12	8			1	2
18	9	25	11	11			1	
19	9	26	10	9			1	2
20	9	27	9	12			1	
Total					19	19	19	19
Number of Observations					19	19	19	19
Number of Declines					1	1	19	9
Probability of Decline					$\frac{1}{19}$	$\frac{1}{19}$	1	$\frac{1}{19}$
Average Magnitude of Declines					19	19	1	$1\frac{9}{9}$
Probable Magnitude of Decline					1	1	1	1

EXHIBIT 17
PACIFIC TELEPHONE AND TELEGRAPH COMPANY
**Relative degree of common equity risk
as calculated by witness Mason in Exhibit No. 9**
(P. T. & T. v. 250 largest companies)

*Median risk of each
group of companies*

50 largest industrials	1.20
50 largest gas	0.76
50 largest banks	0.61
50 largest telephone	0.50
50 largest electric	0.48
P. T. & T.	0.42

*Number of companies
in each group with
risk greater than
P. T. & T.*

Industrials	50
Gas	36
Banks	40
Telephone	30
Electric	31
Total	187

EXHIBIT 18

PACIFIC TELEPHONE AND TELEGRAPH COMPANY

Disparities in operating and financial characteristics among "companies having common equity risk corresponding to that of Pacific Telephone"

	Total operating revenue 1965 (millions) (1)	Type of business (2)	Population served (millions) (3)	Number of telephones served (millions) (4)	Uses accelerated depreciation flow-through (5)	Moody's rating Debentures (6)	Bond (7)	Standard and Poor's common stock rating (8)	* (9)	Common equity average, 1961–65 Percent (10)	Earnings (percent) (11)
1. North Shore Gas..........	$ 16.8	Gas	0.2					—		36	16.9
2. Washington Natural Gas......	34.8	Gas	1.7		x			B+		36	11.3
3. Chenango and Unadilla Telephone.......	4.6	Telephone	0.1	0.04				NR		29	9.3
4. Hawaiian Telephone........	48.0	Telephone	0.7	0.28				A–		44	11.7
5. C. & P. Tel. Co.—Washington, D.C........	102.6	Telephone		0.76		Aaa		—		76	7.3
6. Diamond State Telephone......	33.9	Telephone		0.28		Aaa		—		80	8.9
7. Public Service Electric and Gas.......	528.0	Gas and electric	4.0		x	A	Aa	A		35	12.1
8. Hartford Gas.........	12.2	Gas	0.4		x			—		44	8.2
9. Idaho Power........	52.6	Electric	0.4			A	Aa	A		34	9.6
10. Intermountain Telephone......	14.1	Telephone	0.6	0.15				B+		54	8.9
11. Portland General Electric....	59.5	Electric			x		Baa	A–	3.5	35	11.2
12. Texas Power and Light........	101.9	Electric	1.5			Aa	Aaa	—	4.8	37	19.0
13. New Haven Gas.......	10.2	Gas	0.4					—		61	7.8
14. Gen. Tel. Co. of Southeast.....	24.4	Telephone		0.26				—		38	9.0

15.	Pacific Power and Light......	118.2	Electric	1.4		x	Ba	Baa	B+	8.5	31	11.5
16.	Florida Power...............	99.8	Electric	1.8				Aa	A	2.0	39	12.2
17.	Georgia Power...............	222.8	Electric					Aa	NR	2.5	35	11.6
18.	Harris Trust and Savings Bank..		Bank	3.7							100	12.0
19.	Hartford National Bank and Trust................		Bank								98	9.7
20.	Illinois Power..............	151.1	Gas and electric	1.2				Aa	A	3.7	36	16.1
21.	Mountain States Tel. and Tel...	463.9	Telephone		3.11		Aaa		A		72	9.1
22.	New England Tel. and Tel.....	533.2	Telephone		4.08		Aaa		A		65	9.5
23.	Pennsylvania Electric.........	97.9	Electric	1.4			A	Aa	—		35	12.8
24.	Southern California Edison ...	472.8	Electric	6.8		x	A	Aa	A	3.0	37	11.4
25.	Washington Gas Light........	96.9	Gas	2.3			A	A	B+	0.6	35	9.9
	Pacific Telephone and Telegraph...............	1,344.6	Telephone	14.8	8.50		Aaa	A	A		62	8.0

* Inches of column space in Moody's *Public Utilities* under caption, "Competition."

EXHIBIT 19
PACIFIC TELEPHONE AND TELEGRAPH COMPANY
Rates of return allowed Bell System Companies
1957–66

		Rate of return on commission rate base		
		Net investment		*Other than net investment (percent)*
Date	*State*	*Average (percent)*	*End of year (percent)*	
1957				
4-22..............	Kentucky	*6.60	6.35	
5-31..............	Nebraska	*6.75	6.50	
7-24..............	Wisconsin	*6.25	6.00	
8-6...............	Michigan	6.60		
10-10.............	New York	6.50		
10-15.............	Rhode Island	*6.50	6.25	
10-18.............	South Dakota	*6.15	5.90	
11-22.............	New Hampshire	6.20		
12-23.............	Virginia	*6.63	6.38	
12-30.............	New Jersey	*6.43	6–6.37	
Median....		6.50		
1958				
1-15..............	Delaware			6.19
1-30..............	Massachusetts	*6.70	6.45	
1-31..............	Utah	6.25		
2-11..............	Maryland			6.25
3-4...............	West Virginia	6.35		
3-13..............	Idaho	*6.60	6.35	
3-19..............	Minnesota			6.00
4-18..............	Wisconsin	*6.35	6.10	
4-21..............	North Dakota	6.38		
4-30..............	Maine	6.00		
4-30..............	Montana			5.56
5-29..............	South Dakota	*6.12	5.87	
7-11..............	Washington	6.10		
12-29.............	Ohio			6.16
Median....		6.35		
1959				
1-12..............	Oregon	6.35		
2-5...............	Wyoming	*7.00	6.75	
3-23..............	Delaware			6.19
Median....		6.68		

EXHIBIT 19 (Continued)

		Rate of return on commission rate base		
		Net investment		Other than net investment
Date	State	Average (percent)	End of year (percent)	(percent)
1960				
1-11..............	Montana			5.79
2-16..............	Vermont	6.00		
2-18..............	Michigan	6.62		
5-27..............	Kansas	6.59		
11-17..............	West Virginia	6.45		
11-22..............	South Dakota	6.25		
Median....		6.45		
1961				
4-6..............	Maryland	6.52		
12-28..............	New Hampshire	6.30		
Median....		6.41		
1962				
2-6..............	Connecticut	*6.23	5.98	
4-13..............	Wyoming	*6.92	6.67	
4-16..............	Pennsylvania			5.09
9-14..............	New Hampshire	6.30		
Median....		6.30		
1963				
1-11..............	Alabama			6.20
1964				
8-21..............	Kansas	6.54		
11-13..............	Maryland.........	*6.67	6.35–6.50	
12-22..............	District of Columbia	*6.50	6.25	
Median....		6.54		
1965	—	—	—	—
1966				
3-23..............	Nevada	*6.63	6.38	
6-3..............	Maryland	*6.80	6.55	
10-22..............	Florida	*7.05	6.80	
Median....		6.80		
Median, 1957–66		6.50		

* Reflects an upward adjustment of 0.25 percent to convert approximately the Commissions' allowance on end-of-year rate base to average rate base.
Sources of Data: Table 26, Ex. 5, C-7409; Exhibit No. 55, A-49142; and Volumes 42–65 of "Public Utilities Reports," 3d Series.

EXHIBIT 20
PACIFIC TELEPHONE AND TELEGRAPH COMPANY
Capital costs and ratios imputed to last decision

		Cost (percent)	
	Percent	Rate	Weighted
Long-term debt			
Outstanding....................	34.28	3.67	1.26
Additional.....................	1.74	4.30	0.07
Advances from A.T.&T...........	1.05	4.50	0.05
Total Debt....................	37.07	3.72	1.38
Preferred stock..................	2.93	6.55	0.19
Common stock equity..............	60.00	7.88	4.73
Total...................	100.00		6.30

EXHIBIT 21
PACIFIC TELEPHONE AND TELEGRAPH COMPANY
AND SUBSIDIARY (CONSOLIDATED)
**Common stock earnings and dividends per average share and
payout ratios, 1957–66** (1967 estimated at various assumed intrastate
rates of return)

Year	Price range (in dollars)	Earnings*	Dividends	Payout (percent)
1957........	—	$1.09	$1.00	81.5
1958........	21.375–16.875	1.13	1.00	78.2
1959........	29.875–21.25	1.47	1.07	72.7
1960........	32.25 –26.25	1.39	1.14	79.9
1961........	48.25 –30.25	1.43	1.155	81.0
1962........	39.375–26.125	1.42	1.20	84.8
1963........	35.25 –30.50	1.45	1.20	82.6
1964........	32.50 –28.00	1.38	1.20	87.1
1965........	31.375–25.00	1.30	1.20	92.5
1966........	27.00 –20.50	1.30	1.20	92.6
1967 estimated				
Present rates....................		1.34	1.20	89.7
6.30 percent return†..............		1.40	1.20	86.0
6.50 percent return†..............		1.44	1.20	83.3
6.75 percent return†..............		1.50	1.20	80.05

* On Average shares outstanding
† Based on Commission Staff's "Separated Summary of Earnings"

TSA EQUIPMENT COMPANY

IN EARLY March 1971, Carl Taylor, treasurer of TSA Equipment Company, was preparing for the April meeting of the board of directors. For the last seven years, TSA had experienced a gradual decline in earnings. The company, however, continued to pay dividends and, in fact, paid a steady $1.20 per year for the past four years. Mr. Taylor felt that TSA should investigate several investment alternatives, and he wanted to have adequate cash available to take advantage of any potentially successful opportunities. Therefore, he planned to propose that the regular quarterly cash dividend for the first quarter of 1971 be 25 cents per share, to be paid in April 1971.

Although the board of directors was responsible for dividend policy, any opinions advanced by Mr. Taylor would usually be acted upon favorably.

COMPANY BACKGROUND

TSA Equipment Company was organized in 1927 and maintained its executive offices in Los Angeles, California. The company is an important maker of industrial tractors and heavy construction equipment. They are also a large producer of farm equipment as well as some heavy-duty trucks. The company markets trucks and farm equipment through an independent dealer organization consisting of approximately 2,000 franchised dealers and 200 retail branches maintained by the company. Industrial tractors and heavy construction equipment are marketed primarily through 50 independent distributors. TSA has attained its market position in industrial tractors and heavy construction equipment largely through the vigorous efforts of this highly effective distributor organization.

Sales of trucks and farm equipment have also been sustained by an effective independent dealer organization. The number of dealers has grown rapidly in the past few years as shown in the chart below:

	Number of dealers
1966	1,000
1967	1,100
1968	1,400
1969	1,600
1970	2,000

For the dealers these have been relatively profitable operations.

The retail branches maintained by the company, on the whole, have proven rather successful. The company uses these outlets primarily to test innovative marketing techniques. These branches are located in strategic areas in the United States and are direct competitors of the company's independent franchised dealers. This has created some friction between the two groups in the past, but TSA feels that they should continue with the factory outlets in order to help maintain the market price and improve their marketing techniques.

The company is also engaged in defense work through its wholly owned subsidiary Allen Electronics, Inc. Allen is a producer of electronic components for use in radar guidance systems. The company is also a leading manufacturer of a classified item which has proven to be highly successful in electronic eavesdropping. Defense and related sales counted for 10 percent of TSA's sales volume for the year ended December 31, 1970.

FUTURE EXPANSION

The company has been considering future expansion opportunities and has decided on three alternatives eligible for more serious investigation. The first investment opportunity would be to increase the number of company-owned truck and farm equipment dealerships from 200 to 225. In the past, land acquisition costs for the typical store have approximated $100,000, but this amount is expected to double in the future as desirable sites become more difficult to locate. Building costs have also soared from $10 to $15 a square foot. The typical dealership would require at least 20,000 square feet of building space. Working capital requirements will be 30 percent of sales for the average organization. At the end of the first year, each dealership should add $10,000,000 to the company's sales revenue and this amount should increase 20 percent per year until a maximum of $24,000,000 is reached (Exhibit 1). Cost of sales and other expenses (excluding income taxes) are expected to reach $8,600,000 after the first year and should increase in relation to sales. Strong management is required to operate these businesses efficiently and TSA will have to begin a strenuous management recruiting and training program if this investment alternative is chosen. Because of competitive factors, each dealership is estimated to have a 15-year useful life.

Another investment opportunity involved the construction of a new factory in the Pacific Northwest. Market research has discovered a demand in this area for industrial tractors, which cannot be profitably satisfied by TSA's present plants. It has been estimated that the demand in this area for a certain model of tractor is as follows:

Year	Units
1972	9,000
1973	18,000
1974	27,000
1975	27,000
1976	27,000
1977	27,000
1978	27,000
1979	15,000
1980	0

The average revenue received by TSA is $7,600 per unit.

It has been estimated that a factory capable of producing 27,000 tractors per year could be constructed for $15,000,000. The land which TSA has been considering for this factory is valued at $1,500,000. The factory could be completed by the beginning of 1972 in order to meet the scheduled demand. The tractors produced by this factory are expected to have the same cost coverage and working capital burden as TSA's other lines. Also, the physical plant is expected to be of little or no value in 1980.

The third alternative encompassed the idea of tapping the expanding West European market which seemed to offer exceptional growth, particularly for construction equipment. This was of particular interest at this time due to the uncertainty in the present state of the domestic economy. Mr. Bud Wary, vice president of marketing, felt that the best method for entering an overseas market, considering time, cost, and risk, was to purchase an existing company which showed potential and had an established market position.

Mr. Taylor felt that Kaydean Enterprises, Ltd., headquartered in London, with distributorships in selected areas of western Europe and the British Isles, offered such an opportunity. Kaydean manufactured hydraulic shovels and related equipment, all complementary to TSA's current product lines. All of the stock of Kaydean Enterprises, Ltd., was privately held by the founders. After some negotiations, the owners offered for sale their control in Kaydean for an immediate $35 million in cash. TSA was presently considering a counteroffer of an immediate $30 million in cash plus 20 percent of the net profits of Kaydean for the next five years. It was felt that this would help motivate the management and former owners.

Mr. Taylor had prepared Exhibit 2 for use in analyzing the financial aspects of this purchase. He was particularly concerned about the effect on the market price of TSA stock, their cost of capital, and also the extra overhead required to control an overseas division. Kaydean's sales were estimated to continue to grow at least 12 percent per year in the foreseeable future (Exhibit 1). Because of competitive factors, the useful life of this investment was considered to be 15 years.

FINANCING OPERATIONS

TSA common stock was closely held until 1935. In March of 1936, the company sold 10,000,000 shares to the public at $42.60 per share. In 1941, the company declared a 25 percent stock dividend. A 100 percent stock dividend was declared in 1951 which effectively split the stock. The 25,000,000 shares outstanding were reduced in 1963 when the company repurchased and retired 200,000 shares held by the founder's brother.

The company has always been active in the short-term money market by issuing 90-day notes when funds were needed. In the last five years this method of financing has grown rapidly as shown by the table below:

Year	Notes outstanding December 31	Interest rate (percent)
1966.............	$ 66,500,000	6.0
1967.............	63,100,000	6.5
1968.............	91,400,000	6.5
1969.............	171,000,000	7.0
1970.............	238,400,000	7.5

Long-term debt was obtained by issuing bonds to the public. The company followed a policy of issuing 20-year bonds with no convertible provisions at the rate prevalent in the market.

TSA also had an agreement to borrow $50,000,000 from a group of three life insurance companies. The company had been gradually retiring its outstanding bonds, expecting to issue new ones when the tight money market, beginning in late 1969, took effect. Late in 1970, TSA borrowed the $50,000,000 at 7.5 percent from the insurance companies. This amount was payable in 10 years and the company was able to negotiate the loan without restrictive covenants. These funds were earmarked for future expansion and $15,000,000 was placed in marketable securities and $35,000,000 invested in securities due in more than one year.

RESTRICTIONS ON DIVIDENDS

Due to its negotiating ability, the company was not unduly restricted as to dividend payments. The only restriction imposed by the insurance companies was that TSA's retained earnings not be reduced by the payment of dividends below its total long-term debt. At December 31, 1970, the company's retained earnings of $443,695,000 greatly exceeded its long-term debt of $144,047,000.

DIVIDEND POLICY AND MARKET VALUATION

The company had consistently paid dividends since it first issued its stock to the public, and in order to maintain the best market position for its stock, it had always paid generous dividends. The dividends increased on a step basis from 1961 through 1970, but earnings did not keep pace with this increase. The market value of the stock had historically been more in line with earnings than dividends (Exhibit 5). However, Mr. Taylor felt that it was to the company's advantage to continue paying dividends as high as was reasonable considering the company's financial condition. In preparation for the impending board meeting, Mr. Taylor had developed other supporting exhibits.

EXHIBIT 1

TSA EQUIPMENT COMPANY

Projected sales levels for each dealership

(dollar figures in thousands)

Year

1	$10,000
1–6	20 percent per year
7–10	Constant
11	$19,000
12	$14,000
13	$11,000
14	$ 8,000
15	$ 5,000
16	0

Projected sales levels for kaydean

(dollar figures in thousands)

Year

1	$ 80,000
1–8	12 percent per year
9	$150,000
10	$125,000
11	$100,000
12	$ 70,000
13	$ 40,000
14	$ 20,000
15	$ 5,000
16	0

EXHIBIT 2

TSA EQUIPMENT COMPANY

Kaydean Enterprises, Ltd.

(dollar figures in thousands)

	12 Months ended December 31					
	1966	*1967*	*1968*	*1969*	*1970*	*1971 (Est.)*
Net sales	$50,225	$51,610	$54,454	$62,907	$71,441	$80,000
Cost and expenses	49,136	50,673	53,368	60,550	67,634	74,000
Operating Profit	$ 1,089	$ 937	$ 1,086	$ 2,357	$ 3,807	$ 6,000
Other income and deductions (net)	(24)	58	31	(143)	(183)	—
Income before Taxes	$ 1,065	$ 995	$ 1,117	$ 2,214	$ 3,624	$ 6,000
Income taxes	505	347	390	940	1,654	3,000
Net Income	$ 560	$ 648	$ 727	$ 1,274	$ 1,970	$ 3,000
Depreciation and amortization	$ 1,404	$ 1,528	$ 1,701	$ 1,898	$ 1,971	$ 2,100
Total Assets	$49,020	$50,763	$52,188	$55,231	$60,170	$65,000
Number of shares	400	400	400	400		

EXHIBIT 3

TSA EQUIPMENT COMPANY

Consolidated balance sheet as of December 31, 1966–1970

(dollar figures in thousands)

	1966	1967	1968	1969	1970
ASSETS					
ash....................	$ 56,666	$ 46,864	$ 39,843	$ 48,066	$ 44,221
arketable securities.......	24,906	27,188	384	9,600	29,428
eceivables, net...........	198,937	198,026	219,146	256,329	275,738
ventories...............	530,667	536,838	557,984	574,488	638,388
Total Current Assets..........	$ 811,176	$ 808,916	$ 817,357	$ 888,483	$ 987,775
ther investments, at cost...	15,301	14,430	19,715	21,547	56,829
ther assets..............	9,468	9,680	11,724	4,547	39,576
ant and equipment, net....	336,682	347,823	358,254	383,298	366,248
epaid expenses and deferred charges........	8,164	7,052	10,260	9,100	1,200
Total Assets......	$1,180,791	$1,187,901	$1,217,310	$1,306,975	$1,451,628
IABILITIES AND STOCKHOLDERS' EQUITY					
ccounts payable..........	$ 84,994	$ 99,077	$ 105,088	$ 160,697	$ 201,155
otes payable............	66,516	63,064	91,418	170,957	238,359
ccrued taxes............	42,947	45,397	33,163	34,823	37,742
urrent portion of long-term debt..............	6,136	6,910	14,740	6,475	8,984
ther current liabilities.....	4,653	4,200	4,536	5,498	10,846
Total Current Liabilities.......	$ 205,246	$ 218,648	$ 284,945	$ 378,450	$ 497,086
ong-term debt............	183,984	153,822	142,514	91,023	114,047
ommon stock (no par)	396,800	396,800	396,800	396,800	396,800
etained earnings.........	394,761	418,700	429,051	440,702	443,695
Total Stockholders' Equity........	$ 791,561	$ 815,500	$ 825,851	$ 837,502	$ 840,495
Total Liabilities and Stockholders' Equity........	$1,180,791	$1,187,970	$1,217,310	$1,306,975	$1,451,628

EXHIBIT 4

TSA EQUIPMENT COMPANY

Consolidated profit and loss statements for the year ended December 31, 1966–70
(dollar figures in thousands)

	1966	1967	1968	1969	1970
Sales.....................	$1,549,821	$1,525,138	$1,523,984	$1,591,696	$1,626,921
Cost of sales..............	1,250,255	1,243,580	1,257,946	1,326,201	1,352,479
General and administrative expenses................	98,685	101,726	104,485	107,897	111,601
Selling expenses...........	67,790	65,817	71,657	69,931	76,401
Profit from Operations......	$ 133,091	$ 114,015	$ 89,896	$ 87,667	$ 86,440
Other income.............	17,909	20,859	20,233	24,759	25,748
Total Income.....	$ 151,000	$ 134,874	$ 110,129	$ 112,426	$ 112,188
Interest...................	13,561	13,950	14,775	17,848	25,984
Other expense............	13,987	23,284	23,817	28,421	30,097
Net Profit before Income Taxes...	$ 123,452	$ 97,640	$ 71,537	$ 66,157	$ 56,107
Income taxes..............	58,635	43,941	31,426	24,746	23,354
Net profit.........	$ 64,817	$ 53,699	$ 40,111	$ 41,411	$ 32,753
Retained earnings, beginning..............	358,464	394,761	418,700	429,051	440,702
Dividends................	28,520	29,760	29,760	29,760	29,760
Retained earnings, ending.........	$ 394,761	$ 418,700	$ 429,051	$ 440,702	$ 443,695

EXHIBIT 5

TSA EQUIPMENT COMPANY

Per share data

	Number of shares (000 omitted)	Earnings per share	Dividends per share	Price range
1961................	25,000	1.03	.80	18⅛–14
1962................	25,000	1.31	.80	19–14⅛
1963................	24,800	1.56	.80	21–16⅜
1964................	24,800	2.31	.90	29⅛–19⅛
1965................	24,800	2.28	1.00	32–22⅛
1966................	24,800	2.61	1.15	35⅛–21
1967................	24,800	2.17	1.20	27⅜–22
1968................	24,800	1.62	1.20	25⅞–20
1969................	24,800	1.67	1.20	26⅛–16⅜
1970................	24,800	1.32	1.20	20–14⅞

EXHIBIT 6
TSA EQUIPMENT COMPANY
Financial data for Allis-Chalmers
(dollar figures in thousands)

A worldwide manufacturer of capital and consumer goods. Basic markets are electric utilities, construction material handling, consumer, industrial, defense and agriculture. Stock is traded on the New York Stock Exchange.

	12 months ended December 31				
	1966	*1967*	*1968*	*1969*	*1970**
Sales..........................	$857,215	$821,765	$767,313	$804,737	$870,076
Earnings after taxes...............	26,155	5,002	(54,590)	18,423	15,022
Net earnings per share (average)....	$2.33	$2.67	$0.41	$(3.96)	$1.20
Dividends per share...............	0.8125	1.00	0.625	–0–	.05
Total Assets....................	$665,158	$636,983	$705,613	$702,617	$768,909
Net working capital..............	305,246	259,110	157,723	211,205	231,525
Long-term debt..................	117,000	114,000	111,000	111,404	156,967
Net worth......................	363,166	363,537	304,167	371,071	338,759
Price range of common stock.......	19¼–40¼	21⅝–44	24–38⅛	20¾–32⅝	12⅞–27

* Includes Allis-Chalmers International Finance Corp., a subsidiary not previously consolidated.

EXHIBIT 7
TSA EQUIPMENT COMPANY
Financial data for Caterpillar Tractor Co.
(dollar figures in thousands)

The company's output includes 244 models of 24 prime product classes: crawler tractors, wheel tractors, wheel tractors for scrapers and wagons, track and wheel loaders, pipe layers, off-highway trucks, motor graders, crawler drawn scrapers, rippers, bulldozers, tool bars, hydraulic controls, cable controls, engines, inertia welders, forklift trucks, and straddle carriers. Sales are handled through a network of independently owned dealerships operating throughout the free world. Stock is traded on the New York Stock Exchange.

	12 months ended December 31				
	1966	*1967*	*1968*	*1969*	*1970*
Sales....................	$1,524,036	$1,472,502	$1,707,087	$2,001,637	$2,127,800
Earnings after taxes........	150,086	106,385	121,596	142,474	143,800
Net earnings per share (common)..............	$2.64	$1.87	$2.14	$2.51	$2.53
Dividends per share........	1.20	1.20	1.20	1.20	1.20
Total Assets.............	$1,118,294	$1,340,087	$1,507,232	$1,661,617	$1,813,600
Net working capital........	416,283	448,834	407,422	456,848	489,500
Long-term debt............	145,092	292,910	318,546	306,471	283,900
Net worth...............	733,835	773,084	827,060	902,060	977,800
Price range of common stock.................	33⅛–51⅜	34¼–50	36⅛–48½	37⅞–54⅞	30–44¾

EXHIBIT 8
TSA EQUIPMENT COMPANY
Financial data for Clark Equipment Co.
(dollar figures in thousands)

The company manufactures industrial trucks, straddle carriers, towing tractors, material handling systems, tractor shovels, tractor dozers, conventional and self-loading tractor scrapers, backhoe loaders, industrial loaders, compaction and logging equipment, agricultural implements, truck trailers truck bodies, freight containers, transmissions, torque converters, retarders and winches, differentials axles, axle housings, hydraulic pumps and valves, malleable castings, and commercial refrigeration and food service equipment. Stock is traded on the New York Stock Exchange.

	12 months ended December 31				
	1966	*1967*	*1968*	*1969*	*1970*
Sales................................	$493,919	$489,508	$507,400	$645,446	$671,01
Earnings safter taxes.................	28,213	23,199	28,960	38,605	35,28
Net earnings per share (common).......	$2.53	$2.06	$2.44	$3.21	$2.9
Dividends per share..................	1.25	1.15	1.20	1.40	1.4
Total Assets........................	$330,159	$313,895	$357,194	$444,246	$501,93
Net working capital.................	104,997	110,775	115,694	155,285	179,51
Long-term debt.....................	57,886	58,341	55,309	76,894	102,95
Net worth..........................	154,406	167,093	183,402	214,429	233,55
Price range of common stock..........	19½–32	21–36¼	23–35⅛	30–40¾	24¼–3

EXHIBIT 9
TSA EQUIPMENT COMPANY
Financial data for Deere & Co.*
(dollar figures in thousands)

Manufactures a full line of agricultural implements, various industrial equipment, and lawn an garden equipment. Stock is traded on the New York Stock Exchange.

	12 months ended October 31				
	1966	*1967*	*1968*	*1969*	*1970*
Sales....................	$1,062,062	$1,086,379	$1,030,539	$1,043,033	$1,138,00
Earnings after taxes........	78,709	57,610	42,622	54,135	45,99
Net earnings per share......	$5.46	$3.90	$2.88	$3.67	$3.1
Dividends per share........	1.70	1.95	2.00	2.00	2.C
Total Assets..............	$1,173,225	$1,322,332	$1,376,777	$1,404,847	$1,509,69
Net current assets..........	530,684	587,664	566,147	578,570	597,94
Long-term debt...........	193,629	259,869	249,098	241,333	237,13
Net worth...............	613,155	644,741	658,286	679,846	696,38
Price range of common stock.................	51⅞–75½	50¼–75½	45¾–59½	34¾–56⅞	27⅝–45⅜

* Consolidated (excluding Deere Credit Corp.)

EXHIBIT 10
TSA EQUIPMENT COMPANY
Financial data for Eaton Yale & Towne, Inc.
(dollar figures in thousands)

The company manufactures about 4,000 products in the following categories: truck and off-ghway vehicle components; locks and hardware; automotive and controls products; materials ndling equipment, including industrial trucks, systems and components, and construction and restry equipment, power transmission systems, and general products. Stock is traded on the New ork Stock Exchange.

	12 months ended December 31				
	1966	*1967*	*1968*	*1969*	*1970*
les........................	$795,610	$750,664	$889,826	$1,054,309	$997,434
rnings after taxes............	51,396	31,778	49,198	60,887	47,264
et earnings per share (common).................	$3.45	$2.10	$2.89	$3.46	$2.54
vidends per share............	1.80	1.25	1.32	1.40	1.40
otal Assets..................	$505,929	$529,554	$622,705	$ 735,505	$802,539
et working capital............	$174,431	$211,998	$224,043	$ 237,548	$254,593
ong-term debt................	28,475	65,000	63,750	72,874	99,443
et worth....................	299,622	312,703	361,770	413,214	447,560
ice range of common stock....	22¼–29¾	24⅛–36½	26⅜–43⅜	32¾–46⅞	22¼–40⅝

EXHIBIT 11
TSA EQUIPMENT COMPANY
Financial data for International Harvester Company
(dollar figures in thousands)

The company is one of the nation's largest industrial enterprises, a leader in farm machinery, portant in motor trucks, and also a maker of industrial tractors, engines, and various miscellaneous oducts. Stock is traded on the New York Stock Exchange.

	12 months ended October 31				
	1966	*1967*	*1968*	*1969*	*1970*
les.....................	$2,583,035	$2,541,897	$2,539,974	$2,652,827	$2,711,535
rnings after taxes........	109,679	93,024	75,428	63,786	52,432
et earnings per share (common)..............	$3.86	$3.31	$2.69	$2.30	$1.92
vidends per share........	1.725	1.80	1.80	1.80	1.80
otal Assets.............	$1,793,654	$1,813,117	$1,902,333	$2,026,210	$2,217,571
et working capital........	747,453	757,052	768,696	751,019	766,544
ong-term debt............	278,595	264,427	298,106	312,688	402,198
et worth...............	1,094,007	1,136,439	1,161,448	1,155,153	1,146,843
ice range of common stock.................	32–52⅞	32⅞–41	30⅜–38¾	24⅛–38	22–29⅜

UNIVERSE AIRLINES

Mr. Abernathy, chief financial officer and treasurer for Universe Airlines, was reviewing the 1969 Financial Statements and noted that while year-end earning results were generally favorable (when compared with other major U.S. trunk lines), there was a current slowdown in the U.S. economy and an unfavorable future earnings forecast. In particular, he was concerned with the impact of the government's new tight money policies on future financial requirements of Universe Airlines. As evidence of his concern, he noted that the prime lending rate had edged upward and could be expected to continue upward—thus putting a brake on the U.S. economy (Exhibit 1).

If respectable economic forecasters and government officials could be believed, these actions and ensuing economic events could produce a serious "credit crunch" for Universe as well as the entire airline industry. Mr. Abernathy recalled the last "credit crunch" on the tight markets in 1966. As further evidence of his concern, he noted a gradual downward trend of the Dow-Jones Averages and other leading business indicators (Exhibit 2).

Considering the future financial requirements of Universe, Mr. Abernathy knew that large amounts of new capital would be required to finance the replacement of old aircraft and to expand their route structure. Presently pending before the Civil Aeronautics Board (CAB) was an application for a Miami-St. Louis-Seattle route which permitted intermediary stops in Denver, Atlanta, and Tampa/St. Petersburg. Approval was expected early in 1971. The addition of this new route would require additional aircraft and working capital totaling $228 million. Anticipating this new route, Universe had contracted for the purchase of three new

Lockheed L-1011 aircraft for delivery in 1972. Prior to 1972, Universe would utilize its existing fleet supplemented with leased aircraft, primarily from United, TWA, and Delta.

Universe Airlines has had a long and steady history of profitable operations which allowed them to pay a cash dividend for the past 15 years. However, Universe had never before experienced such a large requirement for incremental financing. In part this was due to equipment purchase commitments and working capital requirements for the expanded route structure. And in part this was due to obsolescence (and subsequent necessary replacement) of aircraft that served the existing route structure.

Mr. Abernathy was considering a recommendation to the board of directors that Universe eliminate the annual cash dividend, or a significant portion of it, as one means of conserving cash and reducing its external financing requirements. He was aware that if dividends were paid to maintain Universe's long-standing dividend policy, a new equity offering would be required and that this external equity would be more costly than financing future requirements from internal equity (retained earnings). If no dividends were paid Mr. Abernathy reasoned that the resultant increase of retained earnings would, in part, provide for future financial requirements in addition to making it easier to finance the remainder through long-term debt. It is anticipated that internally generated funds, together with additional borrowings permissible under existing loan agreement covenants, may not provide adequate cash for these purchase commitments and for payment of outstanding debt in accordance with its normal maturities.

COMPANY BACKGROUND

Universe was incorporated on December 31, 1935, under the laws of the state of Missouri. The state of incorporation was transferred to Delaware effective June 30, 1966. Universe has its principal offices and overhaul and maintenance facilities as Lambert Field, St. Louis, Missouri.

Universe's routes provide transcontinental service across the southern-tier of states, between Missouri, Georgia, Florida, and California, and connect the industrial and distributing areas of the Great Lakes, midwestern and New York-Washington regions with the southern states from Texas to Florida. In addition to traffic originating in its own territory, the company receives business from and delivers to all transcontinental lines and connects with other international carriers at the major international gateway cities served so as to provide connecting service to all major foreign countries.

The present routes certificated to Universe total approximately 15,512 unduplicated miles. Scheduled flights over these routes as of July 1, 1969, have reached 312,465 miles daily.

During the calendar year 1969, Universe ranked within the top 10 in size among the airlines of the United States in terms of revenue passenger-miles flown.

The following tabulation sets forth certain statistics relating to Universe's operations during the five years ended December 31, 1969.

Calendar year	Revenue ton-miles (000)	Revenue passenger miles flown (000)	Passenger load factor	Revenue passengers carried
1965............	375,115	3,209,467	54.64	4,822,422
1966............	406,782	3,616,095	59.78	5,250,831
1967............	486,082	4,149,850	55.85	6,005,061
1968............	573,409	4,797,913	50.72	6,712,437
1969............	598,819	4,998,346	52.48	7,212,158

Universe has on file with the Civil Aeronautics Board a number of applications for various route extensions. These include proposed services between Memphis and Miami; between Atlanta and Nashville; between Atlanta and Cleveland; between Miami and Seattle; and nonstop service between Chicago and Atlanta.

Various other carriers also have applications on file with the Civil Aeronautics Board involving proposed routes and services which would parallel or be competitive with Universe's proposed new routes and with certain segments of Universe's presently certificated routes.

The action which the CAB might take with respect to any of the above-described route proposals, or with respect to the proposals of any other applicants which seek routes competitive with Universe's proposed and existing routes, cannot be predicted with certainty. However, Universe was anticipating approval on the Miami to Seattle route with a stopover in St. Louis.

Universe is subject to competition from surface carriers between virtually all of the cities it serves and to scheduled airline competition over a substantial portion of its system. Direct, single-carrier airline competition exists between such major points as New York, Philadelphia, Baltimore and Washington to Charlotte, Atlanta, Birmingham, New Orleans and Houston; Chicago to New Orleans, Atlanta, Jacksonville and Miami; Chicago to St. Louis, Memphis, Cincinnati, Nashville and Houston; Houston to New Orleans, Birmingham and Atlanta; and Atlanta to Dallas, Los Angeles and San Francisco.

The CAB may create or permit additional competition from time to time. This may be accomplished by award of new route authority or by approval of voluntary mergers. Under the existing laws, as interpreted by the CAB, an air carrier cannot be assured of protection against paralleling competition simply by rendering adequate service.

Substantially all of Universe's land and buildings are leased. Its real property ownership is limited to 70-odd acres of land. Universe also owns a limited number of radio transmitting and receiving sites and fuel farm sites. Its principal offices and operations and maintenance base are located on the Lambert Airport on ground areas leased from the City of St. Louis under long-term leases, with certain renewal options. Universe has constructed various buildings and facilities upon portions of this leased property, and it leases other buildings and facilities on portions owned by the city. In addition, Universe has long-term leases for maintenance hangars with the respective city or airport authorities at Miami, Dallas, Chicago, and Detroit.

Universe also leases ticket counter space and operating areas in most of the airports which it serves. Generally, these leases run for periods of from 5 to 30 years and are based on fixed rental charges per square foot of exclusive floor space occupied, with provisions for periodic adjustment of rates. The airport leases are usually tied in with agreements for the nonexclusive use of ramps and runways, and landing fees are based on the number of schedules and type of aircraft. In addition, Universe leases downtown ticket and reservation offices in the major cities served. These leases normally are for shorter terms than the airport leases.

Universe's total ground property and equipment rental costs and landing fees for the year ended December 31, 1969, were as follows:

Ground property and equipment rentals......	$ 5,536,000
Landing fees............................	6,418,000
Total.......................	$11,954,000

The minimum annual rentals for ground property and equipment under leases expiring more than three years after December 31, 1969, will be approximately $4,750,000.

As of December 31, 1969, Universe owned and operated the following jet aircraft:

Type of aircraft	Number seats per aircraft	Fleet total
DC-8-61................	195	7
DC-8-51................	135	10
Boeing 727-B............	135	11
Boeing 720-B............	96	5
DC-9-32................	89	31
Boeing 737-C............	89	8
		72

In addition, Universe owns and operates three L-100-20 four-engine turboprop all-cargo aircraft.

Universe's aircraft are the same type of aircraft used by many of the other major airlines in the United States. In addition, under an interchange agreement with Pan American, certain through-plane services are operated between Atlanta and Frankfurt, Germany, via London, England, utilizing Boeing 747 aircraft owned by Pan American. Universe leases flying time on these Pan American aircraft for operations between the interchange point, Dulles International Airport, Washington, D.C., and Atlanta, and for certain additional purely Universe operations over its system.

By December 31, 1969, Universe had outstanding commitments for the purchase of one DC-9-32 aircraft for delivery in July 1970; three B-747 aircraft, for delivery in the late fall of 1971; five McDonnell-Douglas DC-10 aircraft, for delivery in late 1972 and early 1973; and it continues its interest in the purchase of the Lockheed L-1011 aircraft. The company originally committed itself for the purchase of 10 L-1011 aircraft, which initially requires total expenditures of approximately $150,000,000, excluding escalation (Exhibit 9).

FINANCIAL HISTORY

Over the past 20 years, Universe has been particularly strong from a financial standpoint. While other airlines often expanded ground facilities, aircraft, and in-flight accouterments in a manner not consistent with their markets, Universe has pursued a policy of limited expansion and efficient use of existing aircraft. This policy was established at the request of former Controller John B. Vella who demanded that Universe maintain a strong financial position, even at the expense of possible revenue loss. This penchant for profitable service, therefore, is a trademark of Universe, and in many ways sets it apart from most of the airline industry. During the 1960s, Universe saw its net income consistently grow from $8,256,000 in 1961 to $26,324,000 in 1969. This resulted in earnings per share of $1.09 in 1961 and $2.67 in 1969. (See Exhibits 3–6.)

During this nine-year period Universe had grown from $59,312,000 of revenue in 1961 to $274,835,000 in 1969. This 363 percent increase in revenue (1961–69) allowed Universe to overtake National, Western, and Continental in trunk revenue size over that period. This revenue growth was also accompanied by a net income increase of 219 percent from 1961 to 1969. (See Exhibit 7.)

Universe has long felt that constant dollar dividends would stabilize the price of their stock and help them float future equity issues for necessary expansion. Therefore, quarterly cash dividends had been paid every quarter since March 31, 1954. (See Exhibit 8.)

Since the investor classes of Universe had been primarily income-oriented individuals and institutions in the past, this dividend policy was deemed satisfactory. (A recent survey, however, showed an influx of growth-oriented investors as Universe shareholders. Considering Universe's traditionally conservative financial and marketing postures, management did not know quite how to evaluate this trend.) Universe's P/E ratio had fluctuated from only 8.54 to 13.48 since 1961 and its stock price had consistently remained high when other airlines were experiencing down markets and sluggish trading.

It had long been characteristic of Universe to remain fairly constant in its capital structure over the years. In fact, Mr. Abernathy often credited Universe's strong financial position to his own personal unwillingness to allow their significant operating ratios to fluctuate. While others in the industry often pointed to Universe's conservative financial posture as a reason for impeded revenue growth (on lost revenue opportunity), no one could argue with their profitability over the years. Before Mr. Abernathy made any decision, he analyzed industry data to see how Universe compared with other trunk carriers (Exhibits 10–17).

EXHIBIT 1
UNIVERSE AIRLINES
Interest rates 1965–69

		Yield in percent per annum				
Class	*Year*	*January*	*March*	*June*	*September*	*December*
Long-term U.S.	1965	4.14	4.15	4.14	4.25	4.43
government	1966	4.43	4.63	4.63	4.79	4.65
bonds	1967	4.40	4.45	4.86	4.99	5.36
	1968	5.18	5.39	5.23	5.09	5.65
	1969	5.74	6.05	6.06	6.32	6.81
Corporate Bonds:	1965	4.43	4.42	4.46	4.52	4.68
Aaa	1966	4.74	4.92	5.07	5.49	5.39
	1967	5.20	5.13	5.44	5.65	6.19
	1968	6.17	6.11	6.28	5.97	6.45
	1969	6.69	6.85	6.98	7.14	7.72
Corporate Bonds:	1965	4.80	4.78	4.85	4.91	5.02
Baa	1966	5.06	5.32	5.58	6.09	6.18
	1967	5.97	5.85	6.15	6.40	6.93
	1968	6.84	6.85	7.07	6.79	7.23
	1969	7.32	7.51	7.70	8.05	8.65
Corporate Bonds:	1965	4.53	4.52	4.59	4.65	4.79
Industrial	1966	4.84	5.06	5.25	5.71	5.63
	1967	5.45	5.39	5.64	5.93	6.39
	1968	6.34	6.33	6.54	6.24	6.72
	1969	6.78	7.02	7.16	7.42	7.95
90-day U.S.	1965	3.81	3.93	3.80	3.92	4.37
Treasury bills	1966	4.69	4.81	4.78	5.80	5.00
(market yield)	1967	4.72	4.26	3.53	4.42	4.96
	1968	4.99	5.16	5.52	5.20	5.94
	1969	6.13	6.01	6.43	7.08	7.81
Corporate Bonds:	1965	4.66	4.63	4.66	4.77	4.91
Railroads	1966	4.97	5.18	5.26	5.65	5.78
	1967	5.63	5.51	5.80	6.03	6.63
	1968	6.65	6.67	6.88	6.70	6.97
	1969	6.98	7.16	7.37	7.68	8.16
Corporate Bonds:	1965	4.52	4.51	4.56	4.64	4.82
Utilities	1966	4.85	5.08	5.32	5.78	5.65
	1967	5.42	5.37	5.80	6.02	6.57
	1968	6.47	6.39	6.60	6.27	6.85
	1969	7.02	7.23	7.38	7.62	8.39
Prime bank rate	1965	4½	4½	4½	4½	5
	1966	5	5½	5¾	5¾	6
	1967	5½	5½	5½	5½	6
	1968	6	6	6½	6¼	6½
	1969	7	7½	8½	8½	8½
Federal Reserve	1965	4½	4½	4½	4½	4½
Bank rediscount	1966	4½	4½	4½	4½	4½
rate	1967	4½	4½	4	4	4½
	1968	4½	5	5½	5½	5½
	1969	5½	5½	6	6	6
4–6 month com-	1965	4.25	4.38	4.38	4.38	4.65
mercial paper	1966	4.82	5.21	5.51	5.89	6.00
	1967	5.73	5.24	4.65	5.00	5.56
	1968	5.60	5.64	6.25	5.82	6.17
	1969	6.53	6.82	8.23	8.48	8.34

EXHIBIT 2
UNIVERSE AIRLINES
Dow Jones closing prices by quarters

		High	*Low*			*High*	*Low*
1960	1..	685.5	599.1	1965	1..	906.3	869.8
	2..	656.4	599.6		2..	939.6	840.6
	3..	646.9	570.6		3..	937.9	861.8
	4..	617.8	566.1		4..	969.3	929.7
1961	1..	679.4	610.3	1966	1..	995.2	911.1
	2..	706.0	672.7		2..	954.7	864.1
	3..	726.5	679.3		3..	894.0	767.0
	4..	734.9	697.2		4..	820.9	744.3
1962	1..	726.0	689.0	1967	1..	876.7	786.4
	2..	705.4	535.8		2..	909.6	842.4
	3..	616.0	571.2		3..	943.1	859.7
	4..	654.0	551.1		4..	933.3	849.6
1963	1..	689.0	646.8	1968	1..	908.6	825.1
	2..	728.6	684.3		2..	919.2	861.3
	3..	746.0	687.7		3..	938.3	869.7
	4..	762.2	711.5		4..	985.2	942.3
1964	1..	820.3	766.1	1969	1..	952.7	899.8
	2..	831.5	800.3		2..	968.9	869.8
	3..	875.7	823.4		3..	886.1	802.0
	4..	891.7	857.5		4..	863.1	769.9

EXHIBIT 3
UNIVERSE AIRLINES
Balance sheet for year ending
December 31, 1967–69
(dollar figures in thousands)

	1969	1968	1967
ASSETS			
Cash..	$ 15,373	$ 15,612	$ 14,906
Accounts receivable...........................	21,197	18,953	18,275
Refund of prior years' federal income taxes........	1,392	628	287
Maintenance and operating supplies (at average cost).......................................	6,738	5,545	4,872
Prepaid expenses, etc..........................	835	1,127	994
Total Current Assets..................	$ 45,535	$ 41,865	$ 39,334
Property and equipment (at cost)			
Flight equipment...........................	$405,726	$362,584	$322,174
Ground property and equipment..............	47,830	36,899	28,223
	453,556	399,483	350,397
Less—Accumulated depreciation..............	152,838	124,400	97,284
	301,718	275,083	253,113
Advance payments for new equipment..........	38,712	29,580	21,075
	339,430	304,663	274,188
Deferred Charges..........................	7,585	5,794	6,362
Total Assets.......................	$392,550	$352,322	$319,884
LIABILITIES AND STOCKHOLDERS' EQUITY			
Current maturities of long-term debt.............	$ 18,778*	$ 16,305	$ 15,540
Short-term notes payable......................	6,785	5,376	2,934
Accounts payable and miscellaneous accrued liabilities...................................	15,092	14,784	10,353
Accrued payroll and vacation pay..............	7,336	6,783	6,209
Tickets outstanding subject to refund or use.......	4,921	3,606	2,138
Air travel plan deposits.......................	747	787	643
Accrued income taxes.........................	539	771	782
Total Current Liabilities..............	$ 54,198	$ 48,412	$ 38,599
Long-term debt*.............................	$134,095	$115,522	$106,345
Deferred credits			
Deferred federal income taxes................	42,250	51,395	54,553
Unamortized investment tax credit............	9,377	6,738	9,206
	$ 51,627	$ 58,133	$ 63,759
Stockholders' Equity			
Common stock, par value $3 per share, authorized 10,000,000 shares, outstanding 9,873,000 shares.........................	29,619	29,619	29,619
Additional paid-in capital....................	8,054	8,054	8,054
Retained earnings..........................	114,957	92,582	73,508
	$152,630	$130,255	$111,181
Total Liabilities....................	$392,550	$352,322	$319,884

* At December 31, 1969, Universe's long-term debt (including current maturities) consisted of the following:

A. Due banks under unsecured notes carrying an interest rate ¼ percent above prime rate, repayable in quarterly installments of $6,000,000 to March 31, 1974, with the remaining $40,535 payable on September 30, 1974... $142,535

B. Due insurance companies under 6 percent unsecured notes, repayable in monthly installments ($210,000) to December 31, 1976.................................... 10,080

C. Due IBM for Universamatic Reservations System, repayable in quarterly installments through December 31, 1970.. 258

Total.. $152,873
Less—current maturities.. 18,778

$134,095

Under terms of credit agreements, $37,350,000 of retained earnings on December 31, 1969, is restricted as to payment of cash dividends.

EXHIBIT 4
UNIVERSE AIRLINES
Income statement
for years ending December 31, 1961, 1965, 1967–69
(dollar figures in thousands)

	1961	1965	1967	1968	1969
perating revenues					
Passenger...................	$55,322	$142,340	$204,408	$231,940	$250,318
Cargo......................	3,726	10,543	16,338	20,281	22,893
Other (net).................	264	736	1,201	1,226	1,624
Total Operating Revenue....	$59,312	$153,619	$221,947	$253,437	$274,835
perating Expenses					
Flying operations.............	$12,116	$ 38,190	$ 52,310	$ 54,352	$ 60,067
Maintenance.................	7,176	20,714	29,266	32,929	38,672
Aircraft and traffic service	7,229	21,576	33,427	41,755	43,935
Permotion and sales...........	4,025	12,038	19,736	23,973	24,374
Depreciation and amortization....	4,952	13,851	22,531	27,116	28,438
Passenger service	3,407	9,639	16,225	20,315	20,478
General and administrative	1,653	4,235	5,873	6,642	6,912
Total Operating Expenses...	$40,558	$120,243	$179,368	$207,082	$222,876
come from Operations before Income Tax..................	18,754	33,376	42,579	46,355	51,959
ther Expense					
Interest expense...............	2,582	4,786	5,912	6,789	7,345
Less—Interest capitalized on advances for equipment........	(315)	(117)	(1,432)	(1,619)	(1,831)
	$ 2,267	$ 4,669	$ 4,480	$ 5,170	$ 5,514
terest income.................	(533)	(812)	(847)	(892)	(947)
ain on disposition of aircraft (net)......................	(223)	(520)	(691)	(2,041)	(445)
	$ 1,511	$ 3,357	$ 2,942	$ 2,237	$ 4,122
come before Income Taxes.......	$17,243	$ 30,019	$ 39,637	$ 44,118	$ 47,837
emium for income taxes					
Federal income taxes...........	2,413	3,771	4,375	4,137	5,336
State income taxes.............	175	308	328	336	433
Deferred federal income taxes....	4,050	7,203	11,051	12,786	13,195
Investment tax credit..........	2,932	5,174	5,933	6,015	5,317
ess—Amortization of investment tax credit...................	(583)	(1,584)	(2,018)	(2,179)	(2,768)
	$ 8,987	$ 14,872	$ 19,669	$ 21,095	$ 21,513
et Income...................	$ 8,256	$ 15,147	$ 19,968	$ 23,023	$ 26,324
er Common Share*					
Net Income..................	$ 1.09	$ 1.66	$ 2.04	$ 2.33	$ 2.67
Cash Dividend................	.16	.24	.40	.40	.40

* 7,545,000 shares in 1961; 9,128,000 shares in 1965; 9,642,000 shares in 1967; 9,973,000 shares in 1968.

EXHIBIT 5

UNIVERSE AIRLINES

Statement of retained earnings

for the three years ending December 31, 1969

(dollar figures in thousands)

	1967	1968	1969
Balance at beginning of year.........	$57,397	$73,508	$ 92,582
Net Income......................	19,968	23,023	26,324
	$77,365	$96,531	$118,906
Deduct cash dividends..............	$ 3,857	$ 3,949	$ 3,949
Balance at end of year..............	$73,508	$92,582	$114,957

EXHIBIT 6

UNIVERSE AIRLINES

Statement of change in financial position

for three years ended December 31, 1969

(dollar figures in thousands)

	1967	1968	1969
Funds Provided by:			
Net income.............................	$19,968	$23,023	$26,324
Add expenses not requiring current outlay of working capital...............			
Depreciation and amortization..........	22,531	27,116	28,438
Deferred income taxes................	11,051	12,786	13,195
Investment tax credit, net of amortization......................	3,915	3,836	2,639
Total from Operations............	$37,497	$43,738	$44,272
Dispositions of property and equipment......	241	335	415
Additional financing under			
Installment purchase agreements........	—	135	—
Bank credit agreement................	25,000	26,000	42,000
	$62,738	$70,208	$86,687
Funds Used For:			
Property and equipment additions			
Flight equipment, including advances.......	31,105	48,915	52,574
Ground property and equipment..........	9,436	8,676	10,931
Reduction of long-term debt..............	16,736	15,950	18,778
Cash dividends.........................	3,857	3,949	3,949
	61,134	77,490	86,232
Increase (decrease) in Working Capital......	$ 1,604	$(7,282)	$ 455

EXHIBIT 7
UNIVERSE AIRLINES
Revenue history

1960...............	$ 48,876,000
1961...............	59,312,000
1962...............	73,605,000
1963...............	93,967,000
1964...............	127,053,000
1965...............	153,619,000
1966...............	196,114,000
1967...............	221,447,000
1968...............	253,437,000
1969...............	274,835,000

EXHIBIT 8
UNIVERSE AIRLINES
Stock price and earnings history, 1960–69

	Price/Share	E.P.S.	P/E	D.P.S.	Yield	Net operating revenue	Price Range
1960..........	8¾	1.02	8.48	.12	1.37	49,876	6⅞–9¼
1961..........	10½	1.09	9.63	.16	1.52	59,312	7¼–12⅛
1962..........	12	1.14	10.53	.16	1.33	73,605	6¼–12⅞
1963..........	17¼	1.34	12.87	.20	1.16	93,967	10⅜–22½
1964..........	16½	1.42	11.62	.24	1.45	127,053	15–23⅛
1965..........	22⅜	1.66	13.48	.24	1.07	153,619	16½–29¼
1966..........	20¼	1.73	8.54	.32	1.58	196,114	19⅝–31⅞
1967..........	25½	2.04	12.50	.40	1.57	221,947	19¼–27¾
1968..........	31¼	2.33	13.41	.40	1.28	253,437	25½–31¼
1969..........	28⅜	2.67	10.63	.40	1.41	274,835	27⅜–35⅞

EXHIBIT 9
UNIVERSE AIRLINES
Future capital requirements
(dollar figures in thousands)

	1970	1971	1972	1973
Ground property*.................	5,200	5,300	5,300	5,300
and equipment..................		8,900	10,600	10,600
Flight equipment†				
Douglas DC-9-32‡..............	2,435			
Boeing B-747§..................	13,970	47,480		
Douglas DC-10‖................	11,500	12,500	31,500	21,000

* Expansion of existing facilities 1970–73; purchase of facilities and equipment for Denver and Seattle 1971–73. High range anticipates new route approval; low range anticipates new route disapproval by CAB.
† Flight equipment purchases subject to agreements made prior to December 31, 1969. No subsequent purchases 1970–73 considered.
‡ Balance due on last Douglas DC-9-32.
§ Balance due on three Boeing 747-Bs. Delivery August–December 1971. Advance of $13,920,000 payable in 1970.
‖ Balance due on five Douglas DC-10s. Assumed three will be delivered in 1972, two will be delivered in 1973.
Advances of $11,500,000 and $12,500,000 to be paid in 1971 and 1972, respectively.

EXHIBIT 10

UNIVERSE AIRLINES

10 airline industry composite data (unweighted averages)

	Sales (millions)	Net income (millions)	E.P.S.	Price/ share	P/E ratio	Dividends/ share	Dividend yield (percent)	Return on equity (percent)	Current ratio (times)	Debt/ total assets (percent)	Total asset turnover (times)
1960	$201	$ 3.0	$ 0.27	$ 6.7	12.9	$0.18	2.2	3.5	1.7	61	.85
1961	212	−0.2	−0.39	7.6	20.8	0.13	2.3	−2.5	1.4	64	.79
1962	240	2.3	0.10	7.4	11.1	0.12	1.7	5.4	1.5	63	.86
1963	271	8.1	0.71	14.2	13.8	0.14	2.0	9.0	1.5	60	.95
1964	308	16.8	1.57	20.4	10.8	0.25	1.8	15.7	1.4	55	.97
1965	363	28.3	2.47	35.1	15.7	0.31	1.7	21.9	1.6	52	.92
1966	410	29.8	2.36	43.9	19.4	0.50	1.4	20.0	1.7	55	.82
1967	507	34.2	2.43	38.0	19.7	0.56	1.3	16.3	1.6	55	.79
1968	571	21.7	1.45	35.2	22.8	0.62	1.7	9.7	1.4	60	.72
1969	655	20.8	1.09	21.8	15.3	0.53	1.6	6.0	1.2	59	.75

EXHIBIT 11

UNIVERSE AIRLINES

Industry data

	Year	American	Braniff	Continental	Delta	Eastern	National	Northwestern	TWA	United	Western
Dividends per share....	1960	$ 0.50	$ 0.05	0	$ 0.08	$ 0.49	$ 0.03	$ 0.10	0	$ 0.20	$ 0.30
	1961	0.50	0.02	0	0.08	0.13	0	0.10	0	0.21	0.30
	1962	0.50	0.02	0	0.09	0	0	0.10	0	0.22	0.30
	1963	0.50	0.04	$ 0.05	0.13	0	0	0.13	0	0.23	0.33
	1964	0.56	0.02	0.13	0.19	0	0.15	0.15	0	0.75	0.59
	1965	0.63	0.02	0.20	0.25	0	0.20	0.20	0	0.88	0.73
	1966	0.66	0.08	0.27	0.32	0.22	0.30	0.30	$ 1.00	0.94	0.91
	1967	0.79	0.08	0.40	0.33	0.40	0.30	0.35	1.00	1.00	0.91
	1968	0.80	0.38	0.50	0.40	0.50	0.30	0.40	1.00	1.00	0.91
	1969	0.80	0.50	0.50	0.40	0.38	0.30	0.45	0.50	1.00	0.45
Price per share........	1960	$ 10.8	$ 1.4	$ 2.1	$ 1.9	$ 11.5	$ 2.5	$ 2.0	$ 13.9	$ 14.9	$ 6.0
	1961	11.1	1.5	2.6	3.2	13.2	3.5	4.0	12.0	17.8	7.1
	1962	9.2	1.8	2.2	5.3	9.7	6.2	4.7	10.5	15.2	9.6
	1963	17.3	2.2	4.5	9.1	14.6	9.7	9.2	31.0	22.5	22.1
	1964	22.4	4.6	6.6	10.3	21.4	16.4	15.9	47.8	29.6	28.8
	1965	30.6	12.2	17.6	23.8	44.5	35.1	31.9	63.5	52.4	39.8
	1966	34.5	23.3	25.8	39.4	38.4	42.9	59.5	73.6	61.0	40.6
	1967	33.8	15.5	24.3	34.1	46.8	34.5	43.3	50.6	66.0	30.9
	1968	35.0	21.1	23.5	37.4	28.4	40.3	43.0	42.6	43.0	38.0
	1969	30.8	10.1	12.8	30.5	14.5	23.8	28.0	23.4	27.0	16.6
Sales (in millions)	1960	$ 429	$ 87	$ 61	$120	$ 294	$ 70	$123	$ 378	$ 379	$ 69
	1961	421	89	63	146	295	65	111	363	502	64
	1962	463	95	66	170	288	90	151	401	594	86
	1963	488	99	78	210	355	109	171	477	623	99
	1964	544	110	88	225	414	122	212	575	669	118
	1965	612	129	117	258	508	148	263	673	793	124
	1966	728	188	158	319	496	182	311	700	857	156
	1967	842	256	188	398	658	180	384	876	1,099	193
	1968	957	294	208	432	745	225	416	948	1,262	222
	1969	1,033	326	256	516	870	260	468	1,098	1,478	240

E.P.S.

Year										
1960	$ 0.70	$ 0.04	$ 0.31	$ 0.17	$ −0.87	$ −0.39	$ .09	$ 0.97	$ 1.11	$ 0.52
1961	0.42	0.04	0.13	0.28	−2.32	−0.98	.28	−2.21	0.29	0.18
1962	0.42	0.14	0.21	0.37	−2.30	0.58	.60	−0.85	0.61	1.18
1963	1.17	0.07	0.27	0.72	−3.04	1.00	.72	2.95	1.07	2.12
1964	1.96	0.34	0.61	0.82	−0.90	1.08	1.47	5.47	2.02	2.83
1965	2.21	0.53	1.26	1.20	3.52	1.91	2.50	5.74	3.27	2.57
1966	3.01	1.01	1.75	1.81	1.57	2.62	2.90	3.29	2.26	3.39
1967	2.38	0.27	1.73	2.57	2.05	2.03	3.21	3.89	3.92	2.27
1968	1.75	0.63	0.41	1.89	−1.09	2.51	2.74	1.90	2.23	1.56
1969	1.90	0.34	0.28	2.05	−0.26	2.25	2.46	1.76	2.39	−2.26

P/E ratio

Year										
1960	15.4	35.3	6.7	11.3	—	—	20.9	14.3	13.4	11.6
1961	26.2	36.7	19.3	11.5	—	—	14.5	—	61.5	38.5
1962	22.1	12.7	10.4	14.6	—	10.7	7.9	—	24.9	8.1
1963	14.8	30.2	16.3	12.5	—	9.7	12.8	10.5	21.0	10.4
1964	11.4	13.7	10.9	12.6	12.6	15.2	10.8	8.7	14.7	10.2
1965	13.9	22.7	14.0	19.8	24.5	18.4	12.8	11.1	16.0	15.5
1966	11.5	23.2	14.7	21.8	22.8	16.4	20.5	22.4	26.9	12.0
1967	14.2	58.3	14.0	13.3	—	17.0	13.5	13.0	16.8	13.6
1968	20.0	33.5	57.2	19.8	—	16.0	15.7	22.4	19.3	24.3
1969	16.2	29.8	45.8	14.9	—	10.6	11.4	13.3	11.3	—

Dividend yield (percent)

Year										
1960	4.0	2.3	0	4.7	3.0	0.7	2.6	0	1.4	3.0
1961	4.7	1.7	0	4.2	1.1	0	5.1	0	1.4	5.1
1962	4.5	1.6	0	2.7	0	0	2.5	0	1.3	4.3
1963	5.4	2.4	2.3	2.5	0	0	2.7	0	1.6	3.5
1964	3.3	0.8	3.0	2.1	0	1.6	1.6	0	3.3	2.7
1965	2.8	0.4	3.0	2.5	0.5	1.2	1.3	1.6	3.0	2.5
1966	2.2	0.7	1.5	1.3	1.0	0.9	0.9	1.4	1.8	2.3
1967	2.3	0.4	1.6	0.9	1.1	0.7	0.6	2.0	1.6	2.2
1968	2.4	2.4	2.1	1.2	1.3	0.9	0.9	1.2	1.5	2.9
1969	2.3	2.4	2.1	1.1	—	0.8	1.1	—	2.3	1.2

EXHIBIT 11 (Continued)

	Year	American	Braniff	Continental	Delta	Eastern	National	Northwestern	TWA	United	Western
Net income...........	1960	$ 11.8	$ 0.7	$ 1.7	$ 2.8	$ -5.6	$ -2.9	$ 1.6	$ 6.5	$ 11.2	$ 2.4
	1961	7.3	0.7	1.1	4.7	-15.0	-7.3	3.7	-14.8	3.7	0.9
	1962	7.1	2.4	1.8	7.0	-14.9	4.3	7.2	-5.7	7.7	5.6
	1963	19.7	1.3	2.4	13.8	-19.7	8.2	10.5	19.7	14.7	10.0
	1964	33.5	6.0	5.7	15.7	-5.8	7.9	26.8	37.0	27.3	13.4
	1965	39.7	9.5	12.1	23.0	29.7	15.1	45.7	50.1	45.8	12.1
	1966	54.1	17.8	17.2	34.6	15.0	21.9	53.1	29.7	38.3	16.0
	1967	48.1	4.7	17.3	49.2	24.1	17.1	58.7	40.8	72.8	12.2
	1968	35.5	10.4	4.1	36.1	-11.9	21.1	50.1	21.5	41.8	8.4
	1969	38.5	6.2	3.2	39.2	-2.3	18.9	51.5	19.9	44.7	-12.2
Return on common equity (percent)	1960	7.9	2.0	9.4	7.2	-5.1	-8.8	2.5	5.1	7.2	7.5
	1961	4.8	2.0	4.5	11.3	-15.0	-27.9	7.2	-16.9	1.9	2.7
	1962	4.7	6.3	6.6	13.0	-17.2	14.1	13.7	-7.0	3.9	15.7
	1963	12.3	3.1	7.9	21.3	-40.1	20.8	15.3	19.4	6.5	23.0
	1964	18.0	13.1	15.5	20.4	-13.5	18.9	21.8	26.4	11.3	24.7
	1965	17.2	17.2	25.5	24.2	24.1	26.0	27.7	21.4	16.4	19.3
	1966	19.2	21.4	27.4	27.9	9.9	27.6	25.0	11.3	9.1	21.4
	1967	13.1	6.3	22.2	29.6	10.5	18.1	22.2	13.9	13.3	13.6
	1968	9.1	12.4	5.3	18.5	-6.2	18.7	16.3	6.5	7.3	9.0
	1969	9.2	7.1	3.3	17.3	-1.5	14.8	12.1	5.8	7.4	-15.4
Current ratio.........	1960	1.6	2.0	1.5	1.5	1.7	1.4	1.9	1.5	1.3	2.5
	1961	1.7	1.9	1.3	1.2	1.5	1.2	1.0	1.2	1.2	1.4
	1962	2.1	1.8	1.7	1.3	1.5	1.1	1.1	1.3	1.2	1.7
	1963	1.7	1.8	1.7	1.6	1.7	1.7	1.2	1.5	1.1	1.3
	1964	1.6	1.9	1.0	1.3	1.7	1.3	1.1	1.2	1.1	1.4
	1965	1.5	2.1	1.6	1.5	1.9	1.5	1.1	1.0	1.8	1.7
	1966	1.8	2.9	1.3	1.8	1.3	1.6	1.3	1.1	2.2	1.8
	1967	2.0	0.8	1.7	1.4	1.7	1.4	1.4	1.6	2.4	1.7
	1968	1.6	1.4	1.1	1.5	1.4	0.8	1.3	1.5	1.2	1.7
	1969	1.3	1.1	0.9	1.2	1.1	0.8	0.9	1.8	1.1	1.4

Debt per total assets
(percent)

Year										
1960	63	54	73	58	60	58	59	67	64	49
1961	68	54	61	58	69	66	65	77	66	59
1962	69	50	65	53	73	62	58	81	63	57
1963	66	48	59	46	84	57	53	79	55	49
1964	62	43	56	39	87	55	35	72	57	42
1965	61	50	53	38	71	51	37	60	62	41
1966	65	73	53	43	70	46	35	63	57	40
1967	65	76	64	37	69	43	29	64	56	47
1968	63	73	72	39	75	51	36	64	61	63
1969	62	72	67	46	77	41	28	68	60	69

Total asset turnover

Year										
1960	.83	.95	.74	.99	.87	.72	.83	.84	.75	.98
1961	.68	.94	.81	1.08	.86	.65	.59	.76	.78	.75
1962	.69	.99	.69	1.07	.88	.88	.81	.75	.94	.87
1963	.69	1.04	.83	1.16	1.11	.95	.87	.93	.98	.89
1964	.75	1.11	.84	1.16	1.13	.98	.89	.92	.92	.95
1965	.75	.99	.86	1.11	1.14	.94	.79	.98	.81	.87
1966	.67	.61	.87	1.01	.91	.96	.74	.84	.71	.91
1967	.62	.68	.65	1.08	.79	.85	.80	.82	.73	.83
1968	.67	.79	.55	0.92	.76	.70	.66	.82	.70	.64
1969	.69	.87	.64	0.81	.84	.81	.63	.77	.76	.65

EXHIBIT 12
UNIVERSE AIRLINES
General business statistics*

Year	GNP	Net profit (billions)	E.P.S. (S & P 500)	Dow Jones averages	P/E ratio (S & P 500)	D.P.S. (S & P 500)	Dividends (billions)	Personal income	Personal savings
1960	$503.8	$26.7	$3.28	$592.0	$17.1	$1.95	$13.5	$401.1	$17.2
1961	520.1	27.2	3.44	716.1	21.1	1.97	13.7	416.6	21.0
1962	560.4	31.2	3.66	602.6	16.7	2.08	15.1	442.5	21.5
1963	590.5	33.1	4.01	739.4	17.6	2.21	16.5	465.5	20.0
1964	632.4	38.5	4.56	874.6	18.1	2.41	17.8	497.5	26.2
1965	684.9	46.5	5.17	949.5	17.1	2.64	19.8	538.9	28.4
1966	749.9	50.0	5.55	782.6	14.9	2.84	20.8	587.2	32.5
1967	793.9	46.7	5.34	891.5	17.5	2.91	21.4	629.3	40.4
1968	865.1	48.2	5.76	963.8	17.2	3.01	23.3	688.8	40.4
1969	931.4	48.6	5.81	816.5	16.6	3.14	24.7	748.9	37.7

* The Dow Jones figures are the average of the highest and lowest closing prices for the fourth quarter of each year. All the other figures are averages of all four quarters for each year. The national economic aggregates (excludes items 3 through 6 above) were obtained from *Survey of Current Business*, U.S. Office of Business Economics. These annual aggregates were derived from averaging each quarter's seasonally adjusted annual figure, which will explain possible slight discrepancies from the true annual figures.

EXHIBIT 13
UNIVERSE AIRLINES
Dividends per share

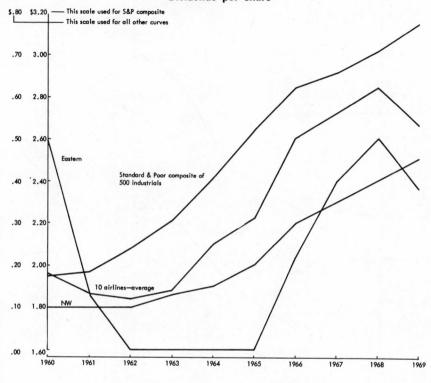

EXHIBIT 14
UNIVERSE AIRLINES
GNP, sales, profits

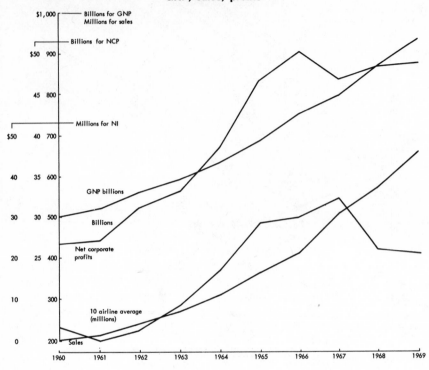

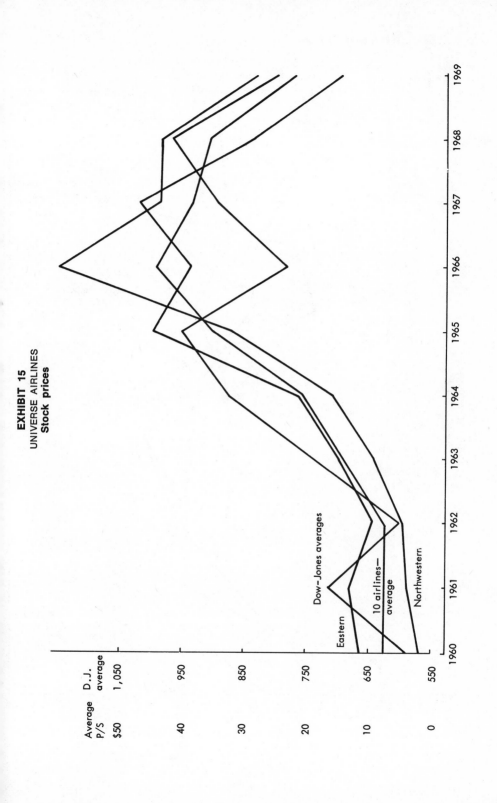

EXHIBIT 15
UNIVERSE AIRLINES
Stock prices

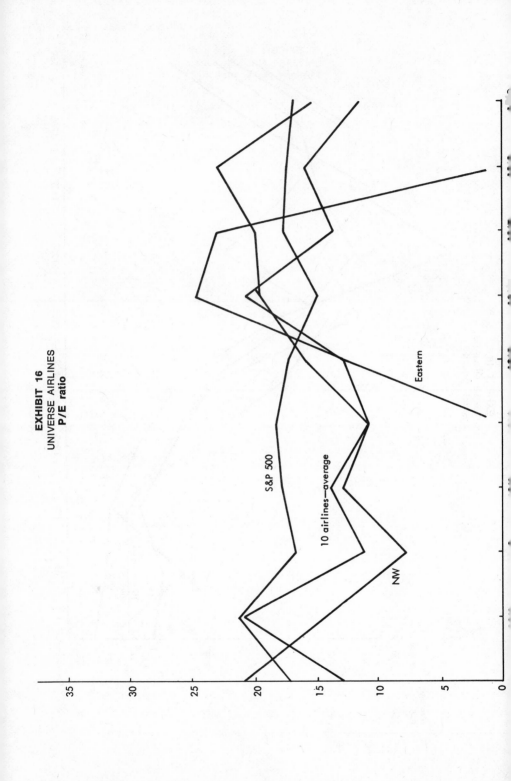

EXHIBIT 16
UNIVERSE AIRLINES
P/E ratio

S&P 500

10 airlines—average

NW

Eastern

35
30
25
20
15
10
5
0

EXHIBIT 17
UNIVERSE AIRLINES
Earnings per share

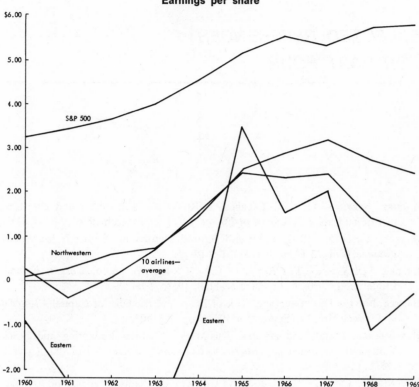

SELECTED REFERENCES
FOR PART FOUR

ARCHER, STEPHEN H., and FAERBER, LEROY G. "Firm Size and the Cost of Equity Capital," *Journal of Finance*, Vol. 21 (March 1966), pp. 69–84.

ARDITTI, FRED D. "Risk and the Required Return on Equity," *Journal of Finance*, Vol. 22 (March 1967), pp. 19–36.

BARGES, ALEXANDER. *The Effect of Capital Structure on the Cost of Capital.* Englewood Cliffs, N.J.: Prentice-Hall, 1963.

BAXTER, NEVINS D. "Leverage, Risk of Ruin, and the Cost of Capital," *Journal of Finance*, Vol. 22 (September 1967), pp. 395–404.

BEN-SHAHAR, HAIM, and ASCHER, ABRAHAM. "Capital Budgeting and Stock Valuation: Comment," *American Economic Review*, Vol. 57 (March 1967), pp. 209–14.

BODENHORN, DIRAN. "A Cash Flow Concept of Profit," *Journal of Finance*, Vol. 19 (March 1964), pp. 16–31.

BONESS, A. JAMES. "A Pedagogic Note on the Cost of Capital," *Journal of Finance*, Vol. 19 (March 1964), pp. 99–106.

BREWER, D. E., and MICHAELSON, J. "The Cost of Capital, Corporation Finance, and the Theory of Investment: Comment," *American Economic Review*, Vol. 55 (June 1965), pp. 516–24.

BRIGHAM, EUGENE F., and SMITH, KEITH V. "The Cost of Capital to the Small Firm," *The Engineering Economist*, Vol. 13 (Fall 1967), pp. 1–26.

CROCKETT, JEAN, and FRIEND, IRWIN. "Capital Budgeting and Stock Valuation: Comment," *American Economic Review*, Vol. 57 (March 1967), pp. 214–20.

ELTON, EDWIN J., and GRUBER, MARTIN J. "The Cost of Retained Earnings— Implications of Share Repurchase," *Industrial Management Review*, Vol. 9 (Spring 1968), pp. 87–104.

FARRAR, DONALD E., and SELWYN, LEE L. "Note on Taxes, Corporate Financial Policy and the Cost of Capital to the Firm." Working Paper. Cambridge, Mass.: Sloan School of Management: Massachusetts Institute of Technology, 1967.

FRIEDLAND, SEYMOUR. *The Economics of Corporate Capital.* Part II. Englewood Cliffs, N.J.: Prentice-Hall, 1966.

GORDON, MYRON J. *The Investment, Financing and Valuation of the Corporation.* Homewood, Ill.: Richard D. Irwin, Inc., 1962.

GORDON, MYRON J. "The Savings Investment and Valuation of a Corporation," *Review of Economics and Statistics,* Vol. 44 (February 1962), reprinted in James Van Horne (ed.), *Foundations for Financial Management.* Homewood, Ill.: Richard D. Irwin, Inc., 1966, pp. 434–59.

HALEY, CHARLES, W. "A Note on the Cost of Debt," *Journal of Financial and Quantitative Analysis,* Vol. 1 (December 1966), pp. 72–93.

HOLT, CHARLES C. "The Influence of Growth Duration on Share Prices," *Journal of Finance,* Vol. 17 (September 1962), pp. 465–75.

LERNER, EUGENE M., and CARLETON, WILLARD T. "The Integration of Capital Budgeting and Stock Valuation," *American Economic Review,* Vol. 44 (September 1964), pp. 683–702.

LERNER, EUGENE M., and CARLETON, WILLARD T. *A Theory of Financial Analysis.* New York: Harcourt, 1966.

LERNER, EUGENE M., and CARLETON, WILLARD T. "Financing Decisions of the Firm," *Journal of Finance,* Vol. 21 (May 1966), pp. 202–14.

LERNER, EUGENE M., and CARLETON, WILLARD T. "Reply," *American Economic Review,* Vol. 57 (March 1967), pp. 220–22.

LEWELLEN, WILBUR G. *The Cost of Capital.* Belmont, Calif.: Wadsworth Publishing Co., Inc., 1969.

LINDSAY, J. R., and SAMETZ, H. W. *Financial Management: An Analytical Approach.* Homewood, Ill., Richard D. Irwin, Inc., 1967.

LINTNER, JOHN. "Dividends, Earnings, Leverage, Stock Prices and the Supply of Capital to Corporations," *Review of Economics and Statistics,* Vol. 44 (August 1962), pp. 243–69.

LINTNER, JOHN. "The Cost of Capital and Optimal Financing of Corporate Growth," *Journal of Finance,* Vol. 18 (May 1963), pp. 292–310.

LINTNER, JOHN. "Security Prices, Risk, and Maximal Gains from Diversification," *Journal of Finance,* Vol. 20 (December 1965), pp. 587–616.

MALKIEL, BURTON G. "Equity Yields, Growth, and the Structure of Share Prices," *American Economic Review,* Vol. 53 (December, 1963), pp. 1004–31.

MAO, JAMES C. T. "The Valuation of Growth Stocks: The Investment Opportunities Approach," *Journal of Finance,* Vol. 21 (March, 1966), pp. 95–102.

MILLER, M. H., and MODIGLIANI, FRANCO. "Cost of Capital to Electric Utility Industry," *American Economic Review,* Vol. 56 (June 1966), pp. 333–91.

MODIGLIANI, FRANCO, and MILLER, M. H. "The Cost of Capital, Corporation Finance and the Theory of Investment." *American Economic Review,* Vol. 48 (June 1958), pp. 261–97.

MODIGLIANI, FRANCO, and MILLER, M. H. "The Cost of Capital, Corporation

Finance and the Theory of Investment: Reply," *American Economic Review*, Vol. 51 (September 1958), pp. 655–69. MODIGLIANI, FRANCO, and MILLER, M. H. "Taxes and the Cost of Capital: A Correction," *American Economic Review*, Vol. 53 (June 1963), pp. 433–43. MODIGLIANI, FRANCO, and MILLER, M. H. "Reply," *American Economic Review*, Vol. 55 (June 1965), pp. 524–27.

PETERSON, D. E. *A Quantitative Framework for Financial Management.* Homewood, Ill.: Richard D. Irwin, Inc., 1969, chaps. 1–3.

PORTERFIELD, JAMES T. S. *Investment Decisions and Capital Costs.* Englewood Cliffs, N.J.: Prentice-Hall, 1965.

QUIRIN, G. DAVID. *The Capital Expenditure Decision.* Homewood, Ill.: Richard D. Irwin, Inc., 1967, Chaps. 5 and 6.

ROBICHEK, A. A., and McDONALD, JOHN G. "The Cost of Capital Concept: Potential Use and Misuse," *Financial Executive*, Vol. 33 (June 1965), 2–8.

ROBICHEK, A. A., McDONALD, J. G., and HIGGINS, R. C. "Some Estimates of the Cost of Capital to Electric Utilities, 1954–1957: Comment," *American Economic Review*, Vol. 57 (December 1967), pp. 1278–88.

ROBICHEK, A. A., McDONALD, J. G., and MYERS, STEWART C. *Optimal Financial Decisions.* Englewood Cliffs, N.J.: Prentice-Hall, 1965.

ROBICHEK, A. A., and MYERS, STEWART. "Problems in the Theory of Optimal Capital Structure," *Journal of Financial and Quantitative Analysis*, Vol. 1 (June 1966), pp. 1–35.

SCHWARTZ, ELI. "Theory of the Capital Structure of the Firm," *Journal of Finance*, Vol. 14 (March 1959), pp. 18–39.

SCHWARTZ, ELI, and ARONSON, J. RICHARD. "Some Surrogate Evidence in Support of the Concept of Optimal Capital Structure," *Journal of Finance*, Vol. 22 (March 1967), pp. 10–18.

SOLOMON, EZRA. "Measuring a Company's Cost of Capital," *Journal of Business*, Vol. 28 (October 1955), pp. 240–52.

SOLOMON, EZRA. *The Management of Corporate Capital.* New York: Free Press, 1959.

SOLOMON, EZRA. *The Theory of Financial Management.* New York: Columbia University Press, 1963.

VICKERS, DOUGLAS. "Elasticity of Capital Supply, Monopsonistic Discrimination, and Optimum Capital Structure," *Journal of Finance*, Vol. 23 (March 1967), pp. 1–9.

WESTON, J. FRED. "A Test of Cost of Capital Propositions," *Southern Economic Journal*, Vol. 30 (October 1963), pp. 105–212.

WIPPERN, RONALD F. "Financial Structure and the Value of the Firm," *Journal of Finance*, Vol. 21 (December 1966), pp. 615–34.

Valuation and the Cost of Capital* for Regulated Industries

Edwin J. Elton and Martin J. Gruber†

MUCH of the theoretical work on cost of capital and valuation has been tested using data from the electric utility industry [1, 5, 7, 9, 10]. Many reasons have been put forth for this choice. Paramount among them has been the desire to find a large sample of firms which are homogeneous with respect to product, technology, and markets and thus hopefully homogeneous with respect to operating risk. In addition, electric utilities employ unusually uniform accounting standards and have earning patterns and rates of return which are reasonably stable over time.

While all of these characteristics make electric utilities suitable for testing cost of capital propositions, the fact that the electric utility industry is regulated introduces a new problem. The very process of regulation might make the appropriate formulation of valuation or cost of capital equations different from those which are appropriate for nonregulated industries. One aspect of this problem which has received wide attention in the literature is the effect of debt on the value of the firm and the cost of capital.

The original discussion of this controversy is contained in the Miller and Modigliani [6] and Gordon [2] articles. In this exchange, and in a subsequent article [1], Gordon stated that the correct formulations were those presented by M & M when they ignored the effect of corporate taxes.[1] Furthermore, he asserts that because M & M incorrectly

---

*Reprinted from *The Journal of Finance*, Vol. 26, No. 3 (Spring 1971), pp. 661-70, by permission of the authors and the publisher.

†Associate Professors of Finance, Graduate School of Business Administration, New York University.

[1] The argument revolves around whether the models proposed by M & M in [7] or those put forth in their tax correction article [8] are more appropriate for regulated industry. We shall refer to the equations put forth by M & M in [7] as the pre-tax equations and those put forth in [8] as the post-tax equations.

tested a model incorporating the tax effect of debt, they misinterpreted their own statistical results. Gordon's argument is based on the belief that regulators set prices in a way that causes the post-tax pre-interest return for a firm to be constant.

This article shows that even if Gordon is correct in his view of the regulatory process, he may very well be incorrect in his choice of the appropriate model to test. Furthermore, it is Gordon rather than M & M who has misinterpreted the meaning of his statistical results. It should be emphasized that it is not only the interpretation of the work of M & M and Gordon that is affected by this controversy. Rather, the resolution of this conflict affects the interpretation of all previous empirical studies and the evidence these studies supply as to the appropriateness of alternative theories of the cost of capital and value of the firm.

I. THE APPROPRIATE DEFINITION OF RISK CLASS

Let us start by examining Gordon's view of the regulatory process in more detail. Gordon has stated that a change in the utilities leverage "may be expected to cause the (regulatory) agency to change consumer rates and $\bar{X}$ (expected earnings before interest and taxes) so as to leave $\bar{X}^\tau$ unchanged."[2]

Since $\bar{X}^\tau$ is earnings after tax but before interest, Gordon's view can be paraphrased as follows. Regulators adjust prices in such a way that after-tax earnings plus interest is a constant independent of the firm's debt-equity ratio. Gordon further argues that because of this regulation the appropriate equations to test are the pre-tax equations of M & M.[3] This position is succinctly stated in Brigham and Gordon: "a utilities earnings on the common equity vary with leverage in exactly the same way that they would if the corporations were not subject to an income tax. Hence, for electric utility companies all the (M & M) equations developed previously on the assumption of no corporate income tax are valid with a corporate income tax."[4] Even accepting Gordon's view of the regulatory process, we disagree with Gordon's conclusions as to the appropriate equations to test.

The value of the firm to Gordon is implied in his second statement and subsequent analysis.[5] Using M & M's notation it is:

$$V = \frac{\bar{X}^\tau}{\rho}. \tag{1}$$

This equation can be used to derive an expression for the value of a firm in terms of the pre-tax earnings of an all-equity firm. Using Gordon's definition

---

[2] Gordon [2], 1272.
[3] Ibid.
[4] Brigham and Gordon [1], 93.
[5] Gordon [2], 1272.

of the regulatory process, we can equate earnings after taxes but before interest for the levered and unlevered firm. Introducing the subscript NL to represent the non-levered firm yields:[6]

$$\bar{X}^\tau = \bar{X}_{NL}. \tag{2}$$

Expressing post-tax earnings as a function of pre-tax earnings for the non-levered firm we have

$$\bar{X}_{NL} = \bar{X}_{NL}(1 - \tau). \tag{3}$$

Substituting (3) and (2) into (1), we have

$$V = \frac{\bar{X}_{NL}(1 - \tau)}{\rho}. \tag{4}$$

Either equation (1) or equation (4) can be used to express the value of the firm according to Gordon.

On the other hand, M & M [8] argue that the value of any firm (regulated or not) is simply

$$V = \frac{\bar{X}(1 - \tau)}{\rho} + \tau D. \tag{5}$$

However, under Gordon's view of the regulatory process, $\bar{X}$ (the earnings on assets) is not a constant but is affected by the amount of debt in the firm's capital structure.

Accepting Gordon's description of the regulatory process (equation 2) and expressing $\bar{X}^\tau$ and $\bar{X}_{NL}^\tau$ in terms of pre-tax cash flows, we have[7]

$$\bar{X} - (\bar{X} - rD)\tau = \bar{X}_{NL}(1 - \tau). \tag{6}$$

Solving for $\bar{X}$ gives:

$$\bar{X} = \bar{X}_{NL} - \frac{rD\tau}{(1 - \tau)}. \tag{7}$$

---

[6] This is the equation Gordon described on 1272 of [2].

[7] $\bar{X}$ is a variable and can be interpreted as the earnings before interest and taxes which the regulatory agency allows a firm to earn. This equation can be derived directly from Gordon's equation (7) in [2]. Equation 7 is

$$\bar{X} = \frac{\bar{X}^\tau - \tau rD}{1 - \tau}$$

or

$$\bar{X}^\tau = \bar{X} - \tau(\bar{X} - rD).$$

If the firm is unlevered, this reduces to $\bar{X}_{NL}^\tau = \bar{X}_{NL}(1 - \tau)$. Equating the post-tax pre-interest earnings for the levered and unlevered firm yields (6).

Substituting (7) into (5) yields:

or
$$V = \frac{\left\{\bar{X}_{NL} - \dfrac{rD\tau}{1 - \tau}\right\}(1 - \tau)}{\rho} + \tau D \qquad (8)$$

$$V = \frac{\bar{X}_{NL}(1 - \tau)}{\rho} + \frac{D\tau(\rho - r)}{\rho}. \qquad (9)$$

Equation (8) or (9) represents the value of the firm according to M & M if we accept Gordon's definition of regulation. The difference between equations (1) and (5) (or the equivalent equations (4) and (9)) arises because of the authors' belief that different variables should be capitalized at the rate ρ. In order to determine the appropriate earnings stream to capitalize at this rate, we must first understand M & M's use of equivalent risk class. M & M define risk in terms of the probability distribution of average possible outcomes divided by expected outcome. Two income streams are subject to the same risk (in the same risk class) if they have identical distributions of average possible outcomes divided by expected outcome. If two income streams are subject to the same risk, they must provide the same yield to an investor and, therefore, be capitalized at the same rate. M & M have shown that if two income streams having the same risk do not yield the same return to the investor, homemade leverage (arbitrage) will take place to insure identical yields.

Therefore, to determine whether Gordon or M & M are correct, we must determine which part of the earnings stream of a company employing debt is subject to the same risk as the earnings stream of a debt-free company. That is, which part of the earnings stream should be capitalized at the rate ρ, the capitalization rate for an all-equity firm. Gordon has capitalized the term $\bar{X}^\tau$ or $\bar{X}_{NL}(1 - \tau)$ by the rate ρ. This is correct if the distribution of $\dfrac{X^\tau}{\bar{X}^\tau}$ is unchanged with different proportions of debt. M & M [8] in their post-tax formulation discount $\bar{X}(1 - \tau)$ or $\left(\bar{X}_{NL} - \dfrac{rD\tau}{1 - \tau}\right)(1 - \tau)$ (using Gordon's theory of regulation) at the rate ρ. This is correct if the distribution of $\dfrac{X(1 - \tau)}{\bar{X}(1 - \tau)} = \dfrac{X}{\bar{X}}$ is unchanged with different financial structures. The resolution of this difference depends on whether the probability distribution of $\dfrac{X}{\bar{X}}$ or $\dfrac{X^\tau}{\bar{X}^\tau}$ is independent of leverage.[8] We will show that under Gordon's assump-

---

[8] As shown in M & M [7], the appropriate way to define a risk class is in terms of the distribution of the ratio of the random variable average future earnings to its mean value. As pointed out above, the debate is whether the pre-tax or post-tax ratio is invariant to a change in the firm's debt-equity ratio.

tions concerning the nature of regulation, $\dfrac{X}{\overline{X}}$ is independent of leverage and correctly defines a risk class and that his use of $\dfrac{X^\tau}{\overline{X}^\tau}$ is incorrect.

Proof that the distribution of $\dfrac{X}{\overline{X}}$ is independent of leverage

Let us consider a utility with no debt in its capital structure which sells a single product.
Let:

M = price per unit of service for the no-debt company,
C = cost per unit of service,
d_i = units of service demanded—a random variable,[9] and
$P(d_i)$ = the probability of the demand level equaling d_i.[9]

The probability distribution of earnings before taxes and interest for the nonlevered firm is equal to:

$$(M - C)\, d_i. \tag{10}$$

The expected earnings before interest and taxes is:

$$(M - C) \sum_{i=0}^{\infty} d_i P(d_i). \tag{11}$$

The probability distribution of $\dfrac{X}{\overline{X}}$ can then be represented by dividing (10) by (11) or

$$\frac{X}{\overline{X}} = \frac{d_i}{\displaystyle\sum_{i=0}^{\infty} d_i P(d_i)}. \tag{12}$$

Consider a second firm identical to the first except for the presence of debt in its capital structure.[10] According to Gordon, the regulatory agencies would set

---

[9] X according to M & M is average future earnings. We have split X into $(M - C) d_1$. The symbol d_1 is used to embody the averaging necessary to determine average future earnings. It is the probability distribution of average future demand and is not necessarily equal to the probability distribution of demand in any one year.

[10] These firms need not be the same size. The only change in the proofs necessary to accommodate differences in size is to define d_i as the number of units of service demanded per unit of assets. The empirical work on cost of capital or valuation hypotheses is based upon a crosssection of firms with different capital structures at a point in time. Our proofs are designed to yield equilibrium relation-

a different price for this firm so that the after tax earnings plus interest is the same as that of the unlevered firm.

Let:

Y = price per unit of service for the firm with debt in its capital structure and

R = interest charges on the debt.

Using Gordon's belief concerning the regulation process, we can equate the expected value of earnings after taxes but before interest for the levered and unlevered firm:

$$(M - C) \sum_{i=0}^{\infty} d_i P(d_i)(1 - \tau) = (Y - C) \sum_{i=0}^{\infty} d_i P(d_i)(1 - \tau) + \tau R. \tag{13}$$

Solving for Y gives:

$$Y = M - \frac{R\tau}{(1 - \tau) \sum\limits_{i=0}^{\infty} d_i P(d_i)} \tag{14}$$

The probability distribution of earnings before interest and taxes for the levered firm is equal to:

$$(Y - C) \, d_i. \tag{15}$$

Substituting equation (14) into equation (15) gives:

$$\left\{ M - \frac{R\tau}{(1 - \tau) \sum\limits_{i=0}^{\infty} d_i P(d_i)} - C \right\} d_i, \tag{16}$$

while expected earnings are equal to:

$$\left\{ M - \frac{R\tau}{(1 - \tau) \sum\limits_{i=0}^{\infty} d_i P(d_i)} - C \right\} \sum_{i=0}^{\infty} d_i P(d_i). \tag{17}$$

The probability distribution of $\dfrac{X}{\bar{X}}$ for the levered firm is thus equal to (16) divided by (17) or:

$$\frac{X}{\bar{X}} = \frac{d_i}{\sum\limits_{i=0}^{\infty} d_i P(d_i)}. \tag{18}$$

---

ships for different firms at a point in time. It is, of course, possible that firms changing their capital structure receive a transitional gain or loss.

For an alternative approach, one which both analyzes change over time in the value of the firm as it changes its capital structure and derives results in terms of the Sharp-Lintner-Mossin general equilibrium model see Hamada [3].

Equation (18) is identical to equation (12) which was derived for the case of an unlevered firm. Consequently, the random variable earnings before interest and taxes is independent of leverage and is appropriate for defining a risk class.

Proof that the distribution of $\dfrac{X^\tau}{\overline{X}^\tau}$ depends on the firm's leverage

Let us perform a parallel analysis in terms of earnings after taxes and before interest to see if such a definition is an appropriate way of defining risk class. The distribution of these earnings for the unlevered firm is:

$$(M - C)\, d_i(1 - \tau) \tag{19}$$

with an expected value of:

$$(M - C)(1 - \tau) \sum_{i=0}^{\infty} d_i P(d_i). \tag{20}$$

The probability distribution of $\dfrac{X^\tau}{\overline{X}^\tau}$ for the non-levered firm can be found by dividing (19) by (20):

$$\frac{d_i}{\displaystyle\sum_{i=0}^{\infty} d_i P(d_i)}. \tag{21}$$

The distribution of earnings before interest and after taxes for the levered firm is equal to:

$$(Y - C)(1 - \tau)\, d_i + R\tau. \tag{22}$$

Using equation (14) yields:

$$\left(M - \frac{R\tau}{(1 - \tau) \displaystyle\sum_{i=0}^{\infty} d_i P(d_i)} - C \right)(1 - \tau)\, d_i + R\tau \tag{23}$$

with an expected value of

$$\left(M - \frac{R\tau}{(1 - \tau) \displaystyle\sum_{i=0}^{\infty} d_i P(d_i)} - C \right)(1 - \tau) \sum_{i=0}^{\infty} d_i P(d_i) + R\tau. \tag{24}$$

Thus, the probability distribution of $\dfrac{X^\tau}{\bar{X}^\tau}$ for the levered firm is:

$$\frac{\left(M - \dfrac{R\tau}{(1-\tau)\sum\limits_{i=0}^{\infty} d_i P(d_i)} - C\right)(1-\tau)\,d_i + R\tau}{\left(M - \dfrac{R\tau}{(1-\tau)\sum\limits_{i=0}^{\infty} d_i P(d_i)} - C\right)(1-\tau)\sum\limits_{i=0}^{\infty} d_i P(d_i) + R\tau.} \tag{25}$$

In order for $\dfrac{X^\tau}{\bar{X}^\tau}$ to be appropriate for defining risk class, equation (25) must equal equation (21). These two equations will be equal only if $d_i P(d_i) = \sum\limits_{i=0}^{\infty} d_i P(d_i)$ for all i, a condition which arises only in the certainty case.[11] Since the distribution of $\dfrac{X}{\bar{X}}$ is invariant with the proportion of debt in a firm's capital structure, $\bar{X}$ rather than $\bar{X}^\tau$ should be discounted at the rate ρ. Consequently, the formulation of the value of the firm presented in (8) (or 5) is appropriate, and Gordon's formulations (1) and (4) are incorrect. Although equation (5) is identical to M & M's valuation equation with the impact of corporate taxes included, Gordon's definition of the impact of regulation does affect its properties. This can be illustrated by examining the derivative of the valuation equation with respect to D. For nonregulated firms $\bar{X}$ is not affected by the firm's debt/equity ratio and the derivative of equation (5) with respect to D yields:

$$\frac{dV}{dD} = \tau.$$

With Gordon's definition of regulation, $\bar{X}$ becomes a function of the firm's debt/equity ratio, and equation (8) becomes a more useful form. Taking the derivative of equation (8) with respect to D yields:

$$\frac{dV}{dD} = \frac{\tau(\rho - r)}{\rho}.$$

Since $\tau > \tau\left(1 - \dfrac{r}{\rho}\right)$, regulation (as specified by Gordon) does reduce the value of the levered firm. However, it does not, as he stated, reduce the differential value of leverage to zero.

The question remains as to whether M & M's use of equation (5) to test the

---

[11] d_i must be single valued for equation (25) to equal equation (21).

value of electric utilities led to biased results as Gordon claims. M & M measured $\bar{X}$ as earnings before interest and taxes for utilities with different amounts of debt in their capital structure. If Gordon is right about the nature of regulation, they were actually observing $\left(\bar{X}_{NL} - \dfrac{rD\tau}{1 - \tau}\right)$ when they measured $\bar{X}$, and were thus testing equation (8), which we have demonstrated is the correct valuation equation. Gordon's assertion of bias in the regression coefficients because of a misspecification of the valuation equation is incorrect.

II. THE COST OF CAPITAL UNDER REGULATION

Most empirical tests of the M & M system have not directly employed their valuation equation. Rather, the tests have been performed on one or more of the propositions regarding the yield to security holders which M & M derived from their valuation equation. In this section of the paper we will derive the appropriate form of these propositions under Gordon's definition of regulation. We will show that these propositions are identical to those put forth by M & M when they included the effect of corporate taxes and that Gordon was incorrect in adopting their pre-tax equations.

As just shown under Gordon's assumption about regulation, equation (9) is the appropriate valuation equation. It is:

$$V = \frac{\bar{X}_{NL}(1 - \tau)}{\rho} + \frac{D\tau(\rho - r)}{\rho}. \tag{9}$$

Multiplying both sides of the equation by ρ, dividing by V, and using equations (2) and (3) yields:

$$\rho = \frac{\bar{X}\tau}{V} + \tau(\rho - \tau)\frac{D}{V}. \tag{26}$$

Solving for $\dfrac{\bar{X}\tau}{V}$, gives:

$$\frac{\bar{X}\tau}{V} = \rho - \tau(\rho - r)\frac{D}{V}. \tag{27}$$

Equation (27) is exactly M & M's equation (11.c) in [7] or the after-tax earnings yield in the nonregulated case.[12]

We can now easily solve for the after-tax yield on equity capital.[13]

---

[12] We have employed the terminology used by M & M in their tax correction article [8]. Many authors (including M & M themselves) have referred to this equation as the after-tax cost of capital.

[13] We have again employed the terminology used by M & M in their tax correction article. Many authors (including M & M themselves) have referred to this equation as the after-tax cost of equity capital.

The after-tax yield on equity capital is equal to earnings available for common stock divided by the market value of common stock:

$$\frac{\bar{\pi}^\tau}{S} = \frac{\bar{X}^\tau - rD}{S}. \tag{28}$$

But from (27) above,

$$\bar{X}^\tau = \rho V - \tau(\rho - r)D. \tag{29}$$

Substituting (29) into (28) and simplifying gives:

$$\frac{\bar{\pi}^\tau}{S} = \rho + (1 - \tau)(\rho - r)\frac{D}{S}. \tag{30}$$

Equation (30) is identical to the form put forth by M & M for a non-regulated firm in [8].

In contrast, Brigham and Gordon [1] propose that for regulated industry the after-tax yield on equity capital should be:

$$\rho + (\rho - r)\frac{D}{S}.$$

They test the equation

$$\frac{D}{P} = \alpha_0 + \alpha_1 br + \alpha_2 \frac{D}{S}.$$

Brigham and Gordon use the size of a regression coefficient which they call α_2 as one test of the M & M theory. They state that if M & M are correct, then α_2 should be equal to $(\rho - r)$ and have a value between .01 and .025. However, if they had used the correct formulation, equation (30), α_2 would be equal to $(1 - \tau)(\rho - r)$ and its value should lie between $(1 - \tau)(.01)$ and $(1 - \tau)(.025.)$[14] Assuming a corporate income tax rate of 50% the critical values for testing M & M would be .005 and .0125, and all of Brigham and Gordon's estimates using market measures would lie in this critical range and thus support M & M. However their estimates employing book measures of debt and equity still fall outside the critical range.

III. CONCLUSION

In this paper we have shown that, even if Gordon's definition of regulation is accepted, M & M have been consistent and correct in applying their post-tax formulation to regulated industry. On the other hand, Gor-

---

[14] To the extent that τ varies between utilities, Brigham and Gordon's use of D/S rather than $(1 - \tau) D/S$ would introduce error into the independent variable which would bias the regression coefficient in a downward direction. See Johnston [4].

don has failed to apply correctly his own definition of the regulatory process and so has incorrectly interpreted his own as well as M & M's empirical results.

REFERENCES

1. Eugene Brigham and Myron Gordon. "Leverage, Dividend Policy, and the Cost of Capital," *Journal of Finance*, Vol. 23, No. 1 (March 1968).

2. Myron Gordon. "Some Estimates of the Cost of Capital to the Electric Utility Industry, 1954–57: A Comment," *American Economic Review*, Vol. 57, No. 5 (December 1967), pp. 1267–77.

3. Robert Hamada. "The Effects of Leverage and Corporate Taxes on the Shareholders of Regulated Industries," in Trebig, Harry M. and Howard R. Hayden (eds.), *Rate of Return under Regulation* (Division of Research, Michigan State University, 1969).

4. J. Johnston. *Econometric Methods*. New York: McGraw-Hill, 1960.

5. Merton Miller and Franco Modigliani. "Some Estimates of the Cost of Capital to the Electric Utility Industry, 1954–1957," *American Economic Review*, Vol. 56 (June 1966), pp. 333–91.

6. Merton Miller and Franco Modigliani. "Some Estimates of the Cost of Capital to the Electric Utility Industry, 1954–57: Reply," *American Economic Review*, Vol. 57, No. 5 (December 1967), pp. 1288–1300.

7. Franco Modigliani and Merton Miller. "The Cost of Capital, Corporation Finance, and the Theory of Investment," *American Economic Review*, Vol. 48 (June 1958), pp. 261–97.

8. Franco Modigliani and Merton Miller. "Corporate Income Taxes and the Cost of Capital—A Correction," *American Economic Review*, Vol. 53 (June 1963), pp. 433–43.

9. Alex Robichek, John McDonald and Robert Higgins. "Some Estimates of the Cost of Capital to the Electrical Utility Industry: Comment," *American Economic Review*, Vol. 57, No. 5 (December 1967), pp. 1278–88.

10. J. Fred Weston. "A Test of Cost of Capital Propositions," *Southern Economic Journal*, Vol. 30 (October 1963), pp. 105–12.

Fund Administration and Dividend Policy[*]

Robert H. Plattner [†]

DIVIDEND POLICY is a widely used term in finance which is fairly universally accepted to mean that policy which determines the amount of dividends to be paid from the earnings of a firm. Fund administration, on the other hand, is a little-used term in financial writing. To my knowledge it has never been defined, possibly because of the relative unimportance of "internal funds" prior to 1954, the date when accelerated forms of depreciation were authorized for general use in computing federal income tax for business firms. The apparent originator of the term fund administration in financial writing is M. H. Waterman.[1] In his writing, however, he does not distinguish between fund administration and dividend policy.

It could be argued that determining dividend policy is fund administration and vice versa. But I believe that there is a benefit to be derived by making a distinction between the two terms in both meaning and usage. Reduced to a simple proposition, there is a process, appropriately called fund administration, which describes how a firm manages its funds, and the dividend decision is only one, although a vital one, of the several decisions which make up the fund administration policies of a firm. Therefore, the term dividend policy alone *should not* be used to describe the *basis* on which decisions that determine the characteristics of a firm's dividend payments are made.

---

[*] Reprinted from *Quarterly Review of Economics and Business*, Vol. 9 (1969), pp. 21–29, by permission of the author and the publisher.

[†] Assistant Professor of Finance, University of Massachusetts.

[1] Merwin H. Waterman and others, *Essays on Business Finance* (Ann Arbor, Mich.: Masterco Press, 1957).

The term dividend policy, an investor-oriented term, should be confined to describing the *results* of fund administration, an internal management process. Used in this manner, dividend policy would be evidenced primarily by a firm's payout ratio—the percentage of earnings paid out in dividends. It can also be used to describe the historical patterns, or regularity, of dividend payments and perhaps to include observations on the use of stock dividends in lieu of cash disbursements.

The purpose of this article is to show that if a firm determined the size of its dividend payment without considering its overall fund administration process it would commit a serious error.

First a concept of fund administration and a description of the funds administered will be presented. The idea will then be advanced that the dividend decision is made in conjunction with other fund decisions. Thus, what might be called dividend policy should more properly be described as a *part* of fund administration policy.

I am not explicitly concerned with the question of how firms determine the amount of dividends to be paid. Therefore, I do not explore the question of what motivates a firm to exhibit a certain dividend payment pattern. Although this is an important question in finance it is beyond the scope of this venture.

There are currently many confusing and inconsistent uses of the term funds; and since ideas concerning fund administration cannot be presented without establishing a concept of the term funds, it necessarily must be clearly understood before fund administration is discussed. I will begin with an attempt to clarify some of the confusing concepts manifest in the usage of the term and then will argue for the inclusion of the dividend decision within the larger framework of decisions constituting fund administration.

FUNDS AND THEIR CONCEPTS

There is an unfortunate latitude of meaning of the term funds as used in financial writing.[2] Some authors use it to mean cash. Others define funds as net working capital, and still others use it to mean all a firm's financial resources. All too often, after an author has defined the term, he uses it in a way which contradicts his definition, and even alternates between different meanings.[3] Writers in accounting literature

---

[2] Perry E. Mason, *"Cash Flow" Analysis and the Funds Statement* (New York: American Institute of Certified Public Accountants, 1961), pp. 11–12; and Hector R. Anton, *Accounting for the Flow of Funds* (Boston: Houghton, 1962), p. 31.

[3] Fourteen recent editions of finance textbooks were reviewed to determine what meaning the author assigned to the word funds and whether he was consistent throughout the book. These books were as follows: Louis K. Brandt, *Business Finance, a Management Approach* (Englewood Cliffs, N.J.: Prentice-Hall, 1956); Gilbert W. Cooke, and Edwin C. Bromeli, *Business Financial Management* (Boston:

have long been critical of the misuse of the term.[4] Apparently their attitude has had little effect upon writers of finance textbooks.

Table 1 illustrates the three most common ways in which funds are defined. It is important to note that the way in which a funds statement is constructed "defines" the meaning of the term funds. This is the basis of most of the errors which occur in financial literature. An author defines the term, then constructs a fund statement which shows funds to be something else.

In practice, very few funds statements are actually constructed on a cash basis, because most firms do not operate on such a basis. Thus, their current assets and revenues are not entirely cash items.

Most funds statements are constructed using funds to mean net working capital. However, in many cases this is not as suitable for financial analysis and planning as a statement constructed so that the term means all the financial resources of a firm.[5] This concept of funds includes not only all a firm's assets, but also its spending or purchasing power. It includes assets which are acquired by the issue of common stock in exchange, a transaction which would not appear in a funds statement constructed on either a cash or a net working capital basis. It should be noted that in Table 1 the item of net working capital may still be used without contradicting the definition of funds as financial resources—since net

---

Houghton, 1967); Carl S. Dauten and Merle T. Welshans, *Principles of Finance* (Cincinnati: South-western, 1964); Charles W. Gerstenberg, *Financial Organization and Management of Business* (Englewood Cliffs, N.J.: Prentice-Hall, 1959); Paul G. Hastings, *The Management of Business Finance* (Princeton, N.J.: Van Nostrand, 1966); Pearson Hunt and Victor L. Andrews, *Financial Management, Cases and Readings* (Homewood, Ill.: Irwin, 1968); Pearson Hunt, Charles M. Williams, and Gordon Donaldson, *Basic Business Finance, Text and Cases* (Homewood, Ill.: Irwin, 1966); William H. Husband and James C. Dockeray, *Modern Corporation Finance* (Homewood, Ill.: Irwin, 1966); Robert W. Johnson, *Financial Management* (3d ed.; Boston: Allyn and Bacon, 1966); Raymond P. Kent, *Corporate Financial Management* (2d ed.; Howewood, Ill.: Irwin, 1964); J. Robert Lindsay and Arnold W. Sametz, *Financial Management, an Analytical Approach* (Homewood, Ill.: Irwin, 1967); Richards C. Osborn, *Business Finance, the Management Approach* (New York: Appleton-Century-Crofts, 1965); Eli Schwartz, *Corporation Finance* (New York: St. Martin's, 1962); and J. Fred Weston and Eugene F. Brigham, *Managerial Finance* (New York: Holt, 1966).

Only one author, Hastings, clearly defines the term funds and maintains consistency throughout the book between his definition and his use of the term in funds statements. He defines the term as all a firm's assets. Two other authors, Osborn and Brandt, are consistent but do not specifically define the term. Osborn uses funds to mean all assets, and Brandt uses funds to exclude working capital. Of the other authors, some define the term, some do not, but all use it in an inconsistent manner, shifting between the choices of cash, net working capital, and all assets throughout their books.

[4] In addition to the works of Mason and Anton, see also William A. Paton, "The 'Cash-Flow' Illusion," *Accounting Review*, Vol. 38, No. 2 (April 1963), pp. 243–51.

[5] Mason, *"Cash Flow" Analysis and the Funds Statement*, p. 54.

TABLE 1
Funds statements using alternative definitions of funds

Funds defined as cash		*Funds defined as net working capital*		*Funds defined as all financial resources*	
Sources					
Cash received from sales....	$100	Net income............	$40	Net income............	$40
		Depreciation..........	30	Depreciation..........	30
Sale of common stock......	10	Sale of common stock......	10	Stock issued in exchange for building............	10
Sale of machinery..........	5	Sale of machinery..........	5	Sale of machinery..........	5
				Increase in current liabilities............	5
Total funds received........	$115		$85		$90
Uses					
Retirement of debt.........	$ 5	Retirement of debt........	$ 5	Retirement of debt........	$ 5
Dividends..................	10	Dividends.................	10	Dividends.................	10
Purchase of fixed assets....	65	Purchase of fixed assets..	65	Purchase of fixed assets...	65
Increase in net working capital............	5	Increase in net working capital............	5	Increase in current assets............	10
Cash expense...............	30				
Total funds used...........	$115		$85		$90

working capital is considered an asset. Furthermore, it is accurate and consistent to define funds as financial resources, yet discuss cash or net working capital transactions as fund transactions. Most financial authors would benefit by adopting the definition of funds as that of all financial resources. This is the definition used in this article.

Fund administration is, of course, the process of administering funds. There are, however, several facets to the process which deserve attention. I will focus primarily on one facet, the interrelation of the dividend decision to other decisions which make up the total process of fund administration.

FUND ADMINISTRATION

Fund administration implies a stream or source of funds which is managed in some way. For example, funds may be used to pay dividends, to purchase assets, to retire debt, or for other purposes. Also, external funds may be used to supplement available internal funds. In a sense, it may be said that a funds statement exhibits the results of a firm's fund administration policies.

A classification commonly used in funds statements distinguishes between internal and external sources. This twofold classification is also useful for the following discussion of fund administration.

Internal funds

It is important to understand the nature of the internal fund stream, for it is the primary source of funds for many firms. When a firm does not make regular large capital expenditures it may have little or no need to resort to external sources.

Internal funds come from revenue, and from a finance point of view, revenue is generally considered an independent variable not subject to control. However, revenue may be divided into three separate elements which *are* subject to some degree of control: (1) current or "cash" expense, paid in the current period, (2) noncurrent or "noncash" expense, which is paid either in a prior period, such as depreciation, or which is expected to be paid in a future period, such as deferred taxes, and (3) net income or earnings. It will be convenient later to subdivide earnings into dividends and retained earnings.

Firm managers generally strive to keep current expenses at a minimum for any given level of revenue. Beyond this, there is little control over the current expense portion of revenue. In contrast, noncurrent expense *must* be controlled. That is to say, the size of noncurrent expense is a result of managerial policy. The appropriate size of noncurrent expense is unknown at the time the relevant revenue is determined. Therefore, the quantity of noncurrent expense that applies to the current period is a matter of managerial judgment. This does not mean that firm managers adjust the size of noncurrent expense to achieve short-run objectives. It does mean, however, that they can adjust the size of noncurrent expense according to policy objectives which may change over time. An example would be the decision of what depreciation rate to use—straight line or some form of accelerated depreciation—or the decision to defer that part of taxes related to the use of accelerated depreciation.

The decision which determines the size of noncurrent expense also affects the size of earnings. That is, for any given quantity of revenue and current expense, a change in the size of noncurrent expense will have an opposite effect on earnings. This relationship may be seen in Table 2. Example A in Table 2 is a base with which alternatives B

TABLE 2
Three elements of revenue

	Alternative income statements showing different sizes of revenue components		
	A	*B*	*C*
Revenue.................	100	100	100
Current expense..........	50	50	45
Noncurrent expense........	30	35	30
Earnings (net income).......	20	15	25
Dividends................	12	12	13.2
Retained earnings..........	8	3	11.3
Net income payout ratio*.....	60%	80%	52.8%
Internal fund payout ratio†....	24%	24%	24%

* Dividends/net income.
† Dividends/net income and noncurrent expense.

and C are compared. Example B shows an increase in noncurrent expense which reduces earnings. Notice that although the dividend payment is not changed, the net income payout ratio *increases*, and also that the internal fund payout ratio, the ratio of dividends to net income plus noncurrent expense, *remains the same*. Example C shows the effect of a decrease in current expense—such as income tax. The net income payout ratio is lower than that of Example A.

When considering the subject of fund administration, only those funds which are subject to control are of importance. Hence internal funds are defined or measured by the sum of earnings plus noncurrent expense. In a general sense the *total* quantity of internal funds is not controllable, but the *relative size* of noncurrent expense and earnings is.

External funds and dividends

Fund administration extends beyond the determination of the relationship between the relative size of noncurrent expense and earnings. The scope of fund administration includes also the decision which determines the relationship between the quantity of dividends paid and the quantity of external funds required. External funds are those obtained from the sale or issue of securities.

Many firms, if not most, follow a practice of paying a regular dividend.[6] That is, regardless of the approximate portion which is regularly paid from earnings (sometimes called a target ratio), the dollar amount of dividends is not decreased unless the firm's liquidity is threatened. In fact, it is not uncommon for firms to obtain external funds in order to make a usual or a reduced dividend payment. Also, the dividend amount is not increased unless it appears that the new level can be maintained. Dividend and other funds data of firms representing total U.S. industry for the period 1955–66 are shown graphically in Chart 1.

It may be seen in Chart 1 that the pattern of aggregate dividends is very steady, moving upward after 1960 when industry earnings begin to increase. Aggregate dividends declined only in 1958 when net income declined sharply. Dividends represent a quantity of internal funds which is not available for capital expenditures. Therefore, annual dividends are plotted below the base line so that quantities above the line represent only funds used for capital expenditures. For the purpose of this analysis capital expenditures include increases in net working capital. Thus capital expenditures are equal to the total quantity of funds used.

When the quantity of dividends paid is deducted from internal funds, the quantity remaining is available for asset expansion, which includes working capital expansion. Internal funds come from revenue, and since the pattern of dividend payments is relatively steady, the pattern of internal funds available for capital expenditures follows closely the pattern of firm revenues—which is not necessarily steady and/or predictable. Relevant revenue data for U.S. industry are not available but internal fund quantities are shown in Chart 1.

Planned fund expenditures do not necessarily coincide with revenue and internal fund expectations.[7] When expenditures exceed internal funds

---

[6] John Lintner, "Distribution of Incomes of Corporations among Dividends, Retained Earnings, and Taxes," *American Economic Review*, Vol. 46, No. 2 (May 1956), pp. 97–113; and John A. Brittain, *Corporate Dividend Policy* (Washington, D.C.: Brookings, 1966). Brittain provides excellent references on the many dividend studies which have been made.

[7] Firms do try to relate capacity to expected volume requirements but, to the extent that forecasting does not produce exact results, capital spending does not correlate closely with internal fund availability. See Maurice W. Lee, *Macroeconomics; Fluctuation, Growth and Stability* (4th ed.; Homewood, Ill.: Irwin, 1967),

CHART 1
Funds data of aggregate U.S. industry

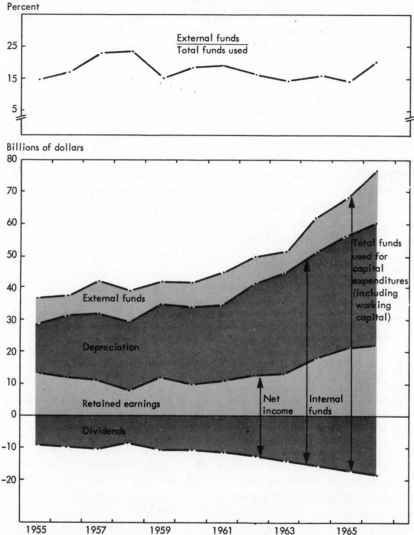

Source: *Economic Report of the President* (Washington: U.S. Government Printing Office, 1967), p. 294. Dividend data estimated from data on p. 290, to be consistent with data on p. 294.

less dividend payments, additional funds must be obtained from external sources. Total funds used (capital expenditures) and the percentage of

and Milton H. Spencer, Colin G. Clark, and Peter W. Houguet, *Business, and Economic Forecasting* (Homewood, Ill.: Irwin, 1961), all of whom discuss a theory of capital expenditures and offer references on studies which have been made in this area.

total funds supplied from external sources are shown at the top of Chart 1. It may be observed that when expenditures rise sharply, as in 1957, 1961, 1964, and 1966, incremental needs are supplied from external sources—external funds as a percentage of the total rises.

After 1961 the relative use of external funds declined (the proportion of internal funds increased). This may be attributed to a relatively decreased level of current expense, the federal income tax. In 1962 federal tax depreciation guidelines were revised, allowing a generally larger depreciation expense which reduced tax liabilities.[8] In 1964 federal income tax rates were reduced.

From the foregoing discussion of various fund relationships it may be concluded that the dividend decision affects the decision to use external funds. It may be clearly seen from Chart 1 that on an aggregate basis the volume of dividends paid regularly exceeds the annual quantity of funds obtained from external sources. This fact raises the question of how U.S. firms make their dividend decisions. It also raises the question as to the basis that should be used to evaluate dividend policy, that is, what data should be used to determine how a firm decides upon the quantity of dividends to be paid.

As mentioned previously, this article does not attempt to explore the question of what motivates a firm to adopt certain dividend payment patterns. My purpose is to illustrate the need for a concept of the dividend decision within a broader concept of fund administration. This requires a demonstration of the existence of important relationships, but not necessarily an evaluation or an explanation of their cause.

In Chart 2 data are plotted which show the relationship of dividends paid to net income (net income payout ratios) and dividends paid to net income plus depreciation (internal fund payout ratios). These data show that during the period 1955–56 firms tended to pay out a relatively constant percentage of internal funds in the form of dividends, despite fluctuations in the internal funds.[9] Even in 1957 when dividends declined, the ratio of dividends to internal funds did not deviate sharply from the 12-year average of 29.2 percent. In contrast, during the same period net income payout ratios not only fluctuated about the 12-year average of 45.7 percent, but tended to rise from 1955 to 1958, remained about 50 percent until 1963, and then declined to less than 45 percent.

Net income payout ratios display more volatility than do internal fund payout ratios because of the relatively large and stable quantity of depreciation expense, which is part of internal funds. But net income payout

---

[8] U.S. Department of the Treasury, *Depreciation—Guidelines and Rules*, Internal Revenue Service Publication 456 (Washington, D.C.: U.S. Government Printing Office, 1962), p. 1.

[9] See Brittain, *Corporate Dividend Policy*, whose work is an extensive statistical study. His results indicate similar findings.

CHART 2
Dividend data of aggregate U.S. industry

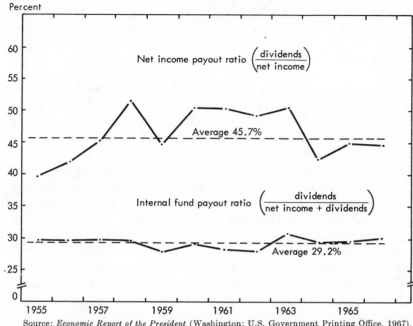

Source: *Economic Report of the President* (Washington: U.S. Government Printing Office, 1967), p. 294.

ratios appear to have shifted from one basic level to another during the 12-year period, whereas the internal fund payout ratios appear to have moved in shorter-term cycles about the 12-year average. The rise in net income payout ratios which occurred from 1954 to 1958 may be explained by the general use of accelerated forms of depreciation by firms after 1954. As stated previously, an increase in noncurrent expense will tend to cause a relative decrease in earnings unless revenue can be increased or current expense reduced. Thus if depreciation expense should increase, and firms adjust dividend payments so as to keep the ratio of dividends to internal funds constant, the accompanying reduction in earnings would result in increased net income payout ratios. The decline in net income payout ratios observed after 1963 may be explained by the reduction in federal income tax rates which became effective in 1961. Both earnings and internal funds increased, but not the proportion of internal funds paid out in dividends. Net income payout ratios declined because earnings increased proportionately more than did dividends. This phenomenon is illustrated in Chart 2.

It may be observed from these occurrences and relationships that if dividend policy were found to be related to net income payout ratios only, during the period 1955–64 many firms in the United States *did make changes* in their dividend policy. On the other hand, in terms of fund administration policy it can be observed that the same firms *made little or no change* in their dividend decisions.

SUMMARY

Fund administration is a term concerned with the total funds stream of a firm—its sources and its uses. Dividend payments are a use of funds which affect fund sources. The dividend decision, therefore, is an integral part of a firms' fund administration policy. And when the dividend decision is made, the most appropriate description of the process which takes place is *fund administration*. Also it seems more meaningful to make observations about a firm's dividend decision by referring to the quantity of dividends paid from the internal fund stream rather than from only the earnings portion of that stream.

In this context the term dividend policy would continue to describe more or less what it has always described—the percentage of earnings paid in dividends (net income payout ratio), dividend payment regularity, and other payment characteristics of interest to investors. It should be recognized, however, that net income payout ratios and other dividend characteristics are a result of fund administrative policies.

Increasing Stream Hypothesis
of Corporate Dividend Policy*
Keith V. Smith†

CORPORATE DIVIDEND POLICY has been examined normatively and empirically in studies of investment behavior and as part of larger works on corporate finance. Dividend decisions are of particular interest because they can be traced to a specific group of individuals within the organizational hierarchy. Decisions on major capital expenditures typically are made at varying levels within the organization depending upon the relative size and importance of each investment project. The responsibility for operating decisions and other policy measures may also be difficult to pinpoint within the complexity of large business organizations. But corporate dividend decisions are made expressly by the board of directors of the business firm. Another characteristic of corporate dividend policy is that a gap exists between the prescriptions of economic and financial theory and the real-world practices of corporate directors. This paper will not attempt to bridge that gap, but will attempt to clarify the empirical side by postulating and testing an alternative hypothesis of corporate dividend policy.

DIVIDEND POLICY RESEARCH

Dividend policy is of theoretical importance because it represents a flow of dollars to investors as a return on their equity investment, and

* Reprinted from *California Management Review*, Vol. 14, No. 1 (Fall 1971), pp. 56–64, by permission of the author and the publisher.

† Associate Professor of Finance and Business Economics, University of California. Research support was provided by the Division of Research, U.C.L.A. Helpful suggestions were made by Frank E. Norton, J. Fred Weston, and Steven A. Lippman of U.C.L.A.

because dollars not paid out to common shareholders are retained within the firm as an important source of long-term financing. Some theoretical models have focused on dividend policy directly, while others have placed dividend decisions within a larger framework. Miller and Modigliani[1], in a corollary to their classic treatment of cost of capital, showed that the total value of the firm is indifferent to the particular dividend policy which is followed. Gordon[2], building on his familiar stock valuation model, postulated functional relationships between the corporate retention rate and the average return earned on that retention, and proceeded to determine the optimal payout ratio for a firm. Walter[3] also developed a stock valuation model which focused on the important comparison between the market capitalization rate and the expected return on reinvested earnings. An informational context was suggested by Michaelson[4] in his diverse policies hypothesis. He argued that dividends are used by management to convey their future expectations for the firm, and thus dividend decisions depend on the recent history of dividend payments. A larger framework was reflected by Weston and Brigham[5] in their residual theory of dividend policy. This theory holds that, because of the higher cost of new equity capital, earnings should be retained as long as it is profitable to invest in capital projects. Lintner[6] also has formalized investment and financing decisions into a theoretical formulation which is a simultaneous solution of capital budgeting, cost of capital, capital structure, and dividend policy.

Alternative approaches likewise have appeared in empirical dividend models. In one type, the researcher has postulated stock values as a simple function of earnings and dividends[7], or has also included other variables[8] and industry factors[9]. A second type of model has attempted to explain dividend payments directly. The target ratio adjustment model of Lint-

---

[1] M. H. Miller and F. Modigliani, "Dividend Policy, Growth, and the Valuation of Shares," *Journal of Business*, Vol. 34 (October 1961), pp. 411–33.

[2] M. J. Gordon, "The Optimum Dividend Rate," *Management Sciences: Models and Techniques* (London: Pergamen Press, 1960), pp. 92–106.

[3] J. E. Walter, "Dividend Policy: Its Influence on the Value of the Enterprise," *Journal of Finance*, Vol. 18 (May 1963), pp. 280–89.

[4] J. B. Michaelson, "The Determinants of Dividend Policy: A Theoretical and Empirical Study" (unpublished doctoral dissertation, University of Chicago, 1961).

[5] J. F. Weston and E. F. Brigham, *Managerial Finance* (3d ed.; New York: Holt, Rinehart, Winston, 1969), pp. 372–97.

[6] J. Lintner, "Distribution of Incomes of Corporations among Dividends, Retained Earnings, and Taxes," *American Economic Review*, Vol. 46 (May 1956), pp. 97–113.

[7] M. J. Gordon, "Dividends, Earnings, and Stock Prices," *Review of Economics and Statistics*, Vol. 41 (May 1959), pp. 99–105.

[8] W. Beranek, *Analysis of Financial Decisions* (Homewood, Ill.: Richard D. Irwin, Inc., 1963).

[9] I. Friend and M. Puckett, "Dividends and Stock Prices," *Review of Economics and Statistics*, Vol. 54 (September 1964), pp. 256–81.

ner, which postulates current dividends as a function of dividends during the last period and earnings during the current period, has been confirmed in subsequent studies. Brittain[10] showed that that model could be improved by substituting cash flow for net earnings as an independent variable. Darling[11] tested a more complex model having dividends as a function of current earnings, prior earnings, depreciation, change in total sales, and a measure of firm liquidity. Findings of these empirical studies indicate that dividend decisions of many firms are not based on a simultaneous determination of investment and financing, as suggested by the more sophisticated theoretical models.

INCREASING STREAM HYPOTHESIS

A perusal of the dividend history of large industrial firms yields two immediate observations.

No single dividend theory, either theoretical or empirical, is likely to succeed in explaining the behavior of all firms; there simply is no consensus.

Many firms evince great reluctance to decrease or cut dividend payments, thus causing a certain stabilization in dividend patterns over time.

Lintner noted that the elements of inertia and conservation have tended to stabilize dividend policies, while Darling postulated that the career goals of top management are an important factor leading to stable dividend policies. The proposed hypothesis of this paper follows directly from such arguments.

The increasing stream hypothesis of corporate dividend policy is that the board of directors deliberately avoids dividend cuts if at all possible and attempts to construct over time an increasing, or at least a nondecreasing, record of cash dividend payments. A corollary of the increasing stream hypothesis is that, when it is no longer possible to avoid a dividend cut, directors will make a single cut large enough so that subsequent cuts are avoided. To illustrate, Figure 1 presents the recent historical dividend record of five well-known industrial firms. The five were chosen to illustrate different dividend policies that are encountered in the real world. Burroughs, to begin with, has paid the same annual dividend over the past decade. Columbia Broadcasting System has increased its dividend each year, although some of the increases were miniscule. Atlantic Richfield appears to follow a practice of maintaining a given dividend level until a higher level can be maintained. The policy of avoiding successive dividend cuts is illustrated by Sunstrand. Their record consists of two

---

[10] J. A. Brittain, *Corporate Dividend Policy* (Washington, D.C.: Brookings Institute 1966), pp. 37–73.

[11] P. G. Darling, "The Influence of Expectations and Liquidity of Dividend Policy," *Journal of Political Economy*, Vol. 65 (June 1957), pp. 209–24.

FIGURE 1

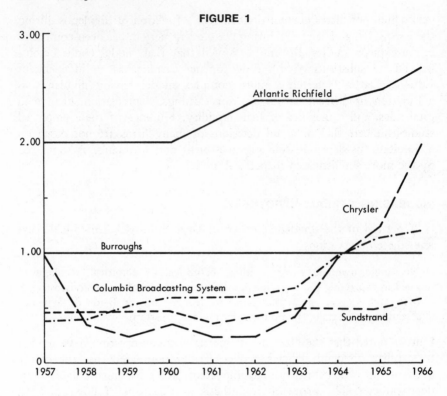

increasing stream segments interrupted by a significant cut of 23 percent in 1961. The first four firms support the increasing stream hypothesis of this paper. An exception to the hypothesis is Chrysler—its dividend decisions appear to be related to considerations other than the amount of prior dollar payments.

It is well to take a closer look at the possible rationale behind such a corporate dividend policy. First of all, the dividend decision is made by the board of directors of the firm. Although some boards have "outside" directors, a majority of power on most boards is wielded by inside directors who, in addition to being among the largest individual sharholders, comprise the top level management of the organization. Apart from the influence of the dividend decision on their personal investment in the firm, the directors undoubtedly are interested in establishing a dividend record which will perpetuate their position of influence and power within the organization. In a word, they will attempt, using dividend policy, to portray their contribution to the continued prosperity of the firm.

From the review of theoretical models, we have seen that certain academicians view dividend policy in a residual or passive context. Instead, they prefer to focus on retention policy as only one of a complex of issues including capital budgeting, capital structure, and cost of capital.

The simultaneous solution of these issues is suggested as being in the best interests of shareholders because it maximizes shareholder wealth. Characteristic of such a theoretical solution is that from year to year the available dividend payments vary inversely with the investment opportunities. An increasing stream of dividend payments would thus not be expected from a board of directors who based their dividend decisions on such theoretical arguments. Both approaches are based on the best interests of shareholders, but directors who follow the increasing stream hypothesis make decisions as they perceive investors would want them to rather than from the viewpoint of theoreticians. Another distinction is that the theoretical solution is a long-run phenomenon while the increasing stream hypothesis recognizes that investors respond to short-run dividend decisions. Existing studies of dividend policy and market prices have not succeeded in separating short-run from long-run effects.

An alternative interpretation of the increasing stream hypothesis deals with the informational content of the firm's dividend policy. We have seen that management can use dividend payments to signal future prospects for the firm. Because corporate directors have great flexibility in establishing the size of dividend payments from year to year, the increasing stream hypothesis may result in misinformation to investors. In other words, an increasing pattern of dividends by no means implies that investment opportunities, hence earnings prospects of the firm, are increasing in such a manner. By avoiding dividend cuts, management may overestimate future expectations. Conversely, one might argue that an increasing stream is just as likely to underestimate future prospects by avoiding large dividend increases that cannot be maintained. Expectations thus may be biased in either direction.

RESEARCH DESIGN

The remainder of this paper is concerned with an empirical test of the increasing stream hypothesis of corporate dividend policy. Although quarterly dividend data are tempting subjects to examine, it was felt that they are highly sensitive to special accounting practices, "extra" dividends, and the particular fiscal year used by different firms. For example, firms use extra dividends in various ways. Although an extra dividend might have a pronounced short-run effect on investors, it was felt that the annual cash dividend, including both normal and extra components, was the relevant datum for investigation since the extra component is probably soon forgotten. Another methodological decision was to limit attention to relatively large, well-established firms whose directors were likely to have had some degree of flexibility in establishing the annual dividend payments for their respective firms.

The Standard and Poor's Compustat Service provides a large sample of almost 900 firms that satisfy the above criteria. The particular tape used provided annual data for 1948 to 1967. Since most of the 1967 data were incomplete, only 19 years could be used. Basic data for the study, therefore, were the annual streams of earnings-per-share and dividends-per-share for all firms on the Compustat industrial tape. Both earnings and dividends were adjusted for all share splits and other effects so that the adjusted data represented consistent schedules over the total horizon of 20 years.

Cash dividends are made available from the earnings generated within the business firm. A first step was to calculate the trend of changes in earnings-per-share *(EPS)* over time. An earnings change for year was defined as

$$\Delta E(t) = \frac{EPS(t) - EPS(t-1)}{EPS(t-1)} \tag{1}$$

which is a simple percentage measurement. It was convenient to divide the possible range of earnings changes into intervals defined by $b_1 \leq \Delta E(t) \leq b_2$ where b_1 and b_2 are, respectively, the lower and upper boundaries of a given interval. Similarly, an annual change in dividends per share *(DPS)* for year t was calculated by

$$\Delta D(t) = \frac{DPS(t) - DPS(t-1)}{DPS(t-1)} \tag{2}$$

TABLE 1
Frequency of dividends per share changes by year and interval

Interval	1949	1950	1951	1952	1953	1954	1955	1956	195?
*..............	0	0	0	0	0	0	0	0	
< −.8.........	11	14	2	4	12	8	10	6	1
−.8 to −.6.....	11	1	3	6	6	5	2	2	
−.6 to −.4.....	21	10	16	16	14	12	8	3	1
−.4 to −.2.....	64	20	55	44	43	31	25	15	2
−.2 to 0.......	69	33	82	96	50	47	38	34	5
0..............	244†	186	238†	347†	364†	313†	238	240	29
0 to 2.........	90	100†	137	115	145	159	208†	240†	25
.2 to .4........	79	144	73	42	49	84	120	136	8
.4 to .6........	25	60	25	6	13	25	36	33	1
.6 to .8........	21	21	12	7	3	8	17	11	1
.8 to 1.0.......	6	13	11	2	1	6	4	3	
>1.0..........	22	56	23	8	12	22	25	34	
‡..............	5	20	17	9	2	11	15	9	
Total........	668	678	694	702	714	731	746	766	79
Cumulative Total........	668	1,346	2,040	2,742	3,456	4,187	4,933	5,699	6,49

* Dividends decreased but negative or zero values involved.
† Interval containing median value for that year.
‡ Dividends increased but negative or zero values involved.

and, again, percentage intervals of the form $b_1 \leq \Delta D(t) \leq b_2$ can be defined.

Another way of studying dividend behavior is to assign particular values to dividend changes and examine the sequence of such assignments over time. For example, let a value of zero (0) represent a dividend cut (of any size), a value of unity (1) represent a "repeated" or same-dividend payment, and a value of two (2) represent an increased dividend payment in a given year. The particular dividend pattern for a given firm could then be traced by observing the firm's sequence of 0, 1, and 2 values over some particular horizon. For example, the steady pattern for Burroughs as shown in Figure 1 could be summarized by the sequences (111111111) while the erratic pattern of Chrysler is given by (002012222). Any sequence, such as (111221122) for Atlantic Richfield, would illustrate an increasing stream policy. The increasing stream hypothesis was tested by examining such sequences for all firms listed on the Compustat tape, as well as with cumulative counts of $\Delta E(t)$ and $\Delta D(t)$ by intervals.

EMPIRICAL RESULTS

We first examine dividend policy by observing the changes in EPS and DPS over time for all firms in the sample. Table 1 presents the

'8	1959	1960	1961	1962	1963	1964	1965	1966	Total	Cumulative Total
0	0	0	0	0	0	0	0	0	0	0
.0	17	9	27	16	6	14	6	4	199	199
.6	1	5	6	1	6	2	2	2	80	279
.5	7	9	11	13	11	3	4	5	211	490
.6	28	12	12	10	24	8	10	12	497	987
.8	35	45	55	43	15	16	15	23	820	1,807
.5†	385†	346	397†	419†	413†	329	267	241	5,630†	7,437
5	238	273†	270	275	299	344†	353†	399†	4,115	11,552
.4	80	82	51	51	64	99	154	128	1,555	13,107
.2	19	29	12	17	10	24	26	27	411	13,518
8	13	8	2	3	5	6	14	12	184	13,702
3	6	5	5	4	4	5	3	6	91	13,793
1	14	20	13	12	10	20	19	14	344	14,137
0	10	24	3	18	18	18	20	15	230	14,367
.3	853	868	876	882	885	888	893	888		
.4	8,187	9,055	9,931	10,813	11,698	12,586	13,479	14,367		

distribution of $\Delta D(t)$ by interval for each year in the period 1949 to 1966. Values of b_1 and b_2 which define each interval are shown in the extreme left column of the table. The interval identified as "zero" includes those cases where the dividend payment was not changed. Numbers in the column for year t (where t = 1949, . . . , 1966) reveal the number of firms whose $\Delta E(t)$ fell into particular intervals. Totals at the bottom of each column indicate the number of firms for which relevant data were available for that year. The number of observations in a given year varied from 668 to 893, while the total number of firm-year observations for the entire study was 14,367. (If attention were limited to only those firms for which data were available across the entire horizon of the Compustat tape, the total number of observations would be greatly reduced. For example, Fama and Balicak[12], who followed that procedure with the same data source, had a total of only 6,246 observations.) The interval containing the median observation is indicated for each year, and also for the total study.

Note in Table 1 the large number of zero or small positive dividend changes. A total of 5,630 (39.2 percent) instances of no change, and 4,115 (28.6 percent) increases of less than 20 percent appear in just those two intervals. The median observation for each year and for the total study also appeared in only those two intervals. Conversely, only 1,807 (12.6 percent) times were dividend payments cut by the boards of directors of the sample firms. That is, the observations in Table 1 are heavily skewed toward positive dividend changes. Finally, the number of observations in each interval tends to decrease as one moves to larger dividend changes, both positive and negative.

Table 2 is a joint frequency distribution of $\Delta E(t)$ and $\Delta D(t)$ by intervals, but where counting is done over all years in the horizon. If most firms followed a constant payout dividend policy, then the majority of observations would have fallen along the major diagonal of the interval matrix in Table 2. Instead, note that many values also fell in cells adjacent to the major diagonal. The three most populated cells of Table 2 were: 1,824 instances when both earnings and dividends increased between 0 and 20 percent; 1,594 cases where earning increased but dividends were not changed; and 1,179 situations when dividends were not changed despite an earnings decrease.

Although a separate exhibit for $\Delta E(t)$ is not included because of space limitations, the row totals in Table 2 portray the aggregate behavior of earnings changes for all firms over the total horizon. Note that the distribution of earnings changes was skewed much less than that for dividend changes. The data in Tables 1 and 2 would thus appear to confirm the increasing stream hypothesis, at least in an aggregate sense,

---

[12] E. F. Fama and H. Balicak, "Dividend Policy: An Empirical Analysis," *Journal of the American Statistical Association*, Vol. 63 (December 1968), pp. 1132–61.

TABLE 2
Frequency comparison of earnings and dividends per share changes by intervals

Earnings intervals	Dividend intervals														Total	Cumulative total
	(1)	(2)	(3)	(4)	(5)	(6)	(7)	(8)	(9)	(10)	(11)	(12)	(13)	(14)	Total	
(1) *	0	71	22	31	30	14	197	8	3	3	0	0	5	3	387	387
(2) < −.8	0	10	8	8	9	12	54	9	4	1	0	0	0	4	119	506
(3) −.8 to −.6..	0	1	4	23	46	25	67	20	10	6	2	0	2	1	207	713
(4) −.6 to −.4..	0	7	8	31	64	78	200	86	31	6	8	2	8	11	540	1,253
(5) −.4 to −.2..	0	9	7	30	101	174	536	254	100	28	5	8	28	15	1,295	2,548
(6) −.2 to 0.....	0	8	5	25	83	219	1,179	698	202	36	21	17	34	24	2,551	5,099
(7) 0	0	2	2	2	6	35	200	144	29	10	2	1	9	1	443	5,542
(8) 0 to .2......	0	10	5	21	61	140	1,594	1,824	485	88	35	14	52	40	4,369	9,911
(9) .2 to .4.....	0	9	1	9	36	57	653	698	376	89	37	18	58	41	2,081	11,992
(10) 4 to .6.....	0	7	0	6	14	24	275	197	167	56	31	12	29	16	835	12,827
(11) 6 to .8.....	0	4	0	3	10	10	173	71	61	30	11	9	20	10	412	13,239
(12) 8 to 1.0....	0	1	0	0	6	6	94	41	30	18	12	2	23	6	239	13,478
(13) >1.0	0	20	12	16	21	18	259	62	54	38	19	8	69	46	642	14,120
(14) †	0	40	6	6	10	8	149	3	3	2	1	0	7	12	247	14,367
Total..........	0	199	80	211	497	820	5,630	4,115	1,555	411	184	91	344	230	14,367	
Cumulative Total..........	—	199	279	490	987	1,807	7,437	11,552	13,107	13,518	13,702	13,793	14,137	14,367		

* Decreased but negative or zero values involved.
† Increased but negative or zero values involved.

by indicating directors' reluctance to cut dividends regardless of what happens to company earnings.

An alternative test of the increasing stream hypothesis is obtained by examining the sequence of dividend changes over time by each firm. This is necessary since each firm-year observation in Tables 1 and 2 is treated independently of all others. Figures 2, 3, and 4 are based on

FIGURE 2

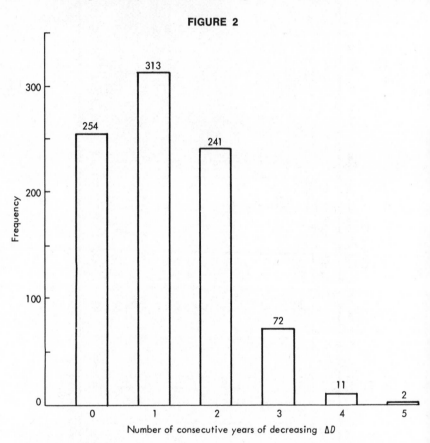

Number of consecutive years of decreasing ΔD

the zero-unity-two method of classifying dividend changes, as explained in the previous section.

Figure 2 has to do with decreasing dividends. The longest consecutive stream of decreasing dividends was observed and recorded for each of the 893 firms in the Compustat sample. A total of 254 firms never cut dividends during the period for which their dividend policy is available. The most frequent policy was connected with the 313 firms who cut dividends, but never in two or more consecutive years. If the increasing stream hypothesis is defined as the absence of two consecutive dividend

FIGURE 3

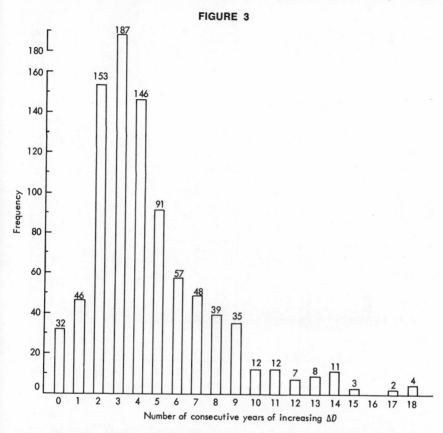

Number of consecutive years of increasing ΔD

cuts, then 567 (63.2 percent) firms followed such a hypothesis. But if the increasing stream hypothesis is defined by the weaker condition of the absence of three consecutive years of decreased dividends, then 808 (90.1 percent) of the firms confirmed that hypothesis.

At the other extreme, only 2 firms cut dividends in five straight years, while 11 firms had four straight dividend reductions. The earnings and dividends history of these firms is presented in Table 3. For each firm the first row of data is annual *EPS*, while the second is annual *DPS*. The first year in the relevant history t_1 is indicated in parentheses for each firm. In every case, the continued practice of cutting dividends is seen to be related to a deterioration in earnings generated by the firm. In several cases, earnings deficits were experienced for one or more years of the period. And for six firms, cash dividends were eliminated completely in the last year.

Since many firms cannot forecast future changes in EPS, it can be argued that certain examples of successive dividend cuts, such as in Table 3, do not violate the increasing stream hypothesis. Except for the last

FIGURE 4

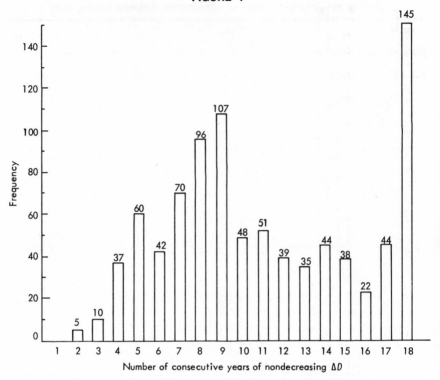

Number of consecutive years of nondecreasing Δ*D*

year of the horizon in which earnings improved, Scovill Manufacturing and Crompton Knowles had decreased earnings in each year that cash dividends were cut. Although a similar pattern was observed for Gulf and Western Industries, it may be attributed to a change of corporate philosophy as the firm became a conglomerate in the late 1950s. Conversely, firms such as Boston Herald Traveler and Celanese did violate the hypothesis since dividends were cut in two years for which earnings increased. Whereas many of the firms in Figure 2 which cut dividends two or three consecutive years can likewise be rationalized in terms of a degraded earnings profile, the relationship is by no means as obvious. One interpretation follows that of Lintner;[13] namely that firms take more than a single year to make the proper adjustment toward a new level of dividends.

Figure 3 has to do with policies of increasing dividends. The longest consecutive streak of increasing dividends was observed and recorded for each of the 893 firms in a manner analogous to that for Figure 2.

---

[13] J. Lintner, "Optimal Dividends and Corporate Growth under Uncertainty," *Quarterly Journal of Economics*, Vol. 78 (February 1964), pp. 49–95.

TABLE 3
Earning and dividend history of consecutive dividend cutting firms

Firm	t_1*	t_2	t_3	t_4	t_5	t_6
National Sugar Refining	$3.30	$3.50	$1.61	$1.14	$0.16	
(1957).................	2.50	2.25	2.00	0.90	0.00	
Pabst Brewing (1954)............	0.50	0.57	(0.19)	(0.70)	(0.60)	
	1.00	0.70	0.53	0.20	0.00	
Bayuk Cigars (1948)............	2.70	1.70	1.70	1.06	1.09	
	1.75	0.98	0.80	0.75	0.60	
Chris Craft Industries (1953).......	2.95	(0.50)	1.97	(1.66)	0.97	
	1.82	1.14	0.91	0.75	0.00	
Boston Herald Traveler (1954).....	1.41	2.01	1.72	2.08	2.99	
	1.20	1.05	1.00	0.50	0.00	
Celanese (1951).................	2.85	0.62	0.81	0.76	1.46	
	2.40	1.80	1.00	0.80	0.40	
Scovill Manufacturing (1955).......	3.66	2.81	1.31	(0.75)	2.37	
	2.50	2.25	2.00	0.75	0.50	
Crompton Knowles (1950)	7.96	6.32	2.25	0.18	0.50	
	6.00	3.00	1.75	0.50	0.25	
General Instrument (1953)	1.13	(0.50)	0.21	0.37	0.74	
	1.00	0.63	0.38	0.25	0.15	
Interstate Host (1952)............	0.67	0.62	0.73	0.69	0.75	
	0.40	0.30	0.20	0.15	0.10	
Gulf & Western Ind. (1951).......	1.29	1.17	1.13	(0.10)	(0.02)	
	0.80	0.70	0.60	0.30	0.00	
Triangle Conduit & Cable.........	1.88	1.70	0.23	0.31	(1.88)	0.28
(1958)..................	1.33	1.20	1.00	0.45	0.23	0.08
Neisner Brothers (1959)..........	0.82	0.18	0.44	(0.29)	0.15	0.51
	0.80	0.75	0.40	0.35	0.05	0.00

* t_1 represents the year indicated in parenthesis after each firm, while t_2, t_3, . . . , t_6 are subsequent years in each case.

Note: Earnings per share data in parenthesis are deficits.

It is seen that this frequency distribution includes longer streaks of increased dividends. Four firms increased dividends in each of the 18 years for which dividend changes could be observed. Although the median category was for four-year periods of increasing payments to shareholders, many firms exhibited relatively long periods wherein dividends were increased.

Recall that the increasing stream hypothesis also was defined in terms of a nondecreasing stream of dividend payments. Figure 4 presents a frequency distribution for the longest stream of years wherein dividends were either increased or held constant. The resulting distribution contains even longer observations than the foregoing. The median observation occurs for a 10-year period. Surprisingly, the mode occurs for the entire horizon of 18 years. That is, 145 firms never cut dividends during the period 1949 to 1966. (The apparent discrepancy between these 145 firms and the 245-firm category in Figure 2 is attributed to a lack of data for all 254 firms across all 18 years; complete data were not available for all 893 firms over the entire horizon.) It is a known fact that many firms proudly advertise their long and uninterrupted stream of increasing (or nondecreasing) dividends over time. The extent of such a dividend policy is documented in Figure 4.

CONCLUSIONS

This study was an empirical investigation of the increasing stream hypothesis of corporate dividend policy. The hypothesis is based on the perceptions of corporate directors concerning the dividend history which their decisions create, rather than being consistent with any of the dividend theories appearing in the literature of finance and economics. The methodology employed was nonparametric, and rigorous statistical tests were not employed. Instead, frequency counts of dividend and earning records over time were used. Although the reader may draw his own inferences, the findings would appear to support the increasing stream hypothesis that firms avoid dividend cuts in favor of uninterrupted streams of nondecreasing dividend payments to common shareholders. Exceptions to the hypothesis were explained partly by the degraded earnings profile of particular firms. As increased sophistication continues to be reflected in various areas of managerial decision-making, it will be interesting to see if future dividend decisions move toward the residual role inherent in simultaneous solution of the firm's financing and investing problems—or continue to reflect the increasing (or nondecreasing) stream hypothesis of corporate dividend policy.

part V
Refining the debt
and capital structure

UNITED STATES STEEL CORPORATION

DURING THE SUMMER and early fall of 1965, members of the Finance Committee of the United States Steel Corporation were reviewing the company's debt and equity structure (Exhibit 1) with the objectives of improving the corporation's earnings and providing for substantially increased capital expenditures which were under consideration by the board of directors. The increased capital outlays were intended to contribute to greater earnings in future years through better operating efficiency by the use of more modern equipment and processes and through regaining a greater share of the market by an improvement in competitive stature. Of particular interest to the committee was Bethlehem Steel Corporation's recent retirement of their 7 percent preferred stock, since U.S. Steel had a similar issue which it was considering retiring.

NATURE OF THE STEEL INDUSTRY

The larger steel companies are fully integrated vertically. That is, their operations extend from mining ore to fabricating products of steel. Full integration results in an above-average investment in fixed assets per dollar of sales. These assets include large holdings of raw materials in the form of coal and limestone reserves, major transportation facilities such as fleets of ore boats, as well as the more commonly thought of melting, rolling, and fabricating operations. For example, when U.S. Steel was formed, it put an estimated $700 million, or approximately 50 percent of its capital into ore reserves.

The steel industry has wider swings in its level of activity than industry in general. This can be seen by Exhibit 3. The reason for these swings is that steel is primarily dependent on the durable goods markets. During recessions, for example, automobile sales drop significantly, machine tools are not replaced as rapidly and heavy construction is deferred. All of these forces tend to cumulatively work together to reduce steel sales. The combination of high capitalization and broad swings in demand produces large fluctuations in earnings. Earnings in the steel industry in recent years have also been affected by the growing competition from foreign steel and other materials and by government pressures to keep steel prices down.

1965 STEEL INDUSTRY LABOR CONDITIONS

Steel production during the first quarter of 1965 ran well ahead of the 1964 rates. This increase was due not only to a stronger economy, but also to a strike-hedge buildup in inventory brought on by a United Steel Workers Union contract expiration date of May 1. Nearly all steel mills were operating at maximum capacity during this period. If there was more finishing capacity, production would be even higher.

The labor situation was somewhat uncertain. I. W. Abel challenged incumbent President D. J. McDonald for the union's presidency in elections held late in February. The contest for union leadership meant that both candidates had to make unusually extravagant demands to the steel companies in order to gain support from the membership. The union's first proposal called for an average increase of at least $1 per man-hour, which amounted to a 20 percent increase. The companies flatly rejected this proposal and stated that they would not go above a 2 percent annual increase, which was the average size of the 1961 and 1963 settlements. However, at this time it was generally felt that they were willing to go as high as 3½ percent. A steel workers' strike would be unpopular on all sides. The administration would probably see it as a threat to the economy and invoke provisions of the Taft-Hartley Act to bring the strikers back to work. The workers and companies would certainly prefer a settlement without a strike.

PROJECTED INDUSTRY TRENDS

Consumption of steel is expected to grow at a rate averaging about 2½ percent annually. Competitive pressure from imports is expected to continue but it is doubtful that there will be an abnormal surge in imports. Alternative materials have cut into several steel markets but new product development in the industry is expected to offset this trend. Because of these pressures and the administration's effort to contain inflation, it is doubtful that the industry will be able to raise prices except on a piecemeal basis. Hence, the industry will give greater attention to technological improvements and cost reduction.

THE SIZE OF U.S. STEEL

U.S. Steel is the largest producer of steel products in the free world. The statistics are impressive evidence of the company's size. Exhibit 4 compares key data for U.S. Steel with those of the next three largest steel companies in the United States. Further evidence of the company's size is an employment level, in 1964, of nearly 200,000 employees who earned nearly $1.6 billion in salaries and wages. U.S. Steel's operations are carried out in over 70 major facilities located in 23 states and five foreign countries. They produce, in addition to basic iron and steel products, coal and coal chemicals, cement, limestone, manganese, prefabricated housing, bridges, and other fabricated products. The company generates about half the electric power it uses, and operates fleets of steamships, barges, and tugs, and owns and operates a number of railroads in areas where it has steel-related operations.

DEBT AND EQUITY STRUCTURE

The capital spending program which the Finance Committee was reviewing projected an increase in capital spending to $600 million annually for the coming three years. This amount is nearly double the annual rate they have spent over the previous five years. Exhibit 4 indicates U.S. Steel's past capital expenditures as well as those of its major competitors.

In the past few years, the company's policy has been to finance sizable portions of its capital expenditure program by issuing debentures. This was the case in 1958 and again in 1961 when they authorized debenture issues of $300,000,000 each of 4s and 4½s, respectively. Information on these issues is shown in Exhibit 1. In each case, the capital expenditures were made and later the issue was floated in order to restore working capital. The committee believed that the proposed expansion program could be conducted without additional financing.

For some time, the corporation has been considering reincorporation in Delaware to take advantage of the state's more lenient corporation laws. Management believed that a change of the state of incorporations could be most easily accomplished by a merger of the New Jersey incorporated parent company into its wholly owned Delaware subsidiary. Accompanying this merger would be a change in the capital structure of the firm. The members of the Finance Committee reached the conclusion that there would be many advantages to the corporation and to its stockholders if the preferred stock were exchanged for some form of long-term debt. Although the preferred stock was noncallable, the laws of both New Jersey and Delaware permit elimination of this provision if two thirds of the stockholders agreed. The preferred stock had six votes per share and was not callable. The $100 par stock currently had a market value of about $150 per share. They realized that the company would have to offer the holders of the preferred stock a price somewhat in excess of the market value at the time of conversion. Last year, Bethlehem Steel had paid its holders of 7 percent cumulative preferred $100 par stock, $175 per share in the form of 4½ percent debentures. The Bethlehem preferred stock was also noncallable and had one vote per share, but had no other restrictive provisions. They expected that U.S. Steel would have to offer 4⅝ percent debentures if it were to convert at the end of this year. It would be issued at the rate of $175 principal amount of debenture for each preferred share. Exhibit 6 presents interest rate data on new corporate bond issues over the last five years.

Dividends on the preferred would be paid through 1965 with interest on the debentures accruing on January 1, 1966. The debentures are non-redeemable for the first 10 years and will receive the benefits from a sinking fund starting in the 11th year. It is estimated that 63 percent of the debentures would be retired prior to maturity.

For the merger and the change in capital structure to become effective, two thirds of the outstanding capital stock must be voted in favor of this proposed plan.

Management plans to call a special meeting of the stockholders on November 24, 1965 to consider this proposal. At that time, it will be important that each shareholder be made aware of advantages and disadvantages of exchanging the preferred stock for convertible debentures both from the corporate as well as from the individual stockholder's viewpoint.

EXHIBIT 1
U.S. STEEL CORPORATION
Schedule of long-term debt and capital stock
DECEMBER 1964
Long-Term Debt

Description	Due	Issued	Authorized (million)	Amount outstanding (million)	Call price
Debenture 4s..........	1983	7-15-58	$300.0	$275.5	104
Debenture 4½s........	1986	4-15-61	$300.0	$300.0	103¾
Subsidiary (various)....				$191.0	

Capital Stock

Description	Votes per share	Shares authorized (million)	Shares outstanding (million)	Pre-emptive rights
7% cumulative preferred (par 100)........	6	4	3.6	No
Common (par 16⅔)....................	1	90	54.1	No

Price Ranges

Description	1960	1961	1962	1963	1964
Debenture 4s					
High.................	98⅜	98¾	98⅜	98⅝	97¼
Low.................	90½	92¼	95	95¾	94¼
Debenture 4½s					
High.................	—	102	104⅛	104	102½
Low.................	—	97½	100¼	100⅜	100
7% Preferred					
High.................	148	147¼	152¾	157⅜	162½
Low.................	139½	141¾	139½	150	147¾
Common					
High.................	103¼	91¼	78⅞	57½	64½
Low.................	69¼	75¼	37¾	43½	50½

Source: Moody's *Industrial Manual.*

EXHIBIT 2
U.S. STEEL CORPORATION
Quarterly price ranges of preferred stock, 1963–65

Quarters	High	Low
1963		
1st....................	157⅜	150
2nd....................	157⅜	152¾
3rd....................	155	152
4th....................	156½	150¾
1964		
1st....................	154¼	149⅞
2nd....................	152½	147¾
3rd....................	160¼	151¾
4th....................	162½	155½
1965		
1st....................	164¾	155½
2nd....................	157⅜	151
1 to August 17.........	154	151¾
18....................	170¼	165½

Source: Proxy Statement for U.S. Steel Corporation, October 15, 1965.

EXHIBIT 3
U.S. STEEL CORPORATION
Steel industry—annual steel production in the United States

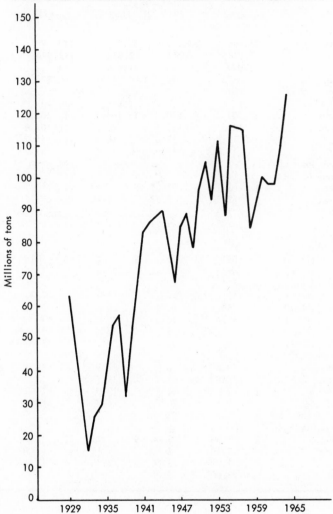

EXHIBIT 4
U.S. STEEL CORPORATION
Comparative financial data for four largest steel producers

	1960	1961	1962	1963	1964
Sales (million dollars)					
U.S. Steel.........	$3,649	$3,302	$3,469	$3,599	$4,077
Bethlehem.........	2,178	2,034	2,072	2,096	2,241
Republic..........	1,054	966	1,050	1,114	1,273
National..........	667	648	745	846	966
Net income (million dollars)					
U.S. Steel.........	$ 304.2	$ 190.2	$ 163.7	$ 203.5	$ 236.8
Bethlehem.........	121.1	122.4	88.7	102.4	147.9
Republic..........	52.8	57.0	40.0	55.5	72.3
National..........	41.9	32.9	35.5	63.7	84.9
Earnings per share of common (dollars)					
U.S. Steel.........	$ 5.16	$ 3.05	$ 2.56	$ 3.30	$ 3.91
Bethlehem.........	2.52	2.52	1.80	2.11	3.11
Republic..........	3.36	3.62	2.54	3.52	4.58
National..........	5.53	4.31	2.32	4.12	5.41
Price range of common stock (dollars)					
U.S. Steel (High)..	$ 103¼	$ 91¼	$ 78⅞	$ 57½	$ 64½
(Low)...	69¼	75¼	37¼	43½	50½
Bethlehem (High)..	57¼	49⅜	43¾	34⅜	43¼
(Low)...	37¼	39⅛	27⅛	28¾	31⅜
Republic (High)..	78¾	65¾	60	44	51¾
(Low)...	48½	53¾	28	34¾	39⅞
National (High)..	98¼	98⅛	48⅛	53	65¼
(Low)...	68	80	29*	34¾	47
Price/earnings ratio					
U.S. Steel.........	20.2	16.1	18.9	19.5	14.6
Bethlehem.........	18.8	17.5	19.7	15.7	12.0
Republic..........	19.0	16.5	19.0	11.2	10.0
National..........	15.1	20.7	16.8	10.7	10.7
Dividends per share on common (dollars)					
U.S. Steel.........	$ 3.00	$ 3.00	$ 2.75	$ 2.00	$ 2.00
Bethlehem.........	2.40	2.40	2.17	1.50	1.50
Republic..........	3.00	3.00	2.50	2.00	2.00
National..........	3.00	3.00	1.60	1.65	1.95

EXHIBIT 4 *(Continued)*

	1960	*1961*	*1962*	*1963*	*1964*
Total assets (million dollars)					
U.S. Steel.........	$4,627	$5,072	$4,983	$5,034	$5,206
Bethlehem.........	2,275	2,303	2,212	2,344	2,407
Republic..........	1,121	1,143	1,128	1,151	1,260
National..........	849	937	899	925	1,025
Net property (million dollars)					
U.S. Steel.........	$2,788	$2,899	$2,820	$2,744	$2,693
Bethlehem.........	980	992	779	980	1,156
Republic..........	611	656	645	646	702
National..........	532	589	564	532	554
Plant expenditures (million dollars)					
U.S. Steel.........	$ 492.4	$ 326.8	$ 200.6	$ 244.7	$ 292.6
Bethlehem.........	169.9	114.3	144.5	177.3	399.0
Republic..........	119.5	85.9	44.7	55.1	112.0
National..........	145.8	102.1	42.8	32.0	91.1
Long-term debt (million dollars)					
U.S. Steel.........	$ 422.8	$ 893.4	$ 833.4	$ 770.6	$ 745.4
Bethlehem.........	140.4	138.7	135.4	128.9	263.4
Republic..........	214.7	219.8	200.2	180.8	210.3
National..........	189.5	249.9	216.7	178.2	172.7
Stockholders' equity (million dollars)					
U.S. Steel.........	$3,302	$3,306	$3,309	$3,379	$3,483
Bethlehem.........	1,649	1,657	1,640	1,668	1,607
Republic..........	728	739	740	764	805
National..........	513	526	538	581	645

* Reflects 2 for 1 common stock split.
Source: *Moody's Industrial Manual.*

EXHIBIT 5

U.S. STEEL CORPORATION

Balance sheet data as of December 31, 1960–1965
(dollar figures in millions)

	1960	*1961*	*1962*	*1963*	*1964*	*1965**
ASSETS						
Cash.....................	$ 276.7	$ 281.4	$ 283.8	$ 279.0	$ 268.3	$ 268.
Marketable securities.......	175.0	360.8	407.5	578.4	314.7	496.
Accounts receivable........	218.5	267.6	252.0	279.3	390.5	345.
Inventory................	725.6	793.3	743.3	641.5	700.4	642.
Total Current Assets.........	$1,395.8	$1,703.1	$1,686.6	$1,778.2	$1,673.9	$1,751.
Sundry investments and receivables.............	43.0	50.9	59.1	71.2	77.6	108.
Property, plant and equipment..............	6,303.0	6,548.5	6,552.7	6,668.9	6,901.6	7,196.
Less: Reserve for depreciation.............	3,515.4	3,649.0	3,732.6	3,925.3	4,208.6	4,482.
Net Fixed Assets..	$2,787.6	$2,899.5	$2,820.1	$2,743.6	$2,693.0	$2,714.
Sundry parts and supplies...	48.9	49.0	48.1	47.6	48.5	51.
Fund for capital expenditures.............	300.0	300.0	300.0	330.0	655.0	655.
Deferred charges...........	51.5	69.5	69.0	62.9	58.1	54.
Total Assets......	$4,626.8	$5,072.0	$4,982.9	$5,033.5	$5,206.1	$5,333.
LIABILITIES AND STOCKHOLDERS' EQUITY						
Current accounts...........	$ 373.1	$ 381.1	$ 341.8	$ 357.4	$ 438.6	$ 453.
Accrued taxes.............	336.2	295.2	297.6	325.4	354.5	352.
Bonds and mortgage due....	31.6	32.4	50.5	50.4	21.0	22.
Dividends payable..........	46.8	46.9	33.4	33.4	33.4	33.
Total Current Liabilities.......	$ 787.7	$ 755.6	$ 723.3	$ 766.6	$ 847.5	$ 860.
Long-term debt............	422.8	893.4	833.4	770.6	745.4	705.
Contingency reserves.......	64.4	67.1	67.1	67.1	67.6	68.
Insurance reserve.........	50.0	50.0	50.0	50.0	50.0	50.
Preferred stock†..........	360.3	360.3	360.3	360.3	360.3	360.
Common stock‡............	900.6	901.9	901.9	901.9	902.2	902.
Earned surplus.............	2,041.0	2,043.7	2,046.9	2,117.0	2,220.3	2,362.
Total Stockholders' Equity..	3,301.9	3,305.9	3,309.1	3,379.2	3,482.8	3,624.
Investment tax reserve......	—	—	—	—	12.8	25.
Total Stockholders' Equity and Liabilities.......	$4,626.8	$5,072.0	$4,982.9	$5,033.5	$5,206.1	$5,333.

* Estimated.
† 4 million shares authorized; 3,602,811 shares outstanding (1964).
‡ 90 million shares authorized; 54,129,987 shares outstanding (1964).
Source: *Moody's Industrial Manual.*

EXHIBIT 6
U.S. STEEL CORPORATION
Corporate bond yields—
Industrial group

Year	Yield
1960	4.59
1961	4.54
1962	4.47
1963	4.42
1964	4.52
1965 (January)	4.53

Source: *Moody's Industrial Manual.*

EXHIBIT 7
U.S. STEEL CORPORATION
Income statements for years ending December 31, 1960–65
(dollar figures in millions)

	1960	1961	1962	1963	1964	1965*
Net sales	$3,648.9	$3,301.7	$3,468.8	$3,599.3	$4,077.5	$4,400.0
Cost of sales	2,469.0	2,327.5	2,530.7	2,548.6	2,914.4	3,203.0
General, administrative, and selling expense	178.8	181.5	176.0	173.4	175.6	186.0
Pension plan payments	87.2	85.5	38.8	42.7	46.0	35.0
Taxes, other than income	154.6	144.5	152.2	154.6	164.5	166.0
Depreciation and depletion	194.6	201.5	261.9	307.2	335.5	325.0
Amortization of emergency facilities	13.8	9.1	3.9	0.6	—	—
Operating Profit	$ 550.9	$ 352.3	$ 305.3	$ 372.2	$ 441.5	$ 485.0
Other income	49.6	34.8	32.1	37.9	51.9	65.0
Total Income	$ 600.5	$ 387.1	$ 337.4	$ 410.1	$ 493.4	$ 550.0
Interest and debt discount expense	16.9	29.9	37.5	35.6	34.4	31.0
Balance	$ 583.6	$ 357.2	$ 299.9	$ 374.5	$ 459.0	$ 519.0
Provision foreign taxes	270.0	161.0	132.0	165.0	215.0	235.0
State income taxes	9.4	6.0	4.3	5.9	7.2	9.0
Net Income to Surplus	$ 304.2	$ 190.2	$ 163.6	$ 203.6	$ 236.8	$ 275.0
Earned surplus beginning year	1,924.0	2,041.0	2,043.7	2,046.9	2,117.0	2,220.0
Preferred dividends	25.2	25.2	25.2	25.2	25.2	25.0
Common dividends	162.0	162.3	135.2	108.3	108.3	108.0
Earned Surplus End of Year	$2,041.0	$2,043.7	$2,046.9	$2,117.0	$2,220.3	$2,362.0
Earnings per share (common)	$ 5.16	$ 3.05	$ 2.56	$ 3.30	$ 3.91	$ 4.60
Dividends per share (common)	$ 3.00	$ 3.00	$ 2.75	$ 2.00	$ 2.00	$ 2.00
Common shares outstanding (000 omitted)	54,033	54,113	54,114	54,116	54,130	54,138
Earnings per share (preferred)	$ 84.82	$ 52.78	$ 45.43	$ 56.50	$ 65.72	$ 74.50
Preferred shares outstanding (000 omitted)	3,603	3,603	3,603	3,603	3,603	3,603
Dividends per share (preferred)	$ 7.00	$ 7.00	$ 7.00	$ 7.00	$ 7.00	$ 7.00

* Estimated.
Source: *Moody's Industrial Manual.*

EXHIBIT 8
U.S. STEEL CORPORATION
Source and application of funds
(dollar figures in millions)

	1960	1961	1962	1963	1964	1965*
Net income..............	$304.2	$190.2	$163.7	$203.6	$236.8	$275.0
Depreciation and						
depletion..............	214.2	212.2	270.9	316.1	339.7	328.0
New debt..............	(31.7)	470.6	(59.9)	(62.8)	(12.3)	(28.0)
New equity.............	2.9	4.0	0.0	0.0	0.6	0.0
Total Sources....	$489.6	$877.0	$374.7	$456.9	$564.8	$575.0
Dividends..............	$187.2	$187.5	$160.5	$133.5	$133.5	$133.0
Capital spending..........	492.4	326.8	200.6	244.7	292.6	353.0
Other investments........	(182.5)	23.4	(2.3)	30.3	324.2	25.0
Increase in working						
capital...............	(7.5)	339.3	15.9	48.4	(185.3)	64.0
Total Uses......	$489.6	$877.0	$374.7	$456.9	$564.8	$575.0

* Estimated.
Source: *Moody's Industrial Manual.*

ASSOCIATED CHEMICAL COMPANY

In January 1971, management was considering the retirement of Associated Chemical's preferred stock. This was a 5 percent cumulative, callable at par, issue with a par value of $100. It was felt that now was an excellent time to adjust the company's inadequate common stock to preferred stock ratio and to realign the debt to equity ratio. Since the company was now considering either an additional plant expansion or an acquisition investment, this would be a good opportunity to reevaluate the company's policy of using preferred stock as an acquisition tool. The company had never retired any of its preferred stock and management felt that it was essential to investigate all of the ramifications of the retirement decision.

COMPANY BACKGROUND

Associated Chemical Company was incorporated in Georgia in November 1922, as Associated Smelting. During a major reorganization of the company, its policies and its goals, the name was changed to Associated Chemical Company. During the late 1950s and through the early 1960s, Associated demonstrated a high rate of growth. Its success continued even through the chemical industry slumps of 1961 and 1962. However, in the last few years they have been troubled by a leveling off of sales and a significant decrease in earnings per share. (Exhibits 1 through 6.)

The majority of Associated Chemical's revenue comes from the sale of industrial chemicals. This accounts for over 70 percent of existing sales. The rest comes from the sale of industrial refrigeration systems and aerosol products. These products are sold directly to customers in the paper and pulp, textile and synthetic fiber, and the chemical industry. There are also many customers in the fields of rubber, plastics, food processing, and pharmaceuticals. The products of the refrigeration department are produced and distributed under contract on a national basis to the air conditioning and refrigeration service industries.

Lately, Associated Chemical has been moving into the field of industrial refrigeration systems. These are usually small refrigeration systems in which the exact control of temperature is important. These systems have been sold to customers in the fields of medical technology and research, computer manufacturing, and chemical processing.

Associated Chemical also packages and sells high-pressure aerosol commercial insecticides. The entire product line is handled by independent jobbers.

The company's main plant is located at Brunswick, Georgia. The plant is located on a 95-acre site with direct access to the port. Other minor facilities are located in Alabama, Wisconsin, and Mississippi. These sites are mainly for local business offices and for distribution warehouses.

It had been the practice of Associated to raise capital and to acquire plants and equipment through the issuance of preferred stock. In 1965, management felt that internal expansion was in order and used preferred stock to raise $1,000,000. Also, in 1966, preferred stock was issued to acquire several small plants. In 1968, 10,000 shares of preferred stock were used for acquisitional purposes. As of December 31, 1970, there were 30,000 shares outstanding of preferred stock out of 35,000 shares authorized.

DIVIDEND POLICY

Associated's management had long held the policy that dividends should be paid only out of net income. The management felt that when earnings declined to a level which could not support the dividends previously paid, dividends would be decreased or eliminated until earnings improved. Dividends should not be financed through borrowing or decreasing retained earnings, cash or other liquid assets.

Prior to 1970, this management policy had not posed any problems, because earnings had generally been sufficient to allow for dividend increases. But when earnings declined by over two-thirds in 1970, management was for the first time confronted with the problem of having to reduce dividends. They felt the recent decline in the price of the common stock resulted from the two-thirds decline in earnings and that the price of the common stock could not be supported by borrowing money to maintain the previously established dividend level. Management also felt that potential investors in the company's common stock would perceive that the dividend level was not being supported by current earnings and would take this into account when evaluating the investment potential of Associated's common stock. (See Exhibits 7–10.)

Management indicated that its major responsibility to their stockholders was to use the resources of the company to improve the earnings of the company, and thereby increase the price of the common stock and not to pay dividends when it was not justified by current earnings. Thus, any further increase in dividends would materialize only when earnings grew sufficiently to support a dividend increase and to support a continued improvement in earnings.

Management's desire to retire the company's preferred stock stems from the fact that it was the payment of the preferred stock dividend which forced management to make the decision to decrease the level of common stock dividends.

INVESTMENT ALTERNATIVES

In the past several years, sales of Associated's refrigeration systems (which are used where the precise control of temperature is often important, such as in the manufacture of chemicals or in the use of medical research) have increased significantly. With the exception of the compressor, most of the components in the refrigeration systems are purchased from other companies and assembled by Associated.

Associated Chemical has recently developed a solid state temperature sensing and control mechanism which should increase the sales level, because the new mechanism provides better temperature control and costs less to produce. Mr. Wheaton has been considering the possibility of either acquiring Thermo-Control Corp. or building a new plant to produce Associated's new control mechanism and the other refrigeration components.

Thermo-Control Corp., a small Detroit-based company, currently supplies components for industrial and automotive air conditioning and refrigeration systems, and has supplied many of the components used in Associated's refrigeration system. In 1970, Thermo-Control Corp. earned $340,000 after taxes (no allowance is made for research) on sales of $4.732 million. The balance sheet for 1970 showed $2.187 million in assets and $580,000 in common equity. Thermo-Control Corp.'s future sales and earnings are projected to continue to grow at an annual rate of 8 percent until a sales level of $8 million is reached, after which sales and earnings will remain constant. The company's equity consists of 58,000 shares of common stock which are held by Mr. Allen Edwards and family.

Mr. Edwards has tentatively agreed to exchange the common stock of Thermo-Control Corp. for $2 million in cash, or he will settle for $200,000 in cash and $2 million in convertible 10-year debentures paying a 6 percent coupon rate. The debentures would be convertible into the common stock of Associated Chemical at $35 a share any time after December 31, 1973.

As an alternative to the acquisition, Mr. Wheaton is considering building a plant to produce the new temperature control mechanism. Suitable land has been located and could be purchased for $135,000. Plans have been drawn up for a $1.228 million plant with a useful life of approximately 30 years. Additional equipment costing $610,000 would be needed to manufacture the new temperature control mechanism. The life cycle of the new product has been estimated to be eight years. During the life of the plant it will be capable of producing a variety of refrigeration components required by Associated.

The plant would be constructed in 1971 and be producing useful sales by 1972. Sales in 1972, 1973, and 1974 are estimated at $1.2 million, $2.2 million, and $3.4 million, respectively. After 1974, sales are expected to increase at any annual rate of 12 percent. The plant will have a maximum sales capacity of $6 million.

Cost of labor and materials of the plant's products are expected to run approximately 62 percent of sales. In addition, there will be a fixed operating expense of $100,000 per year.

FINANCING ALTERNATIVES

In the past, when Associated needed financing, they relied primarily upon equity and short-term loans. In 1961, to finance expansion, Associated went public with an issue of common stock. In 1965, 1966, and 1968 they used preferred stock to finance additional capital needs and acquisitions. Short-term loans and credit had been used to finance asset expansion. The management of Associated felt a need for greater versatility in their financing, especially in light of the recent decline in the price of the common stock due to a poor earnings report for 1970. Associated Chemical has in the past been completely free of any long-term debt, and Mr. Wheaton felt that this policy might prove to be a restrictive factor in the future growth of the company. Because of this, negotiations had begun in mid-1970 with Associated's banker, First National, for long-term debt. An arrangement was reached in December 1970, whereby Associated could borrow $2 to $5 million at 7 percent on the face amount of the loan for a period of 10 years. Interest would be payable in semi-annual installments and repayment of the principle would begin in 1973 with equal semiannual installments.

Under the arrangement with First National, Associated must maintain a net worth position in excess of $10 million, net working capital in excess of $3 million, and unemcumbered net fixed assets in excess of $6 million. Mr. Wheaton feels that Associated Chemical should not have any difficulty in meeting these restrictions.

In order to eventually increase the number of shares of common stock outstanding, management was considering the issuance of convertible debentures to finance not only the possible acquisition of Thermo-Chemical Corp. but the retirement of the preferred stock and the construction of the new plant, if the latter appeared to be more attractive than the acquisition of Thermo-Control Corp. Discussions with a major regional underwriting firm indicated that between $2 and $5 million net proceeds to Associated could be raised through such an issue. The cost of the underwriting would be 6 percent of the net proceeds desired by Associated. For example, if Associated wanted to raise $2 million, the underwriting cost would be 6 percent $\times$ $2 million = $120,000. Therefore, the total value of the offering would have to be $2.12 million to cover the underwriting cost and provide Associated with $2 million in cash.

The convertible debentures would be issued for 10 years and would pay a 6 percent coupon rate. The debentures would be convertible into common stock of Associated at $35 a share any time after December 31, 1973.

The underwriters advised the management that when the price of the common stock reached $45, 50 percent of the debentures should convert and when the price of the common stock reached $50, the remaining 50 percent should convert. One hundred percent conversion would also occur in the 10th and final year if the price of the common stock was $37 or more. The underwriters also advised management that 100 percent conversion could occur if the dividend yield reached 8 percent.

Before management makes a final decision upon the retirement of the preferred, the acquisition of Thermo-Control Corp. or the construction of a new plant, Mr. Wheaton wants to study the possible alternative means of financing these projects.

Some of the alternatives for financing would be a common stock offering, a preferred stock offering, cash and other liquid assets of the company, discounting of receivables, short-term loans, and commercial paper. There may be certain restrictions placed upon the company because of its size, history, and credit rating, which means that certain financing alternatives may not be open to Associated Chemical; thus Mr. Wheaton wants to examine each alternative to determine its feasibility.

Mr. Wheaton knew that Associated would probably have to seek additional financing within the next 10 years in order to produce new products and take advantage of other investment opportunities which would be profitable to Associated Chemical and, of course, maximize the return to the common stockholders. Therefore, Mr. Wheaton wanted to determine what effect each of the financial alternatives would have on future financing. Use of equity now may preclude the use of equity again within a few years but may put the company in a better position to obtain debt financing. Similarly, the use of debt financing now may preclude its use again within a few years and may force the company to use equity or delayed equity in the form of a convertible debenture. Of course, the use of a convertible debenture means that dilution will occur upon conversion and conversion would increase the dividend burden of the company.

GROWTH PROSPECTS

Mr. Wheaton did not perceive any investment opportunities in 1971, other than the alternative of purchasing Thermo-Control Corp. or constructing a new plant to produce Associated's recently developed solid state temperature sensing and control mechanism and other refrigeration components. The leveling off of Associated's sales in 1970 had generally been caused by the national recession that began in the early part of 1969 and, as experts declared the recession was going to be turned back in 1971. The recession may be reversed in 1971, but the management of Associated was not inclined to make capital expenditures for projects which did not provide a higher rate of return than generally returned by the existing products of Associated. The company also had some reserve capacity because of the recession and would rather utilize this reserve to meet any increase in sales in the near future. Management was optimistic that the economy would improve in 1971, but believed that the improvement would be slow in the beginning with some reversals because problems such as inflation in both prices and wages, unemployment, a foreign trade deficit, high interest rates and tight money, the Vietnam War, and many other issues were still not resolved. Therefore, the management of most companies and the general public would hold back until positive events actually occurred.

Mr. Wheaton estimated that if Associated did not either purchase Thermo-Control Corp. or construct a new plant, sales for 1971 would be $32.4 million and the costs associated with these sales would be in the same proportions as existed in the sales to cost relation in 1970. These proportions in 1970 were higher than in previous years because of the recession and the small gain in sales by Associated. Mr. Wheaton did not perceive that these costs would be reduced until the economy improved and the problems mentioned before were being resolved.

Also, Mr. Wheaton forecasted that Associated's sales could grow at an annual rate of 3 percent without major capital expenditures or acquisitions. But higher annual growth rates would require, as they had in the past, sizable expenditures on capital improvements or acquisitions. Obtainment of these higher growth rates would probably require Associated to diversify because the profit margins on its existing products were low, and subject to significant competitive pressure from national and regional chemical companies. Associated's desire to expand its refrigeration business was an attempt to diversify to a greater extent into a more profitable area.

EXHIBIT 1
ASSOCIATED CHEMICAL COMPANY
Balance sheet for years ending December 31, 1967–70
(dollar figures in thousands)

	1967	1968	1969	1970
ASSETS				
Cash.......................................	$ 658	$ 579	$ 422	$ 524
Certificates of deposit.....................	0	392	392	354
Marketable securities......................	0	899	289	389
Liquid Assets.....................	$ 658	$ 1,870	$ 1,103	$ 1,267
Net accounts receivable....................	2,938	3,393	3,808	4,028
Inventory...............................	3,411	3,327	5,075	5,381
Prepayments............................	149	246	274	154
Total Current Assets...............	$ 7,156	$ 8,836	$10,260	$10,830
Net fixed assets..........................	8,987	9,977	11,809	9,977
Patents, etc..............................	196	172	370	273
Total Assets....................	$16,339	$18,985	$22,439	$21,080
LIABILITIES				
Accounts payable........................	$ 1,609	$ 1,566	$ 4,048	$ 3,142
Dividends payable.......................	114	130	143	136
Accruals................................	480	598	500	0
Income tax payable......................	185	508	185	305
Container depreciation....................	375	424	549	421
Current Liabilities.................	$ 2,763	$ 3,226	$ 5,425	$ 4,004
Investment credit........................	331	320	331	280
Deferred income tax......................	821	1,005	1,212	1,325
Preferred stock 5% cum..................	2,000	3,000	3,000	3,000
Common stock par $2....................	1,295	1,295	1,295	1,295
Paid-in surplus..........................	39	42	42	42
Retained earnings........................	9,090	10,097	11,134	11,134
Total Liabilities.................	$16,339	$18,985	$22,439	$21,080

EXHIBIT 2
ASSOCIATED CHEMICAL COMPANY
Income statement for years ending December 31, 1967–70
(dollar figures in thousands)

	1967	1968	1969	1970
Net sales.................................	$22,969	$28,169	$31,369	$31,613
Cost of sales.............................	16,389	19,921	22,342	24,210
Selling expense...........................	2,321	3,052	3,433	4,164
Research expense.........................	709	782	928	954
Depreciation.............................	856	955	1,023	1,159
Total Expenses.......................	$20,275	$24,710	$27,726	$30,487
Earnings before interest and taxes	2,694	3,459	3,507	1,126
Income taxes.............................	1,294	1,858	1,808	561
Net Income..............................	$ 1,400	$ 1,601	$ 1,699	$ 565
Preferred dividend........................	100	150	150	150
Earnings available to common................	$ 1,300	$ 1,451	$ 1,549	$ 415
Common dividend.........................	398	444	512	415
Retained Earnings........................	$ 902	$ 1,007	$ 1,037	$ 0
Shares of common outstanding (thousands)	647	647	647	647
Shares of preferred outstanding (thousands)	20	30	30	30

EXHIBIT 3
ASSOCIATED CHEMICAL COMPANY
Company sales for years end-
ing December 31, 1957 to 1971
(dollar figures in thousands)

1971 (estimate)	$32,400
1970.	31,613
1969.	31,369
1968.	28,169
1967.	22,969
1966.	22,402
1965.	18,649
1964.	15,645
1963.	13,954
1962.	13,170
1961.	12,524
1960.	11,519
1959.	10,830
1958.	8,526
1957.	8,422

EXHIBIT 4
ASSOCIATED CHEMICAL COMPANY
Change in sales from previous year's sales
(dollar figures in thousands)

Year	Dollar change from previous year's sales	Percentage change from previous year's sales
1971.	$ 787	2.5
1970.	244	0.8
1969.	3,200	11.4
1968.	5,200	22.7
1967.	567	2.5
1966.	3,753	20.1
1965.	3,004	19.2
1964.	1,691	12.1
1963.	784	6.0
1962.	636	5.1
1961.	1,005	8.7
1960.	689	6.4
1959.	2,304	27.1
1958.	104	1.2

EXHIBIT 5
ASSOCIATED CHEMICAL COMPANY
**Earnings per share for years
ending December 31, 1962–70**

Year	Earnings per share
1970	$0.64
1969	2.40
1968	2.24
1967	2.01
1966	2.01
1965	1.48
1964	1.43
1963	1.24
1962	1.00

EXHIBIT 6
ASSOCIATED CHEMICAL COMPANY
**Change in earnings per share from previous
year's earnings per share**

Year	Dollar change from previous year's earnings per share	Percentage from previous year's earnings per share
1970	($1.76)	(72.5)
1969	0.16	7.1
1968	0.23	11.5
1967	0	0
1966	0.53	35.8
1965	0.05	3.5
1964	0.19	15.3
1963	0.24	24.0

EXHIBIT 7
ASSOCIATED CHEMICAL COMPANY
**Dividends and payout percentage for years
ending December 31, 1962–70**

Year	Dividend	Payout ratio (percent)
1970	$0.64	100.0
1969	0.79	33.0
1968	0.68	30.7
1967	0.61	30.6
1966	0.44	20.4
1965	0.36	24.4
1964	0.32	22.4
1963	0.28	22.6
1962	0.28	28.4

EXHIBIT 8
ASSOCIATED CHEMICAL COMPANY
Retention rate

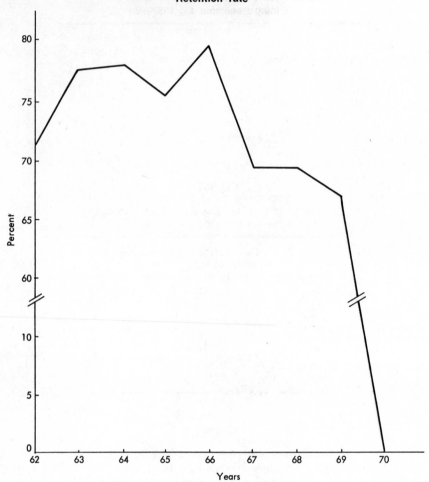

EXHIBIT 9
ASSOCIATED CHEMICAL COMPANY
**High and low prices for common stock and
P/E range common stock prices**

Year	High	Low	P/E ratio range for high and low common stock prices
1970	$37.5	$21.0	15.6–8.8
1969	43.5	25.0	19.4–11.2
1968	42.0	23.0	20.9–11.4
1967	28.5	20.0	14.2–10.0
1966	24.25	16.5	16.4–11.2
1965	20.25	14.5	14.2–10.2
1964	16.5	12.25	13.3–10.1
1963	13.75	9.25	13.8–9.2

Note: P/E ratio range has been calculated by dividing the high and low prices of the common stock for each by the previous years' earnings per share. The bias of this manner of calculating the P/E ratio is to assign higher P/E ratios when earnings per share are increasing and lower P/E ratios when earnings per share are declining.

The above-listed data does show that the market has assigned somewhat higher P/E ratios when earnings have continued to advance particularly after earnings per share went over $2. Mr. Wheaton believes that in the next 10 years a P/E ratio of 10 will probably be the minimum and a P/E ratio of 16 would be near the maximum. When calculating future common stock prices in the next years for the purpose of dividend yield and probable timing for conversion of the convertible debentures if they are used to finance the proposed projects, Mr. Wheaton will use the P/E ratios of 16 and 10 to calculate the possible maximum and minimum common stock prices.

Of course, if the future earnings per share of Associated Chemical either make marked advances or declines, some reevaluation of common stock prices and probable P/E ratios will be required.

EXHIBIT 10
ASSOCIATED CHEMICAL COMPANY
Common stock prices for the years 1963–70

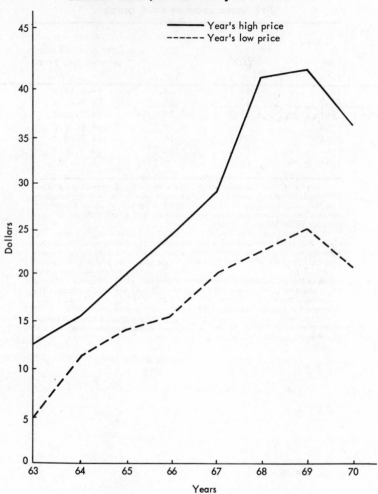

WHITTAKER CORPORATION

ON MAY 13, 1971, Joseph Alibrandi, president of Whittaker Corporation, notified holders of its 4½ percent convertible subordinated debentures that the exchange offer announced on April 16, 1971, would become effective through June 30, 1971. The corporation officers had earlier in May announced the terms of the exchange offer, and were confident that an exchange would improve the corporation's financial position by reducing the principal amount of outstanding indebtedness. The current price of the debenture was $615, up from $550 at the time of the April announcement. Mr. Alibrandi urged each holder to evaluate carefully the exchange offer in view of their individual investment objectives and the current market prices. He also assured them that their acceptance of the offer would prove beneficial to the company.

COMPANY BACKGROUND

The Whittaker Corporation was incorporated in California in 1947 and maintains its principal offices in Los Angeles.[1] From 1964 through 1970, Whittaker grew and diversified into the areas of metals, textiles and chemicals by acquiring 130 companies. Sales grew from around $40 million to over $790 million. This rapid growth brought with it major problems in all areas, from management to marketing to finance. Further complications were brought on by the 1969–70 economic downturn and the resulting liquidity squeeze experienced by many large firms.

In October 1970, Mr. Alibrandi was elected president, and he quickly established a course of action to solve the company's problems. Earlier

---

[1] It is a "Fortune 500" with a sprawling international organization.

in July, Mr. Alibrandi and other officers had redefined three basic corporate objectives:

1. To strengthen the company's balance sheet.
2. To realign the company into specific business areas and to weed out those parts that did not fit [the] chosen areas, or could not be brought to acceptable levels of performance.
3. To structure a lean, hard-hitting operating organization with maximum emphasis on building a solid and continuing earnings capability.[2]

To meet these objectives, the organization was streamlined into five promising business areas, including housing and urban development, industrial chemicals and textiles, recreational products, transportation products, and metals distribution. In addition, a divestiture program was initiated in order to eliminate unprofitable operations. Twenty-two such operations were identified as unprofitable or marginal. Four units with sales of over $62 million and pretax operating losses of almost $7 million in 1969 were discontinued in 1970. Planned for discontinuance in fiscal 1971 were 18 units with sales of almost $68 million and pretax operating losses of $6.5 million, plus two additional operations which had sales of over $68 million and pretax operating income of $1.3 million.

In addition to the divestiture program, a lid was placed on future external acquisitions until at least May 1972. All emphasis was placed on internal improvement and goals were set to improve liquidity. From fiscal 1970 to fiscal 1972, the current ratio is set to go from 1.49 to 2.16; total liabilities to equity to go from 2.72 to 1.75; and the profit margin to go from 2.4 percent to 5.9 percent. The new second-quarter earnings report of 1971 indicated improved operating performance by an increasing return on sales, a decreasing cost of sales despite inflation, and an improved inventory as a percent of sales (Exhibit 3).

EXCHANGE OFFER

Part of the plan to strengthen the balance sheet involved the proposed exchange of the 4½ percent convertible debentures due in 1988. The offer is to issue and deliver to all holders in exchange for each of the $1,000 convertible debentures, $500 in principal amount of a new series of 10 percent subordinated debentures due in 1988 and 40 warrants expiring on May 5, 1979. The new debentures are not convertible and are subordinated to all obligations of Whittaker for borrowed money other than certain outstanding subordinated debentures and notes. A sinking fund, identical to that for the 4½ percent convertible debenture, will be established to provide for redemption. Prior to July 1st in each year

---

[2] A presentation to The New York Society of Security Analysts by Joseph Alibrandi on June 18, 1971.

from 1978 to 1987, they will redeem 7.5 percent of the debentures outstanding on July 1, 1977. Whittaker also has the option to redeem the new debentures at any time as a whole or in part after July 1, 1978.

The warrants are exercisable immediately upon their issuance and they are not attached to the debentures. They entitle the holder to purchase all or any part of the number of shares of Whittaker's common stock specified therein at an initial warrant price of $50 per share at any time before May 15, 1979. After this date the warrants will be void and nonexercisable. Upon exercise of the 40 warrants, the holder can purchase 40 shares of common stock.

LISTING

The 4½ percent convertible debentures are listed on the New York Stock Exchange. The closing price for the $1,000 debenture on May 12, 1971 was $615. Earlier in April when the exchange offer was first announced, the price was $550. The new 10 percent subordinated debentures have been approved for listing on the New York and Pacific Coast Stock Exchanges. The principal amount of the debenture is $500. The warrants are not a new issue, and are presently listed on the American and Pacific Coast Stock Exchanges. The closing price of the warrants on the American Exchange on May 12, 1971, was $6¼. Earlier in April at the time of the announcement, the price was $7½.

Whittaker's common stock is listed on the New York and Pacific Coast Stock Exchanges. The closing price on the New York Exchange on May 12, 1971 was $12. Earlier in April the price was $13.87. A stock price history is presented in Exhibits 7 and 8. Mr. Alibrandi and the other key officers all felt that the exchange offer was structured to increase the equity of the common shareholder, to improve the capital structure, to give the 4½ percent convertible debenture holder a 10 percent premium in the market, and to not endanger the position of the warrant holders. The effects of a substantial number of additional warrants or common shares on the price of the warrants and common stock were not entirely clear.

EXHIBIT 1

WHITTAKER CORPORATION

Balance sheet for years ending October 31, 1969–70

(dollar figures in thousands)

	October 31	
ASSETS	*1970*	*1969*
Current Assets		
Cash...	$ 16,845	$ 15,024
Marketable securities at cost, not in excess of market............	955	9,053
Receivables, less reserves..................................	178,699	161,774
Inventories, at the lower of cost (first-in, first-out) or market (net of $4,900 reserve for loss on operations to be discontinued in 1971)................................	180,034	178,614
Prepaid expenses...	6,968	6,342
Total Current Assets............................	$383,501	$370,807
Land..	$ 21,714	$ 14,720
Buildings..	78,566	56,364
Equipment..	152,688	134,035
	$252,968	$205,119
Less accumulated depreciation............................	89,073	68,799
	$163,895	$136,320
Goodwill (cost in excess of net assets of purchased businesses)...	$ 44,630	$ 45,006
Deferred federal income taxes..............................	3,887	—
Miscellaneous (net of $6,800 reserve for loss on operations to be discontinued in 1971)..............................	14,565	22,277
	$ 63,082	$ 67,283
Total Assets....................................	$610,478	$574,410

LIABILITIES AND STOCKHOLDERS' EQUITY

Current Liabilities		
Notes payable...	$122,401	$ 74,391
Current maturities of long-term and convertible subordinated debt..	19,698	17,391
Accounts payable and accrued expenses......................	114,990	116,203
Federal and foreign income taxes...........................	342	17,073
Total Current Liabilities.................................	$257,431	$225,058
Long-term debt..	$117,957	$106,125
Convertible subordinated debt.............................	$ 70,503	$ 72,898
Minority interest in subsidiaries...........................	$ 7,455	$ 2,611
Stockholders' Equity		
Capital stock		
Preferred stock (entitled to $5,447 in involuntary liquidation...	$ 388	$ 484
Common stock..	19,048	18,735
Additional paid-in capital.................................	68,487	67,393
Retained earnings..	69,209	81,106
Total Stockholders' Equity...............................	$157,132	$167,718
Total Liabilities and Stockholders' Equity.............	$610,478	$574,410

Source: *Annual Reports* 1969, 1970.

EXHIBIT 2
WHITTAKER CORPORATION
Income statement for years ending October 31, 1969–70
(dollar figures in thousands)

	October 31	
	1970	*1969*
Sales...	$792,720	$661,056
Costs and expenses (including straight-line depreciation and amortization aggregating $18,366 and $12,278 in 1970 and 1969, respectively)		
Cost of sales...	$649,797	$510,292
Engineering, selling, and general and administrative...........	104,319	78,765
Interest..	19,911	9,422
	$774,027	$598,479
Income from continuing operations before provision for federal income taxes and extraordinary items...............	18,693	62,577
Provision for federal income taxes........................	8,810	30,685
Income from continuing operations after provision for federal incomes taxes and before extraordinary items........	$ 9,883	$ 31,892
Income (loss) of discontinued operations, Net of Federal income tax benefit.................	(3,627)	(2,876)
Income before extraordinary items........................	$ 6,256	$ 29,016
Extraordinary items, net of federal income taxes		
Disposition of securities held for investment...............	9,481	1,864
Loss of discontinued operations disposed of in 1970.........	(6,950)	(407)
Provision for loss on disposition of operations to be discontinued in 1971...............................	(8,385)	—
Write-off of goodwill (cost in excess of net assets of purchased businesses) in connection with operations to be discontinued in 1971...............................	(8,827)	—
	$(14,681)	$ 1,457
Net Income......................................	$ (8,425)	$ 30,473

Source: *Annual Reports*, 1969, 1970.

EXHIBIT 3
WHITTAKER CORPORATION
Income statements, unaudited
(dollar figures in thousands)

	2nd quarter ended April 30		6 months ended April 30	
	1971	*1970**	*1971*	*1970**
Sales............................	$187,150	$188,962	$355,027	$364,606
Cost of sales.....................	150,762	152,176	286,577	291,809
Gross Profit.....................	$ 36,388	$ 36,786	$ 68,450	$ 72,797
Operating expenses...............	24,829	24,957	48,095	49,174
Income from operations.............	11,559	11,829	20,355	23,623
Other deductions, net..............	4,157	4,526	8,503	8,233
Income from continuing operations before taxes and extraordinary items........................	7,402	7,303	11,852	15,390
Provision for income taxes..........	2,750	3,278	4,743	7,419
Income from continuing operations after taxes and before extraordinary items..................	$ 4,652	$ 4,025	$ 7,109	$ 7,971
Net loss of discontinued operations...	—	(888)	(439)	(795)
Income before extraordinary items...	$ 4,652	$ 3,137	$ 6,670	$ 7,176
Extraordinary items, net of income taxes				
Disposition of securities held for investment.....................	$ 10,935	(93)	$ 10,935	$ 9,505
Loss of discontinued operations disposed of in 1970..............	—	(750)	—	(5,500)
Provision for loss on disposition of operations to be discontinued in 1971.........................	(2,410)	—	(2,410)	—
Write-off of goodwill.............	(952)	—	(952)	—
	$ 7,573	$ (843)	$ 7,573	$ 4,005
Net Income..............	$ 12,225	$ 2,294	$ 14,243	$ 11,181

* Restated to include companies pooled subsequent to April 30, 1970 and year-end 1970 adjustments applicable to the first and second quarters of 1970. The results of operations of discontinued businesses have been segregated and are shown as "Net loss of discontinued operations" (net of income tax benefit).
Source: *Annual Reports*, 1970, 1971.

EXHIBIT 4
WHITTAKER CORPORATION
Indebtedness as of January 31, 1971
(dollar figures in thousands)

Current Indebtedness:
Notes Payable to—
Banks—(includes $78,270 with variable interest keyed to the prime rate
plus ½ percent and $34,678 with interest rates ranging from 7 percent
to 11.5 percent).. $112,948
Others—(interest rates ranging from prime rate to 10 percent)......... 31,357
Current maturities of long-term and convertible debt..................... 19,520

$163,825

Long-Term and Convertible Subordinated Debt:
Long-Term Debt—
Noninterest bearing to 7½ percent notes maturing at various dates to
1983.. $ 26,133
10⅞ percent note due in 1972................................... 2,326
Unsecured note due 1977 with variable interest keyed to the six-month
Eurodollar rate plus 1½ percent................................ 20,000
Unsecured note payable in seven equal semiannual installments due 1974
through 1977 with variable interest keyed to the six-month Eurodollar
rate plus 1 percent... 20,000
Unsecured notes payable in five equal semiannual installments due 1973
through 1975 with variable interest keyed to the six-month Eurodollar
rate plus 1¼ percent... 9,000
4 percent subordinated notes secured by certain real property, equipment
and other assets maturing at various dates to 1974.................. 21,540
2 to 9 percent notes secured by certain real property, equipment and common stock of certain subsidiaries, maturing at various dates to 1993.... 19,377
5 percent subordinated notes due 1984 secured by and convertible into
common stock of Computing & Software, Inc., at $42 per share....... 6,560

$124,936

Convertible Subordinated Debt—
4½ percent convertible subordinated debentures, due 1988, convertible
into common stock at $47 per share............................ 59,998
4¾ percent convertible subordinated debentures, due 1987, convertible
into common stock at $17 per share............................ 2,242
5 percent convertible subordinated promissory notes, due 1971 to 1974,
secured by certain real property, convertible into common stock at $39
per share.. 3,200
5½ percent convertible subordinated debentures, due 1976, convertible
into common stock at $36 per share............................ 1,781
8 percent convertible subordinated debentures, due 1979, convertible into
common stock at $130 per share............................... 340
Convertible subordinated promissory notes, due 1970 to 1973, with variable interest keyed to the prime rate, secured by common stock of certain subsidiary companies and certain receivables, convertible into common stock at $58 per share.................................... 5,390

$ 72,951

Total Long-Term and Convertible Subordinated Debt............. $197,887
Less current maturities.. 19,520

$178,367

Source: *Annual Report,* 1971.

EXHIBIT 5
WHITTAKER CORPORATION
High-low price of $1,000 4½ percent convertible debenture

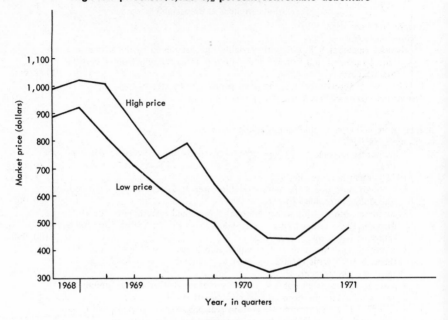

EXHIBIT 6
WHITTAKER CORPORATION
High-low price of warrants

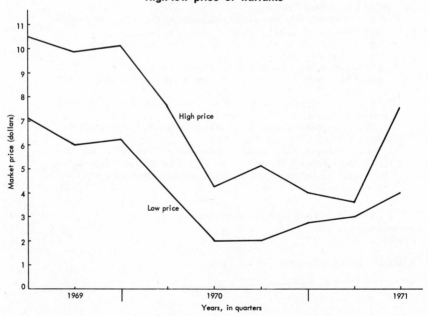

EXHIBIT 7
WHITTAKER CORPORATION
High-low price of common stock

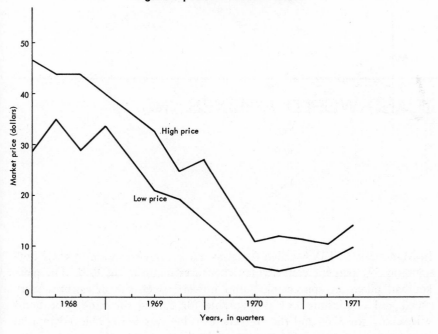

Years, in quarters

EXHIBIT 8
WHITTAKER CORPORATION
Prices of common stock

December 31	High	Low	Close
1962............	$3\frac{1}{2}$	1	1
1963............	$1\frac{1}{2}$	$\frac{3}{4}$	1
1964............	$1\frac{3}{4}$	$\frac{7}{8}$	1
1965............	3	$1\frac{1}{4}$	3
1966............	$7\frac{3}{8}$	$2\frac{3}{4}$	7
1967............	$45\frac{7}{8}$	$6\frac{5}{8}$	$45\frac{7}{8}$
1968............	$45\frac{5}{8}$	$28\frac{1}{2}$	34
1969............	$36\frac{1}{4}$	$15\frac{1}{8}$	18
1970............	19	5	7

TRANS WORLD AIRLINES, INC.

In March 1965, TWA called for conversion or redemption of their outstanding 5¾ percent convertible debentures maturing in 1983. The market had taken an appreciable jump upward since the debentures were issued and conditions looked favorable for calling the issue. The bond was selling for $264 and the conversion value was $230. The redemption price at this time was $105.45 plus accrued interest (Exhibit 7). A highly leveraged capital structure was causing some concern, but rising earnings per share in the past three years gave management an optimistic view that by lowering this leverage somewhat by calling the issue, the financial community would be willing to loan more money for further purchases of aircraft (Exhibit 3). TWA required additional funds to cover the large expenditures needed to expand its fleet of aircraft, which at this time was being converted to jets. (Exhibit 5).

COMPANY BACKGROUND

TWA is the second largest U.S. airline system in scheduled revenue passenger-miles, although it ranks third domestically and is subordinate to Pan-American in international flights (Exhibit 2). Domestically, the greatest competition is from United Airlines and American Airlines, both of which have competitive routes. TWA's domestic flights originate and terminate at Los Angeles and San Francisco on the West Coast and concentrate primarily on the northeast's heavily populated section of the East Coast, plus some flights to Florida. Intermediate cities along this corridor are also served. Internationally, TWA has flights to many countries of Europe, Africa, and the Near and Far East (Exhibit 1).

In 1960 and 1961, scheduled passenger-miles took a downturn for several of the airlines, but in 1962, the trend had turned upward. The decline, in the case of TWA, reflected in part an internal struggle for control of the management, as well as a general decline in traffic. The management struggle was between Howard Hughes, majority stockholder via Hughes Tool Company, and the primary lending institutions. These institutions believed that Hughes Tool Company, as principal vendor of aircraft and parts to TWA, operated for the benefit of Hughes Tool Company rather than for TWA. With this attitude, they would not finance any more purchases until the situation was resolved. To keep TWA viable in the interim, a decision was reached between Hughes Tool Company and the lending institutions to establish a voting trust into which the 78 percent of TWA stock owned by Hughes Tool would be put, with one representative from Hughes Tool and two from the institutions comprising the board. This decision cleared the way for further financing ($165 million) and the acquisition of more jet aircraft.

The aircraft industry is a voracious consumer of capital. New aircraft are designed that are bigger and faster than the current planes, and an airline must purchase in order to remain competitive. This seems to run in 10-year cycles. The Douglas series of airplanes came out in the 1930s, epitomized by the DC-3. After World War II, the DC-4, 6, and 7 followed each other as a general family of airplanes. Then in the late 1950s, the first jets appeared on the scene, initially turbojets, then full jets. It is expected that larger jets and faster jets will follow each other in about the same cyclic pattern. Therefore, a sound capital structure is necessary in order to acquire financing for purchase of these new planes. One move made by TWA was the avoidance of buying turbojets in favor of going directly to full jets.

Two things worked together to improve the company position after 1961. These were: (1) an unexplained increase in passenger travel, experienced by all airlines, and (2) the realization that with the introduction of jets, the break-even load factor dropped tremendously because of the greater efficiency of jets relative to piston aircraft (Exhibit 2). In 1961, TWA had 47 jets in operation and in the course of delivery. By the end of 1964, there were 106 jets in service and 53 more on order. The last of the piston aircraft were also being phased out during this period. The combination of these factors drove the break-even load factor down to 46 percent and placed TWA in a good position relative to the passenger load factor—which was increasing.

FINANCING

To purchase the desired aircraft, TWA has required a considerable amount of funds. In 1961, equipment mortgages and notes totaled $279 million. By the end of 1964, this amount increased to $325 million (Exhibit 3). Included in this latter figure was $38.5 million of 5¾ percent convertible debentures issued in October 1963, and having a maturity date of October 1983. The conversion price was $22 and was set at a time when the stock was selling for $20¾. Just prior to the time of the issue, the average yield on new Baa industrial straight-debt instruments was 4.9 percent. After comparing the present debt/equity position and the amount of 6.7 million shares outstanding, management felt that a debt issue would be the best route to follow. To make the issue more attractive, a higher than market yield had to be realized by the investor plus the opportunity to participate in future growth of the company via the conversion privilege. This could work to TWA's advantage, for if the common stock appreciated above the call price of the bond, an increase in equity base would be achieved by calling the issue. This would lower the debt/equity ratio making the stock more attractive to a certain class of investors and also place the company in a better position to seek more debt.

These factors were discussed with Hughes Tool Company which owned 78 percent of the outstanding common stock. As a result of these discussions, a final agreement was reached on a private basis, and Hughes Tool Company purchased $30 million at par on October 21, 1963. The remaining $8.5 million was offered to the shareholders of record on December 3, 1963 at $101.37 per $100 of debenture, and subscribed. Immediately after the sale to Hughes Tool Company in October, the price rose to $26. There were no underwriting costs.

CONVERSION

Although no target date had been set for the call of this issue, market conditions brought the question to the forefront in mid-1964. The debentures were selling in the vicinity of $200, and the common stock was priced around $46 (Exhibit 6). The conversion value of the issue closely paralleled the market value of the bond (Exhibit 7). Management, represented by Mr. Charles Tillinghast, Jr., president, decided that when the issue was one year old, conditions would be opportune to force conversion by calling. This would enable TWA to avoid impending sinking-fund payments, interest payments, and at the same time broaden the equity base. This latter benefit would put the capital structure in a more favorable light when additional financing was sought. This decision to call was reenforced by a study made by TWA's financial advisors. The sinking-fund payment saved amounted to $1.8 million and the interest charges saved represented $2.2 million. From the investors' viewpoint, a capital gain would be realized in terms of the appreciated stock of approximately 135 percent (assuming that the owner was the original purchaser of the bond). The possible detrimental effects on the price of the stock by calling the issue were believed to be minimal and only of short-term duration. The fact that a nondividend paying stock was being received in lieu of an interest-bearing bond would probably have some effect on the price was considered; but again, it was estimated to be only short term in nature, if any effect did exist. Historically, stock prices do fall after a forced conversion, but in a rising market they recover lost ground in a relatively short time.

Voluntary conversion had already been taking place. As of January 29, 1965, $523,700 worth of debentures had been converted. One of the unknowns in the forced conversion picture was the position that Hughes Tool Company would take. TWA had informed Hughes Tool Company of the interest in forcing conversion of the issue and requested a position statement from them indicating whether they would convert or request redemption. As Hughes Tool did not respond, TWA made plans to cover the possibility of redemption by announcing that if Hughes Tool Company redeemed, TWA would issue equity to raise the necessary funds.

Hughes Tool Company, prior to the possible conversion, owned 5,221,301 shares. If the company converted, they would acquire an additional 1,363,636 shares which would change their ownership from 78 to 76 percent of the outstanding stock.

EXHIBIT 1

TRANS WORLD AIRLINES, INC.
Domestic system as of October 1, 1963

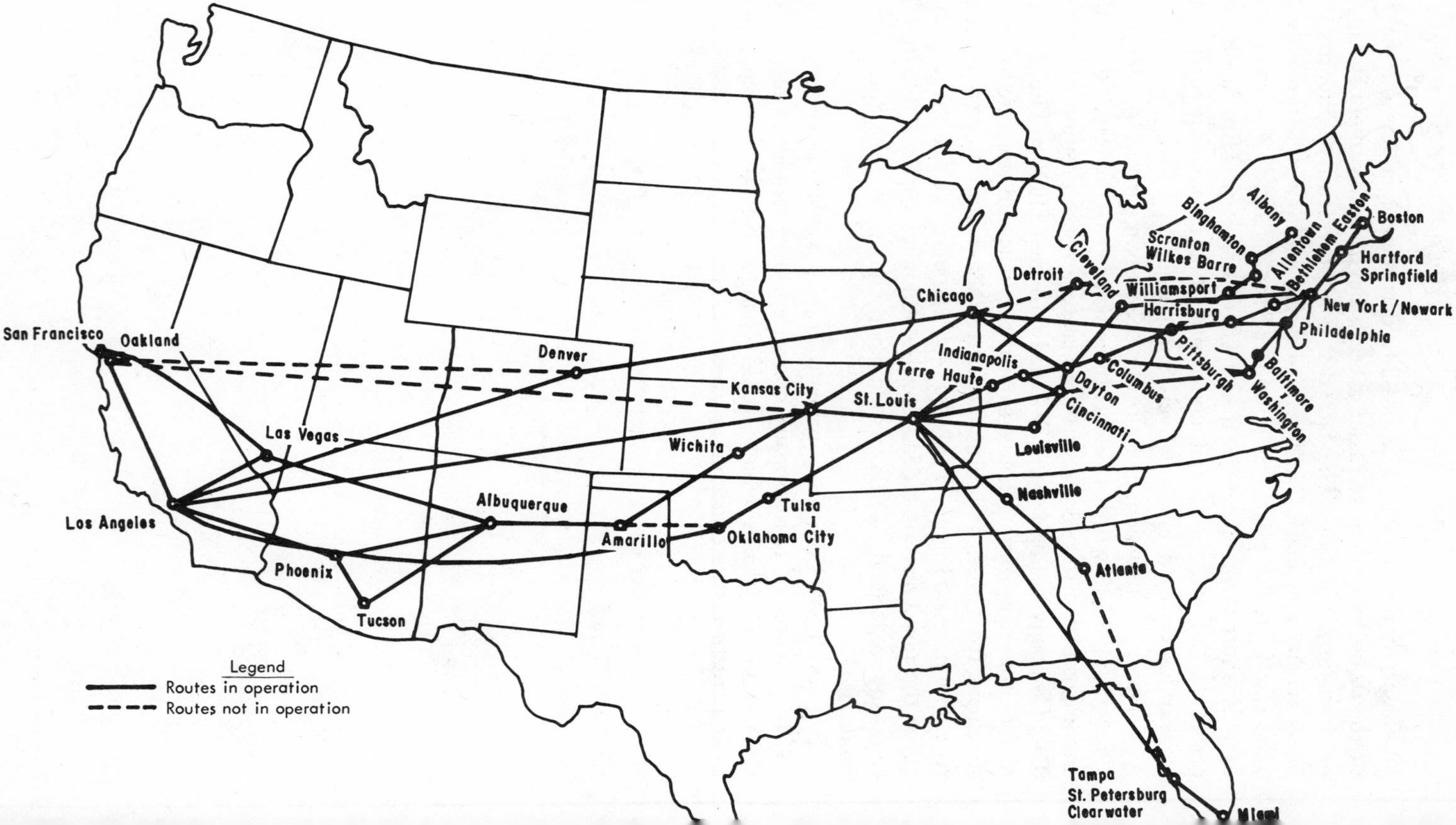

Legend
——— Routes in operation
– – – Routes not in operation

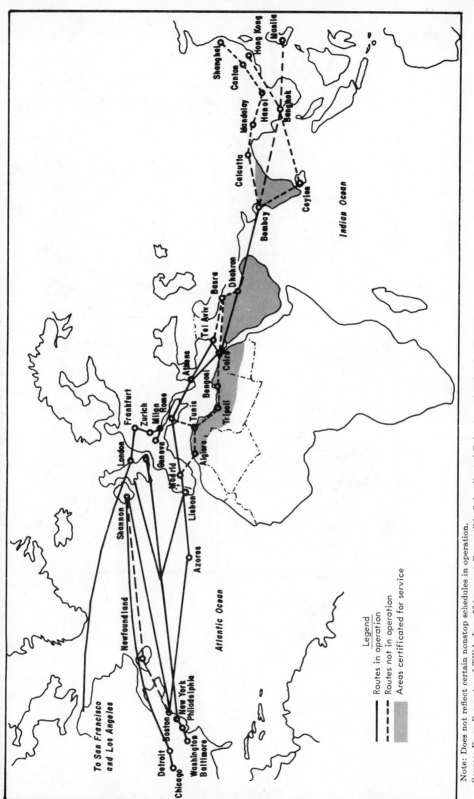

Note: Does not reflect certain nonstop schedules in operation.
Source: From *Prospectus* of TWA, Inc., 5¾ percent Convertible Subordinated Debentures due October 1, 1983.

EXHIBIT 2
TRANS WORLD AIRLINES, INC.
Industry comparisons

SCHEDULED REVENUE PASSENGER—MILES IN BILLIONS

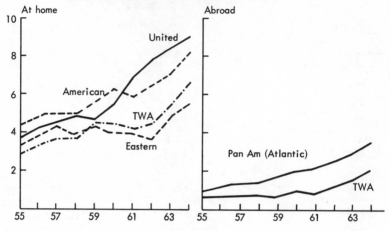

LOAD FACTOR AND BREAKEVEN FACTOR (PERCENT OF SEATS SOLD)

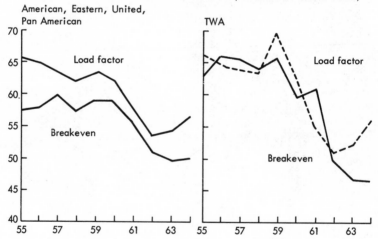

EXHIBIT 3

TRANS WORLD AIRLINES, INC.
Balance sheets for years ended December 31, 1960–64
(dollar figures in thousands)

	1964	1963	1962	1961	1960
ASSETS					
...sh	$ 14,902	$ 25,542	$ 22,432	$ 21,185	$ 47,590
...arketable securities	47,672	45,912	54,081	25,341	16,655
...ccounts receivable	59,819	46,040	41,249	35,865	30,738
...ax claim	–	–	–	8,257	–
...ventories	20,815	16,836	14,641	12,743	15,274
...epaid expenses	4,294	2,426	3,828	5,831	2,726
Total Current Assets	$147,502	$136,756	$136,231	$109,222	$112,983
...operty, plant and equipment	783,045	660,140	626,029	591,934	503,314
...ss: Depreciation, amortization	315,068	296,085	261,896	254,512	208,562
Net Property Account	$467,977	$364,055	$364,133	$337,422	$294,752
...posit on purchase contract	–	3,060	4,221	1,697	17,018
...oncurrent receivables	1,059	1,222	4,245	5,527	4,330
...rcraft integration costs	1,963	1,133	16,987		
...ng-term prepayments	2,805	3,195	3,156	23,352	21,215
...her deferred charges	2,599	2,089	2,285		
Total	$623,905	$511,510	$531,258	$477,220	$450,298
LIABILITIES					
...rrent maturities, long-term debt	$ 11,912	$ 106	$ 32,021	$ 18,551	$ 12,741
...ort-term equipment notes	20,498	–	–	–	–
...ccounts payable	67,603	75,794	43,610	47,900	34,953
...avel deposits	5,087	4,751	4,467	4,197	3,974
...cruals	–	–	13,472	11,841	10,556
...deral, foreign, state income tax	4,082	226	90	111	7,652
...nearned transportation revenue	12,278	10,471	8,051	6,626	7,046
Total Current Liabilities	$121,460	$ 91,348	$101,711	$ 89,226	$ 76,922
...bentures	138,485	138,500	107,024	100,524	–
...uipment, mortgage, sinking-fund notes	187,200	171,800	171,800	114,800	$ 62,800
...uipment, mortgage, serial notes	–	–	49,800	64,600	56,400
...tes payable	–	–	–	–	100,000
...tallment contracts	1,184	512	594	109	180
...nditional sales contracts	–	–	–	1,031	3,862
...ferred federal income tax	33,403	5,919	6,159	10,320	20,292
...serve for overhaul jets	–	–	9,621	7,425	3,801
...ferred gain on aircraft sales	1,855	1,435	2,925	1,857	–
...pital stock ($5 par)	33,831	33,511	33,371	33,371	$ 33,371
...pital surplus	50,316	49,316	48,925	48,925	48,925
...rned surplus	56,171	19,169	dr 672	5,032	43,745
Total	$623,905	$511,510	$531,258	$477,220	$450,298
Net Working Capital	$ 26,042	$ 45,408	$ 34,520	$ 19,996	$ 36,061

Source: *Moody's Transportation Manuals.*

EXHIBIT 4

TRANS WORLD AIRLINES, INC.
Income statements for years ended December 31, 1960–64
(dollar figures in millions)

	1964	1963	1962	1961	1960
OPERATING REVENUE					
Passenger—first class	$ 138,435	$ 115,946	$ 102,919	$ 113,320	$ 149,294
Passenger—coach	360,250	295,957	244,872	198,838	179,935
Mail	22,523	23,058	21,199	16,056	15,600
Freight	31,993	25,200	26,891	18,260	15,283
Other	21,768	16,352	4,990	16,444	17,977
Total	$ 574,969	$ 476,513	$ 400,871	$ 362,918	$ 378,089
OPERATING EXPENSES					
Flying operations	$ 139,003	$ 119,936	$ 103,442	$ 99,577	$ 112,040
Maintenance	82,275	64,419	73,510	69,491	72,728
Passenger service	46,109	36,517	29,847	28,909	27,909
Aircraft and traffic servicing	79,253	68,366	60,262	53,552	51,305
Promotion and sales	73,345	63,524	53,458	47,242	45,891
General and administrative	20,769	18,429	16,070	17,858	14,735
Depreciation and amortization	48,698	68,448	56,402	83,979	37,267
Total	$ 489,452	$ 435,639	$ 392,991	$ 400,608	$ 361,875
Operating Profit (Loss)	$ 85,517	$ 40,874	$ 7,880	$ (37,690)	$ 16,214
NONOPERATING INCOME AND EXPENSE					
Gain, disposal of property	$ 1,798	$ 1,442	$ 940	$ (3,891)	$ 2,033
Interest and amortization	20,693	22,175	19,869	18,027	4,152
Other income	1,939	(330)	1,299	2,495	1,125
Total	$ 16,956	$ 21,063	$ 17,630	$ 19,423	$ 994
Pretax Net Income	$ 68,561	$ 19,811	$ (9,750)	$ (57,113)	$ 15,220
INCOME TAXES					
On operations and capital gain	$ 3,986	$ 171	$ 98	$ 8,434	$ 7,147
Provision for deferred taxes	27,485	240	4,161	9,973	1,592
Total	$ 31,471	$ 69	$ 4,063	$ 18,407	$ 8,739
Net Income	$ 37,090	$ 19,880	$ (5,687)	$ (38,706)	$ 6,481
Retained earnings, end of period	$ 56,171	$ 19,169	$ (672)	$ 5,032	$ 43,745
Earnings per share	$ 5.47	$ 2.95	$ (0.85)	$ (5.80)	$ 0.97
Common stock dividends	—	—	—	—	—
Number of Common Shares	$6,766,222	$6,702,315	$6,674,155	$6,674,155	$6,674,155

EXHIBIT 5

TRANS WORLD AIRLINES, INC.

Source and disposition of funds for years ended December 31, 1960–64

(dollar figures in millions)

	1964	*1963*	*1962*	*1961*	*1960*
SOURCE					
Net income	$ 37.0	$ 19.8	$ (5.7)	$(38.7)	$ 6.5
Depreciation and amortization	49.2	51.9	57.3	83.7	37.5
Deferred income taxes	27.5	(0.2)	(4.1)	(10.0)	1.6
Addition to overhaul reserve	—	—	2.2	3.6	1.7
Deferred interest charge	—	—	6.5	0.5	—
Increase in long-term debt	29.7	40.4	78.7	166.1	229.1
Sale of capital stock	1.3	0.5	—	—	—
Change in working capital	19.4	(10.9)	(13.5)	15.1	(31.0)
All other (net)	5.2	2.7	(4.1)	0.7	(5.0)
	$169.3	$104.2	$117.3	$221.0	$240.3
DISPOSITION					
Capital expenditures	$134.4	29.9	77.2	82.1	171.9
Deposits and advance on aircraft	21.3	16.5	3.1	30.1	29.6
Long-term debt retired	13.6	57.8	37.0	108.8	38.8
	$169.3	$104.2	$117.3	$221.0	$240.3
PRICE RANGE					
Stock	$ 52¼–31¼	$ 31⅞–70½	$ 14¼– 7½	$ 20⅜–10⅞	$ 19–11⅛
PRICE RANGE					
Debentures 6½'s, 1978 (x.w.)	$113¾–94½	$104⅛–70½	$ 80¼–50	$ 72¼–57	—
Warrants	$ 33¾–15⅛	$ 15⅛– 4⅛	$ 6½– 3⅛	$ 5⅜– 4⅛	—
Debentures 5¾'s, 1983	$224–147	$146–130	—	—	—
Net Tangible Assets per Share	$ 20.74	$ 15.22	$ 12.23	$ 13.08	$ 18.89

Source: *Moody's Transportation Manuals.*

EXHIBIT 6
TRANS WORLD AIRLINES, INC.
Prices of TWA common stock and convertible 5¾, 1983 debentures

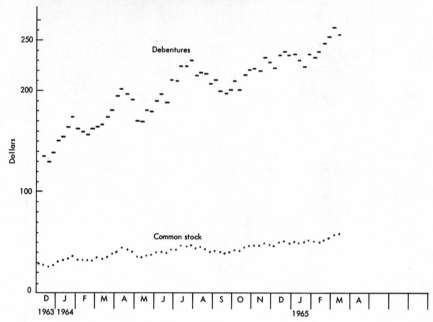

EXHIBIT 7
TRANS WORLD AIRLINES, INC.
Performance of TWA convertible debenture 5¾'s, 1983

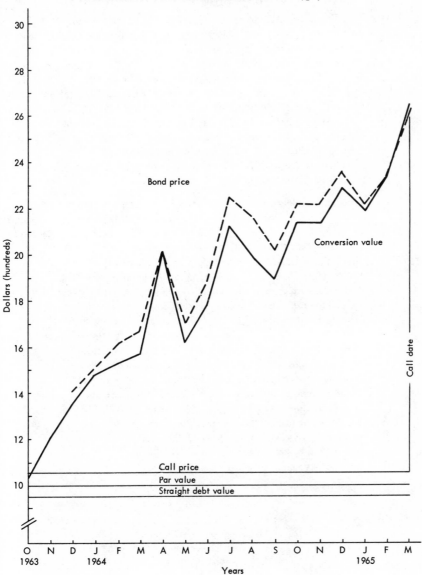

EXHIBIT 8
TRANS WORLD AIRLINES, INC.
Long-term debt

1. TWA, Inc. Equipment Mortgage Sinking Fund 6½'s, Series A, due 1972.
    Outstanding December 31, 1964, $92,800,000 privately held.
    Proceeds for purchase of jet aircraft.
    Dated December 1, 1960, due December 31, 1972.
    Sinking Fund to retire $11,600,000 notes each December 31, 1965–71.
    Special Fund Payments of $6,100,000 each December 31, 1965–69 may be
    used to purchase additional aircraft or to redeem notes at 106 during year
    ending December 31, 1966 and at 1 percent less each year thereafter.
    Secured by first lien on substantially all aircraft, engines, propellers, spare
    parts plus remaining jet equipment to be acquired.
    Company agrees, with certain exceptions to maintain net working capital
    of at least $10,000,000.

    Options: Holders granted to Hughes Tool Company options to purchase,
    after December 31, 1961, all notes at 122 percent of principal
    if purchased on or before March 31, 1962, and at 0.05 percent
    less for each quarter elapsed from January 1, 1962.
2. TWA, Inc. Equipment Mortgage Sinking Fund 6's, Series B, due 1977.
    Outstanding December 31, 1964, $106,000,000 privately held.
    Proceeds, with other funds to purchase 28 jet planes from Boeing Company
    dated July 1961, due December 31, 1977.
    Sinking Fund to retire $10,000,000 notes each December 31, 1967–76.
    Callable from Flight Equipment Fund moneys at 106 to December 31,
    1963, reduced annually thereafter to 100 after December 31, 1976.
    Secured equally with Series A 6½ percent notes due 1972.
    Company may not pay cash dividends on or acquire capital stock in excess
    of 50 percent of consolidated net income after December 31, 1960, or if
    consolidated net working capital is less than $10,000,000.
3. TWA, Inc. Subordinate Income Debenture 6½'s due 1978.
    Outstanding December 31, 1964, $100,000,000.
    Dated June 8, 1961; Maturity June 1978.
    Interest payable to extent of income.

    Interest Payments: Per $1,000 debenture
    December 1, 1961, $31.24;
    June 1, 1962, none;
    December 31, 1962, none;
    June 1 to December 1, 1963, none;
    June 1, 1964, $162.50;
    December 1, 1964, $32.50
    Available Income: Net Income for fiscal year plus interest charges de-
    ducted in computing net income and accrued during
    fiscal year on debentures and other debt subordinated
    to senior debt.

EXHIBIT 8 (Continued)

Unless and until senior notes are paid, indenture prohibits interest payment if after giving effect thereto consolidated net working capital would be less than $10,000,000 if default exists on senior debt or on any other debt. Callable at 105⅜ in 1965 and sliding scale down to 100½ in 1976.

Sinking Fund: Cash or debentures to redeem on each December 1, 1973–77. 10 percent of debentures outstanding on June 30, 1973. Callable for sinking fund.

Warrants: Issued with each $100 debenture for purchase of 2.7 common shares at $20 per share to June 1965, and at $22 per share thereafter to December 1, 1973. Warrants detachable. Traded on American Exchange entitling holder to purchase one share per warrant.

Purpose: Proceeds to pay $100,000,000, 6½'s interim subordinated note issued to acquire jet aircraft.

4. TWA, Inc. Convertible Subordinated Debenture 5¾'s due 1983. Outstanding $38,500,000.

Dated October 1, 1963. Due October 1, 1983.

Callable as a whole or in part on or after April 1, 1964 at following prices (plus unpaid cumulative interest) to each September 30, inclusive:

1964...	105.75	1971...	103.475	1978...	101.200
1965...	105.45	1972...	103.150	1979...	100.875
1966...	105.100	1973...	102.825	1980...	100.550
1967...	104.755	1974...	102.500	1981...	100.225
1968...	104.450	1975...	102.175	1982...	100.125
1969...	104.125	1976...	101.850	1983...	100.000
1970...	103.80	1977...	101.525		

Sinking Fund: Cash or debentures to retire at par $1,800,000 Debentures each October 1, 1973–82.

Convertible: Into common, if called on or before 15th day prior to redemption date, at $22 a share. Conversion protected against dilution. Not secured.

Purpose: Proceeds to purchase jet aircraft.

Offered: $30,000,000 sold at par on October 21, 1963 to Hughes Tool Company. $8,500,000 additional at $101.37 per $100 debenture to common stockholders.

5. *Conditional Sales Contract* Outstanding December 31, 1964, $1,495,593 for purchase of bulk storage and other facilities. Final payment due in 1973.

6. *Bank Credit* Agreement with 15 banks for $145,000,000 revolving credit. Funds to help pay for jet aircraft. Balance to come from cash earnings. Interest rate of 5.5 percent ceiling and 4.5 percent floor and will be 0.005 percent above prime rate. Credit runs until December 31, 1967.

Source: *Moody's Transportation Manuals.*

SELECTED REFERENCES
FOR PART FIVE

AYERS, HERBERT F. "Risk Aversion in the Warrants Market," *Industrial Management Review*, Vol. 5 (Fall 1963), pp. 45–53.

BACON, PETER W., and WINN, JR. EDWARD L. "The Impact of Forced Conversion on Stock Prices," *Journal of Finance*, Vol. 24 (December 1969), pp. 871–74.

BAUMOL, WILLIAM J., MALKIEL, BURTON G., and QUANDT, RICHARD E. "The Valuation of Convertible Securities," *Quarterly Journal of Economics*, Vol. 80 (February 1966), pp. 48–59.

BOWLIN, OSWALD D. "The Refunding Decision," *Journal of Finance*, Vol. 21 (March 1966), pp. 55–68.

BRIGHAM, EUGENE F. "An Analysis of Convertible Debentures: Theory and Some Empirical Evidence," *Journal of Finance*, Vol. 21 (March 1966), pp. 35–54.

BROMAN, KEITH L. "The Use of Convertible Subordinated Debentures by Industrial Firms, 1949–59," *Quarterly Review of Economics and Business*. Vol. 3 (Spring 1963), reprinted in James Van Horne (ed.), *Foundations for Financial Management*. Homewood, Ill.: Richard D. Irwin, Inc., 1966, pp. 219–33.

COHAN, AVERY B. "Yields on New Underwritten Corporate Bonds, 1935–1958," *Journal of Finance*, Vol. 27 (December 1962), pp. 585–605.

DONALDSON, GORDON. "In Defense of Preferred Stock," *Harvard Business Review*, Vol. 40 (July–August 1962), pp. 123–36.

ELSAID, HUSSEIN H. "The Function of Preferred Stock in the Corporate Financial Plan," *Financial Analysts Journal*, July–August 1969, pp. 112–17.

EVERETT, EDWARD. "Subordinated Debt—Nature and Enforcement," *Business Lawyer*, Vol. 20 (July 1965), pp. 953–87.

FISHER, DONALD E., and WILT, GLENN A., JR. "Nonconvertible Preferred Stock as a Financing Instrument, 1950–1965," *Journal of Finance*, Vol. 23 (September 1968), pp. 611–24.

JEN, FRANK C., and WERT, JAMES E. "The Value of the Deferred Call Privilege," *National Banking Review*, Vol. 3 (March 1966), pp. 369–78.

JEN, FRANK C., and WERT, JAMES E. "The Effects of Call Risk on Corporate Bond Yields," *Journal of Finance*, Vol. 22 (December 1967), pp. 637–52.

JOHNSON, ROBERT W. "Subordinated Debentures: Debt That Serves as Equity," *Journal of Finance*, Vol. 10 (March 1955), pp. 1–16.

MCKENZIE, ROBERT R. "Convertible Securities, 1956–1965," *Quarterly Review of Economics and Business*, Vol. 6 (Winter 1966), pp. 41–48.

PINCHES, GEORGE E. "Financing with Convertible Preferred Stock, 1960–1967," *Journal of Finance*, Vol. 25 (March 1970), pp. 53–63.

PYE, GORDON. "The Value of the Call Option on a Bond," *Journal of Political Economy*. Vol. 74 (April 1966), pp. 200–5.

PYE, GORDON. "The Value of Call Deferment on a Bond: Some Empirical Results," *Journal of Finance*, Vol. 22 (December 1967), pp. 623–36.

ROBBINS, SIDNEY M. "A Bigger Role for Income Bonds," *Harvard Business Review*, Vol. 33 (November–December 1955), pp. 100–14.

SOLDOFSKY, ROBERT M. "Convertible Preferred Stock: Renewed Life in an Old Form," *The Business Lawyer*, July 1969, pp. 1385–92.

SPILLER, EARL A., JR. "Time-Adjusted Breakeven Rate for Refunding," *Financial Executive*, Vol. 31 (July 1963), pp. 32–35.

WEINGARTNER, H. MARTIN. "Optimal Timing of Bond Refunding," *Management Science*, Vol. 13 (March 1967), pp. 511–24.

WINN, WILLIS J., and HESS, ARLEIGH, JR. "The Value of the Call Privilege," *Journal of Finance*, Vol. 14 (May 1959), pp. 182–95.

The Function of Preferred Stock in the Corporate Financial Plan*

Hussein H. Elsaid†

A NEW PHENOMENON has developed in recent years—an increasing number of corporations have redeemed their outstanding preferred issues and
a marked decrease has occurred in the portion of capital raised through
preferred stock relative to other sources of financing. This development
has revived interest in preferred stock financing and its future.[1]

This study is based on a survey of 314 issuers of preferred stock representing a sample of 473 preferred offerings since 1945.[2] The findings

* Reprinted from *Financial Analysts Journal* (July–August 1969), pp. 112–17,
by permission of the author and the publisher.

† Assistant Professor of Finance at Southern Illinois University. The author is
grateful to Professors Paul M. Van Arsdell, Ahmad D. Issa, and J. Van Fenstermaker
for helpful suggestions in preparing the manuscript of this paper.

[1] Examples of recent publications: Donald A. Fergusson, "Recent Development
in Preferred Stock Financing," *The Journal of Finance*, Vol. 7, No. 3 (September
1952); Leonard Jay Santow, "Ultimate Demise of Preferred Stock as a Source
of Corporate Capital," *Financial Analysts Journal*, Vol. 18, No. 3 (May–June 1962);
Jean Ross-Skinner, "Will Preferred Stock Come Back?," *Dun's Review and Modern
Industry*, Vol. 80, No. 9 (September 1962); Gordon Donaldson, "In Defense of
Preferred Stock," *Harvard Business Review*, Vol. 40, No. 4 (July–August 1962);
and Donald E. Fischer and Glenn A. Wilt, Jr., "Non-Convertible Preferred Stock
as a Financing Instrument, 1950–1965," *The Journal of Finance*, Vol. 23, No. 4
(September 1968).

[2] In determining the size of the survey, any issue not classified as a preferred
stock was not included; preferred issues by corporations chartered outside the
United States were excluded; and any issue of $300,000 or less was not included
in the survey. To improve representation, all the issues were included in the sample
with the exception of electric, gas, and water issues, from which only 50 percent
was selected at random. A questionnaire was sent to the highest ranking financial
executive of each of the 314 corporations who were responsible for issuing the
473 preferreds over the period 1945–1965.

The response to the questionnaire was extremely gratifying. Two hundred and refute the claim that preferred stock financing is phasing out. This study will attempt to show that: (1) current arguments against preferred stock financing are subject to serious challenge; (2) preferred stock performs a useful function in the corporate financial plan; and (3) management's opinion as to the future course of financing does not verify the supposition that preferred stock will not have a place in the corporate financial structure in the near future.

ANALYSIS OF CURRENT ARGUMENTS AGAINST PREFERRED STOCK FINANCING

The major arguments against preferred stock financing evolve around income and risk. With respect to income, it is argued that preferred stock financing does not compare favorably with debt financing owing to the tax-deductibility of interest but not of preferred dividends.

This argument is challenged on the ground that a more meaningful comparison is between preferred stock financing and common stock financing. From the lender's point of view, preferred and common stocks are equity securities. Additional equity financing may be needed to improve the borrowing base prior to debt financing. If an acceptable borrowing base is not provided, the bond rating of the company may drop, leading to a higher interest rate on new bond issues. It follows that the comparison between debt financing and preferred stock financing tends to mislead and confuse the issue. If the comparison is between preferred and common stock financing, preferred stock would be more advantageous to common stockholders—would have better effect on the income available to them. This is because the return on preferred stock is limited, which makes it a cheaper source of financing assuming that the cost of common stock is measured by the expected return on the funds supplied.

Another weakness of the argument favoring debt over preferred stock financing can be demonstrated by considering a refinancing operation designed to eliminate preferred stock. There are three courses of action available to management: (1) to offer preferred stockholders a subordinated debenture in exchange for their preferred stock;[3] (2) to use cash in retiring the preferred; or (3) to distribute the money to common stockholders as dividends and keep the preferred outstanding. With re-

---

thirty-four financial executives, or about 75 percent of those contacted, answered the questionnaire. These answers represented some 310 nonconvertible preferred issues, or about 80 percent of their total in the sample, and 54 convertible preferreds, or about 64 percent of the total convertible issues contained in the sample.

[3] It should be noted that income bonds may be used in lieu of subordinated debentures. However, only corporations with well established earning power can use this financing device.

spect to the first alternative, the earnings available to common stockholders are increased by the excess of preferred dividends eliminated over the net-after-tax interest on the subordinated debenture and by the potential net-after-tax earnings on funds that would otherwise have been used to redeem the preferred stock. If this increase in earning power is capitalized at a representative earnings-price ratio for this particular corporation and the capitalized value reduced by the capital gains tax, the result is the net gains realized by common stockholders.

It should be noted that offering a subordinated debenture in exchange for preferred stock outstanding may not change significantly a company's borrowing base, while improving its tax position. However, such an exchange may be disadvantageous to corporations holding the preferred stock for investment purposes. This is because these corporations are accorded a special tax status with respect to preferred dividends received. Eighty-five percent of these dividends are tax-exempt. Such tax treatment does not apply to interest received on bond holdings. To be successful, the proposed exchange would have to offer some clear advantages to corporate investors.

With respect to the second course of action, which calls for cash redemption of the preferred stock, the earnings available to common stockholders are increased by the amount of preferred dividends eliminated. The net gains realized by common stockholders can again be determined by the same procedure discussed under the first alternative. On the other hand, if management elects to follow the third course of action and distributes the money to common stockholders, the dividends will be subject to personal income tax. It is suggested that the weighted average tax bracket of common stockholders of this corporation (weighted according to concentration of dividend income) should be applied to the total amount of dividends to reach the comparable net gains realized by common stockholders under this alternative. Thus the issue lends itself to quantitative analysis that could be undertaken to determine the effect on the net gains to common stockholders, and hence the desirability of the retirement of preferred stock.[4]

Considering risk, usually a business firm is subject to two types of risk, namely business risk and financial risk. Business risk is defined as "the probability, expressed as a fraction not exceeding unity, that the firm's prospective business productivity will cease to be compensatory."[5] Financial risk can be defined as the probability that the firm will not be able to meet maturing financial obligations as to interest and principal. Thus, the introduction of debt in capital structure introduces financial risk. A prudent financial management should not superimpose a high de-

[4] Donaldson, "In Defense of Preferred Stock," pp. 123–36.

[5] Robert W. Mayer, "Analysis of Internal Risk in the Individual Firm," *Financial Analysts Journal*, Vol. 15, No. 6 (November 1959), p. 91.

gree of financial risk on an existing high business risk. On the other hand, a low business risk may be associated with a reasonable degree of financial risk in the hope that common stockholders will gain from trading on the equity.

With respect to the element of risk, the argument against preferred stock and in favor of debt financing is based on the allegation that there is no practical difference between the contractual obligations of the two sources of financing. Although legally preferred dividends do not have to be paid regularly, the argument goes, responsible management must behave as if preferred dividends were fixed charges and should be paid. Thus, they conclude that "for all practical purposes, the preferred dividend is like bond interest—but without the advantages that a debt contract provides."[6]

The argument above is subject to serious challenge. Although management plans to pay preferred dividends regularly just as in case of interest payments, there is a significant difference in the degree of risk imposed by the two types of financing. The risk of failing to meet a legal commitment, with the associated chance of becoming insolvent, is far more serious than the risk of having to suspend preferred dividends. In times of adversity, the difference between the contractual obligations of the two financing devices becomes very important—it is a difference between continuation and cessation of the business.

REASONS FOR ISSUING PREFERRED STOCK

The questionnaire stated a number of possible reasons for issuing nonconvertible preferrends and another set of reasons for issuing convertible preferreds. The following is an analysis of the responses received.

Nonconvertible preferreds

As indicated in Table 1, the primary reason for issuing nonconvertible preferred stock is to maintain a balanced capital structure. This finding seems compatible with the goal of an optimum financial plan—a plan that reflects sound financial proportions and minimizes the cost of capital to the particular corporation under study. This factor is most important to utilities because, among other reasons, "many of the regulatory commissions believe preferred stocks belong in every [utility] capital structure for 'balance.'"[7] Statistical evidence shows that the 1961 decision by the Securities and Exchange Commission permitting utilities to substitute debentures for preferred stock in their capital structures has not

---

[6] Donaldson, "In Defense of Preferred Stock," p. 125.

[7] J. Robert Lindsay and Arnold W. Sametz, *Financial Management: An Analytical Approach* (Homewood, Ill.: Richard D. Irwin, Inc., 1967), p. 400.

TABLE 1
Use of nonconvertible preferred stock classified by reason and industry

Percent of total response from each industry

Reason	Manu-facturing	Electric, gas, and water	Com-munica-tion	Financial and real estate	Com-mercial and mis-cellaneous	Percent of total response
To maintain balanced capital structure.................	34.8	93.0	87.5	61.9	56.3	76.1
To improve the borrowing base for subsequent future debt financing.............	52.2	51.9	62.5	95.2	31.3	54.8
To take advantage of favorable market conditions..........	58.7	47.6	50.0	14.3	62.5	47.7
To provide secondary financial leverage.................	41.3	25.9	22.5	57.1	18.8	29.7
To avoid fixity of interest payments attached to debt financing.................	6.5	6.5	—	—	18.8	6.1
To preserve common stock-holders' control............	13.0	1.1	10.0	14.3	18.8	5.8
To facilitate merger or acquisition................	13.0	0.5	2.5	4.8	—	3.2

impaired the relative importance of preferred stock financing to electric, gas, and water utilities.

Table 1 shows that the factor second in importance, as a reason for issuing nonconvertible preferreds, is to improve the borrowing base. It is most important to finance corporations. The response of the executive vice president of a finance company explains his company's use of preferred stock financing to improve the borrowing base as follows:

In 1958 the company experienced a rather substantial growth in its receivables. This growth was financed principally with short term debt. By the end of 1958, the ratio of all debt to underlying equity had reached a point beyond which the company (and probably most of its creditors) would not wish to go. Thus, it was necessary to resort to some form of equity financing, and since there was room in the capital structure for additional preferred stock, this type of issue was selected in preference to common stock."

The third major reason for issuing nonconvertible preferreds is to take advantage of favorable market conditions. As is true of any marketing operation, management may find it desirable to issue preferreds in preference to other securities to meet the varied demands of different types of investors. Table 1 reveals that, with the exception of financial and real estate corporations, favorable market conditions seem to be an important prerequisite for issuing nonconvertible preferreds.

According to this survey, to provide secondary financial leverage is the least important among the four major reasons for issuing nonconvertible preferred stock. This reason is most important to financial and real estate concerns. The other three reasons investigated in this study, namely: (1) to avoid the fixity of interest payment attached to debt financing; (2) to preserve common stockholders' control; and (3) to facilitate merger or acquisition, were found to be of very minor significance for issuing nonconvertible preferreds, as shown in Table 1.

In conclusion, the difference among industries as to the relative importance of reasons for issuing this type of security should be noted. For example, to maintain balanced capital structure is the most important reason for utilities, in contrast to favorable market conditions for manufacturing concerns.

Convertible preferreds

The chief reason advanced for using the conversion feature is to "sweeten" a preferred issue (Table 2). However, a survey of new convertible preferred issues covering the period 1948–1953 brought different findings.[8] Thus it can be concluded that there has been a move towards utilizing the conversion feature as a "sweetener" in recent years. Raising common equity capital indirectly and improving the borrowing base were selected by 68.5 percent of the respondents, which places these two factors second in importance as reasons for issuing convertible preferreds.

Use of convertible preferreds to facilitate merger or acquisition has received much publicity recently. Some writers suggest that a counter trend to the reduced use of nonconvertible preferreds is the use of convertible preferreds in merger. It is argued that "convertible preferred stock has one feature all its own: it makes a prime catalyst in pulling off tricky corporate mergers."[9] A typical response is that of the treasurer of a commercial corporation. He states:

Tax considerations make the preferred stock route very expensive. This would not preclude the use of a convertible preferred in merger. The latter makes a great deal of sense.

Why does the use of convertible preferred stock in merger or acquisition make a great deal of sense? The following reasons are suggested.

---

[8] Sixty-nine corporations were contacted, out of which 53 replied. Out of the 53 respondents, 55 percent stated the reason for issuing convertible preferreds to be the raising of common equity capital indirectly, while 29 percent utilized the conversion feature to "sweeten" the preferred issue. See C. James Pilcher, *Raising Capital with Convertible Securities* (Ann Arbor, Mich.: Bureau of Business Research, School of Business Administration, The University of Michigan, 1955), pp. 59–61.

[9] Ross-Skinner, "Will Preferred Stock Come Back?", p. 35.

TABLE 2
Use of convertible preferred stock classified by reason and industry

Percent of total response from each industry

Reason	Manufacturing	Electric, gas and water	Communication	Financial and real estate	Commercial and miscellaneous	Percent of total response
To use convertibility as a selling point (sweetener)...	85.0	50.0	33.3	80.0	85.7	75.9
To raise common equity capital indirectly..........	85.0	100.0	66.7	20.0	57.1	68.5
To improve the borrowing base for subsequent future debt financing.............	70.0	100.0	33.3	80.0	42.9	68.5
To maintain balanced capital structure................	50.0	90.0	33.3	70.0	28.6	55.6
To take advantage of favorable market conditions.....	60.0	40.0	66.7	50.0	42.9	5.00
To facilitate merger or acquisition..............	5.0	—	—	20.0	14.3	7.4
To avoid the fixity of interest payments attached to debt financing................	—	—	—	—	—	—

1.   Convertible preferred offers common stockholders of the acquired company equity in potential higher earnings as well as in assets. If the combination proves to be successful, they can convert and reap the benefits of higher earnings. If, however, the potential increase in earnings does not materialize, they can keep their preferred stock and enjoy whatever protection it may provide.

2.   Convertible preferred offers the common stockholders of the acquired company a tax-free exchange. This is because if bonds or cash are offered for the common shares of the acquired firm, its stockholders must pay the capital gains tax on the amount received in excess of their cost basis. However, if a convertible preferred stock is used to consummate the acquisition, the transaction is tax-exempt.[10]

3.   Convertible preferred is more advantageous to the common stockholders of the acquiring company as compared with a common-for-common exchange. In the latter case, the earnings per share may be diluted by: (*a*) the premium that may have to be paid to the common stockholders of the acquired company and (*b*) the cost and time it takes to organize and consolidate the activities of the new combination. With a convertible preferred, the dilution effect will be gradual and could be absorbed by the growth in earnings. This reasoning is mirrored in

---

[10] See *Internal Revenue Code*, Sections 351–368.

the response of the vice president of a transportation company. He states:

The advantage of using convertible preferred to consummate an acquisition is that it provides for an immediate contribution to common stock earnings which can be maintained as the preferred is converted and the dilution is absorbed by growth in the earnings of the acquired company over the conversion period.

4. Convertible preferred enables the acquiring company to offer the common stockholders of the acquired company a higher dividend yield than that which would result from a straight common exchange. Such a higher yield is often necessary to bridge the discrepancy between the dividend policies of the two companies. It should be pointed out that this reason is not peculiar to the use of a convertible preferred since a nonconvertible can achieve the same result.

It can be concluded that convertible preferred stock offers the same advantage that can be obtained from the use of a nonconvertible preferred plus some others inherent in the conversion feature, which help in smoothing the path for a merger or acquisition. Despite the reasoning above, the findings of this study do not indicate a significant use of this device for that purpose. Only 7.4 percent of the respondents elected it as a reason for issuing convertible preferred stock.

In conclusion, the different priorities of reasons for issuing convertible preferreds by different industries should be noted. The most important two reasons for electric, gas, and water utilities (each is selected by 100 percent of the respondents) are: (1) to raise common equity capital indirectly and (2) to improve the borrowing base. For manufacturing corporations, the most important two reasons (each is selected by 85 percent of the respondents) are: (1) to raise common equity capital indirectly and (2) to "sweeten" a preferred issue.

FUTURE OF PREFERRED STOCK

Arthur S. Dewing predicted some years ago that preferred stock would not have a place in the corporate financial structure. That is because corporations will seek a simpler capital structure and demand will decline for such "hybrid securities."[11] Owing to the diminishing supply of preferred stocks in recent years, a number of financial writers have hastened to confirm this prediction. The findings of this study do not support Dewing's contention (Table 3).

The majority of the respondents state that they will consider preferred stock financing in the future. Moreover, only one management states that it would prefer a simpler capital structure consisting of common

---

[11] Arthur S. Dewing, *The Financial Policy of Corporations* (5th ed.; New York: The Ronald Press Co., 1953), I, p. 166.

TABLE 3
Percentage distribution of management's opinions as to the future course of financing—classified by industry

Type of financing	Manu- facturing	Electric, gas, and water	Com- munica- tion	Financial and real estate	Com- mercial and mis- cellaneous	Tota
Will consider preferred stock financing...................	35.1	66.7	42.9	69.6	10.0	51.‡
Prefer common equity and long-term debt..................	33.3	11.7	19.0	17.4	30.0	20.‡
Prefer common equity and short-term debt.............	1.8	1.0	4.8	—	—	1.‡
Prefer common equity, long- and short-term debt..........	29.8	20.6	33.3	13.0	60.0	26.2
Prefer common equity only.....	—	—	—	—	—	—

equity only. It should be pointed out, though, that investor demand will play an important role in the future of preferred stock financing. Based on comments received in response to the questionnaire, it seems reasonable to advance the assumption that an increase in demand for preferred stocks will stimulate their supply and reverse their declining trend. The establishment of a stable basis of valuation of preferred stock holdings of life insurance companies—the most important purchasers of new preferred issues—can contribute significantly to such increase in demand.[12]

SUMMARY

Current arguments against preferred stock financing evolve around income and risk. With respect to income, the arguments, while valid in some particular cases, can not be generalized. With respect to risk, on the other hand, the arguments are misleading. Contrary to widely held views, this study shows that preferred stock performs a useful function in the corporate financial plan and, thus, seems to be assured of a continuing place in corporate capital structure.

[12] For a detailed study of this point, see Alden C. Olson, *The Impact of Valuation Requirements on the Preferred Stock Investment Policies of Life Insurance Companies* (East Lansing, Mich.: Bureau of Business and Economic Research, Graduate School of Business Administration, Michigan State University, 1964).

Financing with Convertible Preferred Stock, 1960-1967[*]

George E. Pinches[†]

CONVERTIBLE PREFERRED STOCK has gained substantial popularity in corporate financing during recent years. Prominent academicians [2, 3, 18, 20] have explored the subject of convertible security valuation. Numerous other articles [7, 9, 10] have been written about the growing use of convertible preferred stock in corporate mergers. This study presents data on the volume, usage, and characteristics of 335 convertible preferred stocks issued during the eight-year period, 1960–1967.[1]

Specifically, the following questions will be considered: (1) What dollar volume of convertible perferred stock was issued for cash, or in exchange for outstanding corporate securities? (2) What was the volume

[*] Reprinted from *The Journal of Finance*, Vol. 25, No. 1 (March 1970), pp. 53–63, by permission of the author and the publisher.

[†] Assistant Professor of Finance, Oklahoma State University. The author is grateful to Dr. Roland I. Robinson for his penetrating comments on the dissertation [17] from which this paper is drawn. The primary research was conducted while under a General Electric Doctoral Dissertation Fellowship at Michigan State University. Support for updating and expanding this portion of the study was provided by the Research Foundation at Oklahoma State University.

[1] It should be emphasized that these 335 convertible preferred stock offerings do not represent the universe of such stocks issued during the 1960–1967 time period. The study was limited to those convertible preferred stocks issued by firms that had securities (either common stock or convertible preferred stock) listed on the New York Stock Exchange anytime during the 1960–1967 period. In dollar volume the group should represent at least 80 percent of the convertible preferred stocks issued during this eight-year period. Statistics were gathered by reference to [4, 5, 11, 12, 13, 14, 15, 16, and 19]. Data from these publications provide the source of all tables presented in this article, unless specifically noted otherwise. Further information on data collection techniques will be made available upon request to the author. Lists of the stocks examined and mergers financed with convertible preferred stock are also available upon request.

and trend of financing corporate mergers with convertible preferred stock? (3) Why do corporations employ convertible preferreds as a financing tool? (4) What contractual features have characterized recent convertible preferred issues? and (5) What is the future for convertible preferred stock?

I. THE VOLUME OF CONVERTIBLE PREFERRED STOCK

Total preferred stock played a very limited role in new corporate financing during the 1960–1967 period (Table 1). The cash offerings of all preferred stocks averaged 3½ percent of total corporate offerings, while convertible preferred stock averaged only 1 percent of this total for the eight-year period.

However, data taken from estimates of the Securities and Exchange Commission (Table 1) or from other sources, such as the Corporate

TABLE 1
Cash security offerings of U.S. corporations: 1960–67
(millions of dollars)

Year	Total corporate securities issued* (1)	Total preferred stock issued* (2)	Convertible preferred stock issued† (3)	Convertible as a percent of total corporate securities (3)/(1)	Convertible as a percent of total preferred securities (3)/(2)
1960	$ 10,154	$ 409	$ 74	0.7	18.1
1961	13,165	450	194	1.5	43.1
1962	10,705	422	220	2.1	52.1
1963	12,211	343	97	.8	28.3
1964	13,957	412	133	1.0	32.3
1965	15,992	725	276	1.7	38.1
1966	18,074	574	228	1.3	39.7
1967	24,798	885	328	1.3	37.1
Total	$119,056	$4,220	$1,550		

* Estimates of the Securities and Exchange Commission as reported in the *Federal Reserve Bulletin*, October, 1968, p. A-44.
† Data for 1960–1965 was obtained by subtracting non-convertible preferred stock as estimated by Fisher and Wilt [6, p. 612] from total preferred stock. The data for 1966–1967 were gathered by the author. Refer to footnote 1 for limitations on data for 1966–1967.

Financing Directory of the *Investment Dealer's Digest*, understate the importance of convertible preferred stock.[2] In recent years many convertible preferred stocks have been issued for other securities in corporate mergers, or in exchange transactions during corporate refinancings. This

---

[2] These two sources do not yield identical measures of security issues because of differing populations and data gathering objectives. See [8, p. 14, 17] for an explanation of these differences.

study, by presenting data on both exchange and cash financing, provides the most complete information available on recent convertible preferred stock usage.

The 335 convertible preferred stocks reviewed for this study totaled over $12.1 billion for the 1960–1967 period (Table 2).[3] Merger and acqui-

TABLE 2
Convertible preferred stock issued, by purpose: 1960–67
(millions of dollars)

Year		Purpose		
	Acquisitions	Exchange for securities of issuing firm or stock dividend	Cash	Total
1960................	$ 136.7	$ 16.8	$ 0.2	$ 153.7
1961................	513.1	—	65.8	578.9
1962................	351.2	10.7	160.1	522.0
1963................	543.1	9.2	83.5	635.8
1964................	347.5	63.8	5.0	416.3
1965................	1,696.5	2.7	136.1	1,835.3
1966................	2,464.9	337.9	227.9	3,030.7
1967................	4,489.1	165.7	327.9	4,982.7
Total................	$10,542.1	$606.8	$1,006.5	$12,155.4

sition financing accounted for approximately $10.5 billion of this usage during the eight-year period. Particularly noteworthy in Table 2 are the following points: (1) 87 percent of the convertible preferreds were issued in mergers and acquisitions; (2) approximately 5 percent of the usage was in direct exchange for outstanding securities of the issuing firm, or for stock dividends; (3) cash offerings accounted for about 8 percent of the offerings; (4) 81 percent of all the convertible preferreds issued during this eight-year period occurred in 1965, 1966 and 1967, with 41 percent being issued in 1967 alone; and (5) convertible preferreds issued for cash or exchange did not rise as fast as the quantity of convertibles issued for mergers and acquisitions.

Size

The 335 issues included in the study ranged in size from $50 thousand to $690 million. However, more than 55 percent of the issues were between $5 million and $50 million.

---

[3] Since some firms had more than one convertible issue, the 335 stocks originated from only 230 separate firms. In all cases the dollar amount of the convertible preferred was determined by multiplying the number of shares issued per firm times the involuntary liquidating value of the security. The involuntary liquidating value was normally the redemption value, although in a few cases an arbitrary value had to be assumed.

Industry usage

Firms in the industrial category were, by far, the largest users of convertible preferred stock. During this eight-year period 82 percent of the convertible preferreds were issued by such firms. The public utility industry, which is the stronghold of non-convertible preferred stock [6, p. 613], accounted for only 10 percent of the total volume of convertible preferred stocks. It should be pointed out, however, that this industry accounted for 51 percent of *new* cash issues of convertible preferred stock. The bank and finance industry and the transportation industry used this type of security only infrequently between 1960 and 1967.

II. MERGER FINANCING WITH CONVERTIBLE PREFERRED STOCK

During the study period, 335 convertible preferred stocks were employed to finance 481 corporate acquisitions (Table 3). Three hundred

TABLE 3
Mergers and acquisitions financed with convertible preferred stock: 1960–67

	Securities employed		
Year	*Only convertible preferred stock*	*Convertible preferred stock and other securities*	*Total*
1960...........	12	6	18
1961...........	15	14	29
1962...........	8	6	14
1963...........	19	9	28
1964...........	9	15	24
1965...........	23	18	41
1966...........	87	23	110
1967...........	145	72	217
Total...........	318	163	481

and eighteen of the mergers were accomplished solely with convertible preferred stock, while in the remaining 163 mergers other securities and/or cash were employed in addition to the convertible security.

Total mergers

Data gathered by the Federal Trade Commission and W. T. Grimm & Co., a consulting firm specializing in mergers, indicates that 15,642

TABLE 4
Total number of mergers and acquisitions: 1960–67

Year	Total mergers* (1)	Mergers financed with convertible stock† (2)	Financed with convertible preferred stock‡ (3)	Convertible as a percent of total mergers (3)/(1)	Convertible as a percent of stock-financed mergers (3)/(2)
1960............	1,345	—	18	1.3	—
1961..·.........	1,724	—	29	1.7	—
1962............	1,667	—	14	.8	—
1963............	1,479	—	28	1.9	—
1964............	1,950	702	24	1.2	3.4
1965............	2,125	689	41	1.9	6.0
1966............	2,377	939	110	4.6	11.7
1967............	2,975	1,898	217	7.3	11.3
Total..........	15,642	4,228	481		

* Data for 1960–1963 is based on Federal Trade Commission statistics and was obtained from the Statement of Willard F. Mueller to the Select Committee on Small Business, United States Senate, March 15, 1967, appendix Table 1. (Mimeographed.) Data for 1964–1967 was obtained from "1967 Merger Review." (Chicago: W. T. Grimm & Co., January 1, 1968). (Mimeographed.) The figures collected by W. T. Grimm & Co. indicate considerably more mergers for the 1964–1967 period than the .Federal Trade Commission data. The exact reason for this difference is unknown.
† Obtained from "1967 Merger Review."
‡ From Table 3.

mergers and acquisitions occurred between 1960 and 1967 (Table 4). Convertible preferred stock played a fairly insignificant role in total merger activity; it accounted for only 3.1 percent of total mergers during this time period. However, during 1966 and 1967 convertible preferred stock became more popular in financing corporate mergers. During 1966 convertible preferreds were employed in 4.6 percent of all mergers and this figure increased to 7.3 percent during 1967. Possible reasons for this increase in popularity will be briefly examined in Section III.

Mergers financed with stock

For those mergers financed partially or totally with stock (either common stock, non-convertible preferred stock, or convertible preferred stock) a somewhat different relationship existed. Between 1964 and 1967 approximately 11.4 percent of all stock-financed mergers involved convertible preferred stock (Table 4). During the last two years covered by the study, convertible preferred stock was involved in 11.5 percent of all mergers where stock was employed.

Size of acquisitions

While 481 mergers were examined, there were only 406 separate transactions.[4] Convertible preferred stock was the only security employed in 264 of the transactions, while other securities and/or cash were employed in addition to the convertible security in the remaining 142 transactions (Table 5). When grouped according to size there was a significant

TABLE 5
Number and size of acquisitions, by type of securities employed
(millions of dollars)

					Size						
Financing	*Less than .5*	*.5 to 1.0*	*1.0 to 2.5*	*2.5 to 5.0*	*5.0 to 10.0*	*10.0 to 25.0*	*25.0 to 50.0*	*50.0 to 100.0*	*100.0 to 250.0*	*over 250.0*	*T ac sit*
Only convertible preferred stock*...	15	13	46	39	40	44	31	20	13	3	2
Convertible preferred stock and other securities†........	2	1	10	15	20	34	18	19	18	5	1
Total acquisitions‡...	17	14	56	54	60	78	49	39	31	8	4

* Size of the acquisitions was determined by multiplying the involuntary liquidating value times the num of shares issued. Accordingly, size was taken as of the time the individual mergers occurred.

† Size was determined by adding the value of convertible preferred stock to the value of other securi For common stock the value was determined by multiplying the average market price in the month of merger times the number of common shares involved. For debt or non-convertible preferred stock the v employed was face or par value. An arbitrary value was established where stock warrants were employed.

‡ The chi-square approximation of the Kolmogorov-Smirnov two-sample test was employed. $\chi^2 = 21.45$ df = 2 is significant at the .001 level, which implies that the distribution of acquisitions financed with vertible preferred stock and other securities was stochastically larger.

difference in the distributions according to the type of financing employed. This difference implies that the acquisitions financed with a combination of convertible preferred and other securities were larger than the acquisitions financed solely with convertible preferred stock. Evidently, small mergers can often be financed with convertible preferred stock while larger mergers generally suggest, or necessitate, a combination of securities.

III. REASONS FOR EMPLOYING CONVERTIBLE PREFERRED STOCK

As indicated in Table 2, approximately $10.5 billion in convertible preferred stock was issued in mergers and acquisitions between 1960

[4] In many instances two or more related firms were acquired simultaneously. In these instances it was impossible to determine how much of the total value belonged to any specific firm.

and 1967. In addition, considerable smaller amounts were issued for cash, in exchange for outstanding securities, or as stock dividends. Possible reasons for employing convertible preferred stock for these purposes are reviewed in this section.

Mergers

Eighty-six percent of the convertibles reviewed were issued to finance corporate mergers or acquisitions. In 1966 and 1967 alone, almost $7 billion in convertible preferreds were issued for this purpose. If a merger is non-taxable to the common stockholders of the acquired firm and accounted for as a "pooling of interests," either common stock or convertible preferred stock with voting rights has to be exchanged.[5] Three different, although possibly overlapping, reasons indicate why convertible preferred stock may be favored over common stock as a means of financing some corporate mergers.

If firms are long-run wealth maximizers, the increasing use of convertible preferred stock to finance corporate mergers suggests that acquiring firms *expect* greater returns than could be obtained by employing other types of securities to finance the mergers. This possible expectation of long-run benefits—from employing convertible preferred stock instead of other securities—implies either a declining or "U" shaped cost of capital function. However, a detailed study [17] failed to provide any support for this position. Undoubtedly, further research and different approaches are called for to identify the long-run benefits and implications of financing corporate mergers with convertible preferred stock.

A second reason for employing convertible preferred stock to finance mergers is as a means of reconciling divergent cash dividend policies between acquiring firms and the firms to be acquired, while enabling the acquiring firm to keep its existing cash dividend policy on common stock [10, p. 53]. Inspection of the present 481 mergers verified that many of the acquiring firms paid little or no cash dividends.[6] In such cases convertible preferred stock serves as an expedient means of adjusting divergent cash dividend policies between merging firms.

A third reason for financing mergers with convertible preferred stock could be the desire, on the part of the acquiring firm, for immediate earnings leverage. Under our present accounting convention, an immediate increase in reported earnings available for common stock is normally

---

[5] There are certain (limited) exceptions in accounting treatment and under the Internal Revenue Code. The use of debt, even convertible debentures, and other securities that do not provide for continuity of ownership normally results in a taxable merger transaction. Within certain limits debt and other similar securities may not invalidate the "pooling of interest" accounting treatment.

[6] The size of the acquiring firm did not appear to directly influence the payment or size of the cash dividend.

possible if a merger occurs with convertible preferred stock. As long as the after-tax earnings of the acquired firm are greater than the dividend requirements on the newly issued convertible preferred, and merged firm will show increased earnings. These increased earnings may be temporary or permanent depending on the conversion terms, actual rates of conversion, and the reporting of potential dilution resulting from future conversion.[7] Due to the increased emphasis on earnings performance, this reason, by itself, may largely explain why convertible preferred stock became increasingly important in financing corporate mergers during the study period.

Cash

The public utility industry issued over half of the convertible preferred stock used to obtain new capital. With the regulated rates and relatively predictable income patterns, it is not surprising these firms employ convertible preferred stock as well as non-convertible preferred stock [6, p. 620] in corporate financing. Approximately $376 million of the $483 million of convertible preferred stock issued for cash by non-public utility firms occurred in the following industries: (1) chemical, oil, metal, and tire; (2) heavy machinery; and (3) data processing. All of these industries require substantial capital outlays and convertible preferred stock was employed in addition to other securities to finance these outlays.

Exchange

One firm, which did not pay cash dividends on its common stock, accounted for 46½ percent of the convertible preferred stock issued for purposes of corporate refinancing. This exchange of convertible preferred for common stock enabled the company to offer current cash dividends in exchange for less common stock outstanding in the future. The other issuers of convertible preferred stock—in exchange for outstanding securities—apparently had similar motives except one firm which declared a dividend payable in shares of convertible preferred stock.

IV. CONTRACTUAL FEATURES OF CONVERTIBLE PREFERRED STOCK

The convertible preferred stocks included in this study contained a wide variety of contractual features. All issues were examined to deter-

---

[7] In recognition of the impact of potential dilution, the Accounting Principles Board [1] required in 1966 that clear disclosure must be provided of the possible effects of dilution on reported earnings per share. See [21, pp. 60–63] for a discussion of the impact of accounting changes on earnings. A further refinement of these requirements is contained in: Accounting Principles Board. "Earnings Per Share," *Opinion No. 15*. New York: American Institute of Certified Public Accountants, May, 1969.

mine the following characteristics: dividend provisions, liquidation terms, voting rights, call provisions, conversion restrictions and sinking fund requirements. It was felt that the potential usage of the convertible preferred issue should influence the contractual terms offered. Therefore, the 335 stocks were classified into two groups: (1) those primarily employed in financing mergers;[8] and (2) those employed in cash financing or offered in exchange for outstanding securities of the issuing firm (Table 6).

Most convertible preferred stocks issued between 1960 and 1967 had the following features: (1) they were cumulative, but not participating; (2) they had no sinking or purchase fund; (3) they had a fixed conversion rate; (4) no waiting period before conversion could take place; and (5) the conversion privilege did not expire. However, there were significant differences in four provisions depending on whether the security was intended for usage in merger financing, or was issued for cash or in exchange for outstanding securities of the issuing firm. Those securities intended for merger financing generally had: (1) no premium on voluntary liquidation; (2) full voting right; (3) either a fixed or variable call rate; and (4) a five-year waiting period before they were callable. Convertible preferred stocks intended for cash or exchange financing: (1) had a premium on voluntary liquidation; (2) had contingent or no voting rights; (3) had a variable call rate; and (4) could be called at any time (without a waiting period).

V. THE FUTURE OF CONVERTIBLE PREFERRED STOCK

During the 1960–1967 period, convertible preferred stock has become more popular—especially for financing corporate mergers and acquisitions. Less than 15 percent of the convertible studied were employed for uses other than financing corporate mergers. The findings of this study give no reason to believe that convertible preferred stock will become any more significant as a means of raising new corporate capital. Equally, the use of convertibles as stock dividends or in exchange for outstanding securities óf the issuing firm appears to be of only occasional interest.

However, there is nothing to suggest that companies will lessen their usage of convertible preferred stock in financing some non-taxable mergers that are accounted for as a "pooling of interests." While the ultimate benefits derived from employing convertible preferred stock in merger financing were not the primary subject of this study, it appears that convertible preferred stock: (1) may have certain long-run benefits for acquiring firms; (2) is used as a means of reconciling divergent cash

---

[8] At least 40 percent of the issue had to be employed in merger financing for it to be classified in this group.

TABLE 6

Characteristics of 335 convertible preferred stocks: 1960–67

			For mergers	*For cash or exchange*	*Total*
I. A. Cumulative cash.......	Cumulative		290	43	333
dividends..........	Noncumulative		2	0	2
B. Participating cash.....	Participating		5	0	5
dividends..........	Nonparticipating		287	43	330
II. Premium on voluntary......	Premium		110	32	142
liquidation*.............	No premium		182	11	193
III. Voting rights†.............	Full		257	16	273
	Partial or none		35	27	62
IV. A. Call provision rate‡....	Fixed		151	13	164
	Variable§		141	30	171
B. Call protection‖.......	Years before callable				
	Zero		50	26	76
	1		2	0	2
	2		7	4	11
	3		18	1	19
	4		7	2	9
	5		162	9	171
	6		18	0	18
	7		9	1	10
	8		7	0	7
	10		11	0	11
	15		1	0	1
C. Sinking- (or purchase)..	Sinking fund		42	8	50
fund provision.......	No sinking fund		250	35	285
V. A. Conversion rate........	Fixed		258	34	292
	Variable#		34	9	43
B. Conversion rights......	Years before convertible				
	Zero		262	41	303
	1		10	0	10
	2		8	1	9
	3		6	1	7
	5		6	0	6
C. Length of conversion privilege............	Years before expiration				
	3		4	0	4
	4		3	0	3
	5		11	1	12
	9		3	0	3
	10		19	2	21
	11		1	0	1
	12		2	0	2
	14		1	0	1
	15		3	4	7
	17		0	1	1
	20		3	0	3
	21		1	0	1
	Does not expire		241	35	276

* For two independent samples, χ^2 of 19.25 with df = 1 is significant at the .001 level.
† For two independent samples, χ^2 of 60.82 with df = 1 is significant at the .001 level.
‡ For two independent samples, χ^2 of 6.09 with df = 1 is significant at the .01 level.
§ Four issues had increasing call rates while 167 had a decreasing call rate.
‖ For two independent samples, χ^2 of 37.71 with df = 1 is significant at the .001 level.
Five issues had increasing rates while thirty-eight had decreasing rates.

dividend policies between merging firms; and (3) allows acquiring firms to benefit from immediate earnings leverage.

In the future, convertible preferred stock may continue to play a fairly important role in merger financing, but it will probably be of little use in raising capital—except in the public utility industry. Drastic changes in the present tax structure would appear to be necessary before any significant upswing in the use of convertible preferred stock in raising new corporate capital might occur.

REFERENCES

1. Accounting Principles Board. "Reporting the Results of Operations," *Opinion No. 9.* New York: American Institute of Certified Public Accountants, December 1966.

2. William J. Baumol, Burton G. Malkiel, and Richard E. Quandt. "The Valuation of Convertible Securities," *Quarterly Journal of Economics,* Vol. 80 (February 1966), pp. 48–59.

3. Eugene F. Brigham, "An Analysis of Convertible Debentures: Theory and Some Empirical Evidence," *Journal of Finance,* Vol. 21 (March 1966), pp. 35–54.

4. *Commercial and Financial Chronicle,* various issues.

5. *Corporation Records.* New York: Standard & Poor's Corp. n.d.

6. Donald E. Fisher and Glenn A. Wilt, Jr. "Non-Convertible Preferred Stock as a Financing Instrument, 1950-1965," *Journal of Finance,* Vol. 23 (September 1968), pp. 611–24.

7. Jerome S. Hollender. "Creating a Currency for Corporate Growth," *Financial Executive,* Vol. 34 (November 1966), pp. 22ff.

8. *Investment Dealer's Digest,* Section II, Corporate Financing Directory (February 19, 1968).

9. Hargett Y. Kinard. "Financing Mergers and Acquisitions," *Financial Executive,* Vol. 31 (August 1963), pp. 13–16.

10. Anthony H. Meyer. "Designing a Convertible Preferred Issue," *Financial Executive,* Vol. 36 (April 1968), pp. 42ff.

11. *Moody's Bank & Finance Manual.* New York: Moody's Investors Service, Inc., 1959–1968.

12. *Moody's Convertible Preferreds,* Vol. 11, No. 1 (January 1967) and Vol. 3, No. 1 (January 1968).

13. *Moody's Industrial Manual.* New York: Moody's Investors Service, Inc., 1959–1968.

14. *Moody's Public Utility Manual.* New York: Moody's Investors Service, Inc., 1959–1968.

15. *Moody's Transportation Manual.* New York: Moody's Investors Service, Inc., 1959–1968.

16. New York Stock Exchange Listing Statements, 1960-1967.

17. George E. Pinches. "Financing Corporate Mergers and Acquisitions with Convertible Preferred Stock," unpublished Ph.D. dissertation, Michigan State University, 1968.

18. Otto H. Poensgen. "The Valuation of Convertible Bonds," *Industrial Management Review*, Vol. 7 (Fall 1965), pp. 77–92; and Vol. 7 (Spring 1966), pp. 83–98.

19. *The Value Line Convertible Preferred Stock Service*, Vol. 1, No. 4 (May 27, 1968).

20. Roman L. Weil, Jr., Joel E. Segall, and David Green, Jr. "Premiums on Convertible Bonds," *Journal of Finance*, Vol. 23 (June, 1968), pp. 445–63.

21. Frank T. Weston and Sidney Davidson. "What will Accounting Changes Do to Earnings," *Financial Analysts Journal*, Vol. 24 (September–October, 1968), pp. 59–66.

An Analysis of Convertible Debentures: Theory and Some Empirical Evidence[*]

Eugene F. Brigham [†]

THE PURPOSE OF THIS PAPER is to develop a theoretical framework for analyzing the nature of convertible securities, and then to test it. In the first section, a graphic model is used to describe the essential features of a convertible issue. In the second section, a conceptual scheme for estimating *ex ante* rates of return is developed. Next, interactions between the key variables under the control of the firm—the coupon interest rate and the conversion price—are discussed in detail. Finally, the terms and conditions under which convertible bonds were sold by a sample of large, listed firms during the period 1961–1963 are described.

I. A MODEL OF CONVERTIBLE BONDS

The essential features of a convertible bond may be described by reference to Figure 1. While the graph may be given either an *ex post* or *ex ante* interpretation, at this point it is more convenient to think

[*] Reprinted from *The Journal of Finance*, Vol. 21, No. 1 (March 1966), pp. 35–54, by permission of the author and the publisher.

The paper has benefited greatly from the comments on an earlier draft by Franco Modigliani, Merton H. Miller, Harry V. Roberts, John P. Shelton, Eugene M. Lerner, and especially Myron J. Gordon, who stimulated the author's initial interest in the subject, suggested the graphic model in Section I, and provided valuable comments and suggestions at later stages. T. C. Anderson assisted with the data collection as well as the model formulation. The research was conducted in part while the author was on a Ford Foundation Faculty Research Fellowship, and research assistance was provided by the Bureau of Business and Economic Research, UCLA.

[†] Professor of Finance, University of Florida.

FIGURE 1
Hypotethical model of a convertible bond

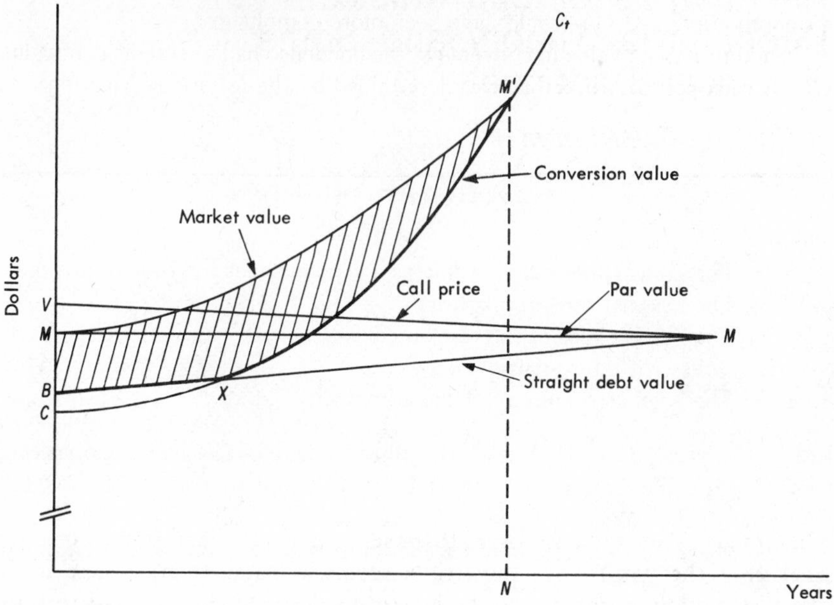

of it *ex post*. In other words, the conditions described are assumed to have already happened.

The hypothetical bond was sold for M dollars in year t_0, and this initial price was also the par (and maturity) value. It was callable at the option of the corporation, with the call price originating at V, somewhat above par, and declining linearly over the term to maturity to equal M at maturity.[1]

The original conversion value (C) was established by multiplying the market price of the stock at the time of issue by the number of shares into which the bond may be converted (the conversion ratio). The stock price grew at a constant rate (g), causing the conversion value curve (CC_t) to rise at this same rate. This established the curve CC_t, which shows the conversion value at each point in time. All of this is expressed by equation (1):

$$C_t = P_0(1 + g)^t R \qquad (1)$$

where C_t = the conversion value at time t; P_0 = the initial market price of the stock; g = the rate of growth of the stock's price; and R = the conversion ratio, or the number of shares into which the bond may be converted. Had

---

[1] Had the bond not been callable for a specified number of years, then the line VM would have been undefined prior to this date.

growth been zero, CC_t would have been horizontal; had it been negative, CC_t would have declined; and had growth been uneven, CC_t would not have been a smooth curve and (1) would have been more complicated.

In addition to its value in conversion, the bond also had a straight-debt value (B_t) at each point in time that was determined by the following equation:

$$B_t = \sum_{K=1}^{(T-t)} \frac{I}{(1+i)^K} + \frac{M}{(1+i)^{T-t}} \tag{2}$$

where:

B_t = The convertible bond's value as a straight-debt instrument at time t

T = The original term to maturity

i = The market rate of interest on equivalent-risk, pure-debt issues

I = Dollars of interest paid each year

M = The bond's redemption value at maturity.

If $I = iM$, then $B_t = M$; but in the illustrative case, as is typically true, $I < iM$ with the consequence that $B_t < M$ prior to the maturity date. In Figure 1, the values of B_t are shown by the line BM.[2]

Note that the conversion value and the straight-debt value combine to establish a lower bound for the price of the bond. Logically, the bond could not sell for less than its value as straight debt (BM), and if it should fall below the conversion value (CC_t) arbitragers would enter the market, short the stock, and cover their short positions by buying and converting bonds. This latter process would continue until the market price of the bond is driven up to its conversion value. The higher of these two floors dominates, with the discontinuous curve BXC' forming the effective market value floor.

The curve designating the market value (MM') lies above the line of basic value (BXC_t) over most of the range but converges with BXC_t in year N. The rationale behind this price action is developed in the following two subsections.

(a) Why the market value exceeds the BXC_t floor

The spread between MM' and BXC_t, which represents the premium marginal investors[3] are willing to pay for the conversion option, may

---

[2] In the graph BM appears to be linear, though in fact it is curved. The construction also implies that the interest rate on the firm's straight debt was constant over a period. Had it changed—either because of a change in the general level of rates or because of a change in investors' appraisals of the firm's risk—BT would have shifted.

[3] Marginal investors, often called "the market," are defined as those just willing to hold the bond at its going price. These investors are, in fact, the ones who actually determine the level of the bond's price.

be explained by several factors. First, since it may be converted into common stock if the company prospers and the stock price rises, the convertible bond usually commands a premium over its value as straight-debt (i.e., the right of conversion has a positive value). Second, the convertible bond usually commands a premium over its conversion value because, by holding convertibles, an investor is able to reduce his risk exposure. To illustrate, suppose a particular bond is convertible into 20 shares of stock with a market price of $70, giving a conversion value of $1,400. If the stock market turns sharply down and the stock price falls to $35 per share, a stock investor suffers a 50 percent loss in value. Had he held a convertible bond, its price would have fallen from $1,400 to the bond value floor, BM in Figure 1, which is probably well above $700. Hence, holding the convertible entails less risk than holding common stock, and this causes convertibles to sell at a premium above their conversion value.

(b) Why the market value approaches the conversion value

The MM' curve in Figure 1 rises less rapidly than the CC_t curve, indicating that the market value approaches the conversion value as the conversion value increases. This empirically validated fact is caused by three separate factors. First, and probably most important, the bond-holders realize that the issue is callable, and if it is in fact called they have the option of either surrendering for redemption or converting. In the former case they receive the call price, while in the latter they receive stock with a value designated by C_t. If the market price of the bond is above either of these values, the holder is in danger of a potential loss in wealth in the event of a call, and this fact prevents wide spreads between MM' and BXC_t whenever the market value exceeds the call price.

The second factor driving MM' toward CC_t is related to the loss protection characteristic of convertibles. Barring changes in the interest rate on the firm's straight-debt securities, the potential loss on a convertible is equal to the spread between MM' and BM. Since this spread increases at high conversion values, the loss potential also increases, causing the premium attributable to the loss protection to diminish.

The third factor causing the gap between MM' and CC_t to close has to do with the relationship between the yield on a convertible and that on the common stock for which it may be exchanged. It is well known that the yield on most common stocks consists of two components—a dividend yield and a capital gain yield. In the next section it is shown that convertibles also have two yield components, one from interest payments and one from capital gains. After some point, the expected capital gain is the same for both instruments, but the current yield on the bond declines vis à vis that on the common stock because dividends on growing stocks typically rise but interest payments are fixed. This causes the gap between MM' and CC_t to close, and eventually would lead to a negative premium except for the fact that voluntary conversion occurs first.

II. YIELDS ON CONVERTIBLE SECURITIES

(a) Ex post convertible yields

Convertible yields may be viewed either *ex post* or *ex ante*. In this section they are considered after the fact; in the next section the more interesting question of *ex ante* yields is examined.

The actual rate of return earned on a convertible is found by solving equation (3) for k, the internal rate of return:

$$M = \sum_{t=1}^{N} \frac{I}{(1 + k)^t} + \frac{T.V.}{(1 + k)^N} \tag{3}$$

where
    M = The price paid for the bond
    I = The dollars of interest received per annum
    $T.V.$ = The terminal value of the bond: the call price if surrendered on call, the maturity value if redeemed, the conversion value if converted, or the market price if sold
    N = The number of years the bond was held
    k = The internal rate of return.

The equation up to this point is purely definitional and has no behavioral content; it simply states that if one paid M for a convertible bond, held it for N years, and received a series of interest payments plus a terminal value, then he received a return on his investment equal to k.[4]

(b) Ex ante yields

The *ex ante* yield on a convertible (k^*) is probabilistic—it is dependent upon a set of variables that are subject to probability distributions, hence it must itself be a random variable. It is possible, however, to define

---

[4] Three simplifications are made in this analysis. First, taxes are ignored. Second, the problem of reinvestment rates is handled by assuming that all reinvestment is made at the internal rate of return. Third, it is assumed that the bondholder does not hold stock after conversion; he cashes out, as would be true of an institutional investor precluded from holding common stock.

each of the determinants of k^* in terms of its mean expected value; $E(g)$, for example is the expected value of the rate of growth in the stock's price over N years. For simplicity, $E(g)$ and other random variables are shortened to $1g$, $T.V.$, et cetera. With the variables defined in this manner, it is possible to work sequentially through two equations to find the expected rate of return on a convertible bond.

Remembering that bondholders are assumed to cash out in year N, presumably reinvesting the terminal value received in some other security, one may establish three determinants of $T.V.$: (1) the corporation's policy in regard to calling the bond to force conversion; (2) the investor's decision to hold the bond until it is called, to sell it, or to voluntarily convert; and (3) the path of the conversion's value curve.

Corporation's call policy. It will be shown in the empirical section that corporations issuing convertible bonds generally have policies regarding just how far up the CC_t curve they will allow a bond to go before calling to force conversion. These policies range from calling as soon as they are "sure" conversion will take place—this generally means a premium of about 20 percent over the call price—to never calling at all. If the policy is to never issue a call, however, the firm generally relies on the dividend-interest differential to cause voluntary conversion. The question of if and when a corporation *should* call its convertible bonds is taken up later in this paper. Here, it is merely necessary to indicate the call policy does have a very direct influence on the *ex post* $T.V.$ figure used in equation (3). Naturally, therefore, expectations about call policy influence the *ex ante* version of equation (3).

Investors' cash-out policy. This factor is similar to the corporate call policy in that it sets a limit on how far up the CC_t curve an investor is willing to ride. The decision is influenced by the interest-dividend relationship, by the investor's aversion to risk (recall that risk due to a stock price decline increases as one moves up the CC_t curve), and by his willingness to hold securities providing low current yields. To simplify, it is assumed that investors are willing to ride higher up CC_t, given the dividend-interest relationship, than the firm is willing to let them ride; hence, corporate call policy supercedes investor cashout policy.

The path of the conversion value curve. As we saw, the path of the conversion value curve is traced out by equation (1):

$$C_t = P_0(1 + g)^t R \tag{1}$$

Recognizing that $R = M/P_c$, where P_c is defined as the conversion price of the shares, equation (1) may be rewritten:

$$C_t = \frac{P_0}{P_c}(1 + g)^t M \tag{4}$$

Setting (4) equal to the $T.V.$ defined by corporate policy (e.g., \$1,200 if a 20 percent premium is used), one finds:

$$T.V. = \frac{P_0}{P_c} (1 + g)^N M \qquad (5)$$

Now, converting to logarithmic form and solving for N, one obtains:

$$N = \frac{(\text{Log } P_c - \log P_0) + (\log T.V. - \log M)}{\log (1 + g)} \qquad (6)$$

Equation (6) may be interpreted as follows. First, an inspection of equation (3), which was used to find the realized internal rate of return (k), reveals that for given values of M, I, and $T.V.$, smaller values of N produce larger values of k. In other words, for a given interest component and a given capital gains component, the internal rate of return is larger the faster the capital gain is realized. From (6) we see that N is smaller the smaller the differentials between log P_c and log P_0, and between log $T.V.$ and log M, and it also declines as the rate of growth increases.[5] P_0, P_c, and M are all known with certainty at $t = 0$, while $T.V.$ (defined by corporate policy), g, and N are expected, probabilistic values.

With these definitions and equations, we may consider how an investor might look upon *ex ante* convertible bond yields. The following is the calculating sequence. First, the investor (or potential investor) has expectations about the variables on the right side of equation (6). Specifically, he knows P_c, P_0, and M, and he has expectations about the values of $T.V.$ and g.[6] This information may be used to solve (6) for N. With N estimated, the potential investor has all the data necessary to solve equation (3) for k^*, the expected yield on the bond.

[5] Since log $X -$ log Y is equal to X/Y, these log differentials could be expressed as ratios of the absolute values. In other words, N is smaller as the ratios P_c/P_0 and $T.V./M$ become smaller.

[6] A word about $T.V.$ and g is in order. It is shown in a later section that corporations do have policies with regard to calling to force conversion, and investors are able to make forecasts about the *minimum* conversion value at which the bond is likely to be called. Further, there are quite strong institutional constraints that tend to prohibit firms from calling bonds until this minimum value has been reached.

The growth rate of the common stock is much less predictable, but it too can be estimated. One approach is simply to extrapolate past share price growth, adjusted in whatever manner the investor thinks appropriate. Alternatively, one can recognize that stock price growth is dependent upon earnings and dividend growth, and that these are dependent upon retained earnings, the rate of return at which retained earnings can be invested, and the amount of leverage employed by the firm (among other things). In this paper no attempt is made to specify the manner in which investors measure expected growth.

(c) Market equilibrium

When convertible bonds are initially offered to the public, they are typically priced at par (usually $1,000).[7] If the terms of the issue, in combination with investor expectations about the other key variables, produce an expected rate of return just equal to the marginal investor's required rate of return on investments with this degree of risk (his opportunity cost, in a sense), then the bond will just clear the market. The price will not run up in the manner of a "hot issue," nor will it fall after underwriters have ceased stabilization. In the unlikely event that investor expectations are borne out exactly, the conversion value will follow a predicted CC_t curve, the market price will follow a predicted MM' curve, the firm will call the bond at the predicted $T.V.$, and investors will realize yield k^*.

(d) An illustrative case

To illustrate the material in this and the subsequent section, it is useful to present an example. Suppose a firm's stock price has been growing and is expected to continue growing by 4 percent per annum; the company is known to have called convertibles in the past when the conversion value exceeded the par value by 20 percent; and its common stock is currently selling for $45 per share. If the company then offers a debenture that pays 4 percent interest and is convertible into 20 shares of stock for sale at par, $1,000 (the conversion price is thus $50, or $1,000/20) and investor could calculate the expected years to conversion by substituting the expected values into equation (6). He would find N approximately equal to 8 years.[8] With this estimate of the years the bond will remain outstanding, the investor could then substitute into equation (3) and solve for k^*. For the values in the example, this would be approximately 6 percent.[9] If this *ex ante* yield is equal to or greater than the investor's required rate of return on investments with the same (estimated) risk, then he would buy the bonds.[10] If the marginal investor's opportunity cost is just met, the issue price will be stable.[11]

---

[7] It must be made very clear that the discussion at this point is related to publicly-offered bonds, not to those offered through rights to existing stockholders. There are quite fundamental differences, which are discussed later, between rights offerings and issues sold to the general public.

[8] $$N = \frac{(\log \$50 - \log \$45) + (\log \$1{,}200 - \log \$1{,}000)}{\log (1.04)} \approx 8.$$

[9] $$\$1{,}000 = \sum_{t=1}^{8} \frac{\$40}{(1 + k^*)^t} + \frac{\$1{,}200}{(1 + k^*)^8} \quad \text{when } K^* = 6\%.$$

[10] Prudent portfolio policy suggests that no single investor should buy the entire issue unless the dollar value of the issue is small in relation to his portfolio.

[11] In the case of rights offerings, bonds are generally under-priced; consequently, they sell at a premium over par immediately after issue.

III. TRADE-OFFS BETWEEN INTEREST AND CAPITAL GAINS

When the corporation negotiates with investors (actually investment bankers, who anticipate the market's reaction to the issue) prior to selling convertible bonds, six key determinants of k^* come into play:

Predetermined Variables: M = Issue price of bond (usually $1,000)
$T.V.$ = Terminal value at which the firm is expected to force conversion
P_0 = Current market price of the shares
g = Expected growth rate of share prices
Decision Variables: P_c = Conversion price
I = Coupon interest rate.

Predetermined variables are defined as those not subject to negotiation. Obviously, the price of the bond could be subject to negotiation, but typically it is not; if the issue price differs from par it is by a small amount and reflects underwriting costs. The terminal value, here defined as determined by the corporation's call policy, could likewise be settled in the indenture, but normally it is not. Similarly, it would be possible to at least partially put g in the decision variable category by limiting the dividend payout, but this is not done. Note that N is not included in the list; it is itself dependent upon the other variables, hence including it would be redundant.

The decision variables—conversion prices and coupon interest rates—are the terms actually negotiated in the pre-issue meetings between the corporation and the underwriters. Equations (3) and (6) may be studied to gain insights into the way in which different combinations of I and P_c interact with the predetermined variables to influence k^*. This, in turn, provides insights into rational trade-offs between the two decision variables.

One way to consider the relationships between the decision variables is illustrated in Figure 2. Here, the vertical axis measures the ratio of straight-debt interest to the coupon rate on the convertible issue, while the horizontal axis gives the ratio of the conversion price to the initial market price of the stock. Limits of 1.0 are set for both ratios on the assumptions that (1) convertible interest yields can never exceed equivalent risk straight-debt yields (if they did, this would indicate that the value of the option to convert was *negative*), and (2) the conversion price is never set lower than the stock's market price at time of issue.[12] The curves are the locus of a set of iso-yield points for given growth (and other) expectations.

---

[12] This latter assumption has, to the author's knowledge, always held true for non-rights offerings. There have been occasions—most notably AT&T's 1949 issue—when stockholders were offered convertibles with the conversion price lower than the initial market price.

FIGURE 2

Six percent yield curves derived under various growth, interest rate, and price combinations

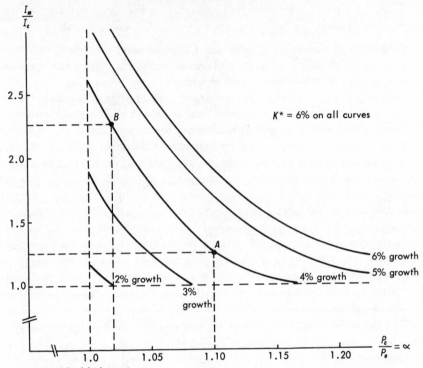

$$\frac{I_m}{I_c}$$

$K^* = 6\%$ on all curves

6% growth
5% growth
4% growth
3% growth
2% growth

$$\frac{P_c}{P_0} = \propto$$

I_m = Straight-debt interest
I_c = Convertible debt interest
P_0 = Stock's initial market price
P_c = Conversion price
Note: All curves assume that the issuing corporation will call when bonds have a conversion value of $1,200.

Points A and B on the 4 percent growth rate curve illustrate the construction of the iso-yield curves. At Point A straight-debt and convertible coupon rates are 4.5 percent and 4.0 percent, respectively, giving a ratio of 1.125, while the conversion price to market price ratio is $50/$45 = 1.100. These values were found in the example above to produce a 6 percent expected yield on the convertible bond. At Point B, the convertible interest rate is only 2 percent, so the yield ratio becomes 4.5/2.0 = 2.250. In order to obtain the 6 percent expected return, given the 4 percent growth rate, conversion must occur faster; specifically, by working through equation (3), one finds that it must occur in five years rather than eight. Solving equation (6) for the conversion price that allows conversion in five years yields a figure of $46.00, or a P_cP_0 ratio of $46.00/$45.00 = 1.02. This completes the derivation of Point

B. Other points on the curves are determined in a similar manner: by arbitrarily setting a convertible coupon rate, then working through the equations to find a conversion price that produces a 6 percent yield.[13]

The expected yield on a convertible bond has two components—an interest yield known with relative certainty, and a yield from capital gains that is considerably less certain. Consequently, the average investor would probably think of a convertible as being less risky than common stock, but more risky than straight bonds.

Assuming that marginal investors are risk averters, expected yields on convertibles should lie between those on stocks and those on non-convertible debt, which suggests that market forces will drive a firm's convertible bonds to a point along an appropriate iso-yield curve. However, this is not necessarily correct. Suppose, for example, that investors require an 8 percent rate of return on the company's common stock, 4½ percent on its straight-debt, and 6 percent on its convertibles. This would mean that the firm could set a 2 percent coupon and a $46.00 conversion price (Point *B*), a 4.0 percent coupon and a $50 conversion price (Point *A*), or any other combination along the 6 percent yield curve. Intuition tells one, however, that the first situation is more risky than the second. With the coupon set at 4 percent, most of the return is from interest, while with a 2 percent coupon the expected yield is derived largely from capital gains. In general, the higher up the vertical axis we go on any yield curve the more dependent the yield is on capital gains, and consequently the greater the risk of not attaining the indicated yield.

This leads to the conclusion that the firm's trade-off opportunity curve is something other than an iso-yield curve, and such a situation is illustrated by Figure 3. Equations (3) and (6) are used to construct a set of yield curves, all under the assumption that the stock will grow at 4 percent per annum and that the bond will be called when its conversion value is $1200. If the coupon rate on the convertible is set close to the straight-debt interest rate, the yield ratio is close to 1.0. In this case the convertible is very much like a regular bond, and the bond could be sold on an expected yield basis just above the 4.5 percent straight bond yield. On the other hand, if a very low coupon is set, the bondholder is relying primarily on capital gains. Under such circumstances, he may require a yield close to the 8 percent return on common stock. The hypothetical trade-off opportunity curve shown in Figure 3 incorporates this hypothesis.[14]

---

[13] Actually, a simple computer program was written to do the calculations.

[14] An alternative hypothesis would be that investors are indifferent between interest and capital gains, hence the trade-off curve should lie exactly on the iso-yield curve appropriate to the firm's risk class. Still another hypothesis would be that investors prefer capital gains because of their tax advantage, hence the trade-off curve should be *steeper* than any single yield curve.

FIGURE 3
Hypothetical trade-off opportunity curves for 4 percent growth rate

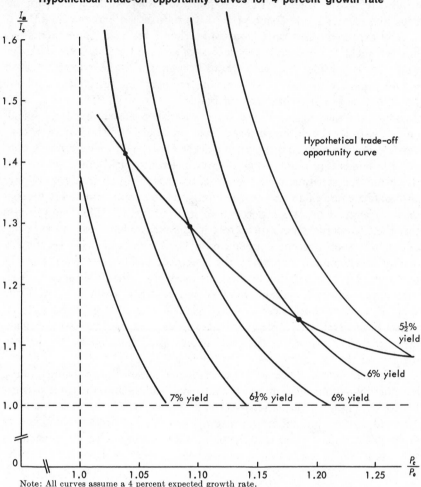

Note: All curves assume a 4 percent expected growth rate.

All the curves in Figure 3 are drawn on the assumption of a 4 percent growth rate. At higher growth rates, the yield curves are shifted to the right, and this in turn leads to higher trade-off curves. Figure 4 shows hypothetical trade-off curves under various growth assumptions; one should note that at higher growth rates the curves are higher.

Actually, of course, trade-off opportunity curves can only be derived empirically, but there are two bits of evidence indicating that, in fact, they do take the shape suggested by the model. First, five companies completed the questionnaires[15] in sufficient detail to permit the construc-

---

[15] The questionnaires are discussed in the next section.

FIGURE 4
Hypothetical trade-off opportunity curves under various growth assumptions

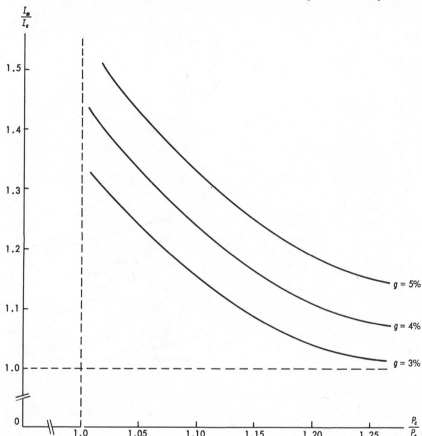

tion of segments of their actual trade-off curves; these are plotted in Figure 5, where they are also compared with the hypothetical curve for a 4 percent growth rate firm. Each of the companies' curves has the proper shape.

Further, their positions are in accordance with their growth prospects and their credit strengths. Companies A and B are the only ones of the five classified as "growth companies,"[16] and of these two A has had the more rapid growth in recent years. The positions of Companies C, D, and E do not appear to reflect differential growth prospects as much as differential credit strengths. Each of the firms is in a basic, "non-glamour" industry, and seems to have about the same expected rate of growth as the economy. They differ markedly in size, however, with C being largest, D next, and E smallest. Also, C's bonds are rated BBB,

---

[16] See the notes to Figure 6 for information on growth companies.

FIGURE 5
Actual trade-off opportunity curves derived from questionable data

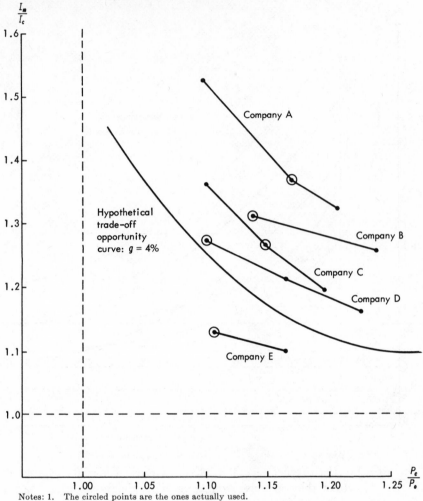

Notes: 1. The circled points are the ones actually used.
2. The hypothetical trade-off opportunity curve was taken from Figure 4 and assumes a
4 percent growth rate.

while those of D and E are rated BB. This suggests that size and credit rating, as well as growth prospects, are influential in determining trade-off opportunity curves.

Another approach to observing actual trade-off possibilities is to compare the I_m/I_c and P_cP_0 ratios of a sample of outstanding bonds at a particular point in time.[17] This approach remedies two problems with

---

[17] For this type of analysis, it is necessary to define I_c and I_m as yields to maturity rather than as coupon rates. Coupon rates are satisfactory so long as the bonds are selling for $1,000, as they were in the case of new issues, but are inappropriate to use for outstanding bonds with their widely differing prices.

FIGURE 6
Relationships between I_m/I_c and P_c/P_m on outstanding bonds

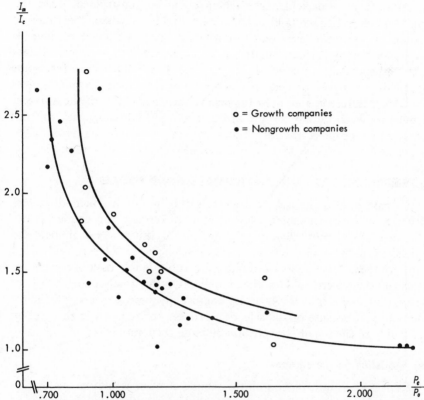

Notes: A. Growth companies were selected as follows:
1. The standard and Poor list of 200 growth companies dated February 22, 1965 was scanned and compared with the list of firms contained in *Moody's Convertible Bonds*. All companies on both lists (20) were initially included in the sample.
2. The value for I_c becomes very small, or even negative, when the market price of the bond is very large. (I_c is the yield to maturity on the bond.) Ten of the growth companies were deleted from the sample because their ratios either became negative or "exploded" as I_c approached zero.

B. Non-growth companies were selected as follows:
1. The first 35 companies in *Moody's Convertible Bonds* not designated as growth companies by S & P were chosen as the basic sample.
2. Companies with negative or very large yield ratios were deleted as in the growth company sample.

C. The curves were fitted free-hand.

Source: The ratios were derived from figures contained in *Moody's Convertible Bonds* dated May 17, 1965.

the trade-off curves derived from questionnaire data: (1) the fact that the sample was far too small to be more than suggestive, and (2) the fact that the bonds were issued at various times during the period 1961–63, while market conditions at any given time undoubtedly exert an influence on the position and slope of tradeoff curves.[18] The theory suggests that,

---

[18] If the stock market is strong and investors are optimistic, convertibles will be more favorably received than if the market is weak. In addition, discussions with investment bankers suggest that convertibles are simply more popular with

other things held constant, a scatter diagram of I_m/I_o against $P_c P_o$ ratios should be approximated by a downward sloping curce that is somewhat flatter than any iso-yield curve which could be constructed. That this condition does in fact hold is shown by Figure 6, where the ratios of groups of "growth" and non-growth companies are compared. The fits are by no means perfect, but this is to be expected in view of the fact that "other things" are not held constant. Credit ratings differ; some of the bonds have stepped-up conversion prices; their remaining lives are widely different; and, most important, the stock prices of the different companies, even within the growth and non-growth categories, are not expected to grow at the same rates. All in all, the fits are reasonably good, and the curves do have the postulated shapes and positions.

IV. EMPIRICAL DATA ON CONVERTIBLE BOND USAGE

To gain insights into the corporate planning that lies behind the decision to issue convertibles, as well as to determine the characteristics of convertible bonds themselves, a sample of issues was examined and a detailed questionnaire was sent to the issuing firms. During the period 1961 to 1963, 215 publicly-offered convertible bonds having a value of $1,080,000,000 were sold to the public.[19] Of this total, $820,000,000 or 76 percent, were sold by 42 listed companies; these 42 were chosen for the sample.[20] Because of the selection process, the remarks in this section refer only to the use of convertibles by large corporations.

(a) Statistics on the sample

Table 1 gives information on the sample companies and on the characteristics of the bonds themselves. Panel A shows that the issues ranged in size from $2.5 to $60 million, with the majority falling in the $5 to $20 million classes. Industrial firms predominated; the fact that convertibles were not used to any extent by utilities, which have been doing much new financing, is significant. Panel C shows that maturities ranged from 15 to 30 years, with 20 and 25 years being most frequent.

The bond ratings ranged from A to B, with 67 percent falling below BBB, the lower limit of "investment-grade" securities.[21] This suggests

institutional and other investors at certain times than at others, somewhat irrespective of the state of the stock market.

[19] "Corporate Financing Directory," *Investment Dealers' Digest*, February 1965.

[20] Interested readers may obtain a list of the firms in the sample by writing to the author.

[21] BB bonds "are regarded as lower medium grade. They have only minor investment characteristics." *Standard & Poor's Bond Guide*. Only BBB or higher rated bonds may be held in national banks' investment portfolios, and, though the permissible holdings of other institutional investors vary from state to state, they, too, are generally restricted to BB or better securities. However, the 33% of the issues rated A or BBB had 45% of the dollar value of bonds issued.

TABLE 1
Statistics on the sample of convertible bonds

A. Size of issues	Dollars (millions)	No. of issues Number	Percent
	2.5– 4.9	3	7
	5.0– 9.9	16	37
	10.0–19.9	11	26
	20.0–29.9	5	12
	30.0–39.9	4	9
	40.0–60.0	4	9

B. Industrial categories	Category	Number	Percent
	Industrial	37	86
	Transportation	4	9
	Public utility	1	2
	Finance	1	2

C. Maturity	Years to maturity	Number	Percent
	15	5	12
	20	25	58
	21	1	2
	22	2	5
	25	7	16
	30	3	7

D. Quality ratings	S & P Rating	Number	Percent
	A	3	7
	BBB	11	26
	BB	20	46
	B	9	21

E. Coupon rate	Rate	Number	Percent
	$3\frac{1}{8}$–$3\frac{1}{2}$	2	5
	$3\frac{5}{8}$–4	4	9
	$4\frac{1}{8}$–$4\frac{1}{2}$	17	40
	$4\frac{5}{8}$–5	16	37
	$5\frac{1}{8}$–$5\frac{1}{2}$	2	5
	$5\frac{5}{8}$–$6\frac{1}{2}$	2	5

F. Rights offerings		Number	Percent
	Offered to stockholders	23	53
	Not offered to stockholders	20	47

G. Stepped-up conversion price		Number	Percent
	Price stepped-up	8	19
	Not stepped-up	35	81

H. Sinking fund provision		Number	Percent
	Sinking fund	38	88
	No sinking fund	5	12

I. Underwriting data	Number of underwriters	Issues per underwriter
	13	1
	5	2
	2	3
	1	5
	1	9

that institutional holders would encounter some difficulties in purchasing most of the convertibles in the sample. However, the fact that the convertible issues were generally rated low *should not* be interpreted as meaning that the firms' straight debt was also low rated. All but two of the convertible issues were subordinated—generally to all existing and future long-and-short-term debt. This clearly caused the convertibles to be rated well below straight-debt.

About half of the issues were sold through rights offerings; 19 percent employed a stepped-up conversion price; and 88 percent had a sinking fund provision.[22] It is not shown in the table, but all of the bonds had essentially the same call provisions—they were callable immediately after issue with the call premium starting at the coupon interest rate and declining by $\frac{1}{4}$ percent per year to par. Relatively high concentration was found from the underwriting data, with Lehman Brothers acting as principal underwriter for 9 issues and Eastman Dillon, Union Securities for 5.

(b) The questionnaire

A detailed, 7-page questionnaire was sent to the chief financial officer of each of the 42 sample firms. Fifty-two percent, or 22 firms, returned the completed questionnaires, often with a two or three page letter elaborating on some of the points and describing their general financial philosophy.[23] This descriptive material is summarized below.

Reasons for using convertibles. When a firm sells convertibles, it does so for one of two primary reasons: (1) it wants equity capital and believes that convertibles are an expedient way of selling common stock, or (2) it desires debt but finds that by adding the convertible feature interest costs are reduced substantially. According to Table 2, 73 percent of the respondents were primarily interested in obtaining equity, while 27 percent used convertibles to "sweeten" debt issues. The bonds of this latter group generally carried the lower ratings, which was to be expected.[24]

---

[22] The typical sinking fund provision does not commence for some 10 years after issue; it requires the corporation to deliver funds to the trustee, who uses the funds to acquire bonds by lottery at par or through open market purchase, whichever is cheaper; and it gives the firm the right to deliver bonds acquired in conversion rather than money. Generally, the sinking fund amortizes from 50 to 80 percent of the total amount of bonds.

[23] Of the 22 completed questionnaires, 15 were in response to the original request and 7 were submitted after a follow-up letter. When the responding and nonresponding firms were compared by the characteristics listed in Table 1, no significant differences were noted.

[24] Recall that the firms in the sample are large, all of them being listed on either the New York or American stock exchange. Had the sample been extended to smaller, financially weaker companies it is likely that a larger percentage would have indicated that convertibles were used to sweeten debt issues.

TABLE 2
Reasons for using convertible bonds

Question: "Which of the following were most important in your company's decision to use convertibles?"

Responses

Number	Percent	
		I. *Primarily interested in obtaining equity:*
15	68	1. You believed your stock's price woud rise over time, and convertibles provide a way of selling common stock at a price above the existing market.
1	5	2. The funds were to be used for a project that would not produce much income for a fairly long period; using convertibles provided a way of preventing an earnings per share dilution during the "start-up" period.
		II. *Primarily interested in obtaining debt:*
6	27	3. At the time of issue, your company wanted debt, but found conditions to be such that a straight bond issue could not be sold at a reasonable rate of interest. (I.e., convertibles were used to "sweeten" a debt issue.)
22	100	
		III. *Applicable to either debt or equity:*
3	14	4. Certain classes of investors, notably institutions, cannot, or typically do not, buy equities. You are attempting to appeal to this group by using convertibles.

Notes: 1. Two companies checked both (1) and (4), and one company checked both (3) and (4).
2. An "other" category was included on the questionnaire but was not used by the respondents.

Financing alternatives. To check the consistency of the responses to Question I, as well as to gain insights into other sources of funds and their costs, the following question was asked:

At the time you decided to use convertibles, what alternatives were available for raising *the same amount of funds as was obtained from selling convertibles?*

All companies indicated that common stock could have been sold at net prices ranging from 2 to 5 percent below the market price, the larger discounts being applicable to small firms and to those needing large sums of money relative to the value of their outstanding shares. It is worth noting that neither in the questionnaire responses nor in subsequent interviews with selected firms was a fear indicated that a common stock issue would have brought on the danger of a break in the market price of the stock. The feeling seemed to hold that the market could absorb a stock issue the size of the convertible debenture offering. All but two respondents indicated that straight-debt could have been sold. When rates on straight-debt were mentioned, they ranged from ½ to 1 percent above those on the convertible issue.

In summary, the relatively large, listed corporations in the sample were by no means forced to use convertibles. They generally had the opportunity of selling either straight-debt or stock, both at "reasonable" costs, but they deliberately chose to employ convertibles.

Conversion price/interest rate trade-offs. To obtain information on the possibility of making trade-offs between coupon rates and conversion prices (used in Figure 5 above), the questionnaires included the following question: Two observations on the answers to this question are in order.

At the time of issue, your common stock was selling for approximately $———; the conversion price was $———; and the interest rate on the bonds was ———%. What opportunities did you have for trade-offs between conversion prices and the bond interest rate?

	Conversion price	Percent rate on bond
Actual...............	$———	———%
Available*............	$———	———%
	$———	———%

* Underwriter actually indicated that these alternatives were available.

First, the responses were poor, as only 5 of the 22 responding companies were able to supply the *actually offered* combinations. The others answered with such statements as "no records at this time," "alternatives discussed, but not actually pinned down," and "not considered." The second observation is that on rights offerings, trade-offs were not thought to be important. As a typical spokesman for a firm issuing bonds to stockholders put it: "Not applicable. Ours was a rights offering, and we simply set an interst rate and conversion price that would give the rights a sufficiently high value to ensure exercise." Several combinations could have been used to produce this "sufficiently high" rights value, but companies offering the bonds to stockholders were evidently less concerned than those selling directly to the public.

Conversion policy. It was pointed out in the preceding sections that a firm's policy with regard to forcing conversion by calling the issue is one of the vital determinants of the rate of return to bondholders. In order that something might be learned about this factor, the firms were asked about their conversion policy on the questionnaire, and the sample of bonds was examined to see when conversion actually was forced.

The question, and the responses to it, are shown in Table 3. Almost a quarter of the companies stated that their policy was to force conversion

TABLE 3
Conversion policies

"*Which of the following most nearly reflects your company's policy with regard to conversion?*"

	No.	%
1. Force conversion by calling as soon as you are "sure" the bonds will actually be converted, not redeemed? (Please indicate by how much conversion value must exceed call price.)	5	23
2. Encourage conversion by increasing common stock dividends, thus making the yield on common higher than that on bonds?	5	23
3. Have not encouraged conversion at all, but would force conversion prior to selling a new debt issue.	2	9
4. Do not plan to force or encourage conversion at all.	7	31
5. Other. (Please explain.)	3	14
	22	100

Note: The three companies checking "other" have no established conversion policy.

as soon as the conversion value exceeded the call price by about 20 percent. Another 23 percent indicated that they would encourage voluntary conversion by raising dividends.[25] The remaining 54 percent of the respondents either did not plan to force conversion at all, or else had no clearly defined policy.

These responses have been borne out reasonably well by actual experience. Of the 43 bonds in the sample, 20 had reached the point where the conversion value exceeded the call price by at least 20 percent. Six of these bonds, or 30 percent, had been called by March 1965.

(c) Institutional factors making convertibles attractive

Questionnaire responses and interviews suggested that two strictly institutional phenomena may serve to make convertibles a relatively attractive form of financing. First, a number of institutional investors—life insurance companies, certain pension funds, banks, and so on—are severely restricted in their ability to hold common stocks. The investment officers of many of these institutions are thought to feel that it would be desirable to have more equities than regulations permit. Convertible bonds provide these intermediaries with a method of indirectly holding more equities than the law permits.

---

[25] One of these firms returned a schedule showing the way voluntary conversion occurred in its case. In September 1964, the common dividend was raised by 25 percent. At this point bondholders would receive about 15 percent more income from dividends on conversion than in interest on the bonds. The conversion value was approximately equal to the market value and exceeded the call price by about 30 percent. Between the time of the dividend increase and the record date of the next quarterly dividend, some 50 percent of the bonds were converted voluntarily, and the company indicated that these conversions were continuing as additional bondholders recognized the income differential.

The second institutional factor has to do with margin requirements. Stock brokers suggest that there exists a class of investors who desire to obtain more leverage than is available under current margin requirements. Many convertible bonds can be bought on a 20 percent or better margin versus one of 70 percent on listed common stocks.

To the extent that high-leverage investors and restricted institutions are important factors in the market, it is possible that this might, in effect, shift the supply curve for funds placed in the convertible market to the right, thus lowering the cost of capital of convertibles. This is, in fact, what many advocates of convertibles suggest.[26] Although it may be true, there is no reason whatever to suppose that the supply shift could not be matched by an equal demand shift on the part of corporate borrowers, thus eliminating the supposed advantage attributed to convertibles. Indeed, is it not possible that corporations could be "over-sold" on the use of convertibles, thus causing them to demand an excessive amount of funds through such issues, and making the cost of convertible capital relatively more expensive than other types? This is completely speculative, of course. There is no evidence to indicate whether these institutional factors create a favorable or unfavorable situation for convertibles. In the author's own opinion, however, the institutional effects are probably favorable on balance but decidedly second-order in importance.

V. CONCLUSIONS

The major findings of the study may be summarized as follows. First, a graphic model was employed to show that a convertible bond has a market value floor which is set by the higher of its straight-debt or conversion value. Typically, the bond will sell above this floor because of (1) a capital gains potential coupled with a degree of protection against losses due to a drop in stock prices, and (2) institutional constraints against the purchase of stock.

A convertible's *ex ante* yield is dependent upon expectations about the following: (1) growth rates, (2) the firm's policy on calling to force conversion, (3) the conversion ratio, (4) the price of the shares at time of issue, and (5) the coupon interest rate. If this *ex ante* yield, as computed by marginal investors, differs from their required rate of return, the bond will go to a premium or discount immediately after issue.

To gain insights into the actual usage of convertible debentures, a questionnaire was mailed to each of the 42 listed firms that had a public offering from 1961 through 1963. While it would be redundant to present

---

[26] For example, see W. S. Skelly, Convertible Bonds: *A Study of Their Suitability for Commercial Bank Bond Portfolios* (New York: Salomon Bros. & Hutzler, 1959), passim.

a detailed description of the sample statistics, it is interesting to note (1) that 73 percent of the firms indicated that they were mainly inter-' ested in raising equity capital when they sold convertibles, and (2) that essentially all of these (large, listed) firms seemed to have had the ability to finance with straight debt or common stock at the time they issued convertibles.

While this paper has not dealt explicitly with the question of whether or not firms *should* use convertibles, it has shown that certain institutional factors may be operating to render convertible financing an advantageous way of selling new equity. To the extent that certain investors who really want to make equity commitments are able to buy convertibles but not common stock, the demand curve for convertibles may be shifted to the right. This, in turn, would lower the cost of convertible capital vis-à-vis that of directly sold common stock. The extent of this phenomenon was not investigated, but it may well be important at times.

The Refunding Decision:
Another Special Case In
Capital Budgeting*

Oswald D. Bowlin†

I. INTRODUCTION

BUSINESS FIRMS may refund their outstanding debt for a number of reasons, e.g., to extend maturity or to eliminate onerous covenants in the indenture. The principal concern here, however, is with refunding for the purpose of reducing interest costs. Techniques used by business firms to measure the interest savings from refunding debt at lower coupon rates vary widely and give very different results. Teachers and researchers in business finance have made little progress in reducing the confusion surrounding this problem, despite the fact that the monetary benefits from refunding are considerably easier to estimate than those obtained from investments in operating assets. Hopefully, this paper will eliminate some of the confusion.

Refunding debt at a lower coupon rate is an anomaly among investments made by business firms, because of the degree of certainty concerning future monetary benefits. Usually most of the savings in financial expenses obtained through refunding with a lower coupon issue are as-

* Reprinted from *The Journal of Finance*, Vol. 21, No. 1 (March 1966), pp. 55–68, by permission of the author and the publisher.

This paper is based on a research project on which the author worked during the summer of 1964 while participating in the Workshop in Research in Business Finance at the Harvard Business School. The Workshop was financed by a grant from the Ford Foundation. The author also received financial assistance for the project from Kansas State University.

The study has benefited from suggestions by Professor Gordon Donaldson of the Harvard Business School concerning the objectives and the research methodology. Professor Eli Shapiro of the Harvard Business School has also made several valuable comments.

† Professor of Finance, Texas Technological College.

490

sured, once the new issue is sold, whereas normally prospective earnings from assets are very uncertain at the time of purchase. This peculiar characteristic of certainty of future savings can and should be taken into account in measuring the net monetary benefits to the firm from refunding. The vehicle that can be employed to accomplish this end should be the rate used to make time adjustments of relevant cash flows.

The objective of this paper is both descriptive and normative. First, the bond refunding operation will be described. Second, some empirical evidence of methods used in measuring interest savings by public utilities that refunded bonds in the 1962–63 period will be presented. Third, several approaches to measuring interest savings in bond refunding recommended in the financial literature will be presented and compared. Next, an attempt will be made to determine the best analytical technique for use in measuring interest savings. The most important question which will have to be answered concerns the rate that should be used in making time adjustment of cash flows resulting from the refunding operation. Last, the profitability of the 1962–63 refundings by public utilities will be determined by use of the analytical technique found to be correct. This part of the study will give some empirical evidence of the extent to which techniques generally used by business firms cause managements to make unprofitable refunding decisions. The practicality of generalizing about refunding policies of business firms also will be considered in this section.

II. THE REFUNDING OPERATION

The decision to refund a bond issue for the purpose of reducing interest costs is an investment decision. The refunding operation requires a cash outlay which is followed by interest savings in future years. The net cash investment equals the sum of (1) the call premium on the refunded bonds, (2) duplicate interest payments, (3) issue expenses on the refunding bonds, and (4) any discount on the refunding bonds less (*a*) any premium on the refunding bonds and (*b*) any tax saving obtained because of the refunding operation.[1] The tax savings occur because the call premium, duplicate interest, and remaining issue expense and discount on the old bonds are tax deductible immediately. An unamortized premium on the old bonds would reduce immediately the tax deductible expenses.

Normally, the tax savings will not be realized at the exact time the initial investment in the refunding operation is made. Thus, the tax

---

[1] Duplicate interest occurs when the bonds which are to be refunded and the refunding bonds are outstanding concurrently. The duplicate interest period is frequently 30 to 60 days because the corporation usually desires to have the refunding cash on hand or assured before the old bonds are called.

savings will have to be discounted back to the date of the investment. The discount rate should be the same rate used to make time adjustments of all cash flows resulting from the refunding operation. The determination of the correct discount rate is the fundamental issue with which this paper is concerned.

Future net cash benefits from the refunding operation are determined by subtracting the annual net cash outlays required on the refunding bonds from the annual net cash outlays required on the refunded bonds. The net cash outlays in both cases are the after-tax annual interest cost of the bonds less the reduction in taxes resulting from the amortization of the bond issue expenses and any bond discount. The amortization of a bond premium would increase taxes. Computation of the amount of interest charges on both bonds must be based on the total par of the refunded bonds.[2]

Usually a firm extends the maturity of the refunding bonds beyond the maturity of the refunded bonds. Thus the new issue replaces not only the refunded bonds, but also other financing that would have been required at the maturity of the refunded bonds. For example, assume that a firm refunds Bond A, maturing in 20 years, with Bond B, maturing in 25 years. Bond B is a replacement for other financing during the last 5 years of the life of Bond B. The cost of the other financing that would have been required to replace Bond A after 20 years, if it had not been refunded earlier, will affect the net savings actually realized from refunding with Bond B. The net savings might be increased or decreased, depending upon future financing costs. Since financing costs in the future are highly uncertain, interest savings, as a practicality, are estimated generally only for the period up to the maturity of the earlier-maturing bonds, normally the maturity of the refunded bonds.[3] Any error that results from this procedure would be fairly small when the maturities of both bonds are 20 years or longer in the future and the difference in maturities is only a few years, as in the above example. However, the probability of significant errors increases, the earlier the maturity of the refunded bonds and the greater the difference in the maturities.

Another problem in measuring future interest savings from refunding can arise if either the refunded or the refunding bonds, or both, are to be retired partially before maturity, e.g., through a sinking fund. The point was made above that interest charges for both bonds should

---

[2] This statement assumes that the new bond issue is of sufficient size to refund all of the old bond issue, which is normally the case. If only part of the old bond issue is refunded with the new issue, the interest savings should be based on the total par of the bonds refunded.

[3] This procedure usually is recommended (sometimes implicitly) in the literature. See Section IV.

be based on the total par of the refunded bonds. If the old bonds were to be retired partially before maturity, future interest savings from refunding will be reduced accordingly. If the rate of retirement of the refunding bonds is such that the amount outstanding at some date after refunding is reduced below the amount of the refunded bonds that would have been outstanding in the absence of refunding, additional financing will be required at that time unless the assets of the firm are to be reduced. The cost of the additional financing, theoretically, should be added to the interest charges on the refunding bonds outstanding in determining the net savings. Usually, however, business firms will find this procedure impractical because of the uncertainty of future financing costs and the relatively small difference in the planned rate of retirement of the two issues.

In summary, debt refunding is an investment on the part of the corporation. The cash outlay necessary to effect the refunding is followed by interest savings in future years. The measurement of the monetary benefits must relate the interest savings to the required investment.

III. THE MEASUREMENT OF INTEREST SAVING BY BUSINESS FIRMS

Little empirical evidence is available concerning procedures business firms actually follow in making refunding decisions. To throw some light on the subject, the author sent a questionnaire to the 33 public utilities that refunded publicly-held bonds with new public bond issues carrying lower coupons during the period 1962–63. A total of 40 bond issues were refunded by these firms during the period.

Thirty firms responded to the questionnaire. These firms included 22 companies engaged primarily in the production and distribution of electricity; 5 companies engaged primarily in the purchase and distribution of natural gas; 1 large holding company whose subsidiaries are engaged primarily in the production, purchase and distribution of natural gas; and 2 telephone companies.[4] Size of the firms ranged from very large companies servicing wide, heavily populated areas to small companies servicing small, sparsely populated areas. Gross revenues ranged from less than $12,000,000 to over $1,000,000,000.

Twenty of the responding firms indicated that the only purpose of their refunding was to reduce interest charges. The ten other respondents listed the reduction of interest charges as the most important reason for refunding. Eight of the ten indicated that the second most important reason for refunding was to lengthen the maturity of outstanding debt.

---

[4] The nonresponding firms included two companies engaged primarily in the generation and distribution of electricity and one pipe line company. Gross revenues of these firms ranged from approximately $20,000,000 to a little over $120,000,000.

The two other reasons listed as being second in importance were "to remove high interest rate issue from balance sheet," and to refund at a time when additional capital was needed. Only one firm listed as many as three reasons for refunding. The third reason indicated by this firm was to improve the appearance of the company's debt structure.

The firms were asked to state as specifically as possible how the interest savings which they had hoped to obtain by refunding were measured. An answer which could be used here required either a good record of a study of the refunding savings or a degree of technical knowledge on the part of the individual who completed the questionnaire.[5] In addition, a sufficient answer required considerable time and effort. Nineteen responses were sufficiently clear and complete to show conclusively that the firms used a wide variety of methods of measuring interest savings in bond refunding. Five firms used more than one method and one firm used several. A tabular presentation of the responses is impractical, but a general summary will indicate the lack of certainty of the "best" method.

Seven firms used some form of payback-period calculation either exclusively or in conjunction with other procedures. Eight firms indicated the use of some form of time-adjusted calculations, but usually the procedures were not equivalent. Other methods used preclude specific classification except that they involved measuring interest savings with indifference to the time of their realization.

The eight firms that used time-adjusted approaches were in general disagreement as to the rate to use in making the time adjustments. One firm used a rate which was "an indication of what over-all money is worth" to the firm. Another firm used the return on equity. A total of three firms used the yield on the refunding bond. A sixth firm used all three of these rates, but prefaced its specific explanation with the following statement:

Anticipated interest savings were measured in several ways; however, the desirability of refunding was based primarily on establishing a "break-even point." This break-even point was calculated by more than one method, as well. . . . Consequently, precise savings were not projected. Rather, anticipated effective cost of money below the range of break-even points indicated that real savings would be achieved. These break-even points ranged from 4.845% to 5.29%, depending upon the method used in their calculation.

The rates used by the two other firms that employed time-adjusted techniques were not defined specifically.

---

[5] The questionnaire was sent to the individual believed to be the chief financial officer of each firm. In at least two cases the responsibility for its completion was delegated to the assistant treasurer. However, in several cases the basis for the answer to this question was a study conducted by an investment bank or a management consulting firm.

Break-even analysis was used frequently in evaluating refunding opportunities. Ordinarily, the net yield on the refunding bonds would have to be well below the "break-even yield" before the firm would seriously consider the possibility of refunding. There was no consistency, however, among the firms that used this type of analysis in the computation of the break-even yield.

In summary, the empirical evidence indicates that neither financial managers of business firms, investment bankers, nor management consultants are certain of the procedure that should be used to measure interest savings in bond refunding. Some form of the payback period calculation is a popular method, but can be adequately defended only in cases in which the firm is more interested in liquidity or avoidance of risk than profitability. Time-adjusted techniques are used by some firms, but in no consistent manner. Other approaches used by firms have little theoretical justification. Thus the uncertainty in this area of finance can and does lead to widely differing results.

IV. APPROACHES TO THE MEASUREMENT OF INTEREST SAVINGS RECOMMENDED IN THE LITERATURE

Academic writers have not been in agreement concerning the procedure that should be used in measuring interest savings in bond refunding. Four approaches recommended in the literature will be presented here in order to depict the major points of disagreement. The disagreement in recommended procedures has not resulted in active debate in the literature. Indeed, not one of the authors has stated why his approach is better than the others.

A few writers have recommended the use of the cost of capital in measuring interest savings.[6] Interest savings are determined for the period up to the maturity of the earlier-maturing bond. Either the net present value or the rate of return technique is employed.

Net present value is determined in the usual manner, by subtracting the net cash investment in the refunding operation from the present value of the interest savings. Future interest savings are discounted at the firm's cost of capital. If the net present value is positive, the refunding operation would be profitable for the firm. Although the literature is

---

[6] See, for example, Robert W. Johnson, *Financial Management* (2d ed.; Boston: Allyn and Bacon, Inc., 1962), pp. 447–51; Pearson Hunt, Charles M. Williams, and Gordon Donaldson, *Basic Business Finance: Text and Cases* (Rev. ed.; Homewood, Ill.: Richard D. Irwin, Inc., 1961) pp. 560–64; Earl A. Spiller, Jr., "Time-Adjusted Break-even Rate for Refunding," *Financial Executive*, July 1963, pp. 32–35. Johnson does not distinguish between the investment opportunity rate and the average cost of future financing when discussing refunding. Hunt, Williams and Donaldson and Spiller use the investment opportunity rate.

not always clear concerning the results of refunding when net present value is negative, the inference is that refunding would not be profitable.

If the rate of return technique is used, the present value of future interest savings and the refunding investment are equated. The discount rate required to equate the two is the rate of return. The rate of return is compared to the firm's cost of capital to determine whether or not refunding would be beneficial.

The use of the cost of capital in the measurement of interest savings in refunding will be referred to hereafter as the cost of capital approach.

Two other approaches are presented by John F. Childs in his book entitled *Long-Term Financing.*[7] Presumably, the first approach is preferred since it is presented in the text, whereas the second approach appears in a footnote.

Childs' example is a refunding decision facing a company with an issue of $10,000,000 principal amount of bonds outstanding. The bonds carry a coupon of 5 percent, mature in 24 years, and are callable on 30 day's notice at 104¾. Interest rates have declined, and the company finds that the bonds can be refunded with a new 25-year bond issue which can be sold at about 100 percent if the coupon rate is set at 4 percent. After underwriters' compensation and expenses of approximately 1.50 percent, the company will net 98.50 percent from the sale of the new issue. Applying this information to Bond Value Tables, the cost of new money to the firm is found to be 4.10 percent.

His first approach is explained as follows:

Now then, we have to decide what to compare the 4.10% cost of our new money with in order to determine the savings in terms of yield. In effect, what we are doing is selling new bonds and reinvesting the proceeds in our old bonds at their call price. Thus, we are interested in the rate to call the outstanding bonds. They have a 5% interest coupon, a 24-year remaining maturity and a call price of 104¾ (call premium 4¾%). The yield at the call price is 4.67%, as shown by referring to Bond Value Tables. On the basis of yield, we would realize a saving of 0.57%, which is a result of subtracting the cost rate for the new bonds of 4.10% from the cost to call the outstanding bonds of 4.67%. This is a gross saving and must be adjusted for the tax effect to get the net savings. Assuming a 50% tax rate, there would be a net saving of substantially one-half.[8]

The second approach suggested by Childs includes the call premium on the refunded bonds in the computation of the cost of the new money.

---

[7] John F. Childs, *Long-Term Financing* (Englewood Cliffs, N.J.: Prentice-Hall, Inc., 1961), pp. 239–41.

[8] Ibid., pp. 239–240.

The procedure is presented as follows:

1.	New bonds—4% coupon, maturity 25 yrs., to be sold	100.00%
2.	Less compensation and expenses	1.50
3.	Net proceeds	98.50%
4.	Less premium to call old bonds	4.75
5.	Net to company after calling old bonds	93.75%
6.	Cost of old bonds: 5% coupon—price 100%	5.00%
7.	Cost of new money: 4% coupon, maturity 25 yrs. Price 93.75 (line 5 above)	4.41
8.	Saving before taxes	0.59

This method produces a slightly greater savings because the call premium is written off at the lower interest rate over a longer period of time.[9]

Both methods suggested by Childs would base a refunding decision on the net interest savings per annum, expressed as a difference in yield, for the period up to the earlier maturity of the two bonds.[10] The net cash investment in refunding, other than the call premium under the first approach, is written off on an annuity basis over the longer period of 25 years.[11] In both approaches, the write-off of the net cash investment reduces future interest savings.

The only difference in Childs' two approaches is the way in which the call premium is handled. In both approaches the write-off of the premium affects the computation of a cost, the "yield at the call price" in the first approach and the "cost of new money" in the second approach.

The significant difference in the cost of capital approach and Childs' two approaches is the rate used to adjust cash flows over time.[12] The cost of capital approach utilizes the firm's cost of capital in making time adjustments. In the example used by Childs, net refunding investment included only underwriters' compensation and expenses pertinent to the refunding bonds and the call premium on the refunded bonds. The compensation and expenses were written off on an annuity basis at the "cost of new money." The call premium was written off on an annuity basis in the first approach at the "yield at the call price," and in the second approach at the "cost of new money." In both methods used by Childs, the call premium affected the computed rate at which it was written

---

[9] Ibid., p. 240.

[10] Note that interest is converted semiannually on both bonds.

[11] In the Childs example, the net cash investment includes only the call premium on the refunded bonds and compensation and expenses on the refunding bonds. The other components of the refunding investment are discussed in Childs' book on pages 240–41. However, the rate at which some of these components should be written off is not clear.

[12] The difference in the format used by Childs and the net present value and rate of return formats used above to explain the cost of capital approach is relatively unimportant. The use of different formats will be discussed in the following section.

off. In the cost of capital approach, the cost of capital is not affected by the call premium on the refunded bonds.

The net difference in the result obtained from using either of Childs' two approaches, or the cost of capital approach, depends upon the difference in the "yield at the call price," the "cost of new money," and the firm's cost of capital. For most firms, the difference in results obtained will be substantial because of the difference in the net interest cost of new debt financing and the firm's cost of capital. This point will be considered further in the following section.

Another approach has been suggested by J. Fred Weston.[13] The essence of his approach is to reduce the future net cash benefits per year from refunding by (1) the interest cost on the additional bonds that would have to be sold to finance the net cash investment plus (2) the amount of money set aside each year which would accumulate to the par of the additional bonds.[14] The formats of the Weston and Childs approaches are similar except that Weston expresses interest savings in terms of dollars per annum whereas Childs expresses them in terms of differences in yield.

Weston's own example will be presented in order to examine his recommendations in the context in which they were made. Later, his approach will be compared with the Childs approaches.

The problem is a company which refunds a $60,000,000 6½ percent bond issue, callable at 106, with a new bond issue carrying a coupon of 5 percent and sold to net 96. The maturity date of neither bond is explicit in the example, but the savings are determined for a 20-year period. A total par value of $66,250,000 would have to be sold at 96 to net the firm the required $63,600,000 ($60,000,000 × 106) to refund the old bonds. The savings per annum are determined as follows:

Interest on 6.5% bonds	$3,900,000
Interest on 5% bonds	3,312,500
Savings per annum	$ 587,500

He points out, however, that the savings per annum should be reduced because an additional $6,250,000 ($66,250,000—$60,000,000) will have to be paid at the end of the 20-year period. The reduction in savings per annum according to his example is the amount of money which set aside each year to increase at the compound rate of 5 percent per annum will accumulate to $6,250,000 in 20 years. This amount is found

[13] J. Fred Weston, *Managerial Finance* (New York: Holt, Rinehart & Winston, Inc., 1962), pp. 147–48.

[14] Reducing the future net cash benefits per year by (1) the interest cost on the additional bonds that would have to be sold plus (2) the amount of money set aside each year which would accumulate to the par of the additional bonds is equivalent to writing off the net investment on an annuity basis against future benefits.

to be approximately $189,000. Subtracting $189,000 from the annual savings of $587,500 gives a net savings per annum of $398,500.

The use of a 5 percent interest rate in determining the amount which would accumulate to $6,250,000 is a minor error. Perhaps the intent was to use the net yield on the bonds as the interest rate. Since the bonds carried a coupon rate of 5 percent and were sold to net 96, the net yield was approximately 5.32 percent. Using 5.32 percent in place of 5 percent to determine the amount of money which must be set aside each year to accumulate to $6,250,000 results in a difference in amount of about $6,250.

Incorporating the minor correction, the Weston method assumes that the net yield on the additional bonds sold to finance the net cash investment in the refunding operation is the total cost of the funds.

The significant difference in the Weston and Childs approaches is the way in which the call premium on a refunded bond affects the results. The call premium was written off against future cash benefits in Childs' first approach at the "yield at the call price," and in his second approach at the "cost of new money." In both methods the call premium affected the computation of the rate at which it was written off. In the Weston approach the call premium was written off at the net interest cost of the refunding bonds, but the write-off did not affect the computation of the net interest cost.

The difference in the Weston and Childs approaches usually will not affect the results significantly. For example, writing off the call premium in the refunding problem used as an example by Childs at the 4.10 percent interest cost of the new bonds results in savings before taxes of approximately 0.59 percent, which was the savings obtained by Childs in his second approach.

In summary, academic writers have not been in agreement concerning the measurement of interest savings in bond refunding.[15] The significant

---

[15] The works of three other authors should be mentioned. See Arleigh P. Hess, Jr. and Willis J. Winn, *The Value of the Call Privilege* (The University of Pennsylvania Press, 1962), particularly Chapter II and Appendix A. Appendix A is entitled "A Technical Note on the Value of the Call Privilege" and was written by Jean A. Crockett. See also Willis J. Winn and Arliegh P. Hess, Jr., "The Value of the Call Privilege," *Journal of Finance*, May 1959, pp. 182–95.

Hess and Winn use the net present value technique in measuring interest saving in bond refunding. However, the two authors do not define the discount rate that should be used in determining the present value of future interest savings. In Appendix A of the book, Jean Crockett uses the current long-term interest rate, even when measuring interest savings from future refunding. She states on page 124 "We assume that the current long-term interest rate . . . is the proper rate for discounting . . . ; but, if desired, some other rate could easily be substituted in the expressions obtained."

The present author feels that the use of the current long-term interest rate in determining the present value of interest savings from future refunding is questionable. However, this problem is beyond the scope of this paper.

difference in the approaches that have been presented is the rate used to make time adjustments of cash flows. In the following section, an attempt will be made to determine the rate that should be used.

V. WHICH PROCEDURE IS BEST IN MEASURING INTEREST SAVING FROM BOND REFUNDING?

The point was made earlier that bond refunding involves an investment of funds which is followed in future time periods by savings in interest charges. If the present value of the future interest savings exceeds the present value of the investment, the refunding operation will be a profitable undertaking for the firm because a net savings has been obtained. The discount rate to apply to future interest savings should be the total cost (including both explicit and implicit costs) of the funds necessary to make the investment.

According to the net present value technique in capital budgeting theory, the cash benefits from an investment should be discounted at the firm's average cost of capital. The crucial fact here, however, is that the cash benefits from a refunding operation are not equivalent to those of the usual investment by a business firm. An investment in an operating asset involves considerable risk because the future cash benefits from its use are uncertain. Refunding a bond issue with another bond issue is entirely different, because the future cash benefits up to the earlier maturity of the two bonds are the result of contractual interest charges on the refunding bonds being less than those on the refunded bonds. Thus, once the refunding bonds are sold, the interest savings up to the earlier maturity are assured to the company.[16]

In the development of the argument that follows, interest savings will be measured up to the earlier maturity of the refunded and refunding bonds. The problem created by differences in the maturities of the two bonds will be considered later.

If a firm is able to make an investment from which earnings are certain, the financing of the investment involves no financial risk to the firm so long as the earnings are sufficient to meet all financial expenses. For example, the investment can be financed by a fixed debt without risk to the firm.[17] Since no risk is incurred, no implicit cost is associated

---

[16] The refunding decision involves a risk that interest rates will rise between the date of the decision and the date the refunding bonds are sold (or if the issue is underwritten, the date the contract with the underwriters is consummated). The management of the firm may require that expected interest savings be sufficient to compensate for this risk before a decision to refund is made. The amount of expected interest savings required to compensate for the risk is a judgment problem for management.

[17] If the assumption of certainty of return on investment is extended to the lender, the net interest cost of the funds to the borrowing firm would be the pure rate of interest. However certainty of earnings on the investment by the borrowing firm does not eliminate all of the risk to the lender. The earnings could be dissipated by the borrowing firm before the lender is paid.

with the debt financing; the only cost of the funds necessary to make the investment would be the net interest cost of the debt financing. The investment would be profitable to the firm if the future cash earnings discounted back to the present at the net interest cost of the debt are greater than the present value of the investment. Any part of the investment not made immediately should be discounted back to the present at the net interest cost of the debt.

Refunding a bond at a net interest savings results in a net reduction in cash outlays rather than an increase in cash inflows. Nevertheless, the refunding will cause the firm's total profits to increase, or its total losses to decrease.

Since the savings are certain, the net cash investment required in the refunding can be financed by debt without necessitating an increase in equity capital to optimize the firm's capital structure. Thus, the net present value of the refunding operation should be determined by discounting the future net cash benefits at the after-tax cost of the source of funds used to finance the refunding investment, presumably the net yield on the refunding bonds. The net cash investment would be subtracted from the present value of the future cash benefits to determine the net present value in the usual manner. The decision to refund when the net present value is positive would be profitable for the firm. Since the interest savings are assured if the new bonds can be sold at the expected rate, the refunding operation will reduce the over-all risk of the firm even though the debt to equity ratio increases. On the other hand, a negative net present value would be unprofitable.

The above procedure in measuring net interest savings will be referred to hereafter as the net yield approach. Of the four approaches discussed in the previous section, only the Weston approach, with the minor correction noted earlier, is entirely correct.

Very different results can be obtained by the use of the net yield and cost of capital approaches. As an example, assume that after a decline in interest rates a corporation finds it can refund its $20,000,000 par 4½ percent bonds, due in 20 years, with 4 percent bonds of the same type, quality, and maturity date. Interest on both bonds is paid semiannually. Assume further that all bonds are sold at par and that the annual amortization of issue expenses amounts to $4,000 for each issue. Using a corporate income tax rate of 50 percent, the refunding operation would result in semiannual after-tax savings of $25,000 for 20 years.

If the corporation's cost of capital is 8 percent, the cost of capital approach would result in a present value of the savings stream of 19.7928·$25,000 = $494,820. Discounting the future savings at 2 percent, the approximate after-tax cost of debt,[18] results in a present value of 32.8347·$25,000 = $820,868. If the net cash investment required to re-

---

[18] The after-tax cost of the bonds is slightly higher than 2 percent because of the issue expenses.

fund is $600,000, for example, use of the cost of capital as the discount rate would lead to the rejection of the operation because a negative net present value results.

On the other hand, the bonds would be refunded if the after-tax cost of debt is the discount rate used because the net present value is $220,868. The $220,868 net present value is a net gain to the common stockholders. No additional equity capital will have to be raised to counterbalance the additional bonds; the refunding operation has reduced the financial risk of the firm.

The discussion above has been concerned primarily with the concept rather than the format of measuring the profitability of refunding. The principle of discounting future interest saving at the cost of debt can be employed in several ways. For example, either the rate of return or the Weston technique can be employed.

The use of the Childs format requires the computation of a synthetic yield on the refunding bonds. The process would be to write off the net cash investment on an annuity basis to future interest periods. The rate used to write off the investment should be the net interest cost of the refunding bonds computed in the conventional manner.[19] The write-off of the investment will serve to increase future interest costs. Then, the synthetic yield on the refunding bond is computed by discounting the future interest costs, which include the write-off of the refunding investment, back to equal the par of the refunded bonds. The yield is synthetic because it is affected by the components of the refunding investment which do not affect the conventional computation of the yield cost on bonds.[20] These components include (1) the call premium on the refunded bonds, (2) duplicate interest, and (3) any tax savings obtained because of the refunding operation.[21] If the synthetic yield on the new bonds is less than the coupon rate on the old bonds, refunding would result in a net monetary benefit to the firm.

The net yield approach recommended here can be adapted easily to a break-even basis. For example, a firm could compute the yield on a new bond at which it would break even from refunding its debt. At lower yields, refunding would be profitable.

---

[19] Recall that Childs writes off the call premium on the refunded bonds at two different rates, neither of which is the net interest cost of the refunding bonds computed in the conventional manner.

[20] The significance of these components for a refunding decision is that they affect the amount of funds that must be obtained to refund the old issue. However, they should not affect the computation of the cost of the new funds, although they do affect the computation of the synthetic yield as indicated above.

[21] Components of the refunding investment that affect the conventional computation of yield include the issue expenses and any discount or premium on the refunding bonds. The refunding investment was discussed in Section II of the present paper.

Another problem with which the management of a firm is confronted is whether to refund now or at some later time. If the net present value from refunding later is greater than the net present value from refunding now, the firm should delay. The difficulty in determining the net present value from a delayed refunding is in estimating future interest rates. Hess, Winn and Crockett have proposed a solution to this problem by the use of probability analysis.[22]

This procedure might be adapted also to refunding cases in which the maturities of the refunded and refunding bonds differ. Thus a probability estimate of the savings in financial costs between the maturities of the two bonds could be added to (or subtracted from, if the estimated savings are negative) the savings up to the earlier maturity. The development of this procedure, however, is beyond the scope of the present paper.

VI. RETURNS FROM REFUNDING BY PUBLIC UTILITIES IN 1962–63

The conclusion has been reached that debt refunding will be profitable to a firm when the rate of return obtained is greater than the cost of the particular funds required to finance the net cash investment. Normally, the cost of the funds would be the net yield on the refunding bonds. Thus the profitability of the refundings by the public utility firms discussed earlier can be seen by comparing the net yield on the refunding bonds with the rates of return obtained.

The yield on every refunding bond included in the study fell somewhere between 4 and 5 percent. The results of computations by the present author of the rate of return earned by the public utilities in their 1962–63 refundings are shown in Table 1.

The procedure followed in the computations of the rates shown in Table 1 was to discount net interest savings for each year to the maturity date of the refunded bonds, at a rate which would equate their present value with the net cash investment. The only data necessary for the computations which could not be obtained from Moody's *Public Utility Manual* were issue expenses on both the old and new bonds. These were estimated from the Securities and Exchange Commission's *Cost of Flotation of Corporate Securities, 1951–55*.[23]

Probably the most obvious observation that can be made from a study of the data in the table is the wide range of rates of return obtained

---

[22] Arleigh P. Hess, Jr. and Willis J. Winn, *The Value of the Call Privilege,* Chapter II and Appendix A.

[23] Securities and Exchange Commission, *Cost of Flotation of Corporate Securities, 1951–55,* (Washington 25, D.C., June 1957), Table 12, p. 51.

TABLE 1
Rates of return earned on 40 bond refundings by public
utilities in 1962 and 1963 (percent)

3.6*	9.1	11.5*	14.7*
5.5	9.5	11.9*	14.8
5.7	9.6*	12.3	15.3*
6.5	9.7	12.3	16.1
6.8	9.9	12.8*	16.1
7.1*	10.1	12.8	17.2
7.3	10.4*	13.0	19.7
8.0	10.4	13.1	23.8
8.2	11.2	13.8	26.7*
8.7	11.3	14.6*	43.4

Note: The forty bonds were refunded by thirty-four refunding bonds.
One new bond was used to refund two old bonds in four cases and three old
bonds in one case.
    One utility refunded bonds at two different times.
    * Denotes that at least one other reason in addition to interest savings
was indicated by the respondent to the questionnaire as a factor causing
the decision to refund. In all cases, interest savings were indicated as the
primary reason for refunding. Ten responding firms indicated more than
one reason for refunding; the 9.6 percent and the 14.6 percent rates of return were earned from refunding two old bond issues with one new bond issue.

by the refundings. Although a little more than 50 percent of the rates
fell between 10 and 20 percent, there is no salient concentration.

Since the rates of return shown in the table are on an after-tax basis,
and the yields before taxes on all of the refunding bonds fell somewhere
between 4 and 5 percent, none of the refunding operations appear unprofitable. The reader should note that the rate of return computations
probably involved some errors because issue expenses for all bond issues
were estimated from the Securities and Exchange Commission's *Cost of
Flotation of Corporate Securities, 1951–55.* While these probable errors
would have had a relatively small effect on the results, too much faith
should not be put in the *exact* figures obtained.

The rates of return obtained by the refundings were plotted graphically against a long list of quantitative variables depicting financial characteristics of the firms, e.g., sales, assets, rates of profits, rates of growth
and debt to equity ratios. No correlations whatsoever were found. Neither
were the rates of return related to the particular type of utility. Furthermore, there was no consistent relationship between the rates of return
and the extension of maturity dates by refunding[24] or the procurement
of additional capital.[25] Thus, no generalization can be made about the

---

[24] All of the maturity extensions except one fell within the range of approximately
two to six years. The one exception was an extension of a little over 17 years.

[25] A total of 33 refunding bonds were sold to refund the 40 refunded bonds.
In 21 of these 34 refunding operations, the firm obtained more capital than was
required to call in the old bonds. In 18 cases, the addition was ten percent or
more of the amount of the old bonds outstanding. In several cases, very large

effect of any factors on the rate of return required to entice the firms to refund.

There are several reasons why rates of return will vary considerably in debt refunding. First, opportunities for interest savings vary among firms. For example, firms with high-yield bonds outstanding will often be able to refund at great savings if interest rates decline, particularly if the financial position of the firm has improved. Second, since firms use methods of measuring interest savings which give different results, the same refunding opportunities will be evaluated differently. Thus, the enticement to refund will vary. Third, management expectations of future interest rates will affect refunding decisions. If a substantial decline in interest rates is expected, refunding will probably be deferred. Management expectations of interest rates will vary among firms and for the same firm at different times. Fourth, refunding often has advantages other than interest savings. Ten firms who answered the questionnaire indicated reasons for refunding in addition to interest savings, although the latter was always given as the primary reason. The wide range of rates which have an asterisk beside them in Table 1 indicates that no relationship existed between the rates of return obtained and the fact that factors in addition to interest savings led to the refunding decision. Nor was any consistent relationship found between any particular secondary reason for refunding and the rates of return obtained. Fifth, firms differ in respect to policies and aggressiveness. Although this factor is difficult if not impossible to measure, doubtless it was of great importance in the case of the refundings that have been examined in this study.

VII. SUMMARY AND CONCLUSIONS

This study has found that the investment required to refund debt should be analyzed differently from ordinary investments in operating assets. Thus debt refunding should join the leasing of assets as a special case in capital budgeting.

Refunding will be profitable for a business firm whenever the rate of return earned on the net cash investment in the operation is greater than the cost of debt capital to the firm. If the net present value method is used as the analytical tool, future interest savings from refunding should be discounted at the cost of debt, normally the net yield on the refunding bond. Use of this rate is better than the use of the cost of capital because debt financing of the refunding investment does not require future additions to equity capital.

Few firms use the method recommended here in measuring interest

---

amounts of additional capital were obtained. Recall, however, that only one firm that answered the questionnaire discussed earlier indicated that the need for additional capital had any affect on the decision to refund.

savings. The great variety of methods in use depicts the confusion and uncertainty concerning the correct procedure.

Some of the procedures used by public utilities that refunded in 1962–63 would have resulted in losses on a time-adjusted basis if the firms had not followed the practice of deferring refunding until a new bond could be sold to yield well below the computed break-even yield. Other firms employed methods of measuring interest savings which could result in passing up profitable refunding opportunities. For these reasons, it is difficult to generalize about the net effect of the widespread use of theoretically incorrect procedures in measuring interest savings. The effect probably has not been great, because most firms that refund primarily to take advantage of lower interest rates do not base their decisions on precise estimates of profits, although these are generally made. The reasonable assurance of considerable profits seems to be much more important.

part VI

Raising long-term funds

SOUTHERN CALIFORNIA
EDISON COMPANY

DURING THE SUMMER OF 1969, the financial vice president of the Southern California Edison Company (SCE) was faced with several financing problems. Money rates for SCE, an Aa rated electric utility, were rising well above their historically normal levels. (See Exhibit 1.) Because of the increase in money rates, both the company's imbedded cost of debt[1] and its imbedded cost of preferred stock[2] were rising at a rapid rate (Exhibit 2). As a result, the SCE cost of capital was believed to have risen above the fixed 7.35 percent return on rate base[3] allowed by the California Public Utility Commission.

Money rates were expected to continue to rise, or at least to remain at the recently attained higher levels, as long as the Federal Reserve Board continued to constrain the growth of the money stock to curb inflation and as long as U.S. companies continued to require large amounts of capital. Both the Federal Reserve's policy of constraint and the companies' need for large amounts for capital were expected to continue for several more months.

Electric utilities, whose franchises demanded they serve all customers upon instantaneous demand, were unable to delay plant expansion because of the five- to seven-year delay between design and placing a generating plant in service. SCE, whose kilowatt-hour sales were expected to grow at a rapid rate during the next decade, would need substantial funds

---

[1] The imbedded cost of debt is the weighted average cost of all outstanding debt issues at the annualized interest and amortization cost rates.

[2] The imbedded cost of preferred stock is the weighted average cost of all outstanding preferred stock at the annualized dividend rates.

[3] Rate base is the electric operating plant at original cost less depreciation for an electric utility in California. The numerator is the electric operating revenues less all the electric operating expenses.

for several years (Exhibit 3). Therefore, not only was the high cost of debt and preferred stock a concern to SCE but the availability of sufficient funds through debt and equity financing was a worry.

The currently high money rates were adversely affecting electric utilities. Times interest coverage, which was used by financial analysts, rating services, and states legal requirements for issuing debt, was declining (Exhibit 4). The rate of returns used by many investors, analysts, and utility commissions were also declining (Exhibit 5). In addition, earnings per share for SCE remained below the 1967 high (Exhibit 6), despite a rate increase in 1969.

The SCE financial vice president wanted: (1) to keep the Aa bond rating, and (2) to assure that the company would be able to meet state legal investment laws, the company's Articles of Incorporation, and indenture coverage requirements. He wondered: (1) if sufficient funds would be available through the traditional debt and equity channels to meet future capital requirements, (2) if the current high money rates would sustain themselves over the long run or if they would diminish somewhat, (3) if the pending rate case would increase the allowed return on rate base to the cost of capital, and (4) if other sources of capital were available for financing?

These financial conditions during the summer of 1969 caused SCE to investigate the potential to lease an entire electric generating station instead of financing the plant through normal debt and equity financing. A large generating plant, which was to be built in or about 1973, was selected as the test site. The plant was expected to cost about $100 million. A consultant was hired to determine the feasibility of leasing and to locate the leasor if the lease proposal appeared feasible.

ELECTRIC UTILITY BACKGROUND

The revenue needs of an electric utility in California are determined by a commission. These revenue requirements include operating costs, book depreciation, income taxes, and return on rate base. Operating costs include not only operating and maintenance costs but insurance costs, property, payroll and other taxes, rentals or lease costs, and fuel and purchased power expenses. Book depreciation is usually straight-line depreciation at original cost less salvage (if any). Income taxes usually include both state and federal income taxes. The return on rate base as explained above is the "reasonable" return allowed by the commission after income tax but before interest costs. This "reasonable" return on undepreciated plant is to cover the costs of keeping enough plant available to serve the needs of the customers. Therefore, return must be comparable to the cost of capital in the long run. The cost of capital is usually considered to consist of debt and equity.

Debt and preferred stock costs in California are considered to be the weighted average, or imbedded costs of all outstanding issues. Both are considered by the California Public Utility Commission at their before tax cost. The reason for this is that the return on rate base allowed is after income taxes. Since debt and equity both comprise parts of this return, the income taxes do not affect them. In addition, income tax is figured to be a part of the revenue requirements as a separate cost from return:

$$RR = OC + BD + DC + EC + T \tag{1}$$

RR = Revenue requirements
OC = Operating costs
BD = Book depreciation
DC = Debt cost
EC = Equity cost
T = Income taxes

The removal of interest from the income tax consideration can be done algebraically. Income tax is computed as follows:

$$T = t(RR - (OC + TD + DC)) \tag{2}$$

T = Income tax
t = Income tax rate
RR = Revenue requirements
OC = Operating cost
TD = Tax depreciation
DC = Debt cost

If the right-hand side of formula (1) is substituted for RR in formula (2) the following takes place:

$$T = t(OC + BD + DC + EC + T - OC - TD - DC)$$
$$T = t(BD - TD + EC - T)$$
$$T = t(BD - TD + EC) + Tt \tag{3}$$

$$T = \frac{t}{1 - t} (BD - TD + EC)$$

If BD and TD are the same, the income tax in formula (3) can be found by multiplying the $\frac{t}{1 - t} (EC)$. Therefore, debt cost for a utility, which is expected to earn an exact return or have its RR changed, is not affected by income tax.

Capitalization for electric utilities consists of long-term debt, preferred and preference stock, and common equity. Some utilities include notes payable because they use these notes as a means of financing in the long term by always having a large amount outstanding. SCE does not use notes payable to finance the plant upon which its return is derived. Therefore, SCE does not include notes payable as part of its capital structure.

Most utility leases up through 1969 were for equipment. Commissions, analysts, and the Internal Revenue Service considered them operating leases. Therefore, they were not capitalized and the full lease payments were considered part of operating costs. However, some analysts included one third of these lease payments as fixed charges in their coverage calculations. Some state legal laws and the SCE indenture also considered one third of the lease payments as fixed charges. These lease "fixed charges" amounted to about $2.4 million for SCE in 1969.

COMPANY BACKGROUND

The Southern California Edison Company, which was incorporated in 1909, is an established electric utility. The company serves much of southern and central California. It has maintained stabile earnings and paid regular dividends since incorporated. During the past few years its capital structure has remained about 53 percent debt, 10 percent preferred and preference stock, and 37 percent common equity (Exhibit 7). Since this structure appears about right for the company's risk class, the company's management planned to maintain the capital structure at about the 53 percent debt level (Exhibit 5).

The imbedded costs of debt and preferred stock are shown in Exhibit 2. Debt cost, which had risen, was expected to reach about 5.13 percent in 1970. The imbedded cost of preferred stock was expected to reach 6.20 percent in 1970. In addition, equity costs which had been placed at 11.8 percent by the California Public Utility Commission in 1969 were expected to be increased to 12 percent in 1970 or 1971. Other utilities in the comparable risk class were earning above 12 percent. Therefore, to compete for equity funds, SCE needed to earn a comparable amount.

CONSULTANT'S LEASE ANALYSIS

In the fall of 1969, the consultant reported to SCE that he felt leasing would provide several advantages. The financing burden would be eased, because leasing would provide a new source of capital. The lease expense would be included in operating costs and be fully expensed. Since the cost of capital was believed to be 9.5 percent by the consultant while the allowed return on rate base was 7.35 percent, direct investment and inclusion of plant in rate base would be disadvantageous. The cost of the lease financing would be cheaper than financing through debt and equity. The cost of the plant would not be included on the balance sheet. While the entire amount of the lease could be deducted as operating expenses for rate-making purposes, the lease payments would not be included in interest coverage calculations by more than one third of their amount under the worst conditions. Therefore, the consultant recommended that the company lease the power plant.

The package the consultant proposed included several assumptions. The entire lease payment would be allowed by the utility commission as an expense. Analysts, rating services, and the Internal Revenue Service would not capitalize the lease. From one third to zero of the lease payments would be computed in interest coverage calculations. The lease would be financed by a limited partnership composed of individuals in high-income by a limited partnership composed of individuals in high-income tax brackets, who would be able to take advantage of accelerated depreciation to make the venture profitable to them. The consultant and a large investment banker would handle the transaction.

The partnership would finance the $100 million through 10 percent equity and 90 percent debt. It was believed that the annual debt cost for the partnership would be about 8.5 percent and that a 7 percent compensation on the $100 million at the end of the lease period would be satisfactory for the equity investment. The lease period was expected to be 30 years, with lease payments being semiannual. The consultant also believed that the debt could be amortized during the last 20 years. While he recognized that the payments would actually be $38,250 during the first 10 years and $47,175 during the last 20 years per million dollars, he computed the lease payments at $38,200 during the first 10 years and at $47,100 during the last 20 years. Therefore, he calculated the expected annual rate of the lease per million dollars as follows:

		Present value at 3¾ percent		Present value at 4 percent	
Periods	Payments	Factor	Total	Factor	Total
1–20..........	$ 38,200	13.8962	$ 530,834	13.5903	$519,149
21–60..........	47,100	9.8417	463,544	9.0332	425,446
60..........	170,000	0.1098	18,666	0.0951	16,167
			$1,013,044		$960,762
			960,762		
			$ 52,282		

Effective semiannual rate $= \dfrac{\$13,044}{\$52,282} (4.00 - 3.75) + 3.75$ percent

$\qquad\qquad\qquad = (.2495)(.25) + 3.75$ percent

$\qquad\qquad\qquad = 3.812$ percent

Effective annual rate $\quad = 2(3.812 \text{ percent}) = 7.62$ percent

Since the consultant believed that the cost of debt to SCE would be 8.1 percent, he believed that company's cost of capital would be

SCE cost of capital (percent)		
Capital structure	Cost	Factor cost
Debt............ 60%	8.1%	4.86%
Equity.......... 40%	11.5%	4.60%
	Cost of Capital = 9.46% = 9.5%	

9.5 percent. As a result, he calculated the ownership payments on a 9.5 percent basis, with the differential of 1 percent from the partnership lease of 8.5 percent increasing the payments by $6,800 per million dollars invested:

Periods	Payments	Present value of 4.5 percent		Present value of 4¾ percent	
		Factor	Total	Factor	Total
1–20..........	$ 45,000	13.0079	$ 585,356	12.7307	$572,882
21–60.........	53,900	7.6301	411,262	7.0216	378,464
60.........	170,000	0.0713	12,121	0.0618	10,506
			$1,008,739		$961,852
			961,852		
			$ 46,887		

$$\text{Effective semiannual rate} = \frac{\$\,8,739}{\$46,887} (4.75 - 4.5) + 4.5 \text{ percent}$$

$$= (.1864)(.25) + 4.5 \text{ percent}$$
$$= 4.547 \text{ percent}$$

Effective annual rate $= 2(4.547 \text{ percent}) = 9.09 \text{ percent}$

Therefore, the consultant implied that the effective annual cost of the power plant, if financed by SCE through normal debt and equity channels, would be 1.47 percent (9.09% − 7.26%), more than if the plant were leased.

REQUEST FOR LETTER OF INTENT

The consultant at the time of presenting his recommendation stated that he had located several high tax bracket individuals who were interested in the lease venture. In addition, other utilities had become interested in the potential of leasing. If SCE would sign a letter of intent, the letter would reserve sufficient funds for the large generating plant lease proposal. However, the letter would not be binding on SCE if it later decided that a lease would not be advantageous. During the fall of 1969, the letter was signed by SCE, and the California Public Utility Commission was informed of the lease proposal.

COMPANY ANALYSIS OF POSSIBLE FUTURE DEBT COST

While the cost of the lease would be fixed once the contract was signed, the cost of capital would not be fixed. Therefore, what was the probable level of long-range debt costs for the company? The financial vice president requested a survey be made of investment bankers to help determine what the company's bond rate level would be over the ensuing decade. While the bankers indicated that they expected interest rates to remain at about 8 percent or higher for a few years, they expected Aa electric utility bonds rates would be between 7 percent and 8 percent in the long run. The survey was conducted during the spring of 1970.

COMPANY PRELIMINARY REVIEW OF LEASE ANALYSIS

The Capital Budget Division was given the responsibility for the analysis of the consultant's lease proposal. Certain assumptions were made by the division's economist. Design and operating rights would be the same for lease as for ownership. Operating, maintenance, insurance, and all other taxes except income taxes would be the same for lease as for ownership. SCE would continue to own the land. The investment involved would be $100 million. No purchase agreement would be included at the end of the lease. For depreciation, SCE would use double-declining balance for tax purposes and straight line for book purposes.[4] The effective state and federal tax rate would remain 51.64 percent[5] throughout

Taxable income	= 1.0000	
Less state rate	= .0700	
Federal taxable income	= .9300	
Federal income tax rate	= .4800	
Federal income tax	= .4464	(.93 × .48)
State income tax	= .0700	
Total Income Tax	= .5200	

the life of the project. Lease payments would be as indicated by the consultant with a lump-sum payoff at the end for the equity investment of the limited partnership.

The division was given until the summer of 1970 to provide an answer. During the summer, investment banker representatives, the consultant, and the economist for the company would present their views to the financial vice president. The decision on a binding contract would be made at that time.

---

[4] While tax life of a generating plant is 28 years, the book life of a generating plant is considered to be 35 years.

[5] The California corporate income tax rate of 7 percent and the federal income tax rate of 48 percent are assumed. The rate is calculated as follows.

EXHIBIT 1
SOUTHERN CALIFORNIA EDISON COMPANY
Interest rate structure

		Short-term interest†		Long-term utility rates‡	
Annual	*Money stock* (billions)*	*90-day treasury bills (percent)*	*4–6 month com- mercial paper (percent)*	*Aa utility bonds (percent)*	*Medium grade preferred stock (percent)*
1964............	$160.5	3.55	3.97	4.44	4.41
1965............	168.0	3.95	4.38	4.52	4.50
1966............	171.7	4.88	5.55	5.25	5.15
1967............	183.1	4.32	5.10	5.66	5.55
1968............	197.4	5.34	5.90	6.35	6.24
1969............	203.6	6.68	7.83	7.34	7.05
Monthly					
1969					
January.........	$198.1	6.18	6.53	6.90	6.60
February........	199.3	6.16	6.62	6.89	6.67
March..........	200.1	6.08	6.82	7.08	6.85
April...........	201.0	6.15	7.04	7.11	6.93
May............	201.6	6.08	7.35	6.99	6.83
June...........	202.4	6.49	8.23	7.25	7.02
July...........	203.1	7.00	8.65	7.38	7.11
August.........	202.6	7.01	8.33	7.34	7.06
September.......	202.8	7.13	8.48	7.50	7.18
October.........	203.2	7.04	8.56	7.71	7.34
November.......	203.5	7.19	8.46	7.75	7.37
December.......	203.6	7.72	8.84	8.23	7.69
1970					
January.........	205.2	7.91	8.78	8.40	7.85
February........	204.5	7.16	8.55	8.30	7.84
March..........	206.6	6.71	8.33	8.17	7.79
April...........	208.3	6.48	8.06	8.16	7.76
May............	209.2	7.04	8.23	8.54	7.92
June...........	209.6	6.74	8.21	8.90	8.35

Sources: * *Economic Report of the President.*
† *Federal Reserve Bulletins.*
‡ *Moody's Public Utility Manual* and *Moody's Bond Survey.*

EXHIBIT 2
SOUTHERN CALIFORNIA EDISON COMPANY
Imbedded cost of debt and preferred stock
(dollar figures in millions)

	Debt			Preferred and preference stock‖		
	Proceeds*	Annualized interest and amortiza- tion†	Rate‡ (percent)	Proceeds*	Annualized dividends§	Rate‡ (percent)
1964.......	$ 850.5	$34.4	4.05	$133.7	$ 6.2	4.64
1965.......	948.0	38.3	4.04	133.7	6.2	4.66
1966.......	1,101.8	47.2	4.28	187.6	9.4	5.02
1967.......	1,181.8	51.9	4.39	187.6	9.5	5.06
1968.......	1,281.0	58.3	4.55	260.8	13.4	5.14
1969.......	1,454.6	71.8	4.93	260.8	13.4	5.14

* Face amount or preferred debt − selling expense ± premium or discount.
† Annual interest on debt ± (premium or discount/number of years of debt instrument).
‡ Annualized interest and amortization or dividends/proceeds × 100.
§ Annual dividends on all outstanding preferred issues.
‖ $73.2 million convertible preference stock with annual dividends of $3.9 million has been included with preferred stock during the 1968–69 period. Preference rate is 5.33 percent during period and preferred rate was 5.06 percent in 1968 and 1969.
Source: Southern California Edison Company, *Financial Characteristics Cost of Money and Required Return*, 1970.

EXHIBIT 3

SOUTHERN CALIFORNIA EDISON COMPANY

Projections, statement of funds, and capital requirements

(dollar figures in millions)

	Recorded						Estimated					
	1964	1965	1966	1967	1968	1969	1970	1971	1972	1973	1974	
Sales												
Total operating revenue...	$449.7	$472.5	$515.9	$552.2	$588.8	$642.1	$724.7	$775.3	$831.2	—	—	
Kilowatt-hour sales...	27,961	30,128	33,687	36,419	39,365	42,602	46,340	50,280	54,800	59,020	64,000	8.5%
Capital Requirements:												
Construction and other investment expenditures...	$162.3	$234.6	$269.8	$325.5	$367.4	$320.1	$315.0	$330.0	$400.0	$495.0	$600.0	
Bond maturities...	30.3	37.9	—	—	—	.2	—	—	—	65.0	—	
Total Capital Requirements...	$192.6	$272.5	$269.8	$325.5	$367.4	$320.3	$315.0	$330.0	$400.0	$560.0	$600.0	
Sources of Capital:												
Internal cash (include salvage)...	$119.8	$116.0	$123.1	$133.2	$133.1	$132.6	$165.0	$175.0	$180.0	$195.0	$210.0	
External Financing Required...	72.8	156.5	146.7	192.3	234.3	187.7	150.0	155.0	220.0	365.0	390.0	
Total Source of Capital...	$192.6	$272.5	$269.8	$325.5	$367.4	$320.3	$315.0	$330.0	$400.0	$560.0	$600.0	
Significant items...												
Interest charged to construction 7½ percent...	$ 2.4	$ 3.3	$ 5.7	$ 6.8	$ 10.0	$ 17.5	$ 16.0	$ 15.0	$ 15.0	$ 20.0	$ 25.0	
Investment tax credit*...	1.6	2.3	3.4	4.4	4.7	5.0	5.4	5.4	3.9	1.9	.2	
Tax deferrals from liberalized depreciation...	11.3	11.5	12.3	12.8	17.2	17.5	16.8	16.9	16.3	15.5	14.6	
Salvage...	11.0	15.6	22.9	16.6	17.0	17.8	20.0	—	—	—	—	

* The Southern California Edison Company applies one fifth of each year's credit over a five-year period. Therefore, if the credit were $1 million in 1960, the company would apply $200,000 credit per year from 1960 through 1964. In 1961 if the credit were $1.1 million, the company would apply $220,000 credit per year from 1961 through 1965. If 1960 was the first year of the credit, the cumulative credit in 1960 would be $200,000 in 1960, and $420,000 ($200,000 + $220,000) in 1961.

Source: Southern California Edison Company, *1969 Financial & Statistical Report.*

EXHIBIT 4
SOUTHERN CALIFORNIA EDISON COMPANY
Times interest earned for 20 electric operating utilities 1965–69

	*Moody's bond rating**	*Times interest earned†*					
		1964	*1965*	*1966*	*1967*	*1968*	*1969*
Boston Edison.	Aaa	4.58	4.18	3.93	3.56	3.20	2.73
Carolina Power & Light	Aa	3.67	3.79	3.47	3.35	2.86	2.49
Cleveland Electric Illuminating	Aaa	5.21	5.79	6.25	6.51	6.10	3.80
Columbus & South Ohio	Aa	3.63	4.01	3.95	3.56	3.04	2.55
Commonwealth Edison	Aaa	4.55	4.87	4.67	4.35	3.68	3.08
Detroit Edison.	Aa	4.34	4.55	4.79	3.82	3.44	2.93
Duke Power	Aa	3.61	3.69	3.64	3.45	2.92	2.40
Duquesne Light	Aa	4.94	4.92	4.37	4.01	3.46	2.85
Florida Power Corporation	Aa	3.86	3.60	3.40	3.45	3.31	3.26
Florida Power & Light	Aa	4.27	3.89	3.91	3.38	2.94	2.64
Houston Light & Power	Aa	5.04	5.74	4.95	3.86	3.35	3.37
Kansas City Power & Light	Aaa	4.59	4.40	4.15	3.78	3.32	2.87
Ohio Edison	Aaa	4.48	4.97	5.19	5.52	5.11	4.85
Oklahoma Gas & Electric	Aa	5.49	4.38	4.35	4.14	3.55	3.56
Pacific Power & Light	Baa	2.78	2.68	2.63	2.50	2.37	2.23
Pennsylvania Power & Light	Aa	3.83	3.91	3.59	3.08	2.68	2.29
Potomac Electric Power	A	2.75	2.96	2.90	2.87	2.49	2.06
Public Service Co. of Indiana	Aa	3.93	4.30	4.64	4.67	4.37	3.63
Union Electric	Aa	3.27	3.21	3.17	2.88	2.64	2.49
Virginia Electric Power	Aa	3.93	3.89	3.65	3.44	3.18	2.80
Mean		4.14	4.19	4.08	3.81	3.40	2.94
Median		4.10	4.10	3.94	3.56	3.25	2.82
High		5.49	5.79	6.25	6.51	6.10	4.85
Low		2.75	2.68	2.63	2.50	2.37	2.06
Southern California Edison Company	Aa	3.34	3.24	3.08	2.97	2.70	2.58

* Includes all electric operating utilities with over $100 million operating revenue and over 90 percent of operating revenue from electric operations.
† (Net income + Interest)/Interest. Does not include extraordinary items.
Sources: (1)   *Moody's Public Utility Manual.*
(2)   *Uniform Statistical Reports* (to Edison Electric Institute).

EXHIBIT 5

SOUTHERN CALIFORNIA EDISON COMPANY

Return and capitalization information for 20 electric operating utilities*

| | 1965–69 5-year mid-year average | | | | | 1969 Mid-year | | | | |
| | Return on: | | Capitalization percent§ | | | Return on: | | Capitalization percent§ | | |
Company	Total capital†	Common equity‡	Debt	Preferred and preference	Common equity	Total capital†	Common equity‡	Debt	Preferred and preference	Common equity
1. Boston Edison	7.29%	10.84%	46.5%	10.0%	43.5%	7.52%	11.43%	53.5%	8.1%	38.4%
2. Carolina Power & Light	7.71	12.59	52.7	9.7	37.6	7.94	11.72	53.6	10.3	36.1
3. Cleveland Electric Illuminating	9.71	14.59	45.8	—	54.2	10.46	14.70	47.6	—	52.4
4. Columbus & South Ohio	8.19	13.25	52.0	7.4	40.6	8.36	12.35	55.5	6.3	38.2
5. Commonwealth Edison	8.49	13.93	51.2	4.6	44.2	8.41	13.82	54.9	6.0	39.1
6. Detroit Edison	7.52	11.63	50.3	3.9	45.8	6.92	10.54	53.4	7.1	39.5
7. Duke Power	8.14	12.75	51.0	8.3	40.7	8.59	12.56	53.7	11.9	34.4
8. Duquesne Light	8.40	16.09	52.2	13.1	34.7	8.16	14.98	56.1	12.0	31.9
9. Florida Power Corporation	7.98	13.60	53.6	7.9	38.5	8.58	15.16	56.3	6.7	37.0
10. Florida Power & Light	8.33	12.61	51.3	4.5	44.2	8.20	11.90	55.0	3.4	41.6
11. Houston Lighting & Power	9.66	15.33	51.4	2.0	46.6	9.32	14.49	53.8	3.1	43.1
12. Kansas City Power & Light	7.50	12.14	45.5	14.9	39.6	7.74	11.74	49.6	12.0	38.4
13. Ohio Edison	8.71	15.23	46.3	10.9	42.8	8.58	14.90	47.1	10.1	42.8
14. Oklahoma Gas & Electric	8.65	16.31	51.8	13.8	34.4	8.80	16.48	53.0	13.8	33.2
15. Pacific Power & Light	6.83	11.11	59.6	7.6	32.8	7.18	10.93	59.6	8.0	32.4
16. Pensylvania Power & Light	7.34	13.10	54.1	13.3	32.6	7.95	12.24	56.2	11.2	32.6
17. Potomac Electric Power	6.72	10.08	54.1	10.0	35.9	6.60	8.14	54.9	11.2	33.9

18.	Public Service Co. of Indiana	8.42	14.00	46.6	10.6	42.8	8.96	13.97	46.8	10.0	43.2
19.	Union Electric	7.51	12.94	55.3	11.1	33.6	7.62	11.97	54.7	11.8	33.5
20.	Virginia Electric Power	7.72	13.28	53.1	9.3	37.6	7.71	12.40	54.3	8.7	37.0
	Mean	8.04%	13.27%	51.2%	8.7%	40.1%	8.18%	12.82%	53.5%	8.6%	37.9%
	Median	8.06	13.18	51.6	9.5	40.1	8.18	12.38	54.2	9.4	37.6
	High	9.71	16.31	59.6	14.9	54.2	10.46	16.48	59.6	13.8	52.4
	Low	6.72	10.08	45.5	—	32.6	6.60	8.14	46.8	—	31.9
	Southern California Edison Company	7.03%	11.21%	53.8%	8.7%	37.5%	6.91%	10.37%	53.8%	10.2%	36.0%

* Includes all electric operating utilities with over $100 million in operating revenues and over 90 percent of operating revenues from electric utility operations.
† (Net income + Interest expenses)/(Mid-year total capital. Total capital does not include notes payable. Net income does not include extraordinary items.
‡ (Net income − Preferred dividends)/Mid-year common equity. Net income does not include extraordinary items.
§ Capital structure consists of long-term debt, preferred and preference stock, and common equity. Notes payable and other current liabilities are not included.
Source: *Annual Reports.*

EXHIBIT 6
SOUTHERN CALIFORNIA EDISON COMPANY
Balance sheet for years 1964–69
(dollar figures in millions)

	1964	1965	1966	1967	1968	1969
ASSETS						
Utility Plant						
Original cost	$2,171.2	$2,369.5	$2,591.1	$2,880.7	$3,188.7	$3,461.8
Less: Accumulated provision for depreciation	426.5	468.9	508.4	559.4	592.4	649.7
Net Utility Plant*	$1,744.7	$1,900.6	$2,082.7	$2,321.3	$2,596.3	$2,812.1
Other Property and Investments	14.7	14.8	13.9	14.7	14.9	16.8
Current Assets						
Cash	7.6	9.0	8.4	9.6	8.4	10.8
Temporary invests	—	—	24.0	—	—	2.1
Accounts receivable	33.0	32.2	36.6	39.4	44.4	48.2
Other	56.0	65.3	71.2	75.4	83.9	99.1
Total Current Assets	$ 96.6	$ 106.5	$ 140.2	$ 124.4	$ 136.7	$ 160.2
Deferred debits	6.3	4.1	8.5	7.4	7.1	13.1
Total Assets	$1,862.3	$2,026.0	$2,245.3	$2,467.8	$2,755.0	$3,002.2
LIABILITIES						
Shareholder Equity						
Common stock and original preferred	$ 312.4	$ 312.4	$ 312.4	$ 312.4	$ 324.9	$ 337.4
Capital surplus	162.8	162.8	161.6	161.8	200.1	241.4
Retained earnings	199.4	231.7	269.4	308.5	342.7	381.0
Common Equity	$ 674.6	$ 706.9	$ 743.4	$ 782.7	$ 867.7	$ 959.8
Preferred and preference stock†	132.7	132.7	176.9	187.8	262.8	262.8
Total Shareholder Equity	$ 807.3	$ 839.6	$ 920.3	$ 970.5	$1,130.5	$1,222.6
Bonds, Debentures, etc.	852.9	950.0	1,105.0	1,185.0	1,285.0	1,459.8
Capitalization‡	$1,660.2	$1,789.6	$2,025.3	$2,155.5	$2,415.5	$2,682.4

Current Liabilities

Notes payable	$ 7.0	$ 28.5	$ —	$ 77.5	$ 84.5	$ 46.0
Accounts payable	24.9	26.6	34.7	43.6	48.5	41.8
Other	63.6	68.8	66.6	64.6	74.1	86.5
Total Current Liabilities	$ 95.5	$ 123.9	$ 101.3	$ 185.7	$ 207.1	$ 174.3
Other reserves, contributions and deferred taxes	106.6	112.5	118.7	126.6	132.4	145.5
Total Liabilities	$1,862.3	$2,026.0	$2,245.3	$2,467.8	$2,775.0	$3,002.2

Capital Structure:

Common Equity	40.6%	39.5%	36.7%	36.3%	35.9%	35.8%
Preferred and Preference†	8.0	7.4	8.7	8.7	10.9	9.8
Long-Term Debt	51.4	53.1	54.6	55.0	53.2	54.4
Total	100.0%	100.0%	100.0%	100.0%	100.0%	100.0%

* SCE's rate of return for rate purposes based on net utility plant with some minor adjustments.
† $4,000,000 original preferred usually calculated as part of common equity.
Source: Southern California Edison Company, *1969 Financial & Statistical Report.*

EXHIBIT 7
SOUTHERN CALIFORNIA EDISON COMPANY
Income statement for years 1964–69
(dollar figures in millions)

	1964	1965	1966	1967	1968	1969
Sales Revenue................	$449.7	$472.5	$515.9	$552.2	$588.8	$642.1
Operating and maintenance expenses*..................	$183.3	$191.0	$216.2	$229.2	$257.1	$291.0
Depreciation expenses..........	55.6	59.4	63.9	68.7	74.6	79.9
All other taxes...............	56.1	59.1	63.0	67.4	71.4	75.3
Income taxes.................	40.9	46.3	45.4	45.7	37.5	36.5
Total Expenses........	$335.9	$355.8	$388.5	$411.0	$440.6	$482.7
Operating income..............	$113.8	$116.7	$127.4	$141.2	$148.2	$159.4
Other income†...............	3.6	5.1	7.1	8.6	10.5	16.7
Income before Interest Charges..	$117.4	$121.8	$134.5	$149.8	$158.7	$176.1
Interest‡....................	35.1	37.4	43.7	50.5	58.8	68.2
Net Income..................	$ 82.3	$ 84.4	$ 90.8	$ 99.3	$ 99.9	$107.9
Preferred dividends§...........	$ 5.6	$ 5.6	$ 5.6	$ 8.5	$ 9.5	$ 12.7
Income Available for Common and Original Preferred‖.......	$ 76.7	$ 78.8	$ 85.2	$ 90.8	$ 90.4	$ 95.2
Common or original preferred dividends..................	$ 41.4	$ 46.5	$ 47.5	$ 51.7	$ 56.2	$ 56.9
Retained Earnings.............	$ 35.3	$ 32.3	$ 37.7	$ 39.1	$ 34.2	$ 38.3
Common and Original Preferred Shares (year end)............	36.8	38.0	38.0	38.0	39.5	41.0
Earnings per share (year end) ...	$ 2.08	$ 2.07	$ 2.24	$ 2.39	$ 2.28	$ 2.32
Dividends per share (year end) ..	$ 1.20	$ 1.25	$ 1.25	$ 1.40	$ 1.40	$ 1.40
Times Interest Covered after Income Taxes¶.............	3.34	3.24	3.08	2.97	2.70	2.58

* Include fuel and purchased power expenses, insurance expenses, lease and rental expenses, and operating and maintenance expenses. It does not include all other taxes (property taxes, payroll taxes, etc.).

† Other income includes income from operations other than electrical including interest from investments, interest charged to nonoperating electrical plant that was capitalized, and income tax credits for nonelectrical operating plant.

‡ Includes interest on long-term debt, short-term interest, and amortization.

§ Excludes 480,000 shares participating original preferred dividends.

‖ Income available for common and original preferred/common and original preferred shares.

¶ Income before interest/interest.

Source: Southern California Edison Company, *1969 Financial & Statistical Report*.

UAL INCORPORATED

In the spring of 1971, management was concerned about the financial situation at UAL. At a recent meeting of the board of directors, they learned that several of their principal lenders had become alarmed at the first quarter results. Despite extensive cost cutting, the losses had continued. These lenders (predominantly insurance companies) felt that UAL should provide more protection for their investment in the form of subordinated debt or equity.

Management felt that UAL was in a satisfactory cash position, but financing for aircraft scheduled for delivery over the next few years had to be assured.

COMPANY BACKGROUND

The roots of United Airlines extend back to the barnstorming days of the middle 1920s. Its growth through the depression years has continued to the present. It is now the nation's largest domestic trunk line in terms of miles flown and revenue earned. The airline presently has the most extensive domestic route system of any airline in the United States.

On December 30, 1960, UAL, Inc. was incorporated as the parent holding company of United Airlines, Inc. Soon thereafter, UAL, Inc. acquired Western International Hotels, an organization which owns and operates hotels throughout the world. Western provides about 6 percent of UAL's consolidated revenue.

INDUSTRY PERSPECTIVE

Since United Airlines is UAL Inc.'s largest subsidiary and provides 94 percent of its revenues, it was felt that an examination of the past trends and future prospects of the airline industry would be appropriate. The investigation was limited to the principal U.S. scheduled passenger carriers, because they were most like United in terms of route structure, size, and competitive environment.

The financial and operational status of this group of airlines is summarized in Exhibit 1. Profits peaked in 1967 at $411.4 million and then sharply declined to a $100.8 million loss at the end of 1970. The loss was the result of smaller than expected traffic growth along with increased competition, increased operating costs, and larger debt burdens.

Because airlines in the United States are closely regulated, they are not free to alter fares or adjust service (i.e., eliminate or add routes) without going through lengthy public hearings. Consequently, a substantial portion of an airline's operating costs are fixed regardless of the number of passengers flown. Since airlines are not free to change prices to attract customers, they can differentiate themselves from their competitors only by varying their services. The passenger is offered an assortment of inducements, including gourmet meals, movies, and larger seats. These marketing strategies are designed to increase a particular airline's share of the existing passenger market as well as to attract new passengers into the market. But it is not clear that the added inducements have stimulated the overall market significantly. The net result has been that the various airlines have maintained approximately the same market share over the years and have added substantially to their costs.

As seen in Exhibit 1, the industry has nearly doubled its total fleet over the past six years. Moreover, the proportion of jet equipment has increased to the point that nonjets have nearly disappeared. The airlines have purchased new equipment not only to meet anticipated market growth but also to establish a competitive advantage by offering the latest equipment. The new equipment thus serves as another nonprice inducement to prospective passengers. This policy of fleet expansion and modernization will continue with future purchases of jumbo jets and SSTs. Presently, the industry has on order 239 new aircraft. Most are jumbos, and the cost will be approximately $4 billion. Delivery will be over the next four years. SST commitments extend farther into the future and are subject to change.

PRESENT COMPANY SITUATION

Exhibit 2 shows that after a peak of $73 million in 1967, United Air Lines' earnings declined to a $40 million loss in December 1970. Over

$33 million was lost in the first three months of 1971. The United Air Lines subsidiary accounted for almost all of the losses of UAL. As a result of the continuing losses and increased borrowings to finance aircraft purchases, United's leverage had increased substantially over the past few years. Exhibit 3 shows that the long-term debt to equity ratio rose from 1.53 in 1965 to 1.93 in 1970. A more detailed picture of United's capital structure is presented in Exhibit 6.

In December 1970, Mr. Edward E. Carlson was named president and chief executive officer of UAL, Inc. He lost no time in instituting measures designed to achieve a turnaround in earnings. These measures included a curtailment or elimination of some unprofitable operations, increased efforts to sell flight training services, aircraft servicing and maintenance to others, a thorough analysis of administrative and staff responsibilities to consolidate functions, a 7 percent reduction in manpower from the March 1970 level, and expanded efforts to establish better employee relations with respect to increasing efficiency and improving the quality of service, and to strengthen United's competitive market position. It was hoped that the cost reduction efforts coupled with an expected increase in overall economic activities would bring about a resumption of profitable operations during the last half of 1971.

FUTURE CAPITAL REQUIREMENTS

Exhibit 7 presents a summary of the expenditures required for future aircraft and equipment commitments. In addition, United has 80 aircraft under long-term leases which expire between 1975 and 1985. Annual rentals total approximately $50,700,000. Included in the allocations shown in Exhibit 7 are the estimated annual lease costs for the first five DC-10s to be delivered in the last half of 1971. This amount is $9,700,000 per year. United has options to purchase 15 DC 10s for delivery in 1972 through 1974, and has made position deposits of $1,008,000 and $1,200,000 for six Concordes and six Boeing SST aircraft, respectively.

ECONOMIC SETTING

The economy had been experiencing a mild recession through the previous year. In order to stimulate economic expansion, the Federal Reserve Board had allowed the money supply to expand at a rate of almost 10 percent. By early 1971, this policy had resulted in a marked reduction of long-term interest rates from their 1970 highs. However, the recent 10 percent growth rate in the money supply was well above the rate desired by the FRB. Accordingly, the FRB was expected to move to a lower rate of expansion in the near future. This in turn could result in a renewal of high interest rates.

Reacting to the recession, stock prices had declined sharply during the early part of 1970. A turnaround in stock prices occurred in May 1970. Since then, stock prices had risen steadily. Investors were increasingly confident that the economy would soon resume its pre-recession growth rate. The market was readily accepting both debt and equity issues.

In spite of the recently favorable marked trends, the feeling was that the economy was not recovering as fast as it could be. Continuing high unemployment and inflation were the main causes of this uneasiness. It was feared that the recently buoyant securities market might be short lived.

ALTERNATIVES

Management was not convinced that UAL would require additional capital in the near future if earnings turned around as expected. However, if losses continued, the airline could become hard pressed for funds for new equipment purchases. Funds might come from UAL's revolving credit arrangement with its banks. However, this arrangement was designed primarily to fulfill short-term operating needs.

Insurance companies, who held the bulk of United's debt, expressed some concern for the safety of their loans in light of United's continuing losses. New equity or subordinated debt financing was being considered as a means of providing additional protection to satisfy the senior debt holders. The best estimate of the level of required financing with which they could get by was $85 million.

In analysing the situation, management wondered if issuing new debt would be advisable or even possible in light of the recent losses. High interest rates and restrictive clauses might possibly accompany a new debt issue under present circumstances. On the other hand, investors would probably support an equity issue if they felt that an earnings turnaround was imminent. (Exhibit 8 presents a price and dividend history.)

EXHIBIT 1

UAL, INC.

Airline Industry Summary—U.S. trunkline carriers* and Pan American—System operations data for airline operations only

(dollar figures in millions)

	1965	1966	1967	1968	1969	1970
Income Statement						
Operating revenues	$4,380.3	$5,030.6	$6,117.5	$6,910.3	$7,764.2	$8,130.8
Operating expenses	3,762.6	4,328.9	5,431.5	6,373.8	7,352.2	8,082.2
Operating Income	$ 617.7	$ 701.7	$ 686.0	$ 536.5	$ 412.0	$ 48.6
Nonoperating income (expense)	(62.1)	(55.2)	(48.6)	(117.5)	(165.2)	(202.3)
Net income (loss) before taxes	$ 555.6	$ 646.5	$ 637.4	$ 419.0	$ 246.8	$ (153.7)
Income tax (expense) credit	(219.0)	(259.6)	(224.3)	(153.0)	(99.1)	52.8
Special items—income (expense)	4.8	—	1.7	3.6	—	—
Net Profit (loss)	$ 341.4	$ 386.9	$ 411.4	$ 262.4	$ 147.7	$ (100.8)
Cash Income						
Net Profit (loss)	$ 341.4	$ 386.9	$ 411.4	$ 262.4	$ 147.7	$ (100.8)
Add: Depreciation and amortization	390.8	443.4	552.5	654.3	774.5	855.2
Deferred taxes	83.1	83.0	105.4	151.4	122.3	24.4
Special items	(4.8)	—	1.7	3.6	—	—
Net cash income before special items	$ 810.5	$ 913.3	$1,071.0	$1,071.7	$1,044.5	$ 778.8
Balance Sheet						
Current Assets	$1,339.9	$1,741.4	$2,018.3	$1,882.1	$2,100.9	$2,137.6
Current liabilities	960.8	1,083.2	1,291.2	1,447.0	1,779.6	1,949.0
Working capital	379.1	658.2	727.1	435.1	321.3	188.6
Investments and special funds	426.3	626.6	908.6	1,164.9	1,418.6	1,205.7
Property and equipment—net	3,139.3	4,036.1	5,205.0	6,406.9	6,950.5	7,915.8
Working capital plus net fixed assets	3,944.7	5,320.9	6,840.7	8,006.9	8,690.4	9,310.1
Less: Long-term debt	1,892.6	2,706.9	3,565.2	4,436.5	4,797.1	5,533.4
Net tangible assets	2,052.1	2,614.0	3,275.5	3,570.4	3,893.3	3,776.7
Deferred charges (credits)—net	(390.0)	(455.2)	(573.8)	(679.5)	(819.2)	(873.4)
Stockholders' Equity	$1,662.1	$2,158.8	$2,701.7	$2,890.9	$3,074.1	$2,903.3

Adjusted Balance Sheet Items

Term debt	$1,936.3	$2,772.7	$3,722.7	$4,591.7	$5,042.8	$5,868.2
Add: Capitalized aircraft leases (estimated)	217.6	243.8	358.1	865.8	1,455.0	2,069.9
Less: Subordinated debt (estimated)	376.2	776.9	1,219.9	1,348.5	1,669.2	1,755.0
Total Senior Debt	$1,777.7	$2,239.6	$2,860.9	$4,109.0	$4,828.6	$6,183.1
Net Worth	$1,659.5	$2,158.7	$2,701.3	$2,890.9	$3,073.9	$2,906.6
Add: Subordinated debt (estimated)	376.2	776.9	1,219.9	1,348.5	1,669.2	1,755.0
Less: Deferred charges	56.7	80.5	88.4	147.7	153.2	179.2
Total Effective Tangible Net Worth	$1,979.0	$2,855.1	$3,832.8	$4,091.7	$4,589.9	$4,482.4

Load Factor

Payload factor (percent)	48.9	51.6	50.9	53.1	45.8	44.6
Passenger Load Factor (percent)	55.7	58.4	57.0	48.0	50.6	50.1
Break even (cash operating expense)	40.7	42.3	42.9	39.7	42.0	43.6
Break even (operating expense plus interest)	47.9	50.2	50.7	45.8	50.3	52.1

Number of Aircraft

Jet	692	934	1,197	1,557	1,774	1,846
Turboprop	173	176	161	114	68	48
Piston	406	303	242	80	52	9
Total	1,271	1,413	1,600	1,751	1,894	1,903

* United, American, TWA, Eastern, Braniff, Continental, Delta, National, Northeast, Northwest, and Western.

EXHIBIT 2
UAL, INC.
Historical summary*
(dollar figures in millions)

	1965	1966	1967	1968	1969	1970
Income Statement						
Operating revenues	$792.8	$ 856.9	$1,099.0	$1,261.7	$1,477.5	$1,501.7
Operating expenses	706.3	785.4	988.5	1,168.6	1,358.2	1,522.7
Operating Income (loss)	86.5	71.5	110.5	93.1	119.3	(21.0)
Nonoperating income (expense)	(9.0)	(8.2)	(2.4)	(15.8)	(31.5)	(27.9)
Net Income (loss) before taxes	77.5	63.3	108.1	77.3	87.8	(48.9)
Income tax (expense) credit	(31.8)	(24.9)	(35.3)	(35.6)	(40.2)	9.0
Net profit (loss)	$ 45.7	$ 38.4	$ 72.8	$ 41.7	$ 47.6	($ 39.9)
Earnings per share	$ 6.52	2.27	3.92	2.35	2.55	($ 2.0)
Cash Income						
Net Profit (loss)	$ 45.7	$ 38.4	$ 72.8	$ 41.7	$ 47.6	($ 39.9)
Add: Depreciation and amortization	61.8	69.7	76.6	100.2	140.3	162.9
Deferred taxes	14.7	9.1	12.7	32.2	—	—
Net cash income before special items	$122.2	$117.2	$162.1	$174.2	$187.9	$ 123.0
Balance Sheet						
Current Assets	$307.1	$ 417.1	$ 514.8	$ 298.3	$ 312.5	$ 327.0
Current Liabilities	170.0	188.9	219.6	252.3	272.2	309.5
Working capital	137.1	288.2	295.2	46.0	40.3	17.5
Investments and special funds	106.1	133.1	175.6	165.0	162.5	170.7
Property and equipment—net	555.3	651.7	798.9	1,288.6	1,434.7	1,515.7
Working capital plus net fixed assets	798.5	1,013.0	1,269.7	1,499.6	1,637.5	1,703.9
Less: Long-term debt	435.8	502.2	623.2	804.7	869.3	987.6
Net tangible assets	362.7	510.8	646.5	694.9	768.2	716.3
Deferred charges (credits)—net	(77.4)	(90.4)	(106.0)	(131.3)	(181.0)	(204.2)
Stockholders' Equity	$285.3	$ 420.4	$ 540.5	$ 563.6	$ 587.2	$ 512.1

Adjusted Balance Sheet Items

Term debt...............	$438.4	$ 512.8	$ 632.7	$ 815.4	$ 878.8	$1,006.3
Add: Capitalized aircraft leases (estimated)...........	132.2	135.5	167.5	154.7	365.0	443.4
Less: Subordinated debt............	81.7	158.2	243.2	242.7	250.2	250.2
Total Senior Debt............	$488.9	$ 490.1	$ 557.0	$ 727.4	$ 993.6	$1,199.5
Net Worth...............	$285.3	$ 420.4	$ 540.5	$ 563.6	$ 587.3	$ 512.1
Add: Subordinated debt.............	81.7	158.2	243.2	242.7	250.2	250.2
Less: Deferred charges...........	6.2	5.8	6.6	15.4	17.5	24.1
Total Effective Tangible Net Worth.......	$360.8	$ 572.8	$ 777.1	$ 790.9	$ 820.0	$ 738.2

Number of Aircraft

Jet....................	148	189	238	331	389	392
Turboprop..............	45	44	43	19	—	—
Piston.................	99	85	81	22	4	1
	292	318	362	372	393	393

* Results for Western International Hotels not included.
† Strike 7/8/66.
Source: Moody's *Transportation, Manuals.*

EXHIBIT 3

UAL, INC.

Balance sheets* as of December 31 for the years 1965–70

(dollar figures in millions)

	1965	1966	1967	1968	1969	1970
ASSETS						
Current Assets						
Cash and equivalent............	$176.8	$ 247.2	$ 300.4	$ 61.3	$ 48.7	$ 30.7
Notes and accounts receivable..	88.4	115.0	137.4	149.8	174.4	193.1
Other current assets..........	41.9	54.9	77.0	87.2	89.4	103.3
Total Current Assets.......	307.1	417.1	514.8	298.3	312.5	327.1
Investments and special funds...	106.1	133.1	175.6	165.0	162.5	170.7
Property and equipment—Net....	555.3	651.7	1,288.6	1,288.6	1,434.7	1,515.7
Deferred charges.............	6.2	5.8	6.6	15.4	17.5	24.0
Total Assets..............	$974.7	$1,207.7	$1,495.9	$1,767.3	$1,927.2	$2,037.5
LIABILITIES AND STOCKHOLDERS' EQUITY						
Current Liabilities						
Notes payable...............	$ 2.6	$ 10.6	$ 9.5	$ 10.7	$ 9.5	$ 18.7
Other.....................	167.4	178.3	210.1	241.6	262.7	290.8
Total Current Liabilities.....	170.0	188.9	219.6	252.3	272.2	309.5
Long-term debt..............	435.8	502.2	623.2	804.7	869.3	987.6
Other.....................	1.4	1.5	1.7	2.0	2.9	—
Deferred credits.............	82.2	94.7	110.9	144.7	195.6	228.3
Stockholders' Equity						
Preferred stock..............	14.0	13.5	13.0	12.5	} 587.2	} 512.1
Common stock—outstanding....	68.8	82.5	91.9	92.1		
Surplus....................	202.5	324.4	435.6	459.0		
Total Stockholders' Equity....	$285.3	$ 420.4	$ 540.5	$ 563.6	$ 587.2	$ 512.1
Total Liabilities and Stockholder's Equity....	$974.7	$1,207.7	$1,495.9	$1,767.3	$1,927.2	$2,037.5
Shares outstanding—common†	6,879,945	16,586,686	18,378,104	18,424,058	18,424,059	18,424,065
—preferred†	139,920	135,150	130,380	125,380	112,239	2,901,232

* Results for Western International Hotels not included.

† Common and preferred shares of U.A.I., Inc. at year end from 1969.

Source: Moody's *Transportation Manuals*.

EXHIBIT 4
UAL, INC.
Consolidated income statement
(dollar figures in millions)

	Three months ended March 31 (unaudited)	
	1970	1971
Operating revenues:		
Airline		
Passenger..	$306,328	$291,753
Cargo...	31,076	33,383
Other revenue, net..................................	2,333	3,634
Hotels...	21,586	19,934
Total Operating Revenues.......................	$361,323	$348,704
Operating expenses exclusive of income taxes...............	380,669	392,524
Earnings (loss) from operations before income taxes...........	$(19,346)	$(43,820)
Other deductions (income) net		
Interest on long-term debt.............................	$ 13,333	$ 15,249
Interest capitalized..................................	(3,151)	(2,722)
Interest (gain) on disposition of property.................	48	31
Other, net...	(371)	(296)
	$ 9,859	$ 12,262
Earnings (loss) before income taxes.......................	$(29,205)	$(56,082)
Provision for income taxes..............................	(6,858)	(22,876)
Net earnings (loss).....................................	$(22,347)	$(33,206)
Preferred stock dividend requirements.....................	$ 154	$ 146
On prior preferred stock..............................	380	380
	$ 534	$ 526
Earnings (loss) applicable to common stock.................	$(22,881)	$(33,732)
Earnings (loss) per share		
Primary..	$ (1.24)	$ (1.83)
Assuming full dilution................................	(1.24)	(1.83)
Cash dividends declared on common stock..................	$ .25	$ —

Source: Moody's *Transportation Manuals*.

EXHIBIT 5
UAL, INC.
Statistical operations†

Statistics	1965	1966	1967
Revenue plane miles........................	242.4	247.7	328.8
Revenue available ton-miles.................	3,127.7	3,375.7	4,619.2
Revenue ton-miles.........................	1,512.3	1,710.9	2,361.8
Available seat miles (ex charter)............	22,226.9	23,045.9	30,980.8
Revenue passenger-miles (ex charter)			
First class..............................	3,135.4	3,463.0	4,137.0
Coach/economy........................	9,114.0	9,746.9	14,259.9
Total Revenue Passenger-miles			
(Ex Charter).........................	12,249.4	13,209.9	18,396.9
Cargo Ton-miles (Ex Charter)			
Freight...............................	228.8	261.0	347.1
Express...............................	20.4	19.1	21.7
Mail.................................	773.1	83.8	123.8
Total Cargo Ton-miles (Ex Charter).......	1,022.3	363.9	492.6
Increase (Decrease) Same Period Last Year (Percent)			
Operating revenue......................	18.4%	8.1%	28.3%
Revenue plane miles...................	17.6	2.2	32.7
Revenue available ton-miles..............	21.2	7.9	36.8
Revenue ton-miles......................	24.2	13.1	38.1
Available seat miles (ex charter)..........	20.0	3.7	34.4
Revenue passenger-miles (ex charter).......	23.2	7.9	32.9
Cargo ton-miles (ex charter).............	28.5	12.9	35.1
Utilization—Average hours per day—Overall..	6:52	5:54	6:58
Payload factor (percent)...................	48.4	50.7	51.1
Passenger Load Factor (Percent)			
Actual.................................	55.1	57.3	59.4
Break even (cash operating expense)........	43.4	46.1	47.7
Break even (operating expense plus interest)..	49.5	53.2	54.5

* Strike 7/8/66 through 8/14/66.
† Results for Western International Hotels not included.

		Calendar year—Cumulative to date			
1968	*1969*	*1st Qtr.* *1970*	*2d Qtr.* *1970*	*3d Qtr.* *1970*	*4th Qtr.* *1970*
386.6	425.3	107.2	213.6	329.3	440.3
5,872.5	7,032.3	1,767.0	3,526.6	5,475.4	7,337.1
2,802.4	3,254.6	729.7	1,537.9	2,489.7	3,285.0
39,650.4	46,000.2	11,533.3	22,782.3	35,147.7	47,045.3
4,402.3	4,164.9	870.5	1,703.4	2,613.2	3,435.9
17,015.1	19,834.5	4,405.5	9,268.4	15,506.6	20,332.0
21,417.4	23,999.4	5,276.0	10,971.8	18,119.8	23,767.9
429.4	514.2	113.4	266.1	407.2	535.4
22.6	23.4	5.1	12.3	17.9	23.2
170.8	184.5	43.9	85.9	130.9	188.6
622.8	722.1	162.4	364.3	556.0	747.2
11.5%	17.1%	5.7%	1.8%	2.5%	1.6%
17.7	10.0	10.1	5.8	4.7	3.5
27.1	19.7	10.4	5.9	5.2	4.3
18.7	16.1	1.0	(.8)	.9	1.6
28.0	16.0	9.5	4.9	3.6	2.3
16.4	12.1	(1.3)	(4.1)	(1.8)	(1.0)
26.6	15.9	(5.3)	1.5	3.4	3.4
7:24	7:15	6:59	6:53	7:02	7:04
47.7	46.3	41.3	43.6	45.5	44.8
54.0	52.2	45.8	48.2	51.6	50.5
44.4	41.5	43.2	43.9	45.2	45.0
51.1	49.0	50.4	51.5	53.0	52.9

Source: Moody's *Transportation Manuals.*

EXHIBIT 6
UAL, INC.
Capitalization as of December 31, 1970
Consolidated

Capital Stock
United Air Lines, Inc.
Common
 Par value   No par value
 Outstanding   200 shares
UAL, Inc.
Preferred, 5½%
 Cumulative (prior)
 Outstanding   106,239 shares (106,239 authorized)
 Dividends paid $5.50 per share paid in 1970
Preferred, Series A,
 $.40 Cumulative
 Par value   No par value (convertible after July 31, 1973)
 Outstanding   4,294,254 shares (16,000,000 authorized). Issued
          on July 31, 1970, in connection with the acquisition
          of Western
 Dividends paid $0.20 per share paid in 1970
Common
 Par value $5
 Outstanding   18,424,065 shares (50,000,000 authorized)
 Dividend restrictions $124,808,000 of retained earnings not available for
          dividends at December 31, 1970

Term Debt
Notes payable: To banks, a revolving credit agreement in the maxi-
          mum amount of $300 million. The funds will be
          available on a revolving basis during the entire term
          of the eight-year agreement with the maximum loan
          amount declining at a rate of $15 million quarterly
          beginning April 1, 1971, and continuing to maturity
          on January 1, 1976. The interest rate will be ¼ of
          1 percent over the prime rate through January 1,
          1975, and ½ of 1 percent over prime thereafter... $ 60,000,0
          To banks and insurance companies at interest rates
          of 5 percent due February 1, 1984. Yearly payments
          of $6,000,000 starting February 2, 1975 through
          February 1, 1984............................ 60,000,0
          To banks and insurance companies at interest rates
          of 5 percent due May 1, 1985. Yearly payments of
          $14,500,000 from May 1, 1976 through May 1,
          1980 and $20,500,000 from June 1, 1981 through
          May 1, 1985.............................. 175,000,0
          To insurance companies at interest rates of 7½
          percent due February 1, 1970. Yearly payments of
          $10,000,000 from February 1, 1981 through Feb-
          ruary 1, 1985 and $20,000,000 from February 1,
          1986 through February 1, 1990................. 150,000,0
          To insurance companies at interest rate of 6½
          percent due April 1, 1990. Yearly payments of
          $13,300,000 from April 1, 1976 through April 1,
          1989 and $13,800,000 due on April 1, 1990....... 200,000,0
          Subordinated notes held privately, at interest rate
          of ¼ percent over prime, due March 31, 1974..... 15,000,0

EXHIBIT 6 (*Continued*)

4% Sinking fund debentures	Held privately—three insurance companies, unsecured.	
Due	February 1, 1981	
Callable	At any time to February 1, at 104 in 1958, reducing to 100, in 1981.	
Sinking fund	$8,000,000 annually on February 1, 1970 through 1981..	88,000,000
5% Subordinated convertible debentures	Held publicly, unsecured.	
Due	December 1, 1991	
Callable	As a whole or in part on at least 30 days' notice, initially at 105 in 1967 declining to 100 in 1991.	
Convertible	Into common stock on or prior to December 1, 1981 at the rate of 20 shares for each $1,000 principle amount of debentures plus $350.	
Sinking fund	To retire annually on each December 1, 1977–1990 equal to $5,000,000........................	93,372,000
4-1% Subordinated convertible debentures	Held publicly, unsecured.	
Due	July 1,1992	
Callable	As a whole or in part on at least 30 days' notice, at 104.25 in 1968 declining to 100 in 1992.	
Sinking fund	To retire annually on July 1, 1978 debentures in amount of $6,500,000 plus optional payments of like amount.	
Convertible	Into common stock on or prior to July 1, 1982 at $84 per share, payable by surrender of 15 shares per $1,000 principal amount of debentures plus $260..	130,807,000
		28,110,115
Miscellaneous Debt	Total Term Debt......................	$1,000,289,115

Source: Moody's *Transportation Manuals.*

EXHIBIT 7
UAL, INC.
Projected capital commitments
(dollar figures in thousands)

	Nine months 1971	Year ended December 31			Total
		1972	1973	1974	
Acquisition of Boeing 747 and DC-10 aircraft and related flight equipment............	$141,848	$177,445	$118,116	$54,542	$491,951
Aircraft modifications and related flight equipment......	3,924	1,815	456	—	6,195
Ground facilities and equipment.................	40,934	36,459	15,531	2,730	95,654
	$186,706	$215,719	$134,103	$57,272	$593,800

EXHIBIT 8
UAL, INC.
Price range of common stock* and cash dividends paid

| | Price | | Dividends | | |
| | Common stock | | Preferred- | Preferred | Common stock |
Year	High	Low	5½ percent cumulative	series A	(per share)
1966...................	74¾	43¾	$754,000	$1,335,000	$0.94
1967...................	87⅜	55¼	728,000	1,338,000	1.00
1968...................	66½	34	694,000	1,441,000	1.00
1969...................					
1st quarter............	48½	37⅜			
2d quarter..........	41⅞	35⅞			
3d quarter..........	38½	26¾			
4th quarter..........	35⅞	26⅛	630,000	1,512,000	1.00
1970					
1st quarter............	28⅜	20			
2d quarter..........	24½	12½			
3d quarter..........	20½	12½			
4th quarter..........	23⅜	15⅝	609,000	1,518,000	0.75
1971					
1st quarter............	33⅞	21⅜			

* UAL's common stock is listed on the Net York, Midwest and Pacific Coast Stock Exchanges.

NATIONAL HOUSING PRODUCTS (A)

EARLY IN 1967, Messrs. Frazier, Jackson, and West were considering various financing packages for a project to which National Housing Products was committed. Frazier, Jackson, and West comprised the executive committee responsible for discovering new areas of expansion. The expansion could be accomplished through merger, acquisition, or broadening of their existing product line. Their self-imposed restriction was that the expansion should be in related fields to enable the concern to remain an integrated company.

National Housing Products was incorporated in Delaware in 1931 and maintains its headquarters offices in Portland, Oregon. Prior to 1957, NHP was solely in the lumber business and was not a major voice in the lumber industry. Since 1957, NHP has been one of the fastest growing businesses in the nation and today their size is roughly comparable to Weyerhauser, Boise-Cascade, and Georgia-Pacific, giants in the field.

This phenomenal growth has been brought about principally through acquisition. When NHP started their expansionary policy in 1957, they first merged with another lumber company. Two years later they brought a third lumber company into the fold. NHP then borrowed $7 million to build a small kraft pulp and paper mill. Also the firm purchased a corrugated box plant to use its product. Then, rushing down the path to integration, NHP acquired a chain of 52 lumberyards in Oregon and Colorado. They have since added paper companies and a home-building company so that today NHP is strong in plywood and lumber sales and is a growing force in such products as fine paper, newsprint, prefab housing, mobile homes, and office supplies. From timberland to finished product, NHP, like its large competitors, is thoroughly integrated.

541

As the result of the ongoing series of acquisitions and an internal expansion program, National Housing Products now has some 63 manufacturing plants and some 108 retail and wholesale distribution centers in the United States. It already has interests in mills and plants in half a dozen countries, and is expanding further abroad.

COMPANY OBJECTIVES

The program of rapid expansion discussed above has been somewhat fueled by the objectives of NHP. In an interview with Mr. West, chief executive officer, he was asked about the overall objectives of the company. He gave the following answer:

We have spent a lot of time on this subject in our company. Our objective is to increase the shareholder's value, and the best way to do that is consistently to increase the earnings per share by 20 percent compounded annually. This concept avoids over-stressing the price of our shares in the market, which would suggest a short-term view. We are much more interested in consistency and permanence. If the basic value is developed by the company in the long term the price of our stock should reflect it. We want a high but not delicate price-earnings ratio. Up to 30 is good. Between 30 and 60 would be fragile. We don't need that. The price itself is a short-term thing, and not in our control, but earnings are. This concept of consistently increasing earnings on a long-term basis is one that we use universally throughout the company, and all of the subordinate objectives of the company obtain their relevance from this basic objective.

FUTURE EXPANSION PLANS

Continuing to strive for their objective of increasing shareholder wealth via increasing earnings per share 20 percent compounded annually, NHP was again searching for an area in which to expand. The field they were searching for had to meet two criteria:

1. It had to be profitable by itself.
2. It had to be of a nature that would enhance the sales of their present product line.

The first alternative they considered was stepping up their involvement in the development and construction of primary housing projects.

Housing market

They considered the data in Exhibit 1 depicting housing requirements versus anticipated housing starts. The graph corresponded to the unit and dollar data through 1970 shown in Exhibit 2.

On the surface, the housing market seemed to present ample opportunity for profit taking by NHP both through the development projects themselves and added sales of lumber and prefab homes. However, this alternative was rejected not only due to other alternatives but because NHP had been receiving financial data on the national economy indicating the strong possibility that the mortgage market would soon be tightening up. Because private housing tracts require a great deal of front loading of debt and sales dependent upon the availability of mortgage money, the executive committee felt that the risk involved was too great.

The second alternative for an expansionary area explored by the committee was again in construction, the particular field being that of office buildings.

OFFICE BUILDING MARKET

Strong growth was indicated in the demand for office space throughout the United States. The indicators of this demand were:

1. The labor force had steadily increased from 72 million in 1960 to 81 million in 1967.
2. As a percent of labor force, white-collar workers had increased from 27 percent in 1960 to 36 percent in 1967.
3. The square footage requirements per office worker had increased from 110 square feet in the late fifties to 200 square feet by the late sixties.

Each of the three indicators showed signs of continuing to increase. This, coupled with the relative ease of obtaining financing for office buildings and the large depreciation benefits that accrue to the investor builder, made the office building market appear, indeed, lucrative. However, even in the light of the potential market the NHP executive committee rejected this alternative for various reasons. One reason was that it did not fit their second criteria; That is, office buildings would not appreciably add to the sales of their present product line, other than possibly office supplies. Second, they had a decided lack of experience in the field and did not want to take the risk of having to pay for an education in office building construction. Third, the measurement of success in this type of endeavor differs quite markedly from the measurements generally accepted by the public (shareholders). In the building industry, profit is measured via the cash flow; Theoretically profit before taxes should equal profit after taxes due to the large depreciation write-off. On the other hand the public and most financial analysts are measuring companies in the terms of maximizing profit after taxes.

The third alternative considered by the executive committee was in the realm of recreation. The particular facet of recreation was in the development of recreation land, the trick here being the purchase of raw land, building of recreational facilities, subdividing the land into individual lots, and selling the lots to the public.

RECREATION LAND MARKET

Many factors led observers to believe that the development and sale of recreation land units would be a dynamic area of growth in the economy for years to come.

Leisure time is one of those factors; for example, in the San Francisco area, leisure time for a working person will increase from 1,726 hours per year in 1965 to 1,873 hours in 1985. The effect of this added leisure time can be illustrated by what happened in California in 1966, when 5,340 families were turned away from public beaches and parks on Labor Day. During that same holiday weekend, 86,630 families were refused admittance to camping sites in California State Parks.

In addition to being able to satisfy the leisure time need of the American public, recreation land units would also appeal to that segment of the population wishing to invest in improved land to capitalize on their increased income. The increasing number of families and the greater affluence of those families was another factor leading to the expected boom in the demand for recreation land. The magnitude of these increases is illustrated in Exhibit 3.

Yet another potentially explosive factor in the American economy to be considered when estimating demand for recreational land units is the propensity of the public to spend their personal savings. As indicated in Exhibit 4, disposable personal income and personal savings are growing at a phenomenal rate. The leveling off and decrease of personal savings for 1968 and 1969 reflected the commonly held belief that the propensity to consume would indeed increase.

To determine the total market for recreation land units, the market research group for NHP pegged families earning $15,000+ per year as comprising the bulk of the market. The number of families in this group is reflected in Exhibit 5.

Utilizing all of the aforementioned data, best estimates of current actual sales of recreation land units, and with assistance from outside real estate consultants, the NHP Market Research group developed a forecast of expected total demand for recreation land units (Exhibit 6).

With the expected increase in recreation homesites, the available land for further development will be decreasing. This phenomena produces a 20 percent per annum gain in land value of recreational land. Ten percent is a normal per annum gain for good real estate so recreational land is anticipated to be more than double in value increase.

After reviewing the information on recreation land, the NHP executive committee agreed that an undertaking of this nature would fit in very well with their expansionary plans and criteria for the following reasons:

1. The analysts have figured that NHP could make a 17.7 percent profit of gross sales; Therefore, it met the first criteria.
2. NHP could have a captive market for sales of their prefab, mobile, and on-site constructed homes, and would also enhance lumber sales. Historically 2 percent of land unit purchasers construct a home on the lot.

In the absence of large organized competition in the recreation land market, NHP further believed that they could gain consumer confidence through the fact that they were listed on the New York Stock Exchange.

PROCEEDING WITH EXPANSION

After having made the "go" decision on the recreation land business, NHP has tentatively agreed to purchase 125,000 acres for development. In addition, they have constructed plans for development, sales, and completion of the projects. Development activities will begin with the letting of contracts for the construction of roads, water and sewer systems, and recreational facilities. NHP would make arrangements with local utilities for electricity and telephone service. It is expected that the roads, sewer, and water facilities serving a lot will be completed within one to two years after a lot is sold, or completed according to a program based on the progress of lot sales.

Recreational facilities will include some or all of the following: manmade lakes, marinas, clubhouses, golf courses, swimming pools, tennis courts, and equestrian facilities.

Sales efforts will begin after access roads are cut, probably within nine months after acquisition of the property. Each project will have its own sales force under the direction of a sales manager.

It will be National Housing Products' policy to construct projects with substantial recreational facilities either included in the project or located nearby and to emphasize in its selling program the development use of the property by the lot purchaser and acquisition of the property for investment.

In undertaking this project, management is aware that there is, of course, risk to the shareholder. Their policy in the past has been to accept a risk of 10 percent capital loss on projects having a possible 15–40 percent gain. In committing themselves to this project they do not want to have their total investment exceed 25 percent of projected year total assets. The salvage value of the land would recover approximately 15 percent.

To assist the executive committee in determining the proper financing package, the sales department prepared sales cycles as shown in Exhibit 7. They have developed four different sales patterns based on possible future economic situations. It is run out for five years, for the company fully expects to have no more than a five-year cycle on the development projects.

The sales department further defined the expected sales patterns by obtaining probabilities for the occurrence of the four states of nature. They were:

	Percent
State of nature 1	5
State of nature 2	35
State of nature 3	40
State of nature 4	20

Additional planning for the nationwide NHP projects indicated that lot size will vary significantly, from one-third acre per lot up to two acres per lot. Due to this variation, as well as the differing desirability of individual lots (proximity to lakes, recreational facilities, and so on) selling price will vary from a low of $5,000 up to as much as $25,000.

Sales will be made pursuant to land sales contracts or notes secured by first deeds of trust. Initial payments (including down payments or prepaid interest or both) should normally be in the range of 10–15 percent of total sales price. The notes will be payable in level monthly installments, consisting of both interest and principal. Effective interest rates will range about 9 percent, and final maturities from 5–10 years.

In their financing package, the executive committee will need a complete analytical process that trades opportunity versus risk as affecting long-term debt planning and an accounting footnote that describes technique for handling income and account receivable/bad debt. In addition, they will need to identify the items of analysis in an annotated outline form that can be used in working with their financial sources.

EXHIBIT 1
NATIONAL HOUSING PRODUCTS (A)
Housing gap

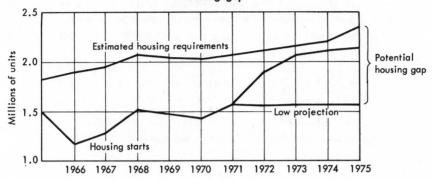

EXHIBIT 2
NATIONAL HOUSING PRODUCTS (A)
Private housing starts in United States

	Year	*Units*	*Dollars*
	1965.......	1,450,600	$20,351,000,000
	1966.......	1,141,500	N/A
	1967.......	1,268,400	$17,885,000,000
	1968.......	1,478,800	$22,423,000,000
Forecast	1969.......	1,445,500	$23,689,000,000
	1970.......	1,414,000	$21,911,000,000

EXHIBIT 3
NATIONAL HOUSING PRODUCTS (A)
Primary families* in United States
(in percent)

Year	*Family income levels in constant (1967) dollars*					
	Under $3,000	$3,000– 4,999	$5,000– 9,999	$10,000– 14,999	$15,000 and over	*Median income*
1950...............	24.2	24.8	39.7	11.3		$5,069
1955...............	19.7	18.5	44.6	12.6	4.5	$6,055
1960...............	16.8	15.0	43.0	17.3	7.9	$6,962
1965...............	13.0	13.3	38.9	22.6	12.2	$8,082
1969 (projected)	9.3	10.7	34.0	26.7	19.2	$9,433

	1950	*1955*	*1960*	*1965*	*1970 (projected)*
* Primary families.............	38,838	41,732	44,905	47,720	51,110

EXHIBIT 4
NATIONAL HOUSING PRODUCTS (A)
Personal income and savings
(figures in billions)

Year	Personal income	Disposable personal income	Personal income
1960...................	401.0	350.0	17.0
1965...................	538.9	473.2	28.4
1967...................	629.3	546.3	40.4
1968 (projected).........	688.7	591.2	40.4
1969 (projected).........	748.9	631.6	37.6

EXHIBIT 5
NATIONAL HOUSING PRODUCTS (A)
Number of families with income greater than $15,000

Year	Primary families	Percent of $15,000+	Families with $15,000+ income
1950..................	38,838,000	N/A	
1955..................	41,732,000	4.5	1,877,940
1960..................	44,905,000	7.9	3,547,495
1965..................	47,720,000	12.3	5,869,560
1969 (projected).......	51,110,000	19.2	9,813,120

EXHIBIT 6
NATIONAL HOUSING PRODUCTS (A)
Recreation land units
(total market)

Year	Annual sales	Cumulative sales
1967..........	500,000	500,000
1968..........	537,500	1,037,500
1969..........	577,813	1,615,313
1970..........	621,148	2,236,461
1971..........	667,735	2,904,196
1972..........	717,815	3,904,196
1973..........	771,651	4,393,662
1974..........	829,525	5,223,187
1975..........	891,739	6,114,926
1976..........	958,620	7,073,546

EXHIBIT 7
NATIONAL HOUSING PRODUCTS (A)
Probability sales range

	Sub	Normal	Good	Super
State of nature / Percent of total units sold	*1*	*2*	*3*	*4*
Year 1	—	—	5%	15%
Year 2	15%	35%	50%	55%
Year 3	35%	35%	30%	20%
Year 4	35%	20%	10%	10%
Year 5	15%	10%	5%	—

EXHIBIT 8
NATIONAL HOUSING PRODUCTS (A)
Estimated project cost factors

A. Raw land—Averaging $500 per acre. One salable lot will be sold out of each acre purchased.
B. Planning and design—20 percent of land price.
C. Administrative—20 percent of land, spread over five years.
D. Improvement costs (including roads, utilities, and recreational facilities)—$6 for every dollar of land costs.
E. Selling costs (including commission and promotion)—10 percent of sales price.
F. Debt for project—Approximately 7 percent interest rate.
G. Improvements to be 80 percent completed after the first year with the remaining being completed by the end of the second year.
H. In addition to amortizing the debt, the firm will make lump-sum payments of 11.7 percent of total debt in the second year, 25.1 percent in the third year, 4.9 percent in the fourth year, and 4.9 percent in the fifth year.

EXHIBIT 9

NATIONAL HOUSING PRODUCTS (A)
Balance sheet data for years ending December 31, 1962–66
(dollar figures in thousands)

	1962	1963	1964	1965	1966
Current Assets	$122,813	$136,374	$233,975	$275,613	$ 301,411
Property and equipment	166,013	169,990	392,887	483,039	459,540
Realty	—	—	—	—	—
Other	7,831	10,123	25,212	45,267	240,807
Total Assets	$296,657	$316,487	$652,074	$803,919	$1,001,758
Current Liabilities	$ 54,244	$ 67,423	$ 91,489	$ 96,264	$ 134,411
Long-term	136,565	121,858	223,661	356,788	473,959
Other	—	3,705	18,966	21,870	25,504
Equity	105,848	123,501	317,958	328,997	368,154
Total Liabilities & Equity	$296,657	$316,487	$652,074	$803,919	$1,001,758

EXHIBIT 10

NATIONAL HOUSING PRODUCTS (A)
Income statement for years ended December 31, 1962–66
(dollar figures in thousands)

	1962	1963	1964	1965	1966
Sales	$334,441	$416,571	$690,656	$802,391	$934,372
Gross profit	74,012	98,002	174,440	203,453	228,570
Earnings before Interest & Taxes	20,895	29,070	58,503	68,034	73,650
Fixed charges	7,678	8,232	10,944	16,483	21,297
Income taxes	4,145	7,640	18,905	17,381	19,864
Net income	$ 9,072	$ 13,198	$ 28,654	$ 34,170	$ 32,489
Preferred dividend	—	—	—	7,029	7,124
Available common	9,072	13,198	21,659	27,141	25,384
E.P.S.	$ 1.14	$ 1.55	$ 2.28	$ 2.96	$ 2.65
Common shares outstanding	7,940	8,500	9,500	9,160	9,590

EXHIBIT 11

NATIONAL HOUSING PRODUCTS (A)
Source and application of funds for years ended December 31, 1962–66
(dollar figures in thousands)

	1962	1963	1964	1965	1966
Net income	$ 9,072	$ 13,198	$ 28,654	$ 34,170	$ 32,489
Depreciation	13,026	19,176	32,623	36,672	37,913
"Cash flow"	22,099	32,374	61,177	70,842	70,402
New debt	73,038	(10,944)	117,083	136,030	120,884
New equity	592	12,415	174,326	(12,778)	17,878
Total Sources	$95,729	$ 33,845	$352,586	$194,094	$209,164
Dividends paid	$ 2,865	$ 3,018	$ 8,442	$ 10,352	$ 11,193
Capital spending	16,044	23,302	114,600	98,365	182,787
Other investments	74,719	7,143	156,009	48,514	27,218
Increase in working capital	2,101	382	73,535	36,863	(12,034)
Total Uses	$95,729	$ 33,845	$352,586	$194,094	$209,164

NATIONAL HOUSING
PRODUCTS (B)

FIFTH YEAR PROGRESS REVIEW

For the operating year 1971, NHP has suffered a net loss of $160.6 million, including a pretax operating loss of $141.2 million on overall realty operations, and a $65 million (pretax) write-down of realty assets. Several factors combined to magnify this loss:

1. The economy has been in a recession for 18–20 months, resulting in
    a) a higher propensity to save, thus withdrawing these funds from the potential market
    b) bad debt jumped significantly, returning recreation land to the company at a time when it was pushing hard to get rid of it
    c) the rate of sales has slowed so that only 60 percent of projected sales have been sold instead of the anticipated 100 percent
2. Several states have brought suits against the company to stop certain sales practices, especially the stressing of investment opportunities in recreation land sales. This has temporarily tied up some 45 percent of the company's unsold lots. The litigation has the possibility of significantly reducing the potential market by restricing purchasers to those more likely to use the lots for a second home.
3. Five class action suits, similar to those charges above, have been brought against the company. The suits involve some $350 million of already completed sales.
4. The rising concern over the ecology has resulted in strong pressure on various governmental agencies. Stricter enforcement of existing rules as well as new regulations have increased development costs and delayed sales.

The executive committee has been requested to analyze what went wrong and submit a Problem Analysis Report to the president. (Specifically, what was wrong with the original study.)

The decision has already been made to get out of the recreation land business and concentrate on what NHP does well. Unfortunately, with the economy coming out of a recession, all indicators show that home and other construction will be one of the strongest activities in the recovery economy. NHP must meet the increased demand or lose their strategic market position. Much of their ease in obtaining finances has been because of the unique combination of product lines. That position will become increasingly important as manufactured homes becomes the primary mode for housing. The profitable economies of scale must be capitalized now. See Exhibit 12 for new capital needs.

In addition, the president wants the committee to prepare a financial recovery analysis. The report should discuss the financial dynamics and ramifications of how NHP can change its capital structure during difficult times. Implicit in that change, is the replacement of long-term debt from a bad to good venture. The report should identify basic assumptions and logic sequences that can be summarized in a flowchart exhibit. Exhibit flow should trace *from* conditions/correcting assumptions *to* the recommended solution and alternatives. (See Exhibits 13, Balance sheet; 14, Income Statement; and 15, source and application of funds.)

EXHIBIT 12
NATIONAL HOUSING PRODUCTS (B)
Capitalization factors

1. *Projected Sales Growth:*   33 percent increase
   (based on commitments from dealers and main product lines forecast model)

2. *Capitalization rates*   *Incremental sales to capital*
   Plants and equipment.......................   2 to 1
   Working Capital...........................   10 to 1

3. *Long-term debt service factors (in millions)*
   (Current, not including above increases)

	1972	1973	1974
Regular operations...........	$ 61.5	164.8	56.9
Realty...................	122.2	—	50.0
	183.7	164.8	106.9

EXHIBIT 13

NATIONAL HOUSING PRODUCTS (B)
Balance sheet data for year ended
December 31, 1971
(dollar figures in thousands)

Current assets........................	$ 933,430
Property and equipment................	1,106,203
Realty...............................	632,731
Other................................	920,505
Notes receivable......................	597,830
Total Assets.................	$4,190,699
Current liabilities.....................	$ 576,933
Long-term debt.......................	2,058,394
Other................................	41,638
Equity...............................	1,513,734
Total Liabilities & Equity.......	$4,190,699

EXHIBIT 14

NATIONAL HOUSING PRODUCTS (B)
Income statement for year ended December 31, 1971
(dollar figures in thousands)

Sales..	$3,500,801
Earnings before interest and taxes................	3,728
Fixed charges..............................	122,664
Taxes..	(47,979)
Net income before extraordinary charge...........	(70,966)
Extraordinary charge........................	(96,000)
Net Income.................................	$ (166,966)
Earnings per share...........................	$ (5.23)

EXHIBIT 15

NATIONAL HOUSING PRODUCTS (B)
Source and application of funds for year ended
December 31, 1971
(dollar figures in thousands)

From operations, net.....................	$ 57,646
Other proceeds, net.....................	41,338
Net new debt..........................	22,297
Total Sources.................	$121,281
Cash dividends.........................	$ 15,157
Capital expense........................	232,781
Decrease in net working capital...........	(143,792)
Decrease in realty, inventory.............	(17,159)
Other, net.............................	34,294
Total Uses...................	$121,281

AVCO FINANCIAL SERVICES, LTD.

MR. H. W. MERRYMAN, the president of Avco Financial Services, Inc., has been aware for some time that the earnings of the company's Australian subsidiary, Avco Financial Services, Ltd., have been growing at an appreciable rate. He knows that if the earnings growth of the Australian subsidiary could be sustained, the profits of Avco Financial Services, Inc. would also increase. However, since the U.S. parent company owned 100 percent of the common equity of the Australian subsidiary it was classified as a foreign investment by both the United States and Australia. This classification imposed several constraints upon the flexibility of both the parent company and the subsidiary with regard to the raising of capital. Thus, Mr. Merryman was faced with the predicament of knowing that earnings could be increased substantially by increasing the debt and equity base of the Australian subsidiary, but also knowing that there were many obstacles opposing the increase in the capital structure of a foreign subsidiary. In May 1972, (halfway through the company's fiscal year) he was examining alternatives to present to the board of directors for the optimum measures to increase the earnings from the Australian subsidiary over the next five fiscal years.

CORPORATE HISTORY

Avco Financial Services became a legal entity on May 5, 1971, when two large consumer finance companies, Avco Financial Services, Inc. (formerly Seaboard Finance Company) and Avco Delta Corporation were legally merged, after operating under common management and a common name for approximately a year.

554

The origins of the two predecessor companies were strikingly similar, as each grew to substantial size during the 1960s. Seaboard was incorporated in Delaware on December 28, 1943, to continue a business begun in Los Angeles, California, in 1927. Seaboard was acquired by Avco Corporation in January 1969. Avco Delta Corporation began in London, England, and Ontario, Canada, as Delta Acceptance Corporation Limited in 1954. In 1964, Delta Acceptance was acquired by Avco Corporation.

Avco Corporation, a Delaware corporation, owns more than 95 percent of all the outstanding voting shares of Avco Financial Services, Inc., including all the issues and outstanding common stock. The company conducts its operations in two major areas of the consumer finance business, namely consumer loans and sales finance. However, under its new name, the company is expanding into wider financial services including second mortgage financing, leasing, and a number of other related activities. In addition, through subsidiaries, it conducts an insurance business, which in part is related directly to the finance activities.

The business of the company requires a relatively small investment in fixed assets, its resources being principally invested in a large number of self-liquidating obligations. On November 30, 1971, approximately 93 percent of its total assets on a consolidated basis consisted of current assets, most of which were installment receivables. The company does not own any substantial amount of physical property other than office furniture and fixtures. Aside from a very few branch office locations, and the Newport Beach corporate headquarters, the real properties occupied by Avco Financial Services are under leases for varying terms to provide space for the various supervisory and branch offices and related service functions.

There were 1,397 branch offices of the company on November 30, 1971 compared to 744 in operation 10 years ago. The offices now in operation are in 3 Australian states, the Australian Capital Territory, and all 10 Canadian provinces and 47 states of the United States.

In 1965, the first Australian branch was opened. A survey had been made in 1964 which considered the different financing possibilities of opening a branch office. They had the opportunity to purchase an existing finance company; however, the problems outweighed the advantages and it was decided to create a new company. The first office was opened in Melbourne. After reaching sufficient size they moved their headquarters to Sydney. At present, there are 60 offices in Australia.

COMPETITION

When Avco went into Australia in 1965, there was virtually no competition because banks did not make personal loans. Large sales finance companies do exist and Australian banks have large holdings in them, but these companies lacked the convenience that the personal loan companies offered. Few other American finance companies are in Australia and the balance-of-payments restrictions now act as a barrier in keeping them out. Avco's biggest competitors at the moment are American banks which have gone to Australia and purchased finance companies. Potential competition also exists from Australian banks changing their policy and making personal loans. This is almost certain to happen in the future; however, Avco feels that by that time they will have established a position that will be difficult for the banks to overtake.

THE AUSTRALIAN ECONOMY

Recent figures show that the GNP rate in terms of real product was 8.6 percent in 1968–69, and 5.5 percent in 1969–70. The percent rate of change in Gross National Product has risen steadily over the past decade and has been similar to the average annual growth rate of the United States. The per capita Gross National Product, ranked by current growth rate, is higher than that of the United States. The total population of Australia is 12,000,000 with over 93 percent located in the six largest cities of Australia.

The Australian government has a policy of low unemployment which is proven by its almost steady unemployment rate in the last 10 years. There has been a steady increase in savings and in bank deposits. The sharp rise in retail sales coupled with an installment credit increase indicates a continued growth potential of consumer financing. Other indicators that support the growth potential of consumer financing are the upward increase in new motor vehicle registration along with a steady increase in the consumer index. Statistical data supporting the above trends can be found in Exhibits 1 through 3.

Avco's experience has been that the Australians are very industrious and meet their obligations. Their payment record is exceptionally good and their default is about 25 percent less than that in the United States.

The Australian banking system follows the Commonwealth system. It is not uncommon for a bank to have hundreds of branches, scattered throughout the country. The banks do not make personal loans to individuals. Permission must be given by the Reserve Bank of Australia to get funds in and out of the country.

BANK LINES OF CREDIT

Avco Financial Services had lines of credit of $605 million with 216 commercial banks as of November 30, 1971, an increase of $125 million since November 30, 1970. The U.S. rates ranged during 1971 and 1970 from 5½–7 percent per annum and the Australian and Canadian rates ranged from 5½–9 percent. During the year ended November 30, 1971, the maximum amount of short-term bank borrowings as determined by month-end balances was $393 million at December 31, 1970 and the minimum amount was $270 million on November 30, 1971.

Australian banks have followed the practice of severely limiting the granting of credit to financial institutions. The Australian operation has bank lines of credit with U.S. banks in the amount of $29 million, all of which in 1971 was guaranteed by Avco Financial Services. Since financial companies by their very nature have a large pyramiding of debt, institutional investors insist on certain covenants in all debt agreements. One of these covenants is that if more than 2 percent of total assets is invested in foreign holdings, the excess must be deducted from the parent's net worth for financial evaluations. All loans to the Australian operation from U.S. banks directly influence the adjusted consolidated net worth of the parent company since they are guaranteed by the parent company. In 1971, $6.99 million was to be adjusted against net worth.

Current plans are to attempt to eliminate the guarantee of the parent company. The Australian subsidiary has established a strong enough financial position, so banks will probably now be willing to make loans directly without the guarantee. (See Exhibits 4 and 5.) In 1971 they were in the final stages of establishing a $5 million line of credit with a U.S. bank whereby no parent company guarantee is required. It is expected that the guarantee will be dropped from all future loans to the Australian subsidiary. Since foreign debt is considered a foreign asset for calculation of total assets invested in foreign holdings, the elimination of these guarantees will immediately put them far enough under the 2 percent level of total assets that this will no longer be a problem.

FOREIGN INVESTMENT CONSTRAINTS

In 1965 when AFS, Ltd., was organized as Seaboard Finance Company, Ltd., the board of directors debated over the amount of the initial equity to be provided. Initial recommendations were for a sum of $5 million; However, the parent company had recently experienced some financial problems. There was the expectation of devaluation of the British pound sterling which could affect the value of the Australian pound, and the recently announced balance-of-payments Guidelines (see Appendix II) clouded the foreign financing picture. As a result of all the uncertainty surrounding a foreign capital venture, the decision was made to start the Australian subsidiary with an initial capitalization of $1 million which was supplied over a period of two years.

Because of the February 1965, Voluntary Cooperation Program to induce business to reduce their overseas capital expenditures, Avco limited the amount of funds transferred to build up the equity base of the Australian subsidiary. (See Exhibit 6.) Then in January 1968, the voluntary plan was made mandatory which severely restricted the outflow of funds from the United States. The net effect was to force the foreign subsidiaries to finance their capital requirements through foreign sources of funds. Some of the normal sources of foreign funds available are:

1. Increase the local borrowing base of the foreign affiliate by capitalizing intercompany debt.
2. Offer assets of the foreign affiliate as collateral for loans instead of depending on parent guarantees.
3. Float Eurodollar bond issues.
4. Sell equity in foreign operations to host country investors.

One of the means of providing capital to the Australian subsidiary was to have U.S. banks loan Eurodollar funds. However, the banks required AFS, Inc., to guarantee these loans. This resulted in a twofold impact on AFS, Inc. First, if the debt (defined as formally borrowed money) to equity ratio of AFS, Ltd., went over 5 to 1, the parent company would be subject to the Interest Equalization tax. Second, any amount of foreign investment including guaranteed loans which exceeds 2 percent of AFS, Inc. total assets reduces the net worth of the parent company for calculation of debt capacity.

A finance company normally has a very high debt to equity ratio which results in a need for continuing debt financing. However, if funds are not available or are limited by various restrictions, the interest rate paid becomes excessive and cuts into profits. Therefore, there is a continuing effort made to evaluate the sources of funds available and their respective charges in order to finance at the lowest possible rate.

It would appear that a simple way to increase the capital of the Australian subsidiary would be to issue stock which would not only increase the equity but would also increase the base for debt financing. However, the growth rate of the Australian company is so great and the potential is so favorable that stock could not be sold at a price which would account for the future increases yet be acceptable to the purchasers.

Avco's wholly owned Australian Insurance Company does invest in AFS, Ltd., by purchasing preferred shares. At present the equity base of AFS Ltd., has been increased by $3,500,000 through the sale of preferred shares. (See Exhibit 6 and Appendix III.) Also $500,000 was sold to a local Australian insurance company.

THE AUSTRALIAN FINANCIAL SITUATION

The money market

A common means of financing in Australia is the bill market. Banks act as intermediaries and charge 1–1½ percent for their stamp and guarantee. The intercompany market (a recent development over the last five years) in Australia is somewhat similar to our commercial paper market in that when company A wants funds it goes directly to company B without dealing through the banks. Avco has used this method from the beginning and has helped to promote it.

Avco also uses what they call "back-to-back" financing through their wholly owned Australian insurance company. They established the insurance company in Australia through their Canadian insurance company. This arrangement allowed Avco to invest in the Canadian company which in turn invested in the Australian company without the balance-of-payments restrictions. The Australian insurance company puts their lendable funds into the money market through a broker who in turn loans it back to Avco. Avco in this way borrows its own money.

Selling to the public requires Reserve Bank approval. Avco, being a small company in the beginning, did not ask for it since they were already active in the intercompany market. In fact, they instinctively stayed away from the Reserve Bank. Beneficial, a competitor, however did go to the Reserve Bank to ask for approval for local borrowing. What they received was approval for a ratio of 9 to 1. In other words for every $9 brought into the country they could borrow $1. They were told this ratio applied to all borrowing including the "Intercompany Market." Beneficial, of course, was disturbed since they were used to working on a pyramid going up, not one going down. Avco followed this development with a great deal of interest and found their instincts had been correct in staying away from the Reserve Bank. As a result such a ratio had never been imposed on them. However, it did hang as a cloud over their heads not to have Reserve Bank approval and occasionally forced them to pay slightly more for their money.

Avco has now (April 1972) gone to the Reserve Bank and asked for approval for local borrowing. (See Exhibit 8.) In the past, the Reserve Bank of Australia has made it very difficult for foreign-owned companies and subsidiaries of foreign companies to get approval to borrow locally. As a result, foreign companies have looked to other places for their money, such as Eurodollars, American dollars, and Canadian dollars. There has been a big influx of investment capital into Australia due to this situation. Now there has been a change in the economy and money is not in as much demand as before and is starting to pile up. The Reserve Bank has decided to liberalize some of its rules to make use of this money.

In the past, the Reserve Bank stipulated that a foreign company could borrow 75 percent of its increase in working capital. Working capital was defined as current assets (receivables) collectible within 12 months. When Avco went to the Reserve Bank and asked for permission to borrow locally, their timing was propitious. The Reserve Bank had changed its attitude and the current thinking now is that current assets include receivables collectible within three years. This includes the entire receivables portfolio for Avco. For next year, 75 percent of the projected increase in working capital means that $10 million will be available for local borrowing.

Having reviewed the limitations imposed on a foreign subsidiary and the conditional and financial constraints imposed by the respective governments and creditors, Mr. Merryman was preparing to go before the board of directors to propose a long-range plan for optimizing the company's ability to increase the capital base for the Australian subsidiary.

EXHIBIT 1
AVCO FINANCIAL SERVICES
Trends of gross national product

A. North America and Oceania: Estimated average annual growth rates

Region and country	Percent change in total Gross National Product				Change for preceding year				Percent change in GNP per capita				Change from preceding year				Current rate of population growth
	1950–1955	1955–1960	1960–1965	1965–1969	1966	1967	1968	1969	1950–1955	1955–1960	1960–1965	1965–1969	1966	1967	1968	1969	1969
Canada	5.5	4.1	5.7	5.0	7.0	3.3	4.8	4.8	2.7	1.5	3.9	3.2	4.6	1.3	3.1	3.3	1.7
United States	4.3	2.2	4.8	4.2	6.5	2.5	4.9	2.8	2.6	0.5	3.3	3.1	5.3	1.4	3.8	1.8	1.1
Australia	3.9	4.0	5.2	4.7	0.9	6.4	3.2	8.6	1.7	1.7	3.1	2.8	-0.1	4.5	1.4	6.6	1.8
New Zealand	3.9	3.8	4.9	2.7	3.9	-0.6	2.5	5.0	1.5	1.7	2.8	1.2	2.0	-2.5	1.6	3.6	1.5

B. North America and Oceania: Trend of Gross National Product in Constant 1968 Prices
Total Gross National Product (billions of dollar equivalents)

		1960	1961	1962	1963	1964	1965	1966	1967	1968	1969
Canada	1.081 C $	43.3	44.5	47.6	50.1	53.6	57.1	61.1	63.1	66.1	69.3
United States		596.8	608.4	648.2	674.1	710.9	755.8	805.1	825.3	865.7	890.0
Australia	0.893 A $	18.7	19.6	19.8	20.9	22.3	24.0	24.2	25.8	26.6	28.9
New Zealand	0.893 NZ $	3.6	3.7	3.8	4.1	4.3	4.6	4.8	4.7	4.9	5.1

C. North America and Oceania: Per Capita Gross National Product in Constant 1968 Prices
(dollar equivalents)

	1960	1961	1962	1963	1964	1965	1966	1967	1968	1969
Canada	2,416	2,436	2,558	2,647	2,780	2,913	3,047	3,087	3,182	3,286
United States	3,303	3,310	3,472	3,559	3,701	3,884	4,089	4,145	4,303	4,380
Australia	1,837	1,886	1,856	1,927	2,016	2,129	2,108	2,202	2,232	2,380
New Zealand	1,524	1,548	1,547	1,615	1,672	1,749	1,784	1,740	1,767	1,830

Source: Excerpts from GNP, by the Agency for International Development, 1971.

EXHIBIT 2
AVCO FINANCIAL SERVICES
Developed countries, 1969
(ranking by current growth rates)

Total gross national product

Country	Rate
Japan	13.8
Germany	7.8
France	6.2
Australia	5.9
Italy	5.6
Portugal	5.5
Netherlands	5.4
Ireland	5.3
Average (Weighted)	5.3
Finland	5.2
Austria	5.0
Belgium	4.9
Canada	4.8
South Africa	4.8
Denmark	4.6
Sweden	4.5
Luxembourg	4.2
Norway	4.2
Switzerland	4.2
New Zealand	3.8
United States	3.8
United Kingdom	2.4
Iceland	−2.3

Per capita gross national product

Country	Rate
Japan	12.5
Germany	7.2
France	5.4
Ireland	4.9
Italy	4.8
Austria	4.7
Finland	4.7
Portugal	4.6
Belgium	4.5
Average (Weighted)	4.4
Netherlands	4.3
Australia	4.0
Luxembourg	4.0
Denmark	3.9
Sweden	3.8
Canada	3.2
Norway	3.2
Switzerland	2.9
United States	2.8
New Zealand	2.6
South Africa	2.4
United Kingdom	2.0
Iceland	−3.2

Source: Excerpts from GNP, by the Agency for International Development, 1971.

EXHIBIT 3
AVCO FINANCIAL SERVICES
Lending operations of finance companies in Australia
A. Summary (dollars in millions)

Period	Amount financed during period	Collections and other liquidations during period			Balances outstanding at end of period		
		Contracts including charges	Contracts excluding charges	Total all contracts	Contracts including charges	Contracts excluding charges	Total all contracts*
Year—							
1965–66	1,916.2	1,062.1	1,065.9	2,128.1	1,471.4	438.7	1,910.1
1966–67	2,302.1	1,163.6	1,359.4	2,523.1	1,630.0	478.5	2,108.5
1967–68	2,724.0	1,250.1	1,549.5	2,799.6	1,850.2	587.7	2,437.9
1968–69	3,239.4	1,418.3	1,912.6	3,330.9	2,105.5	711.7	2,817.2
1969–70	3,805.7	1,612.7	2,206.2	3,818.9	2,401.0	973.2	3,374.3
Quarter ended—							
December 1968	865.3	352.7	509.6	862.3	1,996.2	653.2	2,649.4
March 1969	779.4	361.3	453.9	815.1	2,025.9	694.5	2,720.4
June 1969	842.7	369.8	512.6	882.4	2,105.5	711.7	2,817.2
September 1969	919.4	391.5	517.8	909.2	2,180.7	786.1	2,996.6
December 1969	983.2	406.4	552.2	958.6	2,277.0	860.6	3,137.6
March 1970	907.7	398.1	535.3	933.3	2,326.6	925.4	3,251.9
June 1970	995.5	416.7	601.0	1,017.7	2,401.0	973.2	3,374.3

* Amounts shown in this column are intended to provide a broad overall measure of balances outstanding. It should be noted, however, that movements in this series may be affected by changes in the proportions of the two components of the series to the total.

EXHIBIT 3 (Continued)

D. Amount financed by type of agreement
(dollars in millions)

| Period | Installment credit for retail sales | Wholesale hire purchase | Other consumer and commercial loans | | Commercial loans | | Factoring | Total |
			Personal loans	Mortgage loans	Repayable at call or within 90 days	Other		
Year—								
1965–66	612.7	488.2	70.6	222.6	288.4	153.1	80.7	1,916.2
1966–67	689.2	719.0	95.5	280.4	323.1	127.0	68.0	2,302.1
1967–68	816.1	855.8	116.9	342.0	386.1	132.2	74.9	2,724.0
1968–69	922.7	944.4	124.2	449.5	534.2	188.6	75.7	3,239.4
1969–70	1,037.0	1,059.7	145.2	565.6	636.4	270.1	91.8	3,805.7
Quarter ended—								
December 1968	252.8	248.0	33.9	122.9	135.8	50.7	21.1	865.3
March 1969	218.7	214.0	26.6	101.9	160.9	39.7	17.5	779.4
June 1969	239.9	256.4	33.2	131.5	110.8	52.3	18.5	842.7
September 1969	249.2	269.9	35.2	132.5	151.0	60.1	21.5	919.4
December 1969	273.5	275.7	41.6	146.4	159.7	61.6	24.7	983.2
March 1970	248.1	239.5	33.9	127.0	174.9	62.9	21.3	907.7
June 1970	266.1	274.5	34.5	159.7	150.8	85.5	24.3	995.5

EXHIBIT 3 (Continued)

C. Balances outstanding by type of agreement
(dollars in millions)

At end of—	Contracts including charges			Contracts excluding charges					Total all contracts*
	Instalment credit for retail sales	Other consumer and commercial loans	Total	Whole sale hire purchase	Commercial loans repayable at call for within 90 days	Other consumer and commercial loans	Factoring	Total	
Year—									
1965–66	990.1	481.3	1,471.4	78.4	65.1	273.4	21.8	438.7	1,910.1
1966–67	1,087.4	542.6	1,630.0	100.8	49.3	306.6	21.7	478.5	2,108.5
1967–68	1,222.0	628.2	1,850.2	127.6	69.9	366.6	23.6	587.7	2,437.9
1968–69	1,380.2	725.2	2,105.5	146.7	62.9	479.5	22.6	711.7	2,817.2
1969–70	1,565.1	835.9	2,401.0	167.4	92.5	686.4	26.9	973.2	3,374.3
Quarter—									
December 1968	1,322.0	674.1	1,996.2	140.2	72.5	416.7	23.8	653.2	2,649.4
March 1969	1,332.9	693.0	2,025.9	132.2	106.1	434.2	22.0	694.5	2,720.4
June 1969	1,380.2	725.2	2,105.5	146.7	62.9	479.5	22.6	711.7	2,817.2
September 1969	1,425.4	755.3	2,180.7	157.3	87.7	518.4	22.8	786.1	2,966.9
December 1969	1,487.4	789.6	2,277.0	165.6	104.3	565.4	25.3	860.6	3,137.6
March 1970	1,521.8	804.7	2,326.6	165.9	116.7	615.1	27.6	925.4	3,251.9
June 1970	1,565.1	835.9	2,401.0	167.4	92.5	686.4	26.9	973.2	3,374.3

* Amounts shown in this column are intended to provide a broad overall measure of total balances outstanding. It should be noted, however, that movements in this series may be affected by changes in the proportions of the two components of the series to the total.

EXHIBIT 3 (Continued)

B. Collections and other liquidations of balances by type of agreement

	Contracts including charges			Contracts excluding charges					Total all contracts
Period	Instalment credit for retail sales	Other consumer and commercial loans	Total	Wholesale hire purchase	Commercial loans repayable at call or within 90 days	Other consumer and commercial loans	Factoring	Total	
Year—									
1965–66	778.9	283.2	1,062.1	474.9	271.9	223.6	95.5	1,065.9	2,128.1
1966–67	854.9	308.7	1,163.6	704.6	340.9	237.8	76.2	1,359.4	2,523.1
1967–68	913.0	337.1	1,250.1	836.6	363.6	265.9	83.3	1,549.5	2,799.6
1968–69	1,026.5	391.8	1,418.3	934.8	537.1	352.9	87.9	1,912.6	3,330.9
1969–70	1,150.7	462.0	1,612.7	1,052.9	603.9	445.7	403.7	2,206.2	3,818.9
Quarter ended—									
December 1968	252.7	100.0	352.7	240.4	153.7	93.1	22.3	509.6	862.3
March 1969	267.9	93.4	361.3	224.4	125.9	81.0	22.5	453.9	815.1
June 1969	263.9	105.9	369.8	244.8	152.9	93.1	21.7	512.6	882.4
September 1969	274.9	116.6	391.5	262.7	127.2	102.9	25.0	517.8	909.2
December 1969	285.2	121.2	406.4	270.8	143.5	110.6	27.3	552.2	958.6
March 1970	288.5	109.6	398.1	242.7	160.8	109.5	22.2	535.3	933.3
June 1970	302.1	114.6	416.7	276.7	172.4	122.8	29.1	601.0	1,017.7

EXHIBIT 3 (concluded)

E. Banks, etc., interest rates and security yields
(Percent)

At end of—

At end of	Fixed deposits — 30 days but less than 3 months*	3 months but less than 12 months	12 months but less than 18 months	18 months	Over 18 months to 24 months	Overdrafts (maximum rate) major trading banks	C'wlth Savings Bank deposits (maximum rate of interest)†	C'wealth Govt. securities‡ Theoretical 2 years	Theoretical 10 years	Theoretical 20 years	Private first mortgages registered in N.S.W.—urban and rural securities‡
1966—June	4.25	4.25	4.50	4.50	4.50‖	7.25	3.50	4.94	5.17	5.25	8.8
1967—June	4.00	4.00	4.25	4.25	4.50	7.25	3.50	4.52	5.03	5.25	8.9
1968—June	4.25	4.25	4.50	4.75	4.75	7.25	3.50	4.84	5.11	5.25	9.2
1969—June	4.25	4.25	4.50	4.75	4.75	7.50	3.75	5.01	5.35	5.48	9.3

Month of— (Fixed deposits by deposit size: "Less than $100,000 / $100,000 and over" for 1969; "Less than $50,000 / $50,000 and over" for 1970)

Month of	30 days but less than 3 months*	3 months but less than 6 months — Less than threshold	3 months but less than 6 months — threshold and over	6 months but less than 12 months — Less than threshold	6 months but less than 12 months — threshold and over	12 months but less than 18 months — Less than threshold	12 months but less than 18 months — threshold and over	18 months to 24 months	Overdrafts (maximum rate) major trading banks	C'wlth Savings Bank deposits†	C'wealth Govt. securities‡ Theoretical 2 years	Theoretical 10 years	Theoretical 20 years	Private first mortgages N.S.W.‡
September 1969	4.70	4.50	4.80	4.50	4.90	4.70	5.00	5.00	7.75	3.75	5.27	5.59	5.66	9.3
December 1969	4.70	4.50	4.80	4.50	4.90	4.70	5.00	5.00	7.75	3.75	5.30	5.64	5.72	9.6
March 1970	5.50	4.80	5.50	4.80	5.50	5.00	5.30	5.50	8.25	5.00	5.85	6.00	6.20	9.8
June 1970	5.50	4.80	5.50	4.80	5.50	5.00	5.30	5.50	8.25	5.00	6.40	6.52	6.60	9.8
September 1970	5.50	4.80	5.50	4.80	5.50	5.00	5.30	5.50	8.25	5.00	6.10	6.49	6.55	9.8

* Banks are permitted to accept fixed deposits in excess of $100,000, for periods of 30 days but less than three months at rates not exceeding the maximum rates shown.

† Subject to interest bearing limits:—prior to 1 March 1967—$6,000; from 1 March 1967—$10,000 and from 1 April 1970—$20,000.

‡ Source: Reserve Bank. Income-tax rebate of 10¢ in the dollar has not been taken into account and the effect of brokerage is excluded. Average for the week is centered on last Wednesday of the month.

§ Revised series, including all mortgages for corporations (other than banks and building societies) and individuals, except completely abnormal amounts of $2m or more in months in which large mortgages are few in number. Annual figures are averages of month, quotations.

‖ From August 1966 to May 1968, interest rate on trading bank fixed deposits with a term of 18 months was 4.25 per cent per annum.

¶ Average rate on mortgages registered in 3 months ending with months shown.

Source: Various excerpts from Topical Law Reports, Commerce Clearing House, 1972.

EXHIBIT 4

AVCO FINANCIAL SERVICES
(formerly Seaboard Finance Company Ltd.)
Balance sheet stated in Australian dollars
(000s omitted)

CURRENT ASSETS

	November 30 1971	November 30 1970	November 30 1969	September 30 1968
Cash	$ 44	$ 6	$ 9	$ 9
Amounts owing under precomputed loan and retail sales contracts—Less unearned charges, 1971, $6,152; 1970, $3,522; 1969, $2,041; 1968, $1,125	$24,659	$14,715	$ 8,841	$4,973
Interest Bearing Loans	5,367	5,493	3,105	1,578
Less: Allowance for losses	(825)	(590)	(364)	(158)
Total Installment Receivables	$29,195	$19,618	$11,582	$6,393
Other Receivables and Prepaid Expenses	21	22	19	21
Total Current Assets	$29,260	$19,646	$11,610	$6,423
Property and equipment at cost, less accumulated depreciation and amortization: 1971, $168; 1970, $114; 1969, $69; 1968, $33	564	452	360	272
Investment in Subsidiaries	1	51	—	—
Deferred Income Taxes	354	242	135	42
Total	$30,179	$20,391	$12,105	$6,737

CURRENT LIABILITIES

	November 30 1971	November 30 1970	November 30 1969	September 30 1968
Notes payable (bank loans and commercial): payable within 12 months (unsecured) ... 7,287				
Less: Foreign Exchange Fluctuation account ... 19	$ 7,268	$16,309	$ 7,957	$3,645
Provision for income tax	876	494	274	26
Accrued interest payable	260	173	81	48

Dealers' reserve....................			35		
Provision for dividend..............		52	88	6	
Amounts owing to parent company (unsecured): payable in 12 months....................		2	2	2	2
Other amounts payable...............		116	184	110	36
Amount payable to related companies..			2,504		
Total Current Liabilities........		$17,146	$11,217	$ 8,430	$3,757
Long-term Debt—Unsecured: Notes payable after 12 months.. $13,473					
Less: Foreign Exchange Fluctuation account.......... 246					
		$ 150	$13,227	$ 1,936	$1,936

SHAREHOLDERS' EQUITY

Capital stock: Preferred, par value $100 a Share..	$ 1,500	$ 3,500	$ 500	$ —
Common, par value $200 a Share..	1,150	1,150	1,150	1,150
Earned surplus.....................	445	1,085	89	(106)
Total Shareholders' Equity......	$ 3,095	$ 5,735	$ 1,739	$1,044
Total...........................	$20,391	$30,179	$12,105	$6,737

SEVEN-YEAR COMPARISON

	Year ended November 30			Year ended September 30			
	1971	1970	1969	1968	1967	1966	1965
Receivables (net).................	$30,020	$20,208	$11,946	$6,551	$3,732	$1,293	$444
Gross Income......................	$ 6,001	$ 3,800	$ 2,679	$1,440	$ 671	$ 225	$ 23
Operating Expense.................	$ 2,540	$ 1,677	$ 1,418	$ 867	$ 542	$ 285	$ 57
Provision for Losses (net)........	438	305	254	109	48	14	1
Interest Expense..................	1,446	992	627	330	138	85	6
Total Expense.................	$ 4,424	$ 2,974	$ 2,299	$1,306	$ 728	$ 384	$ 64
Net Income (loss) Before Taxes....	$ 1,577	$ 826	$ 380	$ 134	$ (57)	$ (159)	$ (41)
Income Taxes—Current..............	$ 897	$ 496	$ 272	$ 26			
Less deferred against future years..	(112)	(107)	(93)	(42)			
Net Taxes.........................	785	389	179	$ (16)			
Net Income (loss) After Taxes.....	$ 792	$ 437	$ 201	$ 150	$ (57)	$ (159)	$ (41)

EXHIBIT 5
AVCO FINANCIAL SERVICES
Comparative statistical report for Australia

Receivables outstanding and Gross income

Opened 1965 — Receivables and Yield Annualized for 1965

Year	Avg. no. of accounts (M) IBL	CIL	Sales	Misc.	Total	Avg. net amount (M) IBL	CIL	Sales	Misc.	Total	Gross income (M) — IB loans Amount	IB loans Yield	CI loans Amount	CI loans Yield	Sales Amount	Sales Yield	Other Amount	Other Yield	Insurance
1962																			
1963																			
1964																			
1965	0.1	0.1	—	—	0.2	8	89	20	—	117	3	39.53	17	19.25	3	16.91	—	—	3
1966	0.7	0.8	0.5	—	2.0	154	633	79	—	866	56	36.24	134	21.12	16	20.58	—	—	18
1967	2.9	2.1	1.2	—	6.2	659	1,507	186	—	2,352	228	34.60	362	24.02	40	21.51	—	—	42
1968	6.8	4.3	4.0	—	15.1	1,375	3,151	629	—	5,155	455	33.09	783	24.84	129	20.51	—	—	70
1969	9.5	7.4	8.3	—	25.2	2,032	5,101	1,188	—	8,321	645	31.74	1,243	24.37	240	20.20	—	—	83
1970	13.1	11.3	18.3	—	42.7	4,365	8,691	2,713	—	15,769	1,107	25.36	2,046	23.54	536	19.76	—	—	114
1971	15.3	17.6	29.0	—	61.9	6,088.1	13,852.1	4,751.4	—	24,691.6	1,455.2	23.90	3,418.6	24.68	974.7	20.51	—	—	155.6

Operating costs, Provision, Loss recoveries, Bad debts charged off, Interest

Year	Operating costs (excl. B/D provision) — Operating expenses	Operating ratio	Total cost per account	Control cost per account	Provision for bad debts — Provision	Ratio gross income	Cost per account	Loss recoveries — Loans	Sales	Total	Bad debts charged off — Loans	Sales	Total	Interest — Amount	Ratio gross income
1965	61,094	232.89	305.47	39.35	1,424	5.43	1.84	—	—	—	—	—	—	8,366	31.89
1966	271,953	121.46	135.98	19.67	16,514	7.37	8.36	—	—	—	605	—	605	48,785	21.79
1967	506,144	75.39	81.62	43.40	49,112	7.31	7.24	256	605		1,164	501	1,665	135,000	20.11
1968	815,636	52.05	54.01	28.67	109,898	7.65	6.90	160	757		12,991	3,202	16,193	282,777	19.68
1969	1,098,677	49.69	42.07	23.31	207,117	9.37	7.57	263	672	935	32,046	6,556	38,602	501,247	22.67
1970	1,581,290	41.59	37.03	20.59	311,083	8.18	7.29	1,360	938		68,525	17,318	85,843	1,246,619	32.79
1971	2,318,707	38.62	37.46	21.65	438,082	7.30	7.08	3,816	935		168,917	38,438	207,355	1,641,140	27.33

Net profit, Taxes, Offices

Year	Net profit (Before federal income taxes) — Amount	Ratio net rec.	Ratio gross income	Taxes (Other than federal) — Amount	Ratio gross income	Avg. no. accts. per empl.	Number of offices
1965	(46,472)	(39.31)	(177.15)	2,426	9.25	30	4
1966	(114,159)	(13.16)	(50.99)	3,011	1.34	58	10
1967	(45,831)	(1.95)	(6.83)	27,900	4.15	82	25
1968	184,569	3.58	12.84	44,531	3.10	154	29
1969	353,000	4.24	15.97	53,306	2.41	198	40
1970	634,800	4.03	16.70	34,246		227	51
1971	1,558,399	6.31	25.96	47,711	0.79	241	56

Volume — Loans and Sales

Year	Type of borrower — PB	FB	OSA	NB	(Includes references) amount	Average	Volume—Sales Number	Amount
1965	49	15	—	528	373,313	631	132	28,804
1966	636	137	—	2,418	1,579,130	495	742	139,709
1967	2,573	453	2	6,520	4,551,911	476	2,754	562,307
1968	5,663	1,283	—	9,310	7,504,766	461	6,147	1,230,923
1969	8,340	2,463	6	10,957	11,738,174	539	12,230	2,292,921
1970	10,305	4,214	24	15,593	19,144,279	635	25,373	5,498,988
1971	13,873	5,207	5	18,630	20,810,557	552	32,250	7,819,201

IBL—Interest-bearing loans
CIL—Charges included loans
IB—Interest bearing
CI—Consumer installment
BD—Bad debts
PB—Present borrower
FB—Former borrower
OSA—Other seaboard accounts
NB—New borrower

EXHIBIT 6
AVCO FINANCIAL SERVICES
Capitalization of AVCO Financial Services Ltd. (Australia)

Date	Stockholder	Common	Preferred
		(Australian dollars)	
12-2-64	Avco Financial Serv. Inc.	$ 400	
1-27-65	"	$ 19,600	
2-14-66	"	$ 80,000	
4-30-66	"	$ 150,000	
8-1-66	"	$ 250,000	
11-9-66	"	$ 250,000	
5-29-67	"	$ 250,000	
2-26-68	"	$ 150,000	
9-30-69	Mutual Life & Citizens Assurance Co., Ltd.		$ 500,000
4-1-70	*Hallmark Life Insurance Company, Ltd.		$1,000,000
3-30-71	"		$1,000,000
11-29-71	"		$1,000,000
		$1,150,000	$3,500,000

* Australian Life Insurance Subsidiary of Avco Financial Services, Inc.

EXHIBIT 7
AVCO FINANCIAL SERVICES
(stated in Australian dollars)

Loan volume and net receivables

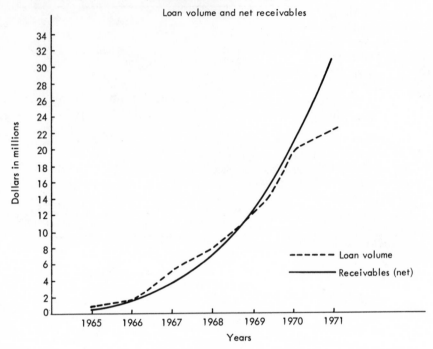

Net income (loss) after taxes

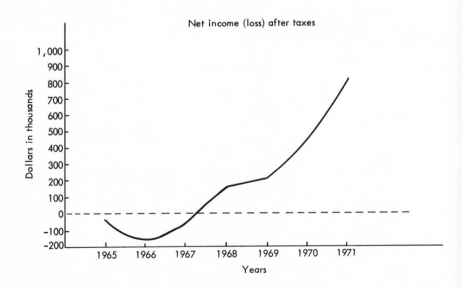

EXHIBIT 8
AVCO FINANCIAL SERVICES

RESERVE BANK OF AUSTRALIA

18 April 1972

The General Manager
Avco Financial Services Ltd.
Australian Area Executive Office
213–219 Miller Street
North Sydney, N.S.W. 2060

Dear Sir,

BORROWING IN AUSTRALIA BY OVERSEAS INTERESTS

Referring to our discussion yesterday we are writing to let you know details of the application of guidelines to finance companies.

All companies which are more than 25 percent overseas owned are requested to consult the Reserve Bank in respect of proposals to increase their borrowings in Australia. In the application of the guidelines to finance companies special provision is made to take account of the relatively high proportion of funds of a working capital nature normally employed in finance company business.

The major principles followed in considering submissions from finance companies generally are:

1. A wholly overseas owned finance company will be considered to have reasonable access to borrowings in Australia to finance increases in working capital requirements provided its local borrowings for this purpose do not exceed 75 percent of the increase in its working capital requirements, which will be defined as the amount required to finance net current assets, i.e., receivables, loans, advances, etc. of not more than three years to maturity (excluding "hard core" loans or advances denominated at call or short term but in fact constituting a continuing or long term line of credit) less current liabilities other than borrowings.

2. Where a company is partly Australian owned the above percentage will be increased by 1 percentage point for each 2 points of local equity, so that a company which is 50 percent or more locally owned would be able to borrow in Australia the whole of the increases in working capital requirements as defined above.

3. The normal guidelines provision will apply in respect of all other increases in local borrowings, including local borrowings to finance receivables, loans, advances, etc. of more than three years to maturity or to finance fixed assets or portfolio investment, i.e., the 2½–10 percent provision as appropriate in respect of increases in funds employed and the 4 for 3 Australian equity provision.

In order to give consideration to any proposal from your company we would need to be furnished with:

(a) consolidated balance sheets at 31 December 1970 and projected forward up to say 12 months, identifying—
   (i) overseas borrowings;
   (ii) local borrowings from each source (type and amount);
   (iii) assets as defined above of not more than three years to maturity (not including income yet to mature and after deducting provision for bad and doubtful debt in respect of such assets);
   (iv) details of current liabilities;
(b) Particulars of the nature and amount of any overdraft limit, e.g., standby or other;
(c) the extent of Australian equity at the time of submission.

APPENDIX I.   EURODOLLARS

Eurodollars can be demand balances in U.S. banks belonging to foreign nationals. No matter how many times they are transferred from one foreign owner to another—they may never leave the United States. The ownership might change—but the dollars themselves never leave the United States. The dollars can be used to purchase goods, finance receivables, repay loans or any other uses to which dollars may be put. The essential difference between a Eurodollar deposit and any other deposit is that the original U.S. owner of the dollars no longer looks to the U.S. banks for repayment but to a foreign bank.

Eurodollar market.   The Eurodollar market is a market located principally in Europe, for lending and borrowing the world's most important convertible currencies. These currencies include the dollar, the Swiss franc, the Deutsche mark, the Netherland guilder, the French franc, and the British pound.

Funds flow into the market from 40 or 50 countries on all continents; these funds are owned by official monetary institutions, government agencies, banks, industrial and commercial enterprises, and private individuals. Funds flow out for investment in a large number of countries, including Japan and the United States. Commercial banks in Hong Kong, London, and Paris are the principal dealers in the market and "make" the market in the sense that they are willing to accept Eurodollars in the form of time deposits or to make loans or investments in Eurodollars.

This market attracts funds because it offers higher rates of interest, greater flexibility of maturities, and a wider range of investment qualities than other short-term capital markets; and the market is able to attract borrowers because it lends funds at relatively low rates of interest. The market operates at low cost because the banks and other firms that use it are well known, because the transactions are for substantial sums, and because dealings are highly competitive.

Uses of Eurodollars.   The process of using Eurodollars and other currencies begins when some bank in the market collects funds in the form of deposits. The bank uses some of these funds in its own operations, and transfers the balance to another bank in the form of a deposit.

Importers have found it useful to borrow Eurodollars and other currencies when this was cheaper than borrowing their domestic currency. When it is cheaper to borrow Eurodollars rather than domestic currency, some agencies or businesses borrow to finance operations or inventories of businesses not directly engaged in international trade.

Who owns Eurodollars?   Only a small part of the dollar deposits in the Eurodollar market at the present time is owned by the residents of the United States. The overwhelming bulk of these deposits represents dollars already owned by foreigners or purchased by them with other currencies. At the end of 1965, foreign holding of dollars totaled $25 billion, of which $14 billion was held by central banks and other governmental agencies outside the United States, $7 billion was held by commercial banks (other than U.S. banks), and $4 billion was held by all other non-U.S. holders.

Risks. The market does not flourish without risk, some more remote than others. Listed below are a few of the potential dangers to the market.

1. The Eurodollar market has spiralled upward and the profit margin has declined. If the volume continues to increase, the potential for trouble also increases if a major bank or creditor should fail.

2. Responsibility for market operations appear to be largely in the hands of the exchange traders. Millions of dollars worth of transactions take place, often with a phone call.

3. The practice of borrowing short and lending long is accelerating.

4. Eurocurrency transactions have made it more difficult to judge the solvency of foreign banks by their balance sheet.

5. The Eurodollar transactions often move through a long chain of banks before reaching the ultimate user. This may result in the ultimate user of the funds receiving a loan even though he has a poor credit rating.

6. If one depository in the chain of Eurodollar fails to pay at maturity, the next depository in line must make good the funds out of other resources.

In short, Eurodollar trading involves a number of risks. But each risk considered alone appears to be either remote or nominal, only when all of the potential risk is considered together does the weight of the exposure warrant concern.

Balance of payments. There is a popular view that portrays the U.S. payments deficit on liquidity basis as a source of funds for the Eurodollar market and thus as a source of funds for U.S. bank borrowing abroad. This tends to be an overgeneralization.

Once a dollar enters the Eurodollar market its movements within that market do not affect the U.S. liquidity balance. Thus when a foreigner decides to deposit with his local bank dollars he holds in, or has received from, the United States—thereby transforming them into Eurodollars—his bank acquires a liquid claim on a bank in the United States. Although the foreign bank may then intitiate a long chain of interbank Eurodollar lending, U.S. liquid liabilities to foreigners are not altered in any way, since the United States remains liable only for the original dollar deposit and not for some multiple thereof.

Similarly, if a U.S. bank borrows Eurodollars from a foreign bank, there is no change in the U.S. deficit on liquidity basis.

To the extent that private foreigners actively acquire dollars for placement in the Eurodollar market and foreign central banks are meeting this demand for dollars, the official settlements balance shows an improvement. For all practical purposes, then, it is generally said that the Eurodollar market has a favorable effect on the U.S. balance of payments to the extent that it reduces, the accrual of dollars in foreign official hands (or even leads to official sales of dollars) and thereby diminishes the danger of U.S. reserve losses.

APPENDIX II. NOTES ON THE UNITED STATES BALANCE OF PAYMENTS

On January 1, 1968, President Lyndon Johnson issued a statement outlining a new program regarding the U.S. balance-of-payments problem. In this statement, the President called for compulsory restrictions of U.S. business investments in Europe and other parts of the world in an effort to combat the continued deficit position of the U.S. balance of payments.

Basically, the balance of payments is a record of the *flow* of international payments and receipts. Transactions other than capital movement and gold movement are included in a nation's balance of payments. Other transactions include export and import of merchandise, tourist travel, transportation, and financial services connected with trade, dividends, and interest received and paid to foreigners, and international gifts or unilateral transfers. Thus, the balance of payments of the United States consists of all transactions that have taken place between the United States and foreign countries in a given year. (See Table 1 for an example of the components making up the U.S. balance of payment for 1969.) In order to balance out a deficit, the United States either reduces its holdings of foreign currencies or pays out the difference in gold at the official exchange rate.

Since 1950, the United States has usually had a balance-of-payments deficit. In the late 1940s and early 1950s, these deficits were needed to help the world recover from World War II. However, after recovery was assured, large U.S. deficits were no longer needed and in fact began to undermine the strength of the dollar. After an improvement in the balance-of-payments position in the mid-1960s, the costs of the Vietnam War, increased private loans and investments abroad, the negative U.S. trade balances, and increasing American tourist expenditures in the late 1960s contributed to a large balance-of-payments deficit and subsequent reduction in the U.S. gold supply.

Thus in 1968, President Johnson, on the advise of his economic advisors, became convinced that further deficits in the balance of payments could not be tolerated since the resulting weakness in the U.S. dollar would threaten the stability of the international monetary system. He, therefore, proposed new action in an effort to bring the balance of pay-

TABLE 1
AVCO FINANCIAL SERVICES
U.S. balance of payments, 1969
(in billions of dollars)

			Receipts		*Payments*		*Balance*
I.	Goods and Services................		55.5		53.6		+2.0
	1.	Merchandise trade (goods).....	36.5		35.8		+0.7
	2.	Services....................	19.0		17.8		+1.2
		a) Military...............		1.5	4.9		−3.4
		b) Investment income........		8.8	4.5		+4.3
		c) Travel..................		2.1	3.4		−1.3
		d) Other..................		6.6	5.0		+1.6
II.	Private Capital..................		4.0		5.4		−1.4
	1.	Long term...................	3.9		4.7		−0.8
		a) Direct investment........		0.8	3.1		−2.2
		b) Portfolio investment......		3.1	1.5		+1.6
		c) Bank and other loans (net)..		—	0.1		−0.1
	2.	Short term..................	0.1		0.7		−0.6
III.	Government....................		1.3		5.4		−4.1
	1.	Loans......................	1.3		3.4		−2.1
	2.	Grans and transfers...........	—		2.0		−2.0
IV.	Other.........................		9.8		6.3		+3.5
	1.	Private transfers.............	—		0.8		−0.8
	2.	Changes in U.S. reserve assets..	0.8		2.0		−1.2
		a) Gold (outflow is receipt)...		—	1.0		−1.0
		b) Convertible currencies.....		0.8	—		+0.8
		c) IMF gold tranche position..		—	1.0		−1.0
	3.	Changes in U.S. liquid					
		liabilities..................	9.0		0.6		+8.4
		a) Foreign official holders		—	0.5		−0.5
		b) Foreign private holders....		9.0	—		+9.0
		c) International organizations					
		other than IMF........		—	0.1		−0.1
	4.	Errors and omissions..........	—		2.9		−2.9
		Total...................	70.6		70.6		—

Sources: Department of Commerce; Federal Reserve Bank of St. Louis.

ments into equilibrium. These actions fell into two categories, temporary measures and long-term measures.

The temporary measures included actions to restrain direct investment abroad, to restrain foreign lending by banks and other financial institutions, to encourage the people to defer all nonessential travel outside the western hemisphere, and a three-step approach to reduce government expenditures overseas.

The long-term measures included plans to increase U.S. exports, to negotiate with foreign authorities to minimize the disadvantages to U.S. trade which arise from differences among national tax systems, and to encourage the flow of foreign funds to the United States by an intensive program to attract greater foreign investment in U.S. corporate securities and to attract more visitors to the United States.

Although extraordinary efforts were taken to reduce the U.S. balance-of-payments deficit it was not sufficient to stop an international monetary crisis which resulted in a devaluation of the U.S. dollar to $38 per ounce of gold.[1]

APPENDIX III. NOTES REGARDING CONTROLS ON DIRECT FOREIGN INVESTMENT

Of particular concern to corporations which own or control foreign subsidiaries is the ability to increase the subsidiaries capital base. Usually this would be a simple matter of just transferring funds from the parent company in the United States to the foreign company. However, in light of the U.S. balance-of-payments problems, the government has taken various steps to limit the outflow of funds to foreign countries.

The first compulsory limitation placed on the outflow of private (i.e., nongovernment) capital to foreign countries was the Interest Equalization Tax Act of 1963. This act imposes on excise tax on the acquisition of foreign stocks or bonds by U.S. persons or companies. The primary purpose of the tax is to aid the U.S. balance-of-payments position by restraining the demand by foreign countries on the U.S. capital market. The tax in effect is designed to bring the cost of long-term financing in the United States into closer alignment with the prevailing costs in foreign markets. Although initially due to expire in July 1965, the tax has been extended and re-extended with the least expiration due on March 31, 1973.

In addition to the Interest Equalization tax, other efforts were made to reduce the outflow of U.S. funds to foreign countries. In February 1965, President Johnson announced the Voluntary Cooperation Program for business firms. Again the purpose was to induce U.S. business firms to make special efforts to participate in attempts to reduce the balance-of-payments deficits. Among other actions, firms were requested to delay or postpone direct investment expenditures in developed countries when such investments were of marginal importance and to make greater use of foreign loans for direct investment.

The January 1, 1968 Presidential statement called for a change from a voluntary program to a mandatory program to reduce the outflow of U.S. dollars to foreign business affiliates. The basic components of this direct foreign investment restriction were:

1. As in the voluntary program, overall and individual company targets will be set. Authorization to exceed these targets will be issued only in exceptional circumstances.

---

[1] Information in this annex is a compilation of several sources, most notably the Commercial Clearing House, Inc., *Balance of Payments Reporter* and a Conference Board Research Report, *Understanding The Balance of Payments,* by John Hein.

2. New direct investment outflows to countries in continental western Europe and other developed nations not heavily dependent on our capital will be stopped in 1968. Problems arising from work already in process or commitments under binding contracts will receive special consideration.
3. New net investments in other developed countries will be limited to 65 percent of the 1965–66 average.
4. New net investments in the developing countries will be limited to 110 percent of the 1965–66 average.

The mandatory program does not prevent U.S. firms from investing in their foreign subsidiaries. It does, however, force them to shift to a greater degree to foreign sources for investment funds. For example, sources of foreign investment funds may come from foreign loans, sale of securities to foreigners, or reinvestment of earnings to the degree allowed under the new program. In March 1968, Canada was completely exempted from the balance-of-payments measures affecting capital outflows. Thus, U.S. firms are able to invest in Canada without restrictions. In summary, the mandatory controls on direct foreign investors (i.e., those individuals or companies in the United States who own at least a 10 percent capital or earnings interest in a foreign business venture) are: (1) annual limits on the amount of positive direct investment, and (2) a reduction of the balances of short-term liquid balances held abroad to the average level of 1965–1966. Subsequent to 1970, positive direct investments to all foreign countries of $2,000,000 or less are exempt from the federal limitations. The positive direct investment must include the direct investor's share of reinvested earnings.

SELECTED REFERENCES
FOR PART SIX

ARCHER, STEPHEN H., and FAERBER, LEROY G. "Firm Size and the Cost of Equity Capital," *Journal of Finance*, Vol. 21 (March 1966), pp. 69–84.

BEECHY, THOMAS H. "Quasi-Debt Analysis of Financial Leases," *Accounting Review*, Vol. 44 (April 1969), pp. 375–381.

BLOCH, ERNEST. "Pricing a Corporate Bond Issue: A Look behind the Scenes," *Essays in Money and Credit*. Federal Reserve Bank of New York, 1964, pp. 72–76. Reprinted from this bank's October 1961 issue of *Monthly Review*.

BLUME, MARSHALL E. "Portfolio Theory: A Step Toward Its Practical Application," *Journal of Business*, April 1970, pp. 152–73.

BOWER, RICHARD S., HERRINGER, FRANK C., and WILLIAMSON, J. PETER. "Lease Evaluation," *Accounting Review*, Vol. 41, No. 2 (April 1966), pp. 257–65.

BIERMAN, HAROLD, JR. "The Bond Refunding Decision as a Markov Process," *Management Science*, Vol. 12 (August 1966), pp. 545–51.

BIERMAN, HAROLD, JR. *Financial Policy Decisions*. New York: Macmillan, 1970, chap. 2 and 12.

BOWLIN, OSWALD D. "The Refunding Decision," *Journal of Finance*, Vol. 21 (March 1966), pp. 55–68.

BROWN, BOWMAN. "Why Corporations Should Consider Income Bonds," *Financial Executive*, Vol. 35 (October 1967), pp. 74–78.

BROWN, J. MICHAEL. "Post-Offering Experience of Companies Going Public," *Journal of Business*, January 1970, pp. 10–18.

BUDZEIKA, GEORGE. "Term Lending by New York City Banks," *Essays in Money and Credit*, (New York: Federal Reserve Bank of New York).

BUDZEIKA, GEORGE. "The Maturity of Loans at New York City Banks," *Monthly Review*, Vol. 49 (January 1967), pp. 10–14. (New York: Federal Reserve Bank of New York.)

BUDZEIKA, GEORGE. "Term Lending by New York City Banks in the 1960's," *Monthly Review*, Vol. 49 (October 1967), pp. 199–203. (New York: Federal Reserve Bank of New York.)

CHAMBERLAIN, JOHN. "Why It's Harder and Harder to Get a Good Board," *Fortune,* November 1966.

"Direct Placement of Corporate Debt," *Economic Review.* Federal Reserve Bank of Cleveland (March 1965). Reprinted in James Van Horne (ed.) *Foundations for Financial Management,* Homewood, Ill.: Irwin, 1966, p. 247.

DOUGALL, HERBERT E. *Capital Markets and Institutions.* 2d ed.; Englewood Cliffs, N.J.: Prentice-Hall, 1970.

EITEMAN, DAVID K. "The S.E.C. Special Study and the Exchange Markets," *Journal of Finance,* Vol. 21 (May 1966), pp. 311–23.

ELSAID, HUSSEIN H. "The Function of Preferred Stock in the Corporate Financial Plan," *Financial Analysts Journal,* July–August 1969, pp. 112–117.

EVERETT, EDWARD. "Subordinated Debt—Nature and Enforcement," *Business Lawyer,* Vol. 20 (July 1965), pp. 953–87.

FERRARA, WILLIAM L. "Should Investment and Financing Decisions Be Separated?" *Accounting Review,* Vol. 41 (January 1966), pp. 106–14.

FERRARA, WILLIAM L., and WOJDAK, JOSEPH F. "Valuation of Long-Term Leases," *Financial Analysts Journal,* Vol. 25 (November–December 1969), pp. 29–32.

FISCHER, DONALD E., and WILT, GLENN A. JR. "Non-Convertible Preferred Stock as a Financing Instrument, 1950–1965," *Journal of Finance,* Vol. 23 (September 1968), pp. 611–24.

FRIEND, IRWIN. "Broad Implications of the S.E.C. Special Study," *Journal of Finance,* Vol. 21 (May 1966), pp. 324–32.

FURST, RICHARD W. "Does Listing Increase the Market Price of Common Stocks?" *Journal of Business,* Vol. 43 (April 1970), pp. 174–80.

GOLDSMITH, RAYMOND W. *The Flow of Capital Funds in the Postwar Economy.* New York: National Bureau of Economic Research, 1965.

HALFORD, FRANK A. "Income Bonds—The Sleeping Giant," *Financial Analysts Journal,* Vol. 20 (January–February 1964), pp. 73–79.

HAMEL, H. G. *Leasing in Industry.* Studies in Business Policy, No. 127. New York: National Industrial Conference Board, 1968.

HAYES, DOUGLAS A. *Bank Lending Policies: Issues and Practices.* Ann Arbor, Mich.: Bureau of Business Research, University of Michigan, 1964, chap. 6.

JEN, FRANK C., and WERT, JAMES E. "The Value of the Deferred Call Privilege," *National Banking Review,* Vol. 3 (March 1966), pp. 369–78.

JEN, FRANK C., and WERT, JAMES E. "The Effects of Call Risk on Corporate Bond Yields," *Journal of Finance,* Vol. 22 (December 1967), pp. 637–52.

JEN, FRANK C., and WERT, JAMES E. "The Deferred Call Provision and Corporate Bond Yields," *Journal of Financial and Quantitative Analysis,* Vol. 3 (June 1968), pp. 157–169.

JOHNSON, RAMON E. "Term Structures of Corporate Bond Yields as a Function of Risk of Default," *Journal of Finance,* Vol. 22 (May 1967), pp. 313–45.

Leasing of Industrial Equipment. Washington, D.C.: Machinery and Allied Products Institute, 1965.

MIDDLETON, J. WILLIAM. "Term Lending—Practical and Profitable," *Journal of Commercial Bank Lending*, Vol. 50 (August 1968), pp. 31–43.

MITCHELL, G. B. "After-Tax Cost of Leasing," *Accounting Review*, Vol. 40 (April 1970), pp. 308–314.

NELSON, J. RUSSELL. "Price Effects in Rights Offerings," *Journal of Finance*, Vol. 20 (December 1965), pp. 647–50.

PINCHES, GEORGE E. "Financing with Convertible Preferred Stock, 1960–1967," *Journal of Finance*, Vol. 25 (March 1970), pp. 53–63.

POGUE, THOMAS F., and SOLDOFSKY, ROBERT M. "What's in a Bond Rating," *Journal of Financial and Quantitative Analysis*, Vol. 4 (June 1969), pp. 201–28.

PYE, GORDON. "The Value of the Call Option on a Bond," *Journal of Political Economy*, Vol. 74 (April 1966), pp. 200–05.

PYE, GORDON. "The Value of Call Deferment on a Bond: Some Empirical Results," *Journal of Finance*, Vol. 22 (December 1967), pp. 623–36.

ROBINSON, ROLAND, and BARTELL, H. ROBERT, JR. "Uneasy Partnership: SEC/NYSE," *Harvard Business Review*, Vol. 43 (January–February 1965), pp. 76–88.

SEARS, GERALD A. "Public Offerings for Smaller Companies," *Harvard Business Review*, September–October 1968, pp. 112–20.

SHAW, DAVID C. "The Cost of Going Public in Canada," *Financial Executive*, July 1969, pp. 20–28.

SOLDOFSKY, ROBERT M. "Classified Common Stock," *The Business Lawyer*, April 1968), pp. 899–902.

SOLDOFSKY, ROBERT M. "Convertible Preferred Stock: Renewed Life in an Old Form," *The Business Lawyer*, July 1969, pp. 1385–92.

SOLDOFSKY, ROBERT M., and JOHNSON, CRAIG R. "Rights Timing," *Financial Analysts Journal*, Vol. 23 (July–August 1967), pp. 101–4.

SPRECHER, C. RONALD. "A Note on Financing Mergers with Convertible Preferred Stock," *Journal of Finance*, Vol. 26 (June 1971), pp. 683–86.

STOLL, HANS R., and CURLEY, ANTHONY J. "Small Business and the New Issues Market for Equities," *Journal of Financial and Quantit tive Analysis*, Vol. 5 (September 1970), pp. 309–22.

SULLIVAN, BRIAN. "An Introduction to 'Going Public'," *Journal of Accountancy*, November 1965.

VAN HORNE, JAMES C. "New Listings and Their Price Behavior," *Journal of Finance*, Vol. 25 (September 1970), pp. 783–94.

VATTER, W. J. "Accounting for Leases," *Journal of Accounting Research*, Vol. 4 (Autumn 1966), pp. 133–48.

WEINGARTNER, H. MARTIN. "Optimal Timing of Bond Refunding," *Management Science*, Vol. 13 (March 1967), pp. 511–24.

Valuation of Long-Term Leases[*]

William L. Ferrara and Joseph F. Wojdak [†]

IN RECENT YEARS significant research efforts of the accounting profession have been aimed at the problem of accounting for lease contracts by lessees. These efforts have been directed primarily toward three major · questions regarding the inclusion of leases in financial statements: (1) what kinds of leases should be *included,* (2) how should these leases be *presented,* and (3) how should capitalized leases be *valued?* This paper deals only with the last of these questions and takes as given, the proposition that long-term leases should be capitalized as assets and liabilities in financial statements.

LONG-TERM LEASE VERSUS PURCHASE-GENERAL

In essence a long-term lease is an alternative to outright purchase of an asset. The lease simultaneously represents a means of acquiring and financing an asset. Thus the lease is different from outright purchase essentially because the lease contract has built into it the financing of an asset's acquisition.

Consider the following offer made by an equipment manufacturer (i.e., the lessor):

A specific type of equipment is offered for sale at a price of $338,000 or the potential buyer may consider leasing the equipment for 10 annual payments

---

* Reprinted from *Financial Analysts Journal,* November–December 1969, pp. 29–32, by permission of the authors and the publisher.

† William L. Ferrara, Professor of Accounting at The Pennsylvania State University and Joseph F. Wojdak, Associate Professor of Accounting at The Pennsylvania State University.

of $50,000 payable at the beginning of each year. The asset has a 10 year useful life, no salvage value and the purchaser (lessee) must agree to pay maintenance, insurance and taxes on the equipment.

The purchaser (lessee) should see this as an offer to sell outright for $338,000 or an offer to sell with built-in financing at an annual interest rate of approximately 10%.[1] The entries on the buyer's books should be as follows depending whether outright purchase or leasing is the method of acquisition.

Outright purchase

Equipment.........................	338,000	
Cash............................		338,000

Lease

Rights to leased property.............	338,000	
Liability for lease payments.........		338,000

Annual lease payment entries would be made in accordance with a debt amortization schedule amortizing a debt of $338,000 with annual payments (including interest of 10%) of $50,000.[2] Illustrative entries for the first two payments are as follows:

Beginning of year 1

Liability for lease payments.........	50,000	
Cash...........................		50,000

Beginning of year 2

Liability for lease payments.........	21,200	
Interest expense[3]...................	28,800	
Cash...........................		50,000

---

[1] The 10% interest rate is the rate of discount which equates 10 annual beginning-of-year payments of $50,000 with an immediate outlay of $338,000.

[2]

Year	Debt balance	Interest at 10%	Payments	Reduction in debt
1...........	$338,000	0	$ 50,000	$ 50,000
2...........	288,000	$ 28,800	50,000	21,200
3...........	266,800	26,680	50,000	23,320
4...........	243,480	24,348	50,000	25,652
5...........	217,828	21,783	50,000	28,217
6...........	189,611	18,961	50,000	31,039
7...........	158,572	15,857	50,000	34,143
8...........	124,429	12,443	50,000	37,557
9...........	86,872	8,687	50,000	41,313
10...........	45,559	4,441*	50,000	45,559
Totals...		$162,000	$500,000	$338,000

* Adjusted for rounding error.

[3] Interest expense should be accrued for interim and annual financial statements.

Entries to reflect depreciation or amortization of the rights to leased property can be recorded in accordance with any of the accepted methods, i.e., straight line, sum of the years digits, etc. The main point here is that amortization of the "rights to leased property" is a process separate and distinct from the amortization of the implicit loan in lease financing.

LEASE VALUATION—SALES PRICE VERSUS DISCOUNT RATES

In Accounting Research Study No. 4[4] Professor John H. Myers agreed with the capitalization of leases similar to the above lease. However, he recommended an alternative approach, based upon discount rates rather than the alternative purchase price, for determining the amount at which "Rights to Leased Property" are to be capitalized.

Professor Myers recommended that the rate of discount to be used in determining the capitalized value of a long-term lease should be:

1. The interest rate used in determining lease rentals and if this rate is not determinable
2. An interest rate equal to the lessee's approximate borrowing cost.

The interest rate used in determining lease rentals may or may not be the same as the 10% rate determined earlier. The 10% rate was determined by finding the rate of discount which equated the $338,000 sale price and the 10 annual $50,000 beginning-of-year payments. It is not clear that this 10% rate is the interest rate used in setting the rentals. The interest rate used in setting the rentals could be the 14% rate of discount which equates the asset's cost, say $298,000, and the 10 annual $50,000 beginning-of-year payments.

The ultimate accounting difference emanating from these two different rates of interest is the difference between the $338,000 sale price of the asset and the $298,000 cost of producing the asset. In one case the "rights to leased property" are capitalized at $338,000 while in the other they are capitalized at $298,000. This $40,000 balance sheet difference is of course accompanied by corresponding differences in periodic asset amortization.

Another way of highlighting the difficulties involved in determining the rate of discount to use is to ask the question,

Should rights to leased assets be capitalized at the lessor's cost ($298,000) or at the amount the lessee would pay for the asset if he purchased it outright (338,000)?

It seems reasonable to conclude that since a long-term lease is essentially a means of financing the acquisition of an asset, the asset should be capi-

---

[4] Published by AICPA in 1962.

talized at what it would have cost if purchased outright and the financing costs entailed in the lease alternative (10%) should be considered interest expense. The lessor's cost and the rate of discount (however determined) used in determining lease rentals appear to be totally irrelevant.

The above approach differs from Professor Myers' in that it focuses attention on the lessee's alternative means of acquiring the asset: by outright purchase rather than on rates of discount. This appears to be quite appropriate especially where the facts are as portrayed above, i.e., the leased property involved is a somewhat standard product available under conditions of outright sale (arms length transaction) as well as a long-term lease.

The above lease transaction would be considered an installment purchase of property under Accounting Principles Board Opinion No. 5 issued in September 1964 (pp. 30–31). However, rather than suggesting sales price for valuation, APB Opinion No. 5 states, "The property and the related obligation should be included in the balance sheet as an asset and a liability, respectively, *at the discounted amount of the future lease rental payments* . . ." (italics supplied).

As in the case of Professor Myers' approach the authors feel that APB made an inappropriate choice by focusing on rates of discount rather than the sales price. If Professor Myers and APB really meant by "an appropriate rate of discount" a rate of discount which would yield the sales price (i.e., the 10% in the above illustration) they both could have removed a great deal of confusion by stating so explicitly. Furthermore, if they were really after the sales price they should have gone to it directly rather than indirectly via a discount rate. A sales price should generally be more susceptible of independent verification than a rate of discount, however determined.

Some modification in the above recommended procedure may have to be made when the sales price used to "book" the "rights to leased property" is not available or if available may not be arms length in nature. This difficulty could arise in:

1. evaluations concerning a "unique asset"
2. evaluations concerning third party lessors
3. evaluations concerning second hand assets

EVALUATIONS CONCERNING UNIQUE ASSETS

A unique asset, e.g., one made to order, could present a problem *if*, in the negotiations concerning construction, the outright purchase alternative is not considered, i.e., a lease is the only method of acquisition considered. This does not appear rational since a purchaser should always consider alternative means of acquiring an asset. However, one must admit that such "apparent irrationality" could arise. Thus, an alternative purchase price may not be available and some other means of determining the capitalizable value of the lease must be used.

Alternatives available consist of discounting the lease rentals at either of the following two discount rates: (1) the rate used in determining lease rentals, and (2) a rate equal to the lessee's approximate borrowing cost. The choice between these two should depend upon which yields the best approximation to an "arms length" sales price. The rate used in setting lease rentals would be appropriate under conditions wherein the negotiations over lease rentals yielded reliable information concerning the lessor's desired rate of return on "cost plus the desired mark-up." This however, would be the equivalent of using the lessor's sales price which as stated earlier is our first choice for a method of determining the amount to use for capitalizing a lease.

Where the negotiations yield no substantive (no information or no reliable information) information or only the lessor's desired rate of return over cost, the lessee's approximate borrowing cost should be used. Discounting by the lessor's desired rate of return over cost would result in capitalizing the lease at the lessor's cost of production which is irrelevant to the lessee. The lessee should capitalize the lease at what it could have purchased the asset for, i.e., at sales price or at the best approximation thereto. The lessee's approximate borrowing cost is better than the lessor's discount rate related to cost since a realistic approximation of the lessee's borrowing cost should yield a capitalized value very close to an approximate arms length sales price.

In reality lease rentals discounted at the lessee's approximate borrowing cost would yield a figure which could legitimately be referred to as the "equivalent sales price" to the lessee. For instance, a lessee who agrees to 10 beginning-of-year $50,000 lease rentals when he has the ability to borrow at 10% is in reality agreeing to pay $338,000 for the asset. Given this line of reasoning one might conclude that the capitalized value of a lease is determinable by discounting the lease payments at the lessee's approximate borrowing cost. The writers admit this, but would prefer to capitalize a lease at the asset's sales price if determinable and if not determinable they would resort to an approximation equal to the lease payments discounted at the lessee's approximate borrowing cost. The reasoning behind this priority of methodology is twofold, viz,

1. the lessee's approximate borrowing cost is usually less susceptible to independent verification than the sales price.
2. the difference between the sales price and the discounted value of the lease rentals (using the lessee's approximate borrowing cost) should be minimal, if a lease is to be considered a logical alternative to purchase.[5]

---

[5] Our tax laws could easily have a tendency to alter this "minimal" difference in specific cases.

EVALUATIONS CONCERNING THIRD PARTY LESSORS AND SECOND HAND ASSETS

A third party lessor is a financial intermediary who provides the financing (via the lease) necessary to get buyer and seller together. A lease arranged in this manner should, for the same reasons mentioned earlier, be capitalized by the lessee at the asset's sale price if it is available. If the sale price is not available then the alternative of discounting the lease payments at the lessee's approximate borrowing cost should be used.

An interesting feature of leases concerning third party lessors is that discounting at the rate used by the lessor in setting lease rentals would not yield the manufacturer's cost. Instead it will yield the lessor's cost which should be the manufacturer's selling price to the lessee or a fair approximation thereto if the third party lessor purchases at a lower selling price. In such cases, if the manufacturer's selling price is not available, use of the lessor's discount rate (if available) might yield a better approximation to sales price than the lessee's approximate borrowing cost.

Second hand assets may or may not have an established market. When leasing such an asset, an established market may yield a reliable selling price for capitalization by the lessee. If with an established market reliable selling prices are not available (second hand assets are normally unique in terms of the amount and nature of accumulated wear and tear) or if there is no established market the lessee's approximate borrowing cost should be used as in the case of unique assets.

LEASES FOR PORTIONS OF AN ASSET'S LIFE

A lease for a portion of an asset's life does not prevent the above analysis from being applied. In preceding illustrations the life of the lease was equal to the physical life of the asset (e.g., zero salvage value). Now we are confronted with a situation where the asset may have a useful life beyond the life of the lease—does this present any difficulties?

As a preliminary we must admit that a difference often exists between the useful life and the physical life of an asset. The basic issue then is, what modifications should there be in the above recommended procedure when the purchase and lease alternative involve less than the asset's full physical life?

Three cases where the lease life is shorter than the asset life deserve comment. In all three cases the initial lease case treated in the first section of the paper will be continued except that the leased asset is assumed to have a residual value of $40,700.

Case I—The lessee has residual rights at the termination of the lease but makes no payment for these rights, above the basic annual lease payments.

The fact that the lessee has residual rights without making additional payments suggests that he has effectively acquired the leased asset for its entire life. Thus, the rights to leased property should be valued at the $338,000 alternative purchase price of the asset. However, total depreciation over the asset's life will be limited to $338,000—$40,700, or $297,300. The following entries may be made to record the asset acquired, to amortize the liability for lease payments and to record the interest expense (10%). These entries are identical to the basic lease case presented earlier.

To record the leased asset

Rights to leased property.............	338,000	
Liability for lease payments.........		338,000

Beginning of year 1

Liability for lease payments...........	50,000	
Cash............................		50,000

Beginning of year 2

Liability for lease payments...........	21,200	
Interest expense....................	28,800	
Cash............................		50,000

The fact that the leased asset has a residual value in no way affects the discharge of the lease liability and the determination of the related interest expense which totals $162,000 ($500,000—$338,000).[6]

Case II—The lessee has no residual rights at the termination of the lease.

When the lessee has no residual rights he is in effect acquiring only part of the leased asset which has a cost equal to the alternative purchase price minus the residual value. The effective alternative purchase price for that portion of the asset's services acquired is therefore $338,000—$40,700 or $297,300. Thus the leased asset is recorded as follows:[7]

Rights to leased property.............	297,300	
Liability for lease payments.........		297,300

Total depreciation over the asset life will be limited to $297,300. Since the ten annual lease rental payments of $50,000 are assumed to be un-

---

[6] See footnote 2.

[7] Some might prefer to book the "rights to leased assets," in this case, at the selling price ($338,000) less the present value of the asset's residual value. This seems reasonable until one recognizes a conflict with the usual method of handling residual values (without discounting) as per Case I. An example of this conflict is the fact that the same asset with the same selling price ($338,000) is being acquired in both Cases I and II. However, less of the asset is being acquired

changed, the effective interest rate being paid by the lessee is considerably higher than the 10% used in Case I. The rate of interest being paid is that rate which equates the ten annual lease payments (totaling $500,000) with the effective alternative purchase price of $297,300. This rate is 14%. The following entries reflect the reduction of the lease liability and recording of related interest expense.[8]

Beginning of year 1

| Liability for lease payments......... | 50,000 | |
| Cash......................... | | 50,000 |

Beginning of year 2

Liability for lease payments.........	15,378	
Interest expense..................	34,622	
Cash.........................		50,000

Case III—For the rights to the residual value of the leased asset the lessee must make a $40,700 cash payment at the termination of the lease contract.

This case is virtually identical to Case II in that at the beginning of year 1 the lessee is only acquiring part of the asset's services for the same ten annual lease payments of $50,000. Thus, the effective alternative purchase price is $338,000 — $40,700 or $297,300. The entries to record the lease and amortize the lease liability are identical to Case

---

8 in Case II since there are no residual rights in Case II. If the Case II "rights to leased property" are valued at $338,000 minus the present value of $40,700, more depreciation will be charged in Case II than Case I even though less of the asset is acquired. Such an ultimate result is difficult to tolerate. Perhaps if the residual value in both Cases I and II are both treated in present value terms via some version of the sinking fund or annuity methods of depreciation the present difficulty inherent in not discounting the residual value in Case II would be resolved.

Year	Debt balance	Interest at 14%	Payments	Reduction in debt
1...........	$297,300	0	$ 50,000	$ 50,000
2...........	247,300	$ 34,622	50,000	15,378
3...........	231,922	32,469	50,000	17,531
4...........	214,391	30,015	50,000	19,985
5...........	194,406	27,217	50,000	22,783
6...........	171,623	24,027	50,000	25,973
7...........	145,650	20,391	50,000	29,609
8...........	116,041	16,246	50,000	33,754
9...........	82,287	11,520	50,000	38,480
10...........	43,807	6,193*	50,000	43,867
Totals...		$202,700	$500,000	$297,300

* adjusted for rounding error

II. When the $40,700 payment is made ten years hence, the asset acquired should be recorded by the lessee at the price paid (i.e., $40,700).

CONCLUSION

Long-term leases should be capitalized by the lessee at the asset's sales price if determinable. If the asset's sales price is not determinable an acceptable approximation would be the lease payments discounted at the lessee's approximate borrowing cost.

To Lease or Not to Lease?*

George L. Marrah †

AN ACCELERATION in the demand for funds early in 1968 found companies paying higher interest rates and accepting more restrictive covenants in debt contracts. Because of this development and other factors many companies turned to lease financing as a way to obtain needed equipment. As a result, a new peak in leasing was reached early in 1968 with approximately $1.3 billion invested in leased equipment. Not only has the amount of leased equipment grown, but the variety of equipment available has expanded dramatically to the point that today almost any type of equipment from trench diggers to machine tools may be leased.

GROWING INTEREST

Despite growing acceptance, many companies refuse to lease because leasing affords the use but not the ownership of equipment. It represents a departure from the traditional idea that ownership of capital is essential to running a business. Other companies shy away from leasing because they are not able to compare the cost and the non-cost factors of leasing with similar factors for installment purchases or for borrowing money and buying equipment. However, the growing acceptance of financial leasing has piqued the interest of many companies which heretofore have never thought of leasing.

*Reprinted from *Financial Executive*, Vol. 36, No. 10 (October 1968), pp. 91–104, by permission of the author and the publisher.

† Associate Professor of Finance at Sacramento State College in the School of Business Administration.

THE PROBLEM

The decision to lease or not to lease is made after the company has decided that the investment represents a wise use of funds. Then the question to be answered is how to finance the equipment.

Leasing is one possibility open to the company. Lease financing is nothing more than an alternative source of funds. The solution of the following problem illustrates one way of making an analytical evaluation and reaching a decision whether or not to lease. The choice is between borrowing funds and buying the equipment, or leasing it. For purposes of the example, let us assume that the equipment costs $30,000, the borrowing rate is 8 percent, and interest will be paid on the unpaid balance. The loan will be for six years and annual principal payments of $5,000 will be made to the financial institution. Lease payments will amount to $7,000 annually.

LEASING

Is leasing more expensive in the hypothetical situation than borrowing and buying? Because lease payments are fully tax deductible, the after-tax cost of leasing is $3,500 a year (Table 1), or $21,000 for the six-year

TABLE 1
Cost of leasing

Year	Lease payments	Tax savings	Net cost leasing	Present value 15%
1.............	$ 7,000	$ 3,500	$ 3,500	$ 3,045
2.............	7,000	3,500	3,500	2,646
3.............	7,000	3,500	3,500	2,303
4.............	7,000	3,500	3,500	2,002
5.............	7,000	3,500	3,500	1,739
6.............	7,000	3,500	3,500	1,512
	$42,000	$21,000	$21,000	$13,247

period. After discounting the net cost of leasing to its present value at an assumed cost of capital of 15 percent, the net cost of leasing is reduced to $13,247. The 15 percent represents the highest rate of return had the funds been invested in other assets of the business.[1]

In order to make the two alternatives comparable, it is assumed that the lease payments are made at the end of the year. If the lease payments

---

[1] Richard F. Vancil, "Lease or Borrow, New Method of Analysis," *Harvard Business Review*, Vol. 39 (September–October, 1961) pp. 122–36.

are made at the beginning of the year, and a cash down payment is required by the lessor, the net cost of leasing would be higher.

Before entering into negotiation with the lessor over the terms of a lease, the lessee should break down the lease payments into component parts. Part of the lease payment represents the lessor's investment in the equipment and interest on his loan. The remainder of the lease payment consists of the lessor's interest return (Table 2). A knowledge

TABLE 2
Breakdown of the cost of leasing

Year	Lease payments	Principal interest return	Imputed interest 8%	Imputed principal
				$30,000
1	$ 7,000	$ 4,600	$2,400	25,400
2	7,000	4,968	2,032	20,432
3	7,000	5,365	1,635	15,067
4	7,000	5,795	1,205	9,272
5	7,000	6,258	742	3,014
6	7,000	6,759	241	0
	$42,000	$33,745	$8,255	

of the breakdown of the lease payments will permit the lessee to bargain more effectively with the lessor. Of course, if the company found itself faced with a "take it or leave it" proposition, the breakdown would be unnecessary.

BORROWING AND BUYING

The net cost of borrowing and buying is $1,929 less than leasing (Table 1, Column 4) for two reasons. First, the assumed average annual repayment on borrowed funds is smaller than the average lease payment. Second, accelerated depreciation can be used to achieve certain tax ad-

TABLE 3
Cost of borrowing and buying

Year	Annual repayments	Interest payments	Depreciation S.Y.D.	Total tax savings	Net cost	Present value 15%
1	$ 7,400	$2,400	$ 8,571	$ 5,485	$ 1,915	$ 1,666
2	7,000	2,000	7,143	4,571	2,429	1,836
3	6,600	1,600	5,714	3,567	2,943	1,936
4	6,200	1,200	4,286	2,743	3,457	1,977
5	5,800	800	2,857	1,829	3,971	1,974
6	5,400	400	1,429	915	4,485	1,929
	$38,400	$8,400	$30,000	$19,200	$19,200	$11,318

vantages. The use of accelerated depreciation (sum of the digits) in writing off the equipment serves to reduce taxes or, to state it more accurately, to postpone them. Also, by the end of the fourth year—using accelerated depreciation—six-sevenths of the original investment in the equipment will have been recovered. Those costs recovered early have a higher time value than those costs recovered later.[2]

It is of historical interest that prior to 1954, leasing had a tax advantage, because companies were not permitted to use accelerated depreciation. The tax advantages of leasing were lessened with the advent of rapid depreciation and a shortening of the allowable useful life of equipment for tax purposes.

A less important factor reflected in the difference in cost is the high cost of capital assumed in the sample problem. If the costs had been discounted to their present value at 4 percent instead of 15 percent, the cost differential between leasing and borrowing would have amounted to $1,878 rather than $1,929. Inasmuch as leasing became less costly than borrowing during the last two years, the high cost of capital penalized these savings.

In this situation the company would obviously pay a premium if it decided to lease the equipment. If the company had borrowed the money at the same rate of interest he would have paid the lessor, it would have cost $38,255, or $3,255 less than the $42,000 in lease payments. Or, if the lease payments of $7,000 a year were discounted to present value at 8 percent, it would amount to $32,361, or $2,361 more than the $30,000 for the equipment. If $2,361 is compounded for six years, it amounts to $3,255. Still another way to look at the premium to be paid if the company leased is as follows: If the leasing payments were discounted down to a present value at 11 percent, the result would be $30,000, and the difference between 8 percent and 11 percent represents the premium paid for leasing. If the company chose to lease under these circumstances the decision would be based on non-cost advantages of leasing.[3]

CASH FLOW

The decision to lease or not to lease may be based on anticipated additional cash flow. The value of cash flow is calculated by subtracting the leasing payments from the added cash flow, and subtracting taxes and discounting to present value. If the annual income before taxes and depreciation is assumed to increase by $12,000 per year for six years

---

[2] Seymour Friedland, "The Economics of Corporate Finance," Appendix A (Englewood Cliffs, N.J.: Prentice-Hall, 1966), pp. 229–34.

[3] For an excellent discussion of the analytic techniques used in leasing, see pages 440–447 of Jerome B. Cohen's and Sidney M. Robbins' *The Financial Manager.* The analytic technique used in this part of the above analysis pretty much follows that used in this text.

after the investment in equipment, the present value of the cash flow, figured at 15 percent, is $9,460.

The annual cash flow for borrowing and buying is shown in Table 4.

TABLE 4
Cash flow—Borrowing and buying

Year	Income	Depreci-ation	Interest payments	Income after taxes	Debt repay-ment	After-tax flow	Present value 15%
1......	$12,000	$ 8,571	$2,400	$ 1,028	$ 5,000	$ 4,086	$ 3,555
2......	12,000	7,143	2,000	2,857	5,000	3,571	2,700
3......	12,000	5,714	1,600	4,685	5,000	3,057	2,012
4......	12,000	4,286	1,200	6,514	5,000	2,543	1,455
5......	12,000	2,857	800	8,343	5,000	2,028	1,008
6......	12,000	1,429	400	10,171	5,000	1,514	654
	$72,000	$30,000	$8,400	$33,598	$30,000	$16,799	$11,384

The present value of cash flow from the borrow-and-buy plan is $1,924 more than leasing. It is greater for the same two reasons listed earlier.

Many firms do not lease because leasing does not build equity. If it is highly probable that the equipment will have substantial value at the end of the leasing period, the company should either buy the equipment or, if it decides to lease, arrange lease payments which reflect the anticipated residual value.

RESIDUAL VALUE

Before entering into a leasing arrangement, the company should make an estimate of the probable residual values of the equipment and convert them into subjective probabilities. For example, the company might calculate that there is a 0.4 probability that the after-tax salvage value would be $6,000, a 0.2 probability that it would amount to $4,000 or $8,000, and a 0.1 probability that it would be either $2,000 or $10,000. The company should then calculate the rate of return using the discounted cash flow method, assuming no residual value at the end of the period.

	Year	Cash flow	15%	Present value
Net Cash Outlay $30,000...............	1	$9,086	0.870	$ 7,905
	2	8,571	0.756	6,480
	3	8,057	0.658	5,302
	4	7,543	0.572	4,315
	5	7,028	0.497	3,493
	6	6,514	0.432	2,814
				$30,309

The third step is to add the probable residual values to the cash flow for the sixth year. If $2,000 is added to the cash flow of the sixth year the cash flow for that year will be $8,514, and the expected rate of return 16 percent (see Table 5). If the cash flow were to be increased by $4,000, the expected rate of return would be 17 percent.

TABLE 5
Standard deviation of expected rates of return

Estimated after-tax residual value	*Expected rate of return*	*Prob- ability*	*Prob- ability rate of return*	*Devi- ation from 18%*	*Deviation*	*2 probability deviation*
$ 2,000	.16	.1	.016	.02	.0004	.00004
4,000	.17	.2	.034	.01	.0001	.00002
6,000	.18	.4	.072	—	—	—
8,000	.19	.2	.038	.01	.0001	.00002
10,000	.20	.1	.020	.02	.0004	.00004
						.00012

Standard Deviation $\sqrt{.00012}$
S.R. = .001
    = 1.1%
.18 + 1.96(.011)
.18 + .02
95% probability that rate of return will be between 16% and 18%

After calculating the probability rate of return, the company should figure the standard deviation. In this problem the best estimate, given the subjective probabilities, is a 95 percent chance that the rate of return will be between 16 and 18 percent. The higher the estimated rate of return, the greater would be the incentive for the firm to buy the equipment. If the company is forced to lease because of a scarcity of working capital, certainly it should use this information to bargain for lower lease payments.

SURVEY OF MANUFACTURERS

During February 1968 a questionnaire was sent to 60 manufacturers to evaluate leasing as a source of capital. Thirty companies returned the questionnaire, which asked them to rank the advantages and disadvantages of leasing on a scale of one through ten. The results are posted in Table 6.

The major reason for leasing—as given by the respondents—was to conserve working capital. The greatest disadvantage was its high cost. A corollary of this disadvantage was the fact that leasing increased the company's fixed costs.

TABLE 6
Advantages and disadvantages of leasing survey of 30 manufacturers

Advantages	*High*	*Med.*	*Low*
Permits greater flexibility in use...........................	5%	68%	27%
Encourages trying new equipment........................	37	37	26
Shifts the risk of obsolescence from user to buyer............	47	37	16
Conserves working capital.............................	53	32	15
Low cost..	5	21	74
Tax advantage......................................	5	20	75
Eliminates problem of equipment disposal..................	47	32	21
Preserves credit capacity..............................	42	37	21
Avoids restrictive covenants in bank loan..................	32	37	31
Eliminates maintenance problems........................	16	42	42

Disadvantages			
High cost..	70%	21%	8%
Does not build an equity...............................	53	26	21
Tax disadvantages...................................	5	53	42
Increases fixed obligations.............................	68	27	5
Difficult to get improvements on leased equipment............	16	37	47
Reluctance to absorb loss if equipment becomes obsolete.......	10	63	27
Forced to use inferior supply items in leased equipment........	0	37	63
Objectionable clauses and limitations.....................	31	47	22
Curtails freedom of the lessee in use of equipment............	21	37	42
Difficult to finance improvements on leased equipment.........	5	47	48

NON-COST FACTORS

In most instances leasing does not offer a cost saving. As a result, justification for the use of a lease arrangement must be based on non-cost factors. Each of the non-cost factors must be analyzed and weighed before a decision is made to lease. The company must prove to its satisfaction that, despite higher costs, leasing is in its best interest. Some of the more important non-cost factors are discussed below.

Respondents to the survey felt the greatest advantage to leasing is that it provides equipment without reducing the level of cash. This is a significant consideration for small and rapidly growing companies in need of cash to pay operating expenses, finance receivables and inventories, and carry on research and development. Companies in strong financial positions do not have to use leasing as a source of working capital.

PRESERVES CREDIT CAPACITY

Approximately 40 percent of the survey respondents felt leasing preserves credit capacity. Their argument is based on the idea that although leasing is a form of debt financing, it is not recognized as such by businessmen. Because the lease arrangement does not appear in the main body of the balance sheet, the debt/net worth relationship remains unchanged. The lack of information on the balance sheet, plus the practice of hiding costs and expenses in the earning statement, may make it possible to stretch borrowing capacity.

Although some companies fail to recognize the true nature of leasing as debt, most financial managers are aware that lease payments are as fixed as interest payments, and have a debt-like impact on credit capacity. Analysis of capital funds following negotiation of a lease generally finds a company in pretty much the same position as if it had issued debt in a sum equal to the capitalized lease payments.

Incidentally, the American Institute of Certified Public Accountants asks for full disclosure of the minimum amount of lease pyaments in the footnotes of financial statements. But even with more complete footnotes in the balance sheet it is still going to be difficult to measure the impact of leasing on credit capacity because of lack of information on the original cost of leased property, its remaining life, and possible salvage value.

There is one special situation in which leasing truly expands a company's credit capacity. A company with temporarily exhausted bank borrowing capacity may lease equipment which it cannot obtain by borrowing and buying. The company can lease equipment because title for the equipment remains with the lessor and cannot be touched by other creditors in bankruptcy proceedings.

It is interesting to note that while four out of five survey respondents considered preservation of credit capacity an important advantage of leasing, many of the same firms also listed increased fixed obligations of a lease arrangement as the greatest disadvantage.

REDUCING RISK OF OBSOLESCENCE

If it is likely that the equipment will become obsolete in the near future, there is an increased incentive to lease and shift the risk of obsolescence to the lessor. However, leasing equipment in an industry where the rate of obsolescence is high is expensive. The lessor will not only demand a premium for the added risk but will make the early lease payments higher to recover his investment quickly.

One factor that does enable a company to reduce the cost of obsolescence by leasing is the lessor's ability to spread the risk of obsolescence among many pieces of leased equipment, and thus reduce the premium charge for the added risk to any one lessee.

A company will substitute an operating lease for a financial lease when it is likely that the equipment will become obsolete a short time after the purchase. The operating lease gives the lessee the right to terminate the contract at will. Thus if better equipment is manufactured the lessee can cancel the lease on the old, and lease the new equipment. Obviously, the leasing payments would be higher for an operating lease than for a financial lease. This assumes, of course, that the equipment is available for leasing. Not all types of equipment can be leased. Equipment that has a very specialized use and may become obsolete in a short time is often unavailable for leasing.

Financial leases stipulate that the equipment will be leased for a specified period of time. During that period the lessor expects to recover his investment and a reasonable profit. If the lessee asks for new equipment to be substituted he will have to pay a premium, the amount of which will depend among other things on the lessor's ability to dispose of the new equipment.

Lessors in some industries encourage lessees to switch to new equipment or to add new peripheral equipment. If the lessor encourages lessees to substitute new equipment for old under the financial lease, leasing does encourage companies to try new equipment. Companies answering the leasing questionnaire seemed to feel that leasing tends to encourage companies along this line.

LOSS OF EQUITY

Approximately half of the respondents to the leasing survey claimed that loss of equity in the equipment was a major disadvantage of leasing. Undoubtedly the idea that a company should own equipment used in its business is one of the biggest obstacles to leasing. That the company will not have any equity in the equipment at the end of the lease is hard to accept. However, because of the time value of money, the value of equity to be received sometime in the future is worth less today, and the loss of equity value resulting from leasing may not be as great as it appears. What is even more important is that the use—not the ownership—of the equipment increases profits.

Terms of a lease should reflect the probability of high terminal value with a large capital gain and a useful life longer than the period over which the equipment is being depreciated. If the terms do not reflect these two factors, by shrewd negotiations the company can reduce its lease payments to reflect the disadvantage of loss of equity and loss of the use of the equipment after the leasing period.

A large number of companies considered that transferring to the lessor the problem of disposing of idle and obsolete equipment is an advantage of leasing. They felt that the lessor is better equipped to dispose of equipment in the used-equipment market. Here again, a knowledge of the state of the used-equipment market may assist the company in negotiating more advantageous terms.

Most of the respondents were aware that leasing offered no tax advantage over buying and that leasing in most instances no longer offers tax shield advantages over ownership.

Leasing does add flexibility to the company's operation. As new equipment is needed it can be leased because the company can use piecemeal lease financing to satisfy its needs for operational growth. Leasing also affords flexibility for companies that use many different types of equipment for a short period.

Lack of restrictive covenants in the contract arrangement is an additional advantage of leasing. The only restrictions in leasing governs use of equipment and does not affect the freedom to manage one's company. Covenants similar to those of intermediate term loans, however, are beginning to creep into contracts as lease financing continues to expand. The fact that ownership of the equipment continues to remain with the lessor, however, should keep the covenants in a leasing contract from being unduly restrictive.

COMPANY BEARS BURDEN

Once the company has decided that the investment in the equipment is a wise use of funds, it must decide on the best form of financing. A financial lease is one way of financing capital. The firm should use leasing as a source of funds either because it costs less or because of non-cost factors. In most instances leasing is more expensive than other alternatives but in some instances may have advantages which add up to financial savings. If a company does decide to lease on the basis of non-cost factors, the burden of proof is on the company to prove it is making a wise choice.

Yield-Risk Performance
of Convertible Securities[*]

Robert M. Soldofsky [†]

How WELL have convertible bonds and convertible stocks performed? How should the performance of convertible securities be measured from the investor's viewpoint? How should the performance of convertible securities be compared with that of other risk classes of securities? Generally, the performance of convertible securities—in terms of the concepts utilized and measurements made—has been poorer than anticipated. The average yields on convertible securities during the 1960's were similar to those on medium grade preferred stock and Baa corporate bonds but the annual fluctuations—and hence the risk—were much greater. These results are shown in Table 3.

ESTIMATED MARKET VALUE OF CONVERTIBLE BONDS

The volume of outstanding publicly offered convertible bonds was estimated at $12.4 billion at the end of 1969.[1] This estimate was based on bond issues listed in *Moody's Manuals* and evidently does not consider

---

[*] Reprinted from *Financial Analysts Journal* (March–April 1971), pp. 61–65, 79, by permission of the author and the publisher.

[†] Professor of Finance at The University of Iowa.

The author wishes to acknowledge the assistance of Mr. Dale Max and Mr. James Gugle, Ph.D. candidates in finance, for gathering and processing the data utilized; Professor Edith Ennis and the staff of the Bureau of Business and Economic Research, College of Business Administration, for their editorial support; and the Computer Center of The University of Iowa for its cooperation.

[1] *Comments on Credit*, Salomon Brothers & Hutzler, June 12, 1970, p. 4. The data for the amounts outstanding by credit rating are from the same source.

the fact that many of the individual issues are selling below par. About 86 percent of the $12.4 billion is in securities rated Baa, Ba, or B. Almost 12 percent were of A quality or better and the remainder was C or lower quality or unrated.

The annual growth in the amount of convertible bonds underwritten and converted beginning with 1960 are shown in Table 1. An amount equal to about 75 percent of the convertible bonds outstanding at the end of 1969 have been issued since 1960. (Table 1 shows the nominal or par value of the convertible bonds issued; no attempt was made to estimate their current market value.)

TABLE 1
Convertible bonds: New issues and retirements
(1960–1969)

Year	No. of new issues	New under-written issues ($1,000s)*	Con-versions ($1,000s)†	Net increase at nominal values ($1,000s)‡	New convertible bond issues as a percentage of total underwritten bond issues§
1959.........	79	514,943	n.a.		13.1%
1960.........	94	347,217	300,000	47,212	6.8
1961.........	82	525,137	200,000	325,137	10.9
1962.........	83	326,494	100,000	226,494	6.9
1963.........	50	228,626	200,000	28,626	4.5
1964.........	49	372,449	200,000	172,449	8.9
1965.........	61	1,183,264	400,000	783,264	19.1
1966.........	96	1,760,690	500,000	1,260,680	20.3
1967.........	230	4,062,278	1,100,000	2,962,278	25.3
1968.........	202	2,698,950	1,000,000	1,698,950	22.9
1969.........	176	3,021,862	1,100,000	1,921,862	22.8
Net Increase...				$9,426,952	

* *Corporate Financing Directory, Investment Dealers Digest.* Several annual issues were used. This series differs slightly from one published by the S.E.C.

† *The Investment Outlook* (New York: Bankers Trust Co.). Various years were used. Conversion given in Memorandum to Table 10. "Financing New Corporate Bond Issues."

‡ Does not represent either the total nominal or book value of convertible bonds outstanding.

§ Based on data published in the *Corporate Financing Directory, Investment Dealers Digest.*

n.a. = not available.

The sharp increase in the relative usage of convertible bonds starting in 1965 might be attributed to the increases in interest rates that began then and to the large increase in the amount of corporate borrowing that year when considerable pressure began to be felt in the capital markets. The distribution of convertible bonds by risk class suggests that many of the issuers were hard pressed for additional funds. Furthermore, many of their financial officers may have believed their corporation's common stock was underpriced at a time when additional funds were needed.

CONVERTIBLE PREFERRED STOCK

Although the demise or disappearance of preferred stock was widely heralded in the early 1960's, Table 2 shows the strong resurgence of *convertible* preferred stock.[2] The reasons are given below. The estimates of the market value of convertible preferred stock listed on the New York Stock Exchange were calculated directly by multiplying the market price for each issue by the number of shares outstanding for the dates given in Table 2. Apparently, the total market value of this type of

TABLE 2*
Straight and convertible preferred listed on the NYSE, 1940–1969

End of year	Number of issues			Market value of issues ($1,000,000)		
	straight	convertible	total	straight	convertible	total
1940.........	312	89	401	$5,345	$ 906	$ 6,251
1950.........	358	75	433	7,311	838	8,149
1960.........	344	58	402	7,267	700	7,967
1965.........	280	93	373	3,434	3,315	6,749
1967.........	277	168	445	3,397	11,482	14,879
1969.........	235†	264	499	4,863	17,777	22,640

* The estimates for 1940 through 1967 were published originally by Robert M. Soldofsky, "Convertible Preferred Stock: Renewed Life in an Old Form," *The Business Lawyer*, July 1969, p. 1392.
† Direct count from published NYSE quotation report for December 31, 1969.
Sources and method of compilation. The total number of issues and their market value are published in the annual issues of the *Fact Book* of the New York Stock Exchange. The number of convertible preferred stocks outstanding at the end of each year and their respective market prices were taken directly from published quotation reports of the NYSE. The market value of each convertible issue was calculated with the aid of the number of shares outstanding as published in *Moody's Manuals*. Numbers and market value of straight preferred stock were determined by subtracting my totals for convertible preferred stock from the totals published by the NYSE.

convertible security ($17.8 billion listed on the New York Stock Exchange, plus such amounts as may be listed on the American Exchange or traded in the over-the-counter markets) is considerably greater than that of convertible bonds. Given the relative and absolute market values for convertible bonds and preferred stock, it is somewhat surprising that the latter has not been the subject of more study.

REASONS FOR ISSUING CONVERTIBLE SECURITIES: CONVERTIBLE BONDS

Convertible bonds are seen as an alternative to the issue of common stock rather than as an alternative to straight bonds. From the corporation's point of view the primary reason for issuing convertible bonds

---

[2]For example see L. Santow, "Ultimate Demise of Preferred Stock as a Source of Corporate Capital," *Financial Analysts Journal*, May–June 1962, pp. 47–54. "The Big Disappearing Act," *Fortune*, December 1963, p. 231.

is effectively to sell common stock at a higher price than that obtaining in the market when the convertible issue is offered. There are various reasons why the issuer might believe that the price of its common stock was temporarily low, such as a general slump in the stock market, a poor earnings performance in the recent past, or the fact that its industry is out of favor. Growth companies may have believed that their stock was favorably priced, but issued convertible bonds anyway in order to gain from the expected continuing rise in the price of their common stock. Furthermore, postponing a new common stock issue avoids temporarily some of the immediate dilution of earnings per share that occurs when new shares are issued. Some companies use convertible bonds to finance new projects during their gestation period. In such cases, it is sometimes argued that convertible securities are attractive to institutions restricted by law in their purchase of common stock. However, the continuing liberalization of legal investments for life insurance companies and for state and local pension funds has probably diminished the force of this argument.

CONVERTIBLE PREFERRED STOCK

The overwhelming reason for the growth of convertible preferred stock since about 1960 is its attractiveness for mergers and the size of the merger movement of the 1960's—the largest in the nation's history. The profound effects of the merger movement on our industrial organization can only be compared with the merger movement in process at the beginning of the century that resulted in industrial combinations such as U.S. Steel.

Three related factors explain why convertible preferred stock is attractive in mergers. First, the stockholders of the acquired firm may insist that a "pooling-of-interests" arrangement be used in order to avoid any immediate income tax payment on capital gains. Only equity securities achieve the required continuity of ownership needed to avoid immediate taxation. Second, among the available types of equity securities, convertible preferred stock enables the acquiring company to meet the expected level of dividend payments of the acquired company's stockholders.[3] Third, until the conversion takes place the use of the convertible form avoids dilution of the earnings per share of common stock and provides additional leverage. Ultimately, of course, the conversion feature permits the shareholders of the acquired company to benefit from expected increases in the market price of the acquiring company's stock.

During 1966 and 1967 almost $7 billion of convertible preferred stock was issued in conjunction with merger financing. Roughly 11 percent

---

[3] For a further discussion of this point, see Anthony H. Meyer, "Designing a Convertible Preferred Issue," *Financial Executive*, April 1968, pp. 42. 44, 51–56, 59, 60, and 62.

of the reported equity-financed mergers utilized at least some convertible preferred stock. Of the convertible preferred stock issued from 1960–1967, 85 percent was utilized in conjunction with mergers; most of the remainder was used to raise new cash for public utilities.[4]

MEANING OF PERFORMANCE MEASUREMENTS

The annual yield or rate of return is defined as the sum of: (1) the dividends received during a year—interest received in the case of bonds—plus (2) the change in the market price from the beginning to the end of the year divided by the market price at the beginning of the year. Obviously, in some years there have been losses or negative returns in terms of this definition. The annual yield concept contrasts sharply with the yield-to-maturity concept on a bond. The latter is a forward-looking concept that assumes that the bond will be held to maturity. All published "historical" bond yield series have this built-in limitation, which glosses over the yield actually achieved each year. These published series also do not satisfactorily display the extent to which bond yields, as defined at the beginning of this section, actually fluctuate. The usual method of determining the current yield on preferred stock by dividing dividends by the market price is also of limited usefulness to investors because it does not give full consideration to the changes in the market prices of the preferred stocks themselves. The new yield series on convertible securities presented here are historical and provide, I believe, a realistic basis for the formation of expected yield distributions.

The annual yield method was discussed in my September–October, 1968, *Financial Analysts Journal* article which developed the yield-risk performance measurements and applied them to a group of 75 common stocks.[5] In that article (page 131), the great advantage of the annual yield method in providing a basis for computing a natural measure of the risk of yield fluctuations was discussed and illustrated. That same measure, the standard deviation of the annual yields, was computed for each group of convertible securities. The yield-risk performance of these convertible securities can be directly related to the performance of other classes of bonds, preferred stock, and common stock.

THE RESULTS

Table 3 shows the yields on Bbb, Bb, and B quality convertible preferred stock from 1960 through 1969 and the yields on Baa and Ba quality convertible debentures from 1957 through 1969. Too few observations

---

[4] The facts in this paragraph were drawn from George E. Pinches, "Financing with Convertible Preferred Stock," *Journal of Finance*, March 1970, pp. 53–63.

[5] Robert M. Soldofsky, "Yield-Risk Measurements of Performance," *Financial Analysts Journal*, September–October 1968, pp. 130–39.

TABLE 3

Yield-risk performance measurements for convertible securities 1957–1969

	Convertible preferred stock*			Convertible debentures*			Medium grade pre-ferred stocks	Baa corpo-rate bonds
			Part 1—Annual Yields					
	Bbb	Bb	B	Baa	Ba	B		
1957...........	—	—	—	−.075	−.149	—	−.002	−.019
1958...........	—	—	—	+.241	+.302	—	+.134	+.084
1959...........	—	—	—	+.005	+.051	—	−.022	+.010
1960...........	−.043	−.019	−.075	+.021	−.007	−.070	+.057	+.070
1961...........	+.075	+.121	+.272	+.140	+.213	+.097	+.080	+.056
1962...........	+.009	−.022	−.071	−.029	−.103	−.214	+.072	+.065
1963...........	+.080	+.052	+.047	+.058	+.069	+.091	+.110	+.066
1964...........	+.095	+.140	−.033	+.134	+.088	+.103	+.122	+.053
1965...........	+.091	+.208	+.308	+.272	+.212	+.220	+.024	+.017
1966...........	−.053	−.048	−.120	−.088	−.094	−.109	−.078	−.075
1967...........	+.277	+.293	+.442	+.157	+.152	+.378	−.025	−.051
1968...........	+.239	+.163	+.089	+.130	+.091	+.104	+.054	+.046
1969...........	−.235	−.198	−.366	−.123	.280	−.311	−.095	−.093
			Part 2—Yield -Risk Measurements					
1957–62								
Ave. Yield......	—	—	—	+.045	+.039		+.060†	+.047†
(Std. Dev.).....	—	—	—	.118	.174		.056†	.037
1960–65								
Ave. Yield......	+.050	+.077	+.064	+.095	+.073	+.028	+.053	+.035
(Std. Dev.).....	.056	.093	.173	.107	.124	.155	.067	.052
1966–69								
Ave. Yield......	+.035	+.035	−.033	+.011	−.049	−.021	−.038	−.045
(Std. Dev.).....	.246	.219	.346	.145	.196	.301	.067	.062

* Standard & Poor's risk classes.
† Seven years from base date.
Note: "+" and "−" signs refer to positive and negative annual yields as described in this text.

were available to permit the satisfactory construction of yields on B quality convertible debentures before 1960. The minus signs in Table 3 represent negative annual yields or losses. For example, the −0.043 yield on Bbb grade convertible preferred stock for 1960 indicates that a $1,000 investment at the beginning of the year would have been worth $957 at the end of the year, including dividends received. The average of the annual yields for the entire period for which the yields were computed is far below what investors may have hoped to earn, and the standard deviations which measure the variability of the performance are very large relative to the yields.

The yield-risk performance measurements for various periods and sub-periods are summarized at the bottom of Table 3. Generally the yields are little higher than for corresponding risk classes of straight bonds and preferred stock, but the standard deviations are much larger. The interested reader may want to refer to the risk-premium curve shown as Chart 2 on page 134 of the September–October, 1968, *FAJ* article, noting where the yield-risk measurement on convertible securities would fall relative to those for bonds, preferred stocks, and common stock given there. The annual yields for medium-grade preferred stock and Baa corporate bonds are shown also in Table 3 as benchmarks because this method of presenting yields is not yet widely used.

CONSTRUCTION OF PERFORMANCE MEASUREMENTS

In gathering the price and dividend—interest data, the minimum number of securities used in each class was set at 10, but that rule was violated 11 times out of the 66 individual yield calculations shown. Most of these violations occurred during the years 1957–1962, because we could not locate enough outstanding, rated issues to meet the conditions. They probably did not exist. From 1963 on, there were only four violations of the 10-security rule, and in each instance nine different securities were used. Eleven Ba and 10 Baa convertible debentures were used for constructing the 1957 yields, which are the earliest presented. The convertible preferred stock series started in 1960, but 1964 was the first year in which the 10-security rule was met for all three grades. No securities with market value outstanding below $5,000,000 were used. A maximum number of 15 securities in each series was used in 21 of the 66 yield calculations. When more than an adequate number of securities were located for a risk class, the smaller issues were not used.

The arbitrary decision was made that any security used should appear in our sample in at least three successive years. In order to qualify therefore, the security had to be outstanding before the beginning of the initial year and still meet the size limitation after being on the market more than three years. This rule may have eliminated some convertible issues that were badly priced or for which a sensational performance by the companion common stock led to an early conversion. Another possible source of bias is the deletion of disappearance from the list of those securities used as the basis of the yield calculation. Over the 10 years for which the convertible preferred stock yield series was constructed, the major reasons for the deletion or removal of individual securities were as follows: 14 were called; 6 became to small because of conversions; 5 had their quality ratings changed; and 2 had their conversion privilege lapse. The reasons for the 57 deletions or removals of individual securities from the convertible bond series were as follows: 35 fell below the minimum 15-year remaining term-to-maturity criterion used for all bonds in these studies; 12 were called; 7 had their ratings changed; and 3 became too small because of conversions. The element most likely to have affected the reported yields were the 26 securities that were deleted because they were called. The price performance of each of these 26 called securities was examined up to call period; in only two instances could it be said clearly that market price performed differently from what would have been expected from the other comparable convertible securities for the same period. On the basis of this detailed examination, the conclusion is reached that the yield series constructed fairly present the results for each risk class. Other investigators using the same measurement technique, would, I believe, report very similar though not identical results.

The annual yields for three classes of convertible bonds and three classes of convertible preferred stock presented in this paper were computed on a basis that is compatible with the yield-risk measurements of performance often applied to common stock, hence lend themselves to Markowitz-type portfolio selection programs.[6]

The performance record of convertible securities indicates that most owners of such securities generally have experienced a combination of low yields and high risk. The currently low prices on many convertible securities may seem to offer astoundingly good opportunities; however, if past performance is any guide when compared with straight bonds and preferred stocks, the yields may be about the same but the risk greater. When compared with common stock directly, the yields on convertible securities have been less, and the risk has been almost as great.

---

[6] Those investors adapting the risk-yield data provided here to such programs may be interested in the fact that the correlation coefficients for the period 1960–1969 between class III (medium quality) common stock and (1) Bbb convertible preferred stock and (2) Baa convertible debentures were 0.75 and 0.47, respectively.

The Euro-Dollar Market:
Some First Principles*

Milton Friedman †

THE EURO-DOLLAR MARKET is the latest example of the mystifying quality of money creation to even the most sophisticated bankers, let alone other businessmen. Recently, I heard a high official of an international financial organization discuss the Euro-dollar market before a collection of high-powered international bankers. He estimated that Euro-dollar deposits totaled some $30 billion. He was then asked: "What is the source of these deposits?" His answer was: partly, U.S. balance-of-payments deficits; partly, dollar reserves of non-U.S. central banks; partly, the proceeds from the sale of Euro-dollar bonds.

This answer is almost complete nonsense. Balance-of-payments deficits do provide foreigners with claims on U.S. dollars. But there is nothing to assure that such claims will be held in the form of Euro-dollars. In any event, U.S. deficits, worldwide, have totaled less than $9 billion for the past five years, on a liquidity basis. Dollar holdings of non-U.S. central banks have fallen during the period of rapid rise in Euro-dollar deposits but by less than $5 billion. The dollars paid for Euro-bonds had themselves to come from somewhere and do not constitute an independent source. No matter how you try, you cannot get $30 billion from these sources. The answer given is precisely parallel to saying that the source of the $400 billion of deposits in U.S. banks (or for that matter the much larger total of all outstanding short-term claims) is the $60 billion of Federal Reserve credit outstanding.

---
* Reprinted from *Morgan Guaranty Survey*, October 1969, and *Federal Reserve Bank of St. Louis*, Vol. 53, No. 7 (July 1971), pp. 16–24, by permission of the author and the publisher.

† Professor of Economics, The University of Chicago.

Assets and liabilities of Euro-Dollar banks*

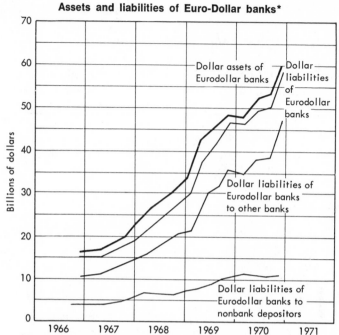

* The reporting Euro-dollars are located in the following countries: Belgium-Luxemburg, France, Germany, Italy, Netherlands, Sweden, Switzerland, and the United Kingdom.

Note: Semiannual data IV/1966, IV/1968. Quarterly data I/1969–IV/1970.

Editor's note: Following first publication of this article, the size of the Euro-dollar market has increased. As the chart shows, liabilities of Euro-dollar banks in eight European countries were $58.7 billion in December 1970.

Source: *Bank for International Settlements*, Annual Report 1971.

The correct answer for both Euro-dollars and liabilities of U.S. banks is that their major source is a bookkeeper's pen.[1] The purpose of this article is to explain this statement. The purpose is purely expository. I shall restrict myself essentially to principle and shall not attempt either an empirical evaluation of the Euro-dollar market or a normative judgment of its desirability.

Another striking example of the confusion about Euro-dollars is the discussion, in even the most sophisticated financial papers, of the use of

---

[1] The similarity between credit creation in the U.S. fractional reserve banking system and in the Euro-dollar market has of course often been noted. For example, see Fred H. Klopstock, "The Euro Dollar Market, Some Unresolved Issues," *Essays in International Finance*, No. 65 (Princeton, March 1968), p. 6. A recent excellent analysis is given in an article by Joseph G. Kvasnicka, "Euro-Dollars—An Important Source of Funds for American Banks," *Business Conditions*, Federal Reserve Bank of Chicago, June 1969. A useful but analytically less satisfactory examination of the Euro-dollar market is Jane Sneddon Little, "The Euro-Dollar Market: Its Nature and Impact," *New England Economic Review*, Federal Reserve Bank of Boston, May/June 1969.

the Euro-dollar market by U.S. commercial banks "to evade tight money," as it is generally phrased. U.S. banks, one reads in a leading financial paper, "have been willing to pay extremely high interest rates . . . to borrow back huge sums of U.S. dollars that have piled up abroad." The image conveyed is that of piles of dollar bills being bundled up and shipped across the ocean on planes and ships—the way New York literally did drain gold from Europe in the bad—or good—old days at times of financial panic. Yet, the more dollars U.S. banks "borrow back" the more Euro-dollar deposits go up! How come? The answer is that it is purely figurative language to speak of "piled up" dollars being "borrowed back." Again, the bookkeeper's pen is at work.

WHAT ARE EURO-DOLLARS?

Just what are Euro-dollars? They are deposit liabilities, denominated in dollars, of banks outside the United States. Engaged in Euro-dollar business, for example, are foreign commercial banks such as the Bank of London and South America, Ltd., merchant banks such as Morgan Grenfell and Co., Ltd., and many of the foreign branches of U.S. commercial banks. Funds placed with these institutions may be owned by anyone—U.S. or foreign residents or citizens, individuals or corporations or governments. Euro-dollars have two basic characteristics: first, they are short-term obligations to pay dollars; second, they are obligations of banking offices located outside the U.S. In principle, there is no hard and fast line between Euro-dollars and other dollar denominated claims on non-U.S. institutions—just as there is none between claims in the U.S. that we call "money" and other short-term claims. The precise line drawn in practice depends on the exact interpretation given to "short-term" and to "banks." Nothing essential in this article is affected by the precise point at which the line is drawn.

A homely parallel to Euro-dollars is to be found in the dollar deposit liabilities of bank offices located in the city of Chicago—which could similarly be called "Chicago dollars." Like Euro-dollars, "Chicago dollars" consist of obligations to pay dollars by a collection of banking offices located in a particular geographic area. Again, like Euro-dollars, they may be owned by anyone—residents or nonresidents of the geographic area in question.

The location of the banks is important primarily because it affects the regulations under which the banks operate and hence the way that they can do business. Those Chicago banks that are members of the Federal Reserve System must comply with the System's requirements about reserves, maximum interest rates payable on deposits, and so on; and in addition, of course, with the requirements of the Comptroller of the Currency if they are national banks, and of the Illinois State Banking Commission if they are state banks.

Euro-dollar banks are subject to the regulations of the relevant banking authorities in the country in which they operate. In practice, however, such banks have been subject neither to required reserves on Euro-dollar deposits nor to maximum ceilings on the rates of interest they are permitted to pay on such deposits.

REGULATION AND EURO-DOLLARS

The difference in regulation has played a key role in the development of the Euro-dollar market. No doubt there were minor precursors, but the initial substantial Euro-dollar deposits in the post-World War II period originated with the Russians, who wanted dollar balances but recalled that their dollar holdings in the U.S. had been impounded by the Alien Property Custodian in World War II. Hence they wanted dollar claims not subject to U.S. governmental control.

The most important regulation that has stimulated the development of the Euro-dollar market has been Regulation Q, under which the Federal Reserve has fixed maximum interest rates that member banks could pay on time deposits. Whenever these ceilings became effective, Euro-dollar deposits, paying a higher interest rate, became more attractive than U.S. deposits, and the Euro-dollar market expanded. U.S. banks then borrowed from the Euro-dollar market to replace the withdrawn time deposits.

A third major force has been the direct and indirect exchange controls imposed by the U.S. for "balance-of-payments" purposes—the interest-equalization tax, the "voluntary" controls on bank lending abroad and on foreign investment, and, finally, the compulsory controls instituted by President Johnson in January 1968. Without Regulation Q and the exchange controls—all of which, in my opinion, are both unnecessary and undesirable—the Euro-dollar market, though it might still have existed, would not have reached anything like its present dimensions.

FRACTIONAL RESERVES

Euro-dollar deposits like "Chicago deposits" are in principle obligations to pay literal dollars—i.e., currency (or coin), all of which consists, at present, of government-issued fiat (Federal Reserve notes, U.S. notes, a few other similar issues, and fractional coinage). In practice, even Chicago banks are called on to discharge only an insignificant part of their deposit obligations by paying out currency. Euro-dollar banks are called on to discharge a negligible part in this form. Deposit obligations are typically discharged by providing a credit or deposit at another bank—as when you draw a check on your bank which the recipient "deposits" in his.

To meet their obligations to pay cash, banks keep a "reserve" of cash on hand. But, of course, since they are continuously receiving as well as paying cash and since in any interval they will be called on to redeem only a small fraction of their obligations in cash, they need on the average keep only a very small part of their assets in cash for this purpose. For Chicago banks, this cash serves also to meet legal reserve requirements. For Euro-dollar banks, the amount of literal cash they hold is negligible.

To meet their obligations to provide a credit at another bank, when a check or similar instrument is used, banks keep deposits at other banks. For Chicago banks, these deposits (which in addition to facilitating the transfer of funds between banks serve to meet legal reserve requirements) are held primarily at Federal Reserve banks. In addition, however, Chicago banks may also keep balances at correspondent banks in other cities.

Like cash, deposits at other banks need be only a small fraction of assets. Banks are continuously receiving funds from other banks, as well as transferring funds to them, so they need reserves only to provide for temporary discrepancies between payments and receipts or sudden unanticipated demands. For Chicago banks, such "prudential" reserves are clearly far smaller than the reserves that they are legally required to keep.

Euro-dollar banks are not subject to legal reserve requirements, but, like Chicago banks, they must keep a prudential reserve in order to be prepared to meet withdrawals of deposits when they are demanded or when they mature. An individual bank will regard as a prudential reserve readily realizable funds both in the Euro-dollar market itself (e.g., Euro-dollar call money) and in the U.S. But for the Euro-dollar system as a whole, Euro-dollar funds cancel, and the prudential reserves available to meet demands for U.S. dollars consist entirely of deposits at banks in New York or other cities in the U.S. and U.S. money market assets that can be liquidated promptly without loss.

The amount of prudential reserves that a Euro-dollar bank will wish to hold—like the amount that a Chicago bank will wish to hold—will depend on its particular mix of demand and time obligations. Time deposits generally require smaller reserves than demand deposits—and in some instances almost zero reserves if the bank can match closely the maturities of its dollar-denominated liabilities and its dollar-denominated loans and investments. Although a precise estimate is difficult to make because of the incompleteness and ambiguity of the available data, prudential reserves of Euro-dollar institutions are clearly a small fraction of total dollar-denominated obligations.

This point—that Euro-dollar institutions, like Chicago banks, are part of a fractional reserve banking system—is the key to understanding the Euro-dollar market. The failure to recognize it is the chief source of misunderstanding about the Euro-dollar market. Most journalistic discussions of the Euro-dollar market proceed as if a Euro-dollar bank held a dollar in the form of cash or of deposits at a U.S. bank corresponding to each dollar of deposit liability. That is the source of such images as "piling up," "borrowing back," "withdrawing," etc. But of course this is not the case. If it were, a Euro-dollar bank could hardly afford to pay 10% or more on its deposit liabilities.

A HYPOTHETICAL EXAMPLE

A Euro-dollar bank typically has total dollar assets roughly equal to its dollar liabilities.[2] But these assets are not in currency or bank deposits. In highly simplified form, the balance sheet of such a bank—or the part of the balance sheet corresponding to its Euro-dollar operations—must look something like that shown below (the numbers in this and later balance sheets are solely for illustrative purposes).

It is the earnings on the $9,500,000 of loans and investments that enable it to pay interest on the $10,000,000 of deposits.

Where did the $10,000,000 of deposits come from? One can say that $700,000 (cash assets minus due to other banks) came from "primary deposits," i.e., is the counterpart to a literal deposit of cash or transfer of funds from other banks.[3] The other $9,300,000 is "created" by the magic of fractional reserve banking—this is the bookkeeper's pen at work.

Let us look at the process more closely. Suppose an Arab Sheik opens up a new deposit account in London at Bank H (H for hypothetical) by depositing a check for $1,000,000 drawn on the Sheik's demand deposit account at the head office of, say, Morgan Guaranty Trust Company. Let us suppose that Bank H also keeps its N.Y. account at Morgan Guaranty and also as demand deposits. At the first stage, this will add $1,000,000 to the deposit liabilities of Bank H, and the same amount to its assets in the form of deposits due from New York banks. At Morgan Guaranty, the transfer of deposits from the Sheik to Bank H will cause no change in total deposit liabilities.

---

[2] Which is why it is not subject to any special foreign exchange risk simply by operating in the Euro-dollar market. The balance sheet of its Euro-dollar operations balances in dollars; if it is, for example, a British bank, the balance sheet of its pound sterling operations balances in pounds. It is operating in two currencies but need not take a speculative position in either. Of course, it may take a speculative position, whether or not it operates in the Euro-dollar market.

[3] Note that even this is an overstatement, since most of the deposits at N.Y. banks are themselves ultimately "created" rather than "primary" deposits. These are primary deposits only vis-à-vis the Euro-dollar market separately.

Euro-dollar Bank H of London

Assets		*Liabilities*	
Cash assets*...............	$ 1,000,000	Deposits...............	$10,000,000
Dollar-denominated		Due to other	
loans.................	7,000,000	banks...............	300,000
Dollar-denominated		Capital accounts........	200,000
bonds.................	2,500,000		
Total assets...........	$10,500,000	Total liabilities.......	$10,500,000

* Includes U.S. currency, deposits in New York and other banks, and other assets immediately realizable in U.S. funds.

But Bank H now has excess funds available to lend. It has been keeping cash assets equal to 10% of deposits—not because it was required to do so but because it deemed it prudent to do so. It now has cash equal to 18% (2/11) of deposits. Because of the $1,000,000 of new deposits from the Sheik, it will want to add, say, $100,000 to its balance in New York. This leaves Bank H with $900,000 available to add to its loans and investments. Assume that it makes a loan of $900,000 to, say, UK Ltd., a British corporation engaged in trade with the U.S., giving corporation UK Ltd. a check on Morgan Guaranty. Bank H's balance sheet will now look as follows after the check has cleared:

Assets		*Liabilities*	
Cash assets...............	$ 1,100,000	Deposits...............	$11,000,000
Dollar-denominated		Due to other	
loans.................	7,900,000	banks...............	300,000
Dollar-denominated		Capital accounts........	200,000
bonds.................	2,500,000		
Total assets...........	$11,500,000	Total liabilities.......	$11,500,000

We now must ask what UK Ltd. does with the $900,000 check. To cut short and simplify the process, let us assume that UK Ltd. incurred the loan because it had been repeatedly troubled by a shortage of funds in New York and wanted to maintain a higher average level of bank balances in New York. Further assume that it also keeps its account at Morgan Guaranty, so that it simply deposits the check in its demand deposit account.

This particular cycle is therefore terminated and we can examine its effect. First, the position of Morgan Guaranty is fundamentally unchanged: it had a deposit liability of $1,000,000 to the Sheik. It now has a deposit liability of $100,000 to Bank H and one of $900,000 to UK Ltd.

Second, the calculated money supply of the U.S. and the demand deposit component thereof are unchanged. That money supply excludes from "adjusted demand deposits" the deposits of U.S. commercial banks at other U.S. commercial banks but it includes deposits of both foreign banks and other foreigners. Therefore, the Sheik's deposit was included before. The deposits of Bank H and UK Ltd. are included now.

Third, the example was set up so that the money supply owned by residents of the U.S. is also unchanged. As a practical matter, the financial statistics gathered and published by the Federal Reserve do not contain sufficient data to permit calculation of the U.S.-owned money supply—a total which would exclude from the money supply as now calculated currency and deposits at U.S. banks owned by non-residents and include dollar deposits at non-U.S. banks owned by residents. But the hypothetical transactions clearly leave this total unaffected.

Fourth, Euro-dollar deposits are $1,000,000 higher.

However, fifth, the total world supply of dollars held by *nonbanks*— dollars in the U.S. plus dollars outside the U.S.—is $900,000 not $1,000,000 higher. The reason is that interbank deposits are now higher by $100,000, thanks to the additional deposits of Bank H at Morgan Guaranty. This amount of deposits was formerly an asset of a nonbank (the Arab Sheik); now it is an asset of Bank H. In this way, Bank H has created $900,000 of Euro-dollar deposits. The other $100,000 of Euro-dollar deposits has been transferred from the U.S. to the Euro-dollar area.

Sixth, the balance of payments of the U.S. is unaffected, whether calculated on a liquidity basis or on an official settlements basis. On a liquidity basis, the Arab Sheik's transfer is recorded as a reduction of $1,000,000 in short-term liquid claims on the U.S. but the increased deposits of Bank H and UK Ltd. at Morgan Guaranty are a precisely offsetting increase. On an official settlements basis, the series of transactions has not affected the dollar holdings of any central bank or official institution.[4]

---

[4] It is interesting to contrast these effects with those that would have occurred if we substitute a Chicago bank for Bank H of London, i.e., suppose that the Arab Sheik had transferred his funds to a Chicago bank, say, Continental Illinois, and Continental Illinois had made the loan to UK Ltd., which UK Ltd. again added to its balances at Morgan Guaranty. To simplify matters, assume that the reserve requirements for Continental Illinois and Morgan Guaranty are the same flat 10% that we assumed Bank H of London kept in the form of cash assets (because, let us say, all deposit changes consist of the appropriate mix of demand and time deposits).

First, the position of Morgan Guaranty is now fundamentally changed. Continental Illinois keeps its reserves as deposits at the Federal Reserve Bank of Chicago, not at Morgan Guaranty. Hence it will deposit its net claim of $100,000 on Morgan Guaranty at the Chicago Fed to meet the reserves required for the Sheik's deposit. This will result in a reduction of $100,000 in Morgan Guaranty's reserve balance at the New York Fed. Its deposits have gone down only $100,000 (thanks to the $900,000 deposit by UK Ltd.) so that if it had no excess reserves before

Clearly, there is no meaningful sense in which we can say that the $900,000 of created Euro-dollar deposits is derived from a U.S. balance-of-payments deficit, or from dollars held by central banks, or from the proceeds of Euro-dollar bond sales.

SOME COMPLICATIONS

Many complications of this example are possible. They will change the numbers but not in any way the essential principles. But it may help to consider one or two.

a) Suppose UK Ltd. used the dollar loan to purchase timber from Russia, and Russia wished to hold the proceeds as a dollar deposit at, say, Bank R in London. Then, another round is started—precisely like the one that began when the Sheik transferred funds from Morgan Guaranty to Bank H. Bank R now has $900,000 extra deposit liabilities, matched by $900,000 extra deposits in New York. If it also follows the practice of maintaining cash assets equal to 10% of deposits, it can make a dollar loan of $810,000. If the recipient of the loan keeps it as a demand deposit at Morgan Guaranty, or transfers it to someone who does, the process comes to an end. The result is that total Euro-dollar deposits are up by $1,900,000. Of that total, $1,710,000 is held by nonbanks, with the other $190,000 being additional deposits of banks (the $100,000 extra of Bank H at Morgan Guaranty plus the $90,000 extra of Bank R at Morgan Guaranty).

---

it now has deficient reserves. This will set in train a multiple contraction of deposits at Morgan Guaranty and other banks which will end when the $1,000,000 gain in deposits by Continental Illinois is completely offset by a $1,000,000 decline in deposits at Morgan Guaranty and other banks.

Second, the calculated money supply of the U.S. and the demand deposit component thereof are still unchanged.

However, third, the money supply owned by the residents of the U.S. is reduced by the $900,000 increase in the deposits of UK Ltd.

Fourth, there is no change in Euro-dollar deposits.

Fifth, there is no change in the total world supply of dollars.

Sixth, the balance of payments of the U.S. is affected if it is calculated on a liquidity basis but not if it is calculated on an official settlements basis. On a liquidity basis, the deficit would be increased by $900,000 because the loan by Continental Illinois to UK Ltd. would be recorded as a capital outflow but UK Ltd.'s deposit at Morgan Guaranty would be regarded as an increase in U.S. liquid liabilities to foreigners, which are treated as financing the deficit. This enlargement of the deficit on a liquidity basis is highly misleading. It suggests, of course, a worsening of the U.S. payments problem, whereas in fact all that is involved is a worsening of the statistics. The additional dollars that UK Ltd. has in its demand deposit account cannot meaningfully be regarded as a potential claim on U.S. reserve assets. UK Ltd. not only needs them for transactions purposes; it must regard them as tied or matched to its own dollar indebtedness. On an official settlements basis, the series of transactions does not affect the dollar holdings of any central bank or official institution.

If the recipient of the loan transfers it to someone who wants to hold it as a Euro-dollar deposit at a third bank, the process continues on its merry way. If, in the extreme, at every stage, the whole of the proceeds of the loan were to end up as Euro-dollar deposits, it is obvious that the total increase in Euro-dollar deposits would be: $1,000,000 + 900,000 + 810,000 + 729,000 + \cdots\cdots\cdots = 10,000,000$. At the end of the process, Euro-dollar deposits would be $10,000,000 higher; deposits of Euro-dollar banks at N.Y. banks, $1,000,000 higher; and the total world supply of dollars held by nonbanks, $9,000,000 higher.

This example perhaps makes it clear why bankers in the Euro-dollar market keep insisting that they do not "create" dollars but only transfer them, and why they sincerely believe that all Euro-dollars come from the U.S. *To each banker separately in the chain described, his additional Euro-dollar deposit came in the form of a check on Morgan Guaranty Trust Company of New York!* How are the bankers to know that the $10,000,000 of checks on Morgan Guaranty all constitute repeated claims on the same initial $1,000,000 of deposits? Appearances are deceiving.

This example (involving successive loan extensions by a series of banks) brings out the difference between two concepts that have produced much confusion: Euro-dollar creation and the Euro-dollar multiplier. In both the simple example and the example involving successive loan extensions, the fraction of Euro-dollars outstanding that has been created is nine-tenths, or, put differently, 10 Euro-dollars exist for every U.S. dollar held as a cash asset in New York by Euro-dollar banks. However, in the simple example, the Euro-dollar multiplier (the ratio of the increase in Euro-dollar deposits to the initial "primary" deposit) is unity; in the second example, it is 10. That is, in the simple example, the total amount of Euro-dollars goes up by $1 for every $1 of U.S. deposits initially transferred to Euro-dollar banks; in the second example, it goes up by $10 for every $1 of U.S. deposits initially transferred. The difference is that in the simple example there is maximum "leakage" from the Euro-dollar system; in the second example, zero "leakage."

The distinction between Euro-dollar creation and the Euro-dollar multiplier makes it clear why there is a definite limit to the amount of Euro-dollars that can be created no matter how low are the prudential reserves that banks hold. For example, if Euro-dollar banks held zero prudential reserves—as it is sometimes claimed that they do against time deposits—100% of the outstanding deposits would be created deposits and the potential multiplier would be in definite. Yet the actual multiplier would be close to unity because only a small part of the funds acquired by borrowers from Euro-dollar banks would end up as additional time deposits in such banks.[5]

---

[5] This is precisely comparable to the situation of savings and loan associations and mutual savings banks in the U.S.

b) Suppose Bank H does not have sufficient demand for dollar loans to use profitably the whole $900,000 of excess dollar funds. Suppose, simultaneously, it is experiencing a heavy demand for sterling loans. It might go to the Bank of England and use the $900,000 to buy sterling. Bank of England deposits at Morgan Guaranty would now go up. But since the Bank of England typically holds its deposits at the New York Federal Reserve Bank, the funds would fairly quickly disappear from Morgan Guaranty's books and show up instead on the Fed's. This, in the first instance, would reduce the reserves of Morgan Guaranty and thus threaten to produce much more extensive monetary effects than any of our other examples. However, the Bank of England typically holds most of its dollar reserves as Treasury bills or the equivalent, not as noninterest earnings deposits at the Fed. It would therefore instruct the Fed to buy, say, bills for its account. This would restore the reserves to the banking system and, except for details, we would be back to where we were in the other examples.

THE KEY POINTS

Needless to say, this is far from a comprehensive survey of all the possible complications. But perhaps it suffices to show that the complications do not affect the fundamental points brought out by the simple example, namely:

1. Euro-dollars, like "Chicago dollars," are mostly the product of the bookkeeper's pen—that is, the result of fractional reserve banking.

2. The amount of Euro-dollars outstanding, like the amount of "Chicago dollars," depends on the desire of owners of wealth to hold the liabilities of the corresponding group of banks.

3. The ultimate increase in the amount of Euro-dollars from an initial transfer of deposits from other banks to Euro-dollar banks depends on:

a) The amount of their dollar assets Euro-dollar banks choose to hold in the form of cash assets in the U.S., and

b) The "leakages" from the system—i.e., the final disposition of the funds borrowed from Euro-dollar banks (or acquired by the sale of bonds or other investments to them). The larger the fraction of such funds held as Euro-dollar deposits, the larger the increase in Euro-dollars in total.

4. The existence of the Euro-dollar market increases the total amount of dollar balances available to be held by nonbanks throughout the world for any given amount of money (currency plus deposits at Federal Re-

serve Banks) created by the Federal Reserve System. It does so by permitting a greater pyramiding on this base by the use of deposits at U.S. banks as prudential reserves for Euro-dollar deposits.

5. The existence of the Euro-dollar market may also create a greater demand for dollars to be held by making dollar balances available in a more convenient form. The net effect of the Euro-dollar market on our balance-of-payments problem (as distinct from our statistical position) depends on whether demand is raised more or less than supply.

My own conjecture—which is based on much too little evidence for me to have much confidence in it—is that demand is raised less than supply and hence that the growth of the Euro-dollar market has on the whole made our balance-of-payments problem more difficult.

6. Whether my conjecture on this score is right or wrong, the Euro-dollar market has almost surely raised the world's nominal money supply (expressed in dollar equivalents) and has thus made the world price level (expressed in dollar equivalents) higher than it would otherwise be. Alternatively, if it is desired to define the money supply exclusive of Euro-dollar deposits, the same effect can be described in terms of a rise in the velocity of the world's money supply. However, this effect, while clear in direction, must be extremely small in magnitude.

USE OF EURO-DOLLARS BY U.S. BANKS

Let us now turn from this general question of the source of Euro-dollars to the special issue raised at the outset: the effect of Regulation Q and "tight money" on the use of the Euro-dollar market by U.S. banks.

To set the stage, let us suppose, in the framework of our simple example, that Euro-dollar Bank H of London loans the $900,000 excess funds that it has as a result of the initial deposit by the Arab Sheik to the head office of Morgan Guaranty, i.e., gives Morgan Guaranty (New York) a check for $900,000 on itself in return for an I.O.U. from Morgan Guaranty. This kind of borrowing from foreign banks is one of the means by which American banks have blunted the impact of CD losses. The combined effect will be to leave total liabilities of Morgan Guaranty unchanged but to alter their composition: deposit liabilities are now down $900,000 (instead of the $1,000,000 deposit liability it formerly had to the Sheik it now has a deposit liability of $100,000 to Bank H) and other liabilites ("funds borrowed from foreign banks") are up $900,000.

Until very recently, such a change in the form of a bank's liabilities—from deposits to borrowings—had an important effect on its reserve position. Specifically, it freed reserves. With $1,000,000 of demand deposit liabilities to the Arab Sheik, Morgan Guaranty was required to keep in cash or as deposits at the Federal Reserve Bank of New York $175,000 (or $60,000 if, as is more realistic, the Sheik kept his $1,000,000 in the form of a time deposit). With the shift of the funds to Bank H, however, and completion of the $900,000 loan by Bank H to Morgan Guaranty, Morgan Guaranty's reserve requirements at the Fed fell appreciably. Before the issuance of new regulations that became effective on September 4 of this year, Morgan Guaranty was not required to keep any reserve for the liability in the form of the I.O.U. Its only obligation was to keep $17,500 corresponding to the demand deposit of Bank H. The change in the form of its liabilities would therefore have reduced its reserve requirements by $157,500 (or by $42,500 for a time deposit) without any change in its total liabilities or its total assets, or in the composition of its assets; hence it would have had this much more available to lend.

What the Fed did effective September 4 was to make borrowings subject to reserve requirements as well. Morgan Guaranty must now keep a reserve against the I.O.U., the exact percentage depending on the total amount of borrowings by Morgan Guaranty from foreign banks.[6] The new regulations make it impossible to generalize about reserve effects. A U.S. bank losing deposits to a Euro-bank and then recouping funds by giving its I.O.U. may or may not have additional amounts available to lend as a result of transactions of the kind described.

If Bank H made the loan to Chase instead of to Morgan Guaranty, the latter would lose reserves and Chase would gain them. To Chase, it would look as if it were getting additional funds from abroad, but to both together, the effect would be the same as before—the possible release of required reserves with no change in available reserves.

The bookkeeping character of these transactions, and how they can be stimulated, can perhaps be seen more clearly if we introduce an additional feature of the actual Euro-dollar market, which was not essential heretofore, namely, the role of overseas branches of U.S. banks. In addition, for realism, we shall express our example in terms of time deposits.

Let us start from scratch and consider the head office of Morgan Guaranty in New York and its London branch. Let us look at hypothetical initial balance sheets of both. We shall treat the London branch as if it had just started and had neither assets nor liabilities, and shall restrict the balance sheet for the head office to the part relevant to its CD operations. This set of circumstances gives us the following situation:

---

[6] The required reserve is 3% of such borrowings so long as they do not exceed 4% of total deposits subject to reserves. On borrowings in excess of that level the required reserve is 10%.

New York head office

Assets		*Liabilities*	
Deposits at F. R.		Time certificates	
Bank of N.Y.	$ 6,000,000	of deposit	$100,000,000
Other cash assets	4,000,000		
Loans	76,000,000		
Bonds	14,000,000		
Total assets	$100,000,000	Total liabilities	$100,000,000
(Note: Required reserves, $6,000,000)			

London office

Assets		*Liabilities*	
	$ 0		$ 0

Now suppose a foreign corporation (perhaps the Arab Sheik's oil company) which holds a long-term maturing CD of $10,000,000 at Morgan Guaranty refuses to renew it because the 6¼% interest it is receiving seems too low. Morgan Guaranty agrees that the return should be greater, but explains it is prohibited by law from paying more. It notes, however, that its London branch is not. Accordingly, the corporation acquires a time deposit at the London office for $10,000,000 "by depositing" the check for $10,000,000 on the New York office it receives in return for the maturing CD—or, more realistically, by transfers on the books in New York and London. Let us look at the balance sheets:

New York head office

Assets		*Liabilities*	
Deposits at F. R.		Time certificates	
Bank of N.Y.	$ 6,000,000	of deposits	$ 90,000,000
Other cash assets	4,000,000		
Loans	76,000,000	Due to London	
Bonds	14,000,000	branch	10,000,000
Total assets	$100,000,000	Total liabilities	$100,000,000

Note: Required reserves, before issuance of new regulations, $5,400,000; since issuance of new regulations, between $5,400,000 and $6,400,000.

London office

Assets		*Liabilities*	
Due from N.Y.		Time certificates	
office	$ 10,000,000	of deposit	$ 10,000,000

Clearly, if we consolidate the branch and the head office, the books are completely unchanged. Yet these bookkeeping transactions: (1) enabled Morgan Guaranty to pay a rate in London higher than 6¼%

on some certificates of deposit; and (2) reduced its required reserves by $600,000 prior to the recent modification of Regulation M. The reduction in required reserves arose because until recently U.S. banks were not required to keep a reserve against liabilities to their foreign branches. With the amendment of Regulation M, any further reduction of reserves by this route has been eliminated since the Fed now requires a reserve of 10% on the amount due to branch offices in excess of the amount due on average during May.[7]

HYPOCRISY AND WINDOW DRESSING

This example has been expressed in terms of a *foreign* corporation because the story is a bit more complicated for a U.S. corporation, though the end result is the same. First, a U.S. corporation that transfers its funds from a certificate of deposit at a U.S. bank to a deposit at a bank abroad—whether a foreign bank or an overseas branch of a U.S. bank—is deemed by the Department of Commerce to have made a foreign investment. It may do so only if it is within its quota under the direct control over foreign investment with which we are still unfortunately saddled. Second, under pressure from the Fed, commercial banks will not facilitate direct transfers by U.S. corporations—indeed, many will not accept time deposits from U.S. corporations at their overseas branches, whether their own customers or not, unless the corporation can demonstrate that the deposit is being made for an "international" purpose. However, precisely the same results can be accomplished by a U.S. holder of a CD making a deposit in a foreign bank and the foreign bank in turn making a deposit in, or a loan to, the overseas branch of a U.S. bank. As always, this kind of moral suasion does not prevent profitable transactions. It simply produces hypocrisy and window dressing—in this case, by unnecessarily giving business to competitors of U.S. banks!

The final effect is precisely the same as in the simple example of the foreign corporation. That example shows, in highly simplified form, the main way U.S. banks have used the Euro-dollar market and explains why it is that the more they "borrow" or "bring back" from the Euro-dollar market, the higher Euro-dollar deposits mount. In our example, borrowing went up $10,000,000 and so did deposits.

From January 1, 1969 to July 31, 1969 CD deposit liabilities of U.S. banks went down $9.3 billion, and U.S. banks' indebtedness to their own overseas branches went up $8.6 billion. The closeness of these two numbers is not coincidental.

---

[7] An amendment to Regulation M effective September 4 established a 10% reserve requirement on head office liabilities to overseas branches on that portion of such liabilities in excess of the average amount on the books in the four-week period ending May 28, 1969.

These bookkeeping operations have affected the statistics far more than the realities. The run-off in CD's in the U.S., and the accompanying decline in total commercial bank deposits (which the Fed uses as its "bank credit proxy") have been interpreted as signs of extreme monetary tightness. Money has been tight, but these figures greatly overstate the degree of tightness. The holders of CD's on U.S. banks who replaced them by Euro-dollar deposits did not have their liquidity squeezed. The banks that substituted "due to branches" for "due to depositors on time certificates of deposit" did not have their lending power reduced. The Fed's insistence on keeping Regulation Q ceilings at levels below market rates has simply imposed enormous structural adjustments and shifts of funds on the commercial banking system for no social gain whatsoever.

CORRECTING A MISUNDERSTANDING

A column that appeared in a leading financial paper just prior to the Fed's revision of reserve requirements encapsules the widespread misunderstanding about the Euro-dollar market. The Euro-dollar market, the column noted, has:

. . . ballooned as U.S. banks have discovered that they can ease the squeeze placed on them by the Federal Reserve Board by borrowing back these foreign-deposited dollars that were pumped out largely through U.S. balance-of-payments deficits. Of this pool of $30 billion, U.S. banks as of last week had soaked up $13 billion. . . .

Thanks to this system, it takes only seconds to transmit money—and money troubles—between the U.S. and Europe. . . . The Federal Reserve's pending proposal to make Euro-dollar borrowing more costly to U.S. banks might make their future demands a shade less voracious, but this doesn't reduce concern about whether there will be strains in repaying the massive amounts already borrowed.

Strains there may be, but they will reflect features of the Euro-dollar market other than those stressed by this newspaper comment. The use of the Euro-dollar market by commercial banks to offset the decline in CD's was primarily a bookkeeping operation. The reverse process—a rise in CD's and a matching decline in Euro-dollar borrowings—will also require little more than a bookkeeping operation.

Euro-Dollars: A Changing Market*

THE LARGE INCREASE in borrowing of Euro-dollars by banks in the United States in the past 2 years has been of major importance for borrowers and lenders in the Euro-dollar market, and has had an impact both on financial markets and on the balance of payments positions of a number of countries.

The rise in outstanding Euro-dollar liabilities of U.S. banks may be measured approximately by the rise in banks' total liabilities to their foreign branches. Such liabilities rose from $4.2 billion on December 27, 1967, to $6.9 billion on December 25, 1968. During the first 7 months of this year the increase was much more rapid, with liabilities to branches reaching $14.4 billion on July 30; in the next 2 months, however, there was only a little further net increase.

The growth in use of Euro-dollars reflected the interaction of rising demand for bank credit in the United States, reduced availability of bank reserves after late 1968, and the maintenance of ceilings on time deposit interest rates under the Board's Regulation Q. Interest rates on newly issued negotiable certificates of deposit reached the permissible ceilings under Regulation Q during the final weeks of 1968. From then until about the end of July of this year, banks increased their borrowings of Euro-dollars with particular rapidity in an effort to meet both rising credit demands from customers and a run-off of maturing CD's. At times in 1968–69, U.S. banks' borrowings of Euro-dollars were also increased by speculative flows of funds out of some European currencies.

Large takings of Euro-dollars by banks in the United States through

* Reprinted from *Federal Reserve Bulletin*, Vol. 55, No. 10 (October 1969), pp. 765–84, by permission of the publisher.

their branches occurred at a time when demands for Euro-dollars by borrowers in the rest of the world were also increasing strongly. For these reasons, interest rates on Euro-dollar deposits rose by mid-1969 to levels which would have been considered highly improbable until this year. Intense demand pressures in the Euro-dollar market helped to accelerate sharply the rapid rate of expansion already experienced by that market in previous years, a development which signaled a growing interdependence among national financial systems.

Flows of funds into the Euro-dollar market from countries other than the United States generally involve a purchase of dollars by a foreign commercial bank or nonbank investor from the central bank of the country whose currency is sold. This year, monetary authorities in some European countries have felt compelled not only to limit further placements of funds in Euro-dollars by their commercial banks, but even to reverse shifts that had already occurred, in order to bolster official reserves. In some countries, such actions were motivated by balance of payments deficits wholly or largely unrelated to Euro-dollar market developments, but even in these cases the strong pull of high Euro-dollar rates was an added consideration in the decisions to impose restrictions on banks' Euro-dollar market activities. Whatever their cause, however, all of the actions taken to force banks to reduce their net lending in the Euro-dollar market were an important additional factor contributing to the steep rise in Euro-dollar rates.

In the United States the Federal Reserve System has sought to moderate borrowings of Euro-dollars by removing a special advantage to member banks that were using Euro-dollars to adjust to domestic credit restraint. Effective September 4 a 10 percent reserve requirement was imposed on net liabilities to foreign branches exceeding the daily-average outstanding amounts in the 4 weeks ending May 28, subject to certain qualifications. The texts of the amendments to Regulations D and M appeared in the *Bulletin* for August 1969, pp. 656–57.

MECHANISMS OF EURO-DOLLAR MARKET

"Euro-dollars" are interest-earning dollar deposits in banks outside the United States; they include deposits in foreign branches of U.S. banks. A bank accepting a Euro-dollar deposit receives, in settlement of the transaction, a dollar balance with a bank in the United States. A bank making a Euro-dollar deposit or loan—other than an advance by a U.S. bank branch to its own head office—completes the transaction with a transfer from its U.S. bank balance.

A bank abroad may take Euro-dollar deposits from nonbanks (that is, from individuals, corporations, or other nonbanking institutions) in its own country or elsewhere. The depositor may have obtained dollars through a current or capital transaction settled in dollars, or through purchase on the exchange market. In either case, the depositor has chosen to acquire a Euro-dollar deposit in preference to alternative forms of short-term investment available to him. A bank may take Euro-dollars also by deposit or by loan from other commercial banks. The lending bank may be redepositing funds which it has itself obtained through Euro-dollar transactions; or it may be using dollars purchased on the exchange market—or through special arrangement directly with its central bank—because it wished to switch out of assets in its domestic currency or some third currency. A bank may sometimes take Euro-dollar deposits directly from some central banks or from the Bank for International Settlements (BIS).

A bank that acquires Euro-dollar deposits may lend dollars to business enterprises in its own country or another country, either to finance dollar payments or for conversion into another currency. A bank itself may switch out of dollars into another currency via exchange market transactions generally covered by forward purchases of dollars. Or it may lend dollars to other banks, including foreign branches of U.S. banks, which in turn may lend either outside the United States or to head offices in this country.

In considering the net effects of Euro-dollar operations on various classes of foreign holdings of dollar balances in the United States, we may disregard redeposits made by banks receiving Euro-dollar deposits since, in the settlement of redeposits, balances pass only from one commercial bank to another. All other Euro-dollar deposit and loan transactions by residents of foreign countries are necessarily associated either with an exchange market transaction (whereby a depositor buys dollars or a borrower of dollars sells them) or with some dollar receipt or payment—for example, for exports or imports—or with withdrawal of dollar balances that had been held in the United States.

Since central banks are the residual suppliers or buyers in foreign exchange markets, it is evident that net market purchases of dollars in connection with the Euro-dollar deposits and borrowings of nonbanks and banks in foreign countries involve a net transfer of balances in the United States from ownership of foreign central banks to ownership of banks operating in the Euro-dollar market. Moreover, the diversion of dollar receipts—such as by foreign exporters—into Euro-dollar deposits makes the reserve gains of foreign central banks smaller than they would otherwise be, whereas the use of Euro-dollar loans to finance dollar payments—for example, for imports—makes those reserve gains larger than if the needed dollars had been bought in the exchange market.

For these reasons, the heavy borrowing of Euro-dollars by U.S. banks through their foreign branches during 1968 and the first half of 1969 served to generate a surplus in the U.S. balance of payments as measured on the official reserve transactions basis. During this period, U.S. liabilities to commercial banks abroad increased, as shown in Table 1, by $11.1

TABLE 1
U.S. Balance of payments on the official reserve transactions basis
(in billions of dollars)

Item	1968 year	1969* Jan.– Mar.	Apr.– June	18- month total
Selected private capital transactions:				
Increase in U.S. liquid liabilities to foreign (private) nonbanks....................	.4	−.0	−.1	.2
Net foreign purchases of U.S. stocks........	2.1	.8	.1	3.0
Net issues of U.S. securities sold abroad by U.S. corporations.....................	2.1	.4	.1	2.7
Increase (−) in short-term foreign claims of U.S. nonbanks......................	−1.0	−.1	.0	−1.0
Balance on goods and services...............	2.5	.7	.5	3.7
Other transactions, not listed below†..........	−7.8	−3.2	−4.0	−15.1
Balance on above transactions................	−1.7	−1.4	−3.4	−6.5
Increase in short-term U.S. liabilities to:‡				
U.S. bank branches abroad................	2.3	2.8	4.5⎫	11.1
Other commercial banks....................	1.1	.3	.1⎬	
Balance on official reserve transactions basis....	1.6	1.7	1.2	4.6
Decrease in U.S. liabilities to foreign monetary authorities...............................	.7	1.7	.9	3.3
Increase in U.S. official reserve assets..........	.9	.0	.3	1.2

* Not seasonally adjusted.
† Includes U.S. private long-term capital outflow, bank credit outflow, U.S. Government grants and credits, remittances and pensions, changes in U.S. liabilities not covered elsewhere, and errors and omissions.
‡ These short-term liabilities are those reported by banks in the United States. Besides demand balances, they include time deposits, other liabilities, and loans and money market paper held in custody.
Source: *Survey of Current Business*, Sept. 1969, pp. 34–38, and partly estimated Federal Reserve data for breakdown of liabilities to commercial banks between U.S. bank branches and other.
Note. Figures may not add to totals due to rounding.

billion, mainly as the result of Euro-dollar transactions. Some minor part of this borrowing recaptured funds that had flowed to the Euro-dollar market out of the dollar holdings in the United States of U.S. residents or foreign nonbanks, but most of the $11.1 billion had its counterpart in net shifts by foreign nonbanks and banks out of foreign currencies into Euro-dollars. Without those shifts foreign central banks would have improved their gold and net dollar asset position vis-à-vis the United States considerably, as the result of other international transactions; instead, the United States had a surplus of $4.6 billion. As Table 1 shows, this provided a decrease in U.S. liabilities to foreign central banks and an increase in U.S. official reserve assets.

STRUCTURE OF EURO-DOLLAR MARKET

The Euro-dollar deposit market is almost entirely a market for short-term funds. The most common initial maturities of deposits, other than call deposits, are for overnight and for 7, 30, 90, and 180 days; very few are for longer periods. A survey of maturities of dollar deposits at foreign branches of U.S. banks has shown that, at the end of July 1969, one-fourth were call and overnight deposits and that the average maturity of other deposits outstanding was 2.7 months. Euro-dollar loans to nonbanks are believed to be of somewhat longer average maturity.

Owners of Euro-dollar deposits and recipients of Euro-dollar loans are spread throughout the world, but most Euro-dollar deposits are in banks in Western Europe. Table 2 shows figures for short-term assets and liabilities, in dollars and certain other currencies, of banks in eight West European countries. It lists banks' assets and liabilities vis-à-vis residents of countries other than their own and includes interbank deposits involving banks in two different countries. (Interbank deposits within the same country are omitted.) At the end of 1968 banks in these eight countries had short-term dollar liabilities, to residents of countries other than their own, amounting to $26.9 billion, and their short-term dollar claims on such foreign residents were $30.4 billion.

The importance of London as a Euro-dollar center is apparent from the fact that at the end of 1968 banks in the United Kingdom accounted for 57 percent of the total dollar liabilities and 49 percent of the dollar assets shown in Table 2. About 80 percent of the dollar deposits in foreign branches of U.S. banks are in London.

The omission from Table 2 of assets and liabilities vis-à-vis residents of the individual country, because data for some countries are unavailable, means that important sources and uses of Euro-dollars are not shown for some of the national banking systems. For example, at the end of 1968, Italian banks had $550 million of deposit liabilities to residents denominated in dollars and other foreign currencies, and on the asset side their outstanding loans of dollars and other foreign currencies to residents amounted to $1.7 billion.

The BIS has estimated the geographic pattern of sources and uses of Euro-dollars for the same eight countries as in Table 2. But unlike that table these estimates, which are shown in Table 3, do include banks' dollar claims on, and liabilities to, local residents. Moreover, the data have been adjusted to eliminate interbank deposits within the eight countries. The term "net size of the Euro-dollar market" has been applied to the totals in Table 3; but the application of any particular geographic boundary to the Euro-dollar market is, of course, arbitrary.

Table 3 shows that in recent years banks in the eight-country area have obtained somewhat more than half of their Euro-dollar resources

TABLE 2
Commercial banks in 8 West European countries' short-term assets and liabilities in certain currencies vis-à-vis nonresidents
(end of year; in billions of dollars)

Country, and item	U.S. dollars		Own currency		Other foreign currencies*	
	1967	1968	1967	1968	1967	1968
Belgium–Luxembourg						
Assets...............	.97	1.46	.19	.33	.47	.81
Liabilities............	.89	1.31	.49	.60	1.05	1.33
Net position........	.08	.15	−.30	−.27	−.58	−.52
France†						
Assets...............	1.89	3.43	.29	.39	.97	1.23
Liabilities............	1.70	3.04	1.07	.70	.89	1.60
Net position........	.19	.39	−.78	−.31	.08	−.37
Germany						
Assets...............	1.03	1.49	1.23	1.50	.12	.12
Liabilities............	.28	.51	1.83	3.03	.06	.06
Net position........	.75	.98	−.60	−1.53	.06	.06
Italy						
Assets...............	2.26	3.20	.20	.30	.68	1.25
Liabilities............	2.14	2.63	.55	.60	.78	1.09
Net position........	.12	.57	−.35	−.30	−.10	.16
Netherlands						
Assets...............	.65	.99	.29	.43	.48	.56
Liabilities............	.81	.97	.52	.62	.30	.50
Net position........	−.16	.02	−.23	−.19	.18	.06
Sweden						
Assets...............	.35	.49	.10	.09	.26	.19
Liabilities............	.17	.21	.19	.23	.09	.09
Net position........	.18	.28	−.09	−.14	.17	.10
Switzerland‡						
Assets...............	3.52	4.39	1.80	2.58	.61	1.02
Liabilities............	2.43	2.82	2.45	3.18	.31	.41
Net position........	1.09	1.57	−.65	−.60	.30	.61
United Kingdom						
Assets...............	9.21	14.98	3.30	4.05	.99	1.80
Liabilities............	9.69	15.38	4.81	4.84	.67	1.59
Net position........	−.48	−.40	−1.51	−.79	.32	.21
Total, 8 countries						
Assets...............	19.88	30.43	7.40	9.67	4.58	6.98
Liabilities............	18.11	26.87	11.91	13.80	4.15	6.67
Net position........	1.77	3.56	−4.51	−4.13	.43	.31

* Sterling, Swiss francs, German marks, Dutch guilders, French francs, and Italian lire.
† Figures for 1967 refer to positions vis-à-vis foreign *banks* only.
‡ Including Euro-currency assets and liabilities of the BIS.
Source: BIS, *39th Annual Report*, June 1969.

TABLE 3
Net size of Euro-Dollar market
(estimated outstanding amounts, end of year; in billions of dollars)

Cumulative sources and uses of Euro-dollars by area	1964	1965	1966	1967	1968
Sources					
Outside area*					
U.S. and Canada.............	1.5	1.3	1.7	2.6	4.5
Japan.....................	—	—	—	—	.1
Eastern Europe..............	.3	.3	.4	.5	.6
Other.....................	2.8	3.3	4.0	4.8	6.6
Total..................	4.6	4.9	6.1	7.9	11.8
Inside area					
Nonbanks..................	1.8	2.2	2.8	3.9	3.2
Banks†....................	2.6	4.4	5.6	5.7	8.0
Total..................	4.4	6.6	8.4	9.6	13.2
Total..................	9.0	11.5	14.5	17.5	25.0
Uses					
Outside area*					
U.S. and Canada.............	2.2	2.7	5.0	5.8	10.2
Japan.....................	.4	.5	.6	1.0	1.7
Eastern Europe..............	.5	.5	.7	.8	.9
Other.....................	.9	1.5	1.9	3.0	4.2
Total..................	4.0	5.2	8.2	10.6	17.0
Inside area					
Nonbanks..................	2.3	3.3	3.7	4.1	4.7
Banks‡....................	2.7	3.0	2.6	2.8	3.3
Total..................	5.0	6.3	6.3	6.9	8.0
Total..................	9.0	11.5	14.5	17.5	25.0

* Banks and nonbanks in all countries except Belgium–Luxembourg, France, West Germany, Italy, the Netherlands, Sweden, Switzerland, and the United Kingdom.
† Amounts converted from other currencies and used for Euro-dollar-type lending, as estimated by BIS; also includes liabilities to central banks and BIS.
‡ Amounts converted to other currencies, as estimated by BIS, excluding Italian banks' conversions to third currencies for relending to nonbank residents (included in nonbank uses).
Source: BIS, *39th Annual Report.*

from within the area. Some of these funds have been acquired through dollar deposits made by nonbanks in the area, but a larger part has come from banks through conversions of other currencies into dollars, whether by exchange market transactions or under special swap arrangements with the Bank of Italy or the German Federal Bank. Among the sources outside the eight countries at the end of 1968 were sharply increased deposits by U.S. and Canadian residents. Of the estimated $1.9 billion increase in 1968 in Euro-dollars provided by sources in the United States and Canada, about $1 billion consisted of the temporary placement in the Euro-dollar market of funds raised by U.S. corporations through bond issues outside the United States, a development that will be discussed later.

From Table 3 it may also be seen that since 1965 banks and nonbanks outside the area of the eight countries have been absorbing a rapidly rising share of the Euro-dollars loaned by banks within the area, with a particularly sharp increase in 1968 in borrowings of Euro-dollars by the United States and Canada. In addition to an increase of over $2 billion in U.S. banks' borrowings through branches and an increase of about $300 million in Euro-dollar liabilities of Canadian banks to banks outside the United States, there were increased borrowings by U.S. and Canadian business firms, partly for use abroad. Table 3 also shows Japan to be an important user of Euro-dollars. Japanese borrowings of Euro-dollars increased in every one of the years 1965–68; this year, there has been some decline since March in the Euro-dollar liabilities of Japanese banks.

EXPANSION OF EURO-DOLLAR MARKET

Rapid growth has been a feature of the Euro-dollar market since its inception more than a decade ago, but the rate of expansion has been much faster since 1967. Dollar liabilities of the banks covered in Table 2 to banks and nonbanks in countries other than their own rose at an average rate of 23 percent a year in the 3 years 1965–67, but the increase was 48 percent in 1968. The totals in Table 3 show a similar acceleration.

In the first 6 months of 1969 the Euro-dollar market expanded even faster than in the same period of last year, according to data (Table 4) for dollar assets and liabilities of banks in the United Kingdom vis-à-vis nonresidents. As was pointed out, the United Kingdom accounts for about one-half of all such assets and liabilities of banks in the eight-country area. There was an increase in assets of 50 percent in the first 6 months of 1969, compared with the 41 percent rise (on a much lower base) in the same period of last year. On the liabilities side the increase was 47 percent compared with 39 percent.

The much more rapid expansion of the Euro-dollar market in 1968 and 1969 has stemmed largely from the effect on the supply of Euro-dollars which the intensified demand has exerted through the pull of higher interest rates. Euro-dollar deposits are a substitute for other financial assets and particularly for time deposits in domestic currency and short-term money market instruments such as Treasury bills. Since 1967 the steep rise in Euro-dollar rates has outdistanced the increases in rates on alternative investments in many countries, thereby enhancing the attractiveness of Euro-dollar deposits.

Because so much of the big increase in the demand for Euro-dollars came from U.S. banks, the increased demand was felt initially in London where activity of U.S. banks' foreign branches is concentrated. However, the impact immediately spread throughout the well-organized and highly

TABLE 4
Banks in the United Kingdom: Dollar assets and liabilities vis-à-vis nonresidents
(end of period; in billions of dollars)

	1967	1968		1969
Assets and liabilities	*Dec.*	*June*	*Dec.*	*June*
Assets (claims against):				
United States.................	4.07	7.13	7.24	13.78
Western Europe..............	2.54	2.61	3.70	4.33
Belgium..................	.23	.25	.34	.46
France...................	.26	.22	.52	.71
Germany..................	.18	.18	.34	.49
Italy.....................	.42	.32	.61	.63
Netherlands..............	.26	.18	.26	.24
Switzerland..............	.30	.46	.50	.78
Other....................	.89	1.00	1.13	1.02
Rest of world..............	2.60	3.22	4.04	4.29
Japan....................	.99	1.32	1.59	1.33
Canada...................	.28	.30	.42	.46
Latin America............	.39	.53	.66	.76
Overseas sterling area.....	.23	.27	.41	.70
Middle East..............	.20	.20	.27	.24
Other....................	.52	.60	.69	.80
Total assets............	9.21	12.96	14.98	22.40
Liabilities (to):				
United States..............	1.38	2.49	2.57	3.35
Western Europe..............	5.19	7.10	8.19	11.76
Belgium..................	.32	.63	.61	1.09
France...................	.63	1.03	.93	1.31
Germany..................	.45	.40	.53	.85
Italy.....................	.74	.98	1.46	1.72
Netherlands..............	.25	.33	.40	.87
Switzerland..............	1.81	2.53	2.82	4.33
Other....................	.99	1.20	1.44	1.59
Rest of world..............	2.62	3.83	4.60	7.55
Japan....................	.04	.07	.06	.14
Canada...................	.77	.92	1.17	2.15
Latin America............	.43	.49	.57	.91
Overseas sterling area.....	.67	1.07	1.21	1.90
Middle East..............	.54	.53	.54	.77
Other....................	.68	.75	1.06	1.67
Total liabilities........	9.19	13.42	15.36	22.66

Source: Bank of England, *Quarterly Review.*

competitive Euro-dollar market. There has been a sharp increase in the movement of nonbank funds to banks in the United Kingdom, but much of the funds moving to London have come from other banks, located in continental Europe or elsewhere.

U.S. banks have not been the only source of rising demand in the Euro-dollar market. Among the special factors affecting demand in recent years have been the voluntary foreign credit restraint program, which has caused foreign borrowers (including U.S. foreign subsidiaries) to look more to U.S. bank branches abroad for credit, and the direct investment control programs, which have encouraged U.S. corporations to borrow abroad. Increases in 1968 in uses of Euro-dollars by nonbanks in the eight countries and also by Japan are shown in Table 3 to have been much greater than earlier, even though Euro-dollar interest rates were moving up; nor did higher rates produce a slowing of the rise in the use of Euro-dollars by the other countries as a group. This year, despite absorption by U.S. banks of a very large part of the addition to Euro-dollar market resources, asset data for banks in the United Kingdom (Table 4) still show a rise in claims on borrowers in countries other than the United States of 11 percent in the first 6 months of 1969. While this was smaller than the 13 percent increase a year earlier, it occurred in the face of much higher lending rates. Dollar claims of U.K. banks on West European borrowers rose faster than a year earlier.

Important forces—some structural and some in response to current developments—have been at work on the supply side of the Euro-dollar market. Structural features which have fostered rapid growth in the past have presumably continued to be operative. Over the past decade the volume of Euro-dollar deposits in major financial centers has increased several times faster than the amount of domestic-currency bank deposits in those centers, probably because of the relatively high degree of competition for Euro-dollar deposits. The monetary authorities of the major industrial countries have never regulated the interest rates that banks might pay for Euro-dollar deposits, and cartel arrangements on interest rates seem to be absent or less restrictive on Euro-dollar deposits than on domestic-currency deposits. Interest rates have typically been higher on Euro-dollar deposits than on domestic-currency deposits of comparable maturity. And as corporations and other large depositors have become more aware of the interest-rate advantages of Euro-dollar deposits, they have become more willing to hold balances in that form.

In 1968 the intensified U.S. controls on the financing of direct investment abroad led to an increase in new issues of securities in foreign markets by U.S. corporations, from about $450 million in 1967 to $2.1 billion in 1968 (Table 1). Outstanding temporary placements of those funds in liquid assets, of which Euro-dollars were a large part, rose from about $400 million to $1.4 billion, that is, by $1.0 billion (Table 1). This year this source of funds has become unimportant, but flows from two other sources seem to have provided fresh supplies to the Euro-dollar market.

First, when foreign net purchases of U.S. securities slowed sharply after the early months of the year—both in new issues abroad and on the U.S. stock market (Table 1)—substantial flows of European and other foreign investment money were undoubtedly diverted to the Euro-dollar market. Secondly, it is clear that unusually large movements of U.S. residents' funds have been generated this year by the attraction of high Euro-dollar interest rates: British and Canadian statistics show increases in U.S. dollar liabilities of banks in those countries to U.S. residents that together amount to about $1 billion for the first half of 1969. The circular flow from U.S. investors through the Euro-dollar market to U.S. banks, brought into motion in this manner, has no net effect on the official settlements measure of the U.S. balance of payments; but it accentuates the deficit as calculated on the "liquidity" basis. (This flow has undoubtedly been an element in this year's unusually large "errors and omissions" item in the U.S. balance of payments accounts.)

Among the forces that contributed to expansion of the Euro-dollar market in 1967 and 1968 were movements out of other currencies motivated by uncertainties about par values. This year, up to September, flows related to currency uncertainties went predominantly into German marks; to some extent, such flows withdrew funds from the Euro-dollar market. On balance, however, there has been a net flow into Euro-dollars in 1968–69 in reflection of such uncertainties—particularly those associated with the French franc and with sterling—in addition to flows in response to high Euro-dollar interest rates.

One result of the large flows to the Euro-dollar market has been to contribute to the decisions taken by monetary authorities in a number of European countries to impose restrictions. These restrictions, which are discussed later, have held back the expansion of Euro-dollar availabilities and thus accentuated the upward push of Euro-dollar interest rates.

INTEREST DIFFERENTIALS WIDEN

Interest rates on Euro-dollar deposits (and on Euro-dollar loans) rose during 1968 and continued to rise—but far more steeply—in the first half of this year, especially in May and June. Movements of the brokers' bid rate on 3-month Euro-dollar deposits in London may be taken as typical of both the movements in rates for other maturities and the changes in rates paid on dollar deposits in centers other than London. The London 3-month rate rose from 6.25 percent at the end of 1967 to nearly 7.5 percent a year later. (Levels are seasonally high in December.) This year the rate climbed to about 11 percent by late June and after some fluctuation was 10.25 percent in mid-October. The primary force pushing rates up this year has been the demand for funds by U.S. banks during a time when the 4- to 6-month commercial paper rate and the day-to-day Federal funds rate have both moved up from around 6 percent in late 1968 to a range of 8 to 9 percent, or even higher, in recent months.

After 1967 the upward movement of Euro-dollar rates outpaced by a wide margin the increases in interest rates in national money markets abroad as well as here, despite sharp increases in 1969 in interest rates in most industrial countries. Because of concern over actual or potential inflationary pressures, the monetary authorities in Germany, the Netherlands, Switzerland, and Canada have allowed market forces to push interest rates higher and have assisted this process by raising central bank discount rates; in Belgium, France, and the United Kingdom the discount rate has been raised and other restrictive monetary measures have been instituted because of both internal demand conditions and balance of payments considerations. Even so, widening gaps between national money market rates and Euro-dollar rates created strong incentives for shifting funds out of domestic-currency assets into Euro-dollars.

For nonbank investors, domestic-currency time deposits are a principal alternative to Euro-dollar deposits. Table 5 compares the rate for 3-month

TABLE 5
Rates of interest on 3-month funds
(at or near end of period; in percent per annum)

		1968		1969		
Type of instrument	*1967 Dec.*	*June*	*December*	*March*	*June*	*August*
Euro-dollar deposit............	6.25	6.25	7.44	8.50	10.50	11.25
Large-size time deposit in domestic currency:						
Belgium....................	4.75	4.25	7.25	7.25	7.38	7.38
France....................	2.75	2.75	3.00	3.00	3.00	3.00
Germany..................	4.00	3.25	4.38	4.25	5.50	6.63
Italy......................	2.75	2.75	2.75	2.75	2.75	2.75
Netherlands...............	5.75	5.63	6.25	7.13	7.81	9.00
Sweden...................	5.25	4.75	4.25	5.25	5.25	6.25
Switzerland...............	4.00	3.75	4.25	4.75	4.00	5.00
United Kingdom...........	7.88	8.00	7.63	8.75	9.25	9.75
Canada...................	6.25	7.00	6.50	6.75	7.00	7.50
Japan.....................	4.00	4.00	4.00	4.00	4.00	4.00
Money market instruments:						
Belgium: Treasury bill.......	4.40	3.75	5.00	6.00	6.55	7.75
Germany: Interbank loan.....	3.96	3.75	4.46	4.50	6.00	6.50
Netherlands: Treasury bill....	4.60	4.87	5.00	5.19	5.72	6.30
Switzerland: Interbank deposit...................	4.00	3.75	4.25	4.75	5.00	5.00
United Kingdom:						
Treasury bill.............	7.26	7.03	6.63	7.61	7.58	7.64
Local authority deposit.....	7.81	8.19	7.81	8.94	9.38	9.69
Canada:						
Treasury bill.............	5.82	6.35	6.06	6.37	6.89	7.42
Finance company paper.....	6.38	7.13	6.50	6.88	7.75	8.38
Premium or discount (−) of 3-month forward dollar against:						
Belgian franc...............	−2.00	2.00	.20	−.72	1.11	10.58

TABLE 5 (Continued)

Type of instrument	1967 Dec.	1968 June	1968 December	1969 March	1969 June	1969 August
German mark:						
Market rate..............	−3.00	−3.46	−4.47	−4.16	−5.63	−5.49
Special rate*.............	†	−4.00	−3.25	−4.50	†	−5.00
Netherlands guilder.........	−1.33	−1.05	−.83	−1.39	−2.32	−.40
Swiss franc................	−2.13	−.65	−1.89	−.91	−1.67	−.24
Pound sterling.............	2.83	5.23	3.79	2.78	3.06	8.13
Canadian dollar............	.49	.95	.45	−.74	−1.70	−.57
Covered interest advantage of Euro-dollar deposit with respect to money market instruments in:						
Belgium: Treasury bill.......	−.15	5.00	2.64	1.78	5.06	14.08
Germany: Interbank loan‡....	−.71	−.46	−.27	−.16	−1.13	−.25
Netherlands: Treasury bill....	.32	.83	1.61	1.92	2.46	4.55
Switzerland: Interbank deposit...................	.12	2.35	1.30	2.84	3.83	6.01
United Kingdom:						
Treasury bill.............	1.82	4.45	4.60	3.67	5.98	11.74
Local authority deposit.....	1.27	3.79	3.42	2.34	4.18	9.69
Canada:						
Treasury bill.............	.92	1.45	1.83	1.39	1.91	3.26
Finance company paper.....	.36	.57	1.39	.88	1.05	2.30

*Special rate offered to German commercial banks by the German Federal Bank on swaps of 3 months or 90 days.

† A special rate is not shown for those dates when swaps were not on offer by the German Federal Bank.

‡ The calculation is based on the special forward rate offered by the German Federal Bank for those dates when swaps were on offer and the rate was more favorable to the banks than the forward rate in the exchange market. Otherwise, the market rate is used.

Source: Domestic-currency time deposit rates: Morgan Guaranty Trust Co., *World Financial Markets;* other data: Federal Reserve Bank of New York and national publications.

Euro-dollar deposits in London with rates on large-size 3-month time deposits in domestic currency at banks in 10 countries. Except in the United Kingdom and Canada, the rate on domestic-currency deposits was below the Euro-dollar rate at the beginning of 1968. The differentials widened during 1968 and have widened further this year in spite of increases in most rates on domestic-currency deposits. At the end of August the interest advantage of the Euro-dollar deposit ranged from 1.5 percent in the United Kingdom to 8.5 percent in Italy.

These calculations are relevant to movements of funds into Euro-dollars on an uncovered basis. But even for movements on a covered basis, 3-month forward discounts on the dollar with respect to other currencies this year have generally not been large enough to offset the interest-rate advantage of the Euro-dollar deposit; the main exception was with respect to covered movements from German marks to Euro-dollars from about the end of April through September. It should be pointed out that in the United Kingdom, Italy, Sweden, and France (since June 1968) shifts of funds of the type considered here have been subject to controls administered with varying degrees of flexibility and effectiveness.

For banks, the standard practice is to keep a balanced position in every currency; that is, in the case of their dollar position, the sum of spot dollar assets and any dollars bought forward would equal the sum of their spot dollar liabilities and any dollars sold forward. The larger part of the spot dollar assets of banks in Europe do not have to be covered forward because a spot liability was already incurred when dollar deposits were accepted from nonbank depositors or other banks. But at times, as Table 2 suggests, the spot dollar assets of banks in a particular country may exceed their spot liabilities. In such cases, banks have acquired dollars by switching out of assets in their domestic currency or some third currency.

Such switching may be done by buying spot dollars in the exchange market and then selling dollars forward—for the appropriate delivery date—in two separate transactions. Or the bank may make a swap with another bank, buying spot dollars from it and selling forward dollars to it in a single transaction. In Italy and Germany swap arrangements of the central banks with commercial banks have been of major importance. Any premium or discount on the forward dollar under the terms of a swap affects the arbitrage calculation just as when a forward sale is made separately.

Covered-interest arbitrage calculations involving the interest rates on 3-month Euro-dollar deposits and 3-month money market instruments, as well as the premium or discount on the 3-month forward dollar, are also given in Table 5. In 1969 the 3-month Euro-dollar deposit has had a covered-interest advantage—usually increasing—relative to money market instruments in Belgium, the Netherlands, Switzerland, the United Kingdom, and Canada. In the United Kingdom, nonresident banks and nonbanks hold large amounts of short-term investments in sterling instruments and are free to shift between these and Euro-dollars. Exchange controls seriously limit the ability of domestic residents to shift funds out of sterling into Euro-dollars. Banks in the United Kingdom may switch between dollars and sterling subject to the restriction of not being allowed to hold spot assets in foreign currencies in excess of spot liabilities.

The swap arrangements between Italian commercial banks and the Bank of Italy carried no premium or discount on the forward dollar until December 1968; from then until February 1969 a 1 percent premium on the forward lira (discount on the forward dollar) was charged the banks. The Bank of Italy has made swaps available to Italian banks since 1959. The availability of swaps was severely restricted from late 1965 until the closing weeks of 1968, but a liberalization of the swap policy in December 1968 and the low level of the premium on the forward lira induced banks to resume making extensive use of swaps. Subsequently, the raising of the swap rate to 5 percent in February 1969 ushered in a new set of policies, to be discussed later.

At various times since 1959 the German Federal Bank has made swaps available to German commercial banks with premiums on the forward mark lower at most times than those in the German foreign exchange market. A comparison of the Federal Bank swap rate or the market forward rate, whichever was relevant, with the uncovered advantage of the rate on 3-month Euro-dollars over the rate on 3-month interbank loans in Frankfurt shows that only infrequently was there a covered advantage favoring Euro-dollars in 1968 and 1969. However, at times when there were large speculative inflows to Germany or shortly thereafter—especially around the end of 1968 and again last June—the German Federal Bank was able to stimulate large placements of Euro-dollars by German commercial banks.

EURO-CURRENCY RESTRICTIONS

Increased borrowing of Euro-dollars by banks in the United States does not appear to have created serious problems of domestic monetary management for most other countries. In 1968, monetary authorities were able to offset any undesired deflationary effects that outflows of funds into the Euro-dollar market might otherwise have had on domestic monetary conditions. Nor were the impacts of these flows on national reserve positions a primary cause of concern. This year, when borrowing of Euro-dollars by U.S. banks has increased much faster, there has been a general tightening of monetary conditions in Western Europe, Canada, and Japan—which, in most cases, has proved to be consistent with the policies desirable from the standpoint of internal economic conditions. However, impacts on reserve positions have caused some concern this year.

Because of reserve losses regarded as unacceptable, banks in France, Italy, Belgium, the Netherlands, and Canada—as well as those in the United Kingdom, long subject to the restrictions mentioned earlier—are now operating under diverse types of regulations designed to limit their lending in the Euro-currency markets. But the actual reserve losses or the prospect of future reserve losses which led to these regulations was by no means the result solely of Euro-dollar market conditions. Domestic economic developments were the main reason in France, while in Italy internal economic and political factors were an important ancillary cause.

The civil disorders and strikes in France in May and June 1968, and the extraordinarily large wage increases that followed, had grave consequences for the French balance of payments. Through most of the year, in fact, official reserve losses exceeded the deficit on current and nonbank capital account, partly because nonresidents were withdrawing funds from franc balances in French banks and partly because French banks were increasing their net spot foreign currency holdings as cover for much enlarged net forward sales of foreign currency to domestic customers. The rise in banks' net spot foreign currency holdings increased the supply of Euro-dollars.

In the fourth quarter, to halt or reverse the drain on official reserves, the French authorities took steps to effect a transfer of foreign currency assets from commercial banks to the Bank of France. One such measure was the cancellation of most of the banks' outstanding forward sales of foreign currencies, which reduced the banks' need to hold spot exchange as cover. In part as a result of these measures, in the fourth quarter there was a decline of $780 million in banks' net assets vis-à-vis nonresidents denominated in dollars and other foreign currencies, as shown in Table 6.

In January of this year, banks in France were instructed to eliminate net foreign currency asset positions vis-à-vis nonresidents by the month-end or, failing this, to deposit the dollar equivalent in a special dollar account with the Bank of France during the next 3 months; banks with net foreign currency liabilities to nonresidents at the end of January were forbidden to reduce them. These instructions explain much of the further reduction of almost $750 million in the French banks' over-all net position with nonresidents during the first quarter of this year. (This figure includes the change in the net position with nonresidents in French francs; for France, as for some other countries, information is not available for 1969 concerning the breakdown of the foreign position as between foreign currencies and domestic currency.)

Thus, between the end of September 1968 and the end of March 1969, banks in France withdrew from the Euro-currency markets roughly $1.5 billion. In terms of pressures on the Euro-dollar market, this was a substantial supplement to the $2 billion of borrowing of Euro-dollars by U.S. banks that occurred in this interval. In the second quarter of this year there was little change in the net foreign position of banks in France.

The Italian monetary authorities took action to restrain Euro-dollar placements by Italian commercial banks in the early months of 1969. The basic balance of payments—on current and nonbank capital account—seemed at that time to be shifting from surplus to deficit, and this soon proved to be the case. During 1968 Italian banks had increased their swaps with the Bank of Italy and had placed funds abroad in large volume, and they continued to do so in January. Moreover, the net outflow of private nonbank capital from Italy, already very large in 1968, began to rise sharply in the early months of 1969, under the influence of uncertainties in the labor and political spheres in Italy as well as the high yields available on investments in the Euro-bond market and

TABLE 6

Commercial banks short-term net assets or net liabilities (—)
vis-à-vis nonresidents

(end of period; in millions of dollars)

Country, and currency	1967 Dec.	1968 Sept.	1968 Dec.	1969 Dec.*	1969 Mar.	1969 June
Belgium†						
Foreign currencies.........	−470	−440	−350	n.a.	n.a.	n.a.
Domestic currency.........	−300	−300	−270	n.a.	n.a.	n.a.
All currencies.............	−770	−740	−620	−736	−680	−662
France						
Foreign currencies.........	260	800	20	n.a.	n.a.	n.a.
Domestic currency.........	−780	−260	−310	n.a.	n.a.	n.a.
All currencies.............	−520	540	−290	−61	−805	n.a.
Germany						
Foreign currencies.........	820	790	1,060	1,347	1,582	1,684
Domestic currency.........	−600	−710	−1,530	−1,112	−167	−300
All currencies.............	220	80	−470	236	1,415	1,384
Italy						
Foreign currencies.........	20	460	740	1,055	1,097	n.a.
Domestic currency.........	−350	−270	−300	−333	−348	n.a.
All currencies.............	−330	190	440	723	749	189
Netherlands						
Foreign currencies.........	80	90	100	n.a.	n.a.	n.a.
Domestic currency.........	−230	−180	−190	n.a.	n.a.	n.a.
All currencies.............	−150	−90	−90	185	334	378
United Kingdom						
Foreign currencies.........	−20	−160	−70	−53	−19	72
Domestic currency.........	−1,510	−930	−790	n.a.	n.a.	n.a.
All currencies.............	−1,530	−1,090	−860	n.a.	n.a.	n.a.
Canada						
Foreign currencies.........	1,130	1,390	1,490	1,482	1,546	1,836
Domestic currency.........	−480	−470	−530	n.a.	n.a.	n.a.
All currencies.............	650	920	960	n.a.	n.a.	n.a.
Japan						
Foreign currencies.........	−650	−486	−413	−413	−497	246
Domestic currency.........	−378	−371	−376	−376	−333	−345
All currencies.............	−1,028	−857	−789	−789	−830	−99

n.a. Not available.

* Figures in this column are comparable with those for subsequent dates, while figures for December 1968 shown in the adjacent column are comparable with those for earlier dates. Where not caused by revisions, differences between series frequently reflect the exclusion of certain foreign currency assets from the figures for the earlier dates.

† Includes Luxembourg through 1968.

Source: BIS, *39th Annual Report*, for 1967–68 except Japan; national publications and O.E.C.D. *Main Economic Indicators* for all others.

in some national capital markets. In addition, Italian business enterprises and other nonbanks have undoubtedly put funds directly into the Euro-dollar market this year in response to high rates of interest. However, for Italy, as for other countries discussed in this article, no accurate measure exists of the amounts of nonbank funds that have gone into Euro-dollar deposits in London or elsewhere.

In February the Italian Exchange Office discouraged further dollar/lira swaps by raising the forward dollar discount to 5 percent. Late in March, banks were instructed by the Bank of Italy that by June 30 they should achieve a zero balance in their over-all net foreign position which, for all the banks together, showed net foreign assets of $750 million at the end of March. This directive was later modified to allow $190 million of net foreign assets to remain outstanding after June. But the reduction of $560 million which did occur meant a considerable net withdrawal of funds from the Euro-dollar and other Euro-currency markets. This was achieved by a rise in the foreign liabilities of the Italian banks rather than by a running down of their assets. Through the first half of this year Italy had a balance of payments deficit of approximately $900 million, but the forced reduction in the net foreign position of banks held the decline in official net foreign assets to about $360 million.

In the first quarter of this year Belgian banks placed a considerable amount of funds in the Euro-dollar market and so added to the drain on official reserves stemming from a deficit on current and nonbank capital account. Belgium, too, seems to have experienced significant out-flows of nonbank funds into the Euro-dollar market. Net foreign assets of the Belgian monetary authorities declined about $330 million in the 9 months from July 1968 through March 1969, of which $110 million was the result of a reduction in the net foreign liabilities of Belgian banks. To prevent further reserve drains, the National Bank instructed Belgian banks to reduce certain assets vis-à-vis nonresidents in the second quarter. Despite this, the banks' over-all net foreign position increased somewhat in that quarter.

Banks in Belgium were instructed to reduce to a ceiling level the sum of: (1) their gross claims on nonresidents in Belgian francs; and (2) the part of their net assets vis-à-vis nonresidents in foreign currencies that had been acquired through the official exchange market. This reduction, equivalent to about $180 million, was achieved largely in the second of these components. However, in the second quarter banks apparently increased their net assets vis-à-vis nonresidents in foreign currencies acquired through the free exchange market. (Under Belgium's dual exchange market system the authorities do not maintain the exchange rate on the free market within the same limits as the official rate.)

Countries in which banks were major suppliers of funds to the Euro-dollar market in the first half of this year included two with very strong balances of payments—Germany and Japan—and also the Netherlands and Canada (Table 6). In three of these four countries, banks increased their gross liabilities to the Euro-currency markets but increased their assets still more. In Japan, part of the increase in the banks' net foreign position came about because banks reduced their gross liabilities in addition to increasing their assets. The Japanese authorities permitted banks to begin financing a portion of Japanese importers' credit needs with loans in yen instead of foreign currency, in view of the high cost of Euro-dollars and Japan's balance of payments surplus.

The circumstances in which the Dutch and Canadian authorities acted to restrict flows of bank funds to foreign markets differed fundamentally from those surrounding the measures adopted in France, Italy, and Belgium, in that the basic payments positions of these two were reasonably good. The Netherlands had a very small deficit on current and nonbank capital account in the first 6 months of this year, while the Canadian balance of payments was in surplus. In the Netherlands, the decline of $185 million in official net foreign assets in the period January–June was almost entirely the result of a rise in net foreign assets of Dutch banks. Nevertheless, to protect official reserves the Netherlands Bank acted in early July to force some repatriation of bank funds. Banks were instructed to reduce their net foreign position in foreign currencies so that the average month-end level in July–December would be 10 percent below the level on May 31 or—at bank option—below the average of the March 31 and April 30 levels. This directive, which required very little reduction of net assets, was followed by another in September that will force substantial repatriation of bank funds by the end of February 1970.

In Canada, official reserves fell nearly $80 million in the first 6 months of 1969 because a rise in banks' net foreign assets—of about $360 million as regards the foreign currency component—exceeded the surplus on current and nonbank capital account. To limit outflows of funds through Canadian banks, in mid-July the chartered banks were requested not to increase further the level of their "swapped deposits," an instrument the use of which has enabled Canadian banks to acquire a large volume of U.S. dollar funds for placement abroad. "Swapped deposits" are U.S. dollar deposits with Canadian banks which Canadian residents place with a bank by selling Canadian dollars spot to the bank and purchasing them forward.

This year, because of very high interest rates in the Euro-dollar market, Canadian banks have been able to attract a rapidly increasing volume of "swapped deposits" by offering high rates of interest on them. Such deposits increased from $650 million in mid-April to more than $1.5 billion in early July, when they equaled more than one-half of total U.S. dollar liabilities of Canadian banks to Canadian residents.

part VII

Valuation, mergers, and acquisitions

TELECTRO, INC.

IN THE EARLY PART OF January 1971, the board of directors of the Telectro Corporation were contemplating further diversification in the light of a national economic downturn. Telectro's sales had not been experiencing the rapid growth they had in the past, and profits took a dramatic fall in 1970. Telectro develops navigational guidance and control systems for aircrafts, surfaced ships, and submarines. The firm also sells components and testing devices for microwave stations. In addition Telectro manufactures hydraulic equipment for aircraft, missiles, industrial machinery, and construction machinery.

The chairman of the board, Mr. Bill Brown, over the past several months had considered a wide variety of companies that could provide Telectro with the sales stability it was seeking. Among these companies, Liquivend was found to be the most attractive because of its remarkable record of growth in the face of stiff competition.

The board of directors of Telectro agreed with Mr. Brown's proposal which called for a merger with Liquivend, they hoped that the company would give added strength to Telectro's weakening financial position. (See Exhibits 1 and 2.) Mr. Brown requested that Robert Knudson, a member of the planning staff, analyze the firm for the purpose of determining a possible purchase price.

LIQUIVEND INCORPORATED

Liquivend had been incorporated in 1954. Its manufacturing facilities and main offices were located in Seattle, Washington. The firm bottles and sells several varieties of soft drinks mainly in the 11 western states.

Also the firm supplies spring water, distilled and fluoridated water in five-gallon bottles, leases electric coolers, and produces exotic fruit drinks. The company had experienced a steady pattern of growth, from sales of $15 million in 1961 to nearly $47 million in 1970. Liquivend's success could be directly attributed to its dynamic and aggressive management which had provided the leadership necessary to compete favorably in a highly competitive industry.

Sales of soft drinks and related products and services attained new highs in 1970, totaling approximately $35 million. The key to this growth, was a new soft drink introduced earlier in the year, coupled with new industry designs for containers and advertising. One of the high points of the previous year was the resurgence of Liquivend's low-calorie soft drinks, following the government's ban on cyclamates late in 1969.

Liquivend became increasingly aware of its responsibilities in dealing with the ecology problem and had therefore taken the initiative in offering productive solutions: antilitter programs, recycling packaging materials, and research into solid waste disposal. Most of the company's products were available in returnable or one-way packages, including the completely reclaimable aluminum container.

The Bottled and Industrial Water Division was quite successful in 1970 with sales and earnings reaching all-time highs. Factors contributing to this success included public concern over water quality, increased per capita consumption, and an aggressive sales program. The sale of pure bottled water to homes and offices contributed the greatest portion of the division's revenues. In 1970, this segment of the operations experienced the fastest growth rate in its history. The division also reached peak performances in its sale of hyper-pure industrial water, a custom-tailored water supplied to a wide variety of users.

FINANCIAL BACKGROUND OF LIQUIVEND

Revenues and earnings achieved record levels in 1970 with revenues increasing 24 percent and earnings exceeding the $2 million mark for the first time as shown in Exhibit 3. The firm had been changing its financial makeup by continuing a policy of retiring long-term debt in favor of equity financing. The most significant event was the public offering of 180,000 shares of common stock, which netted $4.6 million and was used to reduce its unsecured notes with its bank. This had the effect of producing a slight dilution of earnings per share (compared to the expected year-end figure). The refinancing strengthened considerably the company's financial position by reducing long-term debt to less than one third of total capitalization. This debt level provides greater flexibility for financing future growth. However, recent acquisitions increased the current maturity on long-term debt and lead to a reduction in the current ratio. Over the past several years expenditures for property, plant, and equipment were financed by internally generated funds.

LIQUIVEND AND TELECTRO RELATIONS

Bill Brown had been a long-time friend of Herman Bell, president of Liquivend, ever since they first met in college. Mr. Brown became aware of Liquivend through his association with Mr. Bell and became increasingly intrigued with the progress the company had made since its inception. His confidence in Mr. Bell's leadership, combined with the potential of the company, lead him to believe that Liquivend was an ideal acquisition for Telectro.

MR. KNUDSON'S ANALYSIS

In approaching his analysis, Mr. Knudson had decided first to consider the valuation of Liquivend preferred stock. Mr. Knudson determined that there were five basic alternatives:

1. Telectro could purchase the preferred stock in the open market.
2. Telectro could loan Liquivend the cash required to call its preferred stock.
3. Telectro could issue its own common stock in exchange for the preferred stock.
4. Telectro could issue its own preferred stock in exchange for Liquivend's preferred.
5. Finally, Telectro might issue its convertible preferred in exchange for preferred stock.

Among these alternatives, Mr. Knudson concluded that the best course of action for Telectro was to issue the convertible preferred. The existing market price for Liquivend's $5 per preferred stock was $65. Using an exchange ratio based on market price (Telectro's convertible preferred was at $81) Telectro would have to issue 35,700 shares at a total price of $2.68 million to retire Liquivend's preferred shares. Mr. Knudson felt that this price would receive a favorable reaction from the preferred shareholders since they would have the opportunity to equalize their market value and attain possible capital gains through price appreciation on the common stock.

The principle problem then confronting Mr. Knudson was the determination of a price for Liquivend's common equity. Mr. Knudson had already eliminated from consideration a cash purchase of the common equity because of the unfavorable effect of goodwill on Liquivend's earnings. Therefore, the merger would be accounted for on a "pooling of interests" basis. Mr. Knudson first had to determine a price for the common equity and then calculate the number of shares Telectro would have to offer in exchange for Liquivend common shares. He realized that he might have to use the market price of the common stock in several of his calculations; therefore, he considered the possible use of a frequency distribution of the market price as the basis for his exchange ratio. This was only one of several exchange ratios that he would have to evaluate.

EXHIBIT 1
TELECTRO, INC.
Consolidated income statements
for years ended December 31, 1966–70
(dollar figures in thousands)

	1970	1969	1968	1967	1966
Sales and other revenues....	$1,661,781	$1,610,840	$1,564,510	$1,513,608	$1,280,8?
Cost of operations:					
Cost of sales and services.............	1,124,630	1,050,416	1,039,947	1,034,052	931,1
Selling, general, administrative expense........	270,276	254,538	224,813	210,635	157,8
Depreciation............	107,240	90,770	85,217	75,350	36,2?
Rent...................	30,579	27,389	24,902	23,140	13,5
State and local taxes......	21,764	23,799	22,767	19,746	12,1
Interest................	31,234	21,086	18,440	14,681	5,2
Total Cost of Operations......	$1,585,723	$1,467,998	$1,416,086	$1,377,604	$1,156,1
Profit before income tax....	77,058	142,842	148,424	136,004	124,6?
Income taxes.............	31,200	67,200	71,400	62,250	58,5
Net Income.......	$ 45,858	$ 75,642	$ 77,024	$ 73,754	$ 66,1
Dividends on preferred stock					
$3.50 Preferred	294	300	305	319	3
$4.00 Preferred..........	2,472	2,472	2,462	2,452	?
Earnings applicable to common...............	$ 43,092	$ 72,870	$ 74,257	$ 70,983	$ 65,8
Shares of common outstanding............	34,320,570	31,537,950	31,391,526	31,364,490	29,729,1
Per share of common stock:					
Earnings...............	$1.26	$2.32	$2.37	$2.27	$2.
Cash dividends.........	0.98	0.98	0.98	0.40	0.

EXHIBIT 2

TELECTRO, INC.
Consolidated balance sheet
for years ended December 31, 1969–70
(dollar figures in thousands)

ASSETS

Current Assets	1970	1969
Cash...............................	$ 68,242	$ 66,359
Marketable securities..............	43,931	34,972
Receivables, net...................	279,534	272,074
Inventories........................	204,310	213,969
Prepaid expenses...................	144,320	139,048
Total Current Assets.......	$ 740,337	$ 726,422
Fixed Assets		
Receivables due after one year.....	$ 79,242	$ 49,306
Investments in subsidiaries........	70,186	63,772
Land, plant and equipment..........	959,041	869,478
Less: Allowance for depreciation...	(380,742)	(343,130)
Total Fixed Assets.........	$ 578,299	$ 526,348
Total Assets...............	$1,468,064	$1,365,848

LIABILITIES AND STOCKHOLDERS' EQUITY

Current Liabilities	1970	1969
Notes payable......................	$ 37,326	$ 32,500
Accounts payable—Accruals..........	291,934	297,928
Income taxes payable...............	14,821	22,476
Dividends payable..................	9,964	9,328
Total Current Liabilities...	$ 354,045	$ 362,232
Long-term Liabilities		
4⅗% Debenture (due 1986)........	$ 378,886	$ 314,537
8¼% Debenture (due 1993)........	189,444	157,274
Total Long-term Debt.......	$ 568,330	$ 471,821
Stockholders' Equity		
$3.50 Cumulative Preferred*.....	$ 1,366	$ 1,386
$4.00 Convertible Preferred†.....	4,944	4,944
Common Stock....................	22,880	22,714
Additional Paid-in Capital.......	223,767	219,624
Retained Earnings................	292,732	283,127
Total Liabilities and Equity......	$1,468,064	$1,365,848

* 84,460 shares outstanding—1970, 85,660 shares outstanding—1969. Liquidation value $100 per share.
† 617,943 shares outstanding—1970, 617,960 shares outstanding—1969. Liquidation value $100 per share.

EXHIBIT 3

TELECTRO, INC.

Liquivend Company's consolidated income statements
for years ended December 31, 1966–70
(dollar figures in thousands)

	1970	1969	1968	1967	1966
Sales and other revenues.........	$46,389	$37,277	$31,332	$19,705	$17,98
Cost of goods sold..............	23,304	19,306	14,832	10,060	8,78
Gross Margin on Sales.......	$23,085	$17,971	$16,500	$ 9,645	$ 9,19
Selling, general, administrative					
expense.....................	15,818	13,352	11,331	6,622	6,38
Interest expense................	959	922	198	—	—
Income before taxes............	$ 6,308	$ 3,697	$ 4,971	$ 3,023	$ 2,81
Income taxes..................	3,004	1,925	2,516	1,362	1,26
Net Income...........	$ 3,304	$ 1,772	$ 2,455	$ 1,661	$ 1,54
Dividends on preferred..........	514	257	411	411	—
Earnings applicable to common....	$ 2,790	$ 1,515	$ 2,044	$ 1,250	$ 1,54
Shares of common outstanding....	1,246,247	1,066,247	1,064,692	1,055,317	1,053,74
Per share of common stock:					
Earnings after preferred					
dividends...............	2.24	1.42	1.92	1.18	1.4
Cash dividends............	0.48	0.45	0.42	0.34	0.2

EXHIBIT 4

TELECTRO, INC.
Liquivend Company's consolidated balance sheet
for years ended December 31, 1969–70
(dollar figures in thousands)

ASSETS

	1970	1969
Current Assets		
Cash	$ 1,890	$ 854
Marketable securities	250	465
Receivables	4,152	3,901
Less: Allowance for bad debt	(196)	(116)
Inventories	2,216	2,113
Prepaid expenses	630	526
Total Current Assets	$ 8,942	$ 7,743
Fixed Assets		
Land	$ 2,092	$ 1,887
Plant and equipment	20,178	18,377
Less: Allowance for depreciation	(8,866)	(7,764)
Net Plant and Equipment	$11,312	$10,613
Returnable containers*	2,264	2,244
Intangibles		
Goodwill	6,496	6,487
Franchises and patents	1,559	1,164
Total Assets	$32,665	$30,138

LIABILITIES AND STOCKHOLDERS' EQUITY

	1970	1969
Current Liabilities		
Accounts payable	$ 1,642	$ 1,146
Accrued liabilities	1,132	1,286
Current long-term debt	959	372
Income taxes payable	1,042	243
Total Current Liabilities	$ 4,775	$ 3,047
Long-Term Liabilities		
Unsecured note payable†	$ 3,975	$ 8,750
Notes payable, 8¾%	3,380	3,650
Customers' deposits	1,244	1,200
Deferred income taxes	864	788
Total Liabilities	$14,238	$17,435
Stockholders' Equity		
Preferred stock, $20 par†	$ 1,028	$ 1,028
Common stock, $1 par	1,246	1,066
Additional paid-in capital	5,065	1,711
Retained Earnings	11,088	8,898
Total Liabilities and Stockholders' Equity	$32,665	$30,138

* Net depreciation.
† Call price $60.

EXHIBIT 5
TELECTRO, INC.
Price ranges

	Telectro common		Liquivend common	
	High	*Low*	*Bid*	*Ask*
1969				
January	$48¾	$43¾	$41	$41½
February	45	42½	37¼	37¾
March	45	41⅜	37¼	37¾
April	47⅝	41¼	38½	39
May	47½	43¾	37	37⅝
June	45	40½	37⅛	37¾
July	41¼	35	37⅛	37⅝
August	48¾	35⅜	27¾	28¾
September	42⅝	36¼	38½	39
October	44⅞	41⅛	43½	44
November	41⅜	36⅞	47⅝	48
December	37⅜	32½	48	48½
1970				
January	33⅞	30⅛	52¼	52⅝
February	31⅜	30	45¾	46⅛
March	31⅛	29⅞	51	51½
April	33	29¼	46¾	47¼
May	31¼	23¾	38⅝	39⅛
June	25	20	42¾	43¼
July	25	20	38⅝	39⅛
August	23¾	19¼	35¼	35¾
September	27½	23¾	32⅛	32⅝
October	27⅝	23¾	28¼	28¾
November	26⅛	22¼	27⅝	28⅛
December	27½	24⅛	32⅛	32⅕

VOSTRON INDUSTRIES

IT IS March 1968, and the board of directors of Vostron Industries is considering various methods of solving its financing problems. Rapid growth and undercapitalization, demonstrated in Exhibits 1 and 2, have created a very serious liquidity problem for the firm. At present, the members of the board feel that the firm faces four alternative courses of action: two involve the use of debt and convertible securities, and two involve possible merger with larger firms.

In March of 1965, John Vostmyer, Fred Goossens, and Fritz Goossens pooled their electronic knowledge and applied it to the field of printed circuitry. The result was the incorporation of Vostron Industries, a California corporation. For the first year of operations, which ended February 1966, the company proved to be very profitable with printed circuit boards as the sole product line. In March 1966, the president of Vostron, John Vostmyer, was approached by three members of another electronics firm about the possibility of creating a new division of Vostron to produce and sell welded electronics modules on a contract basis. These three, James Gates, Ronald Barnes, and Fran Ross, demonstrated a detailed knowledge of the production and marketing techniques required for the new product line. After careful consideration, Mr. Vostmyer recommended to the board of directors that the formation of a new division, to be known as E.P.I. (Electronic Packaging Industries) was in the best interests of the company. The new division was voted into existence, and each of the new members of the management team was presented with the opportunity of purchasing varying amounts of the company's common stock. These six individuals now own over 96 percent of the common stock of Vostron and also sit on the board of the company. The remaining common shares are held by various operating personnel.

From Vostron's original plant in Santa Ana, California, the company has expanded into two new facilities. The company first expanded to nearby Tustin, California, and then to Page, Arizona. Product lines have been expanded from the original printed circuit boards to include welded electronic modules, cable assemblies, and flexible circuits. At the present time the company employs 120 full-time personnel. The company has been able to grow to this point through the contributions of owners, the plowing back of internally generated funds, and the use of accounts receivable financing.

The firm has enjoyed rapid growth in sales since 1965, as shown in Exhibit 2. These increasing sales required corresponding increases in the asset structure of the firm. As a result, accounts receivable and inventories grew rapidly. At first, the firm was able to finance this expansion through internally generated funds and the increased contributions of owners. However, with sales increasing fantastically, sometimes doubling in three months, management found that these sources would soon be inadequate. Faced with a growing cash flow problem, the management went out in search of short-term borrowing from local banks. These attempts resulted in little success, due to the unwillingness of the banks to extend short-term credit for such long-term needs.

At this point, facing severe cash problems, the board viewed the accounts receivable as being a possible source of funds. They first attempted to shorten the collection period for outstanding accounts. Billings offering better terms to various customers were made, varying from $1/30$ net 60, to $2/10$ net 60, and finally to $2/30$ net 60, depending upon the amount of the receivable and the projected likelihood of collection. This attempt to obtain cash also met with failure due to the makeup of Vostron's customers, of which approximately 95 percent were government subcontractors who were faced with the same types of collection problems.

As an alternative to decreasing the collection period, accounts receivable financing was considered. Taking this action would offer Vostron the use of funds immediately upon the sale of goods. In considering this alternative, management was very concerned with the high interest costs involved with such financing. Several banks were contracted and an arrangement which management felt justified (given the prevailing circumstances and the urgent need for funds) was finally reached with the Bank of America. The bank agreed to advance Vostron 70 percent of the face value of the accounts discounted for a period of 60 days. At the end of the 60-day period, any unpaid accounts would have to be repurchased by the company. Billing was to be handled by the bank; this meant that the bulk of the paper work was their responsibility. The approximate interest rate for the discounting was $9\frac{1}{4}$ percent per annum. The bank put an upper limit on the amount of actual funds advanced at $250,000. Vostron's management was pleased with this arrangement for they felt that this would give them sufficient financing for expected sales growth.

For approximately the next full year, Vostron's cash flow problems were under control. During this time period, the firm added cable assemblies and flexible circuits to their existing product lines. With the rapid growth in sales and with the expansion of inventories and fixed assets required for the two new product lines, Vostron was again faced with a cash flow problem in February 1968. At this point, accounts receivable of $190,000 had been assigned to the Bank of America to secure an indebtedness of $133,038. With anticipated growth in sales to $3.6 million for the fiscal year 1968, the board of directors felt that the $250,000 limit for funds advanced was less than four months from being completely utilized. Accruals at this point had reached a level of $246,000, and the directors of Vostron realized that a decision had to be made about the rate of growth of the firm. They were faced with the dilemma of either slowing growth or seeking some sort of outside financing. The board decided against reducing growth and voted to open a new facility which would require $110,000 in leasehold improvements and $300,000 in new equipment. At this point, the board estimated a need of approximately $1.5 million for increasing fixed assets and for financing the levels of inventory and accounts receivable that would be reached in attaining the 1968 sales projection of $3.6 million.

As a first thought to raising needed funds, the board considered contacting individual investors who had substantial amounts of idle funds. Several members of the board, including John Vostmyer and Fred Goossens, had personal contacts with such individuals. After preliminary discussions with several of them, it was found that the restrictions they would demand under such circumstances would hamper the freedom of the firm. Typical restrictions included maintaining a minimum working capital position, having a minimum current ratio, and restricting amounts of debt financing in the future. These conditions varied according to the individual contacted, but the board felt that they were all too restrictive in nature and ruled them out as possible alternatives. After ruling out this approach to obtaining the needed funds, the board now saw four possible alternatives open to them.

The first two alternatives involved the use of debt and convertible securities. One offer came from the Bank of America and the other from a large brokerage company, Glass and Company. Vostron was interested in discovering what in the line of debt financing was available to the firm and as a first step went to the Bank of America. Upon preliminary negotiations, the Bank made an offer of $500,000, of which $200,000 would be straight debt and $300,000 convertible securities. The $300,000 in convertible securities would be convertible into a 30 percent interest in Vostron's common stock at the option of the bank. The board felt that they could do better than this, and after further negotiations, the Bank agreed, in addition to increase the level of funds advanced for receivables discounting to $750,000.

In an effort to evaluate this proposal in proper perspective, the board decided to look for another source of long-term debt financing. After contacting several sources, Glass and Company has made an offer to supply Vostron with $500,000 in the form of a five-year convertible loan. The agreement stipulates that Glass and Company has the option to convert the $500,000 loan into a 10 percent interest in Vostron common stock within the five-year period. If the brokerage firm did not choose to convert, Vostron would be required to repay the $500,000 principle amount plus accrued interest at 9 percent per annum. This plan was reached after several sessions with representatives from Glass and Company and was believed to be their best offer.

The next two alternatives involve possible merger with larger companies. One offer comes from Salem Labs, an eastern firm listed on the American Stock Exchange. Salem Labs is a research-oriented firm that achieves a high percentage of sales, around 90 percent, from government contracts. Exhibit 7 shows that the company has grown very rapidly, with sales increasing from $1.35 million in 1964 to $10.47 million in 1967. Salem has been searching for a small-growth company that would enable the parent company to maintain its impressive growth record and yet not blemish its scientific image.

The Salem Labs offer involves a certain number of shares that would be transferred to Vostron stockholders immediately for all of Vostron's stock plus an additional number of shares which would be transferred to the Vostron stockholders if certain performance standards are met. Initially, Vostron would receive 30,000 shares of Salem, which is presently selling for $100 per share. At the end of the first year following the merger, Vostron would get one share of Salem for each $4 that their aftertax earnings are over $200,000, up to a limit of 10,000 shares. At the end of the second year, Vostron would receive one share for each $4 that aftertax earnings are over $300,000, up to 10,000 shares. Vostron's directors feel reasonably certain that they will meet the first year's performance standards but are apprehensive about receiving the full 10,000 shares the second year.

If Vostron's board of directors decides to accept the Salem Labs' offer, the new parent company has made it clear that the merger would be complete. Immediately Vostron would be expected to adopt Salem's accounting system and Vostron's management team's performance would be subject to continual evaluation by Salem's management. The consolidated balance sheet for Salem Labs and Vostron is shown in Exhibit 8.

Another merger offer comes from Bell Electronics, listed on the American Stock Exchange. Bell, too, is a rapidly growing firm looking for a growth company to bolster both sales and profits. Bell's sales have increased from $5.3 million in 1964, to $9.06 million in 1967. Unlike Salem Labs, however, Bell is not strictly defense oriented. In early 1968, approximately 60 percent of Bell's sales were achieved through defense-oriented products with the remaining 40 percent being consumer-oriented product sales.

Bell's management is offering to exchange Vostron's 120,000 shares for 120,000 shares of Bell. At the present time, Bell's stock is selling at approximately $30 per share. In addition, since Vostron's personnel must agree not to sell the shares they would acquire for two years after completion of the merger, there would be a value guarantee clause included in the contract. The stock is guaranteed by Bell to have a value of $41.67 at the end of the two-year period. This figure is to be adjusted for stock splits and dividends. If the market value is less than the $41.67, Bell would issue more shares to bring the total value of the company up to this level. A maximum of 30,000 shares, to be adjusted for stock splits and stock dividends, has been placed on this guarantee.

Bell would not step in and completely take over Vostron. The new parent company would gradually change Vostron's accounting system and Vostron's management would continue on its own as long as the proposed subsidiary met mutually agreed upon profit objectives. The plan presented by Bell also stipulates that the present managers of Vostron sign two- or three-year employment contracts. A consolidated balance sheet for Bell and Vostron is shown in Exhibit 5.

EXHIBIT 1

VOSTRON INDUSTRIES

Balance sheets

February 28, 1966 and 1967 and quarters 1968

	February 28 1966	February 28 1967	May 31 1967	August 31 1967	November 30 1967	February 28 1968
ASSETS						
Current Assets						
Cash..................	$17,778	$ 150	$ (2,086)	$ 18,003	$ 6,708	$ 1,719
Accounts receivables......	15,209	155,558	241,854	329,418	296,512	431,703
Notes receivable.........		45,000	22,500	22,500	20,155	
Inventory..............	7,247	53,035	60,725	184,332	299,446	238,114
Prepaid expenses........	3,459	7,499	8,631	11,301	16,755	30,912
Total Current Assets..........	$43,693	$261,242	$331,624	$565,554	$639,576	$702,448
Fixed assets..............	39,918	82,798	109,120	166,927	179,519	203,406
Less: Accumulated depreciation............	3,664	17,912	22,529	29,389	38,973	49,544
Net fixed assets............	36,254	64,886	86,591	137,538	140,546	153,862
Other assets..............	6,034	6,586	5,769	5,738	5,708	5,607
Total Assets......	$85,981	$332,714	$423,984	$708,830	$785,830	$861,917
LIABILITIES AND STOCKHOLDERS' EQUITY						
Current Liabilities						
Accounts payable........	$ 9,939	$ 68,803	$102,671	$176,645	$177,410	$163,549
Notes payable-current....	2,717	43,482	25,572	97,258	72,106	133,038
Accruals...............	17,311	50,252	75,455	144,162	195,890	246,569
Total Current Liabilities.......	$29,967	$162,537	$203,698	$418,065	$445,406	$543,156
Deferrals						
Notes payable...........	3,356	2,564				
Stockholders loans........	14,512	43,513	43,512	43,512	57,513	49,513
Investment tax credit.....		3,759	3,759	3,759	3,759	–0–
Total Deferrals....	17,868	49,836	47,271	47,271	61,272	49,513
Stockholders Equity						
Common stock, $1 par....	15,000	25,000	25,000	25,000	120,000	120,000
Paid-in surplus..........		65,000	65,000	65,000		
Retained earnings........	23,145	30,341	83,015	153,494	159,152	149,248
Total Stockholders' Equity..........	38,145	120,341	173,015	243,494	279,152	269,248
	$85,891	$332,714	$423,984	$708,830	$785,850	$861,917

EXHIBIT 2
VOSTRON INDUSTRIES
Income statement
for fiscal years ended February 28, 1966 and 1967 and for quarters 1968

	February 28 1966	February 28 1967	May 31 1967 3 mos.	August 31 1967 6 mos.	November 30 1967 9 mos.	February 29 1968 1 Year
Net sales...............	$149,330	$636,381	$394,492	$863,319	$1,410,140	$2,148,153
Cost of goods sold.......	87,184	435,075	251,482	518,361	906,259	1,464,525
Gross Profit........	$ 62,146	$201,306	$143,010	$344,958	$ 503,881	$ 683,628
Selling, general and administrative expenses....	34,322	152,302	47,444	107,565	188,882	301,435
Depreciation expense......	3,664	13,807	4,617	11,328	19,654	33,913
Interest expense........	1,259	6,234	2,103	3,994	7,015	11,744
Net Income from Operations.....	$ 22,901	$ 28,963	$ 88,846	$222,071	$ 288,330	$ 336,536
Other income........	246	339	146	2,710	5,172	3,681
Other expenses........		(13,162)	(218)	(428)	(691)	(69,710)
Total Income........	23,147	16,140	88,774	224,353	292,811	270,507
Federal income taxes......		487	36,100	101,200	134,000	121,600
Net Income.............	$ 23,147	$ 15,653	$ 52,674	$123,153	$ 158,811	$ 148,907

EXHIBIT 3
VOSTRON INDUSTRIES
Bell Electronics' consolidated balance sheets
at June 30, 1965, 1966, and 1967

	1965	*1966*	*1967*
ASSETS			
Current Assets			
Cash..............................	$ 371,584	$ 164,327	$ 129,958
Accounts receivable.................	532,215	935,842	1,124,011
Inventory..........................	1,463,872	1,651,932	2,230,500
Prepaid expenses....................	30,353	46,004	49,043
Total Current Assets...........	$2,398,024	$2,798,105	$3,533,512
Plant, Property, and Equipment			
Land..............................	45,000	165,000	165,000
Building and improvement............	168,430	244,293	328,500
Machinery and equipment.............	139,970	389,401	437,571
Less: Accumulated depreciation........	118,071	182,632	211,276
Total Property Plant and Equipment..................	$ 235,329	$ 616,062	$ 719,795
Other Assets			
Notes receivable.....................	51,849	41,289	31,609
Unamortized debenture expense........	36,218	30,401	41,150
Unamortized debenture expense........	36,218	30,401	41,150
Excess of investment over cost........		11,941	161,640
Total Assets................:	$2,721,420	$3,497,798	$4,487,706
LIABILITIES AND STOCKHOLDERS' EQUITY			
Current Liabilities			
Notes payable......................	—	$ 88,000	$ 190,000
Accounts payable....................	$ 320,978	629,617	559,185
Accrued expenses....................	21,306	46,252	127,309
Taxes accrued and withheld..........	13,661	30,084	37,323
Federal income tax payable...........	16,402	127,513	252,755
Total Current Liabilities........	$ 372,347	$ 921,466	$1,166,572
5½%convertible debentures 1977*.......	819,000	767,000	766,000
6% convertible debentures 1982†........			316,000
Stockholders' Equity			
Common stock, $.25 stated value.......	119,590	130,215	135,296
Additional paid in capital.............	630,717	692,892	792,107
Retained earnings...................	779,766	986,225	1,311,731
Total Stockholders' Equity......	$1,530,073	$1,809,332	$2,239,134
Total Liabilities and Stockholders' Equity.........	$2,721,420	$3,497,798	$4,487,706

* Convertible into common stock at $4.72 per share until April 1, 1969 and $5.40 per share thereafter.
† Convertible into common stock at $2.16 per share.

EXHIBIT 4
VOSTRON INDUSTRIES

Bell Electronics' consolidated income statements
for years ended June 30, 1965, 1966, and 1967

	1965	1966	1967
Net sales...........................	$5,305,722	$6,525,311	$9,065,625
Cost of goods sold..................	4,107,064	4,847,528	6,465,292
Selling, general, and administrative expenses.........................	1,031,903	1,200,046	1,889,585
Taxes, other than federal income tax....	74,872	70,985	
Depreciation......................	18,453	28,312	52,986
Interest..........................	53,245	46,630	66,256
Total Expenses................	$5,285,537	$6,193,501	$8,474,119
Income before Federal Income Tax.......	20,185	331,810	591,506
Federal income tax...................	6,000	130,000	266,000
Net income for year..................	14,185	201,810	325,506
Special credit*......................	18,096	3,583	
Net Income.......................	$ 32,281	$ 205,393	$ 325,506
Number of shares outstanding...........	478,360	491,902	535,600
E.P.S. before special credit.............	$0.03	$0.41	$0.61
E.P.S. after special credit..............	0.07	0.42	
Price Range:†			
High............................	6½	9½	33
Low.............................	1⅞	4½	4¾

* Special credit—gain on purchase and retirement of debentures less Federal income taxes of $3,000 in 1966 and $9,000 in 1965.

† Price range:

	1961	1962	1963		1964
High............	3⅛	3⅞	7¾	12 (after listing)	16¾
Low............	1¾	1⅞	3	3 (after listing)	7¼

EXHIBIT 5
VOSTRON INDUSTRIES
Bell Electronics and Vostron Industries
pro forma combined balance sheets

	Bell	Vostron	Combining trans- actions	Pro forma combination
ASSETS				
Current				
Cash..................................	$ 137,643	$ 10,008		$ 147,65▮
Accounts receivables....................	1,186,363	457,610		1,643,97▮
Inventory.............................	2,425,652	269,307		2,694,95▮
Prepaid expenses......................	46,810	46,372		93,18▮
Total Current Assets..............	$3,796,468	$783,297		$4,579,76▮
Fixed Assets				
Plant, property and equipment.............	1,003,729	210,225		1,213,95▮
Less: Accumulated depreciation...........	216,933	53,230		270,16▮
Net Plant Property and Equipment...	$ 786,796	$156,995		$ 943,79▮
Other Assets............................		5,591		5,59▮
Note receivable........................	26,240			26,24▮
Unamortized debenture expense...........	39,310			39,31▮
Excess of investment over cost...........	153,558			153,55▮
Total Assets....................	$4,802,372	$945,883		$5,748,25▮
LIABILITIES AND STOCKHOLDERS' EQUITY				
Current Liabilities				
Notes payable........................		$158,275		$ 158,27▮
Accounts payable......................	$ 622,543	190,264		812,80▮
Accrued expenses.....................	590,193	267,108		857,30▮
Total Current Liabilities...........	$1,212,736	$615,647		$1,828,38▮
Note payable...........................		48,513		48,51▮
5½% Convertible debentures 1977*.........	776,000			776,00▮
6% Convertible debentures 1982†...........	316,000			316,00▮
Stockholders' Equity, Bell				
Common stock, $.25 stated value.........	135,296		$ (40,000)	175,29▮
Additional paid in capital................	792,107		(80,000)	872,10▮
Retained earnings.....................	1,570,233		(161,723)	1,731,95▮
Total Stockholders' Equity, Bell.....	$2,497,636			$2,779,35▮
Stockholders' Equity, Vostron				
Common stock $1 par value.............		120,000	120,000	
Retained earnings.....................		161,723	161,723	
Total Stockholders' Equity, Vostron......................		281,723		
Total Liabilities and Stockholders' Equity.......................	$4,802,372	$945,883	–0–	$5,748,25▮

* Same as in Exhibit 3.
† Same as in Exhibit 3.

EXHIBIT 6

VOSTRON INDUSTRIES

Salem Labs

Consolidated balance sheets

at December 31, 1965, 1966, and 1967

	1965	*1966*	*1967*
ASSETS			
Current Assets			
Cash...........................	$ 95,738	$ 206,479	$ 289,553
Accounts receivable...............	$ 180,690	437,001	1,339,996
Short-term investments.............	227,870	392,387	1,646,528
Inventories......................	298,477	421,151	1,403,169
Prepayments.....................	53,923	57,326	86,860
Total Current Assets..........	$ 856,698	$1,514,344	$4,766,106
Property, plant and equipment..........	236,162	781,789	3,207,189
Less: Accumulated depreciation.......	(42,977)	(175,018)	(335,600)
Other Assets.....................	79,642	122,753	391,320
Total Assets................	$1,129,525	$2,243,868	$8,029,015
LIABILITIES AND STOCKHOLDERS' EQUITY			
Current Liabilities			
Accounts payable..................	$ 78,692	$ 202,246	$ 624,978
Notes payable....................	35,000	250,000	650,000
Accruals........................	21,196	73,566	187,013
Total Current Liabilities.......	$ 134,888	$ 525,812	$1,461,991
Long-term debt (net).................	63,053	92,946	2,470,156
Stockholders Equity			
Preferred stock, 6%...............	16,000	16,000	16,000
Common stock, $1 par.............	272,000	373,239	430,383
Additional paid in capital...........	273,120	592,892	2,418,285
Common stock warrents............	1,000	1,000	1,000
Retained earnings.................	368,834	641,979	1,231,190
Total Stockholders' Equity.....	$ 931,584	$1,625,110	$4,096,868
Total Liabilities and Stockholders' Equity........	$1,129,525	$2,243,868	$8,029,015

EXHIBIT 7

VOSTRON INDUSTRIES

Salem Labs

Consolidated income statements for years ended

December 31, 1965, 1966, and 1967

	1965	1966	1967
Sales..............................	$1,572,293	$3,537,389	$10,471,914
Cost of sales.....................	1,207,678	2,627,380	7,438,926
Selling, general and administrative			
expenses........................	265,848	521,609	2,039,766
Income from operations..............	$ 98,767	$ 388,400	$ 993,222
Other Income and Expense			
Interest income...................	24,852	70,373	106,069
Interest expense..................	(28,445)	(65,728)	(205,595)
Income before Taxes................	$ 95,174	$ 393,045	$ 893,696
Provision for income taxes...........	39,000	153,800	356,885
Income before Extraordinary Item......	$ 56,174	$ 239,245	$ 536,811
Extraordinary item..................	39,000	32,500	62,000
Net Income........................	$ 95,174	$ 271,745	$ 598,811
Shares............................	272,630	373,239	430,393
E.P.S. before extraordinary item.......	$.26	$.64	$1.25
E.P.S. after extraordinary item.......	.35	.73	1.39

	1964	1965	1966	1967
Price Range				
High............................	10¾	19⅛	25½	115¾
Low.............................	10	10	17½	22¾

EXHIBIT 8
VOSTRON INDUSTRIES
Salem Labs and Vostron Industries
pro forma combined balance sheets

	Salem	Vostron	Combining trans- action	Salem combination
ASSETS				
Current Assets				
Cash..............................	$ 299,593	$ 10,008		$ 309,601
Accounts receivable...................	1,248,973	457,610		1,706,583
Short-term investments.................	1,856,373			1,856,373
Inventory............................	1,463,910	269,307		1,733,217
Prepaid expenses......................	89,150	46,372		135,522
Total Current Assets.............	$4,957,999	$783,297		$5,741,296
Fixed Assets				
Plant, property and equipment............	3,273,589	210,225		3,483,814
Less: Accumulated depreciation..........	351,600	53,230		404,830
Total Fixed Assets...............	$2,921,989	$156,995		$3,078,984
Other Assets..........................	357,927	5,591		363,518
Total Assets...................	$8,237,915	$945,883		$9,183,798
LIABILITIES AND STOCKHOLDERS' EQUITY				
Current Liabilities				
Accounts payable......................	$ 760,721	$190,264		$ 950,985
Notes payable........................	750,000	158,275		908,275
Accruals............................	90,173	267,108		357,281
Total Current Liabilities..........	1,600,894	615,647		2,216,541
Long-term debt (net)....................	2,470,156			2,470,156
Notes payable.........................		48,513		48,513
Salem Stockholders Equity				
Preferred stock, $1 par 6%.............	16,000			16,000
Common stock, $1 par.................	430,393		$ (30,000)	460,393
Additional paid in capital................	2,418,285		(90,000)	2,508,285
Common stock warrents.................	1,000			1,000
Retained earnings.....................	1,301,187		(161,723)	1,462,910
Total Stockholders' Equity.........	4,166,865			4,448,588
Vostron Stockholders' Equity				
Common stock, $1 par.................		120,000	120,000	
Retained earnings....................		161,723	161,723	
Total Stockholders' Equity.........		281,723		
Total Liabilities and Stockholders' Equity......................	$8,237,915	$945,883	—0—	$9,183,798

McDONNELL-DOUGLAS

ON JANUARY 16, 1967, it was announced that a proposal of a merger was under consideration by McDonnell and Douglas Aircraft Companies. The merger proposal, which would require approval by shareholders of both companies and by appropriate government agencies, called for the creation of a new company, McDonnell Douglas Corp.[1] McDonnell offered to purchase immediately up to 1,500,000 shares of Douglas treasury stock at $45.80 a share, equal to $68.7 million, "to assist Douglas in meeting its immediate financial requirements." The offer proposed that each outstanding share of Douglas common would be exchanged for 1.75 shares of the new corporation. McDonnell shareholders would receive one share of the new company's stock for each McDonnell share they held (after a 12 percent dividend McDonnell intends to pay before the merger). The offer did not provide details for dealing with the Douglas 4.75 percent convertible and 5 percent sinking fund debentures (see Exhibit 9).

HISTORY OF MCDONNELL AIRCRAFT

McDonnell Aircraft Co. was incorporated in Maryland, July 6, 1939 and changed its name to McDonnell Co. in 1966. The company was founded and controlled by James S. McDonnell.

The firm had subsidiaries located in Texas, California, Colorado, and Missouri. Plant facilities were located on and/or adjoining Lambert-St. Louis Municipal Airport. The main plant is located on airport property

---

[1] *Wall Street Journal,* January 16, 1967.

and has direct access to landing field and runways. McDonnell was chiefly engaged in the production of military aircraft, missiles, space vehicles, and electronic products and systems. The principal military aircraft produced was the phantom jet, of which there were 11 models. McDonnell was currently working to develop additional improved versions of the Phantom II and had proposed advanced versions with a variable sweep wing area and more advanced avionics and weapon systems. Delivery of Phantom II jets had reached a rate of more than two per working day.

Spacecraft production included the Mercury-manned orbital spacecraft project, which McDonnell in conjunction with NASA and numerous subcontractors designed, developed, and manufactured. McDonnell also built the Gemini spacecraft and was working on the design of the Gemini B spacecraft for the air force. On the basis of current planning, it was expected that performance of such work would continue through 1970. McDonnell was also conducting various research and development projects concerning space exploration. Among such projects, McDonnell aimed for an unmanned instrumental spacecraft to land on Mars by the year 1975 as part of NASA's Voyager program. The firm was also engaged in the design and development of an aircraft collision avoidance system, called EROS. The system was designed to warn pilots of converging aircraft which carry the equipment, and to furnish visual instructions to the pilots to climb, descend, level off or hold altitude so as to avoid collision.

Exhibits 1 and 2 provide balance sheet and income statement data for McDonnell from 1962 through 1966. As of December 31, 1966, there were 16,027,266 shares of McDonnell common outstanding. As of January 10, 1967, McDonnell's common stock closed at a price of $35 per share, up $3.125 from the previous day. Exhibit 3 details per share data for the company for the years 1961–66.

HISTORY OF DOUGLAS AIRCRAFT

Douglas was a leading producer of commercial transport airplanes. Its DC-3 type airplane was the workhorse of the air transportation industry until the advent of heavier four-engine types following World War II. In November 1946, the company introduced and began commercial delivery of the DC-6 four-engine commercial passenger transport and in 1953 began production of the DC-7 series. In 1955, Douglas entered the jet transport field. First orders for the DC-8, the company's commercial jet transport, were obtained in October of 1955. In fiscal 1966, 34 DC-8 jetliners were delivered to airlines, making a cumulative total of 280 deliveries. Federal Aviation Agency certificates were obtained in 1960 for two additional versions of the DC-8, increasing the model types in operation to four. Added models were powered by Pratt and Whitney Aircraft engines and others with Rolls Royce turbines. In April 1964, the company announced three new and advanced versions of the DC-8 to be known as the Super Sixty Series. They are all now in production. Total DC-8 orders on January 4, 1967 were 444 including 151 Super Sixty Series DC-8s.

Authorization to start engineering of the DC-9 series, a 56–90 passenger commercial jet transport was given in February 1963. The first aircraft was completed during January 1965. The DC-9 had two aft-mounted Pratt and Whitney Aircraft engines and a sales price of $3.3 million. By January 13, 1967, a total of 446 DC-9s had been ordered by the airlines. Customers for the company's sales included 55 of the major domestic and overseas airlines.

Since its organization, Douglas had been an important designer and producer of military aircraft. Although military production was sharply curtailed after World War II until the Korean War in 1950, several different versions of the Skyraider attack bomber series were developed. In 1964, Dougals was awarded a contract to produce 130 advanced jet training planes for the Navy.

The Douglas Missile Division has been engaged in research and development work on various forms of missiles since 1941. Development of the Spartan antiballistic missile was underway as part of the Nike-X defense system. In April 1960, NASA awarded a contract for development and manufacture of the S-IVB stage of the Saturn, the vehicle for the Apollo mission. Annual missile and space sales and backlog orders as of November 30, 1966 amounted to $409.4 million in sales and $397.6 million in backlog orders. Production facilities are located at Long Beach, Huntington Beach, and Santa Monica, California.

Exhibits 4 and 5 present financial statements data for Douglas for the years 1962–66. Currently there are 5,257,244 shares of common stock outstanding. As of January 10, 1967, Douglas common closed at $47.375, up $2.125 from the previous day. Exhibit 6 outlines per share data for the company from 1961–66.

McDonnell is known to have made a bid for Douglas in 1962. Although this was dropped the following year, rumors continued to circulate. A McDonnell-Douglas merger would be a giant step toward James S. McDonnell's dream to diversify his company, then almost totally dependent on defense contracts. In contrast, Douglas received only about 39 percent of its sales from military and space contracts. However, in June 1966, McDonnell disclosed it had eliminated its holdings of 58,726 shares of Douglas common in the first three months of 1966 at a net gain of $2,567,-287, apparently having given up for good its desire to merge with Douglas.

The issue was reopened later in the year when it became apparent that Douglas was running into problems with production of its DC-8 and DC-9 jetliners. Deliveries of engines and other components from suppliers were behind schedule and Douglas was having production and cost-control difficulties of its own. From 1957 through 1961, Douglas' fortune declined and in 1959 and 1960, the company reported losses totaling $53,250,000 after tax credits. In 1961, the company was back in the black with profits of $5,956,909 and earnings rose to the 1965 level of $14,598,000. The company's troubles became dramatically apparent in 1966 when a loss of $17,061,000 was reported in the third quarter ending August 31, compared with a year earlier profit of $4,009,322 or 76 cents a share.

On January 3, 1967, Douglas announced it had arranged a $75 million loan, 75 percent guaranteed by the government, with a group of banks (see Exhibit 7). Other bank loans and advances from airline customers are believed to total between $200 million and $300 million. It was felt by some observers, however, that Douglas still required more equity.

EXHIBIT 1

MCDONNELL–DOUGLAS
McDonnell Aircraft Company
Balance sheet for years ended June 30, 1961–66
(rounded to nearest thousand dollars)*

	December 31 1966	1966	1965	1964	1963	1962
ASSETS						
Cash	$ 8,121	$ 2,317	$ 2,386	$ 1,775	$ 10,701	$ 7,322
Marketable securities	70,719	43,510	23,200	—	1,361	1,027
Accounts receivable	64,106	67,898	45,258	23,814	42,119	35,706
Contracts in process	544,190	508,739	454,691	506,063	290,755	170,418
Progress payments	cr 368,554	cr 317,774	cr 298,061	cr 323,440	cr 182,442	cr 86,846
Total Current Assets	$318,582	$304,690	$227,474	$208,212	$162,494	$127,627
Investments, other assets	17,727	737	2,839	8,593		
Property, plant and equipment	142,576	129,584	104,671	95,906	78,672	58,422
Reserve for depreciation	69,254	64,595	56,432	48,070	42,898	38,231
Net Property Accounts	$ 73,322	$ 64,989	$ 48,239	$ 47,836	$ 35,774	$ 20,191
Deferred charges	15,402	15,961	10,777	4,188	2,343	1,654
Total Assets	$425,033	$386,377	$289,329	$268,829	$200,611	$149,472
LIABILITIES AND STOCKHOLDERS' EQUITY						
Notes payable	$ 13,050	$ 3,000	$ 1,500	$ 9,000	—	—
Accounts payable	63,423	87,846	78,765	85,748	$ 54,477	$ 28,165
Payroll	25,913	31,463	25,084	20,807	15,895	12,963
Income taxes	17,068	25,247	23,335	19,768	13,923	11,200
Contract adjustments	88,496	36,263	4,934	9,768	15,502	11,372
Dividends payable	1,602	1,623	1,356	940	898	863
Total Current Liabilities	$209,552	$185,442	$134,974	$146,031	$100,695	$ 64,563
Incentive compensation reserve	$ 9,010	$ 7,495	$ 5,204	$ 3,576	$ 2,212	$ 1,522
Minority interest	4,015	3,492	596			
Common stock	20,366	20,303	10,010	9,428	9,017	8,673
Capital surplus	42,326	41,739	38,625	22,887	14,557	7,866
Retained earnings	146,524	127,948	100,125	87,080	74,380	67,120
Total Stockholder's Equity	209,216	189,990	148,760	119,395	97,954	83,659
Less: Treasury shares at cost	6,761	42	205	173	250	272
Net Stockholder's Equity	$202,455	$189,948	$148,555	$119,222	$ 97,704	$ 83,387
Total Liabilities and Stockholders' Equity	$425,033	$386,377	$289,329	$268,829	$200,611	$149,472

* Moody's Industrial Manual, 1967, pp. 2913–19.

EXHIBIT 2
MCDONNELL—DOUGLAS
McDonnell Aircraft Company
Income state for years ended June 30, 1962–66
(rounded to nearest thousand dollars)*

	December 31 1966	1966	1965	1964	1963	1962
Sales.................	$605,401	$1,060,039	$1,007,829	$865,377	$565,339	$390,718
Other income.........	1,384	5,270				
Contract costs.........	559,583	969,106	872,056	785,500	489,173	326,364
General and administrative expenses........			63,388	50,180	36,545	30,875
Depreciation..........	4,976	8,571	8,372	6,152	4,830	5,114
Minority interest......	218	983	301			
Operating Profit...	$ 42,007	$ 81,380	$ 63,712	$ 50,544	$ 34,791	$ 28,365
Interest paid...........	228	208	703	717		
Balance...........	$ 41,779	$ 81,172	$ 63,009	$ 49,827	$ 34,791	$ 28,365
Provision for federal income taxes........	19,778	37,542	30,641	20,071	17,579	14,355
State income taxes......	222	413	355	257	175	130
Net Income.......	$ 21,779	$ 43,217	$ 32,014	$ 24,500	$ 17,036	$ 13,880
Retained earnings, beginning of year......	127,948	100,125	87,080	74,380	67,119	56,679
Dividends (cash).......	3,203	5,242	4,758	3,895	3,790	3,439
Dividends (stock)......			14,210	7,905	5,985	
Stock split...........		10,152				
	$146,524	$ 127,948	$ 100,125	$ 87,080	$ 74,380	$ 67,120

* *Moody's Industrial Manual*, 1967, pp. 2913–19.

EXHIBIT 3

MCDONNELL–DOUGLAS
McDonnell Aircraft Company
Financial and operating data fiscal year ended June 30, 1961–66

Statistical Records:	*December* *1966*	*1966*	*1965*	*1964*	*1963*	*1962*	*1961*
Earned per share	$ 1.36	$ 2.66	$ 4.01	$ 3.26	$ 4.74	$ 4.02	$ 3.54
Dividend per share	0.60	$ .60	$ .60*	$ 1.00*†	$ 1.00*	$ 1.00	$ 1.00
Price range—common§	33¾–20½	33¾–20½‖	69⅞–31¼	39⅝–28‡	60¼–47	61⅛–35	45–22½
Net tangible assets per share	12.27	11.25	12.97	$15.85	$27.19	$24.14	$21.10
Number of shares	16,027,266	16,240,965	7,993,008	7,524,125	3,593,044	3,454,637	3,425,445
Adjusted data for stock splits and stock dividends (common stock data):#							
Earned per share	$ 1.36	$ 2.66	$ 2.01	$ 1.55	$ 1.09	$ 0.90	$ 0.79
Cash flow per share	1.67	3.19	2.53	1.95	1.40	1.27	1.16
Price range§	33.75–20.5	33.75–20.15	34.94–15.63	18.87–11.55	13.79–10.76	13.59–7.78	10.00–5.00
Net tangible assets per share	12.27	11.25	8.99	7.55	6.23	5.37	4.70
Number of shares	16,027,266	16,240,965	15,986,016	15,800,662	15,694,416	15,526,468	15,398,956

* Stock dividends: 1965, 5 %; 1964, 4 %; 1963, 3 %.
† Paid prior to 2-for-1 split.
‡ After 2-for-1 split: before 67½–48½.
§ Calendar year.
‖ After 2-for-1 split; before, 64⅝–50½.
Adjusted for 5 % stock div. in 1965.
Source: *Moody's Industrial Manual*, 1966, p. 2783, 1966. Data from *Moody's Industrial Manual*, 1967, p. 2913–19.

EXHIBIT 4
MCDONNELL–DOUGLAS
Douglas Aircraft Company
Balance sheet for years ended November 30, 1962–66
(rounded to nearest thousand dollars)*

ASSETS	1966	1965	1964	1963	1962
Cash	$ 15,806	$ 6,768	$ 9,345	$ 12,063	$ 17,538
Market securities	6,000	29,858	33,925	11,875	—
Accounts receivables (from U.S. government)	44,733	16,562	22,823	16,718	28,295
Accounts receivables from others	23,506	24,044	25,132	21,208	15,553
Unreimbursed expenditures	—	37,977	37,881	52,997	71,760
Federal taxes refundable	12,315	13,397	—	—	—
Inventories	401,868	233,581	128,853	118,949	128,684
Prepayments	14,071	8,761	6,541	7,263	8,540
Total Current Assets	$518,297	$370,948	$264,500	$241,073	$270,371
Debenture discount and expenditure	—	—	786	521	—
Development costs deferred	127,985	35,788	12,337	9,546	13,685
Leased airplanes	28,407	17,649	15,524	6,792	3,228
Noncurrent trade receivables	39,931	22,489	14,067	18,772	12,573
Property not in operation	—	4,078	—	—	—
Investment in affiliates	8,454	8,179	4,379	—	—
Miscellaneous	2,611	1,316	6,539	10,048	8,704
Property, plant and equipment	242,168	211,471	199,165	181,344	149,270
Less: Depreciation, Expense	117,681	107,148	99,319	89,237	82,165
Net Property Account	124,487	104,323	99,846	92,108	67,105
Total Assets	$850,172	$564,770	$417,977	$378,860	$375,666

* *Moody's Industrial Manual*, 1967, pp. 2913–19.
Columns do not always total due to the error that exists in rounding data.

EXHIBIT 4 (Continued)

	1966	1965	1964	1963	1962
LIABILITIES AND STOCKHOLDERS' EQUITY					
Notes payable to banks..............	$110,783	—	—	—	$ 18,000
Accounts payable...................	183,256	$108,402	$ 48,127	$ 65,290	69,731
Employees' pension trust contribution...	—	13,425	11,800	11,243	10,873
Accrued payroll....................	40,039	30,449	19,727	17,035	18,587
Advances received on contracts........	131,795	91,657	24,536	7,918	4,462
Accrued taxes other than income.......	12,965	9,158	8,071	9,441	5,076
Federal taxes on income..............	—	—	981	6,221	10,606
Development costs..................	—	—	—	—	—
Other current liabilities..............	—	4,397	14,492	2,639	7,546
Current maturity long-term debt........	5,046	4,183	7,469	1,806	1,015
Total Current Liabilities........	$483,884	$261,671	$135,203	$121,593	$145,896
Convertible subordinate debentures— 4¾%..........................	75,000	—	—	—	—
Convertible subordinate debentures— 4%.............................	—	27,900	27,900	27,900	27,900
Sinking fund debenture, 5% 1978.......	41,250	45,000	47,421	52,500	56,047
Purchase money trust deed note........	6,106	6,639	6,752	6,823	7,951
Space systems secured notes..........	30,513	31,594	21,540	22,209	—
Airline financing 5¼% Security Notes..	12,633	15,262	17,529	—	—
Airline financing 4¾% Security Notes..	—	—	472	—	—
Equipment lease, purchase obligation....	4,796	—	—	—	—
Deferred federal income tax reserve.....	21,152	1,637	148	587	2,415
Other reserves......................	—	—	—	—	—
Capital stock......................	43,914	38,617	36,490	34,399	32,762
Capital surplus.....................	59,252	21,676	16,229	13,111	9,294
Earned surplus.....................	71,672	114,774	108,293	99,737	93,401
Total Stockholders' Equity....	174,838	175,067	161,012	147,248	135,457
Total Liabilities and Stockholders' Equity...........	$850,172	$564,770	$417,977	$378,860	$375,666

Columns do not always total due to the error that exists in rounding data.

EXHIBIT 5

MCDONNELL–DOUGLAS

Douglas Aircraft Company

Income statement for years ended November 30, 1962–1966

(rounded to nearest thousand dollars)*

	1966	1965	1964	1963	1962
Net sales.........................	$1,048,012	$766,791	$650,128	$698,341	$749,921
Cost of goods sold................	945,832	632,969	531,822	584,443	645,646
Selling, administrative and general expenses........................	90,818	74,600	58,996	56,696	48,001
Property taxes on inventories.......		2,662	2,645	3,175	3,931
Contribution to employee pension fund...........................	24,479	13,425	11,800	11,175	10,814
Experimental costs................	29,171	17,744	15,985	14,708	16,332
Operating Profit..............	(42,289)	25,390	28,879	28,143	25,196
Other income....................	10,842	7,737	6,627	3,359	7,474
Total......................	(31,448)	33,127	35,507	31,502	32,670
Interest and amortization expense....	16,444	8,110	6,687	5,165	6,112
Other income deductions..........	4,000		2,917	2,030	6,431
Balance.....................	(51,892)	25,016	25,902	24,307	20,127
Provision for federal income taxes....	cr 12,316		2,216	11,279	8,954
Deferred federal income taxes.......	cr 12,017	10,418	9,954	623	879
State income taxes................			38	96	89
Prior years' income taxes..........				518	
Net Income to Surplus.........	(27,560)	14,598	13,695	11,791	10,205
Earned surplus, beginning of year....	114,774	108,293	99,737	93,401	87,089
Dividends (cash).................	3,800	2,723			
Dividends (stock)................	11,741	5,395	5,139	5,455	3,893
Earned Surplus, End of Year....	$ 71,672	$114,774	$108,293	$ 99,737	$ 93,401

* *Moody's Industrial Manual*, 1967, pp. 2913–19.
Columns do not always total due to the error that exists in rounding data.

EXHIBIT 6
MCDONNELL-DOUGLAS
Douglas Aircraft Company
Financial and operating data fiscal year ended November 30, 1961–66

	1966	1965	1964	1963	1962	1961
Statistical Records:						
Earned per share................	($ 5.22)	$ 3.15	$ 3.13	$ 2.86	$ 2.60	$ 1.56
Dividends per share†............	$0.72 + 3% stock	$ 0.60	6% stock	5% stock	3% stock	—
Price range*....................	108½–30	83⅞–29⅛	32¾–21⅜	29¾–20½	37⅜–17½	42⅜–28
Times charges earned						
Before income taxes...........	(9.35)	$ 4.08	$ 4.87	$ 5.71	$ 4.29	$ 2.74
After income taxes............	(4.96)	$ 2.80	$ 3.05	$ 3.28	$ 2.67	$ 1.89
Net tangible assets per share....	33.22	$37.78	$36.77	$35.67	$34.46	$32.82
Price range—debentures 5s, 1978*	100–80	102¾–98¾	101¼–96¼	98⅛–94	98–91	95–86
Number of shares...............	5,269,624	4,634,128	4,378,860	4,127,933	3,931,365	3,816,860
Adjusted data for stock splits and stock dividends (common stock data)						
Earned per share...............		$ 3.15	$ 3.00	$ 2.60	$ 2.25	$ 1.30
Cash flow per share............		$6.76	$ 6.13	$ 5.08	$ 4.71	$ 4.46
Price range....................	83.88–29.13	83.88–29.13	31.48–20.55	25.08–18.59	32.28–15.11	35.53–23.48
Net tangible assets per share....		$37.78	$35.35	$32.35	$29.81	$27.51
Number of shares...............		4,634,128	4,554,014	4,550,633	4,550,633	4,550,633

* Calender years
† Fiscal years
Source: *Moody's Industrial Manual*, 1966, p. 811.
1966 Data from *Moody's Industrial Manual*, 1967, p. 2913–19.

EXHIBIT 7
MCDONNELL-DOUGLAS
Douglas directors will study equity funding offers this week*

Proposals from at least five companies for participating in a Douglas Aircraft Co. $393-million financing program are expected to be ready for consideration by the Douglas board of directors at its meeting this week.

The step follows the reaching of agreement in principle last week between Douglas and a group of eight banks over their participation in the program. One of the understandings is that equity money also will be pumped into Douglas. This means merger or partial control by whichever company supplies the funds.

Though not part of the formal agreement, there is a general understanding among the Douglas board and the various financial groups that there will be changes in top management at Douglas.

A sixth possible participant in the equity program emerged last week: Sherman Fairchild and Fairchild-Hiller Corp. This group has been invited to Douglas to discuss its plan, but its bid is regarded as something of a long shot.

The first three companies invited to make offers—North American Aviation, McDonnell Co., and General Dynamics—all have said they would submit proposals. Martin Marietta, invited later, also plans to submit a plan, and the Signal Oil Co. offer to purchase a $100 million Douglas preferred stock issue has been extended to provide for submission to the Douglas board.

Included in the $393-million program, which would meet financing needs of Douglas through July, are:

- $106 million in advance payments from customers and suppliers, on which interest will be paid. Offsetting payments from overseas will be credits from the U.S. Export-Import bank.
- $125 million in loans for U.S. banks. Security First National Bank of Los Angeles is agent bank for the group.
- $75 million in a federally guaranteed V-loan. It has not been approved yet in Washington, but its signing is expected by the end of this week.
- $46 million from a Canadian bank which is financing a Douglas Canadian subsidiary producing commercial transport subassemblies.

This would leave $41 million to be supplied in equity for the immediate program, but the bank lenders might ask for more to keep debt-equity ratios in line with lending policies.

Some reports have discounted the chances of the Signal Oil offer because of the company's lack of experienced aerospace management, but the proposed terms, which leave the Douglas company intact may make it highly attractive to the Douglas stockholders.

Terms of any equity offer will probably have to be submitted to a vote of the Douglas stockholders, and this process could easily take 30–60 days.

Both North American President J. L. Atwood and General Dynamics President Roger Lewis have conferred personally with Douglas officials. McDonnell

---

* Reprinted by permission from *Aviation Week and Space Technology*, January 24, 1967.

EXHIBIT 7 (*Continued*)

Aircraft has had groups at the Douglas plant, including a team of auditors, over the Christmas weekend.

A negotiating team including three Douglas directors, Donald Douglas Sr., and Stanley de J. Osborne of Lazard Freres & Co., an investment banking and consulting firm hired by the Douglas board, has been named to handle the equity financing proposals. The three directors are Neil Petree, vice chairman of Barker Bros.; Dwight Whiting, vice president of Alexander & Alexander, and Charles S. Jones, a director of the Atlantic Refining Co. Teams from Douglas also have gone to plants of the interested companies to make surveys as part of the merger studies.

North American directors met last week to complete the terms of the North American proposal and planned to submit it by the end of the week. Other proposals also were due in by the end of the week.

Douglas had planned to move its corporate offices to the Century City complex under development in Los Angeles. It has now dropped these plans, citing problems over the lease.

EXHIBIT 8
MCDONNELL-DOUGLAS
Long-term debentures Douglas Aircraft Co.[1]

1. Douglas Aircraft Co., Inc. debentures 5%; due 1978; $60,000,000 authorized; Rating Baa
   Dated—April 1, 1958
   Trustee & Resister—1st National City Bank, New York
   Callable—as a whole or in part, on 30 days' notice at 103 in 1967 graduated
   Sinking Fund—$3,750,000 annually.
   Security—Not secured. Indenture contains covenants restricting sale and lease-pack by company and subsidiaries of any major manufacturing plant or facility for administration, engineering or research, unless net proceeds of the sale at least equal fair value thereof.
   Creation of Additional Debt—Company or any subsidiary may not create funded debt (excepting refunding) unless thereafter, on a consolidated basis, tangible assets after deducting current liabilities at least equal 225% of funded debt.

2. Douglas Aircraft Co., Inc. convertible subordinated debenture 4¾%; due 1991; $75,000,000 authorized; Rating Ba
   Dated—July 1, 1966
   Trustee & Registrar—Chase Manhattan Bank, N.Y.C.
   Callable—as a whole or in part on at least 30 days' notice at 104.75 in 1967 graduated to 100 in 1991.
   Sinking Fund—$4,285,000 annually.
   Convertible—Into Douglas Aircraft common stock at $23.58[2] a share. Protected against dilution.
   Purpose—Proceeds to be added to working capital.

---

[1] *Moody's Industrial Manual*, 1966.

[2] Was $41.27 prior to the merger but was adjusted downward by the 1.75 exchange ratio.

LITTON INDUSTRIES, 1965 (A)

On October 20, 1964, it was jointly announced that an "Agreement of Merger" was signed by a majority of the directors of both Litton Industries and the Royal McBee Corporation. Terms offered to Royal McBee stockholders were as follows: One share of Litton series A $3 cumulative convertible preferred stock would be issued for each share of Royal's 4½ percent cumulative preferred stock. As of October, Royal had 56,813 shares of the 4½ percent preferred stock outstanding. Each of the presently outstanding 1,538,090 shares of Royal's common stock (excluding Royal's treasury stock and shares beneficially owned by Litton) would be converted into a fractional percentage of a share of Litton series A cumulative convertible preferred stock (a percentage equal to the quotient obtained by dividing $17.25 by the average selling price of such Litton preferred stock on the New York Stock Exchange for the first 10 trading days following approval by the stockholders). This finally resulted in Royal's shareholders receiving 0.16875 of a share of Littons series A preferred for each share of common held. Market price data for both corporations are presented in Exhibit 1.

In addition, Litton would lend Royal the sum of $7,675,300 for the purpose of redeeming, by December 2, 1964, all of its outstanding 6¼ percent convertible subordinated debentures due December 1, 1977. The 5 percent series B, 5½ percent series C, and 6 percent series D preferred stock were redeemed October 31, 1964.

Litton Industries was incorporated in the state of Delaware in November of 1953 under the name of Electro Dynamics Corporation. In 1954, after purchasing a firm called Litton Industries located in San Carlos, California, Electro Dynamics changed its name to Litton Industries with home offices located in Beverly Hills, California.

Today Litton Industries is a broadly diversified corporation dealing with products and services in such areas as: data processing, business equipment and supplies, instrumentation and controls equipment, communication and transmission equipment, and shipbuilding. Table 1 indicates the percentage of Litton's net sales accounted for by each of these product and service categories for the fiscal year ending July 31, 1964.[1]

TABLE 1

	Percent
Data processing and business equipment................	40
Instrumentation and controls equipment................	37
Communications and transmission equipment............	11
Ships and other marine vessels........................	12
Total....................................	100

Approximately 22 percent of Litton's sales of $686 million were purchased for use outside the United States, while 20 percent of the products and services were actually manufactured in other countries.

U.S. military products and systems accounted for 46 percent of Litton's total net sales in 1964, while 8 percent was for products for other Free World defense programs. Another 46 percent of sales consisted of a wide variety of commercial and industrial products.[2]

Over the past 10 years, the firm has had tremendous growth in sales, assets, and net income. For the fiscal year ending July 31, 1954, Litton had sales of approximately $3 million, total assets of $4.2 million and net income of $154,000. By 1964, sales had grown to $686 million, total assets had increased to $424 million, and net income had reached $29.8 million. Exhibits 2 and 3 present a seven-year spread of balance sheet and income statement information.

By 1963, Litton ranked 102 in sales, 129 in total assets, and 125 in net profits of the 500 largest U.S. industrial corporations. Much of the firm's growth has been achieved through acquisition of firms with product lines that would complement already existing products or add to its ever-expanding product list.

One distinctive feature of this growth pattern was the accompanying competition from other manufactures. Competition ran from small, one-product (service) companies to some of the largest corporations in the United States. Especially vulnerable to competition were the government contracts. These often called for competitive bidding, profit limitations, and sometimes even cancelation at any time by the U.S. government.

---

[1] Proxy statement issued for the merger with Royal McBee dated November 5, 1964, p. 15.

[2] Ibid.

BUILDING THE BUSINESS EQUIPMENT GROUP

In 1958, Litton entered the business equipment industry with its purchase of Monroe Calculating Machine Company. At that time it was Litton's largest acquisition. Litton's electronic capability provided Monroe with the technology required for the development of electronic calculators. Further growth in the business equipment industry was realized in 1959 with the acquisition of Sweda, a manufacturer of cash registers and point of sales recording equipment.

During this period, competitive forces in the industry were beginning to combine typewriter manufacturers with calculator companies to provide a more viable competitive force in the marketplace. As early as 1958, Litton sought to enter the typewriter market by attempting to acquire Underwood. After a number of meetings, negotiations collapsed and Underwood was later purchased by Olivetti of Italy. Litton's next opportunity to acquire a domestic typewriter manufacturer was with Royal McBee in 1965.

The merger with Royal was undertaken to round out Litton's business equipment product line. Mr. Roy Ash, president of Litton expressed his views on the potential of the typewriter industry when he stated in testimony before the Federal Trade Commission:[3]

Our view at that time was very parallel to that that we had about Monroe at an earlier time and of course what we have had about other industries at earlier times. But to get to that one particularly, at that time we saw, and the public generally saw, the typewriter business as one making free standing products, electro-mechanical in nature, used broadly in a market, but we were absolutely convinced that in the future there would be a major change, a major revolution, not just evolution, in that industry where again the potential of electronics would be brought to bear not in just making another free standing product but making products that even today we haven't yet seen. Word processors of various kinds, composing machines in effect, where the whole process of preparing correspondence, preparing typed documents of various kinds, would be done by a completely different approach than just a free standing desk electro-mechanical product.

That evolution has already begun. In another five or another ten years I think we will see around us in many offices these kinds of different products that will just change the whole nature of what an industry is and what its products are.

In order for the merger to transpire, an affirmative vote by two thirds of the outstanding shares of all Litton voting stock was required. As of October 16, 1964, the record date for notice of the annual meeting, Litton had outstanding 10,906,699 shares of common stock and 492,706

---

[3] *In The Matter of Litton Industries, Inc.*, Federal Trade Commission Docket Number 8778, Initial Decision, pp. 23–24 (February 3, 1972).

shares of series A $3 cumulative convertible preferred stock. Litton's treasury stock consisted of 390,356 shares of common and 594 shares of preferred. Both the common and preferred shareholders voted together as one class with one vote per share.[4]

RECENT ACQUISITIONS

During the 1964–65 period Litton merged with the firms listed below:

1. In March, acquired Data Systems of Los Angeles and Santa Barbara by an exchange of stock (amount not available).
2. In April, acquired Fitchburg Paper Company, Fitchburg, Massachusetts, in exchange for 35,540 shares of $3 cumulative series A preferred stock and 186,177 common shares.
3. Acquired Bruder and Company, makers of infrared food heating equipment (amount not available).
4. In August, acquired Streater Industries for 38,440 common shares and 2,325 series A $3 cumulative preferred.
5. Also in August, acquired Profexray for $590,000 cash and 26,700 shares of series A preferred.
6. Again in August acquired Mellonics Systems Development Inc. of Sunnyvale, California, for 1,795 shares of common.
7. Acquired Magnuson X-Ray for initial consideration of 1,996 shares of series A preferred and $90,000 cash.

Another merger completed in early 1965 was with Hewitt-Robins. The firm designs, engineers, manufactures, and installs conveyer systems to handle bulk materials. Terms of the merger called for the insurance of 161,758 shares of Litton's series A preferred. Litton had already acquired 34 percent of Hewitt-Robins preferred and 46 percent of their common stock.

ROYAL McBEE CORPORATION

The Royal Typewriter Corporation was first incorporated in New York on October 17, 1913 as the successor to the Royal Typewriter Company of New Jersey formed in 1904. During the 1930s and 1940s, Royal was one of the leaders in the manufacture and sale of all lines of typewriters. At that time, competition was brisk between the four traditional typewriter companies of Remington, Underwood, Smith-Corona, and Royal.

In 1954, Royal broadened its product line by merger with McBee Corporation. McBee was a manufacturer of special office equipment and

---

[4] Proxy statement, p. 1, see footnote 1.

office machines, filing and housing equipment for accounting forms and records, and specialized printed products used in accounting statistics and general office record keeping. Under the merger plan, McBee's preferred stock was exchanged share for share for a new preferred series with the same dividend rate, and the McBee common was exchanged at the rate of $\frac{7}{8}$ of a share of new common for each share held.

The bulk of Royal's business (80 percent of net sales) was in the area of typewriters and related products. The other 20 percent was derived from sales of data processing equipment. The company employed over 11,000 persons in 41 states and 8 foreign countries. Even though the field was highly competitive on both a national and international level, at the time of the proposal, Royal was one of the world's largest manufacturers of typewriters. Exhibits 4 and 5 present income statement and balance sheet data for Royal for the five years prior to the merger proposal.

The 1965 merger proposed with Litton Industries was the second major merger that Royal had considered in its history. Acceptance by Royal shareholders required a two-thirds affirmative vote of all the outstanding common stock. As of November, 1964, Royal had 1,538,090 shares of common stock outstanding. The preferred stock shareholders had previously agreed to the merger terms. At this time, Litton owned 394,600 shares of Royal common which amounted to approximately 26 percent of the outstanding shares.

The merger with Litton would benefit Royal in four major areas: (1) It would offer a greater degree of diversification from typewriters and related products; (2) The complementary nature of operations would strengthen Royal's overall position; (3) The merger would assist in the reduction of certain administrative and overhead expenses; and (4) Definite benefits would be achieved through the cooperation of the research groups of both companies.

Exhibits 6 and 7 summarize the financial and capitalization position of both companies as of July 31, 1964. In addition, consolidated pro forma balance sheet and capitalization statements are presented.

EXHIBIT 1
LITTON INDUSTRIES (A)
Market prices of Litton and Royal securities

The following table sets forth the high and low sale prices of Litton Common Stock on the New York Stock Exchange for each quarterly period within the past two years and of Litton's Series A $3 Cumulative Convertible Preferred Stock on the New York Stock Exchange (and, prior to February 3, 1964, the range of bid and asked prices in the over-the-counter market in New York City) for the period during which such preferred stock has been outstanding and the high and low sale prices of Litton's 3½% Convertible Subordinated Debentures on the New York Stock Exchange for each quarterly period within the past two years.

Quarterly period ended	*Common*		*$3 Preferred*		*3½ percent Debentures*	
	High	*Low*	*High*	*Low*	*High*	*Low*
12/31/62.........	69¾	50¾			115	99⅝
3/31/63.........	69	57½			113½	104½
6/30/63.........	78⅞	62½			119¾	108
9/30/63.........	85½	69¼			123¾	110
12/31/63.........	86¾	74½			131½	116
3/31/64.........	79⅝	64	*	*	118	109½
6/30/64.........	72⅞	58¼	90¾	87¾	115¼	104
9/30/64.........	74½	61¾	92¼	87½	114½	104
Period from 10/ 1/64 to 11/ 1/64.........	78	73	97	92¾	118¼	112½

* During the period from January 17 to January 31, 1964, the high bid price on the New York Over-the-Counter market was 88½ and the low bid was 85, while the high asked price was 89½ and the low asked price was 88½. During the period from February 3, 1964 through March 31, 1964, the high sale price on the New York Stock Exchange was 93 and the low sale price was 83¼.

Source: Proxy statement issued for the merger with Royal McBee dated November 5, 1964, p. 14.

EXHIBIT 1 (*Continued*)

The following table sets forth the high and low sale prices of the Common Stock of Royal on the New York Stock Exchange, the range of the bid and asked prices of the 4½% Cumulative Preferred Stock, Series A of the Corporation in the over-the-counter market in New York City, and the high and low sale prices of the 6¼% Convertible Subordinated Debentures of the Corporation on the New York Stock Exchange, for each quarterly period within the past two years.

Quarterly Period ended	*Common*		*4½ percent Preferred*				*6¼ percent Debentures*	
			Bid		*Asked*			
	High	*Low*	*High*	*Low*	*High*	*Low*	*High*	*Low*
12/31/62.......	10¾	7⅛	61½	60	72	68	104½	99
3/31/63.......	10⅞	8⅞	62	60	72	64	105½	102
6/30/63.......	10⅜	9⅛	61	60	72	64	107	103½
9/30/63.......	11⅞	8¾	62	60	67	65	106⅝	102½
12/31/63.......	12½	10½	71½	66	75	72½	107	103½
3/31/64.......	14⅜	11⅛	72	70	77	75	107½	104
6/30/64.......	15⅝	12⅝	None	None	None	None	110	105
9/30/64.......	16	12¾	75	72	None	None	109	104½
Period from 10/ 1/64 to 11/ 1/64.......	16⅜	15⅞	72	72	None	None	3/105	103/8

EXHIBIT 2

LITTON INDUSTRIES (A)

Litton Industries' income statements, years ended July 31, 1958–64

(dollar figures in thousands)

	1964	1963	1962	1961	1960	1959	1958
Sales and service revenues	$686,135	$553,146	$393,808	$250,114	$187,761	$125,525	$83,155
Cost of sales	516,394	413,890	292,017	177,141	132,341	86,050	45,026
Selling, general and administrative expenses	107,424	90,547	67,994	51,084	38,812	27,569	30,190
Provision for doubtful account	—	—	—	—	—	188	107
Net Earnings	$ 62,317	$ 48,709	$ 33,797	$ 21,889	$ 16,608	$ 11,718	$ 7,832
Interest paid	6,167	4,913	2,947	2,202	1,239	895	654
Amortization of debt discounts	—	—	—	—	4	5	7
Other income deductions	—	—	—	—	—	12	129
Balance	$ 56,150	$ 43,796	$ 30,850	$ 19,687	$ 15,365	$ 10,806	$ 7,042
Federal and foreign income taxes	26,384	20,500	14,534	9,529	7,910	5,852	3,342
Minority interest							cr 2
Net Income Before Special Items	$ 29,766	$ 23,296	$ 16,316	$ 10,158	$ 7,455	$ 4,954	$ 3,702
Special items						1,021	—
Net Income	$ 29,766	$ 23,296	$ 16,316	$ 10,158	$ 7,455	$ 5,975	$ 3,702
Retained earnings beginning of year	63,433	49,573	36,559	32,689	21,378	18,808	3,390
Other credits	1,718	3,427	9,359	2,019	3,995	144	17,942
Preferred dividends	637	63	77	125	139	159	58
Common dividends (cash)	—	57	36	—	—	—	168
Common dividends (stock)	17,967	12,547	12,547	8,182	—	3,390	—
Retained earning end of year	$ 72,877	$ 63,433	$ 49,573	$ 36,559	$ 32,689	$ 21,378	$18,808

EXHIBIT 3

LITTON INDUSTRIES (A)

Litton Industries' balance sheets, as of July 31, 1958–64

(dollar figures in thousands)

ASSETS	1964	1963	1962	1961	1960	1959	1958
Cash	$ 56,481	$ 27,695	$ 12,289	$ 8,993	$ 10,948	$ 7,155	$ 5,623
Receivables, net	146,412	141,941	97,941	63,370	40,231	27,681	13,821
Inventories	103,263	86,664	78,549	50,029	33,707	27,982	21,480
Prepaid expenses	3,740	3,455	3,454	2,032	1,631	1,679	1,016
Total Current Assets	$309,896	$259,755	$192,233	$124,424	$ 86,517	$64,497	$41,940
Investment in unconsolidated subsidiaries	1,994	2,578	7,531	7,286	6,620		
Other investments			3,540	1,259			
Property, plant and equipment	175,228	140,975	106,787	60,860	41,546	29,634	22,781
Less: depreciation and amortization reserves	70,560	55,085	43,820	22,987	17,564	11,850	7,916
Net Property Account	$104,668	$ 85,890	$ 62,967	$ 37,873	$ 23,982	$17,784	$14,865
Patents, unamortized cost	365	355	388	394	430	371	361
Goodwill	4,930	4,799	1,245	1,250	817	48	51
Other assets	1,844	1,568	1,587	285	638	553	534
Total Assets	$423,697	$354,945	$269,491	$172,771	$119,004	$83,253	$57,751

LIABILITIES AND STOCKHOLDERS' EQUITY	1964	1963	1962	1961	1960	1959	1958
Notes payable	$ 2,138	$ 17,306	$ 12,626	$ 8,504	$ 2,309	$ 3,025	$ 3,702
Accounts payable	64,749	49,117	37,856	25,867	18,475	7,990	3,259
Federal and foreign income tax	18,070	16,644	9,866	6,534	3,999	4,118	2,724
Deferred service contract income						5,154	4,790
Current portion of long-term debt	1,795	1,138	1,148	950	568	425	435
Other current liabilities	24,884	24,200	17,259	8,937	7,320	5,045	3,913
Total Current Liabilities	$111,636	$108,405	$ 78,755	$ 50,792	$ 32,671	$25,757	$18,823
Deferred service contract income	10,390	9,669	9,018	9,009	6,137		
Long-term debt	137,739	106,142	74,896	49,239	29,629	20,992	10,933
Deferred federal and foreign income tax	9,183	8,762	3,888				
Foreign and other reserves						1,957	
5% preferred stock		1,259	1,280	2,437	2,551	2,847	2,775
Series A preferred stock	2,318						
Common stock	10,508	10,145	4,834	4,368	4,159	179	169
Paid-in surplus	69,046	47,130	47,247	20,367	11,169	10,143	6,243
Accumulated retained earnings	72,877	63,433	49,573	36,559	32,689	21,378	18,808
Total Stockholders' Equity	$154,749	$121,967	$102,934	$ 63,731	$ 50,568	$34,547	$27,995
Total Liabilities and Stockholders' Equity	$423,697	$354,945	$269,491	$172,771	$119,004	$83,253	$57,751

EXHIBIT 4

LITTON INDUSTRIES (A)

Royal McBee's income statements, years ended July 31, 1958–64
(dollar figures in thousands)

	1964	1963	1962	1961	1960	1959	1958
Net sales*	$113,650	$109,231	$106,335	$106,846	$111,073	$103,951	$94,872
Cost of sales	65,795	65,713	64,061	65,913	65,549	60,700	53,925
Operating expenses	43,409	41,050	39,366	41,200	40,516	39,720	39,246
Operating Profit†	$ 4,446	$ 2,468	$ 2,908	dr $ 267	$ 5,008	$ 3,531	$ 1,701
Other income	475	769	1,179	1,132	749	706	493
Total Income	$ 4,921	$ 3,237	$ 4,087	$ 865	$ 5,757	$ 4,237	$ 2,194
Interest paid	937	1,021	1,212	1,470	1,400	1,105	777
Other income deductions	337	301	431	577	561	674	793
Extraordinary charges‡	—	—	—	—	1,972	—	—
Balance	$ 3,647	$ 1,915	$ 2,444	dr $ 1,182	$ 1,824	$ 2,458	$ 624
Provision for income tax	1,749	488‖	663	cr 102	1,053	1,172	237
Net Income	$ 1,898	$ 1,427	$ 1,781	dr $ 1,080	$ 771	$ 1,286	$ 387
Previous surplus	24,280	23,173	28,688	29,180	28,747	28,259	28,912
Special item§			cr 6,938	cr 906			
Preferred dividends	297	320	338	338	338	338	338
Common dividends	—	—	—	—	—	460	1,535
Surplus (July 31)¶	$ 25,881	$ 24,280	$ 23,173	$ 28,668	$ 29,180	$ 28,747	$ 27,426

* Includes all wholly owned foreign and domestic subsidiaries, except RMB Corp., a domestic finance subsidiary.

† After depreciation and amortization: 1964, $2,713,000; 1963, $2,952,000; 1962, $2,684,522; 1961, $2,707,916; 1960, $2,910,765; 1959, $2,257,103; 1958, $1,724,493.

‡ 1960: Mostly due to changes in inventory policy.

§ 1962: After crediting, $185,692 award in litigation (net of taxes) and deducting, $224,011 devaluation of Canadian dollar and $6,900,000 loss on sale of investment in Royal Precision Corp.; balance, $6,938,319.

1961: Taxes (net) refundable as a result of liquidation of wholly owned German subsidiary.

‖ Reduced by $100,000 as a result of net operating loss carry-forward.

¶ At July 31, 1964, $9,100,000 was not restricted as to cash dividends under terms of long-term notes.

EXHIBIT 5

LITTON INDUSTRIES (A)

Royal McBee's balance sheets, as of July 31, 1958–64

(dollar figures in thousands)

ASSETS	1964	1963	1962	1961	1960	1959	1958
Cash	$ 2,147	$ 2,829	$ 4,509	$ 5,140	$ 3,458	$ 3,663	$ 3,833
Marketable securitities	—	—	111	114	994	—	—
Drafts and accounts receivable (net)	20,925	20,038	19,536	21,681	20,369	19,436	15,709
Inventories	24,327	20,015	20,364	23,406	27,603	26,678	19,055
Other current assets*	—	—	—	1,670	—	4,563	—
Total Current Assets	$47,399	$42,882	$44,520	$52,011	$52,424	$54,340	$38,597
Real estate machinery and equipment	37,712	35,837	35,113	34,172	34,572	34,091	29,555
Depreciation	20,520	18,592	16,728	15,492	13,901	12,863	10,258
Net Property	$17,192	$17,245	$18,385	$18,680	$20,671	$21,228	$19,297
Investment in unconsolidated subsidaries	2,017	1,662	1,646	9,275	8,460	7,095	8,543
Long-term note and debenture	—	—	1,750	—	—	—	—
Deferred charges and other assets	3,473	2,916	2,844	2,857	3,188	2,936	2,380
Total Assets	$70,081	$64,705	$69,145	$82,823	$84,743	$85,599	$68,817

LIABILITIES AND STOCKHOLDERS' EQUITY

Notes payable	$ 3,566	$ 538	$ 4,000	$11,778	$ 8,560	$10,548	$ 1,500
Current portion, long-term debt	—	—	536	494	470	470	470
Accrued taxes	1,112	1,022	1,001	1,010	1,310	1,247	961
Accounts payable	4,426	4,274	4,712	4,969	9,051	7,695	2,889
Accrued wages	4,012	4,069	4,060	3,925	3,445	3,749	3,251
Unredeemed coupons	1,033	1,059	1,146	1,141	1,116	1,062	1,000
Provision for income tax	1,743	386	538	321	633	1,061	115
Total Current Liabilities	$15,892	$11,348	$15,993	$23,638	$24,585	$25,832	$10,186
Notes payable	6,671	7,237	7,774	8,312	8,773	8,818	9,060
Subordinated debentures	7,675	7,675	7,675	7,675	7,675	7,675	7,675
4½% Preferred stock	5,681	5,681	5,681	5,681	5,681	5,681	5,681
5% Preferred stock	500	500	500	500	500	500	500
5½% Preferred stock	500	500	500	500	500	500	500
6% Preferred stock	500	50	500	500	500	500	500
Common stock	1,538	1,538	1,538	1,538	1,538	1,538	1,535
Capital surplus	5,811	5,811	5,811	5,811	5,811	5,808	5,754
Surplus	25,881	24,280	23,173	28,668	29,180	28,747	27,426
Total Stockholders' Equity	$40,411	$38,810	$37,703	$43,198	$43,710	$43,274	$41,896
Less: Treasury stock	568	365	—	—	—	—	—
Net Stockholders' Equity	$39,843	$38,445	$37,703	$43,198	$43,710	$43,274	$41,896
Total Liabilities and Stockholders' Equity	$70,081	$64,705	$69,145	$82,823	$84,743	$85,599	$68,817

* In 1961 this consisted of a U.S. Income Tax refund and in 1959 this consisted of advances on plants under construction.

EXHIBIT 6
LITTON INDUSTRIES (A)
Pro forma financial and operating data

Financial Position:

The following summarized statement presents the financial position of Litton and Royal on July 31, 1964, and of Litton on a pro forma basis after giving effect to the acquisition of Royal for cash and preferred stock of Litton, and after giving effect to the repurchase of Royal's 6¼% Convertible Subordinated Debentures and the redemption of the Series B, C, and D preferred stock of Royal.

(thousands of dollars)

	Litton	Royal	Adjustments	Litton pro forma
ASSETS				
Current Assets:				
Cash and marketable securities.....	$ 56,481	$ 2,147	$ (9,457)[1] (5,900)[2]	$ 43,271
Accounts receivable..............	146,412	20,925		167,337
Inventories....................	103,263	24,327		127,590
Prepaid expenses...............	3,740			3,740
Total Current Assets.........	309,896	47,399		341,938
Investments......................	1,994	2,017	5,900[2] (5,900)[3]	4,011
Property, plant and equipment—net....	104,668	17,192		121,860
Other assets.....................	7,139	3,473		10,612
Total Assets....................	$423,697	$70,081		$478,421

LIABILITIES AND STOCKHOLDERS' EQUITY

	Litton	Royal	Adjustments	Litton pro forma
Current liabilities...................	$111,636	$15,651		$127,287
Long-term liabilities................	73,615	6,912		80,527
Deferred income...................	10,390			10,390
Convertible debentures.............	73,307	7,675	7,675[1]	73,307
Excess of net assets over purchase price, to be allocated as appropriate........			(7,886)[3]	7,886
Stockholders' Equity:				
Preferred stock...................	2,318	7,181	1,483[1] 5,698[3] (1,277)[3]	3,595
Common stock....................	10,508	1,538	1,538[3]	10,508
Additional paid-in capital..........	69,046	5,811	30[1] (22,998)[3] 5,781[3]	92,044
Earnings retained................	72,877	25,881	269[1] 25,612[3]	72,877
Treasury stock...................		(568)	(568)[3]	
Total Liabilities & Equity.........	$423,697	$70,081		$478,421

Pro Forma Adjustments:

[1] Repurchase of $7,675,000 of Royal's 6¼ % Convertible Subordinated Debentures at 103½; and redemption of Royal's Series B, C, and D preferred stock with an aggregate par value of $1,483,000 at 102, for a total cash consideration of $9,457,000.

[2] Purchase of Royal common stock, by Litton Industries, for $5,900,000 cash in market transactions.

[3] Issuance of 255,400 shares of Litton Preferred Stock, Series A, with an aggregate par value of $1,277,000, at an estimated market price of $95 a share in exchange for all the remaining outstanding capital stock of Royal; and the elimination in consolidation of the total investment, including the cash investment of $5,900,000.

Source: Proxy statement issued for the merger with Royal McBee dated November 5, 1964, p. 12.

EXHIBIT 7
LITTON INDUSTRIES (A)
Capitalization and changes therein upon the merger

The following table sets forth the capitalization of Litton and Royal at October 31, 1964, and of Litton as the surviving corporation on a pro forma basis:

	Outstanding at October 31, 1964		
Title of Class	Litton	Royal	Litton Pro Forma
Long-term debt[1]:			
4½% Promissory notes, due December 1, 1984............	$50,000,000		$50,000,000
3⅜% Sinking-fund notes, due May 1, 1971................	2,400,000		2,400,000
5.35% Promissory notes, due January 1, 1977.............	2,644,000		2,644,000
4½% Subordinated corporate notes, due January 2, 1969.....	2,675,045		2,675,045
Sundry indebtedness............	5,488,000[4]	$ 497,000	5,985,000
3½% Promissory notes, due November 1, 1974............		6,240,000	6,240,000
Convertible Subordinated Debentures[2]:			
3½% due April 1, 1987.........	64,943,900		64,943,900
5¼% due December 1, 1974.....	4,105,000		4,105,000
4¾% due June 1, 1974.........	4,700,000		4,700,000
6¼% due December 1, 1977.....		7,675,300[6]	
Capital Stock:			
Preferred stock, par value $5 a share (authorized 3,000,000 shares) Series A $3 cumulative convertible.....................	492,706 shs.		749,653 shs.[3]
Serial preferred stock, par value $100 a share, 4½% cumulative preferred Series A................		47,897 shs.[3]	
Common stock, par value $1 a share (authorized 17,000,000 shares)...	10,776,638 shs.[5]		10,776,638 shs.[5]
Common stock, par value $1 a share (authorized 3,000,000 shares)[3]....		1,538,090 shs.[7]	

[1] Includes current maturities of $1,415,000 (Litton) and $66,000 (Royal).

[2] Includes current portion of $470,000 (Litton).

[3] Shares to be issued by Litton have been computed on the basis of one share of Litton Preferred for each share of Royal Series A Preferred and $17.25 of Litton Preferred for each share of Royal common, excluding those shares of Royal common owned by Litton; the market price of the Litton Preferred has been estimated at $95 a share.

[4] Represents several items of indebtedness of consolidated subsidiaries, including both secured and unsecured debts with various due dates to 1979 and interest rates of 3 percent to 6 percent. Several of these debts have sinking-fund provisions and several are payable in currencies other than U.S. dollars.

[5] Excludes 492,706 and 749,653 shares, respectively, reserved for conversion of preferred stock; 1,059,039 shares for conversion of Litton debentures, and an estimated maximum of 250,000 shares which could be issued as additional consideration for acquired businesses. Includes 262,845 shares to be issued November 25, 1964 in payment of a 2½ percent stock dividend.

[6] These debentures have been called for redemption on December 1, 1964.

[7] Excludes 55,250 shares reserved for outstanding stock options but includes those shares of Royal common owned by Litton.

Source: Proxy statement issued for the merger with Royal McBee dated November 5, 1964, p. 8.

LITTON INDUSTRIES, 1965 (B)

SHORTLY AFTER THE MERGER with Royal Mcbee, Litton recognized that there were some major problems with Royal which if not immediately eliminated would lead to financial problems that could largely destroy the efforts Litton had made in broadening its office equipment division.

When Litton acquired Royal, it immediately became the second ranked firm in the office typewriter market with a 19 percent share. IBM was the leader with a 51 percent share. In the portable market, Royal was in second place with a 21 percent share; SCM was the leader with 48 percent of the market. However, changing trends within the typewriter industry were presenting a picture of future competition that would jeopardize Royal's market position—the accelerating change from manual to electric typewriters, a change which had begun some years earlier. During the period 1966 to 1969, shipments of office manual typewriters had dropped from $64 million to $27.5 million—over a 50 percent decline in a three-year period. Unfortunately, this trend was expected to continue, for the usefulness of manual machines was continually diminishing. Commercial offices, universities and financial institutions were systematically changing from office manual to electric typewriters. In the portable market, during the period 1963 to 1969, sales of electric typewriters increased from 15 to 46 percent of total sales of portable typewriters.

Exhibit 8 shows the sharp decline in office manual sales from 1948–65 and the resulting increase in office electric sales. Further evidence indicates that IBM was clearly dominating the market in terms of total office typewriters and heavy duty office typewriters. This information is presented in Exhibit 9.

The reason for the continuing decline in the case of Royal was the fact that, up to this time, the firm had not developed a quality electric typewriter that was competitive with IBM's efforts. From 1948, when Royal first introduced its electric typewriter, through 1966, when the model 660 was introduced, the firm's research and development efforts lagged, and the firm was continually being faced with problems of poor machine performance. Inferior quality had not only led major firms such as E. I. du Pont de Nemours (4,000 typewriters), Union Carbide (5,000 typewriters), and Chase Manhatten Bank (over 4,000 typewriters) to discontinue the purchase and use of the Royal model 660 office electric typewriter, but had also resulted in a negative attitude toward the whole product line of Royal.

This problem was summarized by Mr. Ash when he testified that at the time of the merger, "Royal's product line, factories, management and R.&D. were outdated and its marketing capabilities in need of strengthening."[5]

Failure was not only limited to the office electric typewriter market. In the early 1960s, Royal tried to compete with SCM's new portable electric typewriter. As in the case of the office electric, Royal first attempted to electrify one of its manual portable typewriters; this—as history indicates—did not lead to a successful electric machine. Immediately after the introduction of the Ultronic portable electric in 1966, quality deficiencies were being reported from the field.

Two solutions to the quality problem seemed apparent. One would be the development of a quality office electric typewriter through internal sources, and the other would be the acquisition of another company that had already successfully developed a quality electric. One potential problem with the latter alternative was the negative attitude in the Justice Department and Federal Trade Commission concerning mergers which threatened to lessen competition through the control of too large a market share segment of the industry.

It was estimated that an expenditure of between $5 and $7 million would be needed to develop a type bar office electric typewriter from scratch. After an examination of Royal's research and development personnel it was felt that a whole new R.&D. team would have to be developed. This combined with the actual development of the machine, would take from between five and seven years.[6]

Pressures for a quicker solution mounted with a further examination of Royal's financial statements. From 1960–65 total assets had shrunk by $15 million. The firm had an unfunded pension liability of $9.7 million accompanied by a substantial quantity of unsalable inventory. In addition,

---

[5] Initial Decision, *In the Matter of Litton Industries, Inc.*, p. 147.

[6] Ibid., p. 154.

its marketing organization, which had been a leader prior to World War II, had deteriorated to almost nothing.[7] This was further magnified by an $8 million deficit in 1968.

These factors led Litton to consider a merger with Triumph-Adler, a German manufacturer of typewriters which had already developed an electric office typewriter that would be competitive with IBM. At this time, Triumph-Adler used independent office machine dealers to sell their products in the United States and had approximately a 2 percent share of the U.S. typewriter market. The increased market share Litton derived from this merger was sufficient to cause the Federal Trade Commission to file a suit against Litton Industries on April 10, 1969. The complaint stated that the merger violated Section 7 of the Clayton Antitrust Act. Exhibit 10 presents the statement of complaint issued by the FTC while Exhibit 11 outlines the defense that Litton used in responding to the initial complaint.

As a potential financial manager who one day may be contending with similar problems, you are asked to evaluate the charges against Litton and the response of Litton against these claims.

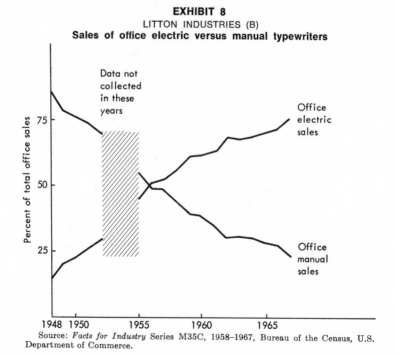

EXHIBIT 8
LITTON INDUSTRIES (B)
Sales of office electric versus manual typewriters

Source: *Facts for Industry* Series M35C, 1958–1967, Bureau of the Census, U.S. Department of Commerce.

---

[7] Ibid., p. 155.

EXHIBIT 9(a)
LITTON INDUSTRIES (B)
U.S. office typewriter market
(sales in percent of market share)

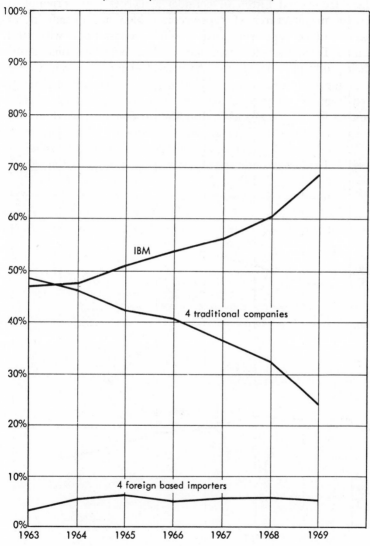

EXHIBIT 9(b)
LITTON INDUSTRIES (B)
U.S. office typewriter market
(sales in percent of market share)

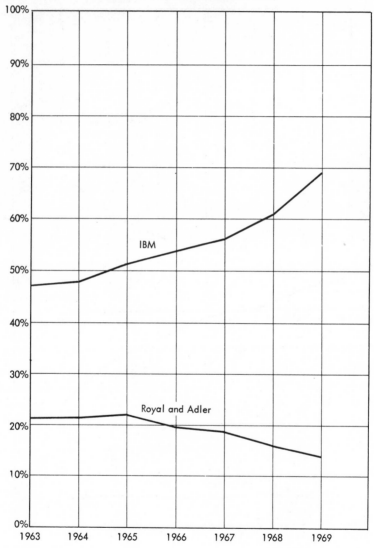

EXHIBIT 9(c)
LITTON INDUSTRIES (B)
U.S. heavy duty office typewriter market
(sales in percent of market share)

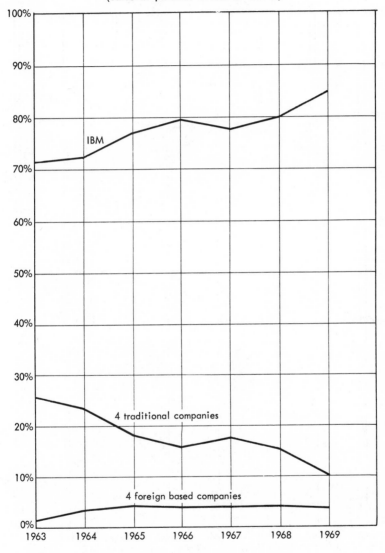

EXHIBIT 9(d)
LITTON INDUSTRIES (B)
U.S. heavy duty office typewriter market
(sales in percent of market share)

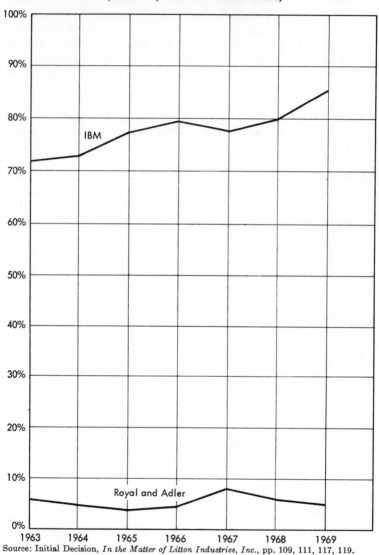

Source: Initial Decision, *In the Matter of Litton Industries, Inc.*, pp. 109, 111, 117, 119.

EXHIBIT 10
LITTON INDUSTRIES (B)
Statement of FTC complaint

The Federal Trade Commission, on April 10, 1969, issued the complaint herein charging that the acquisition, on or about January 3, 1969, by Litton Industries, Inc., a corporation, of 98.5 percent of the stock of Triumph-Werke Nürnberg, A.G., 82 percent of the stock of Adlerwerke, A.G., and all of the stock of their associated companies for a consideration of approximately $51,000,000 violated Section 7 of the Clayton Act (15 U.S.C. §18). The complaint states in part:

4. Litton Industries, Inc. (hereinafter "Litton"), the respondent herein, is a corporation organized and doing business under the laws of the State of Delaware with its principal office and place of business located at 9370 Santa Monica Boulevard, Beverly Hills, California 90213.

5. Litton ranks among the largest industrial corporations in the United States. In the year ended July 31, 1968, its sales and service revenues totaled $1.9 billion and its assets were $1.2 billion. In that year Litton reported profits of $102 million before taxes and enjoyed a cash flow of more than $103 million.

6. Litton's growth has been achieved in large part through a series of mergers and acquisitions. Litton represents that the direct contribution of acquired firm sales accounted for nearly half of its sales in 1967. Acquisitions and mergers secured for Litton leading positions in a number of industries, several of which are concentrated among relatively few firms. Litton ranks among the nation's eight largest sellers of cash registers, office calculating machines, power transmission equipment, A.C. electric motors, trading stamps, military and commercial ships, seismic surveys, store fixtures and refrigeration equipment, medical X-Ray equipment, elementary and high school textbooks, and a number of other products.

. . . .

8. In 1965, Litton acquired Royal McBee Corporation (hereinafter "Royal"), the second largest firm in the typewriter industry with 1964 sales of $114 million. Royal held a strong position in portable typewriters, had made advances in the office electric typewriter market, and dominated the office manual typewriter market. Litton represented that its experience combined with that of Royal in electromechanical technology would facilitate product innovation and development.

9. In 1967, Litton ranked first in domestic sales of office manual typewriters, with 40.8%; second in office electric typewriters, with 11.2%; and second in portable typewriters, with 23.1%. In total typewriter sales, Litton ranked second with a market share of 19.5%.

10. Litton recognized in 1965 a requirement for basic improvement in typewriter products of Royal. Its response was to choose expedients

EXHIBIT 10 (Continued)

that avoided commitment to original research and development. Acquisitions have been among the expedients chosen.

(a) In office electric typewriters, Litton replaced Royal's successful "GA" machine with its Models 550 and 660 typewriters differing from the "GA" largely in style and weight. By 1968, Litton recognized again the unfilled need for original research on a new office electric typewriter. It has estimated that an expenditure of $3.6 million would be required to develop, start and tool for a machine based on patent licenses to replace its existing models. The acquisition of Triumph-Adler is an alternative to original research and to developing a suitable machine based on the present state of the art.

(b) Litton acquired Imperial Typewriter Company, Ltd. in 1966, discontinuing the latter's production of office electric and portable manual typewriters Litton continues to produce as the "Model 80" Imperial's office manual typewriter.

(c) In portable typewriters, Litton introduced in 1966 an all-electric "Ultronic" portable developed by Royal. In 1966, it acquired Willy Fieler, GmbH, to obtain a similar typewriter known as the "All Electric." Litton has also obtained world-wide distribution rights on a low cost manual portable typewriter.

. . . .

12. Triumph-Adler is the collective designation for Triumph-Werke Nurnberg, A. G., a German corporation with its principal office and place of business in Frankfurt, Germany; Adlerwerke, A.G., a corporation owned or controlled by Triumph-Werke Nurnberg, A.G., and subsidiary corporations of each, including Adlerwerke vorm. Heinrich Kleyer A.G., a manufacturing unit, Grundig Burotechnik GmbH., a distributing company, Grundig Business Machines, Inc., USA, Grundig Bureau-equipment SARL, France, and Grundig Business Machine Pty., Ltd., Australia. Triumph-Adler has its principal office and place of business located at Kurgartenstrasse 37 Furth/Bay, Germany, and is headquartered in the United States at 355 Lexington Avenue, New York, New York.

13. Triumph-Adler manufactures office manual and electric typewriters and portable typewriters and ranks among the leading international typewriter companies. Its sales in 1967 were approximately $52 million, and its operations are profitable.

14. Triumph-Adler introduced its standard office typewriter and manual portable typewriters in the United States in the late 1940's. In 1967, Triumph-Adler ranked sixth in typewriter sales in the United States, accounting for about 2.3% of all typewriter sales. Triumph-Adler's share of office electric typewriter sales in the United States has grown to 2.6% of all such United States sales following introduction of its new model.

15. By 1968 Triumph-Adler accounted for 3.8% of manual office typewriter sales, 2.6% of electric office typewriters and nearly 1% of

EXHIBIT 10 (*Concluded*)

portable typewriter sales. Triumph-Adler announced a new portable electric typewriter to the trade in June 1968, and intended to market this product in the United States.

. . . .

24. The effect of acquisition of Triumph-Adler by Litton may be substantially to lessen competition or to tend to create a monopoly in the sale of typewriters generally and in particular kinds of typewriters, throughout the United States, or sections thereof, in violation of Section 7 of the Clayton Act, as amended (15 U.S.C. Sec. 18). These effects may occur in the following, among other ways:

(a) Substantial, actual and potential competition between Triumph-Adler and Litton may be eliminated;

(b) The restraining influence of Triumph-Adler as an actual or potential competitor may be eliminated;

(c) The competitive benefits of internal expansion and innovation by Litton in the development of improved standard office electric and portable typewriters of the kind manufactured by Triumph-Adler may be eliminated;

(d) Litton may be entrenched in its leading position in office manual typewriters;

(e) Already high barriers to the entry of new competition in the typewriter industry, or in segments thereof, may be heightened and increased;

(f) Members of the purchasing public and the ultimate consumer may be denied the benefits of free and open competition;

(g) The cumulative effect of the violation charged, separately and in the context of the series of acquisitions alleged in Paragraph 10 may be to entrench or increase already high levels of concentration by encouraging tendencies for combination and merger by actual and potential competitors.

Source: Initial Decision, *In the Matter of Litton Industries, Inc.*, pp. 2–6.

EXHIBIT 11
LITTON INDUSTRIES (B)
Litton's response to complaint charges

The answer of the respondent filed on June 23, 1969 denied the material charges of the complaint and, as an affirmative defense, states in part:

26. Acquisition by respondent of Triumph-Adler will substantially enhance competition and be in the public interest; disapproval will substantially impede, injure and destroy competition in the typewriter industry.

27. The predominant typewriter market is the office electric market in which the overwhelming bulk of all typing is done. The state of this market is such that without some effective competition, IBM, which now has a virtual monopoly, will increase its lead and will gain a complete monopoly. By all judicially approved antitrust indicia, that company already possesses monopoly power. With the quality of its products, research programs, new product introductions, and the effectiveness of its sales and service organization, it has the power to sweep aside the few remaining weak obstacles to its complete monopoly of the office market. Neither respondent nor Triumph-Adler acting separately is or can become a realistic competitive force in the office market against this dominant concern.

28. Entry barriers to both domestic and foreign companies into the office market are virtually insurmountable.

29. Respondent's Royal Typewriter operations are sustaining heavy losses: $6-½ million in fiscal 1968 and at least $6 million in fiscal 1969 ending July 31, 1969. Its sales organization has been declining through resignations of dealers, salesmen and servicemen. Triumph-Adler's United States business is barely profitable: less than 1-½% in fiscal 1968. Only by the joint efforts of respondent and Triumph-Adler will respondent have any opportunity to continue in the typewriter business.

30. Triumph-Adler has an office electric typewriter which, from a quality standpoint, compares favorably with the older IBM basket-type office electric. Neither Triumph-Adler nor respondent has a machine comparable to or directly competitive with the IBM single element "Selectric" machine or the even newer IBM Magnetic Tape Selectric Typewriter (MT/ST). It is the hope of respondent that, by introducing the Triumph-Adler office electric into the Royal line in competition with IBM, Royal will be able to slow the continuing substantial decline of its sales of office electric typewriters and the decline of its sales and service organization and thereby obtain a base from which to develop products competitive with the IBM Selectric, the new MT/ST and other products inevitably to be introduced.

31. Only in this way can respondent remain in the typewriter business, gain the time required, and justify the expense of attempting to develop machines competitive to IBM's. If respondent is denied this opportunity, it will have no alternative but to withdraw completely

EXHIBIT 11 *(Continued)*

from the typewriter business and leave the market to IBM, thus further enhancing and accelerating the trend towards complete monopoly. Disapproval of the Triumph-Adler acquisition by the Commission will have this effect.

32. Not only does respondent deny that the effects of its acquisition of Triumph-Adler will have a tendency to substantially lessen competition, but it affirmatively alleges that for the reasons herein pleaded to require respondent to divest Triumph-Adler would, itself, substantially lessen competition and tend to create a monopoly contrary to the intent and purpose of Section 7 of the Amended Clayton Act.

. . . .

Source: Initial Decision, *In the Matter of Litton Industries, Inc.*, pp. 6–7.

CROCKER-CITIZENS
NATIONAL BANK (A)

On February 11, 1963, Paul E. Hoover, chairman and chief executive officer of the Crocker-Anglo National Bank in San Francisco announced to the press that merger plans were being discussed with the officers and directors of the Citizens National Bank in Los Angeles. Under the terms of their proposal, all of the assets of Citizens National Bank would be merged into those of Crocker-Anglo National Bank under the latter organization's existing banking charter.[1]

The resulting institution would assume all of the deposit and other liabilities of both banks under the new corporate title of Crocker-Citizens National Bank. The newly formed organization would create a statewide banking operation uniquely suited to serve the growing California market.

Under the terms of the proposal, each share of Crocker-Anglo stock was to become one share of the consolidated bank's common shares outstanding, and each share of Citizens National stock was exchangeable for 1.9 shares of Crocker-Citizens' issue. As a result shareholders of Crocker-Anglo would be owners of 70.15 percent of the bank, holding 6,599,395 shares, while former Citizens National shareholders would retain a 29.85 percent interest, with 2,807,725 shares of the bank's shares outstanding.[2]

The proposed statewide consolidation would be the culmination of the plans and dreams of numerous Californians over the years. The consolidated entity could trace its banking origins back through several major predecessors to the state's early beginnings.

---

[1] "Crocker-Anglo Announces Merger," *Wall Street Journal*, February 12, 1963.

[2] Ira U. Cobleigh, "Crocker-Citizens National Bank," *Commercial and Financial Chronicle*, Vol. 198 (November 11, 1963), p. 1897.

Crocker-Anglo National Bank, with its principal office in San Francisco, was the oldest national bank in California. Its development began before 1925, when the Crocker First National Bank was formed by the consolidation of the First National Bank of San Francisco, the First Federal Trust Company, and the Crocker National Bank of San Francisco. The merged bank began its operations under the First National's federal charter, established on November 30, 1870. The bank continued to be a one-unit operation until 1947, when branches were opened in San Mateo and Oakland through smaller bank mergers. It remained a primarily downtown San Francisco-oriented bank, emphasizing commercial banking and trust operation until its merger with the Anglo-California National Bank in 1956.

Prior to that merger, Anglo-California had maintained a tradition of progressive, vigorous banking policy. It had managed to establish a strong banking system with a network of branch offices centrally located throughout the Bay area for the convenience of the public. In addition, Anglo enjoyed an international reputation as a banker's bank and as an institution for commercial banking, via its foreign branches and through the Anglo-California Trust Company, which specialized in trust and savings functions, serving tens of thousands of San Franciscans. By 1956, the Anglo-California National Bank of San Francisco had expanded its banking services, with a number of new offices and a continuing program of self-improvement.[3]

At that time, Anglo-California's merger with Crocker National was the biggest in California banking history. The result was an institution with 50 offices and total assets of nearly $1.5 billion. The Crocker Bank had been essentially a wholesaler of credit, with approximately half a billion dollars in assets and three branch locations. Its reputation for outstanding commercial and trust facilities was well established. The Anglo Bank had established assets of more than $1 billion and 47 offices, and was noted for its well-developed international banking services and its special experience as a retailer of credit for consumer goods financing. It included among its depositors many of the nation's largest corporations and hundreds of thousands of individuals throughout the northern part of the state.[4]

As a combined operation, Crocker-Anglo had continued to prosper until, in 1962, it ranked among the first 16 banking institutions in the nation in total deposits.[5] At the date of Mr. Hoover's announcement, it employed some 5,500 personnel in 124 offices throughout 29 California counties, from Eureka in the north to Santa Barbara and Bakersfield

---

[3] Monroe A. Bloom, *A Century of Pioneering, A Brief History of Crocker-Citizens National Bank* (San Francisco: Crocker-Citizens, 1970), pages 9–11.

[4] Ibid, page 17–23.

[5] *Moody's Bank and Finance Manual*, 1962, page A33.

in the south, with permits to open 23 additional branch offices in the future.[6]

Further evidence of the strength and growth of the bank can be seen in the comparative financial statements presented in Exhibits 1 and 2. Exhibit 1 shows a growth in Crocker-Anglo's deposits and capital assets, during the five-year period preceding the merger proposal, of nearly 33 percent, or $700 million. Net operating income, as shown in Exhibit 2, increased at nearly twice this rate during the same period, to total $16.5 million for the year ended December 31, 1962.

Mr. Hoover and his associates obviously felt that this strength and growth could be further advanced by the proposed merger with Citizens.

The Citizens National Bank had experienced a recent history of growth and development even more impressive than its proposed partner. The bank was founded in 1890, when Los Angeles was no more than an unpaved town of 50,000. Like the Anglo-California Bank, its initial concern was foreign trade. By 1918, however, the trend towards decentralization was already apparent. In 1928, the Citizens National and the Citizens Trust and Savings Bank were consolidated under the name of Citizens National Trust and Savings Bank of Los Angeles. The bank at this time had 20 branches throughout Los Angeles and its surrounding areas. After World War II, the bank grew as rapidly as the area itself. Branch expansion continued and customer needs were satisfied with the introduction of new services. By 1962, the Citizens National Bank (its name having been shortened in 1959) had grown to seventy-two branch offices serving what had come to be recognized as a major metropolitan area. The bank had completed its conversion to electronic bookkeeping equipment and claimed resources of more than $800 million. With the growth of the bank paralleling that of Los Angeles, and with the outlook for business in California as bright as ever, expansion out of the metropolitan area would have seemed appropriate.[7]

In 1962, Citizens National Bank's management forecasted another period of substantial growth. This was in spite of the fact that banks in general were projected to undergo a prolonged period of relatively easy money conditions through the mid-sixties, with the bank prime lending rate remaining static at $4\frac{1}{2}$ percent after having been reduced from 5 percent in August 1960. This condition of large supplies of available credit at unchanging lending rates, with a sharp increase in the interest rate paid on time and savings accounts (3 percent to $3\frac{1}{2}$ percent) commencing January 1, 1962, would, in most cases, probably result in bank

---

[6] Roy A. Britt, *"President's Letter to the Shareholders of Citizens National Bank,"* May 3, 1963, page 1.

[7] Roy A. Britt, *"Report to the President,"* 1962 Annual Report, Citizens National Bank, January 8, 1963, page 3.

earnings leveling off.[8] Citizens National, remaining highly competitive, easily absorbed the sharp rise in interest requirements and recorded important advances in operating earnings at close of 1962. An analysis of the bank's comparative growth in assets and earnings, detailed in Exhibits 3 and 4, shows that Citizens' growth even exceeded the gains posted by Crocker-Anglo during the 1958–62 period. Higher loan volume and a gain in income from investments were primarily responsible for this increase. In addition, increased efficiency through automation helped lessen the effect of higher interest costs. Competitively, the opening of seven new branch offices to develop new business and the offering of additional services to customers resulted in total resources and deposits both rising by 9.8 percent during 1962.

Based upon this strength in Citizens' financial structure, the management of Crocker-Anglo felt that the proposed merger would make it possible for each bank to take what Roy A. Britt, president of Citizens National Bank, described as "its rightful place in the economy and the financial community of California."[9]

If approved, the merged bank would employ over 7,500 staff members in over 200 offices, with approved permits for the addition of 42 more.[10] Exhibit 5 presents a pro forma combined balance sheet for the companies, assuming that they had been merged as of December 31, 1962. With consolidated assets totaling over $3.2 billion, the merged organizations would have had sufficient deposits on hand at that date to rank as the 12th largest bank in the United States, and second largset in the state of California.[11]

The strong position maintained by Crocker-Anglo in central and northern California, combined with coverage by Citizens in the southern part of the state, rendered both organizations suitable for combination into a unified statewide banking system serving all areas within California. The merger would not only provide increased competition for the three existing statewide banking systems but would also enhance both banks' ability to participate in greater service to growing national and international interests.

The timing of the merger proposal also provided a key element in influencing the banks' directors' discussions. First, the regulatory atmosphere in February of 1963 seemed to be favorable. Mr. James Saxon, the Comptroller of the Currency, had shown a tendency in the past year to approve the applications from national banks for new charters.

---

[8] Paul J. Maynard, "Prospects for Bank Stocks Favorable on Balance at Mid-Year," *The Magazine of Wall Street*, July 13, 1963, page 468.

[9] Britt, "Presidents Letter," page 2.

[10] Ibid.

[11] Cobleigh, "Crocker-Citizens National Bank."

There also appeared to be developing recently a slight liberalization of the Federal Reserve Board of Governor's policy toward acquisitions and mergers.[12]

Second, the merger was to be effected by the issuance of shares of Crocker-Citizens corporation's stock to shareholders of Citizens National Bank in exchange for shares of Citizens during a period which had been judged by Citizens management as favorable for their shareholders. The relative range of prices of the two banks' common stock, and the ratio of earnings on these shares for the period 1958–62, are presented in Exhibits 6 and 7. At the time of the announcement of the banks' merger discussions, Crocker-Anglo stock had been producing an average yield on capital investment of 2.6 percent, which was considered to be about average when compared to the 25 largest U.S. banking institutions of that period.[13]

The past history of both organizations' earning growth led Crocker-Anglo management and market analysts alike to expect future growth in earnings to the benefit of both organizations' shareholders if the merger were consumated.

Discussion between the two institutions' management had been in progress for some time prior to Mr. Hoover's announcement, and agreement in principle had already been secured from the Transamerica Corporation, holder of approximately 40 percent of the outstanding shares of Citizens National Bank.[14]

---

[12] Herbert Bratter, "On the Merger Front," *Banking*, May, 1963, page 147.

[13] "Bank Profits at High Level," *Financial World*, February 20, 1963, page 10.

[14] *Moody's Bank and Financial Manual*, page 380.

EXHIBIT 1
CROCKER-CITIZENS NATIONAL BANK (A)
Crocker-Anglo National Bank
Balance Sheets as of December 31, 1958–62
(dollar figures in thousands)

	1962	1961	1960	1959	1958
Cash	$ 365,473	$ 351,097	$ 305,626	$ 317,744	$ 282,892
Short-term securities	689,135	683,374	524,444	483,004	537,683
Current receivable	—	—	—	—	—
Total Current Assets	$1,054,608	$1,034,471	$ 830,070	$ 800,748	$ 820,575
Long-term securities	4,198	4,258	3,482	8,072	11,727
Land, buildings, etc.	30,366	27,455	21,935	20,682	19,053
Customers acceptance liability	57,069	37,823	37,442	21,834	15,841
Loans and discounts	1,255,397	1,087,029	997,453	987,841	828,447
Long term receivables	11,351	10,003	7,784	7,215	7,553
Other assets	2,808	2,428	2,720	1,364	2,263
Total Assets	$2,415,797	$2,203,467	$1,900,886	$1,847,756	$1,705,459
Reserve for loan losses	$ 23,418	$ 20,987	$ 18,715	$ 16,243	$ 13,544
Reserve for interest, taxes, etc.	12,803	15,560	11,661	9,535	16,544
Bank acceptance liability	57,395	38,212	37,644	22,160	15,841
Unearned income	19,425	16,684	16,330	16,287	13,195
Payables	20,830	12,900	—	—	—
Other liabilities	—	—	—	—	—
Deposits	2,134,493	1,953,841	1,686,757	1,656,680	1,526,989
Total Liabilities	$2,268,364	$2,058,184	$1,771,107	$1,720,905	$1,586,113
Common stock	65,993	65,993	53,066	53,066	50,416
Capital surplus	65,993	65,993	53,066	53,066	50,416
Undivided profits	13,138	10,988	21,790	19,126	17,002
Dividends payable	2,309	2,309	1,856	1,592	1,512
Total Liabilities and Net Worth	$2,415,797	$2,203,467	$1,900,885	$1,847,755	$1,705,459

Source: *Moody's Bank & Finance Manual*, 1962.

EXHIBIT 2

CROCKER-CITIZENS NATIONAL BANK (A)

Crocker-Anglo National Bank

Income statements; years ended December 31, 1958–62

(dollar figures in thousands)

	1962	1961	1960	1959	1958
Operating income:					
Interest and discount on loans....	$ 73,261	$65,019	$63,649	$55,173	$45,660
Interest and dividends on securities...................	21,087	19,142	14,150	13,563	13,724
Other operating income.........	15,730	13,110	11,391	10,741	8,661
Total Operating Income..	$110,078	$97,271	$89,190	$80,017	$68,045
Salaries and wages.............	28,469	25,537	22,715	19,941	17,336
Interest expense...............	34,724	25,309	20,037	19,455	17,667
Federal and state income taxes...	12,139	14,325	16,136	14,218	10,930
Taxes other than on income.....	2,181	1,556	1,425	1,259	1,023
Other operating expenses.......	16,076	14,089	13,064	11,915	9,511
Net Operating Income...	$ 16,489	$16,455	$15,813	$13,229	$11,578

Source: *Moody's Bank & Finance Manual*, 1962.

EXHIBIT 3

CROCKER-CITIZENS NATIONAL BANK (A)
Citizens National Bank
Balance sheets as of December 31, 1958–62
(dollar figures in thousands)

	1962	1961	1960	1959	1958
Cash......................	$157,247	$160,501	$122,647	$164,542	$114,914
Short-term securities.........	255,991	228,318	180,175	139,517	199,924
Current receivables..........	3,580	3,012	2,411	2,365	1,966
Total Current Assets...........	$416,818	$391,831	$305,233	$306,424	$316,804
Long-term securities.........	4,853	4,099	1,869	2,669	1,513
Land, buildings, etc...........	9,501	8,414	8,334	7,437	6,879
Customers acceptance liability..................	3,887	2,443	1,533	1,768	1,449
Loans and discounts..........	373,892	330,108	294,938	271,445	217,156
Other assets................	764	661	511	766	447
Total Assets........	$809,715	$737,556	$612,418	$590,509	$544,248
Reserve for loan losses.......	$ 7,008	$ 5,644	—	—	—
Reserve for interest, taxes, etc......................	3,953	3,401	3,637	2,490	2,359
Bank acceptance liability......	3,887	2,442	1,533	1,768	1,449
Unearned income...........	8,389	7,455	7,110	6,227	4,787
Payables..................	—	—	—	—	—
Other liabilities..............	3,918	3,562	1,753	174	180
Deposits...................	736,082	670,673	555,532	538,450	504,870
Total Liabilities......	$763,237	$693,177	$569,565	$549,109	$513,645
Common stock..............	14,777	13,325	13,325	13,325	7,000
Capital surplus..............	22,523	21,675	21,675	20,675	15,000
Undivided profits...........	9,178	9,379	7,853	7,400	8,603
Dividends payable...........	—	—	—	—	—
Total Liabilities and Net Worth.......	$809,715	$737,556	$612,418	$590,509	$544,248

Source: *Moody's Bank & Finance Manual*, 1962.

EXHIBIT 4

CROCKER-CITIZENS NATIONAL BANK (A)

Citizens National Bank

Income statements; years ended December 31, 1958–62

(dollar figures in thousands)

	1962	1961	1960	1959	1958
Operating income:					
Interest and discount on loans....	$21,116	$18,524	$17,645	$14,292	$12,052
Interest and dividends on					
securities....................	8,414	7,346	5,783	5,713	4,947
Other operating income.....:....	8,143	7,170	6,045	5,299	4,691
Total Operating Income...	$37,673	$33,040	$29,473	$25,304	$21,690
Salaries and wages................	11,177	10,637	9,713	8,192	7,634
Interest expense..................	10,462	7,163	5,853	5,395	4,881
Federal and state income taxes......	3,200	3,950	4,206	3,539	2,370
Taxes other than on income........	990	772	724	587	473
Other operating expenses..........	7,060	5,974	5,004	4,076	3,526
Net Operating Income....	$ 4,784	$ 4,544	$ 3,973	$ 3,515	$ 2,806

Source: *Moody's Bank & Finance Manual*, 1962.

EXHIBIT 5
CROCKER-CITIZENS NATIONAL BANK (A)
Pro forma combined balance sheet
combining Crocker-Anglo National Bank of San Francisco
with Citizens National Bank of Los Angeles at
December 31, 1962
(dollar figures in thousands)

	Crocker-Anglo	Citizens National	Combined trans-actions	Pro forma combination
ASSETS				
Current Assets:				
Cash in banks....................	$ 365,473	$157,247		$ 522,720
U.S. government securities........	495,236	184,575		679,811
State and municipal securities......	193,899	71,416		265,315
Earned interest receivable.........	—	3,580		3,580
Total Current Assets.......	$1,054,608	$416,818		$1,471,426
Other securities.................	238	3,385		3,623
Loans and discounts..............	1,255,397	373,892		1,629,289
Accrued income receivable........	11,351	—		11,351
Federal reserve bank stock........	3,960	1,119		5,079
Stock in commercial fireproof building company..............	—	349		349
Bank premises and equipment......	29,763	9,501		39,264
Other real estate................	603	—		603
Customers' letters of credit and acceptances...................	57,069	3,887		60,956
Other assets....................	2,808	764		3,572
Total Assets..............	$2,415,797	$809,715		$3,225,512
LIABILITIES AND STOCK-HOLDERS' EQUITY				
Current Liabilities:				
Reserve for loan losses...........	$ 23,418	$ 7,008		$ 30,426
Reserve for interest, taxes, etc.....	12,803	3,953		16,756
Unearned income (discounts)......	19,425	8,389		27,814
Letters of credit and acceptance....	57,395	3,887		61,282
Deposits.......................	2,134,493	736,082		2,870,575
Total Current Liabilities....	$2,247,534	$759,319		$3,006,853
Bills payable for federal funds.....	20,830	—		20,830
Other liabilities.................	—	3,918		3,918
Stockholders' Equity:				
Common stock ($10 par value)....	65,993	14,777	$13,299	94,069
Capital surplus.................	65,993	22,523	(13,299)	75,217
Undivided profits...............	13,138	9,178		22,316
Dividends payable...............	2,309	—		2,309
Total Stockholders Equity....	$ 147,433	$ 46,478		$ 193,911
Total Liabilities and Stockholders' Equity.....	$2,415,797	$809,715		$3,225,512

Source: *Moody's Bank & Finance Manual, 1962.*

EXHIBIT 6

CROCKER-CITIZENS NATIONAL BANK (A)

Market prices/earnings Crocker-Anglo National Bank

The following table sets forth the range of prices of the common stock of Crocker-Anglo on the over-the-counter marketing during the calendar years 1958 through 1962.

	Range	
Year ended	*High*	*Low*
12/31/62..............	55¾	33
12/31/61..............	78½	40½
12/31/60..............	40½	31⅝
12/31/59..............	38¼	32
12/31/58..............	39⅝	28¾

The following table sets forth the actual nonadjusted per share earnings for Crocker Anglo during the calendar years 1958 through 1962 and dividends paid to common stockholders from these earnings.

Year	*Net earnings before taxes*	*Net earnings after taxes*	*No. of shares (000s)*	*Earnings per share*	*Dividends paid per share*
1962................	$28,627	$16,489	6,599	$2.50	$1.40
1961................	$30,781	$16,457	6,599	$2.49	$1.40*
1961................	$31,949	$15,813	5,307	$2.98	$1.20
1959................	$27,447	$13,229	5,307	$2.49	$1.20
1958................	$22,507	$11,577	5,042	$2.30	$1.20†

* Also stock dividend of 16⅔ percent.
† Also stock dividend of 25 percent.
Source: *Moody's Bank & Finance Manual*, 1962.

EXHIBIT 7
CROCKER-CITIZENS NATIONAL BANK (A)
Market Prices/earnings Citizens National Bank

The following table sets forth the range of prices of the common stock of Citizens National on the over-the-counter market during the calendar years 1958 through 1962.

	Range	
Year ended	*High*	*Low*
12/31/62..............	67	48
12/31/61..............	71	46
12/31/60..............	52¼	44½
12/31/59..............	54	39½
12/31/58..............	61	44

The following table sets forth the actual nonadjusted per share earnings for Citizens National during the calendar years 1958 through 1962 and dividends paid to common stockholders from these earnings.

Year	*Net earnings before taxes*	*Net earnings after taxes*	*No. of shares (000s)*	*Earnings per share*	*Dividends paid per share*
1962.................	$7,982	$4,782	1,478	$2.82	$1.60*
1961.................	$8,494	$4,544	1,333	$2.74	$1.60
1960.................	$8,178	$3,973	1,333	$2.69	$1.60
1959.................	$7,054	$3,515	1,333	$2.39	$1.80†
1958.................	$5,178	$2,808	700	$3.30	$2.25

* Also stock dividend of 10 percent.
† Also stock dividend of 50 percent.
Source: *Moody's Bank & Finance Manual*, 1962.

CROCKER-CITIZENS
NATIONAL BANK (B)

On May 13, 1963, after consent was obtained between the three parties of Crocker-Anglo National Bank of San Francisco, Citizens National Bank of Los Angeles and Transamerica Corporation as to the terms of the merger, the two banks (not including Transamerica) filed a request for merger before the Comptroller of the Currency. This was just 34 days prior to the decision of the U.S. Supreme Court concerning the case of *United States* v. *Philadelphia National Bank*—a summary of this suit is presented in the readings to this section. Hearings were held in the latter part of July, and after receipt of some 1,605 pages of testimony and exhibits, the Comptroller, on September 30, 1963 approved the merger which was to become effective after November 1, 1963.

On October 8, 1963, the Justice Department filed suit attacking the merger as unlawful under Section 7 of the Clayton Act and Section 1 of the Sherman Act. A preliminary injunction against the merger was denied by the courts on the grounds that the government had not presented a prima facie case as to how the merger would lessen existing or potential competition.

Trial was held during June 1–18, 1965; testimony was taken and time limits set for the filing of briefs and proposed findings. At this time, the U.S. Senate passed a bill which was also passed by the House and signed by the President on February 21, 1966. This bill became known as the 1966 Banking Act. As a result of the passage of this law, the courts were in the unique position of having the laws applicable to a case changed after all the testimony had been received and a decision was pending.

The impact of the 1966 Banking Act upon this merger was to return the application for merger to the Comptroller of the Currency for review under the new regulations of the 1966 act. The Comptroller was instructed by the courts to make specific findings on the possibility of whether the merger would tend to lessen competition, the effect of the transaction in meeting the convenience and needs of the community to be served, and finally, whether—assuming the merger did lessen potential competition as the government contended—the effect would be clearly outweighted in the public interest by meeting the convenience and needs of the community.

Exhibit 8 presents a brief article concerning the merger suit as trial began in June of 1965. Exhibit 9 presents the main arguments of the case, as outlined by the government, opposing the merger.

One of the main arguments of the defense was that the real market to consider in terms of a competitive effect was not the narrow market of commercial banking, but the broader market which included all institutions competing for savings and/or investment dollars. Exhibit 10 presents several tables that provide a prospective view of the Crocker-Citizens position relative to other financial institutions in this broader market.

A second defense contention was that the government did not adjust any concentration ratios for business done in California by out-of-state banks. In *U.S.* v. *Philadelphia National Bank*, the Supreme Court made a 16⅔ percent downward adjustment in the concentration ratios—from 36 percent to 30 percent. Since California is a capital import state and studies have indicated that 38 percent of California home mortgage loans are provided by out-of-state funds, and since California's rate of growth exceeds that of Pennsylvania, this argument has even greater significance in California than in Pennsylvania.

The third area of conflict arose over whether there was a statewide market as the government contended. Defense took the view that banking markets are local, national, and international, but not statewide. For example, the supply of investment dollars is really a national market since California is a capital import state. A major corporation desiring to do business in one state with a bank that had offices throughout that state would in a sense create a statewide market. But the bank would still be competing against banks in Chicago and New York which also wanted to handle the California business. If this did constitute a statewide market, then there were only three banks capable of handling such dealings—Bank of America, United California Bank, and, to a lesser extent, First Western. Thus in reality the merger would create a fourth competitor in this market and would increase, not decrease, competition.

Further evidence was submitted demonstrating the local nature of banking activities within the state of California. Evidence was also submitted showing that in no way were Crocker and Citizens in competition with each other within the state.

As a potential future financial manager who one day may be engaged in merger activity, you are asked to generally evaluate the arguments presented above.

EXHIBIT 8

CROCKER-CITIZENS NATIONAL BANK (B)

Trial to Split Crocker-Citizens Opens Today amid Antitrust Row*

Stanley Strachen

NEW YORK.—While Congress and the Johnson Administration are grappling with the question of the proper role of antitrust law in banking, the Justice Department is moving ahead with its effort to break up the country's 12th largest bank, Crocker-Citizens National Bank, San Francisco.

On Tuesday, a trial begins in US District Court, San Francisco, on a suit filed by the government in October, 1963, to split up the $3.2 billion bank, with 214 branches throughout California.

Not only does the trial come while the role of the Justice Department is being vigorously debated in and out of Congress, but the suit will mark the first time the government has claimed that the merger of two banks in widely separated cities—Los Angeles and San Francisco—would lead to a loss of actual or potential competition.

The suit, moreover, will focus attention on what has become the most controversial implication of the government suits against banking in recent years: that the antitrust law can be applied to 2,000 or so mergers completed in the decade prior to enactment of the Bank Merger Act of 1960.

For in its suit against Crocker-Citizens, the government contends that 14 separate mergers dating back to 1956 were, in fact, consummated in violation of the antitrust laws. While the government says it has no intention of trying to undo all these mergers, the findings of the court on this point would be significant for the many giant banks that carried out major mergers during the 1950s.

Instead of seeking to split all 14 mergers, the government specifically is seeking to invalidate only the last merger in the series—that of Crocker-Anglo National Bank, San Francisco, and Citizens National Bank, Los Angeles, which joined in 1963.

Spokesmen for both sides said last week they expect the trial itself to last only two or three weeks, but the decision could be a long way off. In earlier cases the decisions have been handed down as much as two years after the trials ended.

The Crocker-Citizens trial comes only about two months after the Justice Department won its biggest banking victory—against the $7 billion Manufacturers Hanover Trust Co., New York, fourth largest in the nation.

Although there has been continuing action in other cases, the trial is the first to open since the June, 1963 decision by the Supreme Court—in the Philadelphia National Bank case—applied the antitrust laws to banking.

---

* Reprinted from *American Banker,* June 1, 1965, by permission of the publisher.

EXHIBIT 8 *(Continued)*

Since then the High Court has ruled the merger of First National Bank and Trust Co. and Security Trust Co., Lexington, Ky., illegal, and in March a lower court found against the merger of Manufacturers Trust Co. and Hanover Bank, New York. Both consolidations took place in 1961. The Philadelphia merger was halted by an injunction and never completed.

The Department's attempt to stop the Crocker-Citizens merger in the same fashion failed when the same three-judge panel that will try the case denied a temporary injunction.

Much of the bank's defense will rest on the claim that the original Crocker-Anglo and Citizens National banks did not compete with one another.

In its evidence and the testimony of its witnesses, the bank also will rely heavily on the decision of Comptroller of the Currency James J. Saxon to permit the merger, the material submitted to him with the application, and the public hearing he conducted prior to granting approval.

The bank also expects to show through statistics and records "that concentration has in fact declined" in California banking in the period Jan. 1, 1954 to Dec. 31, 1964.

The bank contends it has "been unable to find any area (of the state) in which the number of banking alternatives has declined during this period."

Crocker-Citizens in order "to show ease of entry and deconcentration" plans to introduce a list of the 137 new banks established in the state from 1953 to 1964 and the financial histories of the 120 of these banks still in existence.

The bank, which plans to introduce voluminous records on branch applications from regulatory agencies, believes it will be unnecessary to call either the Comptroller of the Currency or California Superintendent of Banks John A. O'Kane as a witness.

However, the bank will attempt "to demonstrate by observable fact" that the Comptroller of the Currency was correct when he said, in his decision on the merger, that more de novo branches in the southern part of the state "would seriously over-bank this area." Mr. Saxon said it was "necessary to review most critically applications for de novo branches in this area in order to avoid the evils of destructive competition."

Testimony on branch applications and the ease of entry for new California banks will be given by Harry M. Rhorer, assistant vice president in charge of systemwide branch location at Crocker-Citizens.

The defense will answer the only California bank to object to its merger—Home Bank of Compton—with a filing showing Home Bank's loan and deposit growth between June 30, 1955, and June 30, 1964, to "show that previous mergers have not been 'decisive' as far as this bank is concerned."

The bank will attack the Justice Department's contention that commercial banking constitutes a separate line of commerce for the purposes of antitrust adjudication.

Whether commercial banking is a distinct line of commerce or whether it is interconnected with the multifaceted short-term finance industry has been a point of contention in every bank merger case.

Some attorneys interpret portions of the Philadelphia decision as giving the High Court's approval to the Justice Department version of this relation-

EXHIBIT 8 *(Continued)*

ship. However, the Supreme Court did not specifically rule that commercial banking is distinct from other types of financial institutions.

The bank will submit as part of its evidence the Justice Department's answers to a number of the interrogatories submitted by Crocker-Citizens attorneys.

The purpose of the submission will be to show the government's agreement with several claims of the bank:

- "Crocker-Anglo did not compete with banks in the Los Angeles area."
- "Citizens did not compete with banks in the San Francisco Bay area."
- "No bank customers or banks were injured as a result of the acts alleged in the complaint."
- ". . . Plaintiff is unable to enumerate or locate the banking offices required for a statewide banking."
- "Plaintiff made no complaint over the 1956 consolidation of Crocker First and Anglo-California (to form Crocker-Anglo) at the time, although it did not consider that Section 1 of the Sherman Act was applicable to bank mergers and consolidations in general."
- ". . . Legal restrictions on the opening of de novo branch offices in the relevant markets referred to in the complaint 'make it extremely difficult for any bank to acquire a substantial number of new offices in a reasonable period of time.' "

The bank then offers this conclusion: "It is a mathematical certainty the merger could not have reduced, the number of alternative banking sources in any local market."

The Crocker-Citizens pre-trial document then contends that "in view of plaintiff's admission that the state needs another statewide bank, that it does not know how many offices a statewide bank requires, and that Crocker-Anglo could not have opened such a number as 78 offices [which Citizens brought into the merger] in the five southern counties in the near future, it is apparent that plaintiff cannot sustain its burden of proving that Crocker-Anglo was a potential competitor as a statewide bank without merging."

Also scheduled to testify for the bank in support of points on which the two sides disagree are Emmett G. Solomon, president and chief executive officer; Paul E. Hoover, chairman, and John J. Downes, vice president for special administrative services, along with Oscar Goodman, professor of economics at Northwestern University, Evanston, Ill.

The Justice Department will have 341 separate documents to support its case and "expects that its two witnesses . . . will rely on and testify with respect to all" of them.

The two witnesses the government plans to put on the stand are antitrust division staff economist Dr. John D. Gaffey, and Dr. Joel E. Dirlam, professor of economics, University of Rhode Island.

Much of the government's case will be built around two key points:

- That the two banks were interested in de novo branch expansion that would have brought them into direct competition.

EXHIBIT 8 *(Continued)*

• That the commercial banking business in California, despite the large number of new entrants, has become increasingly concentrated over the past few years.

Significantly, District Judge Lloyd F. MacMahon of New York, in his March 10 opinion on the Manufacturers Hanover case, gave great weight to similar points in the Justice Department case before him.

Judge MacMahon placed the greatest emphasis in his opinion on "the flood tide toward oligopoly" in the New York banking market.

It was his finding that a larger percentage of banking power (both in assets and branches) was being held by the five largest banks in the city. He stressed this in his ruling that the merger was illegal despite the fact that he believes it has served the public interest.

It is apparent from the government exhibits that a similar tack will be taken in the Crocker-Citizens trial. Much of the material attempts to prove that there have been anti-competitive effects from the Crocker-Anglo merger in 1956, and that this trend will be accelerated if the Crocker-Citizens merger is allowed to stand.

For example, two tables that will be introduced by the plaintiff will show the number of banking offices in the San Francisco Bay Area in February, 1956, and in December, 1962.

In 1956, "nine banks together had 91.3% of the 277 offices in the Bay Area and as a result of the . . . consolidation, Crocker-Anglo accounted for about 7.2% of all such offices.

"In December, 1962, Crocker-Anglo had 11%, and eight banks together had 90% of the 370 bank offices in the Bay Area."

Another Justice Department table "shows some important effects of the postwar bank merger trend in California. Notwithstanding the substantial postwar increase in total bank assets and offices, this merger trend has held California banks at, and in many years far below, the number in existence before this growth took place.

"The substantiality of the 166 banks acquired during this period (1954–64) is reflected in the fact that their total assets in the year of acquisition amounted to $5.2 billion, 14% of the total assets of all California banks at the end of 1964."

Also on the "concentration" theme, the government plans to show that "prior to the merger, the Bay Area was still heavily concentrated and that the three largest banks, including Crocker-Anglo, had increased their combined share of total deposits from 70% in 1956 to 79.3% in 1963."

In addition to claiming that competition already has been eliminated, the government contends that "the merger of Crocker-Anglo and Citizens eliminated substantial potential competition."

It will attempt to demonstrate this claim through studies of the premerger branching policies—both past and projected—of the two banks. In New York, it successfully pressed the issue through a study of the banking business carried on by Hanover Bank, the smaller of the two.

Manufacturers Trust Co. was primarily a retail institution, while Hanover's

EXHIBIT 8 (Continued)

operation was almost exclusively in the wholesale area. But the Justice Department proved to Judge MacMahon's satisfaction that the steps toward retail banking which Hanover had taken in the period just prior to the merger agreement were sufficient to justify the finding that the consolidation eliminated a potential competitor from the retail banking field in New York City.

In the Crocker-Citizens case, the government will attempt to show that "in postwar years Crocker-Anglo and, to a lesser extent, Citizens were adding numerous new branches (Crocker had 122 offices at the time of the merger) in California counties where they already had offices, and at the same time steadily moving out into new areas. Each defendant was thereby coming progressively closer to local areas served by offices of the other."

To support its contention that this trend would have continued, and that, but for the merger, the banks would have become direct competitors, the Justice Department will introduce a vast amount of material describing the various areas in which each bank hoped to expand.

Other evidence will include items such as deposits, loans and net earnings of 30 de novo branches of Crocker-Anglo, a bank tabulation, which the government says "summarizes Crocker-Anglo's favorable earnings experience on its de novo branches, a good indication of its interest in and capacity for de novo branch expansion."

Also, a December, 1961, memorandum which the Justice Department says supports its claim "that Crocker-Anglo's branch expansion policy applied to the entire state and did not exclude any particular areas."

A major government exhibit will be a February, 1963, memorandum by Dwight L. Clarke, at the time an executive committee and board member of Citizens, entitled "why shareholders of Citizens National Bank would benefit from an exchange of their stock for that of Crocker-Anglo National Bank in a merger where 'Citizens' would appear prominently in the new bank's name.'"

According to the Justice Department, this memorandum will show:

● "That probably the most fundamental reason for the merger was to combine the two banks at that particular time, before they entered each other's geographic area and became closer and more direct competitors, which was imminent. For if they did not combine at that time, it was unlikely that they ever would, because, in the future, as more obvious competitors, they would be kept apart by the antitrust laws.

● ". . . That Crocker-Anglo's expansion into the Los Angeles area was both inevitable and imminent, regardless of whether or not it combined with Citizens.

● "That if Citizens did not merge with Crocker-Anglo of its own accord at that time, Transamerica Corp., a holding company, would acquire sufficient stock to become the majority stockholder of Citizens and then force Citizens to so merge."

Transamerica owned 41% of Citizens at the merger, and thereby acquired 12% ownership of the new bank, which it agreed to sell as a condition for the Comptroller's approval. The stock is held by a trustee.

EXHIBIT 8 *(Concluded)*

One important factor in the case is the fact that the three judges who must decide it already have written a lengthy opinion on whether "there is reasonable probability of ultimate success by the government," and decided that question in the negative last Fall when they denied the government's request for a temporary injunction against the merger.

The jurists—circuit judge Walter L. Pope, and district judges Alfonso J. Zirpoli and William T. Sweigert—at that time said:

"We are forced to the conclusion that so far as presently existing competition . . . is concerned, there is no showing here that the proposed merger will have any competitive effect. It is not shown that its effect may be substantially, or at all, to lessen any existing competition."

On the government's claim that the merger would reduce potential competition that would arise from the "inevitable" entry of Crocker-Anglo into the Los Angeles area, the court said "the present record leaves us without any evidence that that move would be made absent the merger."

The court also touchd on the oligopoly aspects of the case, pointing out that the merger would mean "that the statewide banks . . . will have competition in that field from Crocker Citizens.

"The present oligopoly resulting from the operations of the three statewide banks . . . would thus be somewhat thinned."

The judges stressed that "if it were possible to point to a lessening of competition as a result of this merger, the fact of an increase of competition with larger institutions would not be a defense." They cited the Supreme Court's Philadelphia decision to substantiate this position.

The series of mergers which the complaint cites began with the Crocker-First and Anglo-California consolidation on Feb. 10, 1956.

Then, in June, 1956, Crocker-Anglo merged the First National Banks of both Scotia and Madera; in September, it acquired Salinas National Bank; in May, 1959, it merged County National Bank and Trust Co., Santa Barbara; in September of that year it added Bank of Carmel, and the first National Banks of Monterey and Pacific Grove.

In November, 1959, Citizens merged Bank of Whittier, and First National Bank, Vernon. In June, 1961, Crocker merged Bank of San Rafael and First National Bank of San Rafael and, finally, Citizens acquired Glendora Commercial and Savings Bank in December, 1962.

The Crocker-Citizens merger took place in November, 1963, following denial of the temporary injunction.

EXHIBIT 9 (B)
CROCKER-CITIZENS NATIONAL BANK
Selected government arguments against the Crocker-Citizens merger

8. The commercial banking business in the State of California, and in various areas within the State, is heavily concentrated in a few banks. As of December 28, 1962 the five largest commercial banks in California accounted for 78.6% of all deposits of individuals, partnerships, and corporations (IPC deposits), 79.6% of total loans and discounts, and 74.7% of all banking offices, of the 123 commercial banks within the State. (See Exhibit 10.)

EXHIBIT 9 *(Continued)*

9. Crocker-Anglo is the fifth largest commercial bank in California and sixteenth largest in the United States in terms of deposits. . . .

10. Citizens is the eighth largest commercial bank in California and forty-third largest in the United States in terms of deposits. . . .

12. Crocker-Anglo and Citizens compete with each other and with other commercial banks in the State of California and in various areas within the State of California in the commercial banking business and in various aspects of the commercial banking business. . . .

15. As a result of the proposed merger of Crocker-Anglo and Citizens alleged below the Resulting Bank would become the fourth largest bank in the State of California (only slightly smaller than the third largest) and twelfth largest in the United States. It would have 9.7% of the IPC deposits, 9.3% of total loans and discounts, and 9.9% of the banking offices of all commercial banks in the State of California. At the same time the percentage of the statewide total for each of these categories held by the five largest commercial banks in California would be increased by 2.5%, 2.1% and 3.8%, respectively.

20. The effect of each of the consolidations and mergers described . . . may be substantially to lessen competition or to tend to create a monopoly in violation of Section 7 of the Clayton Act.

22. The effects of the offences charged in this complaint are, among others:

a) Concentration in commercial banking in California and various parts of thereof has been and may be further substantially increased;

b) the bank which will result from the Agreement to Merge referred to in paragraph 19 will have such vastly increased resources and numerous statewide branch offices that its advantages over smaller competing banks may threaten to be decisive;

c) additional mergers and consolidation may be fostered among other large regional banks now located in northern and southern California in order to achieve the competitive advantages of a statewide branch banking system;

d) additional mergers and consolidations may be fostered among banks in California;

e) actual and potential competition between the defendents will be presently eliminated;

f) actual and potential competition between the banks which participated in the mergers and consolidations alleged in paragraphs 17 and 18 above has been permanently eliminated;

g) existing and potential competition generally in commercial banking in California and various parts thereof may be substantially lessened and a tendency to monopoly may be created.

Source: *United States* v. *Crocker-Anglo National Bank, Citizens National Bank and Transamerica Corporation, Initial Complaint issued by the Justice Department*, before the U.S. District Court for the Northern District of California, Southern Division, October 4, 1963.

EXHIBIT 10 (B)
CROCKER-CITIZENS NATIONAL BANK
Crocker-Citizens' market share in the California banking industry
Relative ranking of California banks
on theory of government's exhibit 32
in United States v. Philadelphia
I
Government's Exhibit 32
Table 32
Relative Ranking of the Five Largest
Philadelphia Banks by Total Deposits
(No. 1 Bank—100)

Before consolidation		*After consolidation*	
Bank No. 1 (1st Penna)	100	Bank No. 1 (Phila-Girard)	100
Bank No. 2 (Phila Nat'l)	97	Bank No. 2 (1st Penna)	62
Bank No. 3 (Girard)	65	Bank No. 3 (Provident Trades)	28
Bank No. 4 (Provident Tradesmen's)	45	Bank No. 4 (Fidelity-Phila)	26
Bank No. 5 (Fidelity-Phila)	42	Bank No. 5 (Central-Penn)	15

Source: Record on Appeal, 2413

II
Relative Ranking of the Ten Largest
California Banks by Deposits

	Before merger		*After merger*	
First Bank.........	B of A	100	B of A	100
Second Bank......	Security First	34	Security First	34
Third Bank........	Wells Fargo	25	Wells Fargo	25
Fourth Bank......	UCB	20	CROCKER-CITIZENS	25
Fifth Bank........	CROCKER-ANGLO	18	UCB	20
Sixth Bank........	Union	8	Union	8
Seventh Bank.....	Bank of California	7	Bank of California	7
Eighth Bank.......	CITIZENS NATIONAL	6	First Western	5
Ninth Bank........	First Western	5	1st Nat'l, San Diego	2
Tenth Bank.......	1st Nat'l, San Diego	2	Hibernia	2

Distribution of Deposits in California Banks as of End of Year 1962 and 1963

	1962			1963		
	Rank in Cali-fornia	% of Total California		Rank in Cali-fornia	% of Total California	
		Each bank	Cumu-lative		Each bank	Cumu-lative
Bank of America...........	1	39.9	39.9	1	40.6	40.6
Security First National.......	2	13.5	53.4	2	12.7	53.3
Wells Fargo................	3	9.9	63.3	3	9.6	62.9
United California Bank.......	4	8.0	71.3	5	8.0	80.1
Crocker....................	5	7.4	78.7	4	9.2	72.1
Union Bank.................	6	3.1	81.8	6	3.2	83.3
Bank of California, N.A.......	7	2.6	84.4	7	2.7	86.0
Citizens...................	8	2.5	86.9	Merged with Crocker (11-1-63)		
First Western..............	9	2.0	88.9	8	1.9	87.9
All Other Banks.............	10–129	11.1	100.0	9–155	12.1	100.0

Source: *United States* v. *Crocker-Anglo National Bank*, 277 Federal Supplement 133 (1967), Civ. No. 41808, pp. 168, 179.

EXHIBIT 11 (B)
CROCKER-CITIZENS NATIONAL BANK
Market position of Crocker-Citizens relative to other financial institutions

(a) In 1962, California savings amounted to $46,057,807,000, only 27.12 percent of which were held by commercial banks and only 2.63 percent of which were held by Crocker and Citizens (BK-E-27):

	(000 omitted)
Commercial Banks	
(IPC time deposits)	$12,493,031
Savings and Loan Associations	
(Savings Capital)	13,400,000
U.S. Savings Bonds	
(Redemption value of bonds held by individuals)	4,644,000
Credit Unions	
(Share capital and member deposits)	814,463
Postal Savings	
(Balance to credit of depositors)	32,137
Life Insurance Reserves	9,646,176
Mutual Investment Funds	
(Market value of net assets)	2,279,000
U.S. Government Marketable Securities With Maturity	
Within 1 Year from Date of Issue	2,749,000

(b) As of January 1962, commercial banks held only 10.01 percent of California farm mortgage loans:

	(000 omitted)
All Operating Banks	$ 138,604
Life Insurance Companies	208,760
Federal Land Banks	187,167
Farmers Home Administration	9,555
Individuals and Others	840,000
Total	$ 1,384,086

As of the closest available date, Crocker and Citizens together held only 1.34 percent of California farm mortgage loans (BK-E-28).

(c) As of January 1962, total California agricultural loans amounted to $2,184,-790,000, only 33.4 percent of which were held by operating banks:

	(000 omitted)
All Operating Banks	$ 730,396
Life Insurance Companies	208,760
Federal Land Banks	187,167
Banks for Cooperatives	92,303
Farmers Home Administration	15,802
Rural Electrification Administration	35,020
Production Credit Associations	75,342
Individuals and Others	840,000

As of the closest available date, Crocker and Citizens combined held only 2.77 percent of California agricultural loans (BK-E-29).

EXHIBIT 11 *(Concluded)*

(d) As of 1962, California mortgage debt on non-farm real estate amounted to $32,150,162,000, only 18.6 percent of which was held by commercial banks:

(000 omitted)

Commercial Banks....................................	$ 5,978,775
Mutual Savings Banks.......................	2,196,000
Savings and Loan Associations..........................	13,941,000
Life Insurance Companies..............................	5,634,387
Others..	4,400,000

As of the same date, Crocker and Citizens held only 1.80 percent of that total (BK-E-31).

(e) In 1962, commercial banks held only 32.74 percent of the total California business loans and credit outstanding. The $21,276,061,000 total amount of such loans and credit was held as follows:

(000 omitted)

Commercial Banks....................................	$ 6,945,861
Commercial and Finance Company Paper..................	598,800
Small Business Administration..........................	76,600
Finance Companies...................................	1,111,700
Life Insurance Companies..............................	2,064,400
Savings and Loan Associations..........................	588,700
Trade Credit..	9,830,000

Crocker and Citizens held 2.85 percent of that (BK-E-33).

(f) In 1962, commercial banks held only 44.36 percent of California's $7,101,896,000 installment and non-installment consumer credit:

(000 omitted)

Commercial Banks	
(Installment credit and single payment loans)	$ 3,150,596
Other Financial Institutions	
(Single payment loans)..............................	87,500
Sales Finance Companies..............................	1,219,400
Credit Unions.......................................	497,300
Consumer Finance Companies..........................	379,900
Others—Installment Credit............................	160,000
Retail Outlets	
(Installment credit and charge accounts).................	1,156,600
Credit Cards..	51,200
Service Credit.......................................	399,400

Crocker and Citizens had 5.56 percent of that total (BK-E-35).

Source: *United States* v. *Crocker-Anglo National Bank*, 277 Federal Supplement 133 (1967), Civ. No. 41808, pp. 158–169.

SELECTED REFERENCES
FOR PART SEVEN

ACKERMAN, ROBERT W., and FRAY, LIONEL L. "Financial Evaluation of a Potential Acquisition," *Financial Executive*, October 1967, pp. 34–54.

ALBERTS, WILLIAM W., and SEGALL, JOEL E. (eds.). *The Corporate Merger.* Chicago: University of Chicago Press, 1966.

COHEN, MANUEL F. "Takeover Bids," *Financial Analysts Journal*, Vol. 26 (January–February 1970), pp. 26–31.

CROWTHER, JOHN F. "Peril Point Acquisition Prices," *Harvard Business Review*, Vol. 47 (September–October 1969), pp. 58–62.

GOUDZWAARD, MAURICE B. "Conglomerate Mergers, Convertibles, and Cash Dividends," *Quarterly Review of Business and Economics*, Spring 1969, pp. 53–62.

HAYES, SAMUEL L., III, and TAUSSIG, RUSSELL A. "Tactics in Cash Takeover Bids," *Harvard Business Review*, Vol. 45 (March–April 1967), pp. 135–48.

HEXTER, RICHARD M. "How to Sell Your Company," *Harvard Business Review*, Vol. 46 (May–June 1968), pp. 71–77.

HOGARTY, THOMAS F. "The Profitability of Corporate Mergers," *Journal of Business*, Vol. 44 (July 1970), pp. 317–27.

JAENICKE, HENRY R. "Management's Choice to Purchase or Pool," *Accounting Review*, Vol. 37 (October 1962), pp. 758–65.

KELLY, EAMON M. *The Profitability of Growth Through Mergers.* Pennsylvania State University, 1967.

KRABER, RICHARD W. "Acquisition Analysis: New Help from Your Computer," *Financial Executive*, March 1970, pp. 10–15.

LARSON, KERMIT D., and GONEDES, NICHOLAS J. "Business Combinations: An Exchange-Ratio Determination Model," *Accounting Review*, Vol. 44 (October 1969), pp. 720–28.

MacDougal, Gary E., and Malek, Fred V. "Master Plan for Merger Negotiations," *Harvard Business Reveiw*, Vol. 48 (January–February 1970), pp. 71–82.

Melicher, Ronald W. "Financing with Convertible Preferred Stock: Comment," *Journal of Finance*, Vol. 26 (March 1971), pp. 144–47.

Mueller, Dennis C. "A Theory of Conglomerate Mergers," *Quarterly Journal of Economics*, Vol. 83 (November 1969), pp. 643–59.

Pinches, George E. "A Reply to Financing with Convertible Preferred Stock: Comment," *Journal of Finance*, Vol. 26 (March 1971), pp. 150–51.

Reid, Samuel Richardson. *Mergers, Managers, and the Economy*. New York: McGraw-Hill 1968.

Reilly, Frank K. "What Determines the Ratio of Exchange in Corporate Mergers?" *Financial Analysts Journal*, Vol. 18 (November–December 1962), 47–50.

Rockwell, Willard F., Jr. "How to Acquire a Company," *Harvard Business Review*, Vol. 46 (May–June 1968), pp. 121–32.

Sapienza, S. R. "Pooling Theory and Practice in Business Combinations," *Accounting Review*, April 1962.

Sapienza, S. R. "Business Combinations—A Case Study," *The Accounting Review*, Vol. 39 (January 1963), pp. 91–101.

Shad, John S. R. "The Financial Realities of Mergers," *Harvard Business Review*, Vol. 47 (November–December 1969), pp. 133–46.

Silberman, Irwin H. "A Note on Merger Valuation," *Journal of Finance*, Vol. 23 (June 1968), pp. 528–34.

Smalter, Donald J., and Lancey, Roderic C. "P/E Analysis in Acquisition Strategy," *Harvard Business Review*, Vol. 44 (November–December 1966), pp. 85–95.

Sprecher, C. Ronald. "A Note on Financing Mergers with Convertible Preferred Stock," *Journal of Finance*, Vol. 26 (June 1971), pp. 683–86.

Weston, J. Fred, and Peltzman, Sam (eds.). *Public Policy toward Mergers*. Pacific Palisades, Calif.: Goodyear Publishing Company, Inc., 1969.

Weygandt, Jerry J. "Financing with Convertible Preferred Stock: Comment," *Journal of Finance*, Vol. 26 (March 1971), pp. 148–49.

Wise, T. A. "How McDonnell Won Douglas," *Fortune*, March 1967.

Woods, Donald H., and Caverly, Thomas A. "Development of a Linear Programming Model for the Analysis of Merger/Acquisition Situations," *Journal of Financial and Quantitative Analysis*, Vol. 4 (January 1970), pp. 627–42.

Wyatt, Arthur R., and Kieso, Donald E. *Business Combinations: Planning and Action*. Scranton, Pa.: International Textbook Company, 1969.

Corporate Growth as Affected by the Federal Antitrust Laws*

George B. Haddock†

ANY COMPANY EXECUTIVE who has responsibility for the development or carrying out of plans for the growth of his company must take into consideration a great number of factors. Most of these probably relate to financing, costs, and probabilities of profits, but some of them involve less tangible things, such as relations with customers and sources of supply, possible reactions of competitors, and the possible application and effect of the federal antitrust laws.

This article deals only with the last named factor. In discussions which the writer has had on this subject with groups of businessmen, the comment has often been made that most companies have lawyers to advise them on matters of law, and there is little point to a busy executive spending time in an effort to gain a meaningful knowledge of such a complex and nebulous matter as antitrust law.

The answer has been that lawyers usually give advice only when they are asked for it, or when they learn of the existence of a legal problem. All too often businessmen apply a lot of ingenuity, time, and hard work in developing and perfecting a proposal that has real merit from the viewpoint of increased efficiency, profits, and good business judgment, only to have the program scrapped because of antitrust consid-

---

* Reprinted by permission from the March 1967 issue of the *Michigan Business Review*, published by the Graduate School of Business Administration, The University of Michigan.

† George B. Haddock was a lawyer in the Antitrust Division of the U.S. Department of Justice for more than twenty years. In addition to trial work, he served at various times as head of the Denver, Chicago, and Los Angeles offices of the Division as Chief of its Trial Section in Washington. For the past several years he has been a partner in the law firm of Morison, Clapp, Abrams, and Haddock in Washington, D.C.

erations. Much wasted effort and frustration might be avoided if business-men would become sufficiently aware of major areas of antitrust dangers to seek the advice of their lawyers before spending too much time in working out the details of a proposed program. Sometimes proposals are carried forward to a point where the company is so committed to a particular policy or program that it is very difficult to withdraw or change to avoid antitrust trouble.

The purpose of this article is to point out a few of the areas of potential antitrust danger in programs involving plans for corporate growth, so that these legal problems can be recognized and resolved before commit-ment to such programs.

MISCONCEPTIONS ABOUT ANTITRUST LAWS

There are certain misconceptions concerning the antitrust laws that contribute to confusion and uncertainty in the minds of many business-men. Contrary to widespread popular belief, the federal antitrust laws were never intended or designed to curb bigness or to limit the size to which a company might grow. Over the years, the government has brought some cases attacking monopoly, but these were not based upon the fact that the defendants were too big. Rather, they attacked the means by which the defendants attained and maintained their positions of power and control over particular lines of commerce, and the uses made of the power so acquired.

There have been proposals for legislation placing a maximum upon the size to which a corporation may grow. Concern has been expressed over the "undue concentration of economic power" in the hands of large companies, and hearings have been held recently on this subject by a Senate Committee. However, as they now stand, the antitrust laws have not been applied to discourage or prevent the growth of any companies, or to limit their size, but instead have been used to prevent certain meth-ods of growth and certain uses that have been made of the power that often accompanies great size.

Many people appear to believe that the antitrust laws are intended to preserve and perpetuate small businesses merely because they are small, without regard to their efficiency or the value to the public of the services they perform. This is also a fallacy. While the antitrust laws are applied to protect small business from unfair competitive practices of larger com-panies and by combinations of companies, they provide no guaranty of survival of inefficient organizations.

There are many means by which a company may increase its size. This article discusses three general types of growth: internal, acquisition or merger, and use of power or leverage to increase the share of a market or to eliminate or lessen competition.

INTERNAL GROWTH

"Internal growth" is used as a short-hand term to include construction of new or additional or modernized facilities, and the entry into new or different areas of activity, by means other than the acquisition of existing facilities. Internal growth may involve *forward vertical integration*—production of more fully finished products, or entry into the distribution of one's own products; or *backward vertical integration*—production of one's requirements of raw materials or parts needed in the original line of activity (to make instead of buy); or *horizontal expansion*—construction of new facilities for products already being made, or related lines of products, or entirely different lines of products (often called diversification).

In the absence of a position of monopoly power over any particular line of commerce or level of activity, such as that which Alcoa was found to have had in the early 1940's with respect to aluminum ingots, no very serious antitrust problems result from growth by internal expansion.

The question has been asked: "What is to protect a distributor of a particular brand or make of products from a decision of the producer to engage in direct distribution, or to protect a producer of raw materials or parts from a decision of a large buyer to produce some or all of its requirements of such raw materials or parts?"

The general answer is: "Nothing, except the efficiency or value of the services of the distributor or the parts supplier." If a small businessman can produce parts or raw materials with greater efficiency or at a lower cost than can the buyers thereof, or if he can perform a distribution function better than can a producer, then he probably will survive and grow. If he is unable to provide a value to his customers or to the producers of the products he distributes, greater than they can provide at equal or lower cost, then the antitrust laws are not going to be much help to him.

Internal growth presents fewer antitrust dangers than do other kinds of growth.

GROWTH BY ACQUISITION OR MERGER

Prior to the year 1950, Section 7 of the Clayton Act set forth restrictions on the acquisition by one company of the *stock*, but not the *assets*, of another company under certain circumstances. Because of this loophole, most acquisitions in recent years have involved assets, rather than stock. In 1950, Congress amended Section 7 of the Clayton Act, to make unlawful the acquisition by one corporation of the *stock or assets* of another corporation, where the effect may be substantially to lessen competition or tend to create a monopoly in any line of commerce.

It was not until the year 1962 that the Supreme Court handed down its first decision interpreting and applying amended Section 7 to an acquisition of assets. Since that time there have been a number of other Supreme Court decisions involving various mergers and acquisitions, and a body of legal precedent is being built up that provides some indications as to how the law is likely to be applied to different kinds of factual situations.

In discussions and writings, acquisitions and mergers have been grouped into three imprecise and sometimes overlapping categories, called horizontal, vertical, or conglomerate. A horizontal merger is one involving companies that are competitors or potential competitors in some line of commerce. A vertical merger is one in which one company acquires another which is either an actual or potential customer or source of supply. A conglomerate merger involves the acquisition of a business or facilities in an area of activity not related to the existing business of the acquiring company.

Not all acquisitions fall neatly into one or another of these categories. A given acquisition may have horizontal and vertical effects. (For example, Brown Shoe Company acquired Kinney Shoe Company. Both companies produced shoes, and Kinney was also a retailer of shoes and thus constituted a market for shoe manufacturers.) A merger that appears on its face to be conglomerate, made for purposes of product diversification, can have horizontal or vertical effects on competition.

HORIZONTAL MERGERS

On the basis of cases which have been decided by the Supreme Court since 1962, it appears that nearly all horizontal mergers involve *substantial* actual or potential competition between the acquired and acquiring companies are likely to be held to be illegal. No precise standards have been established for measurement of the substantiality of the effect on competition, either in terms of percentages of market shares or in terms of dollar volumes of business involved, but any acquisition involving companies which are significant competitive factors in any market is likely to fare badly in the Supreme Court.

It is no defense that at the time of an acquisition the two companies were not actually competitors to any significant extent, if it can be shown that they probably would have become substantial competitors if the acquisition had not occurred. For example, suppose that Company A has given serious consideration to entry into the production of a new line of products that would fit in to the products already being made.

The company could either build new production facilities and acquire or train the personnel to produce and market the new line, or it could acquire an existing company that is engaged in that business and already has a going organization with the necessary facilities, personnel and knowhow. If there is a reasonable probability that Company A would enter the business on its own if the acquisition were not made, and would thus become a substantial new competitive factor, then entry by acquisition probably would be held to be illegal.

Not all acquisitions of competitors are unlawful, if there are numerous other competitors and if the market shares of the acquired and acquiring companies are small. If there is ease of entry into the market by newcomers, or if the number of competitors is increasing, there is less danger of antitrust difficulty. But if there has been a history of concentration in an industry, or a situation in which a few large concerns control most of the business, then an acquisition by a large company of even a small competitor is likely to result in trouble under the antitrust laws.

An exception to the general rule against acquisition of a competitor may exist if the acquired company has been losing money and is likely to go out of business within the near future. Under these circumstances its acquisition by a competitor could be found to involve no substantial lessening of competition. However, the mere fact that a company may be faced with a bleak future, or that its owners may want to sell their business and retire, would not usually be a good defense to an action under Section 7.

Most horizontal acquisitions raise questions sufficiently grave to warrant careful study by counsel before they are carried out.

VERTICAL ACQUISITIONS

The theory upon which vertical acquisitions are condemned is their effect in foreclosing competitors from competitive access to the market or the source of supply represented by the acquired company. For example, a manufacturer of shoes acquires a company that operates a chain of retail shoe stores amounting to a significant part of the total market for shoes, thereby giving to the shoe manufacturer the power to exclude competing manufacturers from competitive access to that substantial market. Or a manufacturer of a finished product is a very large buyer of a semifinished product, and constitutes a substantial part of the entire market for that semi-finished product. He acquires a company engaged in producing the semi-finished product, and thereby excludes other producers from competitive access to that part of the market represented by his requirements. Or a manufacturer needs substantial quantities of a raw material which is in short supply. He acquires a substantial producer of that raw material, and thereby excludes other competitors from competitive access to an important source of the raw material that may be necessary to their operations.

In all of these examples, the acquisition may be found to have the effect of placing competitors of the acquiring company under such a competitive handicap as to substantially impair their ability to compete with the acquiring company, thereby tending substantially to lessen competition in violation of Section 7.

Another type of acquisition that may have vertical effects is where opportunity arises to make effective use of reciprocal dealing. Assume that Company A is a substantial purchaser of containers that require waterproofing by use of a particular type of compound. It buys these containers from companies who in turn buy the waterproofing compound from one or more of several producers. Company A acquires one of the producers of the waterproofing compound and is thereby put into a position to tell the container manufacturers that they must buy the waterproofing compound from Company A's subsidiary in order to sell containers to Company A. If the market for containers represented by Company A is sufficiently substantial and attractive, this demand for reciprocal dealing may result in depriving other waterproofing compound dealers from competitive access to that part of their market represented by the container manufacturers who want to sell to Company A. This could result in a substantial lessening of competition among producers of waterproofing compound.

The foregoing examples illustrate a few of the types of adverse effects on competition that may be involved in vertical acquisitions which could be found to violate Section 7.

CONGLOMERATE ACQUISITIONS

To date, there have been no decisions by the Supreme Court that involve purely conglomerate acquisitions—i.e., acquisitions involving entry into fields of activity unrelated to those in which the acquiring company had been engaged. The acquisition by Continental Can Company of Hazel-Atlas Glass Company has been called a conglomerate merger, involving the entry of a tin can producer into the glass container field. However, the decision of the Supreme Court condemning this merger was based on adverse horizontal effects on competition between metal and glass containers for numerous uses.

There is no basis in decided cases for a conclusion that an acquisition by a company engaged in one field of activity, of a company in an entirely different business, would be held to violate the law, unless the acquiring company is of such size and financial power as to become a giant in a business in which the competitors are pygmies. As to such a situation, the state of the law is still uncertain.

NO TIME LIMIT ON SECTION 7 CASES

The potential dangers involved in growth by acquisition are magnified by the fact that there is no statute of limitations on Section 7 cases. In the case of the acquisition by DuPont of stock in General Motors, some of the stock purchases held to have been unlawful had been made before 1920, and the successful suit for divestiture was not filed until more than twenty-five years later.

This means that an acquisition may not result in an immediate antitrust suit, either because there are insufficient indications that it is likely to result in any lessening of competition, or because persons presently in charge of antitrust enforcement may believe that the possible danger to competition is too uncertain or too unimportant to warrant action. However, developments occurring in future years may demonstrate that the acquisition resulted in a lessening of competition or a tendency toward monopoly; or a new "trust-buster" may have different views concerning the importance of the acquisition. A suit could be brought years after the acquisition which might result in a requirement for divestiture of an important part of the assets of the acquiring company.

WILL AN ACQUISITION RESULT IN A SUIT?

A question sometimes asked by businessmen who are contemplating an acquisition or merger is along the following lines: "The papers are full of stories concerning mergers, and there must be scores that occur without any action by the government. What are the probabilities that this particular acquisition will result in a suit by the government?"

This question is a painful one for a lawyer. In many cases there is uncertainty whether the acquisition would actually violate the law, and different persons charged with the enforcement of the antitrust laws may have different views as to the manner in which the law should be applied. If, in the opinion of the lawyer, the acquisition would be held to violate the law if suit were brought, the question then becomes similar to the following: "On such and such a highway, the speed limit is 60 miles per hour. What are my chances of being arrested if I drive at 65? at 75? At 90?" The lawyer might have personal knowledge that only one traffic cop regularly patrols that road, and that he tends to ignore speeds slightly in excess of the speed limit. He also knows that more patrol cars might be assigned to this road, and that the regular patrolman might be in a bad mood on some particular day because of an argument with his wife, or he might have been bawled out by his superiors for laxity in enforcement, thereby increasing the chances of an arrest.

Speculation as to the chances of being caught in a law violation is more a function of a fortune teller than of a lawyer. Entirely aside from ethical considerations, a lawyer would do disservice to his client by speculations that might encourage a client to engage in a course of action that might well be held to violate the law.

For these reasons, conjecture as to whether or not immediate suit by the government is likely to result from an acquisition is not of as much value as is an opinion on the probable decision of the courts if suit were brought.

Summarizing the foregoing, growth by acquisition or merger raises antitrust questions sufficiently serious to warrant careful study by counsel before any irrevocable decision is made or action taken.

USE OF POWER OR LEVERAGE TO INCREASE SHARE OF A MARKET OR TO ELIMINATE OR LESSEN COMPETITION

There are numerous devices and practices that have been used to promote sales, profits, and growth of companies, the illegality of which is so generally known that no more than passing mention is warranted. These include agreements to allocate territories or fields of activities among competitors, to fix or stabilize prices, to boycott competitors, or to engage in selective price cutting to eliminate competitors.

However, there are a few areas of activity which, under some circumstances, may raise no serious legal problems, but which, under others, may violate the law or at least involve such danger as to warrant cautious consideration. Limitations of time and space prevent more than a bare identification of these sensitive areas in this article.

The courts have consistently condemned use by a company of a position of dominance in one line of commerce or field of activity to eliminate competition or exclude competitors in another market. "Tie-in" sales and "full requirements" contracts violate the antitrust laws if the seller uses dominance or control over one kind of product to force or cause buyers who wish to buy that product to also buy another product from that seller instead of from other sources, or to acquire the buyer to purchase his entire requirements from that seller. This does not mean that a seller cannot agree to supply the full requirements of a buyer for a reasonable period of time if the buyer, and not the seller, seeks such a contract.

The Antitrust Division of the Department of Justice recently has shown a very active interest in uses made of patents as devices for increasing the market share of dominant companies in an industry, through pooling of patents and by patent licenses containing "grant-back" provisions, particularly where exclusive rights to the use of the pooled patents or to improvements or extensions of those patents are allocated among the parties to the agreements, and other competitors are denied the right of use of such patents.

Another practice that appears to be receiving attention by the Antitrust Division and the Federal Trade Commission is "reciprocity," meaning a policy of reciprocal preferential dealing between companies that are both sellers and buyers of each other's goods or services. Reciprocity agreements or understandings have not yet been held to be combinations or conspiracies in restraint of trade, but the existence of such arrangements or the opportunity for increased use thereof have been taken into consideration in appraising the probable effects of mergers (as previously discussed), and the practice may well be found to be an unfair method of competition if the effect is to deprive competitors from access to a substantial market.

This is not to say that the human tendency to give preference to one's friends and good customers is likely to be found to be a violation of law, but a systematic practice of using one's importance as a customer as a lever to obtain preferential treatment from buyers who are also potential sellers raises legal questions that deserve consideration in the formulation of company policy.

Other areas of activity deserving mention are the use of exclusive territorial franchises and the legal perils involved in joint ventures. As to both of these, the present state of the law is uncertain. As to exclusive franchises, an appeal now pending before the Supreme Court may result in needed clarification.

ON WAITING FOR GUIDELINES

There have been suggestions that the government should, and possibly may, issue a statement setting forth standards or guidelines that would inform businessmen what is and what is not permitted under the antitrust laws. It is unlikely that any such guidelines will be issued in the near future.

U.S. SUPREME COURT VOIDS MERGER OF PHILADELPHIA BANKS*

THE UNITED STATES SUPREME COURT, given its first opportunity to consider the application of the antitrust laws to the commercial banking industry, decided that §7 of the Clayton Act applies to bank mergers.

Everyone interested in banking is no doubt aware that the banks involved announced plans for a merger in November, 1960. Approval, as required by the Bank Merger Act of 1960, was given by the Comptroller of the Currency on February 24, 1961. Almost before the ink was dry on the certificate of approval, the Justice Department, on February 26, 1961, filed a civil antitrust action—the first of its kind—to prevent the merger. The Government contended that the merger violated the Sherman Antitrust Act and the Clayton Act. The lower court ruled for the banks. In so doing, it decided that although bank mergers were not exempt from the application of the antitrust statutes, §7 of the Clayton Act did not apply because it only prohibited stock acquisitions where the effect would be substantially to lessen competition. Since this was an assets acquisition case, it did not fall within the prohibition of §7. The lower court also stated that any merger that did not violate the Clayton Act could "hardly be held to violate the more, stringent standards of the Sherman Act."

The United States Supreme Court reversed the lower court and ruled that the merger was forbidden by §7 of the Clayton Act, but it did not consider the question of the alleged violation of the Sherman Act.

The Supreme Court conceded that §7 of the Clayton Act reaches

---

acquisitions of corporate *stock* by any corporation engaged in commerce, but it reaches acquisitions of corporate *assets* only by corporations subject to the jurisdiction of the Federal Trade Commission. The FTC has no jurisdiction over banks. Therefore, if the proposed merger were deemed an *assets* acquisition, it would not fall within the prohibition of §7. The Court then proceeded to show how §7 did apply.

The Government had argued that the merger involved in this case differed from a pure assets acquisition, and the banks had contended with equal vigor that the merger was crucially different from a pure stock acquisition. The Court found merit in both arguments. A merger, it stated, "fits neither category neatly." Therefore, since the literal terms of §7 did not dispose of the question, we must determine, said the Court, "whether a Congressional design to embrace bank mergers is revealed in the history of the statute." The Court did find this design, although it required a considerable amount of judicial legislation to do so.

The Court pointed out that when §7 was first enacted in 1914, it referred only to corporate acquisitions of stock. It was silent as to assets acquisitions, mergers, and consolidations. As interpreted by the courts, mergers were found to be beyond the reach of §7. Congress therefore, in 1950, amended §7 to included assets acquisitions by corporations subject to FTC jurisdiction. The Court noted that the legislative history of the 1950 amendment was silent on the question why the amendment made no explicit reference to mergers and why assets acquisitions by corporations not subject to FTC jurisdiction were not included. Nevertheless, said the Court, there was a basic Congressional design evident in the amendment and it was to bring mergers within the prohibition of §7 and thereby close what Congress regarded as a loophole in the section. In other words, said the Court, Congress contemplated that the 1950 amendment would give §7 a reach which would bring the entire range of corporate amalgamations, from pure stock acquisitions to pure assets acquisitions, within the scope of §7. Thus, said the Court, "the stock acquisition and assets-acquisition provisions, read together, reach mergers which fit neither category perfectly, but lie somewhere between the two ends of the spectrum. So construed, the specific exception for acquiring corporations not subject to the FTC's jurisdiction excluded from the coverage of §7 only asset acquisitions by such corporations when not accomplished by mergers."

The Court also concluded that the Bank Merger Act of 1960 did not immunize mergers from the Federal antitrust laws. No express immunity was conferred by the act, and repeals of antitrust laws by implication are strongly disfavored.

The Supreme Court also disagreed with the lower court's finding that there was no substantial lessening of competition as a result of the merger. The Court stated that a merger which produces an entity "controlling an undue percentage share of the relevant market, and results in a significant increase in the concentration of firms in that market, is so inherently likely to lessen competition substantially that it must be enjoined in the absence of evidence clearly showing that the merger is not likely to have such anti-competitive effects." The Court pointed out that the merger would result in a single bank's controlling at least 30% of the commercial banking business in the four-county Philadelphia metropolitan area. The Court concluded: "Without attempting to specify the smallest market share which would still be considered to threaten undue concentration, we are clear that 30% presents that threat." The Court stated that its conclusion as to percentages was not arbitrary, although neither the terms of §7 nor the legislative history of the act suggests that any particular percentage was deemed critical.

It seems to this observer that the majority opinion starts out with a wrong hypothesis and continues for its entire length without recovering from its initial error.

The minority opinion written by Justice Harlan, in which Justice Stewart concurred, is essential reading. Justice Harlan suspects that "no one will be more surprised than the Government to find that the Clayton Act has carried the day for its case in this Court," because the Government had not urged the applicability of §7 in its oral argument before the Supreme Court, but had based its case on the Sherman Act. The minority opinion points out that Congress never intended that the 1950 amendment to §7 of the Clayton Act should apply to bank mergers, and it was on this explicit basis that Congress enacted the Bank Merger Act of 1960. For ten years, said Justice Harlan, "everyone—the department responsible for antitrust law enforcement, the banking industry, the Congress, and the bar—proceeded on the assumption that the 1950 amendment of the Clayton Act did not affect bank mergers. This assumption provided a major impetus to the enactment of remedial legislation, and Congress, when it finally settled on what it thought was the solution to the problem at hand, emphatically rejected the remedy now brought to life by the Court."

The result is, of course, that the Bank Merger Act is almost completely nullified; its enactment turns out to have been an exorbitant waste of Congressional time and energy. As the present case illustrates, the Attorney General's report to the designated banking agency is no longer truly advisory, for if the agency's decision is not satisfactory a §7 suit may be commenced immediately. The bank merger's legality will then be judged solely from its competitive aspects, unencumbered by any considerations peculiar to banking. And if such a suit were deemed to lie after a bank merger has been consummated, there would then be introduced into this field, for the first time to any significant extent, the threat of divestiture of assets and all the complexities and disruption attendant upon the use of that sanction. The only vestige of the Bank Merger Act which remains is that the banking agencies will have an initial veto.

This frustration of a manifest Congressional design is, in my view, a most unwarranted intrusion upon the legislative domain. I submit that *whatever* may have been the Congressional purpose in 1950, Congress has now so plainly pronounced its current judgment that bank mergers are not within the reach of §7 that this Court is duty bound to effectuate its choice.

In a separate memorandum, Justice Goldberg took the position that §7 did not apply to bank mergers of the type involved here. He pointed out, however, that he did not necessarily dissent from the majority's decision invalidating the merger because, there was a "substantial Sherman Act issue" in the case. *U.S* v. *Phila. Natl. Bk.* (U.S.Sup.Ct. No. 83) 31 U.S. Law Week 4650.

part VIII

Markets and intermediaries

SCREEN VIEW COMPANY

In July 1971, the management of Screen View Company was considering the possibility of a public stock issue. The need for additional working capital and funds for new investment alternatives and expansion was clear. The methods of financing to raise these needed funds was less certain. Of particular concern to the management was the advisability of a public issue for a theatre-chain company with large landholdings. On previous issues of similar firms, the market had not provided an accurate valuation of the firm involved.

COMPANY BACKGROUND

Screen View Company is a privately held company engaged primarily in the exhibition of motion pictures. It was incorporated in California in 1940 with headquarters in Los Angeles. The first several years were very successful, followed by a period of decline caused by the initial explosion in the home television market. The firm continued throughout this period to pick up movie theatres in a buyers' market, and when movies once again regained popularity, Screen View found themselves in a highly advantageous position.

They have total or partial interest in 34 theatres, several bowling alleys and various building and landholdings in the five states of California, Utah, Arizona, Nevada, and Alabama. The theatres, which include both conventional indoor and drive-in operations, are in suburban and rural areas rather than metropolitan areas, and are primarily located on land owned by the company. Theatre operations represent one half of total revenues and are derived from admission charges and from sales at the refreshment centers located at each theatre. The company derives the other half of its revenues from property rentals, partnerships in land investment and interest income. Land valuation is not fully shown on the balance sheet, but is of considerable importance to the firm. For example, land on which one theatre is located was purchased for $150,000, but is now worth around $2 million. The firm hopes to exploit this appreciation in the future.

GENERAL ENVIRONMENT

The motion-picture theatre business has not been as ruthless as the motion-picture production operations of major studios. Within the business, the gap caused by major studio cutbacks has been adequately filled by rising independent productions. Although theatre owners would like more major studio films, there is no serious shortage. Theatre operation involves high fixed costs and small variable costs, since the movie will be shown whether the theatre is full or not. Drive-in theatres have very seasonal sales, but indoor theatres are more consistent.

Television has hurt the theatre business, but to a lesser degree now than when television first appeared. The overall effect directly attributable to television is difficult to gauge, but attendance has at times dropped 50 percent from the high level of 20 to 30 years ago. Theatre owners generally agree that a good product will always offset the detrimental effects of television. Movies have reestablished themselves as an inexpensive and enjoyable way to spend an evening out of the house.

The motion-picture theatre industry is highly competitive, with the key element for competitive edge being the films. Films are leased, with most being distributed by the major film companies. In the early period after their release, the films are generally available to exhibitors on the basis of competitive bids. Thereafter, availability is based on negotiation with the distributor. Film rentals are based either on a percentage of box office admissions or a flat fee. Concessions average 20–25 percent of gross income, and often while the movie operations at some theatres show a loss, the theatre will turn a profit because of these concessions.

RECENT OPERATIONS

Earnings for Screen View have varied over the last four years. In 1968, they hit a high of $35,090 but slid to $11,188 in 1970. Fiscal year ending June 30, 1971, revealed earnings of $23,988, on total income of $864,989 and total assets of $4,352,044. They are somewhat more highly levered than other similar companies (Exhibits 3 to 5). One problem the firm has always faced is a recurring shortage of funds. They have operated from a limited capital base and have hesitated to increase their indebtedness. Basically, growth has been sustained through the retention of earnings. Another problem, more qualitative in nature, has been the variable availability of quality films. Because all they are selling is a shadow cast on a screen, they have no product control, and are at the mercy of another industry.

Plans for expansion entail the opening of several new theatres in the near future. Among those being considered involve the multiple-theatre concept, wherein two or more screens are erected on the same property and one projection booth shows different films on the individual screens at the same time. One concession handles the united theatres. With such an arrangement, costs are greatly reduced. The return, therefore, on a comparably smaller investment is much greater.

PUBLIC ISSUE

Funds from a public offering of common stock could be used to help finance these new theatres as well as retire some of the present debt and improve the working capital position of the firm. Several investment bankers known to the management have often suggested a public issue of common stock. Although a specific dollar amount has never been discussed, the issue would be a reasonably large amount based on projected needs, and would not only strengthen the company's financial position, but would also provide all of the benefits of having a publicly traded security. An issue would be controlled in such a way as to guarantee position maintenance by management. At present the company is privately held by a closely knit group of families who built the company from its beginning. Common stock consists of 2,500 authorized shares with 1,408 shares issued and outstanding at a par value of $100. The two families who own and operate Screen View each have 50 percent ownership. Top management, however, has had reservations about a public issue. Primarily, in examining other similar theatre companies with public stock outstanding, they have noted that many of the stocks are selling far below book value. This observation creates a disenchanting prospect. They believe the reason for this market evaluation is that many theatre companies have a heavy percentage of fixed assets in land. The market has historically never favored this situation. For this reason, management is giving some consideration to establishing a real estate subsidiary to handle its land assets, and making the present company the "operating" subsidiary. This tactic has been applied successfully by several theatre companies as well as by other businesses. It is still uncertain as to how the market might evaluate this move. Thus, management is unsure about how to resolve the questions surrounding a public issue. They presently are weighted down by debt, and future debt will be increasingly more expensive. Yet, reliance on the retention of earnings is restricting growth possibilities. The idea of a stock issue which within a short period of time could be selling at a depressed level below book value is also felt to be of questionable value. One point that is foremost in management's analysis is the fact that the future growth and prosperity of the company relies upon the attainment of additional financing.

EXHIBIT 1

SCREEN VIEW COMPANY

Income statements for the years ending June 30, 1968–71

	1971	*1970*	*1969*	*1968*
Theatre operations.............	$428,277	$640,273	$ 661,835	$605,106
Other income.................	436,712	225,916	138,368	176,204
Total Income.........	864,989	˙866,189	800,203	781,310
Expenses....................	627,567	643,096	544,338	522,654
Depreciation expense...........	203,202	207,516	214,978	210,031
Total Expenses........	830,769	850,612	759,316	732,685
Net income before taxes........	34,220	15,577	40,887	48,625
Provisions for taxes...........	10,232	4,389	10,259	13,535
Net Income...........	$ 23,988	$ 11,188	$ 30,628	$ 35,090
Retained earnings:				
Beginning of period*.........	966,473	961,065	997,246	962,156
End of period..............	$990,461	$972,253	$1,027,874	$997,246

* As adjusted for prior year's taxes.

EXHIBIT 2

SCREEN VIEW COMPANY

Balance sheet, June 30, 1971

ASSETS

Cash..	$ 1,452
Accounts receivable..............................	407,931
Inventory..	12,209
Prepaid expenses.................................	24,512
Total Current Assets......................	$ 446,104
Plant, equipment, and leasehold—net.................	1,183,049
Land...	1,403,532
Investments in other firms........................	1,289,188
Other assets.....................................	30,171
Total Assets.............................	$4,352,044

LIABILITIES AND STOCKHOLDERS' EQUITY

Accounts payable.................................	$ 356,365
Contracts payable................................	5,726
Total Current Liabilities...................	362,091
Long-term notes payable:	
6.25%–7%....................................	313,085
7.50%–8%....................................	1,451,706
9.25%–10%...................................	953,401
Total Notes Payable......................	$2,718,192
Other liabilities.................................	12,779
Total Liabilities..........................	$3,093,062
Common stock...................................	140,800
Paid-in-surplus..................................	46,000
Retained earnings................................	990,461
Surplus from liquidation of subsidiaries..............	66,807
Deferred gain on sale of land......................	14,914
Total Stockholders' Equity..................	$1,258,982
Total Liabilities and Stockholders' Equity.....	$4,352,044

EXHIBIT 3

SCREEN VIEW COMPANY

Selected data

Cinema 5, LTD.

	September 30, 1970
Current assets.............................	$ 5,318,920
Total assets...............................	8,888,492
Current liabilities..........................	3,117,908
Long-term debt............................	471,256
Stockholders' equity........................	4,924,000
Total revenue..............................	12,384,219
Net income................................	1,152,061
Common shares outstanding....................	700,825
Earnings per share..........................	$1.65
Book value per share........................	$7.03
Dividend per share..........................	$0.30
Traded on American Stock Exchange	
High—low price range........................	$15.375–$4
Price coverage for June 1971.................	$8.875

EXHIBIT 4

SCREEN VIEW COMPANY

Selected data

United Artists Theatre Circuit, Inc.

August 31, 1970

Current assets......................	$17,568,335
Total assets.......................	89,850,670
Current liabilities..................	16,771,144
Long-term debt.....................	38,337,967
Stockholders' equity................	30,935,447
Total revenue......................	76,875,274
Net income........................	2,422,209
Common shares outstanding..........	1,617,888
Earnings per share.................	$ 1.50
Book value per share...............	$19.12
Dividend per share.................	$ 0.20
Traded over the counter	
High—low price range..............	$28.5–$6.75
Price (average) for June 1971........	$10.625

EXHIBIT 5

SCREEN VIEW COMPANY

Selected data

Commonwealth Theatres, Inc.

October 3, 1970

Current assets......................	$ 3,037,018
Total assets.......................	13,846,588
Current liabilities..................	2,619,967
Long-term debt.....................	4,185,656
Stockholders' equity................	5,957,847
Total revenue......................	19,081,788
Net income........................	822,886
Common shares outstanding..........	1,248,792
Earnings per share.................	$ 0.66
Book value per share...............	$ 4.77
Dividend per share.................	$0.147
Traded over the counter	
Price (average) for July 1971.........	$8.875

ELI LILLY AND COMPANY

IN JANUARY of 1970, Eli Lilly and Co., was in the process of preparing an analysis as to the feasibility of listing its common stock on the New York Stock Exchange. The firm's common stock is currently listed on the Over-the-Counter Market.

COMPANY BACKGROUND

Eli Lilly is one of the 10 largest firms in the U.S. ethical drug industry. It was incorporated on January 17, 1901 in Indiana, and reorganized in the same state on January 28, 1936. The company produces a broad line of more than 800 pharmaceuticals and biological products such as antibiotics, analgesics, antidiabetic agents, sedatives, vitamins, and hormones. Eli Lilly has also diversified into the agricultural, animal, lawn and garden, veterinary, and packaging products areas.

Through its subsidiaries and affiliates the company has operations in all of North and South America, western Europe, Africa, the Far East, Australia, and New Zealand. Foreign operations account for approximately 25 percent of sales, and they continue to expand. More detailed financial information is provided in Exhibit 1.

INDUSTRY DATA

The ethical drug industry is, by most measures, one of the most profitable in the United States. This is due primarily to the nature of its products, which evolve from extensive research programs designed to fulfill a special need. Also, the demand for the industry's products tend to resist cyclical economic swings as they are essential to the public's well being. Therefore, despite the possibility of further government regulation and the current decline in the number of important new products generated out of research and development efforts, the industry is considered to be a leader in terms of profitability.

Quarterly financial reports published by the Federal Trade Commission and the Securities and Exchange Commission for manufacturing corporations indicate that the drug industry has the second highest profit rate on sales (9.3 percent in the fourth quarter of 1969). The specialized nature of the products, which helps in maintaining a stable price structure, low raw material costs and labor costs below the average for U.S. industry are responsible for the high returns within the industry. Also, fixed asset investment is not a prime consideration as in other industries, i.e., paper, chemicals, and steel.

Generally, drug companies have paid out a larger proportion of earnings as dividends than is customary in most other industries. However, the yields on drug stocks are generally below average, reflecting the high market appraisals and price-earnings multiples associated with these stocks. In view of the favorable earnings prospects and strong financial positions of drug companies, a continuation of these trends is anticipated in the years ahead.

Financing in the drug industry has not been a major problem. As plant investment is relatively small in relation to sales, increasing construction costs and interest rates are not especially damaging. According to the FTC-SEC reports, the ratio of current assets to current liabilities in the drug industry was 2.5 to 1 at the end of 1969 and stockholders' equity to debt was 4.9 to 1, both of which were well above the ratios for U.S. manufacturing corporations. Exhibit 2 provides composite industry data for the years 1964–69.

LISTING CONSIDERATIONS

After carefully considering the listing requirements as shown in Exhibit 3, Eli Lilly and Co. would probably have little trouble in meeting these requirements since the company has previously observed the rules of the Exchange. It appears at this time that the listing fee would be $100,000 with a probable annual fee of $20,000.

Also, listing on the New York Stock Exchange could provide stockholders with better market information as quotations would be received immediately and price information would be published daily. The fact that all of the other major drug firms were listed could make listing desirable from a prestige point of view. Furthermore, certain trusts and funds have been unable to invest in Eli Lilly's common stock due to charter requirements limiting their investments to listed stocks.

COMPARISON OF THE NEW YORK STOCK EXCHANGE
TO THE OVER-THE-COUNTER MARKET

The over-the-counter-market is much like any other market. It is an "inside" market (wholesale) at which brokers buy and a conventional market (retail) at which customers buy stock. A problem with this approach is the lack of a trading price. Rather, an investor is faced with a range of prices bounded on the low end by the bid price and on the upper end by the asking price, whereas on the New York Stock Exchange the broker is not a retailer, but an agent. The price is determined by a public auction on the floor of the Exchange. The latest price of a stock can be readily determined for the New York Stock Exchange while this is not possible on the over-the-counter market.

This situation leads to greater price stability on the exchanges because of the improved market information. Furthermore the specialist on the floor of the New York Stock Exchange further contributes to price stability. It is his function to eliminate price variation due to temporary shifts in supply and demand. That is, he will buy his assigned stocks when they are in temporary oversupply and sell them when they are in temporary undersupply. The theory is that this intervention improves price stability by separating actual price movements from random variations. The over-the-counter market has no counterpart to this control mechanism.

The cost of a stock purchase tends to be predictable on the exchanges as the prices tend to more closely approximate the market. Whereas, on the over-the-counter market the broker is acting both as an agent and as a retailer. An additional problem is that no one broker has inventories in all stocks. Rather, each firm specializes in certain over-the-counter issues. This provides an additional complication to the firm's role of agent and salesman.

THE SECURITIES MARKET—1969

The year 1969 was a bear market year. Throughout the year, common stock prices declined rather steadily and were interrupted only by three short and mild rallies in April–May, August, and October. Compared to the two previous bear markets, 1969 price declines were more moderate. Common stock yields were somewhat higher than in 1968, staying above 3 percent most of the year.

The consolidations of declining stock prices also had a dampening effect on excessive speculation in the market. The high cost of credit and the limited opportunities in either the secondary markets or in new issues made it even less attractive. Due to the lack of speculation and the low volatility of the market, the Exchange only imposed special margin and capital requirements on 67 different common issues as opposed to 140 in 1968. Most of the restrictions were imposed early in the year.

Slower share activity, falling stock prices and high cost of money all combined to sharply reduce stock market credit in 1969. Also, the high initial margin of 80 percent in effect during the year had as much influence on the contraction of market credit as the continued restrictions on free substitution of collateral and on withdrawal and retention of funds.

During 1969 and into January of 1970 stock margin debt shrank by more than $1 billion and collateral securing debt was down by more than $6 billion. Potential purchasing power was diminished by almost $1 billion.

The belief that institutions and financial intermediaries had become the predominant investment factor on the New York Stock Exchange was confirmed by a statistical study of transactions conducted by New York Stock Exchange member firms in 1969, and showed that this group of investors accounted for more than half the public share volume (i.e., excluding members), and for more than 60 percent of the public dollar volume. In view of the downturn in overall volume, major institutional investors increased both their share volumes and activity ratios in 1969.

There were 101 new listings on the New York Stock Exchange during 1969. For various reasons, 64 firms were removed from the list, thus resulting in a net gain of 37 common stocks, the largest increase in a year since 1946.

EXHIBIT 1
ELI LILLY & COMPANY
Financial data for years ending December 31, 1965–1969
(dollar figures in millions)

	1969	1968	1967	1966	1965
Balance Sheet Data					
Cash and equivalents............	$119.20	$113.80	$ 63.80	$ 47.70	$ 65.30
Receivables..................	77.70	64.40	50.60	43.50	38.30
Inventory...................	102.60	82.40	79.50	84.50	70.00
Current assets................	299.50	260.60	193.90	175.70	173.60
current liabilities............	117.50	100.80	73.40	69.50	62.70
working capital..............	182.00	159.80	120.50	106.20	110.90
Net plant....................	225.20	183.70	167.10	133.10	109.60
Other long-term assets.........	13.70	13.00	11.50	11.00	8.60
Total Assets.............	538.40	457.30	372.50	319.80	291.80
Funded debt..................	7.40	6.60	8.20	2.30	0.0
Other long-term liabilities........	17.22	14.47	10.58	4.45	3.45
Preferred stock................	0.0	0.0	0.70	1.10	1.20
Common equity...............	396.28	335.43	279.62	242.44	224.44
Total Capital...........	420.90	356.50	299.10	250.30	229.10
Income Statement Data					
Sales........................	$537.20	$479.60	$408.40	$366.70	$316.60
Cost of goods sold..............	169.99	151.30	135.82	120.44	101.86
Depreciation and amortization....	13.92	12.77	10.62	9.77	8.78
Income tax...................	60.38	56.35	42.03	42.87	38.41
Net Income...................	83.47	70.74	53.71	49.85	41.84
Preferred dividends.............	0.0	0.02	0.03	0.06	0.06
Available for common..........	83.47	70.72	53.66	49.79	41.78
Common dividends..............	35.09	29.65	25.95	25.77	22.41
Other Data					
Capital expenditures.............	$ 56.80	$ 32.00	$ 45.40	$ 33.90	$ 14.90
Shares outstanding..............	33.61	33.21	32.65	32.18	32.10
Book value...................	11.79	10.10	8.56	7.53	6.99
E.P.S. as reported..............	2.50	2.15	1.65	1.54	1.30
Dividends per share.............	1.05	0.90	0.80	0.80	0.70
Stock prices—high..............	102.50	89.00	59.25	46.00	43.75
Stock prices—low..............	68.25	47.50	42.50	36.75	30.50
Stock prices—close.............	102.50	77.50	53.00	43.38	41.88

Source: *Compustat Tapes*, published by Standard & Poors Company.

EXHIBIT 1 (Continued)

Total yield analysis (year end)

Yea.	High price	Low price	Price close	P/E of stock	P/E relative	Change in price	Change in stock P/E	Change in P/E relative	Didenpesha
1960......	21.13	15.25	16.75	28.59	1.51	−15.72	5.36	10.21	0.
1961......	23.63	16.25	21.63	30.01	1.45	29.10	4.98	−3.72	0.
1962......	25.25	15.63	19.94	24.94	1.58	−7.80	−16.91	8.83	0.
1963......	29.00	19.94	29.00	35.89	2.03	45.45	43.92	28.13	0.
1964......	31.75	24.63	30.88	31.10	1.66	6.47	−13.33	−18.23	0.
1965......	43.75	30.50	41.88	32.17	1.82	35.63	3.43	9.88	0.
1966......	46.00	36.75	43.38	28.04	1.90	3.58	−12.86	4.14	0.
1967......	59.25	42.50	53.00	32.25	1.81	22.19	15.02	−4.51	0.
1968......	89.00	47.50	77.50	36.39	2.04	46.23	12.86	12.79	0.
1969......	102.50	68.25	102.50	41.28	2.39	32.26	13.42	16.97	1.
MEAN...	47.13	31.72	43.64	32.07	1.82	21.14*	3.22*	4.39*	0.
Standard Deviation	28.38	17.27	27.59	4.74	0.29	6.23*	3.48*	0.16*	0.
Coefficient of Variation	60.23	54.46	63.21	14.79	15.72	14.27*	10.86*	8 59*	22.

* Trend with stability and C.V. about trend line.
Source: *Compustat Tapes* published by Standard & Poors.

EXHIBIT 2
ELI LILLY & COMPANY
Composite industry per share data
(ten largest firms)

	1964	1965	1966	1967	1968	1969
Sales	35.33	40.41	47.47	44.27	51.04	56.30
Operating income	6.68	7.78	8.87	9.14	10.51	—
Profit margins percent	18.91	18.51	18.69	20.65	20.59	—
Depreciation	0.66	0.73	0.83	0.98	1.12	—
Taxes	2.96	3.33	3.85	3.80	4.65	—
Earnings	3.23	3.77	4.31	4.39	4.73	5.23
Dividends	1.79	2.08	2.31	2.49	2.69	2.93
Earnings as a percent of sales	9.14	9.33	9.08	9.92	9.27	9.29
Dividends as a percent of earnings	55.42	55.17	53.68	56.72	56.87	56.02
Price (1941–43 = 10)—High	82.95	106.88	108.79	136.87	139.63	165.05
—Low	72.62	82.97	88.89	102.71	111.75	127.88
Price/earnings ratio—High	25.68	28.30	25.24	31.18	29.52	31.56
—Low	22.48	22.01	20.62	22.40	23.63	24.45
Dividend yield percent—High	2.46	2.51	2.60	2.42	2.41	2.29
—Low	2.16	1.95	2.12	1.82	1.93	1.78
Book value	15.77	16.25	17.51	18.55	20.92	—
Return on book value percent	20.48	23.20	24.61	23.67	22.61	—
Working capital	9.55	10.35	11.88	14.73	14.67	—
Capital expenditures	1.12	1.45	1.95	2.37	2.32	—

EXHIBIT 3
ELI LILLY & COMPANY
Listing requirements

To be listed on the New York Stock Exchange, a company is expected to meet certain qualifications to be willing to keep the investing public informed on the progress of its affairs. The company must be a going concern, or be the successor to a going concern. In determining eligibility for listing, particular attention is given to such qualifications as: (1) the degree of national interest in the company; (2) its relative position and stability in the industry; and (3) whether it is engaged in an expanding industry, with prospects of at least maintaining its relative position.

Initial Listing

While each case is decided on its own merits, the exchange generally requires the following as a minimum.

1. Demonstrated earning power under competitive conditions of $2.5 million before Federal income taxes for the most recent year and $2 million pre-tax for each of the preceding two years.
2. Net tangible assets of $14 million, but greater emphasis will be placed on the aggregate market value of the common stock.
3. A total of $14 million in market value of publicly held common stock.
4. A total of 800,000 common shares publicly held out of 1,000,000 shares outstanding.
5. Round-lot shareholders numbering 1,800 out of a total of 2,000, shareholders.

EXHIBIT 3 (Continued)

Continued Listing

The appropriateness of continued listing of a security on the Exchange cannot be measured mathematically, and the Exchange may at any time suspend or delist a security where the Board considers that continued dealings in the security are not advisable, even though a security meets or fails to meet any specified criteria. For example, the Exchange would normally give consideration to suspending or removing from the list a common stock of a company when there are:

1. Less than 900 round-lot holders, with less than 1,000 shareholders of record.
2. 400,000 shares or less in public hands.
3. $4,000,000 or less aggregate market value of publicly held shares.
4. $7,000,000 or less in aggregate market value of all outstanding common stock or net tangible assets applicable thereto, combined with an earnings record of less than an average of $600,000 after taxes for the past three years.

Listing Agreement

The listing agreement between the company and the exchange is designed to provide timely disclosure to the public of earnings statements, dividend notices, and other information which may affect security values or influence investment decisions. The Exchange requires actively operating companies to agree to solicit proxies for all meetings of stockholders.

Voting Rights

As a matter of general policy, the Exchange has for many years refused to list non-voting common stocks, and all listed common stocks have the right to vote.

EXHIBIT 4

ELI LILLY & COMPANY

Firm comparisons

Company	Year	Net sales (million dollars)	Net income (million dollars)	Number of common shares outstanding (million)	E.P.S. on common stock	Where traded
Eli Lilly	1969	$537.2	$ 83.5	33.6	$2.50	OTC
	1968	479.6	70.7	33.2	2.15	"
	1967	408.4	53.7	32.7	1.65	"
	1966	366.7	49.8	32.2	1.55	"
	1965	316.6	41.8	32.1	1.30	"
Merck	1969	646.9	100.6	36.0	2.79	NYSE
	1968	583.1	92.9	35.8	2.59	"
	1967	528.1	89.3	35.6	2.50	"
	1966	418.4	75.9	35.6	2.50	"
	1965	332.0	59.6	32.3	1.84	"
Pfizer	1969	895.8	71.6	63.3	1.13	NYSE
	1968	725.8	64.7	62.9	1.03	"
	1967	637.8	58.3	60.9	.96	"
	1966	622.0	61.6	60.3	1.02	"
	1965	542.6	53.4	59.7	.90	"
Upjohn	1969	371.0	37.4	14.7	2.54	NYSE
	1968	333.2	34.4	14.7	2.35	"
	1967	273.0	30.1	14.2	2.11	"
	1966	257.6	36.3	14.2	2.56	"
	1965	242.4	37.2	14.2	2.62	"
Marion	1969	28.4	6.5	4.1	1.03	NYSE/OTC*
	1968	16.7	5.4	4.0	.74	OTC
	1967	10.4	4.3	4.0	.49	"
	1966	7.8	3.0	4.0	.35	"
	1965	4.8	1.9	4.0	.19	"
International Chemical and Nuclear	1969	99.6	4.0	5.2	.78	NYSE/OTC†
	1968	68.6	1.6	4.2	.37	OTC
	1967	29.8	.9	2.4	.36	"
	1966	2.8	.2	1.5	.14	"
	1965	.4	.04	1.0	.04	"

* February 1969.
† July 1969.

EXHIBIT 4 (Continued)

Company	Price range		Long-term debt (percent)	Preferred stock	Common stock surplus (percent)	Other (percent)	P/E	Cash dividends (percent)
	High	Low						
Lilly	103	68	1.8	0	97.7	.5	34.6	1.2
	90	47					32.2	1.3
	59	42					30.9	1.6
	46	36					26.9	1.9
	44	30					28.8	1.9
Merck	115	82	3.5	1.0	94.8	.7	35.4	2.0
	96	73					32.9	2.1
	94	73					33.6	1.9
	81	64					31.4	1.9
	75	48					33.6	1.9
Pfizer	35	23	9.6	0	85.0	5.4	25.9	1.9
	25	18					21.7	2.2
	30	22					28.1	1.8
	25	17					21.1	2.2
	25	16					23.2	2.1
Upjohn	58	37	0	0	93.0	7.0	18.8	3.4
	64	41					22.5	3.0
	69	47					27.6	2.7
	83	61					28.2	2.1
	77	52					24.7	1.9
Marion	58	38	6.7	0	93.3	0	45.5	0.4
	64	31					63.5	0.2
	36	10					46.0	0.3
	14	7					30.5	0.3
	11	4					38.5	0.1
International Chemical	31	12	33.3	0	67.7	0	27.0	0
	30	12					56.5	0
	NA	NA					NA	0
	"	"					"	0
	"	"					"	0

ANHEUSER-BUSCH

ANHEUSER-BUSCH is the largest brewing company in the United States. This company and its two major competitors, Schlitz and Pabst, are recognized as the Big Three of the brewing industry. In 1971, they accounted for 40 percent of the beer industry's sales and this share is expected to increase. Because of the present strength of the three companies and their anticipated growth rate, their common stock issues are fairly attractive.

Almost all large industrial companies, including most brewers, list their stocks on the New York Stock Exchange. Anheuser-Busch and Pabst, two of the three largest brewers, have chosen to trade their shares over-the-counter. Since so many other large companies have decided to list, it seems appropriate for Anheuser-Busch to conduct a thorough analysis of the respective merits of the major stock exchanges versus the over-the-counter market.

THE BREWING INDUSTRY

The brewing industry in the United States consists of approximately 150 breweries operated by 90 brewing companies. The total sales of these companies was $9.7 billion in 1970, but 69 percent of the sales were made by 10 companies. Forty percent of the industry sales were made by the "Big Three."

While numerous family-owned brewing operations remain, most U.S. beer production is accounted for by publicly held companies. The ranking of the top 10 in 1970 was as follows: Anheuser-Busch (stock sold over-the-counter), Schlitz (listed on NYSE), Pabst (sold over-the-counter), Coors (privately owned), Schaefer (listed on NYSE), Falstaff (listed on NYSE), Miller Brewing (subsidiary of Philip Morris which is listed on NYSE), Carling (subsidiary of Canadian Breweries which is listed on NYSE plus Toronto, Montreal, Vancouver, and Amsterdam Stock Exchanges), Hamm Brewing (subsidiary of Heublein, listed on NYSE and Pacific Coast Stock Exchange), and Associated Brewing (listed on NYSE and Detriot Stock Exchange).

Anheuser-Busch has led the industry in sales every year since 1959. In 1970, it sold over 22 million barrels of the 121.8 million sold by the industry. Schlitz sold some 15 million and Pabst sold nearly 11 million. Of the remaining seven major brewers, each sold between four and seven million barrels, together accounting for another 36 million barrels.

There are several reasons for the highly concentrated nature of the brewing industry. Among them are the following advantages that the large, national brewers have over the regional companies: (1) Unit cost savings resulting from high-volume production, (2) Financial ability to adopt new, large, and efficient machines as they become available, and (3) Benefits of nationwide advertising programs.

The brewing industry is a steadily growing industry, but there is a large difference between the growth rates of the national brewers and the small brewers. In the decade ending in 1970, barrel sales for the industry rose at a compound annual rate of 3.5 percent. During this period barrel sales for the Big Three brewers grew at over a 10 percent rate. Exhibits 1 and 2 show how the net sales and net income for the Big Three have grown between 1961 and 1971. The percent returns on invested capital and common equity for the same period are shown in Exhibits 3 and 4.

Per capita consumption of beer has risen from 14.9 gallons in 1961 to 18.3 gallons in 1970. Sixty-nine percent of this beer was consumed by the 21 to 39 age group. With this prime beer drinking age group expected to grow at least through 1980, beer consumption should grow at a rate close to 4.5 percent annually during this period.

The national brewers have an advantage over the regional companies in their ability to meet this increase in demand. Their growth will probably have to come through building new plants and increasing the capacity of presently owned plants. Recent attempts at mergers and acquisitions have been reversed by the U.S. Justice Department. In 1969, Schlitz was ordered to sell its Burgermister operations in California and Pabst was forced to sell its Blatz brand.

COMPANY BACKGROUND

The company was founded in 1852. Adolphus Busch, Sr. became president in 1880, and the Busch family has controlled the company to a large extent ever since. August A. Busch, Jr. is the current president and his family controls 16 percent of the company's common stock. Beer accounted for 94 percent of Anheuser-Busch sales in 1970. Its four brands of beer are the premium-priced Budweiser which accounts for most of its sales; Michelob, a super-premium priced beer; Busch Bavarian, a popular-priced beer; and Budweiser Malt Liquor, a newly introduced malt liquor beverage.

Breweries are located in St. Louis; Newark; Los Angeles; Tampa; Columbus; Houston; Jacksonville; Merrimack, New Hampshire; and Williamsburg, Virginia. The nine plants have a total capacity of 27 million barrels per year. The company also sells bakers supplies, corn products, and animal feeds. Through the 1967 acquisition of Adolphus Busch Estate, Incorporated, controlling interests in Manufacturers Railway Company and St. Louis Refrigerator Car Company were obtained.

Two of the company's profit-making endeavors also have a high publicity value. The St. Louis Cardinals baseball team provides valuable Budweiser publicity. There are also three animal sanctuaries called Busch Gardens. They were originated as promotion attempts and operated at a loss in Los Angeles, Houston, and Tampa. Now the animal gardens are beginning to earn profits and continuing to create beneficial publicity.

Anheuser-Busch plows 10 percent of its sales dollars back into plant improvements. It has had to borrow fairly extensively to finance its rapid growth. Exhibit 5 presents balance sheet information for the last five years. Almost all the long-term debt consists of four issues of debentures which came out in 1952, 1964, 1966, and 1967. All four issues are listed on the New York Stock Exchange.

Although the earnings growth for the Big Three has been strong, the rise in their stock prices has been faster. This is indicated in Exhibits 6, 7, and 8, which show the adjusted prices and price/earnings ratios from 1961 through 1971. Exhibit 9 compares the payout ratios of the three companies over the same period.

Anheuser-Busch has reduced the par value of its stock from $4 to $1 through 2 for 1 stock splits in 1965 and 1968. There was also a 10 percent stock dividend in 1966 and a 2 for 1 stock split in 1971 which did not alter the par value. Pabst stock was split 2 for 1 in 1969. Schlitz split 2 for 1 in 1966 and 3 for 1 in 1972.

At the end of 1971, Anheuser-Busch had 44,975,996 shares outstanding, held by 27,539 shareholders. Eighty-three institutions held 1,395,700 shares. Pabst had 9,524,238 shares outstanding, held by 6,030 shareholders. Thirty-seven institutions held 1,956,350 shares. Schlitz had 9,615,269 shares outstanding, held by 4,990 shareholders. Thirteen institutions held 185,200 shares. Sixteen percent of Anheuser's stock was held by the Busch family and 87 percent of the Schlitz stock was held by the Uihlein family.

CRITERIA FOR A LISTING DECISION

Most large industrial firms list their stock on one or more national or regional stock exchanges. Major U.S. corporations are listed on the New York Stock Exchange with few exceptions. Two prominent exceptions are the first and third largest U.S. brewers, Anheuser-Busch and Pabst. Schlitz, the second largest company in the brewing industry, is listed on the New York Stock Exchange.

There are numerous considerations for both stockholders and managers when attempting to determine the desirability of listing the corporation's stock. Some of the advantages and disadvantages of listing are discussed below.

Advantages of listing to the corporation

1. The market for shares is wider and more stable.
2. New large stock offerings can be sold more readily.
3. Greater coverage by the financial press can provide beneficial publicity.
4. The investing public views listing as an indication of company strength and stability.

Advantages of listing to investors

1. Costs of trading are lower for listed stocks.
2. Improved liquidity, wider distribution, and price stability can result in higher prices.
3. Investors are assured that stock exchange standards have been met.
4. Company and trading information is more readily available.

Disadvantages of listing

1. Cost of listing and annual stock exchange fees are incurred.
2. Accounting and reporting regulations of the Securities and Exchange Commission are more stringent for listed companies.
3. Over-the-Counter dealers' "market-making" services are not available.

Difficulty in obtaining quotations, varying quotes, and restricted availability of shares have been important reasons that some investors have preferred listed stocks to those traded over the counter. These problems have been overcome to some extent since the February 1971 introduction of the National Securities Dealers Automated Quotations System (NASDAQ). This computer-based system provides instant quotes on the prices of 2,700 unlisted stocks. Practically every broker has a terminal machine through which he can obtain quotations instantly. One indication of increased acceptance of over-the-counter stocks is the increase of institutional participation in this market from 30 percent to 50 percent of all transactions in the last five years.

Usually, trading volume is higher for listed stocks and prices are less volatile. Exhibit 10 shows volume and price figures for the three largest U.S. brewers for the first quarter of 1972.

EXHIBIT 1
ANHEUSER-BUSCH
Net sales

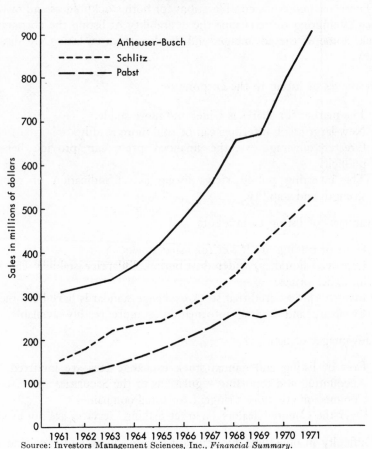

Source: Investors Management Sciences, Inc., *Financial Summary.*

EXHIBIT 2
ANHEUSER-BUSCH
Net income

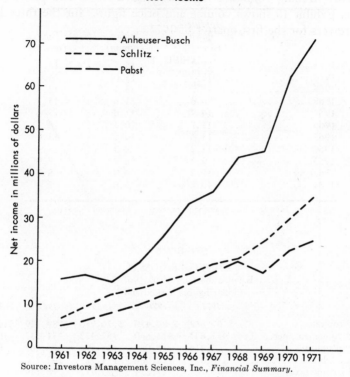

Source: Investors Management Sciences, Inc., *Financial Summary.*

EXHIBIT 3
ANHEUSER-BUSCH
Return on invested capital

	Anheuser- Busch (*percent*)	Schlitz (*percent*)	Pabst (*percent*)
1971................	10.9	13.4	13.2
1970................	13.1	.12.5	13.2
1969................	10.4	11.7	11.6
1968................	11.0	10.4	14.7
1967................	10.3	10.2	14.4
1966................	12.0	10.0	13.3
1965................	10.8	9.8	11.7
1964................	9.6	9.2	10.3
1963................	·8.6	8.8	8.8
1962................	9.8	6.9	7.5
1961................	9.6	5.0	6.3

Source: Investors Management Sciences, Inc., *Financial Summary.*

EXHIBIT 4
ANHEUSER-BUSCH
Return on common equity

	Anheuser-Busch (*percent*)	*Schlitz* (*percent*)	*Pabst* (*percent*)
1971	17.3	15.3	13.2
1970	18.6	15.0	14.0
1969	15.2	13.1	12.1
1968	16.6	11.6	15.3
1967	14.9	11.0	15.4
1966	15.7	10.3	14.5
1965	13.6	10.1	13.0
1964	11.2	9.3	11.4
1963	9.4	8.9	9.9
1962	10.8	6.9	8.3
1961	10.8	5.0	7.0

Source: Investors Management Sciences, Inc., *Financial Summary.*

EXHIBIT 5

ANHEUSER-BUSCH
Balance sheet for years 1967–71
(dollar figures in thousands)

	1971	*1970*	*1969*	*1968*	*1967*
Working capital	$ 87,662	$ 80,430	$ 76,950	$ 89,829	$104,252
Plant and equipment, net	453,647	416,660	387,422	351,537	306,476
Capital expenditures	73,214	65,069	66,396	76,467	85,415
Long-term debt	116,571	128,080	134,925	142,720	147,898
Deferred income taxes	34,103	27,274	23,212	18,149	14,191
Deferred investment tax credit	14,276	13,563	12,577	10,790	8,823
Shareholders' equity	413,974	358,476	314,121	285,318	255,359

Source: Anheuser-Busch, Inc., *1971 Annual Report.*

EXHIBIT 6
ANHEUSER-BUSCH
Stock prices—Anheuser-Busch

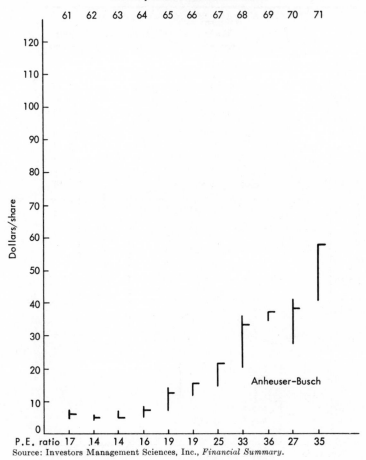

Source: Investors Management Sciences, Inc., *Financial Summary.*

EXHIBIT 7
ANHEUSER-BUSCH
Stock prices—Schlitz

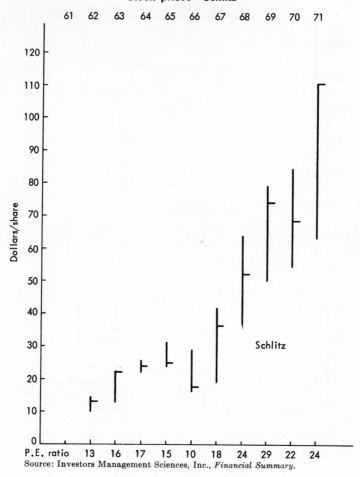

Source: Investors Management Sciences, Inc., *Financial Summary.*

EXHIBIT 8
ANHEUSER-BUSCH
Stock prices—Pabst

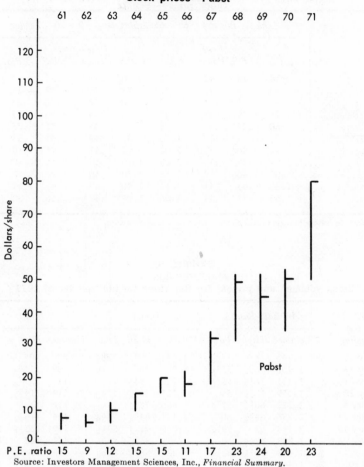

Source: Investors Management Sciences, Inc., *Financial Summary.*

EXHIBIT 9

ANHEUSER-BUSCH

Earnings per share, dividends per share, payout ratio

	Anheuser-Busch			*Schlitz*			*Pabst*		
	E.P.S.	*D.P.S.*	*Price Range*	*E.P.S.*	*D.P.S.*	*Price Range*	*E.P.S.*	*D.P.S.*	*Price Range*
1961	.38	.18	.42	.71	.60	.85	.55	0	0
1962	.40	.18	.45	1.01	.73	.72	.69	.25	.36
1963	.37	.19	.51	1.35	.70	.52	.86	.25	.29
1964	.46	.19	.41	1.47	.70	.48	1.06	.25	.24
1965	.60	.22	.37	1.68	.75	.45	1.31	.25	.19
1966	.77	.25	.32	1.80	.85	.47	1.61	.38	.24
1967	.82	.30	.37	2.02	.95	.47	1.91	.50	.26
1968	1.01	.37	.37	2.20	1.10	.50	2.15	.50	.23
1969	1.02	.40	.39	2.58	1.30	.50	1.90	.58	.31
1970	1.40	.43	.31	3.13	1.40	.45	2.44	.65	.27
1971	1.60	.53	.33	3.66	1.55	.42	2.66	.80	.30

Source: Investors Management Sciences, Inc., *Financial Summary*.

EXHIBIT 10

ANHEUSER-BUSCH

Stock volume* and prices† for Big Three for first quarter of 1972

1972 For the week ending	*Anheuser-Busch†*			*Pabst†*			*Schlitz*		
	Volume*	*High*	*Low*	*Volume**	*High*	*Low*	*Volume**	*High*	*Low*
January 7	1,948	58	$55\frac{5}{8}$	1,153	$79\frac{1}{4}$	$75\frac{5}{8}$	800	$108\frac{1}{2}$	$103\frac{1}{2}$
January 14	1,907	$56\frac{3}{4}$	$55\frac{1}{8}$	981	$78\frac{7}{8}$	$77\frac{7}{8}$	149	$114\frac{3}{4}$	111
January 21	1,371	$56\frac{1}{4}$	$55\frac{7}{8}$	726	$78\frac{1}{2}$	$77\frac{1}{4}$	156	$115\frac{1}{4}$	$111\frac{3}{4}$
January 28	1,659	$57\frac{1}{8}$	55	721	$78\frac{1}{8}$	$77\frac{1}{2}$	214	$114\frac{3}{4}$	$108\frac{1}{4}$
February 4	1,222	$60\frac{3}{4}$	$57\frac{7}{8}$	680	$78\frac{1}{4}$	77	116	113	$108\frac{1}{4}$
February 11	2,276	$63\frac{3}{4}$	$60\frac{1}{8}$	1,121	$84\frac{3}{4}$	$78\frac{5}{8}$	125	$116\frac{1}{4}$	109
February 18	2,333	62	$59\frac{5}{8}$	1,059	$91\frac{1}{4}$	$84\frac{1}{2}$	199	$122\frac{1}{2}$	$115\frac{3}{4}$
February 25‡	1,833	$62\frac{1}{2}$	$60\frac{1}{8}$	835	$86\frac{5}{8}$	$86\frac{5}{8}$	453	122	$120\frac{3}{4}$
March 3	1,393	$66\frac{1}{4}$	$62\frac{7}{8}$	823	$88\frac{3}{4}$	$86\frac{3}{4}$	158	$126\frac{1}{4}$	$123\frac{1}{4}$
March 10	1,440	69	65	1,053	$91\frac{1}{4}$	89	99	128	127
March 17	881	$66\frac{1}{4}$	$63\frac{3}{4}$	646	$88\frac{7}{8}$	88	86	$127\frac{1}{4}$	$124\frac{3}{4}$
March 24	1,551	$64\frac{7}{8}$	$62\frac{7}{8}$	1,223	$87\frac{1}{2}$	84	151	$124\frac{3}{4}$	$121\frac{3}{4}$
March 31‡	767	$66\frac{7}{8}$	$65\frac{1}{4}$	493	$88\frac{1}{4}$	$87\frac{3}{8}$	79	$122\frac{1}{4}$	$188\frac{1}{2}$
Total	20,581	69	55	11,514	$91\frac{1}{4}$	$75\frac{5}{8}$	2,785	128	$103\frac{1}{2}$

* Volume equals sales in 100s.
† For Anheuser-Busch and Pabst, bid prices are indicated. Daily closing prices are listed for Schlitz.
‡ Four-day week.
Source: Compiled from daily Wall Street Journal quotations.

EXHIBIT 11
ANHEUSER-BUSCH
Stock exchange minimum listing requirements

	American	*New York*
Publicly held shares........	300,000 shares (exclusive officers, directors or concentrated holdings)	1,000,000 shares outstanding 800,000 publicly held
Number of shareholders....	900 with 600 round lot holders	2,000 1,800 holders of round lots
Market value (publicly held shares).............	$2,000,000; $5 minimum market value per share	$14,000,000
Earnings.................	$300,000 after all charges in last fiscal year $500,000 pretax and before extraordinary charges	$2,500,000 pretax (fiscal year preceding listing) $2,000,000 each preceding two years
Assets...................	$3000,000 net tangible	$14,000,000 net tangible
Voting rights.............	No nonvoting common	No nonvoting common nor unusual voting provisions
Stockholder approval.......	1. Certain options or renumeration plans 2. Change in control of a company 3. Acquisitions: *a*) from a director, officer or substantial security holder *b*) potential issuance of a 20 percent increase in the outstanding common *c*) consideration paid has fair value of 20 percent of market value of outstanding common	1. Certain options or renumeration plans 2. Change in control of a company 3. Acquisitions: *a*) from a director, officer or substantial security holder *b*) potential issuance of a 20 percent increase in the outstanding common *c*) consideration paid has fair value of 20 percent of market value of outstanding common
Original listing fees (shares)	1 cent first 500,000 $\frac{3}{4}$ cent second 500,000 $\frac{1}{2}$ cent third 500,000 $\frac{1}{4}$ cent fourth 500,000 $\frac{1}{8}$ cent— balance	1 cent first 1 million $\frac{1}{2}$ cent second million $\frac{1}{4}$ cent 3 to 300 million $\frac{1}{8}$ cent — over 300 million
Additional listing..........	1 cent per share to a maximum of $3,500 Minimum $250	Above rates applicable for additional shares
Annual fee...............	$\frac{1}{10}$ cent per share first 2 million $\frac{1}{20}$ cent for balance Maximum—$3,500 Minimum—$500	$1,000 minimum or $250 per issue, whichever is higher (annually for 15 years)

SELECTED REFERENCES
FOR PART EIGHT

BORDEN, ARTHUR M., and BALL, JOHN H. "Introduction to Going Public," *Datamation*, Vol. 14 (August 1968), pp. 50–57.

BROWN, J. MICHAEL. "Post-Offering Experience of Companies Going Public," *Journal of Business*, January 1970, pp. 10–18.

CAHN, B. D. "Capital for Small Business: Sources and Methods," *Law and Contemporary Problems*, Vol. 24 (Winter 1959), pp. 27–67.

CHAMBERLAIN, JOHN. "Why It's Harder and Harder to Get a Good Board," *Fortune*, November 1966.

COHAN, AVERY B. *Private Placements and Public Offerings: Market Shares since 1953.* Chapel Hill, N.C.: School of Business Administration, University of North Carolina, 1961.

COPELAND, RONALD M., and FREDERICKS, WILLIAM H. "Reasons for Subsequent Listings of Common Stocks," *Commercial and Financial Chronicle*, Vol. 205 (May 4, 1967), p. 1756.

DOUGALL, HERBERT E. *Capital Markets and Institutions.* 2d ed. Englewood Cliffs, N.J.: Prentice-Hall, 1970.

EITEMAN, DAVID K. "The S.E.C. Special Study and the Exchange Markets," *Journal of Finance*, Vol. 21 (May 1966), 311–23.

FISHER, MILTON. "Listed and Unlisted Stocks—A Realistic Comparison," *Commercial and Financial Chronicle*, Vol. 212 (October 8, 1970), p. 1012.

FLINK, S. J. *Equity Financing for Small Business.* New York: Simmons-Boardman, 1962.

FRIEND, IRWIN, HOFFMAN, G. W., and WINN, W. J. *The Over-the-Counter Securities Market.* New York: McGraw-Hill, 1958.

FURST, RICHARD W. "Does Listing Increase the Market Price of Common Stocks?" *Journal of Business*, Vol. 43 (April 1970), pp. 174–80.

HERSHMAN, ARLENE, and MURRAY, THOMAS J. "The Pitfalls in New Issues," *Dun's Review*, Vol. 99 (March 1972), pp. 38–41.

LEFFLER, G. L., and FARWELL, L. C. *The Stock Market.* 3d ed. New York: Ronald, 1963.

"Listing Standards," *Commercial and Financial Chronicle*, Vol. 214 (July 29, 1971), p. 311.

MERJOS, ANNA. "Market Lure—Plans to List on the Big Board Can Do Wonders for a Stock," *Barrons*, Vol. 51 (April 12, 1971), pp. 9–20.

MILLER, BEN. "Essential Ingredients for 'Going Public' Successfully," *Commercial and Financial Chronicle*, Vol. 212 (September 10, 1970), pp. 731–35.

MILLER, G. R. "Long-Term Business Financing from the Underwriter's Point of View," *Journal of Finance*, Vol. 16 (May 1961), pp. 280–90.

NAIR, RICHARD S. "Investment Banking: Judge Medina in Retrospect," *Financial Analysts Journal*, Vol. 16 (July–August 1960), pp. 35–40.

ROBINSON, ROLAND, and BARTELL, H. ROBERT, JR. "Uneasy Partnership: SEC/NYSE," *Harvard Business Review*, Vol. 43 (January–February 1965), pp. 76–88.

SAMETZ, A. W. "Trends in the Volume and Composition of Equity Finance," *Journal of Finance*, Vol. 19 (September 1965), pp. 450–69.

SEARS, GERALD A. "Public Offerings for Smaller Companies," *Harvard Business Review*, September–October 1968), pp. 112–20.

SECURITIES AND EXCHANGE COMMISSION. *Annual Reports*. Washington, D.C.: U.S. Government Printing Office, various years.

SECURITIES AND EXCHANGE COMMISSION. *Cost of Flotation of Corporate Securities, 1951–1955*. Washington, D.C.: U.S. Government Printing Office, 1957.

SHAW, DAVID C. "The Cost of Going Public in Canada," *Financial Executive*, July 1969, pp. 20–28.

SMITH, HAROLD T. *Equity and Loan Capital for New and Expanding Small Business*. Kalamazoo, Mich.: W. E. Upjohn Institute for Employment Research, 1959.

STEVENSON, HAROLD W. *Common Stock Financing*. Ann Arbor, Mich.: University of Michigan, 1957.

STOLL, HANS R., and CURLEY, ANTHONY J. "Small Business and the New Issues Market for Equities," *Journal of Financial and Quantitative Analysis*. Vol. 5 (September 1970), pp. 309–22.

STUEBNER, E. A. "The Role of the Investment Banker in Arranging Private Financing," *Business Lawyer*, Vol. 16 (January 1961), pp. 377–85.

SULLIVAN, BRIAN. "An Introduction to 'Going Public'," *Journal of Accountancy*, November 1965.

WALTER, J. E. *The Role of Regional Security Exchanges*. Berkeley, Calif.: Bureau of Business and Economic Research, University of California, 1957.

WATERMAN, M. H. *Investment Banking Function*. Ann Arbor, Mich.: Bureau of Business Research, University of Michigan, 1958.

WHEAT, F. M., and BLACKSTONE, G. A. "Guideposts for a First Public Offering," *Business Lawyer*, Vol. 15 (April 1960), pp. 539–64.

WINTER, E. L. "Cost of Going Public," *Financial Executive*, Vol. 31 (September 1963), pp. 30–32.

VAN HORNE, JAMES C. "New Listings and their Price Behavior," *Journal of Finance*, Vol. 25 (September, 1970), pp. 783–94.

Does Listing Increase
the Market Price
of Common Stocks?*
Richard W. Furst†

SINCE 1960 over 230 companies have moved the trading of their common stock from the over-the-counter market to the New York Stock Exchange. Many others have moved from the over-the-counter market to the American Stock Exchange. It is reasonable to assume that the financial managers of these corporations must have felt that listing would somehow increase the market price of their common stock due to improved marketability, prestige, or some other factor.

THE TRADITIONAL ATTITUDE

Most of the literature on the subject of listing encourages this belief. In an article published in *The Commercial and Financial Chronicle* this viewpoint was expressed in clear and precise terms. The article stated: "For one thing, the basic fact is that the price of over-the-counter stocks is not swollen by the premium the public is ordinarily willing to pay for exchange listed stocks."[1]

Typical of the research advancing this viewpoint is a series of articles by Anna Merjos which appeared in *Barrons*. In the January 29, 1962 issue she noted that the majority of stocks rise in price from two or

* Reprinted from *The Journal of Business*, Vol. 43, No. 2 (April 1970), pp. 174–80, by permission of the author and the publisher.

† The author is an Assistant Professor of Finance at the University of South Carolina.

This paper is based on part of the analysis included in the author's dissertation, which was written at Washington University.

[1] "Difference between Listed and Over-the-Counter Trading," *Commercial and Financial Chronicle*, October 10, 1963, pp. 1415–16.

three months before the date of listing but seem to fall back in price in the thirty-day period after listing.[2] In a later article, however, she stated that "listing adds, sometimes appreciably," to the market price. of a common stock.[3] And, finally, in the May 1, 1967 issue she stated that "generally speaking listing on the American Stock Exchange or on the New York Stock Exchange pays off in the form of higher market prices."[4]

In each article she compared the market prices of the newly listed stocks three months before listing with market prices thirty days after listing. The changes in price during this span were then compared with the changes in the typical market averages.

The belief that listing increases market price is not universal, however. There are many people who argue that listing does not have the same effect on all stocks, that is, its effects vary with the size and other characteristics of the company. These people feel that the true effects of listing have been misinterpreted and that while listing may be beneficial to some companies, it can be detrimental to others.

THE OTC INFORMATION BUREAU STUDY

Probably the most detailed study advancing this latter point of view has been conducted by the Over-the-Counter (OTC) Information Bureau of New York. The bureau's major study was published in 1965, and a supplement was added during 1966. The study compared the performance of the forty-two stocks that were newly listed in 1963 with that of the thirty-five companies which comprise the National Quotation Bureau's industrial average. The time period covered included prelisting dates during 1963 and market prices through June 30, 1965.

The OTC Information Bureau found that of the forty-two companies newly listed in 1963, twenty-eight declined in price from the date of listing and only seven rose in price as much as the Dow-Jones Industrial or Standard and Poor's stock averages. By June 30, 1965 more than half of the forty-two stocks had declined to a price below their price sixty days prior to listing. Of the forty-two, only eleven showed a gain in price from sixty days before listing which was equal to the increase in the market averages. During this same period, the bureau reports that of the thirty-five companies which comprise the National Quotation Bureau's averages, twenty-seven advanced in price and twenty-one

---

[2] Anna Merjos, "Going on the Big Board: Stocks Act Better before Listing than Right Afterward," *Barrons*, January 29, 1962, pp. 5 ff.

[3] Anna Merjos, "Like Money in the Bank: Big Board Listing, the Record Suggests, Is a Valuable Asset," *Barrons*, July 8, 1963, pp. 9 ff.

[4] Anna Merjos, "Going on the Big Board," *Barrons*, May 1, 1967, pp. 9–10.

showed larger gains than either the Dow Jones Industrial or Standard and Poor's stock averages.[5]

WEAKNESSES OF THE STUDIES

Both the series of studies by Anna Merjos and the research by the OTC Information Bureau suffer from the same primary weakness. Neither study separates the effects of listing from the effects of other variables which influence market price. If the market price of a common stock increases (decreases) after listing, this may or may not be due to the listing factor. For example, assume a company was earning $1.00 a share and sold for ten times earnings while being traded over the counter. After listing, the stock's earnings jump to $2.00 a share, but the stock now sells for eight times earnings. The price has increased from $10 to $16, but listing did not cause the increase. The increase was primarily a function of the increased earnings per share. Both the study by the OTC Information Bureau and the series of studies by Anna Merjos would have implied that listing was the causal factor behind the increase in price.

In order to correct this weakness the effects of other variables should be taken into account before it is deduced that listing has or does not have a specific effect. This paper reports the results of a study that used a multiple-regression valuation model to take into consideration the changes in the "other" variables which occurred between the pre- and postlisting dates, and then studied the additional impact of listing. While it is impossible to quantify and measure all the variables which affect market price, it is possible to identify and measure most of the important influences.

THE VALUATION MODEL

The valuation model used to perform this function was developed from prior work by Myron J. Gordon.[6] Whereas much of the terminology used in defining the variables and their relationships will be that used by Gordon, the actual calculations of the values for all but the size variable differ slightly. It is important to recognize that the model closely resembles other theoretical models which state that value is a function of income and the capitalization rate applied to that income. The model states that price is a function of the income stream (the

---

[5] OTC Information Bureau, *Considerations in Listing on a Stock Exchange* (New York: Arthur Schmidt & Associates, 1965), pp. 5–6.

[6] Myron J. Gordon, *The Investment, Financing and Valuation of the Corporation* (Homewood, Ill.: Richard D. Irwin, Inc., 1962).

dividend and the rate of growth in that dividend) and the capitalization rate (the rate being influenced by leverage, size, and the instability of earnings). In logarithmic form the (base 10) regression model is

$$\log P = \log \alpha_0 + \alpha_1 \log D + \alpha_2 \log (1 + br)$$
$$+ \hat{\alpha}_3 \log (1 + \sigma/A)$$
$$+ \hat{\alpha}_4 \log (1 + h - ih/k)$$
$$+ \alpha_5 \log S,$$

where $\hat{\alpha}_3 = -\alpha_3$, $\hat{\alpha}_4 = -\alpha_4$, and $\alpha_0 =$ the regression constant. The variables are defined as follows:

1. $P =$ the closing market prices as of a specific date. If the stock was listed from March 1 to October 30 of any year, then the prelisting price was the closing price on the last day of trading of the preceding year, and the postlisting price was the closing price on the last day of trading in the year of listing. If the stock was listed in the first sixty days of the year, the prelisting price was the closing price on the last day of trading of the year two years previous, and the post-listing price was the closing price on the last day of trading in the year in which the stock was listed. If the stock was listed during the last sixty days of the year, the prelisting price was the price on the last day of trading of the previous year, and the postlisting price was the closing price of the year after listing. For example, assume that listings took place on January 15, April 7, October 24, and November 30 during 1962. If we assume that December 31 was a trading day in each year, then the pre- and post-listing market prices would have been determined as follows:

Company	Date of listing	Price date (prelisting)	Price date (postlisting)
1............	1/15/62	12/31/60	12/31/62
2............	4/7/62	12/31/61	12/31/62
3............	10/24/62	12/31/61	12/31/62
4............	11/30/62	12/31/61	12/31/62

This method was followed for two primary reasons. First, there is a tendency for the market price to rise from about sixty days prior to listing; then the price falls back to about its prior level approximately sixty days after listing. This characteristic was discovered by Merjos, and the preliminary research to this study supported her findings. Second, since prices as of a specific date are being used, it seems advisable to use the same date for as many companies as possible. In addition, the prelisting price date for some stocks will be the same as the postlisting price date for others, and this should add to the overall validity of the results.

2. D = dividend per share paid during the year. Stock dividends were not included, and when no dividends were declared, \$.20 was used as the value.[7] In addition, whenever there was a dividend change during the year, the dividend was adjusted to reflect the new annual rate.

3. The variable br = average growth rate. The average growth rate was obtained by the following method. Let Y_t = actual earnings in year T, D_t = actual dividend in year T, W_t = actual book value in year T, b_t = retention rate defined as $(Y_t - D_t)/Y_t$, r_t' = return on common equity defined as $Y_t/(W_{t-1})$, and $b_t'r_t'$ = actual growth rate. Then

$$b_t'r_t' = \frac{Y_t - D_t}{Y_t} \times \frac{Y_t}{W_{t-1}} = \frac{Y_t - D_t}{W_{t-1}}$$

The actual growth rate was modified to allow for the possibility that the investor may view an unusually good or bad year with some skepticism and is likely to calculate an average or expected growth rate. The average growth rate for the first year was set equal to the actual growth rate, and for each subsequent year the growth rate was calculated by choosing weights which gave 30 percent of the total weight to the most recent year and 70 percent to all prior years' earnings as presented by the smoothed figure. Thus $br = .3\ b_t r_t + .7\ br_{t-1}$.

4. The variable σ/A = earnings-instability index. The earnings per share in year t expected at the end of year $t - 1$ were defined as $Y_t^* = Y_{t-1}(1 + br_{t-1})$, or, in words, the expected value was the present earnings per share times the average growth rate. The difference between the actual and expected earnings per share could thus be defined as $Y_t^* - Y_t$. The expression $(Y_t^* - Y_t)/A_t$ (where A = total assets per share) is thus an approximation of the instability of the leverage free rate of return. By adding 1 to the absolute value of this figure, an index number is obtained which represents an earnings-instability index.

5. The term $(1 + h - ih/k)$ = the leverage variable. In the expression h is the ratio of the long-term debt and preferred stock to common equity, i is the corporate bond rate (Baa) for the appropriate year, and k is the firm's cost of capital, which was defined as $k = D/P(1 + h)^{-\alpha_1} + br$, where α_1 was set equal to 0.03, the value Gordon used, and P was the firm's market price.

6. The variable S = corporate size, defined as total assets minus current liabilities.

---

[7] Initially \$.01 was used in order to avoid having a zero in the logarithmic equation. However, when \$.01 was used as the value, it distorted the anticipated income flow $[D \times (1 + br)]$ and therefore yielded a low regression coefficient. When \$.20 was used as the value (an anticipated minimum dividend was determined), the regression coefficient increased in size and significance.

THE RESEARCH POPULATION

The population for the research study consisted of 198 companies which were newly listed on the New York Stock Exchange from 1960 through 1965.[8] During these six years a total of 239 companies were actually listed, but, for the reasons discussed below, forty-one were eliminated from the population. Table 1 lists these totals by years.

TABLE 1
The research population

Year	Total no. of companies listed	Companies not used	Companies used
1965	50	6	44
1964	42	7	35
1963	41	7	34
1962	30	4	26
1961	35	8	27
1960	41	9	32

The first group of companies to be eliminated from the investigation were those six companies that had been a party to a merger which changed the characteristics of the newly listed company. Some companies (e.g., Pacific Hawaiian Products) were merged into larger companies, while others were the surviving company in the merger but with their fundamental characteristics significantly altered.

Finance companies, savings and loan associations, and closed-end investment companies were also eliminated from the study. These companies have an asset and liability structure that does not fit the standard valuation models. For example, savings and loan associations have time deposits which greatly inflate their debt-equity ratios. In addition, the asset structure of these companies is unique in that all three groups of companies have predominantly financial asset rather than the traditional real assets of the industrial corporation. The asset structure of these firms then leads to the highly levered capital structures. Rather than have these companies distort the data of the rest of the population, they were eliminated from the study.

Nine companies had to be eliminated due to a lack of published financial data. These were extremely small companies, and most of them were listed in 1960 and 1961.

---

[8] The study covers only those companies that moved from the over-the-counter market to the New York Stock Exchange. It therefore excludes any new listings on the New York Stock Exchange when the company had previously been traded on the AMEX or on a regional exchange. Companies that moved from the over-the-counter market to the AMEX were also not included in the study.

The Chase Manhattan Bank was not included in the study since it was the only bank that has become listed. Great American Insurance was eliminated since it was the only insurance company that was listed during the period of the study. Florida East Coast Railway was eliminated since it went bankrupt and was reorganized in the year in which it was newly listed.

THE USE OF A DUMMY VARIABLE

The multiple-regression valuation model was used to perform two different tests. The first test was designed to ascertain whether listing on the New York Stock Exchange had a significant beneficial or detrimental effect on market price. A zero-one dummy variable was added to the valuation model to measure the effect of listing. A pre- and a post-listing observation was taken for each company; a value of zero was assigned to the listing variable for the prelisting observation, and a value of one was assigned to the postlisting observation. All the observations were then combined, and regression coefficients and standard errors were calculated for each independent variable. The results of this test are presented in Table 2.

TABLE 2
Regression coefficients, standard errors, and T-ratios for the independent variables

Variable	Coefficient (S.E.)	T-ratio
Dividend................	0.218 (0.035)	6.23
Growth rate.............	3.836 (0.451)	8.51
Earnings instability........	−1.125 (0.526)	−2.14
Leverage................	−0.653 (0.093)	−6.99
Size....................	0.215 (0.026)	8.23
Listing.................	−0.017 (0.018)	−0.99

Note: Multiple coefficient of determination = .27; degrees of freedom = 389; regression constant = 1.081; S.E. of market price variable = 0.172.

It is readily apparent from the results of this initial test that listing did not appear to have a significant effect on market price. The t-ratio for the listing variable was not significant, whereas the t-ratios for the rest of the variables were highly significant—all were significant at 5%, and all but the earnings-instability index were significant at 1%. However, the multiple coefficient of determination wae quite low (only 27% of the variation in market price was explained) and thus weakened the reliability of the measure.

In order to increase the performance of the model through making the population more homogeneous, the companies were divided into eight industry groups. The same test was then conducted for each industry. The results once again indicated that listing did not significantly affect the market prices of common stocks, since in each industry the listing variable was not significant. The *t*-ratios for the listing variable appear in Table 3; the number of companies appears in parentheses after each industry.

TABLE 3
Zero-one dummy-variable test using eight industry groups

Industry	*T-ratio for listing variable*	*Significant value at 5%*	*Coefficient of determination (R^2)*
Utilities (15)	0.027	2.06	.62
Transportation (9)	−0.415	2.18	.57
Nonindustrial manufacturing (41)	−1.034	1.96	.62
Manufacturing (industrial) (37)	0.196	1.96	.39
Food, drug, beverage, and retail (34)	−0.637	1.96	.39
Basic industries (29)	−0.509	1.96	.18
Building and home (11)	−0.003	2.12	.34
Electronics (22)	0.007	1.96	.25

THE TEST FOR COINCIDENCE

The second test was designed to determine whether the stocks were valued in a different manner after listing than before listing. To perform this task a prelisting regression equation and a postlisting equation for the combined group of companies were determined. These two equations were then compared to see if they were coincident, that is, if they lay on the same hyperplane and would therefore give the same value for the dependent variable given a certain set of values for the independent variables.[9]

---

[9] If the equations were coincident, then the error sum of squares for the overall regression resulting from the combination of the pre- and postlisting equations should have been equal to the sum of the error sums of squares for the separate equations. The difference between the error sums of squares thus became a measure of the degree of coincidence. If the equations did not give the same value for the dependent variable (they were not coincident), it could be concluded that listing had an effect on the market prices of the common stocks. If we let E_1 designate the error sum of squares for the combination of equations, and E_0 the sum of the error sum of squares for the two separate equations, then it can be

The regression coefficients and standard errors for each variable for the prelisting, postlisting, and combined pre- and postlisting observations appear in Table 4. When the test for coincidence was applied, the calcu-

TABLE 4
Regression coefficients and standard errors, cross-industry data

Variable	Prelisting observations	Postlisting observations	Pre- and post-listing observations combined
Dividend.................	0.221	0.219	0.218
	(0.048)	(0.052)	(0.035)
Growth rate...............	3.142	4.508	3.827
	(0.634)	(0.654)	(0.451)
Earnings instability.........	0.353	−1.318	−1.185
	(1.023)	(0.614)	(0.522)
Leverage.................	−0.585	−0.706	−0.648
	(0.134)	(0.130)	(0.093)
Corporate size.............	0.173	0.254	0.212
	(0.038)	(0.036)	(0.026)
Multiple R^2...............	.239	.311	.266
Mean of market price variable......	1.445	1.443	1.444
S.E. of market price variable.......	0.174	0.170	0.172
Degrees of freedom...........	192.000	192.000	390.000
Regression constant...........	1.160	0.962	1.078

lated value for F was 0.866. With 6 and 384 degrees of freedom for the numerator and denominator, respectively, the required significant value at the 5 percent confidence interval was 2.10. The equations were therefore coincident, a listing once again did not appear to affect market price significantly.

When the companies were divided into industry groups, the equations for seven of the eight industries were coincident at the 5 percent confidence interval (see Table 5). The pre- and postlisting equations for the electronic industry were not coincident, since the calculated value of F (3.29) exceeded the significant value.

---

shown that $(E_1 - E_0)/\sigma^2$ and E_0/σ^2 have independent χ^2 distributions with $p + 1$ and $n + n^* - 2p - 2$ degrees of freedom, respectively. The hypothesis could thus be tested by an f-distribution test where

$$F = \frac{(E_1 - E_0)/(p + 1)}{E_0/(n + n^* - 2p - 2)},$$

where n and n^* were equal to the number of observations in each equation and p was equal to the number of independent variables. See K. W. Smillie, *An Introduction to Regression and Correlation* (New York: Academic Press, 1966), pp. 72–73; or J. Johnson, *Econometric Methods* (New York: McGraw-Hill Book Co., 1963), pp. 136–38.

TABLE 5
Tests for coincidence for the industry-wide analysis

Industry	R^2 *for the prelisting observations*	R^2 *for the postlisting observations*	R^2 *for the combined pre- and postlisting observations*	*Calculated value for F*	*Significant value for F at 5%*
Utilities	.72	.65	.62	0.60	2.66
Transportation	.60	.96	.57	1.85	4.28
Nonindustrial manufacturing	.58	.70	.62	0.63	2.24
Manufacturing (industrial)	.46	.25	.39	0.11	2.25
Food, drug, beverage and retail	.42	.53	.39	1.26	2.25
Basic industries	.29	.29	.17	1.24	2.31
Building and home	.45	.62	.34	0.89	4.26
Electronics	.54	.53	.25	3.29	2.40

CONCLUSIONS

The widely held belief that a company will benefit from listing on the New York Stock Exchange through obtaining a higher market price was not confirmed. To the contrary, when one methodology was used (the dummy-variable test), listing had an insignificant effect in all the tests conducted. When the equations were tested for coincidence, in only one instance did the equations appear to be significantly different. Generally speaking, little evidence was found that would support the belief that listing pays off with higher prices. This is not equivalent to stating that market price will not increase after listing. The results simply showed that, generally speaking, market price after listing was not significantly higher than it would have been if the stock had remained on the over-the-counter market. This does not eliminate the possibility that listing may benefit some companies while being detrimental to others. However, the research does indicate that, when other variables are considered, listing per se does not significantly affect the market prices of common stocks in general.

An Introduction to
"Going Public"*

Brian Sullivan †

THE OWNERS of a closely held corporation frequently turn to the independent accountant for financial and business guidance. One of the most important decisions that these owners may face if the business is highly successful is whether or not to "go public." This introductory look at the complex process of going public hopefully will point out some guidelines that the accountant may follow in advising clients who are considering a public sale of stock.

Normally, the independent accountant will have neither time nor inclination to become an expert on anything but the accounting aspects of "going public," but he should be able to describe for his clients the mechanics of a public offering and to give them a critical and disinterested appraisal of its advantages and disadvantages. To do this properly, the accountant should have at least some general understanding of the usual reasons for "going public," and some familiarity with the registration process. He should also be aware of the roles played by the underwriters, the underwriters' attorney, the client and the client's attorney.

Like most catch phrases, "going public" requires definition. It may be defined as the process of converting the closely held corporation into a publicly owned firm through the sale of its stock to the public through underwriters. While the slogan "Why go broke? Go Public!" is an exaggeration, it has become easier during recent years to sell stock of smaller companies to the public.

---

* Reprinted from *The Journal of Accountancy*, Vol. 120, No. 5 (November 1965), pp. 48–53, by permission of the author and the publisher.

† Brian Sullivan is a partner in the law firm of Dykema, Wheat, Spencer, Goodnow & Trigg, Detroit.

Not every closely held corporation, of course, qualifies for a public offering of stock. Earnings—actual and potential—must be sufficient in the judgment of the underwriters to support a public issue of reasonable size. But even if earnings are adequate, the industry may not be considered attractive by investors, and this may as a practical matter rule out a public offering. Discussion of the standards normally applied by underwriters is beyond the scope of this article, but obviously the initial inquiry by the owners of the closely held corporation should be whether or not reputable underwriters would take on the issue and sponsor it in the market.

With his knowledge of the financial condition and prospects of the business, the accountant is in a favorable position to know whether the corporation will qualify for a public offering and, if so, to initiate a program of preparation years in advance of the proposed sale. For the local firm without experience in public offerings, knowledge of the registration process may also lead to retention of clients who might otherwise be lost. If the members of the firm have developed some knowledge of the technicalities of a public offering, the firm may be successful in convincing the client and, equally important, potential underwriters that it can perform the auditor's functions in the registration process.

REASONS FOR "GOING PUBLIC"

The primary reason for "going public" from the corporate standpoint is to raise additional working capital or to finance an expansion or diversification program. Subsidiary reasons include recognition that a public market for stock may facilitate mergers, acquisitions and future financing as well as attract managerial talent through the lure of potential stock options.

From the standpoint of the shareholders, the principal motive for "going public" is to obtain the advantages that flow from creation of a public market for their stock. This market provides liquidity and an opportunity for diversification of investment and avoids the risk faced by shareholders in a close corporation of excess valuation for estate tax purposes without assurance that this value can be realized through redemption or sale. In addition, shareholders who sell part of their stock in a "secondary offering"—a sale by the shareholders rather than by the corporation—frequently discover that the market will value their remaining stock at a price substantially in excess of what could have been realized on sale or redemption of all of their closely held stock.

DISADVANTAGES OF "GOING PUBLIC"

Disadvantages of "going public" involve financial, psychological and business factors. A public offering is a high cost method of raising funds—at least where the amount involved is not large—and expenses, fees and commissions may represent a significant portion of the proceeds of sale. Pressure for dividends after the public offering may involve a drain on working capital although management may be able to convince the shareholders that the "growth" nature of the investment makes the payment of cash dividends a confession of lack of confidence in the future rather than a benefit to shareholders.

Management should recognize the need for adjustment to life in the goldfish bowl following a public offering. Such sensitive matters as executive compensation and fringe benefits will no longer be only the personal concern of management, and conflict of interest situations—such as the selling or leasing of property to the corporation—may have to be discontinued even if fair to avoid exposure to a shareholder's suit.

The most important disadvantage to public ownership of stock is the requirement of disclosure of confidential business information. The registration statement and prospectus must reveal such matters as the relative profitability of different product lines, manufacturing capacity, selling and distribution methods, transactions with insiders, competitive position in the industry, and similar facts that management may be reluctant to parade before competitors or customers.

Until the Securities Acts Amendments of 1964, corporations whose securities were listed on an exchange were subject to more stringent disclosure requirements after the offering than were corporations whose securities were traded only over-the-counter. Now, however, if the corporation has total assets of more than $1 million and a class of equity securities held of record by more than 750 persons (500 after July 1, 1966), the registration, periodic reporting, proxy solicitation and insider reporting and trading provisions of the Securities Exchange Act of 1934 will, in general, be applicable. Probably the most significant result of the Amendments is the requirement that most issuers whose securities are traded over the counter disclose to shareholders at least annually the information required by the SEC's proxy rules. This continuing obligation of disclosure may be considered by the owners-executives of many corporations to be a serious disadvantage of public ownership.

INDEPENDENCE OF ACCOUNTANTS

The SEC's Regulation S-X spells out various criteria applied by the SEC in determining whether or not accountants are in fact "independent." Any accountant who has been a promoter, director, voting trustee or officer of the registrant during the period covered by the certified financial statements included in the registration statement is automatically disqualified, as is any accountant who had any direct financial interest in the registrant. While the recent adoption by the American

Institute of Certified Public Accountants of "independence" rules similar to those of the SEC will tend to eliminate the practice of accountants serving as directors or officers of their clients, other less obvious relationships with the client could still result in disqualification. When the accountant foresees the probability that the client will "go public," he should in the words of revised Rule 1.01 of the Institute's Code of Professional Ethics assess ". . . his relationships with an enterprise to determine whether in the circumstances he might expect his opinion to be considered independent, objective and unbiased by one who had knowledge of all the facts." Familiarity with the Accounting Series Releases of the SEC relating to the "independence" concept is also important.

CONFLICT OF INTEREST SITUATIONS

Frequently, owners of the closely held corporation will have the corporation transact business with them or with firms owned directly or indirectly by them. The office building or plant, for example, may be owned by the shareholders through a realty corporation and leased to the business; sales may be made through a sales company organized by the shareholders; insurance may be placed with an agency owned or controlled by some or all of the shareholders, or products may be acquired from suppliers in which shareholders or executives of the corporation have an ownership interest. With the prospect of public ownership, however, conflict of interest situations become a matter of more urgent concern. Underwriters are acutely sensitive to arrangements of this kind and frequently require that they be eliminated prior to the offering. Since the prospectus must disclose any material transaction with insiders occurring within three years of the effective date of the registration statement, the accountant who looks ahead to public ownership may be in a position to advise his client to avoid arrangements which require disclosure and which might cause an adverse reaction on the part of underwriters, dealers or investors.

ACCOUNTING PRACTICES

The price of a new issue is normally negotiated as a multiple of per share earnings, and the higher the earnings, the higher the price. The accounting practices of many closely held corporations, however, are aimed primarily at minimizing or deferring taxes. Inventories, for example, may consistently be stated on an extremely conservative basis. Equipment costs which should be capitalized may be taken as current expenses. Depreciation methods may be dictated by the client's desire to reach for immediate tax savings rather than by other business considerations. Similarly, the owner-executives may take high salaries and charge rather questionable expenses to the corporation. These and other practices—whatever their merit from a tax standpoint—depress per share earnings during the period preceding the offering and usually reduce the proceeds of sale received by the corporation or the selling shareholders. The sole shareholder, for example, who is in a 60 percent income tax bracket and who takes an additional $30,000 in salary the year before he sells a portion of his holdings in a secondary offering at a price equal to 10 or 15 times per share earnings, usually is not making an intelligent decision. The accountant who recognizes the probability of a public offering and who is aware of these considerations can perform a valuable service for his client by suggesting elimination of practices which unduly depress earnings or which the accountant believes conflcit with generally accepted accounting principles.

AUDIT REQUIREMENTS

The SEC requires certified profit and loss statements for three years and almost invariably the underwriters will want the certification to cover the full five years of the summary of earnings section of the prospectus. Not infrequently the client may limit the scope of an audit so that procedures such as observation of physical inventories or confirmation of accounts receivable which are required for an unqualified opinion will not be followed. Accounting Series Release No. 90 (March 1, 1962) affirms the SEC's position that the opinion paragraph of the accountant's certificate cannot contain exceptions or qualifications relating to the scope of the audit. If the accountant is not in a position to express an unqualified affirmative opinion as to the fairness of the presentations of each year's earnings, the registration statement will be considered defective. While alternative procedures may permit the accountant to express an unqualified opinion even where, for example, opening inventories were not observed, substantial expense and considerable time may be saved at the time of the offering if full audits were conducted for at least five years. The accountant should point out to a client, who may "go public" within five years or less, that restricting the scope of the audit now to cut down costs could result in significantly higher expenses at the time of the offering.

POLICY MATTERS

Prior to "going public," management should review its executive compensation and benefit program. If management wants to create stock option, pension, profit-sharing or other benefit plans or to sell stock to key employees at a bargain price, it is better to do so several years before the public offering rather than shortly before or shortly after "going public."

Frequently, changes must be made in the capital structure of the issuer to facilitate the public offering. For example, a stock split may be required to increase the number of shares outstanding and to bring the price down to a more attractive level from a selling standpoint. Classification of shares into two classes with different voting or dividend rights is common, particularly where there is to be a secondary offering. Tax problems such as constructive receipt or the effect of Section 306 of the Internal Revenue Code may arise as a result of reclassification of shares with different dividend or other rights, and these must be analyzed by the buyer and the accountant.

Related businesses are frequently operated through affiliated corporations under common ownership, and merger or consolidation may be desirable before stock is offered to the public. This will require careful planning and timing, and frequently advance rulings from the Treasury Department may be desirable. Foresight by the lawyer or accountant may avoid last minute delays which are frequently expensive and occasionally fatal to an offering if there is a dramatic change in the market.

Co-operation between the accountant and the lawyer is essential in preparing the corporation for the transition from a close corporation to a publicly held concern. The laywer should have some familiarity with the functions of the accountant, and the accountant should understand the lawyer's role in the registration process. In some cases, the accountant may be able to point out to the lawyer areas of inquiry or significant facts which might not otherwise come to his attention.

LEGAL MATTERS

Prior to preparation of the registration statement the minute book should be reviewed by the lawyer, and any deficiencies in holding meetings or in other corporate formalities should be corrected. Stock records should be reviewed, and the lawyer should make whatever examination is required to establish that all outstanding stock is validly issued, fully paid and nonassessable. Restrictions on voting and dividend rights should be analyzed, and any agreements between the shareholders restricting transferability or voting of stock should be rescinded.

Pre-emptive rights are seldom, if ever, appropriate for a publicly held corporation and should normally be eliminated by shareholder action prior to filing of the registration statement. Special attention must also be paid by the lawyer to sales of stock by the corporation within three years preceding the proposed offering. These sales must be disclosed in the registration statement, and the issuer must explain why the stock was not registered under the Securities Act of 1933. This can be a rather delicate matter, particularly where stock has been sold to a fairly large group such as key employees. If there is no reasonable basis for a claimed exemption from the Act, the SEC may require that the issuer's financial statements reflect any contingent liability that may exist in the form of rescission rights of purchasers of the stock.

Perhaps the most important step that the lawyer can take in preparing the client for the public offering is to review at an early stage all contracts or documents that may have to be filed as exhibits to the registration statement. The accountant should become familiar with the kind of exhibits required to be filed and should not hesitate to point out to his client that proposed contractual arrangements may become a matter of public record. Not only may management be reluctant from a business standpoint to reveal certain purchase, sales, distributorship or similar arrangements, but these contracts may also have antitrust implications that management would prefer not to have brought into sharp focus. Awareness of these problems before the contract is signed is obviously important.

COSTS OF "GOING PUBLIC"

Costs, principally underwriters' compensation, are usually higher for an initial public offering and are proportionally higher for a smaller issue. The risks assumed and expenses incurred by the underwriters do not decrease proportionally for smaller issues.

The compensation to be received by the underwriters is usually measured by the discount or spread; that is, the difference between the price at which the underwriters purchase the stock from the issuer or the selling shareholders and the price at which they propose to offer the stock to the public. While the underwriters' discount will vary with the quality and size of the issue, the nature of the industry, the reputation of the issuer and, of course, market conditions, a typical discount from the offering price on a first offering of, for example, $3 million would be 8 to 10 percent. This discount covers the allowance to the selling group, the management fee of the managing underwriter, expenses, and the market risk assumed by the underwriters. Other costs, principally legal and accounting fees and printing costs, normally would total about an additional 2 percent.

In a secondary offering, costs may be allocated between the issuer and the selling shareholders. While the SEC no longer requires that the selling shareholders pay any part of the expenses, registration of the issue under the Blue Sky laws of some states may be blocked unless the selling shareholders pay their fair share.

TIMING THE OFFERING

Proper timing of the offering is of crucial importance. Not only are there cycles in the appeal of new issues to investors, but, more important, the issue should be brought out when the issuer can show a consistently rising earnings curve with substantial improvement in the most recent fiscal year or interim period. To go public prematurely may mean an offering at too low a price; to delay may be to risk a reversal in the earnings trend which may dampen the enthusiasm of the underwriters and depress the offering price. While the accountant should be cautious about hazarding a prediction of future earnings, he certainly can alert his client to the importance of timing and suggest the factors to be evaluated in deciding when to make the public offering. If the client is considering a material merger or acquisition, he should also realize that the disclosure requirements of the Securities Act of 1933 may force him to reveal the existence of negotiations prematurely, and this could require a postponement of the offering.

NEGOTIATIONS WITH UNDERWRITERS

After balancing the various factors involved and deciding to "go public," the corporation or the selling shareholders must now select the underwriters and negotiate the underwriting arrangements. For all but the smallest and most speculative offerings, and arrangement whereby the underwriters are obligated to purchase the entire issue from the corporation or the selling shareholders—as contrasted with an undertaking only to use their "best efforts" to sell the issue—is usually negotiated.

The standing and reputation of the underwriters will influence the investing public's response to a new issue. As a practical matter, the choice is frequently between underwriters located in the area where the issuer's business activities are concentrated although the size of the issue and the reputation of the issuer may suggest looking for a national underwriter as managing underwriter, either alone or with a local firm. The accountant normally will either have personal knowledge of various underwriters or will have valuable sources of information and can be helpful to the businessman in selecting the underwriter. Not only do the underwriters assist in preparing the offering for market, organize the underwriting and selling groups and assume the market risk after purchase from the issuer or selling shareholders but, equally important, they may create an orderly and active "after market" by wide distribution of the issue and by sponsoring the stock in the market.

Pricing the issue is the principal subject for negotiation with the underwriters. The public normally values stock in the light of its present and potential earnings, and the offering price must bear a reasonable relationship to earnings when compared with stocks of similar corporations in the same industry. While the issuer or the selling shareholders will understandably aim at receiving the highest price reasonably attainable, they should recognize that an excessive price may result in an unsuccessful offering and a weak "after market" which would be a serious barrier to subsequent offerings. The accountant is usually in a position to offer valuable assistance to his client, not only in the form of information relating to the price of comparable issues but, more important, by pointing out the considerations the client should weigh in proposing the offering price.

THE REGISTRATION AND DISTRIBUTION PROCESS

Detailed description or analysis of the registration and distribution process would expand this article beyond reasonable limits. The basic prohibitory effect of the Securities Act of 1933 is to make it unlawful to sell or offer a security for sale in interstate commerce until a registration statement has been filed with the Securities and Exchange Commission or to sell the security in interstate commerce until the registration statement has become "effective." The Act is a disclosure statute; the underlying philosophy is that investors should be adequately protected if relevant financial and other information is presented to them. The SEC does not have statutory authority to pass on the merits of an issue or to block issues of a speculative nature or of dubious investment value.

The disclosure required by the Act is made through the registration statement, particularly the prospectus which forms part of the registration statement and which must be delivered to each purchaser of the security. While certain securities and transactions are exempt from the registration requirements of the Act, none of these exemptions are applicable to a public offering of the kind discussed in this article.

Unless the issue is quite small, the underwriter selected by the issuer will form an underwriting group. In addition, selected dealers will be organized into a selling group and will be given an opportunity to purchase shares from the underwriters at a stipulated discount. The prospectus in the form first filed with the SEC—the preliminary prospectus—is usually circulated to dealers who will be part of the selling group as well as to rating services, institutional investors and investment advisers. Careful records of the distribution must be maintained since all who receive copies of the preliminary prospectus must also receive copies of any amended prospectus reflecting the changes made in response to the letter of comments—frequently called the "deficiency letter"—issued by the SEC after review of the registration statement as it was originally filed.

The first reaction of the typical businessman after reading the initial draft of the prospectus is usually dismay at the manner in which the exciting potential of the business has been clouded over by dull and legalistic writing and concern over disclosure of information that he thinks should not be volunteered. During the arduous process of rewriting, however, he will discover that the prospectus is not really a "selling" document but rather a formal and stylized disclosure of material facts aimed, to a large extent, at insulating the client from any kind of liability.

Although responsibility for preparing the text of the prospectus is on the lawyer rather than the accountant, the accountant should understand the importance of full disclosure of material facts and should carefully read each successive draft of the prospectus so that he can point out any inaccurate or misleading statements.

Prefiling conferences with the SEC staff are frequently required for difficult or novel auditing or accounting matters. Arrangements may be made with the office of the Chief Accountant of the Division of Corporate Finance. It is usually desirable to cover the subjects to be discussed by letter several days before the meeting.

Prefiling promotional activities on the part of the client—even if unintentional—violate the Securities Act of 1933 and may result in the SEC delaying the effective date of the registration statement. Rumors frequently circulate as soon as work starts on the registration statement, and officers of the issuer may find it difficult to resist the temptation to condition the market by optimistic projections of earnings or glowing descriptions of operations. An early warning from the accountant or lawyer may block this kind of activity.

Shortly before the registration statement becomes "effective," usually about the time of filing the amendment in response to the SEC's letter of comments, the underwriters will hold a "due diligence" meeting with the issuer. The basic purpose of the meeting is to afford members of the underwriting group an opportunity to ask questions of officers of the issuer. In addition to its information value, the ritual of holding the meeting may permit the underwriters to avoid liability for alleged misrepresentations in the registration statement by showing that after a "reasonable investigation" they had "reasonable ground to believe" that the statements were true. Normally the accountant attends the meeting.

When an amendment is filed, the 20-day period before the registration statement becomes effective starts to run again, unless, of course, the SEC exercises its discretionary power to fix an earlier effective date. This right to accelerate the effective date is the principal control of the SEC over the form and content of the registration statement and the conduct of the issuer and underwriters in marketing the issue. Its importance is underscored by the fact that the "price amendment" to the registration statement is not filed until the day of or the day before the offering so as to hold to a minimum the time during which the underwriters are committed to purchase the stock.

The accountant should request a copy of the initial draft of the underwriting agreement to determine the scope of the representations the underwriters will want from him at the closing. This is the so-called "comfort" letter. Usually the accountant will be requested to represent that the financial statements which are part of the registration statement comply with the requirements of the Securities Act of 1933 and that on the basis of a limited review nothing has come to his attention to indicate that any unaudited statements were not prepared in accordance with generally accepted accounting standards on a basis consistent with the certified statements or that there has been any material adverse change in the financial condition of the issuer. Obviously the accountant will want to eliminate from the underwriting agreement any representations required to be included in the comfort letter which he thinks are unreasonable or which he is not willing to make. This can be accomplished with a minimum of difficulty if the accountant raises his objections before the underwriting agreement is shaped into final form.

The closing is usually held about a week after the offering. This is a rather formal procedure but, when it is over, the issuer or selling shareholders will have a check for the net proceeds of sale as tangible and welcome evidence that the corporation has indeed "gone public."

CONCLUSION

The principal theme of this introductory survey of "going public" is the importance of early preparation for a public offering. The accountant who believes that the corporation can reasonably look forward to "going public" can perform a valuable professional service by exploring with his clients the advantages and disadvantages of a public offering and by guiding them in initiating a comprehensive program of preparation.

Appendix of tables

TABLE A
Compound sum of $1

Year	1%	2%	3%	4%	5%	6%	7%
1	1.010	1.020	1.030	1.040	1.050	1.060	1.070
2	1.020	1.040	1.061	1.082	1.102	1.124	1.145
3	1.030	1.061	1.093	1.125	1.158	1.191	1.225
4	1.041	1.082	1.126	1.170	1.216	1.262	1.311
5	1.051	1.104	1.159	1.217	1.276	1.338	1.403
6	1.062	1.126	1.194	1.265	1.340	1.419	1.501
7	1.072	1.149	1.230	1.316	1.407	1.504	1.606
8	1.083	1.172	1.267	1.369	1.477	1.594	1.718
9	1.094	1.195	1.305	1.423	1.551	1.689	1.838
10	1.105	1.219	1.344	1.480	1.629	1.791	1.967
11	1.116	1.243	1.384	1.539	1.710	1.898	2.105
12	1.127	1.268	1.426	1.601	1.796	2.012	2.252
13	1.138	1.294	1.469	1.665	1.886	2.133	2.410
14	1.149	1.319	1.513	1.732	1.980	2.261	2.579
15	1.161	1.346	1.558	1.801	2.079	2.397	2.759
16	1.173	1.373	1.605	1.873	2.183	2.540	2.952
17	1.184	1.400	1.653	1.948	2.292	2.693	3.159
18	1.196	1.428	1.702	2.026	2.407	2.854	3.380
19	1.208	1.457	1.754	2.107	2.527	3.026	3.617
20	1.220	1.486	1.806	2.191	2.653	3.207	3.870
25	1.282	1.641	2.094	2.666	3.386	4.292	5.427
30	1.348	1.811	2.427	3.243	4.322	5.743	7.612

Year	8%	9%	10%	12%	14%	15%	16%
1	1.080	1.090	1.100	1.120	1.140	1.150	1.160
2	1.166	1.188	1.210	1.254	1.300	1.322	1.346
3	1.260	1.295	1.331	1.405	1.482	1.521	1.561
4	1.360	1.412	1.464	1.574	1.689	1.749	1.811
5	1.469	1.539	1.611	1.762	1.925	2.011	2.100
6	1.587	1.677	1.772	1.974	2.195	2.313	2.436
7	1.714	1.828	1.949	2.211	2.502	2.660	2.826
8	1.851	1.993	2.144	2.476	2.853	3.059	3.278
9	1.999	2.172	2.358	2.773	3.252	3.518	3.803
10	2.159	2.367	2.594	3.106	3.707	4.046	4.411
11	2.332	2.580	2.853	3.479	4.226	4.652	5.117
12	2.518	2.813	3.138	3.896	4.818	5.350	5.936
13	2.720	3.066	3.452	4.363	5.492	6.153	6.886
14	2.937	3.342	3.797	4.887	6.261	7.076	7.988
15	3.172	3.642	4.177	5.474	7.138	8.137	9.266
16	3.426	3.970	4.595	6.130	8.137	9.358	10.748
17	3.700	4.328	5.054	6.866	9.276	10.761	12.468
18	3.996	4.717	5.560	7.690	10.575	12.375	14.463
19	4.316	5.142	6.116	8.613	12.056	14.232	16.777
20	4.661	5.604	6.728	9.646	13.743	16.367	19.461
25	6.848	8.623	10.835	17.000	26.462	32.919	40.874
30	10.063	13.268	17.449	29.960	50.950	66.212	85.850

TABLE A (Continued)

Year	18%	20%	24%	28%	32%	36%
1	1.180	1.200	1.240	1.280	1.320	1.360
2	1.392	1.440	1.538	1.638	1.742	1.850
3	1.643	1.728	1.907	2.067	2.300	2.515
4	1.939	2.074	2.364	2.684	3.036	3.421
5	2.288	2.488	2.932	3.436	4.007	4.653
6	2.700	2.986	3.635	4.398	5.290	6.328
7	3.185	3,583	4.508	5.629	6.983	8.605
8	3.759	4.300	5.590	7.206	9.217	11.703
9	4.435	5.160	6.931	9.223	12.166	15.917
10	5.234	6.192	8.594	11.806	16.060	21.647
11	6.176	7.430	10.657	15.112	21.199	29.439
12	7.288	8.916	13.215	19.343	27.983	40.037
13	8.599	10.699	16.386	24.759	36.937	54.451
14	10.147	12.839	20.319	31.691	48.757	74.053
15	11.974	15.407	25.196	40.565	64.359	100.712
16	14.129	18.488	31.243	51.923	84.954	136.97
17	16.672	22.186	38.741	66.461	112.14	186.28
18	19.673	26.623	48.039	85.071	148.02	253.34
19	23.214	31.948	59.568	108.89	195.39	344.54
20	27.393	38.338	73.864	139.38	257.92	468.57
25	62.669	95.396	216.542	478.90	1033.6	2180.1
30	143.371	237.376	634.820	1645.5	4142.1	10143.

Year	40%	50%	60%	70%	80%	90%
1	1.400	1.500	1.600	1.700	1.800	1.900
2	1.960	2.250	2.560	2.890	3.240	3.610
3	2.744	3.375	4.096	4.913	5.832	6.859
4	3.842	5.062	6.544	8.352	10.498	13.032
5	5.378	7.594	10.486	14.199	18.896	24.761
6	7.530	11.391	16.777	24.138	34.012	47.046
7	10.541	17.086	26.844	41.034	61.222	89.387
8	14.758	25.629	42.950	69.758	110.200	169.836
9	20.661	38.443	68.720	118.588	198.359	322.688
10	28.925	57.665	109.951	201.599	357.047	613.107
11	40.496	86.498	175.922	342.719	642.684	1164.902
12	56.694	129.746	281.475	582.622	1156.831	2213.314
13	79.372	194.619	450.360	990.457	2082.295	4205.297
14	111.120	291.929	720.576	1683.777	3748.131	7990.065
15	155.568	437.894	1152.921	2862.421	6746.636	15181.122
16	217.795	656.84	1844.7	4866.1	12144.	28844.0
17	304.914	985.26	2951.5	8272.4	21859.	54804.0
18	426.879	1477.9	4722.4	14063.0	39346.	104130.0
19	597.630	2216.8	7555.8	23907.0	70824.	197840.0
20	836.683	3325.3	12089.0	40642.0	127480.	375900.0
25	4499.880	25251.	126760.0	577060.0	2408900.	9307600.0
30	24201.432	191750.	1329200.	8193500.0	45517000.	230470000.0

TABLE B
Present value of $1

Year	1%	2%	3%	4%	5%	6%	7%	8%	9%	10%	12%	14%	15%
1	.990	.980	.971	.962	.952	.943	.935	.926	.917	.909	.893	.877	.870
2	.980	.961	.943	.925	.907	.890	.873	.857	.842	.826	.797	.769	.756
3	.971	.942	.915	.889	.864	.840	.816	.794	.772	.751	.712	.675	.658
4	.961	.924	.889	.855	.823	.792	.763	.735	.708	.683	.636	.592	.572
5	.951	.906	.863	.822	.784	.747	.713	.681	.650	.621	.567	.519	.497
6	.942	.888	.838	.790	.746	.705	.666	.630	.596	.564	.507	.456	.432
7	.933	.871	.813	.760	.711	.665	.623	.583	.547	.513	.452	.400	.376
8	.923	.853	.789	.731	.677	.627	.582	.540	.502	.467	.404	.351	.327
9	.914	.837	.766	.703	.645	.592	.544	.500	.460	.424	.361	.308	.284
10	.905	.820	.744	.676	.614	.558	.508	.463	.422	.386	.322	.270	.247
11	.896	.804	.722	.650	.585	.527	.475	.429	.388	.350	.287	.237	.215
12	.887	.788	.701	.625	.557	.497	.444	.397	.356	.319	.257	.208	.187
13	.879	.773	.681	.601	.530	.469	.415	.368	.326	.290	.229	.182	.163
14	.870	.758	.661	.577	.505	.442	.388	.340	.299	.263	.205	.160	.141
15	.861	.743	.642	.555	.481	.417	.362	.315	.275	.239	.183	.140	.123
16	.853	.728	.623	.534	.458	.394	.339	.292	.252	.218	.163	.123	.107
17	.844	.714	.605	.513	.436	.371	.317	.270	.231	.198	.146	.108	.093
18	.836	.700	.587	.494	.416	.350	.296	.250	.212	.180	.130	.095	.081
19	.828	.686	.570	.475	.396	.331	.276	.232	.194	.164	.116	.083	.070
20	.820	.673	.554	.456	.377	.319	.258	.215	.178	.149	.104	.073	.061
25	.780	.610	.478	.375	.295	.233	.184	.146	.116	.092	.059	.038	.030
30	.742	.552	.412	.308	.231	.174	.131	.099	.075	.057	.033	.020	.015

Year	16%	18%	20%	24%	28%	32%	36%	40%	50%	60%	70%	80%	90%
1	.862	.847	.833	.806	.781	.758	.735	.714	.667	.625	.588	.556	.526
2	.743	.718	.694	.650	.610	.574	.541	.510	.444	.391	.346	.309	.277
3	.641	.609	.579	.524	.477	.435	.398	.364	.296	.244	.204	.171	.146
4	.552	.516	.482	.423	.373	.329	.292	.260	.198	.153	.120	.095	.077
5	.476	.437	.402	.341	.291	.250	.215	.186	.132	.095	.070	.053	.040
6	.410	.370	.335	.275	.227	.189	.158	.133	.088	.060	.041	.029	.021
7	.354	.314	.279	.222	.178	.143	.116	.095	.059	.037	.024	.016	.011
8	.305	.266	.233	.179	.139	.108	.085	.068	.039	.023	.014	.009	.006
9	.263	.226	.194	.144	.108	.082	.063	.048	.026	.015	.008	.005	.003
10	.227	.191	.162	.116	.085	.062	.046	.035	.017	.009	.005	.003	.002
11	.195	.162	.135	.094	.066	.047	.034	.025	.012	.006	.003	.002	.001
12	.168	.137	.112	.076	.052	.036	.025	.018	.008	.004	.002	.001	.001
13	.145	.116	.093	.061	.040	.027	.018	.013	.005	.002	.001	.001	.000
14	.125	.099	.078	.049	.032	.021	.014	.009	.003	.001	.001	.000	.000
15	.108	.084	.065	.040	.025	.016	.010	.006	.002	.001	.000	.000	.000
16	.093	.071	.054	.032	.019	.012	.007	.005	.002	.001	.000	.000	
17	.080	.030	.045	.026	.015	.009	.005	.003	.001	.000	.000		
18	.089	.051	.038	.021	.012	.007	.004	.002	.001	.000	.000		
19	.030	.043	.031	.017	.009	.005	.003	.002	.000	.000			
20	.051	.037	.026	.014	.007	.004	.002	.001	.000	.000			
25	.024	.016	.010	.005	.002	.001	.000	.000					
30	.012	.007	.004	.002	.001	.000	.000						

TABLE C
Sum of an annuity of $1 for N years

Year	1%	2%	3%	4%	5%	6%
1	1.000	1.000	1.000	1.000	1.000	1.000
2	2.010	2.020	2.030	2.040	2.050	2.060
3	2.030	3.060	3.091	3.122	3.152	3.184
4	4.060	4.122	4.184	4.246	4.310	4.375
5	5.101	5.204	5.309	5.416	5.526	5.637
6	6.152	6.308	6.468	6.633	6.802	6.975
7	7.214	7.434	7.662	7.898	8.142	8.394
8	8.286	8.583	8.892	9.214	9.549	9.897
9	9.369	9.755	10.159	10.583	11.027	11.491
10	10.462	10.950	11.464	12.006	12.578	13.181
11	11.567	12.169	12.808	13.486	14.207	14.972
12	12.683	13.412	14.192	15.026	15.917	16.870
13	13.809	14.680	15.618	16.627	17.713	18.882
14	14.947	15.974	17.086	18.292	19.599	21.051
15	16.097	17.293	18.599	20.024	21.579	23.276
16	17.258	18.639	20.157	21.825	23.657	25.673
17	18.430	20.012	21.762	23.698	25.840	28.213
18	19.615	21.412	23.414	25.645	28.132	30.906
19	20.811	22.841	25.117	27.671	30.539	33.760
20	22.019	24.297	26.870	29.778	33.066	36.786
25	28.243	32.030	36.459	41.646	47.727	54.865
30	34.785	40.568	47.575	56.085	66.439	79.058

Year	7%	8%	9%	10%	12%	14%
1	1.000	1.000	1.000	1.000	1.000	1.000
2	2.070	2.080	2.090	2.100	2.120	2.140
3	3.215	3.246	3.278	3.310	3.374	3.440
4	4.440	4.506	4.573	4.641	4.770	4.921
5	5.751	5.867	5.985	6.105	6.353	6.610
6	7.153	7.336	7.523	7.716	8.115	8.536
7	8.654	8.923	9.200	9.487	10.089	10.730
8	10.260	10.637	11.028	11.436	12.300	13.233
9	11.978	12.488	13.021	13.579	14.776	16.085
10	13.816	14.487	15.193	15.937	17.549	19.337
11	15.784	16.645	17.560	18.531	20.655	23.044
12	17.888	18.977	20.141	21.384	24.133	27.271
13	20.141	21.495	22.953	24.523	28.029	32.089
14	22.550	24.215	26.019	27.975	32.393	37.581
15	25.129	27.152	29.361	31.772	37.280	43.842
16	27.888	30.324	33.003	35.950	42.753	50.980
17	30.840	33.750	36.974	40.545	48.884	59.118
18	33.999	37.450	41.301	45.599	55.750	68.394
19	37.379	41.446	46.018	51.159	63.440	78.969
20	40.995	45.762	51.160	57.275	72.052	91.025
25	63.249	73.106	84.701	98.347	133.334	181.871
30	94.461	113.283	136.308	164.494	241.333	356.787

TABLE C (Continued)

Year	16%	18%	20%	24%	28%	32%
1	1.000	1.000	1.000	1.000	1.000	1.000
2	2.160	2.180	2.200	2.240	2.280	2.320
3	3.506	3.572	3.640	3.778	3.918	4.062
4	5.066	5.215	5.368	5.684	6.016	6.362
5	6.877	7.154	7.442	8.048	8.700	9.398
6	8.977	9.442	9.930	10.980	12.136	13.406
7	11.414	12.142	12.916	14.615	16.534	18.696
8	14.240	15.327	16.499	19.123	22.163	25.678
9	17.518	19.086	20.799	24.712	29.369	34.895
10	21.321	23.521	25.959	31.643	38.592	47.062
11	25.733	28.755	32.150	40.238	50.399	63.122
12	30.850	34.931	39.580	50.985	65.510	84.320
13	36.786	42.219	48.497	64.110	84.853	112.303
14	43.672	50.818	59.196	80.496	109.612	149.240
15	51.660	60.965	72.035	100.815	141.303	197.997
16	60.925	72.939	87.442	126.011	181.87	262.36
17	71.673	87.068	105.931	157.253	233.79	347.31
18	84.141	103.740	128.117	195.994	300.25	459.45
19	98.603	123.414	154.740	244.033	385.32	607.47
20	115.380	146.628	186.688	303.601	494.21	802.86
25	249.214	342.603	471.981	898.092	1706.8	3226.8
30	530.312	790.948	1181.882	2640.916	5873.2	12941.0

Year	36%	40%	50%	60%	70%	80%
1	1.000	1.000	1.000	1.000	1.000	1.000
2	2.360	2.400	2.500	2.600	2.700	2.800
3	4.210	4.360	4.750	5.160	5.590	6.040
4	6.725	7.104	8.125	9.256	10.503	11.872
5	10.146	10.846	13.188	15.810	18.855	22.370
6	14.799	16.324	20.781	26.295	33.054	41.265
7	21.126	23.853	32.172	43.073	57.191	75.278
8	29.732	34.395	49.258	69.916	98.225	136.500
9	41.435	49.153	74.887	112.866	167.983	246.699
10	57.352	69.814	113.330	181.585	286.570	445.058
11	78.998	98.739	170.995	291.536	488.170	802.105
12	108.437	139.235	257.493	467.458	830.888	1444.788
13	148.475	195.929	387.239	748.933	1413.510	2601.619
14	202.926	275.300	581.859	1199.293	2403.968	4683.914
15	276.979	386.420	873.788	1919.869	4087.745	8432.045
16	377.69	541.99	1311.7	3072.8	6950.2	15179.0
17	514.66	759.78	1968.5	4917.5	11816.0	27323.0
18	700.94	1064.7	2953.8	7868.9	20089.0	49182.0
19	954.28	1491.6	4431.7	12591.0	34152.0	88528.0
20	1298.8	2089.2	6648.5	20147.0	58059.0	159350.0
25	6053.0	11247.0	50500.0	211270.0	824370.0	3011100.0
30	28172.0	60501.0	383500.0	2215400.0	11705000.0	56896000.0

TABLE D
Present value of an annuity of $1

Year	1%	2%	3%	4%	5%	6%	7%	8%	9%	10%
1	0.990	0.980	0.971	0.962	0.952	0.943	0.935	0.926	0.917	0.909
2	1.970	1.942	1.913	1.886	1.859	1.833	1.808	1.783	1.759	1.736
3	2.941	2.884	2.829	2.775	2.723	2.673	2.624	2.577	2.531	2.487
4	3.902	3.808	3.717	3.630	3.546	3.465	3.387	3.312	3.240	3.170
5	4.853	4.713	4.580	4.452	4.329	4.212	4.100	3.993	3.890	3.791
6	5.795	5.601	5.417	5.242	5.076	4.917	4.766	4.623	4.486	4.355
7	6.728	6.472	6.230	6.002	5.786	5.582	5.389	5.206	5.033	4.868
8	7.652	7.325	7.020	6.733	6.463	6.210	6.971	5.747	5.535	5.335
9	8.566	8.162	7.786	7.435	7.108	6.802	6.515	6.247	5.985	5.759
10	9.471	8.983	8.530	8.111	7.722	7.360	7.024	6.710	6.418	6.145
11	10.368	9.787	9.253	8.760	8.306	7.887	7.499	7.139	6.805	6.495
12	11.255	10.575	9.954	9.385	8.863	8.384	7.943	7.536	7.161	6.814
13	12.134	11.348	10.635	9.986	9.394	8.853	8.358	7.904	7.487	7.103
14	13.004	12.106	11.296	10.563	9.899	9.295	8.745	8.244	7.786	7.367
15	13.865	12.849	11.938	11.118	10.380	9.712	9.108	8.559	8.060	7.606
16	14.718	13.578	12.561	11.652	10.838	10.106	9.447	8.851	8.312	7.824
17	15.562	14.292	13.166	12.166	11.274	10.477	9.763	9.122	8.544	8.022
18	16.398	14.992	13.754	12.659	11.690	10.828	10.059	9.372	8.756	8.201
19	17.226	15.678	14.324	13.134	12.085	11.158	10.336	9.604	8.950	8.365
20	18.046	16.351	14.877	13.590	12.462	11.470	10.594	9.818	9.128	8.514
25	22.023	19.523	17.413	15.622	14.094	12.783	11.654	10.675	9.823	9.077
30	25.808	22.397	19.600	17.292	15.373	13.765	12.409	11.258	10.274	9.427

Year	12%	14%	16%	18%	20%	24%	28%	32%	36%
1	0.893	0.877	0.862	0.847	0.833	0.806	0.781	0.758	0.735
2	1.690	1.647	1.605	1.566	1.528	1.457	1.392	1.332	1.276
3	2.402	2.322	2.246	2.174	2.106	1.981	1.868	1.766	1.674
4	3.037	2.914	2.798	2.690	2.589	2.404	2.241	2.096	1.966
5	3.605	3.433	3.274	3.127	2.991	2.745	2.532	2.345	2.181
6	4.111	3.889	3.685	3.498	3.326	3.020	2.759	2.534	2.339
7	4.564	4.288	4.039	3.812	3.605	3.242	2.937	2.678	2.455
8	4.968	4.639	4.344	4.078	3.837	3.421	3.076	2.786	2.540
9	5.328	4.946	4.607	4.303	4.031	3.566	3.184	2.868	2.603
10	5.650	5.216	4.833	4.494	4.193	3.682	3.269	2.930	2.650
11	5.988	5.453	5.029	4.656	4.327	3.776	3.335	2.978	2.683
12	6.194	5.660	5.197	4.793	4.439	3.851	3.387	3.013	2.708
13	6.424	5.842	5.342	4.910	4.533	3.912	3.427	3.040	2.727
14	6.628	6.002	5.468	5.008	4.611	3.962	3.459	3.061	2.740
15	6.811	6.142	5.575	5.092	4.675	4.001	3.483	3.076	2.750
16	6.974	6.265	5.669	5.162	4.730	4.033	3.503	3.085	2.758
17	7.120	5.373	5.749	4.222	4.775	4.059	3.518	3.097	2.763
18	7.250	6.467	5.818	5.273	4.812	4.080	3.529	3.104	2.767
19	7.366	6.550	5.877	5.316	4.844	4.097	3.539	3.109	2.770
20	7.469	6.623	5.929	5.353	4.870	4.110	3.546	3.113	2.772
25	7.843	6.873	6.097	5.467	4.948	4.147	3.564	3.122	2.776
30	8.055	7.003	6.177	5.517	4.979	4.160	3.569	3.124	2.778

TABLE E
Area under the normal curve

z	.00	.01	.02	.03	.04	.05	.06	.07	.08	.09
0.0	.0000	.0040	.0080	.0120	.0160	.0199	.0239	.0279	.0319	.0359
0.1	.0398	.0438	.0478	.0517	.0557	.0596	.0636	.0675	.0714	.0753
0.2	.0793	.0832	.0871	.0910	.0948	.0987	.1026	.1064	.1103	.1141
0.3	.1179	.1217	.1255	.1293	.1331	.1368	.1406	.1443	.1480	.1517
0.4	.1554	.1591	.1628	.1664	.1700	.1736	.1772	.1808	.1844	.1879
0.5	.1915	.1950	.1985	.2019	.2054	.2088	.2123	.2157	.2190	.2224
0.6	.2257	.2291	.2324	.2357	.2389	.2422	.2454	.2486	.2517	.2549
0.7	.2580	.2611	.2642	.2673	.2704	.2734	.2764	.2794	.2823	.2852
0.8	.2881	.2910	.2939	.2967	.2995	.3023	.3051	.3078	.3106	.3133
0.9	.3159	.3186	.3212	.3228	.3264	.3289	.3315	.3340	.3365	.3389
1.0	.3413	.3438	.3461	.3485	.3508	.3531	.3554	.3577	.3599	.3621
1.1	.3643	.3665	.3686	.3708	.3729	.3749	.3770	.3790	.3810	.3830
1.2	.3849	.3869	.3888	.3907	.3925	.3944	.3962	.3980	.3997	.4015
1.3	.4032	.4049	.4066	.4082	.4099	.4115	.4131	.4147	.4162	.4177
1.4	.4192	.4207	.4222	.4236	.4251	.4265	.4279	.4292	.4306	.4319
1.5	.4332	.4345	.4357	.4370	.4382	.4394	.4406	.4418	.4429	.4441
1.6	.4452	.4463	.4474	.4484	.4495	.4505	.4515	.4525	.4535	.4545
1.7	.4554	.4564	.4573	.4582	.4591	.4599	.4608	.4616	.4625	.4633
1.8	.4641	.4649	.4656	.4664	.4671	.4678	.4686	.4693	.4699	.4706
1.9	.4713	.4719	.4726	.4732	.4738	.4744	.4750	.4756	.4761	.4767
2.0	.4772	.4778	.4783	.4788	.4793	.4798	.4803	.4808	.4812	.4817
2.1	.4821	.4826	.4830	.4834	.4838	.4842	.4846	.4850	.4854	.4857
2.2	.4861	.4864	.4868	.4871	.4875	.4878	.4881	.4884	.4887	.4890
2.3	.4893	.4896	.4898	.4901	.4904	.4906	.4909	.4911	.4913	.4916
2.4	.4918	.4920	.4922	.4925	.4927	.4929	.4931	.4932	.4934	.4936
2.5	.4938	.4940	.4941	.4943	.4945	.4946	.4948	.4949	.4951	.4952
2.6	.4953	.4955	.4956	.4957	.4959	.4960	.4961	.4962	.4963	.4964
2.7	.4965	.4966	.4967	.4968	.4969	.4970	.4971	.4972	.4973	.4974
2.8	.4974	.4975	.4976	.4977	.4977	.4978	.4979	.4979	.4980	.4981
2.9	.4981	.4982	.4982	.4983	4984	.4984	.4985	.4985	.4986	.4986
3.0	.4987	.4987	.4987	.4988	.4988	.4989	.4989	.4989	.4990	.4990

Note: This table presents probabilities for only one-half of the normal curve distribution.